INDIAN ETHICS

This is a remarkable achievement both in scope and organization and in the outstanding quality of some essays. The editors have earned the gratitude of all Western students of Hindu and Buddhist thought and of comparative ethics. New possibilities of dialogue have been opened up.

Alasdair MacIntyre.

Indian ethics is one of the great traditions of ethics in world-historical philosophy. Indian ethical insights have influenced a wide spectrum of thinkers ranging from the early Greeks and Goethe to Emerson and Thoreau. Yet there have been few systematic studies of the broad range of Indian ethical reflections in contemporary philosophical idiom.

This comprehensive compendium explores the scope and limits of Indian ethical thinking. Thirty distinguished writers engage orthodox and heterodox schools of thought from the Vedas, Upanishads, the Mahābhārata and Bhagavad-Gītā to Buddhist, Jaina, and Sāṃkhya-Yoga philosophies, and reflect on the interpretation of their teachings and practices in contemporary contexts and modern secular sensibilities.

The General Introduction examines the distinctive nature of moral philosophy in India as compared to the West. Part A analyzes classic texts dealing with such themes as: Hindu values, virtues and statecraft, the 'ends' of living, rites and gifting, acts and duties, the implications of karma and dharma, caste issues, law, the ethic of yoga and discipline, and the reality of evil and suffering. Part B focuses on Buddhist and Jaina ethics through such topics as emotions, action, consequences, virtue-ethics, renunciation, enlightenment, human rights and ecology. Part C extends and adapts these traditional moral thinking and praxis to modern and postmodern worlds, encountering contemporary thinkers such as Gandhi and Aurobindo, and tests them against present-day issues such as rights, citizenship and democracy, religious tolerance, environmental and animal ethics, and the challenges posed by the imperatives of peace and nonviolence, justice and freedom. Finally, Volume II will pay special attention to post-colonial developments and feminist and applied ethics – on such questions as the gendered self, gender equity, *satī* and abortion, health care and biomedical ethics.

Given the range of topics covered and the eminence of the featured authors, this volume offers an invaluable resource to a wide variety of readers in the fields of philosophy, religion, sociology and cultural studies, and to lay seekers and activists in pursuit of Indian ethical wisdom and South Asian responses to contemporary moral dilemmas.

This volume has been dedicated to the memories of

the late Bimal K. Matilal, Renuka Sharma, Ninian Smart, Bernard Williams

for inspirations and contributions of each in their own way to the genesis and completion of this project.

Indian Ethics

Classical Traditions and Contemporary Challenges

Volume I

Edited by
PURUSHOTTAMA BILIMORIA
JOSEPH PRABHU
RENUKA SHARMA

ASHGATE

Published by
Ashgate Publishing Limited
Gower House
Croft Road
Aldershot
Hampshire GU11 3HR
England

Ashgate Publishing Company
Suite 420
101 Cherry Street
Burlington, VT 05401-4405
USA

Ashgate website: http://www.ashgate.com

British Library Cataloguing in Publication Data
Indian ethics : classical traditions and contemporary challenges: An anthology
1.Ethics – India 2.Hindu ethics 3.Buddhist ethics I.Bilimoria, Purushottama II.Prabhu, Joseph III.Sharma, Renuka
170.9'54

Library of Congress Cataloging-in-Publication Data
Indian ethics : classical traditions and contemporary challenges : An anthology / edited by Purushottama Bilimoria, Joseph Prabhu, and Renuka Sharma.
p. cm.
Includes index.
ISBN 0-7546-3301-2 (hardback)
1. Ethics–India. 2. Social ethics–India. I. Bilimoria, Purushottama. II. Prabhu, Joseph. III. Sharma, Renuka M.

BJ122.I63 2004
70'.954–dc21

2003063853

ISBN 978-0-7546-3301-3

Printed and bound in Great Britain by MPG Books Ltd, Bodmin, Cornwall.

Contents

Preface

Kuryād vidvāṃs tathā 'saktaś cikīrṣurlokasaṃgraham

The disinterestedly wise ought to desire for the holding together of all being
(*Bhagavadgītā* III 25)

Our aim in undertaking this compendium is to provide an account of Indian ethical traditions from early antiquity to the present and to do so in contemporary philosophical idiom. Scholars of comparative philosophy who resist the temptation of an easy relativism, acknowledge that there are three great traditions of world philosophy, those of India, China, and the West. Likewise, students of comparative civilizations have documented the vast influence of the Indian tradition on figures and groups as diverse as the early Greeks – starting with the Orphics and the Pythagoreans – the German Idealists, and Emerson and Thoreau in the Americas. And yet academic philosophy, at least in the West, has not registered either the intrinsic importance or the influence of Indian ethics. From a philosophical standpoint this curious omission has had baleful effects insofar as it has severely narrowed the scope and range of ethical discussion. At a time when there is much talk of pluralism, cross-cultural sensibilities, multiculturalism, and globalization such a gap is doubly unfortunate because it hinders the conversation between cultures that is much needed in a complex contemporary environment.

Given this lacuna, it is strange that there have not been more efforts made by scholars of Indian philosophy to fill this gap. There have indeed been fine and significant books on Indian metaphysics, epistemology, and logic, but sadly very few systematic and wide-ranging studies of Indian ethics. These volumes, we hope, go some way towards meeting this need.

Anyone who has worked within a classical philosophical tradition of such longevity and complexity knows that it demands a number of skills. One needs not only linguistic, philological, and historical knowledge, but also philosophical competence and the ability to interpret ancient wisdom in contemporary contexts. When we conceived of this project we had three purposes in mind: first, to provide a faithful account of the great texts and major schools of both the orthodox and heterodox traditions; second, to relate such an account to present-day concerns and contexts; and third, to highlight what we felt might be distinctive about the Indian ethical traditions in terms of both content and style, text and context. We have expanded more fully on these aims in our general introduction.

With a project as ambitious as this, it is inevitable that there will still remain defects of omission and commission. We are aware of some of them and will, of course, be grateful if others are brought to our attention. Within the limits of our abilities and time, we have done our best, but to finish such a volume is by no means to complete it – the work goes on in what Hegel once called *ewige Arbeit.*

Acknowledgments

What remains now is a very pleasant task. Our contributors one and all have been quite wonderful. Some of them submitted their essays promptly as our first invitation went out about ten years ago. They have displayed almost saintly patience with, and understanding of, the inevitable delays involved in such an ambitious enterprise. Others very generously agreed to write essays at short notice, even if it meant pushing aside some of their own work. Yet others, even if they were not able to contribute directly, aided us with their sage advice and suggestions, or offered us their published essays that would not otherwise have come to notice. At the end of such a large, collaborative undertaking, our overwhelming feeling is one of gratitude and gladness.

Yet that gladness has also been severely tempered. One of our co-editors sadly passed away (at barely 45 years of age) while this volume was lumbering to the finish line. Dr Renuka Sharma had been with this project from its inception and made sure through all the delays and near derailings that it stayed on track. Her own professional credentials were in medicine and psychiatric psychotherapy. However, her knowledge of philosophy, the humanities, and feminism was profound, and the editorial team greatly benefited from her wisdom, sharp mind and compassion. It was characteristic of her and an indication of how seriously she took this volume that she worked on her introduction to Part D (now in the second volume) and other editorial responsibilities till a few days before her death. Her great and generous spirit hovers over this work and continues to bless it.

The late Professor Bimal K. Matilal is also dearly missed as he is remembered for the 'originary' suggestion, back in Oxford, and his role in an initial planning of the volume (*maṅgalam gurave*). And so is Professor Ninian Smart, with his gentle reminders of the kinds of problems we might focus on in the context of 'World Philosophy and Religion'. We record his unrepentant insistence, over numerous shared dinners, that utilitarianism when applied properly to animals and their welfare should, paradoxically, turn all Indians into carnivorous non-vegetarians! The same principles of utilitarianism (albeit of a rule-based variety), that his brother Jack (J.J.C.) Smart swears by on another continent, would not, however, persuade Jack to barrack for India in the cricket match against Australia!

We are very grateful to Professor J.N. Mohanty (of Temple University, PA and Calcutta) for suggestions on how we might approach such a volume and for his own contribution, as well as his constant interest in the progress of the project.

William Jackson read an early draft of the manuscript and made very helpful suggestions towards a more accessible structuring of the essays in the way that the organization of the volume now stands. Sally Percival Wood's assistance with editing and research on gender and certain applied issues, for the chapters that now appear in Volume II, warrant an acknowledgement.

Particular mention also needs to be made of Sarah Lloyd of Ashgate Publishing for seeing the need for such a work and for her constant encouragement and help, particularly for seeing the volume through the various stages of production; Nitasha Devasar, senior publisher with Oxford University Press, New Delhi, for similar strong interest in an Indian edition so that this work could also be made available to scholars and readers in the subcontinent; the editor for Ashgate, Ann Newell, for an equally laborious task.

Closer to home, we (P.B. and on behalf of R.S.) should like also to mention Professors Max Charlesworth (the Founder-Editor of *Sophia* with his cross-cultural sensitivities in the areas of morality and religion), Peter Singer (with whom there has been long association since the days of Animal Liberation and Bioethics in Melbourne), Patrick Hutchings (a colleague and associate at the two universities in Melbourne and with *Sophia*), Shivesh Thakur (with whom studies in philosophy really started); as well as Ramchandra Gandhi, Smt Vishalakshi, Naani Indirani, Gayatri Chakravorthy Spivak, Ashis Nandy, and Dr Peter G. Smith, among others – from whom at least two of us learnt much good analytical, moral and critical thinking. Last but not least, we note Dewi and Rasa, whose canine presence intermittently provided much good company in Venus Bay (a site of the final editing), and indeed timely 'extra-human' ethical reflections.

For my part (J.P.), there are a few other people I want to mention. As already noted, this volume is largely dedicated to the memory of some of our teachers and friends, but it is also dedicated to my mother, Nellie Peris, in celebration of her ninetieth birthday. She too has watched over this volume and inquired frequently about it. But beyond that, she has been for me an exemplar of courage and responsibility. Through all the vicissitudes of a long and eventful life, she has steadily encouraged my efforts, and my work on this volume is offered to her in grossly inadequate thanks for her love and guidance. Still closer to home, I want to thank Betty Bamberg, who has been my Beatrice, leading me not through the heavens (at least not yet) but through the challenges of this life; and my daughter Tara, a Doctor of clinical psychology who will undoubtedly appreciate the psychological wisdom of the Indian traditions.

I want also to thank two great teachers of mine, who alas have passed on: Bernard Williams, who taught me philosophy in Cambridge, and John Findlay, who supervised my doctoral work in Boston. They were both remarkable men and scholars: Williams, brilliantly quick, subtle, and insightful; Findlay, a true sage, erudite, wise, and gracious. Williams's writings on ethics are justly renowned. Findlay was a *compleat* philosopher, who in addition to a commanding knowledge of Western philosophy had read widely in the Indian classics. He shared with me a long poem he had composed to the Buddha as a sixteen-year-old youth in South Africa. As it turns out, he was a senior colleague at the University of London to both Williams and Ninian Smart. We feel privileged to be part of this, as it were, *paramparā* (lineage).

I should also like to mention Alasdair Macintyre, who thankfully is still with us, and has been generous in encouraging and endorsing this work. He too was a teacher of mine in Boston and expressed great interest in this volume. In addition to his widely-admired writings on Western ethics, he has contributed significantly to the enterprise of comparative ethics. I trust he will be pleased by this work.

Thanks also go to institutions in Australia – the School of Social Inquiry and International Studies in Deakin University; the Department of Philosophy, and *Sophia* and its able staff, of the University of Melbourne, and the Monash Asia Institute – and in the US, particularly California State University at Los Angeles, which generously granted J.P. periods of leave; and the State University at Stony Brook (Center for India Studies, and Philosophy), and Columbia University, which provided P.B. facilities, support and secretarial assistance for as long as the project has been current. Science and Spirituality Research in India (SSRI – a Templeton Foundation sponsored centre in Bangalore) provided Sanskrit textual resources.

Sanmaṅgalā sarvasamaṣṭihitam,
astitvānāmanāstitvānāmca maṅgalam,
viśvaśānti maṅgalam
ānṛśaṃsya.

Wishing Wellness, Non-coercive Peace and Blessing to All Beings, and Non-Being.

General Introduction

Thinking Ethics, the West and India[1]

Human beings have long worried about how they should live, and act; often they make decisions about good and bad ways of acting; they form views about good and bad ways of living. In other words, they engage in what they consider to be worthwhile moral living, i.e. in action and ethical thinking. Or they take morality for granted, as a 'given' in their culture and religious or mythological heritage. What then is 'ethics' and the task of ethical thinking?

Now there are at least three well-worn ways of introducing ethics, which are worth revisiting before we say anything at all about Indian ethics.

First would be to begin by describing how people as active agents in a culture have gone about living a life they consider to be worthwhile, in terms of the norms, mores, moral prescriptions, rules and regulations, intuitions and emotions, they adhere to and enjoin upon other members of their community. Some account of how these variegated normative patterns hold together in a coherent whole is also suggested; this too in the larger context of cosmology, metaphysics, ideas of human nature, theology or some transcendental ontology informing their view of the moral world. It might also be asked how far does the culture cast the net of moral regard: does it stop with the individual as the principal subject, or is equal if not more weight given to a concern for the other, i.e., other persons, members of the community, the society as a whole? Do such concerns encompass or extend also to non-human species (gods, ancestors, animals, non-animate things) as deserving subjects (not simply as objects) of a morally fulfilling life? Studies by historians, religionists and anthropologists, especially of distant cultures, provide rough guidelines for such a descriptive, non-intervening, taxonomy.

A second, more detached, approach would be to trace and map the kinds of philosophical reflections thinkers in the tradition have made on the ideals and processes by which people have engaged in the prescribed or agreed-upon ethical living. What kinds of accounts can one give of their ethics, and more specifically what sorts of principles and theories have they evolved to deal with conflicts between, say, rules and practices, and certain moral dilemmas that may arise in the course of determining decisions and acting upon them, or not acting. Some reflections

1 This General Introduction was originally intended for such a volume in hand suggested by the late Prof Bimal K. Matilal in Oxford to P. Bilimoria (circa 1984); an early framework, commended by many towards encouraging the completion of this project, was published as an essay, 'Indian ethics', in Peter Singer (ed.), *A Companion to Ethics*, Oxford: Blackwell, 1992, pp. 43-57.

may have a self-critical edge too, with the intention of advancing the quest for the ethical within the confines and trajectory of the traditional framework, or different accounts thereof, without radically transforming the essentials on which this ethics is founded.

A third way would be to draw up from the writer's vantage-point what 'ethics', understood in more universal, culture-free, and paradigmatic terms would amount to, and the best theory or theories that give a persuasive account of what is good and bad, right and wrong, moral and immoral. The armchair philosopher of morals would articulate a well-constructed, internally (i.e. logically) coherent moral system, that does not bow to the contingencies of external authority, be that of mythology, tradition, religion, church, or some political ideology. Against this he examines any culture's claim to ethical thinking, with a view to evaluating the strengths and weaknesses, desirability and undesirability, of the principles and judgments, theories of good and bad, that determine choices and actions, and their consequences for practical living in the greater interest (of humankind, global world, and so on). It might then be adjudged whether there is ethics, or at least systematic thinking on ethics, worthy of the name.

Each approach has its merit; or each might turn out to be unsatisfactory in respect of what can or cannot be captured under the terms set out; the exercise might prove to be too banal and academic, as is sometimes said of the attempt to encapsulate the aesthetics, music and other art-forms of ancient and so-called primitive, perhaps even of high, cultures. The 'vocabularies' on the two sides tend to be mutually incommensurable. More technically, the difficulties besetting such approaches might rest with methodological and epistemological issues – i.e. with the methods and modes of analyses utilized and the assumptions underpinning how knowledge is obtained in this encounter, such as the proper subject of the ethical discourse. Or it might simply speak of a failure to adequately understand the plurality of the moral domain in other times and cultures from the safe distance of a theory-sensitive contemporary milieu, that takes the economy of logic and universalism more seriously as its grounding basis than the contingencies and ambivalences of lived realities. Thus the third approach especially might be rejected, or heavily qualified, as the proper task of ethical thinking, while placing more trust in the second approach supplemented with the first approach and other mitigating considerations that might be deemed relevant, for instance, in the cross-cultural context.

However, such caveats might be frowned upon as a strategy toward freezing out or foreclosing the possibility of any sustained critical appraisal and problematizing of the presumed relativity in ethical thinking (a position often dubbed as 'ethical relativism'). The question then is not just one of 'what is ethics?', but also of 'how is ethics gone about?' 'how is the ethical thinking itself justified?' 'does it get us very far, morally speaking?' And the answers can, as they have indeed evinced in philosophical inquiries, vary and be at odds with each other. The ethical enterprise, then, is replete with such disputations and disagreements.

Our objective in this Introduction (and subsequent Introductions to each Part) is to provide the reader with a set of sign-posts for studiously engaging the vast and assorted reflections on the ethical in the broad and diverse Indian tradition, from ancient times to some contemporary moments. The bare wherewithal is provided, and the reader is expected to do some at least of the groundwork. The difficulties adverted to above notwithstanding, we – along with the bulk of the contributors to this volume it would seem – are partial toward drawing a little, perhaps a fistful, from each of the three approaches, and even interacting them in the meta-philosophical forays that intersect the inquiry at various points. Inevitably this involves drawing on a comparative vocabulary and making links, where appropriate, with Western explorations of the ethical. So this latter would seem to be a congenial place to begin, again, on a somewhat different note: by way of presenting a definition and overview of 'ethics' prominent, at least, in some quarters of the academic concerns within this discipline in the West. There have been serious criticisms of even this sanguine picture; and alternative positions have been advanced, which too will be briefly noted. Later (under II below) we shall also raise and discuss the question whether this way of casting the broad parameters of ethics bears any resemblance or relevance to the ethical discourse in the Indian context; but for now this preliminary inquiry should suffice for a general orientation.

I. Thinking Ethics in the West

'*An unexamined life is not worth living*'
(Socrates)

The term 'ethics' is derived from the Greek *ethōs* via *ethikōs* (literally 'habit' or 'custom') connoting the 'usage', 'character', 'moral rules'; as a branch of philosophy it pertains to the analysis of concepts such as 'duty', 'ought', 'obligations', 'right' and 'wrong'. In other words, ethics is an inquiry into the nature of morality and its foundations, particularly the way in which human conduct is ordered, guided and appraised. The task of ethics is to give an account of the ways in which human beings ought to act, and to describe the sorts of actions that are, at any given time, morally permissible (or obligatory or justifiable, or perhaps reprehensible) to perform. Ethics also involves reflecting on and evaluating a given set of values, particularly if they are translated into action, often unselfconsciously or as a matter of 'habit'. Some moral philosophers are content simply to ponder over what it means to say that something (value or action) is 'right' or 'wrong', 'good' or 'bad', etc., and under what precise conditions it would seem justifiable to say so. That is to say, they are concerned to clarify the language or discourse of the judgments, and not to lay down what one ought or ought not to do, i.e. prescribe or proscribe action. The latter enterprise is known as meta-ethics, again, bringing conceptual clarity to the usage of moral language.

Applied ethics on the other hand, seeks the application of rules and principles discerned in ethical thinking at a practical, 'hands-on' level in situations and contexts where it is not self-evident as to what is the appropriate moral course of action to be pursued. Public ethics and bioethics would be two instances of applied ethics.

All cultures are thought to have evolved or adopted an ordered moral system and practices or set of norms to guide proper conduct and behaviour of its citizens. While often the moral insights, their origins and justifications have remained unarticulated or passed into legalistic codifications within the culture, the theories buried underneath the actual practices, the underlying assumptions and presuppositions have evaded or defied analysis. Most cultures however show some evidence of having developed some means or instruments by which there can be reflection and an on-going enquiry into both the nature of morality (in the broad sense) and the culture's own moral repertoire. Religion and theology have traditionally played this dual role, and while concerned to preserve a given moral order they have also added their own reflections, 'fine-tuning' or postscripts to the prevailing normative framework. In the West this role has largely fallen within the ambit of philosophy, although the Judeo-Christian tradition has moulded part of the West's moral history. Religion and theology have also been actively involved in the enterprise, often providing a rival background to the early Greek approaches and trajectories for the ethical life – and vice versa. Certain movements in recent times have sought to return to the ancient Greek insights (from Aristotle to the Stoics) to avert the crisis some writers, such as Foucault following Nietzsche, argue has been precipitated by the codes of Christian moralism and rationalism of the (European) Enlightenment. Be that as it may, much effort has been concentrated in philosophical theorizing to:

- inquire into the rules and principles that govern our conduct
- investigate and clarify meanings of moral terms and statements
- analyze and explain moral judgments or positions
- establish criteria and methods for validating ethical judgments
- develop ideal patterns of behaviour or rules for ethically sound praxis (e.g. virtues, principled action, practical reasoning, self-formation, care for the other) towards some greater end states (be that self-actualization, social integration, global harmony, or other-worldly salvation)

By and large the Western efforts have tended towards the construction of a rationalistic system of moral principles, and moral theorizing in contemporary philosophy has been concerned in the main with establishing an objective set of norms, i.e. a normative framework which to all intents and purposes is independent of subjectivist or individual and culture-specific values as say would be the case with a moral system based on emotions, intuitions, or subjective feelings, or historical and historicized traditions. That there might be just such a rationalistic conception of the moral order which yields a consistent set of rules and principles and basic pattern of conduct is a belief shared from the eighteenth-century German philosopher, Immanuel Kant to John Rawls closer to our time. A class of moral philosophers within this group specializes in developing a theory of moral realism, according to which it is possible to define moral terms by reference to real properties that answer to the description, i.e. in an objective realist sense. The arbitrariness and wooliness of terms such as the 'good' can be overcome by identifying in a precise way the property referred to in the context of a moral judgment. This theory is developed in part as an attempt to meet the challenges of ethical relativism that we had occasion to mention earlier, which questions whether moral judgments can be anchored in 'objective', necessary or absolute criteria independently of the mores, customs and practices of a given culture, society or civilization. Of course, not everyone who disagrees with the 'objectivist' position is by definition an ethical relativist; there may be other ways of arguing for ethical stability without falling prey to either extreme, such as in the 'inter-subjective' approach, the skeptical stance, and 'ethics without foundations or high theory' that philosophers such as Wittgenstein, Nowell-Smith, S E Toulmin,[2] John Findlay, Bernard Williams have argued for.

In any event, philosophers are painstakingly aware that a theoretical determination or position need not be matched by an appropriate practical outcome, especially in situations where such a determination or position would seem to suggest more than one course of action or outcome. Inconsistencies may arise or tensions may become manifest in a number of places; between two principles or rules; between a principle and its determination (action or higher order rule); between one determination and another; between the principle and the unexpected consequences. Alternatively, a moral action determined by a moral rule or theory may run counter to or conflict with our moral intuition or ethical conscience. To give a stock example, it is not inconceivable that a theory X would determine two sets of actions, Y and Z, as the right outcome in a given situation. Y and Z viewed separately appear to be consistent with, since derived from theory X, but between themselves they are not compatible and the theory is not able to tell us which action is to be preferred in exactly that situation requiring an ethical resolution. More concretely, imagine a large house is burning down and two individuals, a mother and a child, are trapped in different parts of the house, but due to the failure of the rescue operations equipment and the sheer force of the blaze, only one of the two individuals can be saved, or neither if an attempt is made to save both. Theory X which determines that an effort must be made under such threatening circumstances to save life, is not able to tell us which of the two individuals should be saved. Another principle – or simply 'gut feelings' which articulate no apparent motivation or reason for the choice – might need to be invoked to resolve, or dissolve, the obvious dilemma.

Take another example. A theory in respect of stealing might suggest that it is never proper to covet another person's goods, for people deprived of their possessions would suffer adversely and unfairly. Let us apply this theory in a situation where famine has struck a township which is however overrun with well-stocked supermarkets patronized for years by the townsfolk, but whose proprietors are reluctant to dispense free food. If food is not taken by force by the townsfolk then the children will starve and suffer from malnutrition, thereby increasing suffering in the community. In another reading, however, the rule against stealing is upheld as being absolute or non-negotiable. Indeed, non-coveting is looked upon as a virtue,

---

2 Stephen Toulmin, 'Is there a Fundamental Problem in Ethics?', *Australasian Journal of Philosophy*, **33** (1), May 1955, pp. 1-19.

and so the embarrassing outcome has to be borne regardless. But what considerations would determine which of the two readings you would settle for?

People are not generally aware (or made aware) of the fact that the two alternatives suggested actually appeal to two very distinct and hotly contested ethical frameworks that between them – alongside or after Aristotle's work on ethics – have perhaps carried the most influence in modern Western thinking, namely, utilitarianism (associated with the names of Jeremy Bentham and J S Mill) and deontological ethics (associated with Kant). It is worth mentioning here that there are parallels to resolving such dilemmas in similar ways in the Indian traditions as well, although the theoretical implications one derives from these may well be different to the Western analogues. There is, for example, the story (discussed by Matilal in Chapter 2) of not telling a lie that in one of his earth-bound births had Kauśika reprimanded for causing the death of an innocent deer fleeing from its predator; while in a subsequent birth telling the lie in the recurrent situation to save the fleeing deer cost him gravely the salvation he had all but earned through his stoical moral practices.

Aristotelian virtue ethics and practical wisdom

The defining moment in ethics – or the genealogy of ethics – in the West is said to have arisen with Aristotle's effort to break up philosophy (*logos*) and social matrix with traditional (Mycenenaen) forms of religious and mythical speculations (*mythos*) of the fifth and fourth centuries B C Athenian polis. He worked instead to ground thought in a practical mode of reasoning that looks for justification for our ideas of how we should live, what is good and bad action, and what is our purpose in life. Thus was born the discipline of ethics, best represented in Aristotle's opus *Nicomachean Ethics*, which presents what is taken to be the first systematic treatment of ethics in Western civilization. Here he sets out the conceptual basis for the enquiry into the 'good', 'happiness', 'end states' of human beings; in short, what it is to live a worthwhile, well-developed, all-rounded and fulfilled life. The goal of life, Aristotle argued, is in achieving all of one's potential or the flourishing of all of one's capabilities; to describe this end-state, he used the technical term '*eudaimonia*', which is often (mis)translated as 'happiness', 'pleasure', 'contentment', implying a flourishing in order to make the question of human well-being more a matter of how well a person carries out acitivities in life than how he is merely feeling as in happiness. *Eudaimonia* for Aristotle is an activity (*energeia)* of the soul, something to be sought for its own sake, an intrinsic end-in-itself. Thus Aristotle's ethics is predicated on the goodness of action, the supremacy of rational nature (beyond the animal side) of human beings and the purposive nature (*telos*) of the universe in which humans find meaning for their existence. The former is directed towards the cultivation of 'virtues' as a means of realizing human characteristics to the full and bringing out certain 'excellences' in the person. These traits, which help us discern choices and therefore determine the actions for which we each are ultimately responsible, need not be strictly matters of personal morality but occur against the background of a social and legal structure. Thus there are shared intellectual and political skills as well, which are cultivated as 'excellences' of character. Temperance, honesty in business dealings and courage in the battlefield, we might say, are virtues appropriate to our social life. Moral virtues, then, are described as dispositions toward actions (*aretē*) and emotions in accordance with judgments of practical wisdom (*phrōnēsis*): and this for him is the most important part of the ethical process. Practical wisdom endeavours to grasp principles that are more general in their application or relevance to the particular situation. It is one consequence of Aristotle's theory of ethics that an individual steer the mean between the opposite extremes of virtue and vice in practical life. Thus even unrelenting courage has to be bridled or 'capped' sometimes. In sum, Aristotle's philosophical ethics is described as 'naturalistic' since it is mostly based on certain broad, psychological and biological facts about human nature.[3]

In this regard, we might note in passing, that G E Moore criticized Aristotle for committing what is called the 'naturalistic fallacy': that is, defining one thing in terms of something else by straining the terms of the former. Thus defining moral values in terms of biology and psychology places undue strain on something that is essentially indefinable. 'Good' is another — indeed Moore's favourite — example, that lands us in just such a conceptual soup in much ethical thinking, from the ancients to the moderns. Aristotle has also been criticized, particularly by Continental philosophers (such as Kierkegaard), for placing far too much faith or emphasis on reason in the tenuous area of the ethical, without providing a separate justification for the necessity of 'rational justification' or reasoning from principles for our actions and emotions. (Imagine, he said, trying to reason out love.) Sometimes we get things right as a matter of 'luck'; at other times the accumulated wisdom of a culture might provide the beacon, without the agony of persistent reflection, on what is the best course of action in a particularly demanding situation. Ethics as among the highest achievement of Western culture has been turned into a rational anthropocentric discourse dealing with the ought, and the individual's experience of being obligated and responsible as though cast in an island where there are no other species but images of himself as the other.[4]

Another problem commonly raised with this kind of derivation in ethics is whether it is legitimate to ask in the inquiry as to what is the case, or describing how things happen or work, to then move to make an evaluation and say what one should or *ought* to do, what is to be done. Put another way, can 'ought' be derived from 'is'? Is it valid to deduce an ethical conclusion from premises containing only factual statements? Against the views of the naturalists, the intuitionists have therefore argued for the autonomy of morals, which they believe cannot be reduced to any other kind of discourse, much less a purely theoretical discourse centred on

---

3 For further discussion see, Gerard J Hughes, *Aristotle on Ethics*, Routledge Philosophy Guidebook, London: Routledge, 2001, pp. 41-45.

4 Alphonso Lingis, 'The Immoralist', Edith Wyschogrod and Gerald P. McKenny (eds), *The Ethical*, Oxford, Blackwell, 2003, pp. 197-217 ; see also Edit Wyschogrod (ed.), *Emmanuel Levinas The Problem of Ethical Metaphysics,* New York: Fordham University Press, 2003. p. 198.

logic. Although Kant also raised the same problem concerning the 'ought/is' or 'fact-value' distinction, he would not side with the intuitionists in rejecting logic out of the ethical court. Another outcome of this rejection of the 'fact-value' distinction, which again Kant insisted upon, is that the individual human being should not be looked upon as just a means but as an *end* in his or her own right; and that human life is not reducible to just a set of *facts* from or toward which we tailor certain moral behaviour and laws to keep the order in some balance, but that there is a defined purpose, a *telos*, a higher end or greater good that life moves us towards. And so we move to discuss Kant.

Kantian deontological ethics

Kant's two passions were to explain nature and to explicate the laws of morality. In this pursuit he wrote the most influential works in Western philosophy in the post-Enlightenment period. In his search for the grounds of validity for morality he rejected empirical data such as human desires or inclinations, as these vary from individual to individual. (In other words, he moved the domain of ethics away from Aristotle's 'naturalistic' framework.) Instead, Kant looked to the purely rational nature which is universal in all human beings, although he called it 'practical reason', simply because it deals with the world of practical living and our actions. More significantly, Kant finds the validity of moral precepts in their universalizability and necessity, i.e. a moral principle must be such that it can be willed without inconsistency that all rational agents should act upon it. The test of consistency as the core of fundamental moral law is called the 'categorical imperative'. Since it is the best that reason can come up with, it is binding on human beings. It is in conformity with this principle or maxim that we determine our duties and obligations. As such one acts in conformity with and out of regard for the 'law' and not out of desire or expectation of rewards or with regards to the consequences of the actions.

This is the trust of what is often called the 'deontological' position in ethics identified with Kant. Some have argued for its parallel in the *Bhagavadgītā*'s teaching of 'duty for *dharma's* sake' without regards to the fruits thereof; however, the basis and presuppositions of the two positions are radically divergent and perhaps even mutually contradictory.[5]

Utilitarianism

John Stuart Mill, an early nineteenth century English philosopher, is associated with the principles of utility formulated by Jeremy Bentham and his father James S. Mill (who, incidentally, wrote a manual on the 'History of India' for East India Company officials). John Mills extends this principle to the domain of ethics and economics. According to utilitarian ethics, since as a universal fact human beings favour pleasure

---

5 See discussion in Mohanty (Chapter 1 that follows), Part I (III-V); see also note 41 below for reference to Bilimoria & Hutchings on 'Kant and the *Gītā*'.

over pain, the best system of morality is one that seeks to maximize pleasure for the greatest number of its citizens (in formulaic terms: the principle of greatest good for the greatest number). How one goes about measuring and balancing pleasure (or happiness) and pain (or suffering) is a vexed question, but most utilitarians have been content to extend the theory in practical dealings and life on a calculus based variously on interest, desired goals, preferences or choice of goods deemed necessary for sustaining an individual or social group.

This turn in ethics has moved past the erstwhile concerns over the 'fact-value' distinction. A simple example of the latter would be making a rule or mandatory injunction of carrying a lethal weapon whenever there is a seeming threat in the environment to one's life. One might instead concern oneself with the consequences of carrying a lethal weapon and its potential or accidental misuse, or look at other ways of dealing with the perceived threat, perhaps through some non-violent means. The question of individual agency, responsibility and the intrinsic worth of the action with an eye to the consequences become crucial considerations.[6]

There are different forms of utilitarianism today, some more sophisticated and extensive (or expansive in terms of their spheres of moral concern) than the classical version we have outlined here. For instance, negative utilitarianism has the explicit aim of seeking to minimize pain and suffering among sentient creatures for the greater good; it may not place animals and plants above human beings, or even ahead of the future generation of one community, but it will attempt to strike a balance between undue pain and suffering brought upon by human intervention – for example, with caged and battery-farmed animals – serving merely selfish human consumption drives. Vegetarianism might be one consequence of such an ethical stance; and this has been a popular move in recent times (where new-found commitment to vegetarianism is also unwittingly a conversion to negative utilitarianism). Utilitarianism itself is one of the forms of a broader ethical theory called Consequentialism, and there are again a variety of consequentialisms (an extensive discussion of which we shall encounter in de Silva's chapter on Buddhist ethics). The appeal of consequentialism in areas of applied ethics, such as bioethics should be apparent. Our purpose in mentioning these theories here is to alert our readers that contemporary discussions of aspects of Indian ethics – indeed of colonial Indian history and modern liberalism more widely – cannot avoid but make reference to these dominant paradigms, along with Aristotelian and Kantian ethics. And hence some familiarity with these predominant theories will be helpful for the novice in either of the two traditions in dialogue here.

Natural Law Tradition

All three moral systems considered so far hold that rationality is necessary in order to achieve what ought to be the outcome of ethical actions – happiness, duty,

6 For critical discussion see, J J C Smart and Bernard Williams, *Utilitarianism and Beyond: For and Against*, Cambridge: Cambridge University Press, 1973.

welfare, the greatest good of the greatest number. But whether the longing for these things and the reasons or rational justifications we supply for them actually serve to augment well-being, welfare, talent in effecting an action, or love, are questions that still remain open to debate.[7] One departure from this approach, but equally weighted towards the rational project, is to be found in the so-called Natural Law tradition, which we shall discuss briefly now. This theory in part goes back to the early Greeks who understood that everything had its own nature (*phusis*), and that the nature of each thing endured in a way that no thing endured, since the gods shaped the world according to this ideas or forms (in the sense in which Plato spoke of in his work, *Timaeus*).[8] The nature of each thing then came to be understood as its *logos*, and the various *logos* could properly be apprehended by thought. The Stoics believed that 'all processes are governed by cosmic reason (*logos*) and that law (*nomos*) is what this universal rational principle dictates concerning the spheres of human activity,' and so is no longer a matter for practices established in a society, whether positive law or customs.[9]

This belief was taken up into the medieval Christian tradition which interpreted natural law as the set of rules promulgated by God to mankind and revealed in conscience. Given God's design and the nature of things, an action is good because it is fitting. Conformity to God's moral law is a natural motivation underpinning meritorious actions, claimed St Augustine. For Aquinas, influenced by Aristotle, a law-like character of natural law which is in accord with human nature is so because it is 'an ordinance of reason for the common good,' and since the 'rule and measure of human acts is the reason.'[10] One implication of this theory is that goods can be derived from theoretical and practical reason prior to considerations of human activity and its consequences. Recent thinkers have attempted to extend the natural law doctrine to provide non-normative foundations for moral theory; that is to say, utilize practical reason to identify the goods of a human life prior to the invocation of any moral or normative notions.[11] Despite this flexibility a basic problem haunts the doctrine, which as Buckle notes, lies in translating 'abstract claims about the existence of natural law, rational solutions to questions of proper governance of human conduct into usefully specific practical rules or maxims… what does natural law imply in practice?'[12]

Two things are to be kept in mind at this point of the discussion. One is that ethics can be a highly abstract, ahistorical and meta-critical or a meta-narrative

---

7 See Lingis, op cit, p 204.

8 Jacques Maritain, *Natural Law Reflections on Theory and Practice,* ed. with Introduction by William Sweet, South Bend, Indiana: St Augustine's Press, 2001, pp. 14-17.

9 John Haldane, 'Medieval and Renaissance ethics', in Peter Singer (ed.), *A Companion to Ethics,* Oxford: Blackwell, pp. 133-146, p. 137. (See also next note.)

10 Cited in Stephen Buckle, 'Natural Law', in *A Companion to Ethics*, p. 165.

11 In the work, for example, of Germain Grisez, Joseph Boyle, and John Finn, for which see Ian Gold 'Does Natural Law Have Non-normative Foundations?', in *Sophia*, **41** (1), May 2002, pp. 1-18.

12 Op cit, p. 166.

pursuit inasmuch as the concerns remain within, as it were, the bounds of theory and are expressed in the form of stories about the motivation or reasons why someone has thought doing 'x' was right and doing 'y' was wrong, or vice versa, and such considerations as might change one's thinking about the theory or presuppositions involved. One could think of hermeneutics or jurisprudence as an apt analogy. Secondly, ethics can also become a very practical concern, grounded in day-to-day dilemmas that demand close attention to the lived context and conditions through which moral thinking *per force* proceeds or through which it *ought* to proceed, for otherwise the consequences would be too onerous and no theory could be summoned up for rescue. One then discovers and tests principles, rules, and the stories themselves about how one should, would or might be cautioned against doing x or y. The *Mahābhārata* in the Indian tradition and the *Book of Job* in the Judeo-Christian tradition are good examples of the latter.

Furthermore, it would appear that two developments have helped put ethics, as it were, firmly back on the map in recent times: the revival of classical moral thinking (including a whole new approach to reading Aristotelian ethics, virtue ethics, stoicism, and Kant's moral and aesthetic critiques) and, more significantly, the forays made into the broader academe from the side of applied or practical ethics that have taken upon its mantel wider ethical confrontations, ranging from the more mundanely practical spheres of human treatment of animals to bioethical dilemmas (i.e. advancement of medical technology impacting on the life-processes of the fetus, the mother, the severely disabled, and the incapacitated elderly, a process which in recent times has spawned much differently nuanced debates on abortion, euthanasia, mercy-terminations, rights of patients, ethical responsibilities of the treating professions, codes of professional ethic, and so on). Then, of course, there are the areas of ecological and environmental challenges, business-commerce developmental strategies, discrimination, gender and minority treatment, and most recently cyber-sensibility issues (e.g. unsecured access to virtual pornography), on which moral philosophers have had quite a bit to say, at least in way of clarifying what it would *mean* to say when something is right and when something is wrong, without necessarily pronouncing their own judgments on these issues. A good example of such an influential theorizing is evident in the now-popular gospel on 'Animal Liberation' by the Australian moral philosopher Peter Singer (now relocated to Princeton) who in recent years has gone on to artfully tackle, in very practical and accessible terms, some of our century's most difficult and daunting bioethical challenges, which centre around the prolonged suffering of the elderly or terminally ill, disabled infants, genetic reproductive technologies, responsible living, ecological and environmental degradation, developmental iniquities across the first and third worlds, and other such global concerns.

Does Ethics have to extricate itself from history and religion?

A question that hovers over all the different permutations that have gone on in the field of ethics is in a way of a more fundamental nature, namely: Is there a fixed, transcendentalized understanding or foundational system of ethics *per se*? In other words: Is it possible to conceive of an ethics that neatly crosses the boundaries of histories and cultures and intra-religious developments, and which radically places itself at a safe remove or distance from all historical genealogy of the moral discourse anywhere and everywhere? Is such a grounding of ethics affordable and possible? This is considered by some philosophers to be the first question of philosophy proper, before its application – or *practicum* – to the wide range of human phenomena can become a serious concern. This question took on a particular force with the rise of modernity. The medieval philosophers developed but also transformed most of the moral thinking they had inherited from the ancients; and all this was to be rapidly overhauled within a two hundred year period with the advent of the Enlightenment in Europe, especially in the hands of thinkers such as Rousseau, Locke, Hume, Kant and the Mills. Few philosophers after the Enlightenment have thought of looking to mysticism for a source or origins of ethics, except for 'compatabilist' theories such as the Divine Command Theories, that attempt to reconcile theistic beliefs with intuitions about morality and God's goodness in these matters.[13] In fact, moral thinking in modern times has remained dominated in one form or another (either in articulation or in terms of the responses made to this) by one or the other major strands of an Enlightenment-driven agenda of freeing ethics from its erstwhile theological and ecclesiastical involvement and making it more responsive to the well-being of individuals and the community within a determined set of human goals or goods.

This has been a hallmark of modernity where the question of the highest good or well-being of the individual and community to be attained is – as we have severally noted – settled by *reason* and not by faith or some order of monastic isolation as the means by which the ultimate limits could be realized. One might call this moral realism. Since individuals live and grow in a more complex system of relations with other human creatures, notions such as virtue, social ethic, pleasure, harm, love, sympathy, civil entitlement, privilege, and so on, emerge as the touchstones of such an ethics now separated from its mystical idealism and theological dimensions. Which is of course not to say that the two approaches – reason and mysticism – cannot be compatible or made to interact, but this emerges usually as an after-thought or as a result of reform within a threatened paradigm, as when the Thomists and scholasticism of medieval Christendom responded to the dominance of ecclesiastical morality of the 'Dark Ages'; or, in the Indian subcontinent, when the Buddha, Jaina's Mahāvīra and the *Mahābhārata* reacted to an outworn Brāhmaṇical sacrificial ethics.

In between there were revivals of even more unsettling varieties of ethical positions, ranging from the revival of the austere asceticism of the Stoics (which Foucault in his later work tended towards), to ethical hedonism (based on Epicurean

13 See Mary Midgley, 'The origin of ethics', and also Jonathan Berg, 'How could ethics depend on religion?', (both) in *A Companion to Ethics*, pp. 3-13, and pp. 525-33; Midgley claims that Christianity, by postulating God as the source of the 'Law' or ethics, simply postponed the problem rather than resolved it. By making God the highest value gets us no further.

and Phyrronic tendencies of living for the pleasures of the day), altruism (doing good to others), free-willing egoism (self-interested freedom), its rivals in determinism (mechanistic pre-set behavioural causes), pessimism, transcendentalism, to naturalism (drawing from Natural Law and the rise of Social Darwinism).[14] The controversies and alternative approaches that arose within the individualist-sensitive ethics of what could still be called the modern period in the Anglo-European landscape introduced positions and shifts of often incommensurable kinds. It created problems and tensions between traditional or pre-modern patterns of thinking ethics and modernity's appeal to a set of terms that takes the rational individual as its starting point and shuns the metaphysical web of a bygone era. If the sacrificial trope was the burden of being gods (or like-unto God) and moral responsibility the burden of being human or 'natural,' what would be the burden of being post-rational? Was this sort of question already anticipated at the dawn of the Enlightenment?

However, even within the Enlightenment paradigm itself there were clashes and conflicts or oscillations between different views on ethics. For instance, the more psychologically-attuned theory of moral sentiments formulated by David Hume and Adam Smith clashed with the calculative ethics of utilitarianism. The latter claimed to be much more rational and community-sensitive, measured in a practice that succeeds in delivering the greatest possible happiness for the greatest number. Kant, as we saw, had dealt a severe blow on much of the pre-modern thinking by developing a moral system that steered clear of the above two alternatives by insisting that the morality of an action is to be judged not by its consequences (although these may have a bearing on the decision) but on how well disposed one is towards carrying out the duty incumbent upon one. Now Kant's deontological ethics remains in its numerous incarnations in late modernity the major rival to utilitarianism. Nonetheless, both these dominant paradigms have come under heavy attack from more liberal moral thinkers, such as Bernard Williams, Robert Nozick and Thomas Nagel, and in the revived (Aristotelian-Thomistic) virtue ethics pioneered by Alaisdair MacIntyre.[15] Shifting the focus cross-culturally, at one time it was Kant's deontological ethics that was held up as the beacon for the Eastern perspective on ethics, for which the *Bhagavadgītā* was promoted, first by German idealists and later by Indian thinkers, such as Aurobindo, Tilak, Gandhi and Radhakrishnan.

A third player, as it were, in this field is postmodernism, which in turn questions modernity's self-assured faith in its own terms of grounding ethics, be that ground reason, propositional statements, scientific realism with a human face, or analysis and argumentation. The alternative model of postmodern ethics is brought out most poignantly in the work of Emmanuel Levinas, who develops his own 'phenomenology of alterity' (which we shall come to later).

---

14 For an introductory discussion of these varieties of ethical approaches and some problems within them, see other articles in Singer (ed.), *A Companion to Ethics*.

15 See his, *After Virtue, A Study in Moral Theory*, London: Duckworth, 1981 (revised 1985).

Postcolonial theory for its part questions the legacy of imperialism and colonialism in the ruthless political systems imposed on other cultures, as well as the destruction of indigenous resources for self-understanding, transformative perceptions and moral economy.[16] Postmodernism (along with feminism, a/theology and postcolonial theory) might even permit a recall or retrieval of some aspects of the pre-modern insights and wisdom in such deliberations, leaving certain inquiries open-ended without the kind of *foreclosure* one tends to see forced upon by modernity's haste. We need not fear the anxieties of relativism and alleged post-modernist ethical anarchism in asking deeper questions, for it may indeed be possible to settle provisionally on one theory of ethics over others, at a particular point in time, if we are prepared to provide adequate reasons and arguments for such a determination. This has been the experience in India's long history. A complete account of ethics is neither necessary nor possible at this stage in world scholarship, short of noting resemblances, points of agreement and mutual reinforcements on certain basic virtues and values across the wide tapestry of ethical thinking anywhere. Does any tradition, for instance, deny universal love, unabashedly valorize baseless killing of living creatures, withdraw compassion and sympathy for the suffering, afflicted and dead, and so on? Even the most difficult moral situations have been thought about, quite often resolved in practical ways, and returned to time and again for further reflections with remarkable degrees of convergence on at least what the basic issues are across traditions and cultures.

In other words, ethical insights can arise from a number of different quarters, and they need not be confined to one or the other tradition of moral thinking preceding or contemporaneous with an ethicist. Whatever the source of the insights or ethical intuition, one must be able to articulate, argue, defend with good reason and be reflexive about one's presupposition, position, and judgments without betraying the dogmatism that was so characteristic of by-gone authorities or ethical priests (and their current versions in some quarters or cultures). But this is not necessarily the view held in the Indic tradition, nor unanimously accepted by all the contributors to this volume, the editors among them included.

Thus the debates and what might likely count as ethics in the rest of the new millennium is more than likely to be radically transformed.

II. Thinking Ethics from the *topoi* of India

Given the kinds of ethics or the ethical terrain we have considered in I. above, representing the predominant patterns of thinking on 'ethics' in the West, when we move to the Indian context, the following scenario comes naturally to mind. When intellectuals in India, or scholars working on Indian thought, come together to talk about ethics in the Indian tradition, they ask questions such as: 'Has there ever been 'ethics' in India?' 'Can one meaningfully speak of '*Indian ethics*'?' 'Isn't the idea of

16 See, Gayatri Chakravorty Spivak, *Critique of Postcolonial Reason Toward A History of the Vanishing Present*, Cambridge/London: Harvard University Press, 1999.

'*ethics*' itself a Western invention – like anthropology?' Others may ask: Is there a formal discipline within Indian thought which has an 'internally consistent rational system in which patterns of human conduct are justified with reference to ultimate norms and values?'[17] Or, alternatively, it will be questioned whether the Indian preoccupation with mysticism, and its supposedly 'life-denying' theology, rules out altogether the condition for the possibility of ethics, suggesting that morality in India is so inextricably founded on religious belief and imperatives, that there can be no space for a rationally grounded ethical tradition. Perhaps too, its excessive concern with metaphysics might be thought to deflect away from the proper work of moral philosophical thinking, as indeed of reason and emotion. However, the early twentieth century doyen of Indian and Comparative Philosophy, Sir Sarvepalli Radhakrishnan, did not think there was anything excessive about looking for theological and metaphysical grounds for ethics. He wrote: 'Any ethical theory must be grounded in metaphysics, in a philosophical concept of the relation between conduct and the ultimate reality. As we think the ultimate reality to be, so we behave; vision and action go together.'[18]

In this context, Saral Jhingran invokes Kant on the inexorability of certain unproven ontological beliefs regarding the world (immortality, freedom, and sublime providence), in defending the close relation between the study of Hindu metaphysics ('religio-philosophy') and the domain of ethics: 'man's metaphysical beliefs do seem to condition his entire approach to life and conduct'.[19] But Radhakrishnan and his defenders might appear to some critics to be a trifle apologetic about the virtues of the Indian moral tradition, underscoring a sort of universality about ethics: 'ours is as good as yours';[20] or a tendency that Spivak elsewhere calls 'civilizationalism'.[21]

---

17 Cited in *Bibliographical Guide to the Comparative Study of Ethics,* John Carmen and Mark Juergensmeyer (eds), Cambridge: Cambridge University Press, 1991. p. 12; for a more balanced account, cf. P V Kane, *History of Dharmaśāstra* vol. 2, part 1, pp. 3-11, Poona: Bhandarkar Oriental Research institute, 1974, and Bernard Williams, *Ethics and the Limits of Philosophy*, Cambridge, MA: Harvard University Press, 1985.

18 S. Radhakrishnan, *Eastern Religions and Western Thought*, London: Allen & Unwin, 1958, p. 80.

For similar early works in Hindu ethics (against charges of its complete absence, or world-denying tendencies, lack of theory of social cohesiveness, and so on), see discussion in Patton's chapter (4) in Part A (*circa* third page).

19 Saral Jhingran, *Aspects of Hindu Morality*, Delhi: Motilal Banarsidass, 1988, pp. 1-2; she refers to the supplement to the Second Critique: *Groundwork of the Metaphysic of Morals*, although ostensibly Kant's theory of ethics is based only on reason and acceptable *a priori* principles.

20 Austin B. Creel, 'The Modern Study of Hindu Ethics', chapter in his *Dharma in Hindu Ethics*, Columbia: South Asia Books, 1977; see also Creel, '*Dharma* as an Ethical Category Relating to Freedom and Responsibility', *Philosophy East and West*, **22** (1972). pp. 155-68.

21 Spivak's 'Response' to Panel Discussion on this work, in *Interventions International Journal of Postcolonial Studies*, London: Francis & Taylor, **4** (2), 2002, pp. 205-211.

Spinoza might side with Radhakrishnan, at least in John Findlay's reading. However, other modern Indian thinkers have raised doubts over this visceral view, wondering whether this traditionally presupposed linkage has paid off in realistic terms. The late Bimal Krishna Matilal articulated the conundrum rather perspicuously:

> Certainly, there exists a lacuna in the tradition of Indian philosophy. Professional philosophers of India over the last two thousand years have been consistently concerned with the problems of logic and epistemology, metaphysics and soteriology, and sometimes they have made very important contributions to the global heritage of philosophy. But, except [for] some cursory comments and some insightful observations, the professional philosophers of India very seldom discussed what we call moral philosophy today. It is true that the *dharmaśāstra* texts were there to supplement the Hindu discussion of ethics, classification of virtues and vices, and enumeration of duties related to the social status of the individual. But morality was never discussed as such in these texts. On the other hand, the tradition was very self-conscious about moral values, moral conflicts and dilemmas, as well as about the difficulties of what we call practical reason or practical wisdom'.[22]

The world might present other challenges that do not fall easily within the provenance of a neatly-articulated moral philosophy (as Weber discerned); or it might be inherently morally ambiguous, as Wittgenstein worried; or maybe we can't speak of ethics after the 'failure of morality' as Levinas would put it.[23] But scholars will proceed regardless, dilating on the 'supreme ethic', for example, of the *Bhagavadgītā* or the eight-fold path in the *sīla* teachings of the Buddha (although there are those argue that *sīla*, although of moral import, does not pair off with our (Western) words 'ethics'or 'morality').[24] Or as Matilal tends to do himself, agonize over the exemplary moral dilemmas presented in narrative literature, particularly the epic *Mahābhārata*, and suggesting how there was always a rational solution around the corner or possibly missed, even by Krishna. Matilal was airing the suspicion that Indian philosophy, particularly during what he calls the Indian Middle Ages, did not break away sufficiently from preoccupations with theology and mysticism, and that without 'logic' any branch of philosophy is bound to flounder at its core. The Epics embed and exemplify a myriad of moral issues which are thought through rationally; but the Epics no more than the tradition at large, quite succeeded in articulating a *sui generis* thesis that we would call 'ethics' or 'morality', without their own cultural, theological and historical overtones and baggage.

---

22 Bimal K. Matilal, 'Moral Dilemmas: Insights from Indian Epics', *Philosophy, Culture and Religion Collected Papers of B K Matilal*, ed. J. Ganeri , vol. I. *Ethics and Epics*, Delhi: Oxford University Press, 2000, p. 21.

23 For Weber, see Pratap Bhanu Mehta's chapter (17) in Part C; Levinas makes this judgment in the context of the aftermath of the Holocaust, but we believe it is generalizable to the larger discursive context, for which also see Bernard Williams in his Preface to *Morality An Introduction to Ethics*, Cambridge: Cambridge University Press, 1972.

24 See David E. Cooper and Simon P. James, *Buddhism, Virtue and Environment*, Aldershot: Ashgate Publishing Ltd, 2005, p. 47.

Despite the reservations expressed, these gestures nonetheless are welcome as they are also indicative of the ethical reflections that have proceeded in the tradition. And this is what we have set out to demonstrate in this volume, the salient features of which may be outlined with several qualifications and caveats – as we shall now do in the remainder of this Introduction and continue in the Introductions to each Part.

There is no gainsaying that the Indian tradition had concerned itself with a quest for the 'morally good life' and the attendant principles, laws, rules, etc. that might help achieve this goal. Its thinkers may not, of course, have gone much further than describing or codifying the prevailing and dominant 'ethos', mores, customs and habitual traditions – that is to say, giving expression to what in Sanskrit is termed '*dharma*', very roughly, the social and moral order.

Nevertheless, the questions cited earlier do advert to one issue – namely, the difficulty of locating within the Indian tradition the sort of ahistorical, abstract and formalistic theorizing in ethics that we have become accustomed to in Western philosophical circles, from an ethics based purely on natural law (God's Reason) and Kant's project to construct a pure moral philosophy based solely on principles of reason and not on particular facts about human beings or human history. But it is not unreasonable to suppose that a group of people somewhere could come to believe that morality *has* an important place within human life and that it commands a particular primacy wielding an authority that – if not absolute and *sui generis* – is at least 'architectonic'.[25]

Hence, Indian thinkers, like their counterparts elsewhere, recognized morality's pervasiveness throughout human life and culture, and did not shy away from inquiry into the nature of morality, of 'right' and 'wrong' or 'good' and 'bad'. Reflecting upon the meanings or applications of these judgments has been their way of putting theory, if *theory* it is, into practice. In much Indian philosophy, one does not start with discursive, critical theory, or theoretical reflection on first principles, axiomatic propositions, intuition, emotive judgments, and so on. Rather one begins with the practices that are embedded or grounded in all human cognitive and, perhaps, aesthetic efforts. Over time these practices may come to be embodied in a tradition, in comprehensive doctrines, or articulated in texts foreshadowed by, and prefiguring, other texts. They do not ask questions about their own beginnings – historical or conceptual.[26] The subsequent hermeneutic and critical exegesis of these practices via texts, may yield interpretations, protocols or laws in the sense of practical wisdom (akin to Aristotle's *phrōnēsis*), but not in the sense of *theoria* or purely discursive judgment as, for example, in Kant's prolegomenon for all future thinking on science

25 As Aristotle argued, see, Robert B. Louden, *Morality and Moral Theory, A Appraisal and Reaffirmation*, NY/Oxford: Oxford University Press, 1992, p.4; P. Bilimoria, *Ethics – The Philosophical Tradition*, A Guide for Medical Ethics, Community Medicine, Clayton: Monash University,1994; Some discussions also in: P. Bilimoria, 'Ethics of Emotion : Some Indian Reflections', in Roger Ames and Joel Marks (eds), *Emotions in Asian Thought A Dialogue in Comparative Philosophy,* Albany: SUNY Press, 1995, pp. 65-84.

26 See J.N. Mohanty, 'Theory and Practice in Indian Philosophy', *Australasian Journal of Philosophy*. **73** (1), March 1995, pp. 1-12, p. 8.

and morality. In the latter case, detached thinking about morality – as on Science and Logic – seems to be more important than *living* precariously by the rules and principles one believes in, or which are part of the community's repertoire into which an individual has been born, educated and raised. One does not live by *theory* alone, if one lives by theory at all. Spinoza reminded the West of its first 'calling' to Ethics in this regard and his method was not one dictated by science but by the human imaginary of natural reason and the full range of human interests, desires, feelings and passions. More recently Levinas has argued for the primacy of ethics over ontology, ethics seen as a concrete response to the other.

On the other hand, it could be argued that there are 'pure' theories embedded deeply within the very practices that tradition, as a vehicle, helps to transmit across a range of time and collectives. It was left, however, to the *darśanas*, the reflective philosophical systems and Indian *philosophes* (orthodox and heterodox), to unearth the theoretical insights and, with a modicum of arguments, bring them to the expressive surface, while also delineating the practical path that would yield the goal discerned. Thus for instance, the ultimate ends of a 'good life' and 'spiritual freedom', generally considered, are already inscribed in the scriptural texts. A second-order hermeneutic theory, much like jurisprudential interpretation, is suggestively developed for an 'archeology' of the texts. The theory is then considered for its wider application in particular cases. Professor Mohanty reminds us, however, that '*the applicability itself is a matter of second-level theory*'[27] supposing that the first-order theory bears an analogue to *sui generis* discursive judgments, axioms, first propositions, and so on. However, the broad consensus in contemporary Indian thinking is that such a purely theoretical position in respect of the Indian ethical tradition is untenable. Professor Mohanty, in his inimitable way, champions this attack – in respect, not of the second-level theory, but of the first-order theory, *theoria* per se.

The disagreements over the primacy of theory over practice, or of practice over theory notwithstanding, the dialectic is undoubtedly important and it is this tension that will foreground the remainder of this Introduction. Following, there will be a short discussion of the structure of the present compendium and what it hopes to achieve.

In light of the foregoing, we are left with the conundrum: How has the Indian tradition responded to questions considered to be of primary concern in contemporary ethical inquiries? Namely: (a) the conception and presuppositions underpinning the system of ethics advanced or its analogue; (b) its origin or source and how it developed; (c) the standards or criteria of right conduct proposed and their justification; (d) ways in which the 'entropy effect' or wearing down of traditional values and inscriptions have been addressed; (e) prospects for revisions or reforms to rectify perceived deficiencies; and (f) practical realizations of capabilities of participating citizens, and the flourishing of community.

As with any other major civilization whose roots recede into antiquity, one can naturally expect there to be a variety and diversity of ethical systems within

27 Ibid.

the Indian tradition. To cover all of these positions would be an impossible task. Even to speak of an 'Indian tradition' is to loosely identify an incredibly diversified congeries of social, cultural, religious and philosophical systems, and appropriations from the hoary Vedas, through Jaina and Buddhist tracts, to colonial, post-colonial and feminist responses to the earlier traditions. And they have each changed over time. The present volume attempts to expose at best a few of the systems that have informed Indian ethical discourse slanted towards the kind of questions which might interest a modern philosopher. Before we move to the chapters proper treating of such systems and issues, some further conceptual preliminaries would seem to be in order.

III. The terms of ethics reconsidered

Terms and concepts are not static entities encapsulated by fixed, unchanging meanings. The notion of ethics in India has undergone significant shifts in meaning and emphasis over the long history of Indian philosophical speculation. The same is true in the history of Western ethics. Thus, Henry Sidgwick in his *Method of Ethics* sharply distinguishes between classical and modern moral philosophy.

The chief characteristics of ancient (Greek and Roman) ethical controversy, as distinguished from modern, may be traced to the employment of a generic notion (of good), instead of a specific one such as rightness in expressing the communal moral judgments on action. Right action is commonly regarded by the Greeks as only a species of the Good and – the first question – when we endeavor to systematize conduct is how to determine the relation of this species of the good to the rest of the genus.

As writers such as Alasdair MacIntyre and Bernard Williams have reiterated, the very concept of ethics, 'ethos' deriving from the Greek '*ethikē*' which means character, has more to do with various features of human excellence than with the modern preoccupation with rules governing right actions or rights and obligations.

It is important to start with terminological and historical remarks because the understandable tendency in Western discussions of Indian ethics is to start positivistically with an unthematized notion of ethics slanted towards its own, specifically modern, usages and then to assess Indian ethics in terms of its meanings and normative criteria. Thus, in modern Western ethics, the term ethics is used to cover: (1) reflection on the bases and justifications of moral guidelines (normative ethics) and on the meaning of moral terms like 'right' or 'good' or 'obligation' (metaethics); (2) specific moral guidelines in different areas of life, both professional and quotidian (applied ethics); and (3) how people actually behave (descriptive ethics).

Given these norms and standards, there are usually two summary judgments made by Western or Western-oriented commentators on Indian ethics: (a) that it consists primarily of descriptive and applied ethics, and perhaps normative ethics, but that is largely lacking in metaethics, and (b) given that Indian notions of ethics cover such a large variety of different phenomena, from ritual obligations and social custom to religious sacrifice and positive law, it is difficult to extract much from this morass that is distinctively ethical in the modern Western sense. The ahistoricity and ethnocentrism of such judgments should be obvious.

At the other end of the scale are those philological and textual scholars, who are careful to point out the linguistic and conceptual nuances of terms and ideas, and who occasionally reconstruct the specific contexts that underlie such notions. This is obviously very important work, not only for clarifying the provenance and semantic density of certain ethical expressions, but also for indicating how different such expressions are in meaning and significance from what look like similar terms in Western ethical discourse. But while overcoming ethnocentrism, such approaches by themselves do not do much to further philosophical activity, given that for the most part they simply describe rather than analyze or evaluate linguistic expressions.

It is clear, therefore, that what is needed is a fully-fledged hermeneutic approach that: (1) pays attention to philological details and historical-cultural contexts in which concepts and categories are situated; (2) attempts to analyze such concepts and underlying contexts in terms of an endogenous philosophical discourse; and then (3) tries to mediate and build bridges between Indian ethical discourse reconstructed on its own terms to correspond with Western ethical discussion. The value of such an approach is that it might yield interesting similarities and differences between the two philosophical traditions.

Simply looking at, or *for*, Indian ethics from the perspective of contemporary Western philosophy, as analytic philosophers are prone to do, reduces it to a species of Western philosophy with Indian examples. One recent effort that understandably grew skeptical as it progressed, set out unselfconsciously to map what the author perceived to be the basic essentials of 'Ethics'. But these were more like text-book entries in Western ethics cleverly re-drawn to represent an apparently non-foundationalist logic of (European) Enlightenment connections between the standard topics of virtues, utility, deontological, self- and other-regarding equity-based ideas of justice, moral realism and so on, without regard to the deeper textual narratives or sources and contexts within the Indian traditions. Not only does this sort of exercise distort the Indian traditions by fitting them willy-nilly within an alien, impersonal logic or an apparently comprehensive template, but what is as serious, it deprives philosophy in the West of new possibilities suggested by alternative modes of ethical theorizing. Such efforts at mapping even bypass the salient and powerful alternatives from within the larger Western or European critical tradition itself – e.g. contemporary Continental moral discourse in Habermas, Derrida, Irigaray and Foucault, and Levinas who we discuss at some length under *Postmodern ethics* (on p. 22).

Suppose one were to set up, without much argument as to their universality (actual or desirable), an ethics – 'as ethics *should* be'– on the primacy of *dharma, karma, svadharma, karuṇa and nyāya*, etc., and proceeded to look for these in analytical Western ethics? (A reductive move once proposed by the late Ninian

Smart: so '*Dharma* is ethics, and *ethics* dharma' or 'Dharma as Justice'[28]) There would not be much left of Western, especially modern, ethics; and all the worse for the impasse! Conversely, just pointing out the differentia without further analysis of the philosophical reasons for such differences ends up setting one system against another without any dialogue, actual or imputed, between the two traditions. These issues of meta-philosophical claims, the impasse, the economy and limits of ethics, and reverse judgments on what might or might not conceivably pass off as 'Indian ethics', even by those who wish to doubt the very possibility (but remain comfortable writing smaller commentaries on 'Morals and Mysticism'[29] or 'Hindu Ethics[30])', are discussed in more practical and applied contexts in the Introductions to each Part; and each essay in its own way addresses this issue; or on which the authors speak for themselves.

For example, the question arises in the context of cross-cultural Environmental ethics: If Indian philosophy does not have a theory and practice called 'Ethics', normative or otherwise than as 'first philosophy', and if the requirement that the application of moral beliefs logically cohere to the truth of certain factual beliefs it presupposes is flaunted,[31] how are we then to make sense of any claims on the part of the tradition that there is a viable theory of environmental moral philosophy, ecology, animal rights (*paśvadhikāra*), natural law, and so on?

---

28 See his Introduction with Shivesh Thakur in their (eds), *Ethical and Political Dilemmas of Modern India* (see References at the end). But Smart as anyone else would have been all too aware that only the Hindu Right would be capable of insisting on this complete symmetry, or isomorphism without qualification. '*Dharma* as Justice' is roughly taken from the title of paper by Austin Creel, presented at the Sixth East-West Philosophers' Conference in Honolulu, 1984.

29 For an example of such an evocation of Orientalism in Moses Halls of Philosophy, see Arthur C. Danto, *Morals and Mysticism and Morality – Oriental Thought and Moral Philosophy*, NY: Basic Books, 1972. There have been numerous refutations of Danto; it is almost an old hat. Frits Staal had issued the first salvo, back in 1973 with a review of Danto's book as soon as it is came out (sighted typescript), which was incorporated in his splendid book, *Exploring Mysticism A Methodological Essay*, Berkeley: University of California Press, 1975; in Bilimoria & Hutchings (see note 41 below), and Perrett, 1998, pp. 87-93 (next two notes).

30 See, Roy Perrett, *Hindu Ethics,* Honolulu: University of Hawaii Press, 1998; and abstract of his 'high theory' concerns in the Indic Colloquium 2002, www.Infinityfoundation.com. Despite himself, see Perrett's more descriptive essay on Sāṃkhya-Yoga ethics in this volume.

31 Danto virtually rehearses these counterfactuals in the Indian context, if the ubiquitous appeal to doctrines of *karma, sat (*existence), and *mokṣa* (zombie-like liberation) turn out to be factually false, as the available empirical evidence appears to show, then the entire foundational edifice of *dharma*, its caste-based hierarchy of obligations and meagre rights it seems to grudgingly dish out, etc. etc. all collapse under the weight of this unproven presupposition (p. 21). That philosophy never became independent of religious speculations in India, is a sign, for Danto, of the failure of meta-philosophical criticism and separation of ethics from customs and normative practices; pragmaticism and normative ethical theory that might be based on the latter notwithstanding.

Is it, though, enough to submerge oneself in the normative practices and moral judgments, actions and outcomes, or let oneself swim through the vast narratives of the Epics, The *Mahābhārata* and *The Rāmāyaṇa*, or engage in abstracted discussions of meta-ethics[32] ('what does it mean for something to be right, and wrong?'), 'ought/is', 'emotivism' versus 'objectivism', and so on, to get a grip on the meta-philosophical issue being addressed here? It is clear that certain basic principles constitute ethics: Russell and Moore argued that these principles pertain to the irreducible terms *good* and *bad*. For Moore, knowledge, pleasure and virtue are self-evidently 'good'; and those actions are deemed good that tend to maximize good outcomes for all concerned. That is, Moore holds, in good utilitarian spirit, that judgment of right and obligation are justified by some judgment of overall *good* (and not vice versa); while others argue that a judgment about a given thing being good are self-justifying.[33] Whichever direction one takes, discerning principles, justifying them (not necessarily with reference to 'ultimate rules and values'), deriving duties and obligations, and passing judgments about actions and persons, and so on, right up to working up principles of justice, is the preeminent task of ethics as 'first philosophy'.

Postmodern ethics

Doubtless there is another – or rather a different kind of – task of ethics as 'first philosophy'. This brings us to the third player in the field, namely, postmodernism, which in turn questions modernity's self-assured faith in its own terms of grounding ethics, be that ground reason, propositional statements, scientific realism with a human face, or analysis and argumentation. A model of postmodern ethics finds its early articulation in Emmanuel Levinas, who develops his own 'phenomenology of alterity and its transcendence' from Husserl's ideal of axiologial intentionality and Heidegger's overdetermined relation of Being to knowledge. For Levinas ethics – and not just philosophy or other forms of knowledge – is inseparable from consciousness (and 'consciousness-of' the other), that is to say, from ontology. But the knowledge and relation with the Other is not in the same manner one considers a known object, or communicates a knowledge to her. Levinas argues that that relation occurs irreducibly in the 'face to face of humans, in sociality, in its moral signification.' Morality for him comes not as a secondary layer, 'above an abstracted reflection on the totality and dangers; morality has an independent and preliminary range. [Rather] First philosophy is an ethics'.[34]

In more prosaic terms, Levinas's view is that all morality is grounded in a heteronymous will; and yet the moral agent has freedom. The face of the other opens

32 For a curious foray into this discourse, which leaves Indian ethics seemingly even more wanting, see Ved Prakash Varma, *Some Contemporary Meta-Ethical Theories*, Delhi: University of Delhi, 1978. Varma concludes in favour of an 'emotivist', 'subjectivist-rule' theory as advocated by C L Stevenson, following G E Moore, with modifications.

33 See, Bernard Rosen, *The Centrality of Normative Ethical Theory*, NY, Bern: Peter Lang, 1999, p. 2.

34 Levinas, *Ethics and Infinity: Conversations with Phillippe Nemo*, trans. R A Cohen, Pittsburgh: Duquene University Press, 1985. p. 77.

the realm of the sublime in transcendence[35]: meaning that, nothing is of significance or value that does not transcend the portals of the ego and attends towards the other,[36] becomes the other, and so is not-Being,[37] making evident the emptyness of the 'I-consciousness'. Nothing in my life has meaning but for the other, as when one is deeply or madly in love: 'An amorphous non-I sweeps away the I into an absolute future where it escapes itself and loses its position as subject'.[38] But one might also narcissistically hold on to the other and not allow the freedom, heteronomy, to the other as if an *outsider, stranger*. The other's advent in the horizon of my expectation sets off a whole new trajectory of ethical metaphysics. As Bernet notes: 'Levinas stresses convincingly that the Other's existence is something else than an intuitive fulfilment of my anticipations. The ethical egoism that goes with this consists in turning the other into a field of application of a form of responsibility that first concerns what I owe to myself as a rational ethical agent. For Levinas, responsibility is, quite to the contrary. A matter of response, of obeying a command that comes from the Other and not from me, my superego, or a universal law that has no face.'[39] And

---

35 See Edith Wyschogrod (ed.), *Emmanuel Levinas The Problem of Ethical Metaphysics,* New York: Fordham University Press, 2000. pp. 132-35

36 See in this context, Luce Irigaray, *The Fecundity of the caress',* in R A Cohen (ed.), *Face to Face with Levinas*, Albany: SUNY Press, 1986, pp. 231-45. Although in Levinas the early preoccupation with the erotic and the feminine gives way later to a concern with the ethical qua *ethics*.

37 Levinas is moving past Heidegger's Being to return phenomenology to beings and extend Husserlian intentionality – 'consciousness of' – to the affective : *agapē* and *eros* and *pathos* and *thanatos.*

38 Emmanuel Levinas, *Totality and Infinity,* trans. A. Lingis. Pittsburgh; Duquesne University Press, 1969, *259.* Although for a critique of how Levinas shifts his position in the later work, *Otherwise than Being,* and works up a Derridean 'supplement' to Heideggerean ontology of Being, but more significantly for the religious, 'Jewish', and theistically authoritarian tropes that hide more than reveal Levinas's ambivalences between an ontological horror and ethical passion, see Jeffrey L. Kosky, *Levinas and the Philosophy of Religion,* Bloomington: Indiana University Press, 2001. To be sure, there is no equivalence to the 'Jewish' preeminence in Levinas's ontology in contemporary Indian Philosophy – as distinct from whatever one might mean by 'Hindu' Philosophy, – as *Indian* (or better still, *'Indic')* must encompass the intellectual-critical traditions of the non-Brāhmaṇic gendered Vedics, Śramaṇas, Gymnosophists – 'naked philosophers' – Jainas, Buddhists, Parsis (or Zoroastrians), and secular nominal, a/theistic and naturalist, eclectic or ecumenical Hindus, if *Hindus* they be.

The issue of locating the fundamentals of morality, much less ontology, within a group of people as a fixed community (as Gershom Sholem seemed also to move towards later in his career) is far too complex to go into here. Our isolating 'Indian' ethics here from Western and other locations of the discourse is a discursive-heuristic device, for it registers merely a location in *culture* rather than necessarily in a *people* (not even in the mythic ancestors or descendants of the equally mythic Bharat or the legendary Manu, *et al*).

39 Rudolf Bernet, 'The Encounter with the Stranger: Two Interpretations of the Vulnerability of the Skin', in *The Face of the Other and the Trace of God*, Ed. Jeffrey Bloech, NY: Fordham University Press, 2000, p. 53

still, I can never give the other precisely what she needs, because of my own finitude and imperfections. The Good is not in the constitution of the ego but in the disposition of its self-effacement towards the other; and this is ethics as *prima philosophia*. At least two essays in the volume (Patton, Heim) attempt to understand ancient Indian ethics in the light of the Levinasian modality, or in dialogue with it, where the 'hidden face of the other' serves as a metonym for the 'gift', giving, of oneself as sacrifice.

The hermeneutic approach proposed in this volume is primarily a dialogical approach between traditions in which philosophical conversation flows both ways. Not only is there a juxtaposition of the two or three traditions, each constituted in its own terms, but the model of a dialogue highlights areas of agreement and divergence, permitting a self-consciousness and self-criticism, very rarely found in the absence of such genuine dialogue.

Comparative dharma

Take, as an example, one term in Indian ethical discourse that is perhaps the crucial one, serving as it often does for the closest Indian equivalent to the notion of ethics – and a subject that rightly attracts much attention in the pages of this volume – namely, the idea of *dharma*, as it figures in classical discussion.[40] *Dharma* is the fixed position of duty and of right, in the sense of what is proper and normative. It is by no means restricted to the realm of personal ethics, but it also designates religious observance and secular law, prescribing the individual's social and legal standing within the wider domains of community, caste, and station. Expanding its range even further, *dharma* connotes a general principle or law of nature to which the individual is bound in a two-fold sense, both in terms of supporting the cosmic, social, and personal orders and deriving from them a corresponding obligation. Thus, as universal order, it assigns to each entity, personal or impersonal, its specific place within the wider community. A final consequence of this conception of *dharma* is found in Buddhist logic, where all phenomena in their fixity and quiddity are called *dharmas*.

In its cosmic, and not simply personal, range, however, and because of its dual meaning of ethical duty and right, *dharma* cannot easily be identified straightforwardly with any of the Western conceptions of duty, much less with the Kantian maxim of the necessity to do an action 'from respect for law' (and not out of any consideration for the moral worth, purpose, end served, or the fruits resulting from the action qua action).[41] For while the imperative of *dharma* imposes upon human beings obligations towards both fellow humans and non-human beings, it

---

40 See Vasudha Narayan, '*Dharma* and Hindu Ethics', in Joseph Runzo and Nancy M. Martin (eds), *Ethics and Religion in India*, Oxford: One World, 2001, pp. 177-196.

41 See P.A.E. Hutchings and P. Bilimoria, 'On disregard for fruits – Kant and the *Gītā'*, in P. Bilimoria and P. Fenner (eds), *Religions and Comparative Thought*, Delhi: Satguru Publications. 1988, pp. 353-368. See also Joseph Prabhu, 'Dharma as an Alternative to Human Rights' in *Studies in Orientology: Essays In Memory of Prof. A.L. Basham*, Agra: Y.K. Publishers, pp. 174-180.

is by no means akin to the Christian idea of obedience and humility towards God, or in its secular version, obedience toward a supreme lawgiver, even if, as in Kant, that lawgiver is oneself. It is not categorical in any one particular direction. *Dharma* prescribes the acknowledgment of obligations not only towards a higher or supreme being, but also towards lower beings and, this again, not as a creaturely duty but as a cosmic responsibility. *Dharma* is not only a negative obligation in the shape of the restraints of duty, but it is equally the sustaining power of *right* in the sense of righteousness. Self preservation and the preservation of all things, animate and inanimate, are equally sacred aspects of this mutual cosmic contract: this system of reciprocal duties and rights is geared towards maintaining the cosmic, social, and structural orders of the universe. The unity of duties (obligations, 'rites') and rights ('right') is captured succinctly in the age-old concept of *adhikāra* (which is discussed in the Introduction to Part A).[42]

Human beings are thus not merely the Aristotelian *zoon politikon* or political animal, but *zoon kosmikon* as well, and thus the range of dharma is wider and deeper than any of its Western equivalents. *Dharma* embeds the idea of universal justice involving responsibility in its widest sense, a responsibility for the whole cosmos, not in the form of any external compulsion, but as immanent necessity, so that all that has ever come into existence produces its specific reaction or effect—the law of action and reaction as laid down by the principle of *karma*, which is more a metaphysical than an ethical doctrine in the usual Western interpretation.

Dharma, with its roots in *dhṛ (*sustaining) and Vedic *ṛta* (order), can open up a more holistic, organic and ecologically enlightened perspective as a contrast to the more nature-subjugating, individualistic and competitive environment within which we conceptualize ethics. *Karma*, and even the ideas of *āśrama* (life-cycles) and *puruṣārthas* (end-states), may suggest other possibilities for integrating the disparate elements of human life into this organic whole. And last, but not least, the principle of disinterested, nonviolent action might not go astray in the continuing struggle for justice and peace in the world.

It is clear that contemporary ecological discussions searching for an ethical language that articulates the essential interconnectedness and interdependence between humanity and nature have much to learn from such a cosmic notion of *dharma*, whatever the logical difficulties of deriving definite and justifiable rules of conduct from such a broad concept might be.

Under the impact of ecological, feminist, and communitarian critiques, the long dominant Western ethical models which sought to legitimize and ground moral beliefs and actions in fundamental principles, such as Kantian universalizability or utilitarian happiness maximization, are beginning to give way to more ancient and classical emphases on the virtues and on various aspects of human excellence. A correlative shift from a stress on rules of action to an appreciation of modes of being might then proceed. As indicated, *dharma* is an omnibus term with multiple nuances

42 For analytical discussion, see P. Bilimoria, 'Is *Adhikāra* good enough for 'Rights'?' *Asian Philosophy* (Nottingham). IV (1), Winter 1993, pp. 3-13.

covering a variety of disparate and loosely connected ideas – rules of conduct, individual and social, a combination of both Kantian Moralität or individualized duty and Hegelian Sittlichkeit or community life, a theory of virtues and religious duty oriented toward the transcendent goal of *mokṣa* or liberation. The challenge becomes one of differentiation of specific notions within this totality applicable to particular situations and contexts.

Concluding remarks

The major systems of ethics are examined in greater detail in the volume, including of course Jaina and Buddhist ethics, which have not been discussed above but to which a whole section is devoted in Part B accompanied with an Introduction to this area of thought.

What our enquiry reveals is that Indian civilization, like any other, strives towards normative ethical rules and endeavours to articulate the basis upon which those rules and principles are grounded. It may not succeed in achieving its goal, it may lose sight of the goal, or even fail to reach a point of clarity and sophistication which meets the expectations of modern discourse. But some important ideas and principles emerge which facilitate India's social survival, progression and growth. For those of us ensconced in the modern, post-modern, postcolonial era, India's ethical tradition may appear inadequate. It nevertheless provides some useful analogues and points of contrast with which to engage our notions, ideas, theories and analytic apparatus.

Echoing Foucault's proclivity and Nussbaum's insight that late modernity – now deep in a moral crisis according to some – is turning its ethical gaze towards the ways of the ancients,[43] the major differentiations between Indian ethics and modern Anglo-American efforts to ground moral philosophy are found in tradition and concrete particularity gaining emphasis over abstract, ahistorical universality, and its respect for deeply-rooted practices, customs, mores, laws, values and lived wisdom, which are seen as more important than purely theoretical concerns. Reflection and rational justification embrace alternative possibilities and critiques (*Śrāmaṇic* or Jaina-Buddhist versus Brāhmaṇic categories) and prioritizes the wider community or social whole over the unmitigated interests of the individual as the basis for ethical and moral care until, perhaps, later in the life-cycle (for example, the added value of *mokṣa* or spiritual liberation). The importance of emotions, aesthetics and virtues is also fixed within the Indian ethical framework and so is never far from its thinking on normative principles and their applicability.[44] There have, of course, been serious oversights, which are continually addressed with varying degrees of success,

---

43 Foucault, *The Care of the Self* (1984), 'On the Genealogy of Ethics' (1983); Nussbaum, 'The Softness of Reason: A Classical Case for Gay Studies', *The New Republic* 207, ¾ July 13 (20), 1992, pp. 26-35.

44 See P. Bilimoria, 'Perturbations of Desire: emotions disarming morality in the Great Song of the *Mahābhārata*', Robert Solomon (ed.), *Thinking about Feeling: Contemporary Philosophers on Emotions,* NY: Oxford University Press, 2004, pp. 214-232.

as evidenced in nineteenth-century reform movements, Gandhian and nationalist-inspired moral strategies, egalitarian justice and rights discourse which shaped the Indian Constitution, women's initiatives and various struggles to articulate the entitlements of the mute, unborn and subaltern.

IV Plan of the Work

The work which is presented in two volumes is intended to introduce Indian ethics through the consideration of various strands of thought, issues and perspectives which have exercised moral actors within the Indian philosophical tradition. There is, however, no attempt to represent every possible school of thought, its views and critiques, and so comprehensiveness is not attempted. Such would be the task best held over for an encyclopedia of Indian ethics. A scholarly work can only hope to bring together a smattering of material approximately representative in imagining what it is to think ethics *with* the tradition, rather than *for* it. Only then does one begin the painful task of critical evaluation, deconstruction and reformulation of the traditional and classical offerings or, for that matter, modern alternatives within an Indian context. The volume moves towards the latter task in the second half, perhaps achieving a gesture, rather than a definitive, tightly argued position, of just what Indian ethics is or ought to be in the twenty-first century.

Another aim of this volume and the volume to follow is to be inclusive of the expanding circle of cross-disciplinary interests and responses to problems in ethics, whether from theological, literary, political, economic, developmental, legal or constitutional areas of concern and application. While widening the range of problems and issues considered, and extending the disciplinary and conventional resources of analysis, we nevertheless decided against offering a grand narrative or favouring one 'frame' or perspective on Indian ethics, theoretical or otherwise, over others, extant and possible, or improbable.

In fact, the volume as structured moves through most of these tropic 'traditions', in a loose chronology, even though our aim was to balance this mapping with equal if not more weight given to certain *problems* and questions in moral thinking emergent and perhaps urgently pursued within the representative texts and literary productions of the particular period, say, for example, in Manu or Kauṭilya. But significantly, the project (particularly volume II) concludes with a select application of the preceding discussions to instantiations of certain erstwhile, on-going, and also newer, problems of larger magnitude than simply staying with concerns within theories of personal ethics, virtues, and 'kingdom of ends'. Such problems and issues may have also come to sharper focus since Independence or in the post-colonial era – with globalization knocking at India's door. In other words, on the moral frontiers of environmental and animal treatment, gender justice, infanticide, *satī*, public health and the biomedical challenges, which will be pursued in the next volume.

As remarked in the Preface, this project is a product of some ten years of planning and soliciting essays for the compendium. Over this prolonged timeframe new ideas, suggestions and issues have emerged that have led to the expansion of the volume from the slim and simple idea that was seeded in a conversation between one of the editors and Professor Bimal K Matilal in Oxford quite some time back. From essays that would have fitted into one Part, the volume in its published form has expanded into three Parts, each representing a cluster of concerns that could, even if tendentiously, find a grouping under one cluster.

Part One is intended to cover the early Indian period, mostly classical, through to the second Part, which could be called the *Śrāmaṇic* systems, Jaina and Buddhist ethics. Broadly, a 'school' or system-based discussion is pursued for the majority of the essays, while we have attempted to intersperse the discussions with conceptual and analytical concerns addressing challenging issues, such as the role of reason in negotiating the terms of *dharma*-based normative ethics, the place of a monastic worldview in Buddhist ethics, caste and gender considerations in conceptions of justice, natural law sensibilities in ecological thinking, and so on.

Essays from what was originally intended to be Part Four, covering issues in gender, contemporary ecological (and eco-feminist) and bioethics as well as related applied areas, will appear in a separately dedicated volume, with the title *Indian Ethics Gender, Justice and Ecology Vol II*. Each of the Parts, we thought, should have its own introductory outline to highlight some of the issues taken up in greater depth within the chapters. These introductions include remarks and allusions to the general tenor of the chapters, but it was not thought desirable to repeat the thesis and argument of each chapter in the preliminary pages (though this may be deemed appropriate for a particular Part). Rather, we present an overview of the issues addressed, and what is intended in each of the respective Parts. Each chapter makes a unique contribution to the system or issues taken up by the respective author/contributor.

It is our hope that the two volumes as a whole will give the readers an idea of what Indian ethics is like. There will be those who will object that the volume is far too ambitious, or that it covers too much, or too little. Others might baulk at its lack of pure theorizing on ethics of the kind one finds in discussions of moral philosophy and meta-ethics in the Western academic scene; another class of critic is prone to complain that the philosophical preoccupation verges on the parochial. In other words, there is too much theory that all but obscures the very real, on the ground and lived moral practices of the people. The judgment would go on to urge that, given the many contradictions within institutionalized patterns of conduct and rules (under 'the incessant drone of *dharma* and anvil of *karma*,' as one commentator ruefully put it), immorality, antinomianism, and bizarreness are rife in the tradition, as should be evident for instance in the culture's sexual-homoerotic (*tantra*) and alchemical (yogi-mystical) perversions, preferential gender selection, dowry practices, etc.: one has to live with the anomalies or at best the manifest amorality, or non-ethics. But to concede to such charges would be to fall prey to the kind of prejudices and closures to which Indian thought in more general terms has been subjected since the dawn of Orientalism. This goes back to Hegel who said of Indians that they did not raise their intuitions to the level of concepts, and so did not quite, in the true sense, *think.*[45] Husserl and Heidegger, likewise, held the belief that a certain kind of theoretical thinking, to the utter exclusion of mythical-magical-intuitive practicality, was alien to the Indians.[46] The consequence of such provincialism has been the constant attempt to force the Indian modes of thinking – in the area of ethical thinking as much – into the strait-jacket of Western philosophy and intellectual trends, modern and postmodern. This tendency has to be resisted. We should let our esteemed contributors speak to the issues pondered here.

V. Selected References

Some Select Resources for Indian and broadly Asian Ethics (Selected Bibliography, with additions from Arti Dhand); for more issue-specific resources, see references in notes and/or bibliography to respective chapters.

Ames, Roger T., 'Rites as Rights: The Confucian Alternative', in Larry May, Shari Collins-Chobanian, and Kai Wong (eds), *Applied Ethics: A Multicultural Approach*, New Jersey: Prentice-Hall, 1998 (2nd edn), pp. 90-102.

Barnhart, Michael G. (ed.), *Varieties of Ethical Reflection: New Directions for Ethics in a Global Context,* New York: Rowman and Littlefield, 2002.

Bilimoria, P., 'Indian Ethics', in Peter Singer (ed.), *Blackwell Companion to Ethics,* Oxford: Blackwell Publications, 1991, pp. 43-57.

Brannigan, Michael C., *Striking a Balance: A Primer in Traditional Asian Values*, New York: Seven Bridges Press, 2000.

Card, Claudia, *Feminist Ethics*, Kansas: University Press of Kansas, 1994.

Carmen, John and Juergensmeyer, Mark (eds), *Bibliographical Guide to the Comparative Study of Ethics*, Cambridge: Cambridge University Press, 1991.

Chapple, Christopher Key, *Nonviolence to Animals, Earth, and Self in Asian Traditions*, Albany: SUNY Press, 1993.

Cheng, Chung-ying, 'On the Environmental Ethics of the Tao and the Ch'i', in *Applied Ethics: A Multicultural Approach*, New Jersey: Prentice-Hall, 1998 (2nd edn), pp. 151-159.

Cooper, David E. and James, Simon P., *Buddhism, Virtue and Environment*, Aldershot: Ashgate Publishing Ltd, 2005.

Coward, Harold G., Young, Catherine and Lipner, Julius (eds), *Hindue Ethics: Purity, Abortion, and Euthanasia*, Albany: SUNY Press, 1989.

Crawford, S. Cromwell, 'Hindu Ethics for Modern Life', in *World Religions and Global Ethics*, New York: Paragon House, 1989, pp. 5-35.

Creel, Austin, *Dharma in Hindu Ethics*, Calcutta: Firma KLM, 1977.

---

45 J.N. Mohanty, 'On Interpreting Indian Philosophy', in his *Essays in Indian Philosophy*, edited with introduction by P. Bilimoria, New Delhi: Oxford University Press, 2002, p. 213 (emphasis added).

46 Ibid, 214-215.

Dasgupta, Surama, *Development of Moral Philosophy in India*, Delhi, Munshiram Manoharlal, 1961.

Deutsch, Eliot (ed.), *Culture and Modernity: East-West Philosophic Perspectives*, Honolulu, University of Hawaii Press, 1991

Gudorf, Christine E. and Wolfe, Regina Wentzel (eds), *Ethics and World Religions: Cross-Cultural Case Studies*, Maryknoll, NY: Orbis Books, 1999.

Hindery, R. *Comparative Ethics in Hindu and Buddhist Traditions*, Delhi: Motilal Banarsidass, 1978.

Ilchman, Katz, and Queen (eds), *Philanthropy in the World's Religions*, Bloomington: Indiana University Press, 1998.

Inada, Kenneth K., 'A Buddhist Response to the Nature of Human Rights', in Christine Koggel (ed.), *Moral Issues in Global Perspective,* Toronto: Broadview Press, 1999, pp.22-30.

Jayatilleke, K., 'The Ethical Theory of Buddhism', *The Mahābodhi,* **78**, July 1970, pp. 192-97.

Jhrinran, Saral, *Aspects of Hindu Morality*, Delhi: Motilal Banarsidass, 1989.

Keown, Damien, *The Nature of Buddhist Ethics*, London: Macmillan, 1992.

Lai, Karen, *Moral Cultivation, Self and Community: Learning From Confucian and Daoist Philosophies*, Aldershot: Ashgate, 2006.

Lawton, Clive, and Morgan, Peggy (eds), *Ethical Issues in Six Religious Traditions*, Edinburgh: Edinburgh University Press, 1996.

Li, Chenyang, 'Confucian Value and Democratic Value', in Christine Koggel (ed.), *Moral Issues in Global Perspective*, Toronto: Broadview Press, 1999, pp. 74-81.

May, Larry, Collins-Chobanian, Shari and Kai Wong (eds), *Ethics: A Multicultural Approach*, New Jersey: Prentice-Hall, 1998 (2nd edn).

Morgan, Peggy, and Braybrooke, Marcus, *Testing the Global Ethic: Voices from Religious Traditions on Moral Values*, Oxford: Co-Nexus Press, 1998.

Perrett, Roy W., *Hindu Ethics: A Philosophical Study*, Honolulu: University of Hawaii Press, 1998.

Podgorski, Frank R., 'Paths to Perfection: Yoga and Confucian', in Brian Carr (ed.) *Morals and Society in Asian Philosophy*, Surrey: Curzon Books, 1996, pp. 125-144.

Prabhu, Joseph, 'Dharma as an Alternative to Human Rights' in Narain, A.K. (ed.), *Studies in Orientology, Essays in Memory of Prof. A.L. Basham*, Agra: Y.K. Publishers, 1988, pp.174-180.

Prabhu, Joseph (ed.), *Human Rights in Cross-Cultural Perspective* (Forthcoming, Hackett Publishing Co).

Shanahan, Timothy and Wang, Robin, *Reason and Insight: Western and Eastern Perspectives on the Pursuit of Moral Wisdom*, Belmont, CA: Wadsworth Publishing, 1996.

Sharma, I.C., *Ethical Philosophies of India*, New York: Harper and Row, 1965.

de Silva, Padmasiri (see Bibliography in chapter 10 of this volume).

Singh, Balbir, *Hindu Ethics, An Exposition of the Concept of Good*, New Delhi: Arnold Heinemann, 1984.

Smart, Ninian, and Thakur, Shivesh (eds), *Ethical and Political Dilemmas of Modern India*, NY: St Martins Press, 1993.

Tse, Chung M., 'Confucianism and Contemporary Ethical Issues', in *World Religions and Global Ethics*, S. Cromwell Crawford, (ed.), New York: Paragon House, 1989, pp. 91-126.

Wei, Xiao, 'The Characteristics of Confucian Ethics', in Brian Carr (ed.), *Morals and Society in Asian Philosophy*, Surrey: Curzon Books 1996, pp. 145-155.

Williams, Paul, *Altruism and Reality*, Surrey: Curzon Books, 1998.

Editors:
Purushottama Bilimoria
Joseph Prabhu
Renuka Sharma

Introduction to Part A:

Early Indian Ethics – Vedas to the *Gītā; dharma*, rites to 'Right'

Thus we begin, again, with the most general remark that the early Indian people – perhaps like human beings everywhere in their practical moral judgments – placed on the side of the 'good', such things as: happiness, health, survival, progeny, pleasure, calmness, friendship, knowledge and truth. On the side of 'bad' were, more or less, their opposites or disvalues: misery or suffering, sickness and injury, death, barrenness, pain, anger, enmity, ignorance or error, and untruth. These positive and negative qualities are universalized, in principle at least, for all sentient beings, for it is felt that the highest good is possible when the whole world (gods included) can enjoy the good things that the cosmos has to offer. The highest good (*summum bonum*), however, expresses itself in the total harmony of the cosmic or natural order characterized as *ṛta*: this is the *telos*, the creative purpose that underpins human behaviour. The prescribed pattern of social and moral order is thus conceived as a correlate of the natural order. This is the ordered course of things, the truth of being or reality (*sat*) and hence the 'Law'.[1]

One's actions are therefore consistent with that which promotes the good so perceived, and desists from doing that which promotes or stimulates the bad so that the *ṛta* is not unduly disturbed. An act is therefore right if it conforms to this general principle, and an act is wrong if it contravenes it (and so is *anṛta*).[2] Since to do what is right safeguards the good of all qua *ṛta* (the factual/descriptive order), it is assumed that it is more or less obligatory to do or perform the right acts (the 'ought' or moral/prescriptive order). This convergence of the cosmic and the moral orders is universally commended in due course in the all-embracing appellation of *dharma* (from its earlier sense of 'religious ordinances and fixed principles').[3]

The 'right' or rightness is simply identified with 'rite': it is formalized, taking in varying contexts (i.e. the obligation that is derived from a value, say, survival of the race, becomes the *sui generic* value itself; for example, sacrifice, regardless of what is offered in the act). Rite now comes to possess an intrinsic moral worth. (Of course, not every moral value entails a duty.)

Thereafter rite tends to assume, as it were, an imperious power all of its own, and people forget the original motivation or rationale underlying the imperative.

---

1 *ṚgVeda* I.123.9; IV.51.5; V.8; X.300.1.2. *The Hymns of the Ṛgveda*, trans. R.T.H. Griffiths, Delhi: Motilal Banarsidass, 1973.

2 *ṚgVeda* X.87.11; X.125.5.

3 *ṚgVeda* IV.53.3; VII.89.5.

Rites become increasingly pursued for egoistic ends, optatively, and are adjudged in respect of their utility. One group claims knowledge and therefore privilege over others in accordance with the (prescribed) rites, their correct performance, utility, and so on. This leads to the establishment of differential duties and moral codes for the different major groups or 'classes' in society. Each 'class' constitutes a needful functional unit in the larger complex. The stages or lifecycles an individual goes through may entail distinct or differently arranged moral rules, roles, and goals or values for the group or sub-group he or she belongs to. Likewise for kings and rulers, with added responsibilities and advantages. *Differentia* are superimposed on the organic unity of nature. A kind of oblique distributive justice is assumed, and in time the question of moral *choice* is categorically left out: one either does it or one does not, and enjoys the rewards or suffers the consequences thereof. Herein lie the rudiments of the idea of *karma*, which we develop later.

What counts as *ethics* then is largely the normative preoccupations; the justification is usually that this is the 'divine' ordering of things (in the sense of locating the order in some transcendental plenum or law, depicted in the imageless and, later, iconic gods, not necessarily in an absolute or supremely existent being, as God). This is akin to the ancient, especially in the Stoics', conception of Natural Law in the Western tradition. This may also provide a basis for belief in the absoluteness of the moral law from which the rules and norms are supposed to have been derived. But virtually no attempt is made, until perhaps much later, or elsewhere in the broad tradition, at self-reflexively analyzing the logic of the ethical concepts and reasoning used. Indeed, questions such as: 'What do we *mean* when we say of an action that it is morally right (or morally wrong)?' can hardly be said to have attracted the kind of critical attention attended upon (meta-)ethical thinking in recent times.

That is not to say, however, that genuine issues, concerns and paradoxes of ethical relevance are not raised, even if they are couched in religious, mystical or mythological ideas or terms. To give an illustration: Scriptures proscribe injury to creatures and meat-eating, but a priest would wrong the gods if he did not partake of the remains of a certain ritual animal sacrifice. With the gods wronged, *ṛta* cannot be maintained: what then should he do?[4] It also follows that meat-eating is not unambiguously decried in the Scriptures, as more recent studies have attempted to show.

What we have presented above is, admittedly, a sweeping account that essentially covers the very early period (*c.* 1500-800 BCE) during which time the Brahmanical tradition grew and flourished. It provides a general framework within which we can continue to see how moral consciousness, certain ethical concepts and various, albeit conflicting, moral schemes are developed and articulated in later periods, which may collectively be identified as the 'Hindu' tradition. (For this account we shall have to use more Sanskrit terms as their exact English equivalents, and the converse, is wanting.)

---

4 See, P.V. Kane, *A History of Dharmaśāstra: Ancient and Medieval Religious and Civil Law in India Vols I-V*, Poona: Bhandarkar Oriental Institute, 1968-69, vol. I.i. pp. 1-3.

I. Brāhmaṇical-Hindu Ethics

First we shall make three concrete observations about Brāhmaṇical society.

1. The Vedas, the canonical collection of texts, are regarded to be supremely authoritative. (The usual Judeo-Christian idea of a God to whom the source of the scriptures is owed is lacking here.[5]) Their contents are simply 'seen' or 'heard' (*śruti*); and their principles are embodied in the gods, who are models for human conduct. How far this idea of 'authority' unpacks in real moral terms, and impacts on the social lives of people, is an issue taken up in the ensuing chapters in Part A.

2. A particular principle of social ordering is adopted (probably introduced into India by the Aryans around 2000 BCE), according to which society is organized into a fourfold (but originally threefold) functional division or 'class', called *varṇa* (literally, 'colour' or 'category'). These are, namely, *brāhmaṇa* (brahmin), for religious and educational tasks; *kṣatriya*, for sovereign and defence tasks; *vaiśya* for agriculture and economic tasks; and *śūdra*, for menial tasks. (One is reminded here of Plato's 'stations-of-life' division.) Overall, the sources of power get distributed evenly at different places, and ideally differences in function need not entail differences in interests, rights and privileges; but the outcome in practice shows otherwise. A system of sub-divisions or 'castes' (*jāti*) further proliferates the class functions, gradually turning *varṇa* into a discriminatory hereditary-based institution. In any event, the brahmins certainly enjoy the better end of the system and they wield enormous power. A life-affirming but rigidly casuistic morality develops. In Max Weber's judgment, the Vedas 'do not contain a rational ethic' – if such an ethic did exist anywhere that far back![6]

Exactly who the Aryans are and who the non-Aryans, is a discussion that strays into anthropology and history, but it has some relevance in the context of 'oneself and the other', which is indeed an issue within the purview of ethics.

3. Despite the overall ritualistic *Weltanschauung*, the Vedic hymns are evocative of certain humanistic virtues and ethical ideals, such as being truthful (*satya*), giving (*dāna*), restraint (*dama*), austerities (*tapas*), affection and gratitude, fidelity, forgiveness, non-thieving, non-cheating, giving others their just desert, avoiding injury or *hiṃsā* to all creatures, and being responsive to the guest/stranger.[7] As the gods, who portray these ideals, recede from the people's consciousness, the people are encouraged to take

---

5 For further discussion and a hermeneutic-linguistic basis of the philosophical thesis underpinning the claim see P. Bilimoria, 'Testimony in Indian Philosophy', *Encyclopaedia of Philosophy*, Routledge: London, 1998, pp. 315-19; and P. Bilimoria, 'J.N. Mohanty's Critique of Word as a Means of Knowing and "Authorless Tradition"', in Bina Gupta (ed.), *The Empirical and the Transcendental: A Fusion of Horizons*, NY: Rowman & Littlefield Publishers Inc., 2000, pp. 199-218.

6 Max Weber, *The Religion of India*, Glencoe: The Free Press, 1958, pp .261, 337. See also chapter by Mehta in Part C.

7 *ṚgVeda*, II.28.11; V.85.5; X.10.4; X.113.4; X.117; cf. Kane, op cit, vol I.i, p. 4.

more responsibility upon themselves, and transform these ideals into virtues, habits and dispositions, with corresponding moral 'objects' in the world. Old ethical problems achieve new meaning. Thus the question of whether the princely god Indra should slay the obstructive demon Vṛtra becomes a question for the king: should he vanquish the ascetics who stand in the way of his sovereignty?[8]

Vedic authority becomes normative in the later periods; the Vedas are invoked as the source of ethics (but there is now much more to the Vedas than the earlier hymnal and ritual texts might appear to suggest). To be noted is one other important institution, where three morally significant concepts emerge, namely, *āśrama*, *dharma*, and *karma* (or *karman*), culminating in the ethical concept of *puruṣārthas*, all of which are central to classical Hindu ethics. These concepts are extensively discussed in at least the first three chapters. But before giving a thumbnail overview of these concepts, one further point awaits mentioning.

There are doubtless other ways of appraising ethics in the Vedas, rudimentary as this might appear to be. In this context, Laurie Patton's chapter is suggestive of a rather creative interpretation. This sample summary is offered here by way of illustrating how individual authors have taken up the themes for this section and engaged the texts and tradition on a range of issues central to such a discussion. Hence, Laurie Patton's chapter, 'The Fires of Strangers: A Levinasian Approach to Vedic Ethics' begins by briefly tracing the recent move away from the absolute and toward the contextual and situational in the study of Hindu ethics. This intellectual environment presents an ideal moment for the engagement of a Levinasian approach which takes seriously the complexity of attitudes toward alterity. Recent studies of the Veda have focused on the 'other,' but more exclusively on the non-Aryan other, rather than on the Levinasian 'other' who makes moral obligations on the self. Hoping to add this more phenomenological approach to the study of the 'other' in the Veda, she turns to read Vedic passages as Levinas has read the Talmud. And for this, the chapter begins with a review and 'word-studies' of the basics of the Vedic world, – the more well known *ārya/dāśa*, or noble-slave; *ārya/anārya*, Aryan/non-Aryan being the obvious starting points. However, following Levinas, Patton goes on to look at Vedic ideas of 'face' (*mukha* and related phrases) and the face that makes a claim upon one's attention, as well as 'presence' and 'being in the presence' of someone ('*prati*', and related words). She ends by examining the notions of the moral obligations of the Vedic guest, or stranger (*atithi*) at the threshold. There is obviously complexity in the idea of the Vedic 'other'; while the Vedic attitude expresses the kind of 'annihilation' of the other that we see in the Aryan/non-Aryan discourse; it nevertheless contains the very basic understanding that strangers can have a kind of infinite moral claim upon the Vedic self, and that this claim can structure certain ethical understandings in the Vedic world.

---

8 Wendy Doniger O'Flaherty, 'Separation of Heaven and Earth in Indian Mythology', in Robin W. Lovin and Frank E. Reynolds (eds), *Cosmology and Ethical Order*, Chicago: University of Chicago Press,1985, pp. 177-99, p. 192.

This act of being present to the guest, or stranger, is also connected with the idea of the 'gift' (*dāna*), of giving; there is the 'gifting' by way of sacrifice (*yajña*) to the gods, to the cosmos, to the 'act of gift' itself (the non-transitive *gifting*: the sacrifice sacrificing itself in sacrifice in the primordial creation of the cosmos and gods also from non-existence). But the conceptual finesse of the idea of the 'gift' (*dāna*), it is argued in Maria Heim's chapter, had to await the articulations in the Medieval texts of the *Dharmaśāstras*. A further connection is made between the act of giving, making the 'gift' to the spontaneity of virtuous performance which is not mediated by some principle ('ought I or ought I not do this?').

* * *

Āsŕama. Now we turn to the concepts that become somewhat seminal to classical Hindu ethics.

Life is conceived as progressing through four relative stages in concentric circles, each with its own code of conduct. Namely, period of study (*brahmācārya*), which entails discipline, continence and service to the teacher; householder stage (*gṛhasthya*), which entails marriage, family, provisions, offerings and friendliness; semi-retreat stage (*vanaprasthya*), which entails gradual withdrawal from worldly cares and pleasures; and renunciation (*sannyāsa*), which entails ascetic practices and contemplation. The last marks the preparation for the final liberation and frees the individual both from egoistic and altruistic pursuits, since he has to exercise extreme disinterestedness in this stage. This is as far as the circle expands.

Dharma. '*Dharma*', as noted in the General Introduction, is an all-embracing concept and is perhaps unique to Indian thought. But the term is also rather diffuse as it has many and varying meanings, ranging from 'ordinance, usage, duty, right, justice, morality, virtue, religion, good works, function or characteristics' to 'norm', 'righteousness', 'truth' and much else.[9]

The word is derived from the Sanskrit root *dhṛ*, meaning to form, uphold, support, maintain, sustain, to hold together. It certainly connotes the idea of that which maintains, gives order and cohesion to any given reality, and ultimately to nature, society and the individual. As will be noticed, *dharma* takes over from organic unity the idea enshrined in *ṛta* and shifts more toward the human dimension. In this respect it parallels Hegel's idea of *Sittlichkeit* (the actual ethical order that regulates the conduct of the individual, family, civil life, and state) more than it does Kant's ideal conception of the Moral Law, which is more individualistic and could even be said to place value on self-regarding above all else.

Law writers such as Kauṭilya and Manu bring the notion of *dharma* even more down to earth by devising a comprehensive system of social and moral regulations for each of the different groups, sub-groups (caste, rulers, etc.) within the Hindu social system, as well as specifying certain universal duties encumbent on all. Vocational niches, duties, norms, and even punishments are differently arranged for different

9 Kane, op cit, vol I.I, pp. 1-8.

groups, and the roles and requirements also vary in the different *āśrama* stages for the different groups. Thus, while a wife of a 'twice-born' (the three higher classes) may take part in a Vedic rite, a *śūdra* would be risking punishment if he so much as hears the Vedas recited – what to say of those who fall outside the caste structure (*caṇḍāla*), and other aliens.[10]

More often than not though, *dharma* is invoked as though it were an utterly objective possibility. In fact, it merely gives an overall form to a system of positive law and regulations of individuals and of groups, the specific contents of which are determined by various different factors, among which the voice of tradition, convention or custom, and the conscience of the learned, might be predominant. *Dharma* then provides a frame that, as it were, could flick through different pictures of what is ethically proper or desirable at any one time. What gives coherency to the conception itself is perhaps its coveted appeal to the need to preserve the organic unity of being, to 'make' justice where justice is due, and to minimize the burden of *karma*, if not also to free the individual from its encumbrances. But what do we understand by the term *karma*, which is even rather popular nowadays outside India?

Karma. The basic idea behind *karma* is that every conscious act (cognitive, speech, etc.) and volitional action (physical, psychical, etc.) an individual engages in generates causal conditions for more than the immediately visible effect, such that the net effect, N, of an action X may manifest itself at a later time t_1, or perhaps its traces (*vāsanās*) get distributed over time t_2. Action X may combine the residual effects of action Y to generate a compounded, or even a reduced, effect in some future moment. And this in turn becomes a critical determinant of another action, Z, or a state of affairs pertaining to that particular individual (perhaps even a collective). The effect of Z might be pleasurable (*sukha*) or it might be painful and induce suffering (*duḥkha*), but this is the *retribution* entailed in the causal network that is itself an inexorable manifestation of *dharma*.

Further, the idea of an infinite possibility of action-retribution suggested to the Indian mind the idea of rebirth, for merit or virtue (as Kant also was to recognize), appears to be in need of being rewarded, and demerit punished. This is the Law of Karma. Thus merit or demerit achieved in one life-time could well continue to determine one's constitution (capacities, temperament) and circumstances (relative placement and status) in another birth. Hindu thought espoused the idea of a more substantial theory of rebirth, meaning that something like the 'soul' (*jīva*) carries intact with it the latent potential (*karma*) of all that constitutes the individual, from one existence to another. However, some Hindu philosophers, such as Śaṅkara (8th C. CE) did away with the idea of a self-subsistent soul by asserting the identity of the individual self, *ātman*, with the ultimate reality, Brahman; hence what really transmigrates is a self-deception (*māyā* or *avidyā*) of a constituted self, while it has lost sight of its true identity, namely being one with Brahman!

---

10 Manu II.16.67, X.127, in *The Manusmṛti*, ed. Satya Bhushan Yogi, Delhi: Motilal Banarsidass, 1975.

This linkage of *dharma* and *karma* has the following consequences: there are no 'accidents of birth' determining social inequities; mobility within one lifetime is excluded; one has one's *dharma*, both as endowment and as a social role. One either accumulates an improvement in *karma* aiming toward a higher re-birth, or one tries to sunder the Gordian knot and opts to step off once and for all from the circus of cyclic existence or *saṃsāra* as this condition is known in Indian religious thought. But this is not achieved as simply as it is willed. Indeed, this freedom is placed as the fourth and the most difficult of goals in the fourfold, categorical ends or *puruṣārthas*, literally, 'the ends sought by human beings'.

Puruṣārtha. Very simply the idea is that there are four avenues of volitional pursuits in life which are of intrinsic value, namely: *artha*, material interests; *kāma*, pleasure and affective fulfilment; *dharma*, again, social and individual duties; and *mokṣa*, liberation. They may or may not be continuous with each other, though one goal might prove to be of instrumental value for achieving another, as is often thought of *dharma* in connection with *mokṣa*. But *mokṣa* is *a fortiori* the plenum of *freedom* without which *dharma* as morality – along with the 'ethical ends' of *artha* and *kāma* – is all but baseless, or mere means, i.e. utility, to some instrumentally conceived end. Still, an ascending scale might well be admitted; and the determination of the relative status of each category could lead to the next; but *mokṣa* as freedom in this sense is a presupposition, the *pre-theoretic* possibility, more than an 'end' in the cumulative sense, as is often thought. This contention, however, is a subject of much vigorous debate in Indian philosophy – as the chapters by Mohanty and Daya Krishna forcefully illustrate.

What is significant is that the above conception of human ends provides a distinct backdrop for the detailed working out of the rules, conduct and guidelines in respect of the institutions of *varṇa* and *āśrama* that we considered earlier, in as much as any individual will want to strive toward achieving the best in terms of these 'ends' within the limits of his or her temperament, circumstances, status and so on. Sometimes it is a question of balance; at other times it is a question of which interests or preferences take priority over which. For example, a brahmin in the third stage might consider that he has discharged his social obligations (*dharma*), so that his remaining interest (even challenge) is to edge toward liberation, by becoming a full-time ascetic. As to what he should do and what he should not do in pursuit of this end is left entirely to his own determination, for which he relies on his meditative and cognitive insights. His *dharma* is the correlate of his innate constitution of which he alone is the master: thus an inward-attentive praxis is the source of the principles for his ethic. Here, it may be observed, the gap between intuition and ethics is very nearly closed over. This is another salient feature of Indian ethics.

Daya Krishna's chapter tackles the concept of *puruṣārtha* head-on, and raises a large number of questions about its shifting meaning and functional trope from one period and representative texts to the next. Just how many categories does *puruṣārtha* embrace, retain, tolerate and the order in which these are graded, have been much debated in Hindu philosophical inquiry. Whether in the end this framework has any moral signification, or whether it is a myth (but also in Plato's sense of 'half-truth'), are among the questions that Daya Krishna with his sharp philosophical acumen does not leave unturned. This chapter presents a classic piece of writing by a modern philosopher in India.

II. Upaniṣadic ethics

The *Upaniṣads* (post-500 BCE), perhaps the key philosophical texts of the Hindus, while they presuppose in principle the authority of the earlier Vedas (yet harboring a deep cynicism about Vedic utilitarianism), develop this alternative scheme with much finesse and in great detail for a more universal application. Here metaphysical knowledge is placed over and above worldly pursuits. But this scheme also allows for the possibility of, if not positively encourages, a detached and asocial pursuit of spiritual ends, removed from the vicissitudes of living-in-the-world. That this tendency does develop in the hands of yogis and ascetics, and that it influences Indian ethical thinking, cannot be denied. It appears almost as though *dharma* could be dispensed with. As the restless Yājñavalkya, justifying his decision to leave behind his wealth, home and two wives, puts it: It is not for the sake of the husband, wife, sons, wealth, gods, Vedas, *brahmin*hood, *ksatriya*hood, etc., that these are dear, but for the sake of the Self, all these are the Self, one knows all in the Self ... Work cannot increase nor diminish the greatness of this knowledge.[11]

The Socratic dictum, 'knowledge is virtue' rings through here also, with the added emphasis: 'without virtue there is no knowledge'. Yājñavalkya begins as a Humean (for whom morality is primarily a play of emotions or passions over reason) and like the Stoics (with which the yogic disposition has some deep conceptual if not also historical connection) proceeds to, as it were, conquer and transcend all emotions, feelings, inclinations and sentiments in pursuit of a higher, nonetheless self-centred (or self-regarding in the sense of *svadharma*), 'calling'. But of rules there are few. It is for these sorts of reasons that there have been charges, from within and without the tradition, that all we have here is an ethically bankrupt quietistic and mystically-grounded morality. In one account this is attributed principally to the grave errors in the 'factual' or metaphysical account of the world proffered by the tradition (echoed loudly, it is said, in its doctrine of *māyā*), illusory or dreamlike world, caste hierarchy, a flawed theory of fatalistic or automated action-reward mechanism qua law of *karma*, and other brooding or scientifically unassailable speculative tendencies, that Danto highlighted in his damningly unredemptive critique of Indian Philosophy, which thankfully has since come to pass.[12]

Valid as such broad-brush charges might be, there is a list of three comprehensive virtues extolled in the *Upaniṣads* which is worthy of mention (as it also excited T.S. Eliot), namely, *damyatā*, *datta*, *dayadhvam*: self-restraint, giving or self-sacrifice, and compassion respectively. But there are no rules other than exemplars, and no virtues

---

11 *Bṛhadāraṇyaka Upaniṣad* IV.5.6.7; IV.4.24. *The Principal Upaniṣads*, ed. trans. by S. Radhakrishnan, New York: The Humanities Press, 1974. For Eliot's 3-D's, see V.2.1-3, ibid.

12 Danto 1972, p. 99; see General Introduction for details and discussion (p. 21, n. 29).

after attaining liberation, though it might be a blissful state, or it might not. Still, one moral ramification of the Upaniṣadic worldview is that all life, indeed the entire world, is to be looked upon as one whole, where the ego sets aside in its own narrow self-interests and even effaces itself. Doubts are also raised about the conventional morality of such caste divisions as a story makes one wonder, one suspects, whether a stranger who tells the truth about his unplaceable origin does so because he is a *brāhmaṇa* (brahmin), or is he a *brāhmaṇa* because he tells the truth etc.?[13]

III. Smārta ethics

There occur however parallel and later developments in circles of the more doctrinaire and legalistic advocates of the rule of *dharma*, what we shall call *smārta* ethics. The school known as Mīmāṃsā champions a more rigidly categorical reading of the imperatives prescribed in the Vedas, with the implication that all duties – religious as well as secular – could be divided into those that are optional or 'optative' and those obligatory, and that all ensuing actions are instrumental toward some result or end (even if it is not indicated). But if there is a mandate (*niyoga*) one does it out of a sense of obligation. The Mīmāṃsā develops a whole hermeneutic of *dharma* for which the school is best known, and it proved instructive for later ethical and legal discourse.

The more populist texts known as *Dharmaśāstras*, of which the most relevant are Manu's 'Law Books' and Kauṭilya's treatise on politics, overstress the legalistic side. Thus Kauṭilya – whose contribution and edicts we go on to examine in the next few paragraphs – at a superficial reading appears to justify the rigid reign of the 'rod' (*daṇḍa*) wielded by the king. One plausible ground for this edict is that, unless there are calculated controls, the (natural) law of the small fish being swallowed by the big fish would prevail. Jurisprudence, ordinances for regulating civil life, and the governance and security of the state are the monarch's chief objectives. But Kauṭilya (*circa* 321-296 BCE), also highlights the use of ratiocination (*ānvīkṣikī*) in the study and deliberation on these matters.[14] And both he and Manu make it mandatory for the king to attend to the welfare of the citizens first, by seeking to protect the rights and interests of the individual within a group framework, although not in the most egalitarian manner. Manu even admits that there are different *dharmas* in different epochs (*yugas*), which is suggestive of relativity in ethics.[15] Manu decrees some ten virtues, namely contentment, forgiveness, self-restraint, non-anger, non-appropriating,

---

13 *Chāndogya Upaniṣad*, 4.4.5.

14 Kane, op cit, vol. I, p. 225; Kauṭilya's *Arthaśāstra*, trans. by R. Shamasastry, Mysore: Mysore Printing and Publishing House,1960; R.P. Kangle, (1986, 1988, 1922), The Kauṭilya Arthaśāstra, Part I, Sanskrit text, Part II, English trans.; Part III, A Study. Delhi: Motilal Banarsidass. See also P. Bilimoria, 'Kauṭilya', *Encyclopaedia of Philosophy*, London: Routledge, 1998, pp. 220-22.

15 *The Manusmṛti*, 1, 81-86, ed. by Satya Bhushan Yogi, Delhi: Motilal Banarsidass. 1975.

purity, sensual-control, wisdom, self-knowledge, and truth. Again, these are common to all Indian ethics.

Kauṭilya's ethic of the state

Kauṭilya is one of those curious Indian moral and political thinkers whose contribution to philosophy is marred with contentions and debate: which usually opens with a question of his motive for writing the famed political treatise known as the *Arthaśāstra.*[16] The compendium is often compared with the *Prince* of Machiavelli, and its influence on subsequent political and literary writers (though only marginally on Manu), including Jaina thinkers, is noted. Tradition too has remained somewhat ambivalent about the text, especially in respect of subjecting people to the 'rule of the rod' (*daṇḍanīti*) by the monarch and the seemingly ruthless prescriptions for the most efficacious governance, although this did not prevent certain important teachings, especially on the province of law, from being appropriated later by the *Dharmaśāstras.* These apprehensions, in any case, are arguably misplaced as on closer reading Kauṭilya is assiduously concerned to secure the welfare and wealth of the citizens of a state under a just government of which the king is one among seven, albeit the sovereign, *prakriti* (institutes). Upon the learned and disciplined king falls the duty of safeguarding the commonweal (cashed out in terms of *artha*, *kāma*, and entitlements) of the people in as best and *dharma*-sanctioned way as it is possible, within the constraints of the tradition and prevailing conditions.

Kauṭilya however proffers no arguments and justification for the main principles grounding his political precepts, or even as to why the *varga* of *artha* (literally wealth and livelihood) is made the principal 'kingdom of end' over and above those of *dharma* and *mokṣa*, as traditionally conceived. While the signifiance of *kāma* (enjoyments and sensuality) is laudably underscored (in the life of the king as of the people), and *dharma* or law is upheld as the immemorial beacon of socially ordered conduct, *mokṣa* or the end of spiritual enlightenment and escape from the material world, warrants no place in the *Arthaśāstra.*

In this regard, the *Arthaśāstra* sets out to create a secular ethos, in which nevertheless religious life and spiritual wisdom continue unfettered, if not given due prominence in the immediate appointment of the *purohita*, the brāhmaṇical priest-chancellor, who is consulted by the monarch at every decisive step in the affairs of the state. It could be said, however, that the posture of the *purohita* is simply a means of securing the highest privileges and hieratic dispensation for the brahmin, the uppercrust in the *varṇāśrama* (or 'caste-birth') system, which once again stakes its erstwhile position in the Indian life-world. Laws pertaining to restriction in the forms of marriage or extra-marital relations are allowed for; the urban location of each of the major caste-groups and their respective duties, and other causes for inter-caste mixing (*varṇasaṃkara*), are inscribed. There are consequences for property claims, inheritance rights and succession with each determination in this respect.

---

16 See note 14 herein (the discussion here is in part derived from P. Bilimoria, 1998).

Nonetheless, beyond this Kauṭilya could not be said to be an apologist or even an advocate for an inward-looking Hindu *rāṣṭra*, of the kind that has surfaced, say, in post-Independent India that seeks to set back the sagacious Buddhist Aśokan through to Gandhian approaches toward a pluralist Indian polity. To be sure, the idea of a nation-state, loosely federated or unified, or even of a representative democratic state, never took root in pre-modern Indian political thinking.

It turns out that Kauṭilya is quite conscious of the diversity from ancient days of the Indian regions and accordingly allows for a degree of flexibility in matters of law and justice (*dharmasthya*). Indeed, the king is expected to attend each morning to pleas and petitions from subjects who may come from all walks of life and different caste or subregional groups, including women, the sick, aged and handicapped. When meting out justice, the king or the state is not in a position to make laws; rather the sovereign court's jurisdiction is to negotiate between *dharma* (law), custom or settled community law (*vyavahāra*), transactions or commercial and personal practice and written edicts (*śāstras*). The king may overrule the latter two sources of law, but he cannot put himself above *dharma*, in accordance with which all instances of disputes and contradictory judgments are to be decided (3.1.40-44). This precept entails that the king maintains detailed codes of law and precedents, and judges each case by its merit or otherwise in law, and he metes out punishment proportionate to the offence of violation of the codes, but not in whimsical excess. His ministers (*amātyas* or *mantrins*), the *purohita*, the ascetics, even the queen and prince, the gods and above all *dharma* maintain a check and are witness to any possible deviation. Kauṭilya is also credited with having been among the first to set down codes of law (which come close to the secular codification toward which Hindu Code Bills have been moving in recent decades), as distinct from re-inscripting desirable prescriptions and diverse customary rules, regardless of their moral or philosophical merits, etc.

It should not come as a complete surprise then to see Kauṭilya according an unusually high role to philosophy in the training of the king. He calls this art *ānvīkṣikī*, here understood as the art of reasoning (*naya*) and learning in traditional disciplines (notably, Sāṃkhya, Yoga, Lokāyata), alongside the three Vedas, economics and politics. This king is initiated into, and is expected to maintain a regime of study throughout his life in these lores. The usefulness of *naya* is obviously more in the realm of law than its concerns in logic (*tarka*). Despite this positive register for philosophy, the author does not involve philosophy per se in thinking through deeper moral issues and problems in politics, in the way that Plato and Aristotle did. Perhaps the idealistic tendencies of philosophy in the *Upaniṣadic* tradition made Kauṭilya cautious about philosophy's true worth in the more realistic pursuits of state-making. Clearly, a pure life of detached or reclusive asceticism was not worthy of the philosopher, whose life of practical activity is accomplished if it culminates in providing further *upāyas* or instruments by which the state could provide for the protections (*pālana*) and prosperity (*lābha*), and sovereign stability – in short, the end of *artha* – of the people, for there is no state without happy people.

Following a comprehensive treatment of topics connected with internal administration, Kauṭilya devotes a substantial discussion on foreign policy and diplomacy, intended to fulfil the king's aspiration to be a *vijigīṣu* or would-be world conqueror. More usually the king through his emissaries and envoys maintains harmonious bilateral relations with the neighbouring kingdoms; however, he is cautioned to be vigilant and be alert to possible threats to his kingdom. To that end he is advised to deploy intelligence, spies, and secret agents disguised as ascetics who through spells of magic and progaganda create dissension among people and eventually insurgency in the neighbouring territory. In case the enemy proves to be rather powerful, then the king enlists the help and sanction of the other neighbouring allies, in a roulette of diplomacies common in international relations anywhere.

The Epics and the Gītā

The voluminous epics of the *Rāmāyaṇa* and *Mahābhārata*, through their moving narratives and anecdotes, explore the struggles, the paradoxes and the difficulties of coming to a firm grip with the evolving idea of *dharma*. The *Rāmāyaṇa*, which presents the heroic Rāma and his chaste Sītā as the paragons of virtue, is somewhat dogmatic on its stance of 'righteousness', while the *Mahābhārata* is less sanguine about exactness in matters of duty, as it turns over every conceivable ethical stance the culture has hitherto known. For instance, the sage Kauśika, who in the *Mahābhārata* courts censor for his insistence on telling the truth to a bandit, but which leads to the killing of an innocent man, may well be acclaimed in the *Rāmāyaṇa* for his uncompromising adherence to a principle, as Rāma indeed is for giving priority to his father's promise over his royal and family obligations. (Peter Brook's stage production, and later a six-part video, 'The Mahabharata' vividly re-enacts some of the classic ethical themes depicted in the epic.)

Bimal Matilal's chapter is focused largely on ethics in the *Mahābhārata*, even though its strategy is to pick through a narrative retelling of the disparate tensions, conflicts and dilemmas that arise in the moral world inhabited by the characters in the epic, calling for resolution, rather than offering the 'grand ethics of the epic narrative'. Matilal, in much the same way that Mohanty in his chapter, is concerned with addressing some of the fundamental questions in ethics, anywhere, looking to see how the tradition of these texts and culture deal with them. Mohanty looks for a theory of action in the Indian moral philosophy, wondering just what it would look like, and how it might compare with Hegel's grounding concepts of Moralität and Sittlichkeit, and with Kant's concerns with categorical imperative, the law, and the role of principles. Both writers make extensive reference to the *Bhagavadgītā*.

The *Bhagavadgītā*, however, which is part of the *Mahābhārata*, appears to be more decisive in its ethical pronouncements, and perhaps for that reason has had an extraordinary impact on the Hindu and modern Indian mind. And so we want us to move quickly to the *Bhagavadgītā* (*Gītā* for short) and outline one or two of its outstanding features. The *Gītā* places itself right in the middle of two opposing traditions: *Nivṛtti*, austere path of anti-action (echoing pre-Vedic asceticism), and *Pravṛtti*, the doing of social and moral duties. Each had ethical ramifications for its time and their respective codes and rules were in competition and conflict.

While the *Gītā* is recognized for the ingenuity with which it raises a host of ethical issues (for example: Should I kill my own kith and kin for the sake of regaining my rightful sovereignty?), its judgments have not satisfied all and sundry. The *Gītā* resolves the deep traditional conflict by working through a synthesis of asceticism and activity in its unique concept of *niṣkāma karma* or disinterested action, which implies that one does not forsake one's apportioned duties but performs them with complete disregard for the fruits or consequences. An agent only has a 'right' (*adhikāra*) to the performance of the action and not to its fruit (*phala*) (II.47), or paradoxically, 'inaction in action, and action in inaction'. This is an act-cum-motive based ethic.

This may sound much like Kant's ethic of 'duty for duty's sake', or acting from respect for the Law (hence the Categorical Imperative), but the precise rational-universalizable formulation of Kant is absent here; although there are suggestions of universalizability in the larger epic, the *Mahābhārata*, where it is proclaimed that 'one should not behave toward others in a way which is disagreeable to oneself'.[17] Śaṅkara echoes this sentiment also in his commentary on the *Bhagavadgītā*. The *Gītā*'s motivation is not so much to make the 'Good Will' the sole determinant of moral actions but to conserve the Brahmanical cultural pattern (the *pravṛtti* ideal) and integrate the threatening asocial ethic of ascetic-renunciation (the *nivṛtti* ideal), by appropriating the growing influence of an ideology of devotionalism (*bhakti*) with its theistic predilection, a trait hitherto not found to that extent (or outside of polyandric polytheism) in the larger tradition, into its body-ontology. The *Gītā*'s ethics is both formal and material: one must do one's duty (*svadharma*) according to his or her 'nature' (*svabhāva*), or the moral law and disposition within. However, this duty is determined by virtue of the individual's configuration in the larger social constellation outside (and the starry heavens above), i.e. the caste form of life to which one belongs and the stock of *karma* one brings from other or past life-worlds. Thus the maxim: Better one's duty (though) imperfect, than another's duty well-performed (III.35). But the specific content of the duty and the criteria by which they are to be judged remain obscure. Still, the promise of liberation lies in disinterestedly pursued action (*niṣkāma karma*) (II.14) and a crude 'work ethic' (*karmayoga*), denuded of egoism (doing x as an *end* rather than in one's own self interest) which, it is suggested, might appear to justify ritual activity (*askesis*, sacrifice, austerities and giving) (XVIII.5) and killing alike (XVIII.18). The general scholarly consensus has been that the *Gītā*'s doctrine of disinterested ethic has little, if anything, substantially in common with Kant's Rational 'asceticism', a view discussed in Mohanty's chapter.[18]

But the *Gītā* does not overlook the significant role that a quasi-rational discerning capacity plays in the process of determining what falls either within the ambit of self-interest or disinterested action or non-action. For this task it develops, along the

---

17 *Mahābhārata, Anuśāsana Parvan*, 113.8. *The Mahābhārata*, Books 1-5, trans. by J.A.B. van Buitenen, Chicago: University of Chicago Press, Chicago, 1978-1980; also contains *The Bhagavadgītā*.

18 See also, P. Bilimoria and P. Hutchings, 'The *Gītā* and Kant' (referenced in General Introduction, note 41).

lines of the *Upaniṣads*, the *yogas* (paths) that help sharpen the *buddhi* or intelligent-willing, evaluative emotions, and *jñāna* or knowledge, inclusive of factual and moral information. That the will with emotions could at once be intelligent and practical (socially-attuned), making for moral autonomy of conscience, and even disarming traditional morality when tensions and conflicts with or within normative systems run high, is itself an interesting idea canvassed here.[19] Apart from these teachings, truth, continence and nonviolence (*ahiṃsā*), (XVI.2; 17.14) as well as 'holding together of all' (*lokasaṃgraha*) and 'desiring the good of every living creature' are underscored in the *Gītā*.[20]

The ethics of the *Gītā* is more or less summed up in the picture Kṛṣṇa paints of the ideal ethical person, in the following passage:[21]

> Without hatred of any creature, friendly and compassionate without possessiveness and self-pride, equable in happiness and unhappiness, forbearing, contented, always yoked, mastering himself, resolute in decisions, with his mind and spirit dedicated to me ... he who does not vex the world and is not vexed by it, and is free from joy, intolerance, fear, and vexation ... who is dependent on nothing, pure, capable, disinterested, unworried, and who renounces all undertakings ... who neither hates nor rejoices, does not mourn or hanker, and relinquishes both good and evil.

But as to why one should follow these principles, and what if the consequences of one's action or duty is detrimental to the interests of another, the *Gītā* seems to have nothing to say. This has been said of Kant as well. Also, if good and evil are transcended, and the distinction obliterated, can there any longer be an ethic to speak of? Can we all be like Nietzsche's Superman? Modern Hindu reformers and Indian thinkers have attempted to countenance some of the difficulties raised in the *Gītā*'s ethical teachings, as in the entire tradition itself. One such individual was Gandhi. (We look at Gandhi in Part C, and also make some comments in the context of Jaina Ethics in the Introduction to Part B.)

IV. Does Classical Indian ethics have a concept of 'Rights' over Rites?

Finally, we wish to examine a concept in modern ethics that has been singularly endemic and powerful (except perhaps in utilitarian discourse). The concept has not only set the agenda for reframing not only the many ancient, 'primitive', classical, and pre-Enlightenment moral and political modes of thinking, but also impacted on state policies, democratic frameworks, individualism, economic rationalism, and so on. And that is the concept of 'rights'. It is often juxtaposed with duties or

---

19 See P. Bilimoria, 'Perturbations of Desire: Emotions Disarming Morality in the Great Song of the *Mahābhārata*. See General Introduction, note 44, p. 26.

20 *Bhagavadgītā (=Bhg)*, III.20; V.25; and see, S.S. Rama Rao Pappu, 'Detachment and Moral Agency in the *Bhagavadgītā*', in his (ed.) *Perspectives on Vedānta Essays in Honor of P.T. Raju*, Leiden E.J. Brill, 1988, p. 151.

21 *Bhg*, XII.13-17.

obligations, and the value or weight of the latter is circumscribed in relation to the force and (logical) pervasion of the former. But if it could be argued that a tradition does not have a concept of 'right/rights' in its originary insights or as it develops in subsequent historical times, would it mean that the tradition is that much the worse for not underscoring one of the more fundamental insights and markers of human *qua* human morality? Perhaps the emphasis on duties, obligations, rites, and even the ubiquitous *dharma* pale into insignificance in the absence of the neutralizing, negotiative and empowering instrument of the 'rights' discourse. Let us test this claim against the classical Indian ethical discourse.

So we begin with the question: Is there a theory or doctrine of rights in the Indian tradition? How does one even begin to think of rights in the context of ancient and classical Indian moral thinking? But, given the foregoing ruminations and the discussions in the General Introduction, would it be legitimate to speak of rights as entitlements without reference to the fundamental moral conceptions such as *ṛta*, *dharma* and *vidhi* or scripturally sanctioned actions? It would appear that, just as in contemporary moral discourse, it becomes extremely difficult to speak of duties without giving priority to rights in the traditional Indian context. One cannot speak of rights – if one can speak of rights at all – without giving priority to duties. Hence, we begin, again, with the concept of 'duties'.

Kartavya (Duties)

Duties, it is often said, is the primary concept in Indian social and ethical thought. Even so, there is almost no possibility of considering or determining duties and obligations simply with regard to the natural entitlements of the individual, for a human being is only ever conceived in the total context of the social order as sanctioned by tradition (with the possible exception of the *sannyāsin*). An isomorphism is supposed between *ṛta* (the cosmic or natural order, later referred to as *sat*, 'existence') and the right as righteousness (*satya*) and those actions of human beings that promote this harmony. This isomorphism is expressed in the comprehensive conception of *dharma*, which gradually becomes the touchstone of Indian life and the transcendental framework for determining the legitimacy or otherwise of the normative culture, of the gods, kings and subjects alike, at any point in time. As the root *dhṛ*- suggests, *dharma* is that 'law' that sustains and gives cohesion to the three worlds of nature, society and human beings. The discourse of *dharma* does with time, however, shift more toward the human dimension and forms the basis for a comprehensive system of social and moral regulations for each of the different groups and subgroups that comprise the broad Hindu fold, as well as specifying certain universal norms encumbent upon all human beings (in the horizon of the three worlds). What appears to give coherency to the conception is its appeal to the organic unity of being or existence (i.e. *sat*), to the 'just' (*iust-ice*) where it is due, and in its promise to minimize the burden of *karma* (individually and collectively).

Puruṣārthas' rights

Now the *puruṣārthas* or the deontological ends structured in the framework of *dharma*, it may be argued, circumscribe certain rights or entitlements to the person, albeit, within the context of a tightly-knit social relationship, whose systematic discharge (i.e. enjoyment in the sense of fulfilment) prepares a person for ultimate freedom (the 'end' of ends). But here again, while certain interests are secured, the function of the *puruṣārthas* is to specify duties and obligations (*kartavya*) which a person is expected to fulfil as he or she progresses through stages of the life-cycle (*jīvanāśramas*). These duties and obligations neither entail, nor are they entailed by, any correlative rights on the part of another human being. Of course, under the *puruṣārtha* scheme *kāma* or enjoyment appears as one of the 'ends'. But how can one speak of duties in respect of enjoyment? Is it my duty to enjoy? Does one have an obligation to enjoy, or does one have a *right* to enjoy? The traditional response is that one is free (i.e. exercises one's right) to enjoy as long as the duties encumbent upon the individual under the other 'ends', namely, *artha* or livelihood (which implies welfare of one's family) and *dharma* (which determines the social duties and other obligations of the individual) are being concurrently attended to. Hence *kāma* is not something to which one has, as it were, an automatic or unqualified 'right' at the expense of the other pursuits, including the duty toward one's own health, well-being and fortitude. The question is not one of ordering the 'ends' in a hierarchy (as some philosophers have endlessly argued), but one of establishing their correct relationship and inter-dependence.

* * *

Mokṣa, construed as absolute inner freedom, appears to be the only natural right one has any claim to, but again not without prior fulfilment of duties and obligations implied in the preceding stages of the life-cycle. These may comprise obligations toward offspring and kin as well as the performance of obligatory rites prescribed in the *dharma* manuals, in terms of what is owed (or in old English '*ought*') to them for their contributions toward the continuing welfare of human beings. In addition one has the obligation of making gifts (*dāna*) and offering libations (*homa*). Duties and obligations, in this cosmic perspective, are what make the world go round.

The king, too, has certain obligations, namely, to protect the citizens and their interests and to do right by them. Whether the law-makers who laid down these particular regal obligations had in their mind the correlative rights of citizens (as distinct from their interests) remains a matter of interpretation. For, if *dharma* sets the limits and constraints on the action of citizens and kings alike, then one cannot say that obligations are entailed by the corresponding rights of others. In Kauṭilya's case it is more likely that he was concerned to build up the kingdom of the prince, by the rule of *daṇḍa* ('the rod'), if necessary, than he was concerned with the rights of the citizen. Nevertheless, Kauṭilya does grant certain rights to the citizen in order to protect the people against the king's Machiavellian tyranny.

It may also be argued that the ordinances of Manu set down certain rights for the brahmin, for are his entitlements and privileges not protected and do they not entail correlative duties on the part of non-brahmins? It should not be overlooked here, however, that the brahmin claims his entitlements *qua* being a brahmin, not *qua* being a human being *per se* (which others are also); it is simply his good fortune to have been born a brahmin. Besides, these entitlements are set down by positive law or, if one wants to stretch the metaphor, by a natural law which was applicable in that particular epoch or *yuga*. It may be that Manu was merely giving assent to the status quo in the interest of some higher end that he alone could (fore)see. But the lowly social status and servility of the śūdra is quite categorical in Manu. The śūdra is literally the 'child of misery', though he has a few more entitlements relative to people of mixed caste and the 'untouchables'. At least the śūdra has a certain desert in virtue of his duties that cannot be easily forfeited.[22] One may rightly argue, however, that this has nothing to do with natural rights, for the duties are really those of the marketplace, or rather in the interest of his master (in deference to the well-worn cliché of Nietzsche's 'master-slave' morality, for which he relied upon Manu).

One may nevertheless ask, how is it that the brahmin claimed or appropriated certain rights with respect to the performance of rituals? Rituals have to be performed in certain prescribed ways for them to be binding and effective. But this is a procedural requirement, i.e. the claim is that whoever is qualified should perform this according to the rules. It is therefore an impersonal entitlement, although later literature fixes the brahmin as the most qualified instrument or agent for the task. And this entitlement soon becomes a matter of inheritance. For the law-makers like Kauṭilya and Manu, the *varṇas* (vocational groupings or 'castes') are arranged in a descending order and it is this scale that determines the claimable entitlements, privileges and obligations, as well as punishments and violations, encumbent upon each member of the group.

The brahmin, for instance, who keeps a non-brahmin maiden will jeopardize the inheritance rights (to property) of his sons born through the maiden; but a śūdra's infringement of a brahmin's prerogative could lead to the dispossession of all that he has in his possession courtesy of the brahmin master (VII.417). The brahmin's prerogative extends to cover his control over his own wife, son and any servant or slave, their property, earnings and so forth. The brahmin has no calling to serve anyone other than himself (and perhaps the gods), while it is a śūdra's natural and normal duty to serve the brahmin and illustrious householders, which is not something that can be enforced on the other *varṇas*. The king and his ministers (and a band of clandestine spies in Kauṭilya's state) are under obligation to safeguard these prerogatives, privileges of the 'twice-born' *varṇas*, and indirectly those of the monarch; although this latter calling is not strictly an entailment of a further entitlement claimable by the 'twice-born'. But the question still remains: can we speak in terms of the brahmin's *rights*, even if in a derivative sense? For if we can, then we might be coming close to finding a traditional Indian counterpart to

22 Also, Chitra Tiwari, *Śūdras in Manu*, Delhi: Motilal Banarsidass. 1963.

the (Western) concept of rights. We will return shortly to the specific issue of the brahmin's 'natural' entitlement(s) on which the derivation of the idea of rights would seem to depend.

Adhikāra

Is it possible now to locate a term in Sanskrit that is perfectly cognate with the modern term 'rights'? Austin Creel cites B.N. Chobe saying that there is no Sanskrit word that means rights, and goes on to make the following observation: 'Rights are present in the system, but as the obverse of duties, the reciprocal duties of groups and individuals to each other, and never in any sense separated in status. To the extent that one not only owed duties to another but was owed duties by others, rights are bound up with duties, any duty involving a corresponding right or claim.'[23] The observation is fair as far it goes, but we believe both Chobe and Creel (for citing him) have taken a rather conservative stance in not having looked into Mīmāṃsā ethics and the enormous impact it has had on Hindu jurisprudence over the centuries (to the present). It is the Mīmāṃsā that gave the term, which has become the standard signifier for both the early references, however inadequate and unsophisticated, and the modern adoption of the notion of rights in India (e.g. the 'Fundamental Rights' in '*Adhikāra-patra*' or the Indian Constitution). The term in question is *adhikāra* (in its Sanskritic and not so much in the popular vernacular usages, which simply means 'authority'; the Urdu term *haqq* is probably closer still, and it has been current in Hindustani). It may be noted that the verbal form of 'having right to' does appear as '*arh, arhati*', but there appears to be no corresponding nominal or gerundive form from this root.

Again, although a direct translation is not possible, the term can be construed through a series of derivations as coming closest to our current use of the term 'rights'. It has its genesis in Mīmāṃsā hermeneutics and its *phala* (or fruition) in the *Bhagavadgītā*.

In considering the question as to who is the proper subject of the *vidhi* or injunctions regarding sacrificial performances, the master of Pūrva Mīmāṃsā, Jaimini, speaks of the *adhikāra*, i.e. the criteria for eligibility on the basis of which one's entitlement to the act can be stamped. Four major criterial requirements are highlighted, namely *ārthītva, sāmarthya, agniman* and *vidvan*.[24] The first criterion opens up the eligibility to anyone who has the desire (*kāmanā*) for such and such a reward (*phalārtha*). Jaimini, so Śabara opines in his commentary, counts women as being eligible on the same grounds as men (though possibly restricted to wives to safeguard the classical (*Mahābhārata*) ordinance that a woman is not to act

23 Austin B. Creel, *Dharma in Hindu Ethics*, Columbia: South Asia Books, 1977, p. 19; Creel, Austin, '*Dharma* as an Ethical Category Relating to Freedom and Responsibility', *Philosophy East and West*, 22 (1972). pp. 155-68.

24 From *Jaimini Mīmāṃsā Sūtra, adhyāaya* 6 *pada* I. The entire chapter is devoted to establishing who has the *adhikāra* or 'right' to perform *yajñas*.

independently (*na strī svātantryamarhati*)). The second criterion specifies the fit and able condition of the desirer's body (*samartha*) to carry out and complete the performance. The third specifies the resourcefulness of the performer in terms of obtaining *agni* (sacrificial fire) and other instrumentations (*dravya*) in the prescribed way; and the final criterion supplements the second by specifying the requisite intellectual status of the would-be performer in respect of the knowledge, ritualistic formulae, *mantras*, and such details as are necessary for taking the sacrifice to its logical conclusion. (Only with the correct performance of any act can the connected fruit via the *apūrva* or 'unseen potency' be obtained long after the *yajamāna* has completed the *yajña*.) But such knowledge, etc. occurs only in the Vedas and anyone to be admitted under this criterion must know the Vedas and have access to Vedic *mantras* or *Saṃhitās* and the *Brāhmaṇas*. In the case of *kāmya* (optional rites) and *naimittika* (occasional rites), all the four criteria must be fulfilled, while in the case of *nitya* or obligatory rites (such as the morning and evening prayers) the first need not be present (for the *phala* should not even be an incentive here) and the second may well be deficient.

Now it would appear that just about anyone who is capable of having or expressing a desire for some *phala* – (such as a heavenly state, cows, progeny, etc.) – can claim entitlement under these terms. But when one looks closely at the fourth criterion, which is a sufficient condition for all variety of rites, it strikes one that the requirement of *vidvata* is intended to drastically curtail the scope of eligibility, by surreptitiously introducing two more strictures which are implied in this criterion. These strictures are, namely, that the subject must be a *dvijā* or 'twice-born' and an *upanīta*, i.e. one who has undergone the sacred-thread initiation ceremony (*upanayana*).

It should be obvious to any Indian that not all 'twice-born' persons undergo the initiation rite which is reserved for the brahmin and it goes without saying that a śūdra can never ever be considered eligible under this requirement. Hence, the further strictures serve the purpose of placing constraints on other groups that *prima facie* meet the eligibility criteria (with the help of the attendant unspoken strictures), thereby protecting the interest of the brahmin and, by default, naming him as the subject of the entitlement. Note, however, that the limiting conditions are invoked almost as though these were part of a 'natural' order or law, for what determines that a person X is a 'twice-born' and that another is a śūdra? Once birth as the determinant of this status is accepted, could a brahmin help being born a brahmin, and a śūdra a *śūdra*? Hence, within the terms of this framework, a natural process is believed to function that restricts the scope of the eligibility, against which a śūdra can have no grievance or argument to the contrary. The notion of *adhikāra*, then, is utilized in the thinking of the Mīmāṃsā for establishing the ground rules for entitlement which a brahmin might legitimately claim in respect of the performance of Vedic sacrifices; going further backwards, and somewhat circumspectively, one can delineate the morally transparent 'right' of the brahmin. This dignity is thereby virtue of the special birthright accorded to the brahmin; in principle, however, it may be stretched – as in the case of the first criterion above and in Jaimini's own words – to *sarvādhikāram* (universal entitlement).

On a similar tack, the Mīmāṃsaka treat a text in the *Mahābhārata, śrāvayet caturo varnān*, stating that the four castes have the *adhikāra* to acquire knowledge of the *smṛti* scriptures (*Itihāsa* and *Purāṇas*). This establishes the concessional entitlements which the non-'twice-born' castes can claim in respect of performing rituals which are derived from non-Vedic injunctions. Śaṅkara also repeats this (*śrāvayet caturo varṇān iti ca itihāsapurāṇādhigame caturvarṇasya adhikārasmaranāt*).[25] The more liberal procedure of interpretation of moral codes instigated by the Mīmāṃsā on the basis of the concept of *adhikāra* had far-reaching impact on later jurisprudence and handling of delicate moral issues, such that the Mīmāṃsā *itikartavyatā* (criterion) would be invoked on occasions, in Mīṭakṣara and in the Penal Code in the last century, to decide on issues that arose, say, in relation to *anuloma* (the inheritance rights of the son of the śūdra wife of a brahmin), which effectively overturns Manu (who, if we recall, proscribed such inheritance rights).[26]

Bhagavadgītā's 'adhikāra'

The Brāhmaṇical encoding of the discourse of entitlements in respect of the fruits of religion – such as heaven, *mokṣa*, Hari, Brahman, etc. – is challenged from time to time. Jaina and Buddhist critiques rallied against the foreclosure of this discourse, and while decrying the Brāhmaṇical proclivity toward ritualistic action they continued to place strong emphasis on the necessity of carrying out one's duty in all spheres of life. This *śrāmaṇic* critique of the Vedic ideology was to have a powerful influence on the *smṛti* (the 'recollected' tradition), wherein the seeds of the internal subversion of the Brāhmaṇic discourse are planted. The *Bhagavadgītā* embodies perhaps the earliest such critique.

The *Bhagavadgītā* seeks to consolidate the myriad of petty rewards and fruits promised in the Vedic rites into a single end (here following the Upaniṣads and Sāṃkhya), namely, of spiritual freedom; but on the orthopraxy side the *Gītā* takes over the Mīmāṃsā groundwork of *dharma* (and reconciles this with the practice of *yoga* and emergent *bhakti* or devotion). This is reflected in its rhetoric of single-minded purpose (*vyavasāyātmikā buddhirekeha* II.42) For the *Gītā*, as for the Mīmāṃsā, the rightful discharge of *dharma* entails the performance of certain duties. But the categorical imperative we find in the Mīmāṃsā is considerably weakened in the

25 *Brahmasūtrabhāṣya*, I.iii.38.

26 Manu VII.416. For discussion see, A.S. Nataraja Ayyar, *Mīmāṃsā Jurisprudence (The Source of Hindu Law)*, Allahabad: Ganganath Jha Research Institute, 1962, p. 37. Ayyar cites a case from the Full Bench in Madras (Case I L R 41 Mad. 44) on the question of whether an illegitimate son of a permanently kept concubine could legitimately succeed to his father's putative properties. (p. 78). Mīmāṃsā *nyāya* or principles of interpretation is often invoked to apply Hindu Mīṭakshara Law that recognizes heritable blood lineage between a śūdra and his son. Apparently, the presiding judge of the High Court in Madras during the period, Justice V. Krishnaswamy Ayyar, retained in his court a team of Mīmāṃsā pandits to pronounce on the likely Mīmāṃsā ruling in the cases he dealt with. This shows the regard he had for Mīmāṃsā juris-hermeneutic.

Gītā's discourse of *niṣkāma karma*, or disinterested action, for such a class of actions is still of a type intended variously to purify the mind (*sattvaśuddhi*), to please the gods (*īśvaraprīti*), and to contribute to the welfare of all beings (*lokasaṃgraha*). These actions are not necessarily prescriptive as Vedic acts are, but they stem from one's own *svadharma*.

Now the notion of *svadharma* which in the *Gītā* receives a gallant endorsement, on the face of it, appears somewhat akin to Kant's notion of moral autonomy. However, the *Gītā*'s notion, while it forms the basis of moral action, is not an abstract consequence that results from its critical method, but is a quasi-subjective category referring to the innate characteristics of the individual, which she has according her nature, here termed *svabhāva*.

In a sense the above combines both a formal and a material function. *Svadharma* tells one that one ought to do what one ought to do with regard to whatever is true to one's nature (*svabhāva*); and this is formal, as Kṛṣṇa pronounces: 'Better one's duty (though) imperfect, than another's well-performed' (III.35). But the content of this duty with regard to what is one's nature is promptly specified by the *Gītā* in terms, not of the psychological properties of the individual, but rather of the empirically-determined social placement or status of the individual. In other words, *svadharma* is ascertained by reference to the normative rules of that society, and that may be, as is certainly the case here, the particular class division and its encumbent duties and obligations. Hence one's *svadharma* is determined within the web of the *dharma-karma* dynamic, that is to say, the prescribed role in the interrelated network known as *dharma*. And one does this without regard to consequences or rewards, that is to say, in a spirit of detachment by rescinding the fruits of the action. Surely again, the Kantian maxim, 'duty for duty's sake' rings true here as well, but the difference is precisely in the way in which these duties are determined and legitimated. (Kant, in the final analysis, resorts to utilitarian considerations, the *Gītā* to a transcendental *telos*; in fact, it would be better restated as 'duty for *dharma*'s sake').

The *Gītā*, however, is not bound simply to the discourse of duties, for the idea of *adhikāra* had already opened up other possibilities and claims that might run counter to the 'rites ethic' it attempts to rescue, albeit in a broader context of socially beneficial action. In this regard the *Gītā* presents an interesting variance on the nuance attached to *adhikāra* in its own rather deceptive and delicate use of the term. It does this in a single verse (II.47): *karmaṇyevādhikāraraste mā phaleṣu kadācana*, which we believe is best read as: 'You have entitlement indeed to actions, never though to the results.' Arjuna here is being told that since he (Arjuna) belongs to the warrior group his *adhikāra* is to the act (which a warrior performs), and he has no claim on the results that may or may not follow. He is further told, by implication, that he has no entitlement *not* to do the act that has to be done, that is to say, he has no right to desist from what is (by his self-nature) encumbent upon him as a kṣatriya or of the warrior caste. While it may appear that the *Gītā* is confusing the locution of duties with that of rights (understood as entitlements, let us concede), the move is deliberate, because the author(s) here is attempting to introduce the idea of 'negative rights', which effectively states that no one, including oneself, can rightfully interfere with what is one's due or desert by virtue of the law (of *dharma*); if action Z is one's due, then so be it, this is one's entitlement and nothing should be permitted to erode its fulfilment. By shifting the focus from results or fruits to action, the weight of the entitlement is also shown to fall rather on the side of action than on the side of the fruit. It is almost as though to say that the *Gītā* was tempted to speak of the 'right to duty' (just as we speak of the right to employment).

But the *Gītā* is not that explicit, possibly because the idea was too novel and its application to the wider context of action may have met with understandable demur from the persistent ritualistic and ascetic critics alike. And the *Gītā* also wants to disabuse people of the false idea that they have any entitlement to the fruits of action – which is the reason for asking Arjuna to renounce the fruits (*phalatyāga*) and not the other way round. This notion of *tyāga* is not borrowed, as generally said, from the *sannyāsa* tradition, but in a qualified sense from the Mīmāṃsā, which stressed the giving up of (or abandoning from one's own hand) the *dravya* or substances (such as *soma*) used in the sacrifice. The discourse of duty which the *Gītā* wants to legitimate would gain greater strength from the locution of *adhikāra* which the Mīmāṃsā had got going than it would through any borrowings from the *sannyāsa* direction. But scholars and commentators, especially of the Vedānta-bhakti ilk, have concentrated far too exclusively on *tyāga* (which does not appear in this verse) than on *adhikāra* (which has had the same plethora of variant translations and readings as most other difficult or specialist terms in the *Gītā*).

We would venture to suggest that the *Bhagavadgītā* came very close to opening up the earlier notion of *adhikāra* toward a notion of *rights* in the Brahmaṇical context (for it certainly stretches the erstwhile concept of entitlements beyond the scope intended in earlier texts). It draws its guiding impetus from Mīmāṃsā hermeneutics (or *nyāya*), and seeks to apply it beyond the framework of sacrificial and religious rites to the broader context of social *dharma* (and in war scenarios also). But beyond this it could not go, for good historical reasons. The *Gītā* would have to accept the fundamental idea that all persons are born equal and that nature does not endow differential markings on the individual which immediately translate into social differentiations. It does, though, concede another kind of *adhikāra* to all people (one presumes) in the art of *bhakti* or devotion, for Kṛṣṇa promises to heed whosoever comes to him with a flower, a leaf, water, and a mind fixed on him alone, etc. But this overture toward a more universal *adhikāra* is constrained in the social context by the overbearing weight of *varṇāśramadharma* ('caste' structure) and an orthodoxy that could barely face reconciling itself with the challenges of the insipient individualism inherent in the systems of yoga-asceticism and Buddhism (through its denial of the caste structure if not of *ātman* also). Thus the response of the *Gītā* is restrained and calculated; it merely suggests the possibility of a discourse of universal human rights (*mānava-sarvādhikāra*) but does not develop it.

The medieval *bhakti* sants, especially Kabīr and Nānak, Raī Dās and Tukarām, Mīrābāī and Narshi Mehta, appealed to some notion of universality on the issue of the eligibility to devotional practice. This more humanistic strain helped to cut across caste and gender barriers and overcome the prejudices or prerogatives of the 'twice-born'. Just as for the Buddha a brāhmaṇa (brahmin) is one who is noble by disposition rather than by birth, for the medieval sants anyone who gives herself to Hari (the Lord) has the *adhikāra* to devotion and will undoubtedly find Him.[27] Kabīr added further momentum to this universality by proclaiming that, i) the real *sanctum sanctorum* is not in the enclosure of the temple, or by the Gaṅgā, or in Dwārka, as most paṇḍits would have people believe, but it is in the heart (*hṛdaya*) of each individual, and ii) there is no difference between the *Īśvara* of the Hindu and *Allāh* of the Muslim. By implication and in principle the Muslim has as much *adhikāra* as the brahmin has, and vice versa.

There will be further discussion of the 'rights' discourse in the Buddhist tradition in Part B, and in the modern context in Part C.

Purushottama Bilimoria

27 *Kabīr Granthāvalī (Doha)*, ed. and trans. Charlotte Vaudeville, Pondicherry: Institut Francais d'Indologie, 1951, pp. 41-42.

Chapter 1

Dharma, Imperatives, and Tradition: Toward an Indian Theory of Moral Action

J.N. Mohanty

There are two connected parts to this chapter: *dharma* and imperatives; *dharma* and *mokṣa* (freedom), as discussed in classical Indian thought, with a view to exploring the possibility of a Theory of Action (*karmavāda*) in Indian Moral Philosophy. The argument is critically examined in the light of cognate theorizing in European Philosophy as exemplified, in particular, in Hegel and Kant. Before we discuss some general definitions of *dharma* and their implications for ought-decisions and action, let me say something about the concept of action.

Theory of action forms the cornerstone for practical philosophy, and this is true of Indian thought as well. Legal thought and ritualistic speculations, ethical and spiritual philosophies centre around theory of action. Even those spiritual philosophies which recommend inaction or transcendence of action in any of a whole variety of senses make use, in doing so, of certain widely held ideas about what action is all about. Some clarification about the concept of action is fundamental to understanding Indian thought, and yet it is still one of the neglected topics in modern writings in this field. A theory of action would inevitably cut across psychology, semantics and ontology before it takes us into practical philosophy. A philosophy of action may take various forms. Besides the psychological analysis, philosophy of action may be either phenomenological or metaphysical. I will begin with the Hindu thinking on action and later return to Kant and Hegel, using them as foils.[1] A rather preliminary

1 A phenomenological account, given in Hannah Arendt's *The Human Condition*, distinguishes action from labour and work. While labour is 'the activity which corresponds to the biological process of human body' and work produces an 'artificial world of things, different from all natural surroundings', action (in the sense of Arendt) goes on amongst men. Labour assures maintenance of life; work produces human artifacts (tools, works of art), only action makes politics and history possible. Action also presupposes a community, it is not done in isolation; and it requires speech. Without speech, action cannot reveal its doer, and an action without its doer is meaningless (while an artwork remains what it is whether or not we know the artist's name). To act, further, is to take an initiative, to begin (*archein*), to set something in motion. Each action makes a new beginning (for Arendt, this corresponds to the 'fact of birth'), starts a new process 'which eventually emerges as the unique life story

schematic analysis of an action in the first of these yields the following factors:

i. Agent (*kartā*), knowledge, desire to act (*cikīrṣā* or *icchā*) and the effort or *pravṛtti*. We can begin with looking at each of these:
ii. Agent or *kartā*: Pāṇini defines the (grammatical) agent or *kartā* by the idea of independence. He is independent, who is *kriyānukūlakṛtimān*, i.e. possesses *kṛti* or will which is conducive to the action. He is the locus of that *will* to act (*vyāpāra*) which is the meaning of the verbal root. In the sentences 'the jar arises', 'the jar will be destroyed', the jar is not the primary (*mukhya*) agent even if it is the grammatical subject, for it does not possess independence in the sense defined;
iii. the knowledge that is relevant in the context of action theory consists of the cognition that something is to be done (*kāryatājñāna*);
iv. desire to act, or *icchā* (it is what is directly conducive to volition, (*pravṛtteḥ sākṣādanukulatvam*): 'desire is due to the self (*ātmajanya bhavediccha)* while volition is due to desire *(icchājanya bhaverkṛtiḥ*)');
v. volition or *kṛti*, it moves the will to put forth actual effort unless there is a powerful counteracting aversion (*dveśa*): effort is due to volition ('*kṛtijanya bhavechesta*');
vi. this leads to *yatna* or motor effort, whose general meaning is 'cessation of passivity' (*udāsīnatva-viccheda)* – resulting in the action itself or *kārya*; 'the action is due to effort *(ceṣtajanya bhavet kriya*)'.

---

of the newcomer.' Although each action aims at a purpose, 'the existing web of innumerable conflicting wills and intentions' make it unlikely that it ever achieves its purpose. The 'stories' that it does produce however go beyond the intention of the actor. As a consequence, the eventual outcome of one's actions is never the agent himself. It is as though 'an invisible hand behind the scenes' determines the outcome, so that the human being often seems to be a plaything of a god (as Arendt quotes from Plato). The doer is also a sufferer. In view of the endless consequences beyond human foresight, the old virtue of moderation makes sense. One truly understands an action at the end – when, as Arendt puts it, all participants are dead. To put it in another way, human essence comes into being only with death – not for the agent herself but only for those who will tell her story.

Arendt's account emphasizes the intersubjectivity of action as well as the intention and will of the agent – but at the same time reminds us of the unforeseeable causal chain that an act releases, of the tragedy of being responsible for consequences one did not anticipate, and the hope that with death one's life-story will be complete and thereby one's essential being 'constituted' for the first time.

Contrast with this Hegel's remarks on action in the *Jena Phenomenology*. Hegel, *The Phenomenology of Mind*, trans. J.B. Baillie, London: George Allen & Unwin, 2nd edn, 1966, Ch.VI A a, pp.467-86.

Again, Hegel is talking of action in the sense of ethical action (which we discuss shortly). The Hindu philosophy of action appears to embrace or embody both such accounts, while looking to ground it in metaphysics and psychology (among its variant treatments).

Part I Dharma and Imperatives

With this general introduction we may now turn to the concept of *dharma*, and begin with some classical definitions:

1. Jaimini's *Mīmāṃsāsūtra: dharma* is of the nature of an injunction;
2. Kanāda's *Vaiśeṣikasūtra: dharma* is that from which prosperity and the highest good come about;
3. Gautama's *Nyāyasūtra*: *dharma* is the agent's cognitions: that something is to be done (*kāryatājñāna*); that it can be done (*kṛtisadhyatajñāna*); that some good will come out of doing it (*iṣṭasādhanatājñāna*) – *ought implies can*;
4. Āpadeva: *dharma* is that which is enjoined in the Veda, specifying the goal to be attained.

'*Dharma*' is defined by Jaimini (i) thus: '*codanālakṣaṇo'rtho dharmaḥ.*'[2] This definition makes it incumbent on any theory of *dharma* to undertake an analysis of imperative sentences (*vidhivākyas*). This neither implies that the domain of ethics coincides with that of ought-sentences, nor should we assume that all ought-sentences are sentences about what one ought-to-do (or ought-to-decide).[3] Needless to say that in dealing with imperatives, we are dealing with an important segment of moral discourse.

The sūtra states that *dharma* is that which is known by the *codanā* sentences.[4] What is meant by '*codanā*'? The commentator Śabara explains as follows: *codanā* is that sentence which incites a person to act.[5] The sūtra 1.1.2 thus is supposed to have said what *dharma* is and is not; *dharma* itself is being determined as that which is not known by any other means of knowing except through the appropriate kind of discourse. This is not the only definition of *dharma* available in the philosophies or even in the Mīmāṃsā works. Another one is this: '*dharma* is sacrifice, etc.'.[6] The 'etc.' includes chanting (*japa*), austerity (*tapas*) and charity (*dāna*). But since not all sacrifices are desirable (in fact, some are positively undesirable), the same author adds: '*dharma* must be a desirable matter which serves some purpose.'[7] A second definition along the same lines of the just preceding ones runs as follows : '*dharma* is that from which well being (*abhyudaya*) and the highest good (*niḥśreyasa*) come about'.[8] An answer to the question 'What is *dharma*?' which abandons the project of

2 Jaimini, *Mīmāṃsāsūtra*, 1.1.2.

3 One may, for example, want to distinguish between moral values which are not duties, i.e. between ought-to-be's and ought-to-do's. For this, see Nicolai Hartmann, *Ethics*, vol I.

4 '*lakṣaṇa*' = *lakṣyate jñāyate anena iti.*

5 *codanā iti hi kriyāyāḥ pravartakaṃ vavanamāhuḥ.*

6 *yāgadireva dharmaḥ (*Laugakṣi Bhāskara, *Arthasaṃgraha*).

7 *prayojanavadārtho dharma iti.*

8 *yato'bhyudayaniḥśreyasasiddhiḥ.* (Kanāda, *Vaiśeṣikasūtra*).

defining it is this: '*dharma* is that which the cultivated persons (*āryāḥ*) praise when it is done, and *adharma* is that which they condemn when it is done'.[9]

Let us now return to the definition given by Jaimini. *Dharma* is that which is known by such sentences as incite one to act. What are these sentences? Obviously, these cannot be indicative sentences, sentences which purport to state facts. A sentence whose very meaning consists in asking the auditor to perform a certain action is an imperative which commands or gives an order. By '*codanā*' then must be meant imperatives which prescribe a course of action. These are also called '*vidhi*'. *Nyāyasūtra* 2.1.64 explains a *vidhi* as that which makes a person put forward the effort to perform an action.[10] But not any and every imperative sentence indicates a *dharma*; the sentence must be valid or *pramā*. Only the imperatives enjoined by the scriptures possess the unquestionable validity – either because their author is free from any defect or because they just are authorless (*apaureșeya*). I will return to this issue at a later stage in this chapter. For the present, let us focus on how an imperative sentence is able to incite a person to act.

I think, the common structure regarding 'incitement to action' – a structure that is accepted by all thinkers in the Indian tradition – may be represented thus:

Knowledge—	—desire—	—will to—	—motor effect—	—the action
(*jñāna*)	(*cikīrṣā*)	(*pravṛtti*)	(*ceṣṭā*)	(*kārya*)

Knowledge produces desire, desire produces the will-to-do, this in turn produces actual motor effort, the consequence of which is the action as a completed performance.

Within this general framework, there was however considerable difference in theories that were developed. The differences concerned the precise nature of each member of this causal chain. Beside these differences in interpreting the causal chain, philosophers also differed in their interpretations of the verbal form in which imperatives are expressed. Let us begin with the causal sequence formulated above.

What must be the precise object of a cognition, such that the cognition can produce the will-to-do through the mediation of producing the appropriate desire? Several answers are forthcoming to this question. The older Naiyāyikas held that the object of this cognition is nothing other than achievability of the desired good (*iṣṭasādhanatā*). The idea '*iṣṭa*' or 'the desired goal', for the Naiyāyikas, entails that the performance of the action will bring about some good to the agent: the good will consist in acquiring *sukha* or happiness and getting rid of *duḥkha* or pain.

Consequently, the Nyāya view amounts to saying that three cognitions jointly bring about the desire, namely, (i) that he can achieve the desired good by performing the action; (ii) that he can perform the action; and (iii) that no greater harm will befall the agent in performing the action (*balavadaniṣṭānanubandhitva*). In the absence of

9 *yam tu āryāḥ kriyamānam prașansanti sa dharmaḥ yam garhante so'dharmaḥ.* (*Āpastambadharmasūtra* 1.30.7).

10 *vidhirvidhāyakaḥ.*

any one of three cognitions there would be no desire in the person. Hence (i) and (ii) are cases of the general principle that *ought implies can*. The new (later-day) Naiyāyikas, such as Udayana, tried to simplify the matter by suggesting that all that is required to produce the appropriate desire is knowledge of the meaning of the imperative sentence. The imperative verb contains a suffix ('*tavya*' etc., in general the ending '*liṅ*') which indicates the intention of a competent speaker (*āptābhiprayaḥ*).[11] It is this knowledge of the intention of a competent speaker (possibly, of God) which assures the auditor of the achievability of the desired good by doing the action, and so produces the appropriate desire. The new Naiyāyikas thus retain (i) and (ii) but question if the cognition 'I can do this' is necessary.

Back on the Mīmāṃsā front, Kumārila Bhaṭṭa simplifies the matter a great deal by insisting that the object of the cognition which would be able to cause desire is nothing other than the *vidhi* or prescribed course of action itself. The imperative sentence causes this cognition. The Bhāṭṭas call this cognition *śābdībhāvanā*. Some explanation is needed of this key Mīmāṃsā concept.

A distinction is drawn in the Mīmāṃsā literature between two kinds of causal efficiency (*bhāvanā*), one exercised by words, the other exercised by the things designated by the words. The former is called '*śābdībhāvanā*', the latter is called '*ārthībhāvanā*'. In general, '*bhāvanā*' means – to follow Maṇḍana Miśra[12] – 'cessation of passivity' (*udāsīnatvaviccheda*). This change comes about in three ways: in the case of conscious beings, by effort (mental *yatna*), in the case of unconscious agents by physical motion (*parispanda*). These two fall under what is called '*ārthībhāvanā*'. There is a third mode of cessation of passivity, which is called '*preraṇā*', exemplified typically in the way a verbal injunction inspires a person to act. This is called also '*śābdībhāvanā*'. The suffix of an imperative verb has the power to produce this inspiration – which on its part produces in the person the mental effort (*yatna*) to reach the goal. One can then say:

> Knowledge of an imperative produces *śābdībhāvanā* (inspiration by the mere verbal form) the latter produces *arthibhavana* (mental effort to work toward achieving the goal).

Another way of getting clear about this important Mīmāṃsā distinction is to begin with a definition of '*bhāvanā*', in general. The following definition will serve our purpose.

> *Bhāvanā* is a particular activity of an agent, conducive to the coming-into-being of that which is to come into being.[13]

In the present case, that agent whose activity is called *bhāvanā* is a Vedic injunctive sentence. Now the sentence has a verb in the imperative mood ('One ought to Ø'). Typically, in Sanskrit, this verb would consist of a verbal root and

---

11 *Kusumājali* 5.6.

12 *Bhāvanāviveka* V.

13 *bhāvanāma bhaviturbhavanānukūlo bhāvayaturvyāparaviśeṣaḥ. Arthasaṃgraha.*

an appropriate suffix. The effect which is produced by the suffix is a tendency on the part of the auditor to undertake the action denoted by the verb 'Ø'. The suffix generates in the auditor a thought of the form 'This person/edict wants me to Ø; *ayam mām pravartayata*'.[14] The verbal root (Ø in 'One ought to Ø'), on the other hand, refers to a specific action which is to be undertaken as a result of desire for some goal.[15] This is *ārthībhāvanā*.

Suppose that Yajñadatta orders his son Devadatta to bring a cow. In this case, the sentence uttered by the father expresses his intent, understanding of which institutes to the son to become *inclined* toward action. Such is the function of the mere suffix – this is the *śābdībhāvanā*. This disposition then arouses in the son the tendency to *undertake* the action designated by the verbal root – this is *ārthībhāvanā*. Note that in the case of the Vedic injunction, there is no speaker's intention, for the Vedic texts are, on the Mīmāṃsā theory, authorless (*apauruṣeya*) (a concept to which I will return later). Consequently, in that case, the words *themselves* produce the inspiration in the prospective agent.

The Bhāṭṭa theory then amounts to this: an injunctive sentence gives rise, in the auditor, to its own knowledge. This cognition of the *vidhi* is itself the so-called *śābdībhāvanā*, which by generating *ārthībhāvanā* causes the will-to-do. The thought of conduciveness to a goal is implicated in the latter i.e. the *ārthībhāvanā*. Thus the object of *ārthībhāvanā* is not merely the action Ø, but the goal to be achieved, in the long run the *puruṣārthas*[16] which are the ultimate goals humankind pursue (and which, according to a well-known list, are four: *artha*, i.e. material wealth, *kāma*, i.e. sensuous pleasure, *dharma*, i.e. virtue and *mokṣa*, i.e. *spiritual* freedom).

* * *

To complete this brief sketch, let us recall that the Bhāṭṭa Mīmāṃsakas distinguished between two kinds of volition (or *pravṛtti*): those that are spontaneous or self-caused (*svārasikī*) and those that are imposed (*prairasikī*). The self-caused ones are the ones that are caused by the cognition of what is to be done as conducive to good; the imposed ones are: in ordinary contexts (*loke*), commands of secular authorities such as the king and in the religious contexts (*vede*), the imperative sentences of the scriptures. It is only the last which are strictly ethical. Those that are caused by the knowledge of conduciveness to a good are hypothetical imperatives, rules of prudence. Those that are 'imposed' by commands of secular authorities (such as the sovereign) are in accordance with law; only those that are imposed by the imperatives of the scriptures are strictly speaking 'ethical'.

In the latter two cases, what prompts a person to act is the simple 'imperative' form of the sentence. The imperative sentence or *vidhi* is often defined as the sentence which brings about volition. There is ample discussion in the Mīmāṃsā literature as

---

14 *puruṣapravṛttyanukūlo bhāvayiturvyāparaviśeṣaḥ śābdībhāvanā* (ibid.).

15 *prayojanecchājanitakriyāviṣayavyāpāra ārthībhāvanā* (ibid.).

16 *vivaraṇaprameyasaṃgraha* (Basumati Edition), vol. 1, p. 59.

to how the grammatical form of an imperative is conducive to volition as we have seen in the analysis of the *bhāvanās*. Now this rather complicated theory of the Bhāṭṭas seems to have unnecessarily multiplied entities. For Vācaspati on the other hand agency or *kartṛtva* is the co-inherence of cognition, desire, volition and effort. One who desires and even wills without knowledge of the means adopted and its operations should not be called an agent; nor should one be so called, if he desires, but owing to laziness, makes no effort. Does this above analysis of action – agreed upon in its general outline by the various schools of Indian philosophy – entail 'freedom or will'? The cognition 'I can do', which is a cause of the appropriate desire may be regarded as psychological evidence for freedom. But at the same time, the desire and the volition are also caused by the cognition of the proposed action's conduciveness to good, or simply by the force of the imperative command of the sovereign or of the scriptures. The Nyāya theory which postulates the three cognitions for the production of desire and effort is no less of a multiplication of causes.

The Prābhākaras accordingly proposes a much simpler theory. On this theory, conduciveness to achieving a goal is not a sufficient condition for desire and effort. Things past and things present may be conducive to producing good, but there is no incentive to act with regard to them. Likewise, future rain will be conducive to bringing about good, but there cannot be any incentive to act with regard to it; neither is conduciveness to bring about a good necessary for activity. Only when an action is painful that doing it needs the belief that it is conducive toward a good. Even when the two – being something to be done, and being a means to a good – are here one and the same thing, they are still different entities. One is being a means to bring about a certain result. The other is the propensity of owing its existence to effort. The Prābhākara point is, even if an action is conducive to a good result, its conduciveness to that result, i.e. its being a means to some end, and its being something to be done, are two quite different aspects.[17] An action ought to be performed if it is enjoined by a Vedic imperative – not because it will bring about a desired result. What brings about effort on the part of the auditor is the cognition of *kāryatā*,[18] the cognition, namely, that this should be done ('*idam kāryam*'). In effect, the Bhāṭṭa *śābdībhāvanā* is rejected, only the *ārthībhāvanā* remains. The imperative sentence, by its very form, denotes *kāryatā*, i.e. that this action ought to be done. One who apprehends this latter, is impelled to put forth the effort to perform the action prescribed. This 'ought to' is directly signified, on the Prābhākara theory, by the appropriate suffix: it cannot be established by any other *pramaṇa* or means of knowing.

The Prābhākara view, reminiscent of a Kantian-type theory of categorical imperative whose power over the will should not be mediated by thought of reward or punishment, stands at the other end from the Nyāya view. The latter renders confidence in one's ability toward conduciveness of the recommended course of

---

17 *anyā kāryatā, anyā ceṣṭasādhanatā....phalaṃ prati upāyatvaṃ phalasādha-natvaṃ, kṛtiṃ prati pradhānatvaṃ tadadhīnasattākatvaṃ ca kāryatvaṃ* (*Tantrarahasyam* by Rāmānujācārya, ed. K.S.R. Sastri, Baroda: Oriental Institute 1956, p. 57).

18 *loke kriyākāryatājñānātpravṛttāvapi kāryatājñānameva pravṛttinimittaḥ*.

action to produce a desired good and an assurance that no great evil will befall. This leads a person, upon hearing the imperative, to have the appropriate desire and will-to-do which then results in actual performance. The Bhāṭṭa view stands midway between these extremes: it recognizes that the imperative, by its very grammatical form, has the power to 'inspire' the hearer toward acting. This 'power' (*śakti*) of the words generates the objective urge in the hearer motivated by the thought of conduciveness of the recommended action to bring about a desirable result.

It is generally agreed that the Bhāṭṭa view is in consonance with the views of Jaimini, the author of the *Mīmāṃsāsūtras* and of Śabara, the commentator on Jaimini's *Sūtras*. The sūtra 3.1.4 explicitly says that actions have their purpose in the result and that one's action 'extends' up to the achievement of the result. Performance of *dharma* is motivated by the thought of result: dissolution of *pāpa* or demerit.

However, there seems to have been around an older view ascribed to Bādari who held that the Vedic injunctions impose duties on men quite irrespective of whether they bring about desirable results or not. It is this view of Bādari which Prabhākara revived and improved upon. While agreeing that the thought of the result is not what can lead a person to act in accordance with an imperative, he nevertheless asserted a causal link between the actual performance and the supersensible result by positioning the idea of a supersensible action (*apūrvakārya*). It is this latter, the *apūrvakārya*, the idea of duty, which is conveyed by the imperative suffix – no matter what the verbal root may be (it may be to offer sacrifice, or to practice austerity, or to give in charity). The Kantian strain comes out all the more in this seemingly metaphysical doctrine.

It is important to note that Śri Kṛṣṇa in the *Bhagavadgītā* revived Bādari's understanding of *dharma* when he taught that duty should be done without thought of the consequences of one's action.

Authorlessness of Dharma

Our knowledge of *dharma*, of what ought to be done, derives according to the Hindu tradition, from the Vedas. The Vedas, according to that tradition, are authorless, *apauruṣeya*. It is important to understand the significance of this last belief. So we have to ask, how after all are we to understand the claim that the Vedas are not composed by any human author? Here I will make use of an earlier discussion.[19]

There are two general ways of understanding the claim that the Vedas are authorless. One is to take it literally: they just are not composed. The other is to take it as meaning that their author is God Himself. They do not have any human author. Without giving any reasons, and seemingly arbitrarily, I want to reject both these contentions. But I can only say this much in defence of my rejection: the first does not make any sense to me, the second makes a large presupposition about the existence

19 This was my Presidential Address at the Indian Philosophical Congress, Calcutta, 1987. Parts of the address are incorporated in my *Reason and Tradition in Indian Thought*, Oxford: Clarendon Press, 1991.

of God and furthermore about God's poetic talent and also about his need to produce hymns in praise of lesser deities. There is another way of understanding that claim – one that is consistent with either of the first two – which for me shows a certain insensitiveness to the nature of Hindu thought: this is to hold that the scriptures are revealed texts. One needs to ask: revealed by whom and to whom? In response, when one realizes that certain familiar responses available to some other religious traditions are not available here, one construes that claim regarding 'revelations' as nothing but the claim that the scriptures express the spiritual experiences of their presumed authors. (Note that 'revelation' does not mean 'to be given in a spiritual experience'.) To me this last thesis is very muddled. Without wanting to deny that there are some experiences which are called 'spiritual experiences', I feel puzzled over the claim that sentences express experiences (of whatever sort). Sentences may be occasioned by experiences, they may point to, and announce the occurrence of experiences. But what they express, I take it, are thoughts. Even poetic language does not express poetic experiences. Contrary to Wordsworth, poetry is not emotion recollected in tranquility. It is rather, as T.S. Eliot would have it, personal emotion transformed into public concepts. When a mystic reportedly experienced the identity of Ātman and Brahman, I take it that he was not just reporting his raw experience, but his experience as interpreted by the concepts and vocabulary provided by the *Upaniṣads*.

The authorlessness of the *śruti* (the Vedic texts) means for me minimally the following: in the case of the texts such as the *śruti* the intention of the author is not relevant for understanding the texts. The text itself is primary and autonomous. (This is why the Mīmāṃsā held that the imperative sentences themselves by virtue of their grammatical form should be able to generate in a person the desire to act accordingly.) Secondly, the *śruti* constitute the founding texts for the Hindu world by opening up the horizon – the understanding of Being, as Heidegger would say somewhat obfuscatingly – within which the tradition has understood itself and we who belong to that tradition have understood ourselves. As I have put it elsewhere, the very words of the *śruti* have been taken up by us, the inheritors of that tradition, to interpret our experiences, and thereby we have also interpreted for ourselves the words themselves. Third, the *śruti*, has exhibited – contrary to the *smṛti* and the law books – a plasticity of meaning, an inexhaustible reservoir of meaning which is not exhausted by any system, but has made room for new interpretations. These three features, to my mind, capture the essential core of the belief that the *śruti* is authorless (*apauruṣeya*). The rest are pictures that are dispensable.

The Hindu understanding of *dharma* as embodied in the imperatives laid down in the *śruti* preserves the idea of ethics as rooted solidly in that tradition which was founded by those texts, but which those texts have permitted us to reinterpret ever anew.

The Nature of Hindu Ethics

We are now in a position to take a fresh look at the nature of Hindu ethics. And this we can do by way of letting a familiar point made against the idea of Hindu ethics guide our thinking. It has often been said that the Indian philosophies did not develop a moral theory. The task of a moral theory, one may continue, is not merely to produce a catalogue of do's and don'ts, of virtues and vices, rights and duties, but also to (i) unify them in a system, and (ii) ground them either (a) in the nature of things (i.e. in a metaphysics) or (b) in the nature of humankind (i.e. in a philosophical anthropology) or (c) in a supreme moral principle from which they all, in their systematicity, can be derived. Obviously, the Hindu philosophers did not quite do any of these.

There are two general ways of responding to this critique. One would consist in looking at the various ways the moral teachings were sought be grounded. Implicit in the first part of this chapter is one sort of attempt at grounding: in a grammatical-hermeneutic-psychological construct of the imperative sentences found in the texts that founded the tradition. In effect, what we looked at is a part of a large hermeneutic of the tradition. There may be attempts at other sorts of grounding. For an example of a metaphysical grounding, recall the way Kṛṣṇa supports the thesis of non-attachment (*anāsakti*) by drawing a distinction, *à la* Sāṃkhya, between nature (*prakṛti*) and self (*puruṣa*) in such a manner that all action (and agency) actuated by the three *guṇas*, belongs to the former while the latter, the self, in its essence, is a neutral (*madyastha*) onlooker (*sākṣi*).

There is, in the *Bhagavadgītā*, the large picture of the scheme of things as a system of sacrifices (*yajña*). In more recent times, authors have provided a metaphysical grounding to some of the concrete duties (both positive and negative) by seeking to derive them from a Vedāntic idea of the oneness of all beings. Thus, if we all possess, in the innermost core of our beings, the same Self, then, it seemed, virtues such as love of all beings and non-injury are in consonance with the very nature of things. 'Seeing one self in all beings and all beings in oneself", as the *Gītā* puts, it, becomes – not merely imagining things to be so but recognizing what they are in truth. Not infrequently one comes across an anthropological grounding of the virtues in the nature of the human person, reminiscent of the platonic tripartite division of the soul. One such doctrine follows the implications of the doctrine of the three *guṇas*, arranges them in a hierarchy with *sattva* at the top, *rajas* in the middle and *tamas* at the lowest rung of the ladder so that a virtuous life becomes a life dominated by *sattva*, *tamas* held in check by *rajas* but both under the guidance of *sattva*. There are also in the literature, a teleological grounding of a life of *dharma* (note the double meaning of '*dharma*': what one ought to do and what the nature of a thing is) – which purports to give an extra-linguistic and extra-textual legitimation to the code of duties, by maintaining that a life in accordance with them is conducive to a higher good. When performed 'without attachment', *à la Gītā*, the *dharmas* bring about 'purification of the mind' (*cittaśuddhi*) and prepare a person for the long and arduous path to the attainment of *mokṣa*. *Dharma* prepares the path to *mokṣa*. Ethical life is a preparation for what completely transcends it.

I do not intend here to develop and examine these varied attempts at providing the ethos of the people with a foundation. My own inclination is to recognize what was sought to be done, but to set them aside as being, in the long, run, unsatisfactory. They embed ethical life in a much larger scheme whose acceptance itself is an issue. I would here like to raise only one doubt: what is at most legitimized by these attempts is the very idea of *dharma*, but not the concrete contents of *dharma*, the idea of 'duty' and 'virtue' but not what these duties and virtues are, or why they are what they are. And yet the *dharmaśāstras* gave not merely a general idea, but a wealth of details.

Can such a 'material ethics of values' – recalling an appropriate expression from Scheler, Kant, and Hartmann – be deduced from, or legitimized by an appeal to some highest metaphysical, anthropological or soteriological principle? As Nicolai Hartmann has argued, the lower goods cannot be derived from the highest (should there be one such) or from the Idea of the Good, and it is more likely that the domain of values is not structured like a pyramid with a higher at the top. The *niḥśreyasaḥ*, *mokṣa*, the highest good, is not an ethical concept. And I doubt if it helps us to understand the way the Hindu Sittlichkeit was structured and conceived. The Mīmāṃsā saw this as clearly as any good moral philosopher would, and provided a foundation that is textual-hermeneutic and so 'tradition'-based, without raising it to the level of abstract universality. If Hegal and MacIntyre are right, this is as it should be. What we have in the picture of *dharma* is a concrete Hegelian Sittlichkeit. The *Gītā* built upon it and sought to raise it to the level of Moralität (in the sense in which Hegel imputed Moralität to Kant). Does Sittlichkeit need Moralität, unless the latter is inserted as a mediating link between the former and the grand soteriological finale?

The Destiny of Indian Dharma

In this last section under Part I, I will briefly respond to the question raised at the end of the preceding section, and then conclude with a few remarks about the nature of the Hindu Sittlichkeit.

Drawing on an insight of Hegel in *Jena Phenomenology*, although the Sittlichkeit of a people provides the concrete ethical life, the actual norms, duties and goods that a community needs for its integrity, there is no guarantee that it can be a perfectly coherent whole without internal contradictions and systemic limitations. In other words, one part of it may come into conflict with another, just as the system as a whole may lack sensitivity to certain goods and values.

Consider the destiny of the Indian *dharma* from a Hegelian perspective. Let us think of the conflict of Arjuna in the opening chapter of the *Bhagavadgītā*.[20] The great hero, who for the Indian antiquity typifies courage and heroism, finds himself

20 *Bhagavadgītā*, 4.16-17.

torn between the law of the family (*kuladharma*) and the social law specifying the duties attaching to one's 'station'. In a step that is unusual for him, he rejects the unnecessary violence that will ensue from his performing his social duty. Kṛṣṇa, in his initial response, considers this an obstinacy on the part of the ignorant and the scared. But the crack which has appeared within the texture of the traditional *dharma*, between its two parts, between *kuladharma* and *varṇadharma*, could not just be patched up even by Kṛṣṇa by simply opting for one of the sides: the very idea of *dharma* had to be transcended. The ambiguity and unsatisfactory character of Kṛṣṇa's teaching is precisely due to an attempt, on the one hand, to save the *varṇadharma* as against Arjuna's skepticism, and, on the other, to suggest a way beyond *dharma* toward quite another goal (which had not entered Arjuna's mind) i.e. *mokṣa*.

But the point of this detour via Hegel is to draw attention to the fact that no Sittlichkeit can be such a perfectly harmonious totality that time would not wear it out and history would not change it. A Sittlichkeit is all the stronger, if it admits such change from within, and if it contains within itself the seeds of self-criticism. The Hindu Sittlichkeit satisfies both these requirements. It undergoes continuous transformation from within, and it engages itself in a continuous process of theoretical self-criticism. Change from within is a change by new interpretations of one's basic texts (particularly in as textual a culture as the Hindu). This sort of change through new interpretation is rightly characterized by Vinoba Bhave as 'non-violent revolution in thinking'. Examples of such changes are: a re-interpretation of the term '*yajña*', from a ritualistic to an ethical sense in the *Bhagavadgītā*, and Mahatma Gandhi's re-interpretation of '*varṇa*' from caste to a hereditarily specialized economic and production group. As regards the seeds of self-criticism, Hindu culture exhibits three such: continuing questioning of the claims to legitimacy of the *dharma*s by developing a theory of *pramaṇas*, devaluing the *dharmaśāstras* (*dharma* texts) as *smṛti* as compared to the *śruti*, and, in close proximity to this, the almost pervasive tendency (excepting in the Pūrvamīmāṃsā) to make *dharma* a means to a higher goal, i.e. *mokṣa*.

Part II *Dharma* and *Mokṣa*: Sittlichkeit and Moralität

What then is the relationship between *dharma* and *mokṣa*? The former is what ought to be done (as well as not doing what ought not to be done). The latter is 'spiritual' freedom, freedom from the cycles of birth, freedom from the clutches of karma, freedom from that ignorance about the real nature of things which is the source of all bondage and suffering. It is the highest amongst the goals that human beings pursue, the goal to which all other goals lead, where they are all transcended, transformed and transmuted. The same happens to *dharma* too: the person who achieves *moksa* is not bound by the rules of *dharma*. He has no family, no caste, no position in the network of relations which constitute society and so no 'duty'. What is after all this lofty ideal which has loomed large on the horizon of the Hindu mind? The ethical idea of a virtuous man we understand. But do we really understand the idea of a 'freed' (*mukta*) person, freed from all suffering all ignorance, all misconceptions, also from all obligations and duties? No other culture has placed such an ideal at the highest pedestal amongst its goals.

If *dharma* is Sittlichkeit and *mokṣa* is 'spiritual' freedom (and wisdom what mediates between them) – according to the very influential *Bhagavadgītā* – is what, again in the Hegelian locution, can be called Moralität. It is the ideal of 'inner freedom', of doing one's duty for its own sake without attachment to the consequences, being moved by the sheer concept of what ought to be done, the idea of non-attachment, *anāsakti*. The contrast is between two kinds of individuals. The first of whom is a member of a family and of the society, and who does what the scriptures enjoin him to do and does not to do what they ask him not to do, all with the goal of reaping good consequences (*puṇya*) or merits for himself in this life or the next; he is moved by sanctions of reward and punishment, even by the pleasure and self-satisfaction of leading a life in accordance with the scriptures or even by distinctly altruistic ideals. The second is a person whose inner life is so completely at peace with itself that no thought of consequences of his action enters his mind – consequences whether for himself or for others – no thought of praise or blame, of pleasure or pain, of success or failure, disturbs his inner tranquility. Yet he does what the tradition wants him to do, not because if he did not conform to it he will be censured or punished in this life or the next but only because that is the best he can do in society (and he cannot just not do anything), so that in the midst of a life that to all outward observation is in accordance with the ethical laws, he is yet in his inner life *free*.

How are we to understand this contrast? There is one anxiety that must be squarely confronted and set at rest. Is the inner freedom, the spirit of non-attachment, the total unconcern for possible consequences for oneself or for the other, and all that is sought to be conveyed by the *Gītā* by the word *anāsakti* a merely empty form that can be affixed to any content? In other words, can anything whatsoever be done either with 'attachment' or with 'non attachment'? If 'anything' in the above question is too vague and too wide, shall we rather say that any Sittlichkeit (and note merely the Brāhmaṇic) can be transformed into Moralität simply by transforming one's inner attitude? If that is so, the Moralität has nothing to do with the content of action, its sole concern is the spirit in which one does what one does. Clearly such a separation of form and content is hardly satisfactory.

Kant and the Gītā

Let me again briefly return to Kant. In his ethics, Kant is on the side of those who put the emphasis on the form of morality, on the spirit in which actions are to be done rather than on the content. He did not want to give a new set of duties, but assumed that men, especially those amongst them who have a highly developed moral sensibility, already knew what their duties were. His own work was so to develop the very concept of 'duty' that in true morality would consist in doing one's duty for its own sake. It does appear likewise that for Kṛṣṇa in the *Gītā*, the *dharma* is taken to be already known. What Kṛṣṇa adds is that *dharma* is to be practiced in the true spirit, i.e. with non-attachment. Not unlike Kant, then, Kṛṣṇa does not preach a new ethical code; he reinterprets some older concepts, highlights some, and places the emphasis, following Bādari, on the true spirit of detachment with which one ought to do his duty if he aims at *mokṣa*.

Kant, however, does something which Kṛṣṇa does not. Kant contends and tries to show with appropriate examples, that the idea of universalizability (which follows from the very concept of duty) can yield to a nice test to settle any doubt whether a certain course of action is moral or not. We all know the limitations of this principle of universalizability as a test. Nothing like this is attempted by Kṛṣṇa. If Kant's attempt may be construed as showing, in case he succeeds, that the content is in fact determined by form; in the *Gītā*, it would appear the form is simply prefixed to the already available content. The *dharma* already laid down that a kṣatriya (of a warrior caste group) ought to fight a battle if the cause is righteous. Kṛṣṇa seems only to add: if he also aims at *mokṣa*, he ought to do that with non-attachment. The content in no way is shown to follow from the form. In order to be able to show that it does, one needs to show that only certain actions, and not all, can be done with non-attachment. Furthermore, one needs to show that there are actions which can be performed only with non-attachment. If these two propositions can be substantiated, then there would be a Kant-like deduction of the content of duty from the form.

That the *Gītā* intended something like this, is suggested by Vinoba Bhave. There is a rather puzzling contrast in the *Gītā* between '*karma*', '*akarma*' and '*vikarma*'. Even the wise men, we are told, are confused about this distinction. Commentators have differed as to the exact meaning of the three terms. Vinoba Bhave explains them in the following manner : '*karma*' means all those actions which can be performed with attachment or without attachment, '*vikarma*' stands for all those actions which can be performed only with attachment, while '*akarma*' stands for those actions which can be performed with non-attachment and are so performed. There is a certain intuitive plausibility for drawing such a distinction. One does not want to say that it must be at least possible for someone to commit murder or rape with non-attachment.

Clearly, non-attachment on the part of the agent in such cases would amount to nothing less than horrible indifference, a cold-blooded act of committing the most despicable crime. There are actions such as religious rituals and altruistic deeds like charity which may be done either out of selfish motives or out of a sheer sense of duty. Such actions when performed unselfishly and out of sheer sense of duty amount of '*akarma*'. But is there any action which is such that by its very nature it can be performed only out of a sense of duty, i.e. with non-attachment? I am not sure if there is any. This only shows that there is a limit within which the mere form can help us to decide what to do, and not merely how to do it? Here we again fall back on a given Sittlichkeit, as Kṛṣṇa did on the Hindu Sittlichkeit of that age. Hegel then was right that mere Moralität is not enough: without a Sittlichkeit there cannot be concrete freedom. But which Sittlichkeit? One inevitably falls back on one's own.

There is another place in Kant's thinking where we can look for some help to understand the relation between the ethical submission of the will to a given Law, and the rational need for moral freedom. This may, within limits, help us to think, at least in one way, about a possible relationship between *dharma* and *mokṣa*. Whereas in the first formulation of his Categorical Imperative Kant emphasizes the ideal of universalizability in the third and last formulation, he connects the form of morality to the idea of the moral will as self-legislative. One can trace here a route of moral development. One begins with unconditionally obeying the moral Law out of a sense of duty and ends up with the recognition that the moral law, being the law of practical Reason, has its source in one's own rational Will – not in an external authority however sublime and majestic. Thus at the end of this moral development, one may be still acting in accordance with the Law, out of a sense of duty, but without that sense of constraint which attends submitting one's will to an external authority, but rather with a sense of freedom arising out of recognizing that the Law is but the law of one's own rational nature. With this recognition, moral life becomes spontaneous, not a perpetual conflict to tame the will. Can we say that it is this which comes closest to the idea of *mokṣa*?

The spiritually perfected individual, in the language of the *Gītā*, is 'beyond the three *guṇas*'. The simply virtuous man who abides by the laws of *dharma* as enjoined in the scriptures is one in whom the *tamas* and *rajas* have been perfectly under the control of *sattva*. But on the metaphysical theory of the Sāṃkhya which Kṛṣṇa accepts and amply uses, *sattva*, like the other two *guṇas*, is still a feature of nature (*Prakṛti*), it also binds the self. The attachment to virtue can be as strong as attachment to vice. The theory holds however that there is a core of my being which I reach only when I strip away all the products of nature in me, my body, the sense organs, the inner sense or the mind, the ego-sense, intellect which it calls *Puruṣa*, whose nature is pure consciousness, and which is an uninvolved spectator. It is only by installing myself in that stance, by discovering as a matter of fact that I, in the innermost core of my being, am not an agent at all, that all agency – be it of virtuous or of vicious deeds – belongs only to *Prakṛti* and is actuated by the three *guṇas*, that I can be truly free. But the laws of the scriptures, the law books, do not flow from my rational nature as Kant would have said. Rather, these are social conventions which it is better to abide by than to flout; but more than this they do not have any more hold on myself. Thus *dharma* still is transcended as a contingent other and if the perfected individual still abides by *dharma* that is only to hold out to the other and large mass of 'imperfect' individuals who need the social ethic for their and the community's survival and should not be misled by the wise person's example of the latter freely flouting the conventions of the society. *Dharma* remains a contingent means for a high goal and has no more necessity than what characterizes a community's factually handed down tradition.

Hindu Moralität, again

While my purpose in the just preceding discussion has been to bring out the status of Sittlichkeit in Hindu thinking, nothing that I have said should give the impression that I consider the idea of Moralität as both a viable and desirable goal. But that is a topic which I did not set out to deal with in this chapter. One other issue remains however: that of the place in Hindu ethics of the concept of 'free will'?

It is indeed difficult to ascertain whether the Hindu philosophers subscribed to freedom of the will or not. In order to be able to decide this issue, we must first have to ascertain whether the Hindu philosophers had the western concept of will or not. One cannot just assume that this latter concept was available, that it is a purely phenomenological-descriptive concept without theological-metaphysical and historico-cultural determinations. One thing appears undeniable: the Hindu and the Buddhist philosophers did not have the tripartite faculty psychology so familiar in classical western thought. Volition was often a function of *buddhi* (intelligence), often of *manas* (mind) or *antaḥkaraṇa* (the inner-sense). If the same concept of will was not available, the problem of freedom could not have been the same – also because the problem of freedom arose in western thinking in the context of the theological idea of divine omnipotence (and foreknowledge).

Karma and phenomenology

In the light of this caveat, we may turn to the Hindu idea of *karma*. It is well-known that the idea of *karma*, with its associated ideas of rebirth and *mokṣa* as deliverance from rebirth, constitutes one of the most distinctive features of Hindu religious and philosophical thinking. What I am here trying to do is to understand some fragments of this deep conceptual structure, and to interpret its bearing on such familiar concepts as freedom. Strictly phenomenologically, an action has for its agent what Schutz called 'subjective meaning'. The agent knows what he is doing, what his intention and intended consequence are. He may even have the consciousness of having chosen to do what he does. However, this phenomenological consciousness, though valid within limits – e.g. within the 'reduced' domain of how the action is presented to the agent in his consciousness and with the real existential constraints bracketed out – soon comes to grief. Not only does the most rational of agents fail to anticipate – and even retrospectively to rationally reconstruct – all the consequences of his action, but the story cannot be complete before he is dead, and his own actions may turn back upon him as an alien power, as destiny, owing to the complicated web of other people's wills and intentions, or owing to the so-called divine law and the laws of unconscious human nature of which the actor is unaware. The point however is that, the chain of consequences of one's actions recede linearly into the remote horizon never to be recovered by the agent, in his own life time, but also vertically into dimensions from where they can surface recognized only as alien powers.

The Hindus, as also the Buddhists, realized this more clearly than any others. They also realized this situation in its extreme logical consequence, and sought to understand and bear with it in all its fearful and awesome possibilities. We have, however, gone beyond phenomenology into metaphysics.

How does this metaphysics of action and that phenomenology tie together? The connections are not difficult to see. If all action is caused by desire – as our preliminary analysis pointed out, if all desire to act is caused by the belief that it will bring about a satisfying state (*iṣṭasādhanatā*), the only consequences that the Hindu thinkers admitted into their theory were states in which desires are either fulfilled or frustrated. All other consequences are reduced to these, not denied. Actions bring about either *sukha* or *duḥkha*. The chain of consequences that recede beyond the reaches of phenomenological inspection are such states. But such states cannot float in the air, they need a habitat that is capable of conscious experience and one which is, in some sense, identical with the agent.

While such is the connecting link, the conceptual ties are not all that tight. There are indeed loose ends. For example, why assume that all consequences, even those that follow the death of the agent, are of the nature of *sukha* and *duḥkha* without covertly presupposing that an identical self survives as the habitat of such experiences? But nowhere in the transition from a phenomenology to a metaphysics, are the conceptual links so tight that one expects rational intelligibility, but not rational acceptance. The *karma* theory is a metaphysical theory *par excellence* based upon a phenomenology of action, not following from it deductively. As a metaphysical theory, it is capable of neither empirical confirmation nor empirical disconfirmation. Its appraisal has to be practical; how does the belief transform one's overall view of life, what meaning does it impart to one's vocations, decisions and choices, to one's rights and obligations and aspirations, to one's relations to others and to the world at large? These are issues into which I cannot enter, but before returning to the allied concepts of *dharma* and *mokṣa*, let me take this opportunity to warn against certain hasty and easily available misjudgments.

One such view is that the theory of *karma* involves determinism. If one's actions in their past lives determine one's situation in this, then, it may seem as though one is not free to change one's situation, one is already pre-determined to be what one is. This, however, is only seemingly so. In truth, what determines one's situation is one's own past actions, and likewise what gives shape to one's future is one's present choices. These latter however – and this is the truth about the charge of determinism – are not totally free choices as though they are made by a transcendental ego. At any time, my situation, determined by my past choices, has already been carved out, and the present choices are from within this determinate horizon. If I can never be totally free, neither am I totally determined. My life is an interplay of determination and freedom.

Karma and determinism

Even as I say this, I must add several remarks so that we do not jump to hasty conclusions. In the first place, the standard (western) deterministic theories have in view such objective impersonal and collective determinants as physical and cultural environments, historical and economic conditions, bodily processes etc. It is only the psycho-analytic determinism which has some inkling of the way one's own past but infantile experiences, operating within one's own psyche, may give shape to one's present mental life, but most philosophers who have thought about it in the context of the problems of freedom and responsibility have satisfied themselves that this sort of determination is compatible with freedom, moral responsibility and legal culpability. Karmic determinism is along this line, but radicalizes it still further and should be much less repugnant to the idea of freedom and responsibility.

There is one point, however, with respect to which comparison of karmic with psychoanalytic determinism is misleading. The point of the comparison was that both are internal (i.e. 'intra-psyche') determinisms. In both cases, it is my past experiences and their 'traces' within my psyche which determine my present. However, while this is clearly true (within limits) of psychoanalytic determinism, it is not that clearly true of karmic determinism. For one thing, in the case of karmic determination there is a systematic ambiguity in the applications of the words 'I' and 'my' across different lives. 'I' applies to each member of the series of lives in a unique sense, and there appears none who calls them all 'mine'. If I am J.N.M, and the past life which was 'mine' by A.N.B., I cannot now say that A.N.B. was I in the same sense in which J.N.M. is so; I cannot say A.N.B. was 'my' (past life) in the same sense in which the infancy of J.N.M. was my infancy. It is only if someone could remember all those past lives as having been 'his', then he would have a sense of 'I' and 'mine' which is different from the way we use those indexicals in sundry, mundane occasions. If that is so, then even if 'my' past life determines my present, that determination is ambiguous as between a purely external determination and a purely intra-psychic determination. The nature of this determination, the causation involved, is also different from naturalistic causation on the one hand and intentional causation on the other. The Indian theoreticians had to take recourse to the idea of suspensible 'traces' (or *saṃskāras*) to make sense of trans-life causality; what is important, then, is to keep in mind that this could not be causal explanation in the sense of a covering law nor could it have been arrived at by an inductive generalization (for ordinary experience could not provide data regarding the causation involved). My purpose is not to make the situation, along with its mystery, any more intelligible than it is; I wish to be able to say how it is not to be understood. There is no karmic science, there is a karmic metaphysical point of view, and this point of view – unless misconstrued as a scientific or pseudo scientific determinism – is compatible with the introspective sense: 'I could have done otherwise'.

Duties vs. Rights

It is often said that the Hindu ethics knows only of duties, but not of rights. If this is a limitation, it characterizes much ethical thinking in the West as well, e.g. the Kantian. You cannot remedy it simply by saying that once you have duties, you can derive right from them. If it is one's duty to respect life, a living being must have a *right* to life. Only that this deduction does not work always. (It is the duty of a *kṣatriya* to defend a righteous cause – from which no right accrues to anyone.) Even where it does work, consciousness of duty need not entail consciousness of right. Rights such as are embodied in the American constitution are products of modern consciousness.

The Hindu thinkers of antiquity assigned duties to ethics and right to law. The word '*dharma*' includes both. *Dharmaśāstra* includes both ethics and law. The latter is often demarcated as *vyavahāra*, but that is applied specifically in the context of court action. I will first say a few words about Hindu law, before submitting my conclusion.

Law

Let me begin by recalling one exemplary misinterpretation of oriental thought (which has had a great influence on subsequent ways of looking at the orient) and which we owe to a philosopher for whom I have great admiration. In the Orient, Hegel held, only one is free (i.e. the despot). Professor Tambiah of Harvard has gone into interesting details about the source of Hegel's information. To see how mistaken Hegel could have been, just note that according to the best authorities on ancient Hindu law, the king was not the source of the law. Rather, the judicial authority of the king lay not in the fiction of his divinity but upon positive law and in the king's role as military chief. The Austinian conception of positive law as command of the sovereign was never recognized. Every law, as Sengupta urged, was *dharma* and had its alleged justification in the supposedly eternal principles as well as in right conduct according to current conceptions of 'right'. The king was supposed to be the guardian of law, rather than the source of it. The sources of law are said to be the scriptures, tradition, good custom and *ātma-tuṣṭi* (inner contentment, approval of conscience). As Lingat notes, there is no reference in any of the commentaries and digests to the laws or ordinances passed by any historical monarch. The king cannot interfere either with *dharma* or with custom (*ācāra*). He can – according to *Nārada*, XVIII.9 – reform unreasonable laws, and – according to *Kātyāyana* 42 – abolish customs repugnant to reason. However, *Bṛh* II 28 wants the king not to touch custom.

In saying that in legal theory the sovereign had no power over law, I do not imply that powerful, despotic kings did not surpass their authority. What I wish to emphasize is that the one alone was not free. If the concrete medium of freedom was law, as Hegel himself held to be the case, the Hindu society had a good measure of that objective freedom.

As an example of philosophical concern with legal right, I will briefly take one example – i.e. 'property right'. The Hindu legal philosophers wrote extensively on this concept. The classic work is the logician Raghunātha Śiromaṇi's *Svatvavicāra*. An English exposition of this work is to be found in J. Duncan M. Derrett's work.[21] A familiar definition with which one begins is: '*svatva*' or being one's own property

21 *Classical and Modern Hindu Law*, vol. I, Leiden: E.J. Brill, 1976, pp. 333-57.

– *yatheṣṭa-viniyoga-yogyatva.* i.e. the capacity for using the thing at one's own pleasure. However since law did not permit any and every use, others amended the definition to run: the fact that a thing is morally and legally fit to be used at pleasure. Going through a series of such definitions, Raghunātha settles upon a subjective one: it is an impression produced in the mind by the cognition 'This is mine'. There were obvious problems, for property rights may belong to infants and lunatics – which needed rejecting a purely subjective concept in favour of an objective, relational definition. I need not pursue this fascinating exercise any further. This brief sketch, I hope, will suffice to displace many a persistent misunderstanding.

Conclusion

I began by giving a series of definitions of *dharma* as they are presented in the classical philosophical and *Dharma*-literature; to rehearse:

1. Jaimini's *Mīmāṃsāsūtra: dharma* is of the nature of an injunction. (*codanālakṣaṇo 'rtha*)
2. Kanāda's *Vaiśeṣikasūtra: dharma* is that from which prosperity and the highest good come about;
3. Gautama's *Nyāya-sūtra*: knowledge on the part of the agent that such is desirable and can be attained – *ought implies can*;
4. Āpadeva: that which is enjoined in the Veda, specifying the goal to be attained.

Thus according to the Hindu tradition, *dharma* in the strict sense (i.e. excluding the law codes and rules of policy) are expressed by injunctive (prohibitive) sentences of the Vedas. The later *dharmaśāstras* clarify, expound and explain them. These injunctions embody rules that are of various sorts: they may be obligatory or occasional; they may pertain to one's *varṇa* (rendered 'caste') or to one as a number of a family (*kula*), or they may be for all humans (*sādhāraṇa*). Of many of them, it is true to say that they pertain to a person's role and status in society – but this is not true of all of them: the so-called *sādhāraṇa* or common *dharma*s are not so. What is common to them all is that they are all expressed in imperatives.

The question in the context of this interrogative volume arises: Are they ethical rules? Was there a Hindu ethics? Even if we leave out legal, political and economic rules (i.e. rules conducive to maximizing self-interest) and focus on the core of traditional Hindu moral/spiritual codes, do we have there what should be called an ethics?

Two considerations weighed against an affirmative answer: in the first place, many of the rules have the form of hypothetical imperatives (recall the standard form '*svargakāmo yajeta*'). Only the so-called *sādhāraṇa dharma*s are not formulated in hypothetical form. Secondly, what we have is a seemingly motley crowd of codes, but no attempt is made to unify them in a system or deduce them from a principle.

I would like to make the following remarks by way of summary on these two arguments.

First, the core codes, if hypothetical in form, are correlated to consequences which are trans-worldly (such as: if you desire heaven, then you must perform x...) The philosophers who thought about these injunctions came up with alternative answers as to whether they are to be construed consequentialistically or deontically. Bādari and, following him, Kṛṣṇa in the *Gītā*, gave deontic interpretations: the injunctions are to be followed as duties, the consequences stated are not intended to be motivating factors. Jaimini gave a consequentialist reading: if you desire such and such consequence, then .... Thus, while a very important strand in Hindu thinking is Kantian (or, quasi-Kantian, for reasons given), the mere presence of consequentialism should not be construed as ruling out the idea of a Hindu ethics, for the idea of ethics does not analytically imply Kantian deontic theory.

Second, an important feature of the Hindu thinking on *dharma* is that the injunctions embodying *dharma* were never theologically grounded. The *dharma*-imperatives are not commands of God or gods; nor are they commands of political sovereign (even secular laws were not so). They are rather autonomous in the sense that they have their source in verbal instructions, not in any premise about facts that obtain. They 'ought' is kept independent of 'is'. This is the basis of the oft-advanced claim that the *dharma*s are grounded in *śabda-pramāṇa* (testimony). This is indeed a much larger claim that goes beyond Hindu thought: the claim, namely, that the only source of our cognition of moral rules is language, i.e. imperative sentences.

Third, not all moral theories are monistic, i.e. not all of them unify all rules into a system or deduce them from a principle. It is only in modern times that this mode of thinking came to prevail. The ethics of virtue of antiquity was pluralistic.

Fourth, I distinguished, following Hegel, between Sittlichkeit and Moralität, and maintained that, in Hegel's sense, Hindu ethics concerned Sittlichkeit; it was not Moralität in the modern, Kantian sense. Read Hegel's account of the Greek ethical world where every one knew for certain what he had to do: the laws are known to everybody, 'familiar and recognized', in the form of 'particularity' in a natural ethical community. The Hindu Sittlichkeit, as expressed in the scriptures, was meant to be such.

However, as Hegel pointed out, so also here, this seamless unity of Sittlichkeit is soon broken asunder by internal conflicts – not only between *dharma* and the idea of spiritual freedom (*mokṣa*), but between different domains of *dharma* (as the *Gītā* illustrates: between *varṇāśramadharma* and *kuladharma*.) Just as it was also the conflict between the social ethos and the laws of family that broke the unity of the Greek ethical world.

Given that the ideal of *mokṣa* transcends the claims of *dharma*, the conflict between the two pervades the history of Hindu thought as much as attempts to resolve the conflict. '*Mokṣa*' itself is construed differently in different systems of Hindu thought, but no matter what concept of it one takes into account, the conflict and the tension remain. One may want to resolve the conflict in any of the following ways:

Make *mokṣa* itself into a *dharma*, and give it a higher rank in comparison with the other *dharma*s.

i. Make *dharma*, or a life in accordance with *dharma*s, a means to a preparation for, even if not the immediate antecedent of, the attainment of *mokṣa*.
ii. Take away the claim of *dharma* to be absolute. *Mokṣa* transcends the realm of *dharma*, of moral good and evil. There is a radical cleavage separating the two discourses.

Orthodoxy chose either or both of (i) and (ii). It argued that *dharma* as embodied in the words of the scriptures had absolute validity even for the person who attained *mokṣa*. Without it, there is no *mokṣa*. Śaṅkara gave good arguments why *mokṣa* is not a *dharma*: it is not an action whose performance could be enjoined. It is rather a state of being, consequent upon knowing the truth. The philosophical issue turns around: can knowledge be the subject matter for an imperative ('You ought to know.')?

Liberalism rejected (i) and (ii), and opted for (iii). Morals are relative and changeable. You need some *dharma* or other for social cohesion. But there is no absolutely valid set of *dharma*s. The *varṇāśrama dharma*, or Sittlichkeit based on *varṇa*, has played out its role, and needs to be replaced by another. There is no direct transition from *dharma* to *mokṣa* – but rather a Kierkegaardian 'leap'.

Orthodoxy, however, did perceive a truth. You do not want a person who has achieved *mokṣa* to be an unrighteous person. You would reasonably expect his actions to be in conformity with some reasonable ethical system – perhaps with a system that is more internally coherent than that in common use.

What then is the point of saying that the person who has achieved *mokṣa* is beyond the distinctions between good and evil? Kṛṣṇa says this in the *Gītā*. To say that such a person can do anything whatsoever – for example a heinous crime – with impunity or rather with spiritual splendor is counter intuitive. One expects such a person to be righteous in an important sense. He may not be in conformity with the caste-*dharma*, or family-*dharma*, but he – we expect – will continue to abide by the universal *dharma*s such as truth, nonviolence and doing good to others. Why is he beyond good and evil? Would the Kantian distinction between 'good will' (seeking to overcome sensibility) and 'holy will' (with no such hindrance to overcome) help us? The ordinary person follows *dharma*s because the scriptures command them. The 'liberated' person follows only that *dharma* which is consistent with his self knowledge, and practices it with inner spontaneity – not as following rules.

Chapter 2

Dharma and Rationality[1]

Bimal Krishna Matilal

Introduction: Primitive form of rationality and free-riders

I wish to confess to my readers at the outset that some of the stories I heard in my childhood still hold a certain fascination for me. Although this may be tantamount to bias, I nevertheless wish to start with such a story, which is often heard in the rural parts of Bengal. For I believe that the morals of this story and other similar tales often contain rudiments of some primitive theory of rationality.

One day, a king wanted to create a lake of white milk, because he was tired of looking at pools and lakes full of muddy water. He imagined what it would be like to watch the beauty of the milky waves glittering in the sunshine. Besides, people would be able to have milk to drink whenever they wanted. So the order was given, and thousands of diggers got busy digging in order to create the lake. The digging was successfully completed, but the final ingredient was still missing: the milk. Where could one locate a quantity of milk huge enough to fill the lake? But, since the king wanted it, an order was given that, on a certain day, every citizen had to pour a bucketful of milk into the lake so that the lake that had been dug would be filled with milk. This meant that about one hundred thousand bucketsful of milk were expected to come from the citizens. But, what happened the next day? Each citizen thought to himself, 'Since milk is so dear and so scarce, I will pour a bucketful of water into the lake in the darkness of the night, and when my little bit of water is mixed with all the milk the others will pour in, nobody will be any the wiser'. Next morning, when the king woke up he went to take a look at his new lake of milk, but what he saw instead was a huge lake full of muddy water. Why? Because not a single drop of

1 Although a version of this chapter appears in print, spread across two chapters, in Matilal's *Collected Works*, vol. I (*Ethics and Epics*, New Delhi: OUP, 2002 – with due permission), I have tried to recreate the chapter here in the spirit (indeed to the narration from my notes) of the lectures Matilal gave on this theme in Oxford at various times (during my fellowship with him in All Soul's College, 1983, and seminar visits, 1987, shortly after a symposium on *Śabdapramāṇa* and Testimony). I am grateful to Jonardon Ganeri for sharing with me the papers as these were being collated, and to Professor Gayatri Spivak for reminding me of the importance of the 'Epic and Ethic' work of Bimal-da, which he or they never quite managed to complete. For which see my notes in P. Bilimoria, 'Postcolonial Critique of Reason: Spivak between Kant and Matilal', in *Interventions Journal of Postcolonial Studies*, London: Routledge, Taylor & Francis, vol. **4** (2), 2002, pp. 160–67.

milk had come from any of the citizens, since everybody had thought that the others were dealing with the milk and that he could therefore silently slip into their group without paying the price. In other words, everybody wanted to be a 'free-rider'! But everybody acted with rational self-interest in mind.

Let us assume that everybody wanted the lake of milk to be created because it would have been 'good' for the society in general – since it would create a common resource from which 'free milk' would be distributed to everybody – and not just because it would fulfil the king's whim. Then, one could say, at least from the point of view of this primitive theory of rational behaviour, that, by pouring in water instead of milk, every citizen acted not only immorally but also irrationally. For, based upon this so-called rational self-interest, the argument of each citizen was in fact irrational, since, among other things, everybody knew that everyone else could take the same line of action – based on the same argument – and that, if everybody did this, nobody's self-interest would be served because nobody would receive the intended benefit.

From the moral point of view, we cannot say anything very different. If it is assumed that each citizen was reasonably capable of making the sacrifice – contributing a bucketful of milk – and that in making that contribution none would have been subjected to unbearable hardship or a great deal of suffering, then, according to any moral theory, it would be considered immoral to be a 'free-rider'. Indeed, in accordance with one of the most well-entrenched and widely-held views of morality today – Utilitarianism – 'free-riders' such as those described in the story are clearly immoral because this action is irrational. In spite of many objections that have been raised against classical Utilitarianism, it unquestionably enjoys popularity and the support of many today because of the prime importance it gives to reason or rationality. In the past, Utilitarianism fought against the 'intuitionists' in political and moral fields, by emphasizing an impartial rational test for judging the existing moral principles and traditional social institutions. In many modern, modified versions of Utilitarianism, there is one common thread, that is, adherence to the principle that moral issues must be decided by rational tests. In fact, it has been even claimed that any theory of morality should itself be part of a general theory of rational behaviour.

By the term *dharma* in the title of this essay, I understand nothing short of moral virtue, or rather, a theory of moral behaviour, as it is found implicit in India's traditional wisdom. Thus, I prefer to call the attempt to be a 'free-rider' an *a-dharma*, or a violation of *dharma*. For, in the wider tradition of India, *dharma* stands for neither 'religion' nor the narrower caste-oriented duties. The best evidence for my claim are the frequent discourses on *dharma*, found throughout the two great Indian Epics, the *Rāmāyaṇa* and the *Mahābhārata* – in all their different versions, composed at different periods of history and in different regional languages – as well as in many folktales, stories and fables told at different times.

Dharma and its rational critique

Dharma is a popular subject of inquiry, often found in all such folklore and narrative literature. The nature of *dharma* is often hotly debated and argued about; no other principle has been regarded as sacred and yet open to disputation and argument. This need not be very surprising, for neither in Buddhism nor in Jainism, nor even in Hinduism, was God cited as the authority on *dharma*. (We will come to 'God'-talk shortly.) Hence the search for a rational basis of *dharma* is often compatible with these religious traditions. There were, of course, the Hindu scriptures. But these scriptures proved to be flexible, sometimes to the point that they seemed to have meant whatever their interpreters chose to make them mean. Furthermore, even when the literal text of the scriptures was taken seriously, the interpreters of the Mīmāṃsā undertook to make a rational examination (*mīmāṃsā* means rational examination) of the meaning of the Vedic (scriptural) statements.

It is true, of course, that, in those days, the search for a rational basis for mental or social behaviour was not free from unconscious bias and inherited prejudices; very few are unbiased, even in our own day. The supposedly rational argument often turned into a form of 'rationalization' or 'apologia'. The point, however, is that the tradition did not have to wait until something like the Age of Enlightenment came in order to question the basis of moral and religious beliefs. Even some of the actions of Kṛṣṇa and Rāma – who were regarded as incarnations of God on earth – were subjected to rational criticism over the ages. There is enough textual evidence to prove it and we will discuss some instances in the course of this inquiry.[2]

My claim so far has been that the *dharma* tradition developed through an attempt at rational criticism of itself. Another piece of evidence in support of this claim can now be briefly cited. Consider the caste-hierarchy that is almost as old as Vedic Hinduism. The *Śramaṇa* tradition provided a rational critique from outside. But, even within the domain of Vedic Hinduism, there occurred a search for a rational basis. What resulted was an interpretation of the *karma* doctrine that was intended to provide a 'rational' basis for the apparently irrational practice of caste-hierarchy or social inequality.

It was Max Weber who, in 1920, characterized the caste-*dharma* as 'anti-rational', because it denied the 'natural' equality of man.[3] But, Weber then went on to pay a glowing tribute to the *karma* doctrine of Hinduism, for he saw how the latter provided the rational basis of the caste-hierarchy. For him, the *karma* doctrine of Hinduism was 'the most consistent theodicy ever produced in history'.[4] The caste-hierarchy was, it may be assumed, historically prior to the development of the fully-fledged *karma* doctrine with its rebirth hypothesis. There is some justification for this conjecture, for the *Puruṣa-sūkta* in the *ṚgVeda* clearly refers to the caste-hierarchy.

---

2 B.K. Matilal, 'Kṛṣṇa: In Defence of a Devious Divinity', *Essays in the Mahābhārata*, in A. Sharma (ed.), Leiden: Brill, 1991, pp. 401–18.

3 M. Weber, *The Religion of India*, Glencoe: The Free Press, 1958, p. 144.

4 Ibid., p. 121.

But, although the rudiments of the notion of *karma* or 'just deserts' may be found scattered in various places in the Vedic hymns, it was explicitly referred to as a doctrine (although still deemed an esoteric or secret doctrine) in the *Bṛhadāraṇyaka Upaniṣad.* It was Yājñavalkya, the well-known philosopher of the day, who mentioned the *karma* doctrine in the court of King Janaka, in reply to a question from Ārtabhaga. Yājñavalkya did not, of course, expound the doctrine publicly.

This is how it is supposed to have happened. All the well-known brahmin scholars (both men and women) and priests assembled in the court of Janaka, and the one who could prove himself to be the best among the scholars gathered would win a prize of one thousand cows and ten thousand coins.[5] When Yājñavalkya claimed supremacy, a very tense session of debate, a form of question-and-answer session among the brahmin scholars, took place, all the others asking questions that tested the depth of Yājñavalkya's knowledge, and the latter endeavoring to satisfy them. When Ārtabhaga rose, he started asking questions on matters concerning various rituals.[6] But then he asked a very important question: 'Assuming that the person survives his bodily death, what substratum would the person have when his material body dies and dissolves into all its [material] ingredients?' Yājñavalkya replied: 'Hold my hand and let us go to a secluded place. Only two of us will consider [and know] the answer, not the others present here.' Then the two retired to a secluded place for a while. What they discussed has not been reported in the text. Only a brief account of the meeting has been given, in four lines. It is said that they talked about *karma* – a doctrine that should be admired by everybody, 'For good deeds earn merit for the person while bad deeds earn demerit' (or, the person becomes good in his next life through good deeds, and he becomes evil through evil deeds).[7] This was the outline of the primitive *karma* theory which was later developed in the tradition. And this is how the tradition itself rationalized the ever-persistent caste-hierarchy in Hinduism: the birth of each individual is predetermined by his or her *karma* in previous births. Such rationalizations, however, are not often seen as very rational from our modern point of view (they often amounted to apologias). But the point that I wish to insist on is that the search for a rational basis was considered, at least implicitly, necessary for supporting an existing moral principle, and the caste-*dharma* unquestionably had a moral dimension since it legitimized social inequality.

It should be mentioned here that, while people like Louis Dumont 'valorized' the Hindu caste-system and considered it to be a 'value',[8] Max Weber hailed the linkage between caste and *karma* as a pure product of 'rational ethical thought', even quoting from *The Communist Manifesto*, for he was struck by the obvious similarity in logic: the pious Hindus of low caste were in the same situation as the

5 *Bṛhadāraṇyaka Upaniṣad* 3.1, in *The Principal Upaniṣads with Śaṅkara Bhāṣya*, Delhi: Motilal Banarsidass, 1964.

6 Ibid., 3.2.

7 Ibid., 3.2.13.

8 L. Dumont, *Homo Hierarchicus: The Caste System and Its Implications*, Complete Revised English Edition, Chicago: The University of Chicago Press, 1980.

proletariat; they had nothing to lose, and it was open to them to climb up the ladder of caste-hierarchy gradually, and even to become a god in future life, through good deeds in this one. Although I hesitate to share Weber's enthusiasm regarding the implication of the *karma* doctrine, it cannot be denied that the doctrine did have that sort of significance. I also disagree with Dumont when he considers the Hindu caste-hierarchy as a 'value' and also a 'rational' practice.[9]

* * *

Another illustration of the linkage between *dharma*-ethics and the search for a rational basis may be in order here. I shall refer to another ancient text, the *Chāndogya Upaniṣad*, for another story. Satyakāma grew up with his mother Jabālā, and he wanted to have an education. He approached the well-known teacher of his time, Sage Gautama, for initiation and to join the groups of pupils. For the initiation ritual, Gautama wanted to know the name of Satyakāma's father or his *gotra*, that is, his family name. Unfortunately, Satyakāma did not know who his father was. He said that he would come back after asking his mother. But Jabālā had been a maid who had had to sell her body in order to survive. Thus, she did not know the name of Satyakāma's father. Jabālā told this to Satyakāma, who went back to teacher Gautama and told the truth about his birth in the presence of all the other young pupils. There was a ripple of suppressed laughter out of contempt from the assembled pupils. But Gautama had to make a decision – a moral decision. He got up, embraced the boy and announced: 'Now I have no doubt that you belong to the highest caste, that you are a brahmin, for such courage, firmness and truthfulness can only be the constitutive qualities of a brahmin. I would accept your mother's name as your family name. You will henceforth be called Satyakāma Jabālā. Come, I will initiate you.'[10] Jabālā Satyakāma became a famous Upaniṣadic sage. Here, again, a moral decision was made on the basis of a rational argument. Caste-*dharma* does not always depend upon birth; possession of moral virtues should also be a criterion for one's claims to supremacy.

The above is reminiscent of an episode in the epic, the *Mahābhārata*, where a similar problem of *dharma* was posed, and the decision or rational preference was made on similar grounds. I shall refer to it only briefly, as I have already discussed it elsewhere.[11] In the *Vanaparva* of the epic, a discourse on *dharma* took place between Yudhiṣṭhira and King Nahuṣa who, under a curse, took the form of a huge python. (As I have already noted, such discussions on *dharma* are frequently found in the

9 B.K. Matilal, 'Images of India: Problems and Perceptions', in M. Chatterjee (ed.), *The Philosophy of N.V. Banerjee*, Delhi: Indian Council for Philosophical Research, 1990.

10 *Chāndogya Upaniṣad* 4.4, in *The Principal Upaniṣads with Śaṅkara Bhāṣya*, Delhi: Motilal Banarsidass, 1964.

11 B.K. Matilal, 'Moral Dilemmas: Insights from the Indian Epics', in B.K. Matilal (ed.), *Moral Dilemmas and the Mahābhārata*, Shimla: Indian Institute of Advanced Study, 1989, pp. 1–19.

epic literature, which only showed the arguability of any *dharma*-preference.) When asked to define brahminhood, Yudhiṣṭhira said emphatically that what constituted brahminhood was not birth but a collection of moral virtues such as truthfulness, generosity, forgiveness, goodness, kindness. For, each birth was accidental due to the copulation of a man and a woman out of lust (*rāga*), over which the person born had little control.[12] This, too, shows the ambivalence of the later tradition to accept as entirely rational the prevalent resolution of caste-hierarchy in terms of the *past karma* of the individual. In the *Bhagavadgītā*, Lord Kṛṣṇa says, 'I have created the four *varṇas* (castes) in reliance upon the division of qualities and actions.'[13] This can be read more as a critique of the birth-based division of caste rather than as an endorsement of it.[14]

Dharma, its non-theistic basis

I have said above that, in the Indian *dharma* theory of ethics, authority was seldom ascribed to God. Let us now turn briefly to the *dharmaśāstras* to examine their version of what the authorities had to say about *dharma*. I shall use the most well known: *Mānava-dharmaśāstra*, or *Manu-saṃhitā* for reference. Verse 1 of chapter 2 says:

> Listen [my pupils], I shall describe *dharma* – it is always honoured by the honest and the wise [of the learned]; it is followed by those who are above attachment [greed] and aversion [hatred]; and it is approved by their hearts.[15]

Different commentators have given varying interpretations of some of the epithets, but all have agreed that they constitute a general definition of *dharma* (Kullūka, e.g. *dharma-sāmānya-lakṣaṇa*). In those days, any 'learned' person would have to be, among other things, an expert in Vedic studies. Hence, the commentators, being eager to connect the basis of *dharma* with the Vedas in some way or other, interpreted *vidvān*, or 'the learned', as *vedavit*, or 'versed in the Vedas'. However, the later (commentarial) tradition was aware already that everything enjoined in the Vedas was not a moral duty or a *dharma*. Commenting upon this verse, Kullūka, for example, quoted from the *Mīmāṃsā-sūtra* 1.1.2 of Jaimini, where *dharma* was defined as '*codanā-lakṣaṇo'rtho dharmaḥ*'.[16] But he noted immediately that, although *codanā* means Vedic injunctive statements by which the *dharma* duties

---

12 See my 'Images of India', ibid., (note 9).

13 Chapter IV, verse 13.

14 See also B.K. Matilal, 'Caste, Karma and the Gītā', in R.W. Perrett (ed.), *Indian Philosophy of Religion*, Dordrecht: Kluwer, 1989, pp. 195–202.

15 *Manusaṃhitā*, with Kullūka's Commentary, ed. Narayana Rama Acarya, Bombay: Nirnay Sagar Press, 1946. For reference to the commentaries of Govindarāja and Medhātithi, see also Kullūka's commentary.

16 *The Mīmāṃsā-Sūtra of Jaimini*, with Śabara's Commentary, M. Nyayaratna (ed.), Calcutta: Asiatic Society, 1889.

would be signified (*lakṣaṇaḥ lakṣyate anena*), there is the word *arthaḥ*, which means *śreyaḥ-sādhanam* or 'that which is conducive to good'. Hence Kullūka explains:

> Both are meant by 'injunction in the Vedas' [*codanā*]: good acts that bring about good, e.g., the *jyotiṣṭoma* ritual, and evil acts [*an-artha*] that bring about evil or moral lapses [*pratyavāya*], e.g. *śyena*, or ritual. Hence the meaning of the [Jaimini's] *sūtra* is this: only such Vedic injunctions signify *dharma* as are conducive to good, such as the *jyotiṣṭoma* ritual.[17]

It should be noted that, although they were enjoined in the Vedas, since rituals such as *śyena* or *abhicāra* were meant for harming others, it was immoral to perform them. This is another piece of evidence on how a rational critique developed within the tradition itself to separate the morally unjustifiable injunctions or action-guides from those that were morally justifiable or even morally neutral, for example, the quest for personal good such as perfect bliss, without harming others. This last type of action-guide may, therefore, be put among those that were rationally justifiable.

The other qualifications in the verse of the *Manusaṃhitā* quoted above are somewhat self-explanatory. For our point of view, it is significant to note that *dharma*-ethics, or the *dharma*-prescriptions, cannot be based upon personal greed or hatred. Impartiality is an essential ingredient in the constitution of *dharma*, as it should be in any viable theory of rational behaviour. *Dharma*-morality can hardly be assessed from a self-centred or emotionally biased, partisan point of view. We need the viewpoint of an impartial observer, just as equity and justice are commonly symbolized by a lady blindfolded and holding a scale.

The last qualification in the verse quoted is also important. It enlightens us about the human side of *dharma*-morality. Whatever action is prescribed by *dharma* must also meet the approval of the heart of the honest and the wise; hypocrisy can never be a part of the *dharma* behaviour. Traditional commentators, however, suggest several explanations. Kullūka thinks that the prescribed action must lead to something good (*śreyas*), for then it will be the natural inclination of the mind to perform such acts. Govindarāja interprets it as an absence of any doubt in the mind of the learned with regard to a particular action. Kullūka gives a taunting reply in rejecting this interpretation. He says that, according to this interpretation, if a Vedic scholar decided to travel to the countryside and had no doubt in his mind for reaching such a decision, then that would also be called *a-dharma* – an absurd consequence. Medhātithi first agreed that it meant 'approval of the mind', but then suggested a queer alternative: he interpreted 'heart' (*hṛdaya*) as the Vedas (for the Vedas had to be learnt by *heart*), and then – in an awkward manner – claimed that the phrase meant that *dharma* was approved by the Vedas. This was somewhat embarrassing to the commentators, for the verse, while giving an almost impeccable definition of *dharma*, did not make any explicit reference to the scriptures or the Vedas. Hence various exegetical devices were used to establish the connection between the Vedas and *dharma*. (It may be that the definition was intended to be general enough to

17 Op cit (note 15).

be acceptable to the Vedic and the non-Vedic people.) Medhātithi's alternative explanation, however, was too far-fetched to be true. As I have already explained, I believe that this last epithet was intended to establish the vital connection between *dharma* and the role of moral emotions, as well as the moral inclination of the person in determining the *dharma*. In this way, it supplements the impartiality criterion of rationality with the requirement of sympathetic understanding of the situation under which a moral decision is taken.

We may pursue this point a little further. As I will note presently, it was widely recognized that there was a strong connection between the dictates of moral conscience and *dharma*. Life presents us with many moral conflicts, some of which even amount to genuine moral dilemmas. In genuine moral dilemmas, rational arguments in favour of either prescriptions or actions (where both cannot be done, for the doing of one is the undoing of the other) are equally balanced. Hence if the rational agent is forced to take action, it is usually under unresolved conflict, and the agent may suffer from such emotions as regret and remorse. The Indian epics, especially the *Mahābhārata*, supply numerous illustrations of such genuine moral, or *dharma*, dilemmas, as I have argued elsewhere in greater detail (and will draw on a few instances shortly).[18] Some moral conflicts may be resolvable, but due to lack of sufficient information or informational constraints in the situation, a rationally arrived at decision may seem difficult or even impossible. But, since a decision has to be taken, for the situation demands it (and human beings cannot, like Buridan's ass, show an asinine preference for death by starvation over reaching a decision under unresolved conflict and picking either haystack, not *neither*), the agent may appeal to his or her own moral conscience, being impartial and not biased by any baser emotions such as greed, and his mental inclination will reveal his preference. I believe many moral (as well as other) conflicts are resolved in this way, through the 'heart's approval', and this is exactly what is implied in the last qualification found in the general definition of *dharma* in the verse quoted from the *Manusaṃhitā.* It is easy to support the above interpretation by referring to the original text itself. In verse 6 of the same chapter of the *Manusaṃhitā*, five authorities on *dharma* are cited (where, by the way, Manu did not forget to mention the Vedas):

> The roots of *dharma* are (1) the entire Vedas, (2) the *dharmaśāstras* as well as the (3) virtues cultivated by the Vedic scholars, (4) the good conduct of the honest, and (5) satisfaction of the mind (of the agent).

Six verses later, in verse 12, the same idea is repeated; this time, however, four authorities are mentioned instead of five, for, as the commentaries explain, the virtues cultivated by the Vedic scholars and the good conduct of the honest are merged into a single authority:

> The following, they say, are the direct characteristics of *dharma*: (1) the Scriptures, (2) the *dharmaśāstras*, (3) the conduct of the good, and (4) satisfaction of the mind.

18 See my 'Moral Dilemmas', op cit., (note 11).

In both lists, our interest lies, of course, in the last item, which is similar to the 'heart's approval' of the previous general definition in verse 1. In his commentary on verse 6, Kullūka says clearly that this authority is appealed to where a conflict of *dharma* duties arises. He even quotes a line in support of his claim from Garga, another author of *dharmaśāstras*:

> Satisfaction of the mind is the only authority in cases of conflicting alternatives.

Thus, it is clear that the tradition accepted several other authorities on *dharma*-morality besides the scriptures and the *dharmaśāstras*. This openness bespeaks of the rational stream of the tradition as well as the lesser importance accorded to blind faith. Appeal to the mental inclination of the generally upright person in conflict-situations that are not rationally resolvable due to informational or other constraints, should not be confused with an appeal to inherent bias or blind faith. In his play, *Abhijñāna-Śākuntala*, the poet Kālidāsa put a similar argument in the mouth of his hero, King Duṣyanta: In matters where doubt intervenes, the [natural] inclination of the heart of the good person becomes the *pramāṇa*, 'authority' or the decisive factor.[19]

Dharma and skepticism

I have said that *dharma* was a subject of rational inquiry, not a matter of blind faith, except in the case of the Hindus, where the Vedas were given the supreme authority. But even these Vedas were subjected to rational investigation. (cf. *mīmāṃsā*). Two further points need to be made here. First, the Vedic injunctions cover only a very small part of our normal behaviour at the social and personal level. Hence the necessity arose for guidelines – from the conduct of the good as well as from appeal to good conscience – to achieve rational resolution of conflict-situations. The second point is that medieval authors of the *dharmaśāstras* such as Manu and Yājñavalkya were fully aware of the role of rationality in determining various moral or *dharma* preferences. This may sound a bit odd to some of us moderners, since these authors achieved notoriety for their narrow-mindedness, for 'irrational' rationalization of the same existing unjust social institutions such as inequalities in caste discrimination, and for resisting the change that was bound to come along with the change of time and environment. However, it is undeniable that these same authors also realized that the full extent of *dharma*-morality can be sustained only if it can be given a rational basis. Besides, the stream of critical rationality in the tradition was already alive and active. There were dissident voices not only from the low castes but also from the higher strata of the society, the brahmin priests, etc. We hear frequent stories in the epics and the *purāṇas* of a certain Cārvāka – an adherent of a philosophy skeptical of religious tradition – who, having entered the assembly of the brahmin priests (he

19 Kālidāsa, *Abhjñāna-Śākuntala*, Narayana Rama Acarya (ed.), Bombay: Nirnaya Sagar Press, 11th edn, 1947, I.22.

was sometimes described also as a brahmin), used to ask questions and challenge the validity of the Vedic rituals, using *tarka* or *hetuśāstra*, the 'science of reasoning'. Some of his questions were so radical that satisfactory answers were hard to find. The episode usually ended in turning him away from the assembly. He probably represented the radical rebels of those days.

In the *Rāmāyaṇa* we read the story of Sage Jābāli, who was one of the brahmin-advisers of King Daśaratha.[20] He came to see Rāma in exile along with Bharata and others from Ayodhyā, and tried to persuade Rāma to return to his kingdom, for he claimed that it was a false *dharma* (according to Jābāli) to abandon his kingdom in order to keep some old promise that his dead father had made to Kaikeyī. The sage expounded elaborately a philosophy of materialism and a hedonistic ethic in support of his argument. Of course, Rāma rejected the advice, but that is not the point here. Even traditional authors of *dharmaśāstras* occasionally referred to such a hedonistic ethic as well as to the arguments of those who challenged the authority of the Vedas. Manu, for example, recognized the persistence of such brahmins who used to condemn the Vedic rituals by using reasoning, when he said (chapter 2, verse 11):

> Such a 'two-born' [= brahmin, *dvija*] person as would condemn the root of *dharma* [i.e., the Vedas], having recourse to the 'science of reasoning' [*hetuśāstra*], should be turned away by the good people, for he vilifies the Vedas and is a 'Negativist' [*nāstika.*]

The commentators pointed out that logic, or the science of reasoning, can be used in two ways: (1) to support and give a rational explanation of the Vedas, and (2) to reject it and thereby overthrow its authority. Obviously, it was claimed that the first was 'right' or 'the good way', which was acceptable to followers of the *dharma*-ethics, and the second was 'bad' and hence unacceptable.

Toward the end of the *Mānava-dharmaśāstra,* the rational basis of *dharma* was again emphasized. Chapter 12, verse 105, says in unambiguous language:

> *dharma*-ethics must be very well-acquainted with such *pramāṇas*, 'means of knowledge' as perception, inference and various *śāstra* and texts [sources of verbal testimony].

The commentators noted that the three well-known *pramāṇas* – perception, inference and verbal testimony – are mentioned here as essential requirements for determining any controversy regarding *dharma*. The next verse (106) makes it clearer:

> Only he comes to know the *dharma* – he who examines in the light of reason (*tarka*) any instruction of *dharma* by the sages, and examines them so as not to contradict the Vedas – not anybody else.

In the case of dispute over *dharma*, where it is not easy to decide which course of action should be followed, or by which action *dharma*-morality would be sustained,

---

20 *The Rāmāyaṇa*, Critical Edition, Baroda: Baroda Oriental Institute, 1960–75.

Manu suggested another method which undoubtedly foreshadowed the upholding of the 'rational-democratic' principle. In verse 110 of chapter 12, it was said:

> ["What is to be done?" if such a doubt arises with regard to a conflict of *dharmas* where the texts such as the scriptures of the *dharmaśāstra* have not laid down anything – verse 108 supplies this context] an assembly of not less than ten persons, or [if ten are not available] not less than three persons, should deliberate and reach a decision on *dharma*, and that *dharma* [thus arrived at] should not be transgressed.

In verse 111, a selection procedure for these ten members was given:

> The ten-member assembly will be constituted by three scholars versed in the three Vedas (Ṛg, Yajur, and Sāman), one logician [*haituka*, versed in *hetu-vidyā*], one dialectician or arguer [*tarkī*, versed in *tarka* 'dialectics' or hypothetical reasoning], one expert in semantics and etymology (*nairukta*), one scholar of the *dharmaśāstras*, and three laymen from three different groups, one celibate student [probably a young man studying under a teacher], one house-holder [a married man or a man with a family] and one *retired* person [a considerably senior man who has retired into the forest after leading a full family life].

This seems to be a good combination of people, whose collective wisdom will usually be an effective way to decide the *dharma* in a more democratic frame in matters of dispute. Both terms, *haituka* and *tarkī*, may stand for 'logician'. Obviously, they were talking about two types of 'logician', one who was expert in the science of evidence, or *pramāṇaśāstra*, and the other who was expert in the *prasaṅga* or *reductio* type of argument. Kullūka, however, took one to mean a Naiyāyika, versed in Nyāya-type thinking, and the other to be a Mīmāṃsaka, versed in the Mīmāṃsā-type cogitation. My own interpretation is, however, not very different.

Dharma and moral weakness

Admission of moral conflicts or genuine moral dilemmas (or *dharma*-dilemmas; they are given various names: *dharmasaṃkaṭa*, *dharmavikalpa*, *kṛtyākṛtya-viveka-nirṇaya*, *kiṃkartavya-vimūḍhatā*) requires using some method toward making a rational choice. It is obvious that some sort of pre-ordering or ranking of principles helps such rational deliberation. In matters of ritual-orientated *dharmas*, when conflict arises, the Mīmāṃsā school has determined a fixed rule of pre-ordering, and has given a rational argument in favour of such ordering. Unfortunately, in all practical cases of value conflict or ordinary *dharma*-orientated conflict, it is extremely difficult to establish priorities in the same way. Many epic stories that illustrated such practical *dharma*-conflicts show that the practical resolution of such conflict does not always fix priorities according to the same pattern. It appears to me that this respect for the difficulties encountered in real life is not a mark of irrationality or inconsistency, but emphasizes that we sometimes face moral predicaments for which we cannot find a simply rational solution.

One kind of moral conflict or *dharma*-conflict is the struggle against temptation, or what is called weakness of the will. It is typified by the oft-quoted verse that follows:

> *jānāmi dharmaṃ na ca me pravṛttiḥ/*
> *jānāmy-adharmaṃ na ca me nivṛttiḥ*
>
> *I know what is* dharma, *but I cannot persuade myself to act accordingly. I know what is* adharma *[bad], but I am unable to refrain from it.*

This type of struggle is well illustrated in the ancient epic, the *Mahābhārata*, which tells of a struggle between two families, the Pāṇḍavas and the Kauravas. The leader of the Pāṇḍavas, Yudhiṣṭhira, was addicted to gambling, while the leader of the Kauravas, Dhṛtarāṣṭra, had a blind affection for his son Duryodhana, an affection which led him to allow (by not discouraging) the latter to go to war against the Pāṇḍavas. Yudhiṣṭhira was called Dharmarāja, 'the King of *dharma*', for his righteousness and moral behaviour. But his addiction to gambling was almost proverbial – a fatal flaw in his character. He lost everything, his kingdom, his four brothers, his wife (Draupadī, was publicity humiliated while he himself was present, at the first of his gambling matches). Rescued from this situation, when the second invitation (or challenge) for gambling came, he had the option to refuse. Now, in those days, gambling was explicitly recognized as a vice among the princes, and it was not unknown to Yudhiṣṭhira that it was an *a-dharma*. Besides, he had the fresh experience of the humiliation and shame after his first defeat – not to speak of the immorality of placing his beloved and innocent wife, as well as his four brothers, in a morally unbearable situation of shame. But he was like the celebrated gambler of the *ṚgVeda.*[21] This proverbial gambler said:[22]

> Vainly I decide not to go gambling even when all my [gambling] friends left, but at that very moment I listen to noise made by the throw of dice, and then I have to rush to reach there just as a fallen woman runs [to meet her paramour].

Yudhiṣṭhira's behaviour was in no way different. The second invitation came, and he ran to accept it. The temptation was great. Of course, he gave a reason in favour of this: as a prince, he must accept the so-called challenge. But a man under temptation can always argue himself into finding reasons that support his action. Thus, a bank-employee about to embezzle funds may indeed find reasons for his action (e.g. to counteract the injustice done by the capitalistic system to poor and middle-class people like himself). And there was no moral (or *dharma*-centred) obligation on the part of Yudhiṣṭhira in this case, as he himself admitted much later on, in the *Vanaparva* of the *Mahābhārata*. In the *Vanaparva*, Bhīma once raised the question: 'What is the use of our gaining the kingdom back even though we would have to

---

21 *The ṚgVeda*, with various commentaries, Vishva Bandhu (ed.), Hosiarpur: Vedic Research Institute, 1965.

22 Verse 5, 'The Gambler's Hymn', 10th Maṇḍala.

fight for it? For, my dear brother, I know you well, and I believe you will again be tempted to gamble away everything if the challenge comes for the third or the fourth time, and so on.' To this blunt accusation of Bhīma. Yudhiṣṭhira gave a significant reply: 'Yes, he would'. He admitted that he would again be unable to check his temptation, for in this matter he had no control over himself.

There was a challenge all right – a challenge of a different kind – in the case of Yudhiṣṭhira. The challenge to him was to do what he himself (as Dharmarāja) recognized he ought to have done when desire, fear, temptation and the irrational hope that this time he might win after all, all inclined him to do the opposite. There was not the slightest doubt about what he ought to have done.

Dhṛtarāṣṭra's case was similar. He knew that his son Duryodhana was doing something completely immoral. Duryodhana's conspiracy to kill the Pāṇḍavas by setting fire to their house while they were asleep was quite serious, although even this might be ignored as an instance of the young prince's foolishness. Dhṛtarāṣṭra always looked the other way. He never tried to control his son or teach him any moral lesson. The father knew very well what his son had been doing, and he did not lack knowledge of the *dharma* or moral understanding of the situation. Each time he felt the pangs of his conscience, he would call upon Vidura to explain the *dharma*-ethics to his son. But he seldom listened to Vidura's advice. Anyway, in the two cases of gambling described, Dhṛtarāṣṭra made restitution to the Pāṇḍavas. He returned all their gambling losses to them. He also gave Yudhiṣṭhira Pandu's share of his kingdom after he learnt that the Pāṇḍavas and their mother were alive and in exile. But Duryodhana could not reconcile himself to this outcome. The last act of Duryodhana was unpardonable. According to the conditions of the gambling match, he should have kept his part of the bargain and returned the Pāṇḍavas' share of the kingdom. But he wanted an all-out war with the Pāṇḍavas. Although there were several attempts to negotiate a deal in order to prevent a most devastating war between two lines of the same royal family, Dhṛtarāṣṭra could not do anything to persuade his son to listen to the voice of reason. He just let it happen. His blind affection for his son led him to ignore the advice of all well-meaning persons. It was not until almost the end of the war, after almost everybody was killed except for ten warriors (seven on the side of the Pāṇḍavas and three of the Kauravas), that Dhṛtarāṣṭra admitted his weakness and regretted it.

Philosophically speaking, this moral weakness or weakness of the will may require some explanation, for it may be argued that it is impossible for rational beings knowingly to do wrong. In fact, Plato made such a claim in the *Protagoras.*[23] And, in *Ethica Nicomachea*, Aristotle raised the question again, to discuss it:

> Now we may ask how a man who judged rightly can behave incontinently.[24]

---

23 *Collected Dialogues of Plato*, E. Hamilton and H. Cairns (eds), New York: Pantheon Books, 2nd printing, with corrections, 1963, *Protagoras*, 352b–56c.

24 *The Basic Works of Aristotle*, R. Mckeon (ed.), New York: Random House, 1941, *Ethica Nicomachea*, 7.2.

Aristotle argued that the Socratic (Plato's) claim that there is no such thing as 'incontinence', and that people act so only by reason of ignorance, was indeed a puzzle that needed some philosophical explanation. For, according to Aristotle, this view plainly contradicted the observed facts. Of the several explanations suggested by Aristotle, one may be stated as follows: it is observed that a person behaves incontinently with knowledge, but perhaps, here 'knowledge' is used in a slightly different sense – 'for both the man who has knowledge but is not using it and he who is using it are said to know'.[25] Thus, one might say that the incontinent person has 'knowledge', but is not exercising it. Some philosophers put the matter more strongly. Human beings (and not lower animals, as Aristotle reminded us),[26] are able to, and often do, act against their sincerely held moral principles, with full knowledge and deliberation, and this is simply a fact about ourselves. As I have already noted, the predominant view in classical India is that people do, in fact, act against their moral convictions.

Another point should be made before we leave the subject. In the New Testament (Romans 7), our weakness of the will is seen as a consequence of our sin, and hence it is not philosophically puzzling. Indeed, the following quotation sounds almost similar to the Sanskrit verse I have quoted a few pages earlier: 'For I do not do the good I want, but the evil I do not want is what I do. Now if I do what I do not want, it is no longer I that do it, but sin which dwells within me.'[27] Here, the first part of the sentence coincides with the meaning of the Sanskrit verse. But the attitude the sentence conveys is not prevalent in the Indian tradition. Let me give an example. When the author of the *Mahābhārata* dwelt upon the similar cases of Yudhiṣṭhira and Dhṛtarāṣṭra, he did not refer to the question of sin. Also surprisingly, there was no explicit mention of the *karma* doctrine in this connection, to explain the obvious puzzle. Both Yudhiṣṭhira and Dhṛtarāṣṭra were fully aware of the weakness of their own character and occasionally felt bewildered by it. It may be contended that, according to classical Indian wisdom, weakness of the will is part of human nature (*svabhāva evaiṣa bhūtānām*), and is not ascribed to sin. Here, we can refer back to the *Manusaṃhitā* for an insight.

> It is not a vice to eat meat, to drink liquor, or to have sexual intercourse, for they constitute the natural inclination of the creatures; but (judicious) refraining from such acts generates good consequences.[28]

Kullūka explains *pravṛtti* as the 'natural *dharma*'. This, I believe, illuminates a great deal about the attitude of the classical Indians towards the issue.

---

25 Ibid., 7.3.

26 Ibid.

27 *The Holy Bible* (Revised Standard Edition), New York: Oxford University Press, 1962.

28 *Manusaṃhitā* V.56; ibid. (note 13).

Philosophical issues in dharma dilemmas

We may now turn to the other kind of moral conflict: genuine moral dilemmas. Although several well-known philosophers today may disagree here, I believe that, in cases of moral dilemmas, weakness of the will does not have a large part to play in the philosophical analyses of such situations. Genuine dilemma arises when what ought to be done, all things considered, is as yet unsettled or even unsettlable. It may argued that if the informational constraints are removed and impartial rationality is allowed its full play, then such dilemmas will never arise, provided the agent is not suffering from *akrasia*, or weakness of the will. As opposed to this, one may hold that there may be equally strong and equally admired moral principles which prescribe actions that are in conflict, so that the doing of one is the undoing of the other, so that there is no third choice, for example, the complete withdrawal from action. This, then, would be a case of genuine dilemma, where, we may add, decisions are no doubt made, but such decisions are *ad hoc* and not arrived at fully rationally.

First example

A well-known case of moral dilemma is, I think, the *Bhagavad-Gītā* situation. We all know the story. Should Arjuna fight the bloody battle and kill his venerable grandfather, teacher, uncle, brothers, etc., etc.? Or, should he not? It is obligatory, I should say, morally obligatory, for Arjuna as a man, as a human being, as a member of a family and a human society, to feel revulsion about a bloody battle that would lead to the senseless killing of his own venerable relatives, his near and dear ones. At the same time, as a *kṣatriya*, as a royal prince, it is his duty to fight wars when challenged, to recover the lost throne, and to see that his elder brother Yudhiṣṭhira wins the war. It is what we call an 'impossible' situation, an apt illustration of the 'action-guide' dilemma that I am talking about. He must kill and must not kill.

> Alas! We have resolved to commit a great sin, inasmuch as we endeavour to slay our kinsmen out of a craving for the pleasures of dominion.[29]

But could we really condemn Arjuna for showing such moral concerns? Was he merely acting? Was it a sort of a melodrama? My answer is *no*. For this only typifies the moral dilemma of an agent. Arjuna, by showing this side to his mind, becomes before our eyes more of a human being, not a gigantic killing machine. He had to do the killing, for the die was already cast and all was over, but he had also to weep for those he was killing. His dilemma was genuine, but the resolution was only through a pragmatic concern forced upon him by the situation in which he found himself, and for which he was also partly, if not fully, responsible.

---

29 *Aho bata mahat pāpaṃ kartuṃ vyavasitā vayam*
yadrājyasukhalobhena hantuṃ svajanamudyatāḥ. Bhagavadgītā, I.45.

> Justice reaches its noblest height when, in meting out punishment to a wrong-doer, the punisher sheds tears, being as much hurt as the one punished.

Why would such a situation arise and why would the agent not be fully responsible? My answer would be in terms of human limitations, human imperfections, and human frailties. We humans sometimes do bargain for more than what we expect and can take. This is an imperfect world.

Second example

My next example is from a story related by Kṛṣṇa to illustrate a similar point. A hermit, Kauśika by name, once took a vow of telling the truth throughout his life. One day he faced the following dilemma. Some bandits were chasing several travelers with the intention of killing them. Kauśika was sitting nearby at the crossroad. The travelers passed by, and requested him not to show the miscreants which way they had fled. Kauśika did not answer. Soon the bandits arrived, and, knowing that the hermit would not lie, asked him about the travelers; and Kauśika told the truth. As a result, the travelers were caught and killed. Kṛṣṇa added that Kauśika did not reach heaven after his death (his much-coveted reward) just because of this act of cruelty. Although he abided by his principle of truth-telling throughout his life, it came to no effect. The major point was that, under situational constraints, there might be stronger grounds for rejecting truth-telling as a duty and accepting the stronger duty of saving an innocent life. This encapsulates a very strong moral insight, although it is not Kantian.

For Kṛṣṇa, *dharma* is at least sometimes dictated by the constraints or the contingency of the situation (*Avasthika Mahābhārata*, xii.36.2). But this is no defence of opportunism. Truth-telling has been extolled as one of the highest virtues in the tradition. We should not have any illusion, despite frequent criticisms to the contrary, that the tradition of the *dharma* or the religious texts of India underplayed the importance of truth-telling as a virtue and a value. Āpastambha says plainly that every perjurer goes to hell. Thus, there does not seem to be any religious, textual or *dharmaśāstras* support for sweeping comments such as 'all Hindoos are compulsive liars' (Lord Curzon). But it must be admitted that excusable untruths were permitted by such writers of *dharmaśāstras* as Gautama and Manu. Thus, perjury to save life was permitted as a *dharma*. Hence Kṛṣṇa's story is compatible with the general dictum of *dharmaśāstras* (*dharma*-ethics).

Third example

The above story, told and re-told many times, once generated a very well-publicized controversy, toward the end of the last century in our country, between two great minds, Bankimchandra and Rabindranath Tagore. At the centre of the controversy there was a genuine moral dilemma, and the dispute was about how best to resolve it. The problem however cannot be so easily resolved. It may be that Kṛṣṇa again gave a pragmatic solution depending upon the situational constraints. Hence when Bankimchandra depicted Kṛṣṇa thus in his *Kṛṣṇa-caritra*, young Rabindranath protested with the zeal of a religious purist:

> Falsehood can never be true under any circumstances – even if respected Baṅkimbabu or Śrīkṛṣṇa himself says it can be.[30]

What Tagore insisted upon here was curiously sufficiently in agreement with a strange and tortuous argument of Immanuel Kant in support of truth-telling. Kant talked about a situation which had an uncanny similarity with the *Mahābhārata* story (Kṛṣṇa's story). I quote from Kant's essay 'On a Supposed Right to Tell Lies Benevolent Motives'. [31]

> The moral principle that it is one's duty to speak the truth, if it were taken singly and unconditionally, would make all society impossible. We have the proof of this in the very direct consequences which have been drawn from the principle by a German philosopher, who goes so far as to affirm that to tell a falsehood to a murderer, who asked us whether our friend, of whom he was in pursuit, had not taken refuge in our house, would be a crime.

Both Kant and Tagore, I must admit, are my heroes. Kant was a great moral philosopher, perhaps the greatest of them all. But here, in this particular respect, I would beg to disagree with both of them. The above seems to give the impression of a tortuous argument, a desperate attempt to show that truth-telling is a 'moral absolute'. It would be comparable to the religious absolutes of religious people. Kant continued and concluded: 'To be *truthful* (honest) in all declarations is therefore a *sacred unconditional* command of reason, and not to be limited by any expediency.' Despite the reference to the 'sacred', Kant was the first and foremost to take morality away from religious sanction. Tagore was a little more resourceful here. He argued that Kauśika should have said, 'Yes I know, but I won't tell you.' Bankimchandra, in reply, asked, 'It was possible. But was it probable?' Given the fact that Kauśika was a human being with human frailties and imperfections, he could have been subjected to inhuman physical torture, and, truth, in this way, could have been elicited from him in the end. If the gangsters said, 'We will kill you, if you do not tell', in that case Tagore's suggested way out would have been appropriate. Kauśika could have saved the lives of the innocent men by giving his own life. But that was not the case.

I have already indicated that my inclination here is to support Bankimchandra, and not Kant or the stance of a religious purist that was represented by Tagore. On being truthful and keeping promises regardless of consequences, Bankimchandra commented:

---

30 *Konokhānei mithyā satya hay nā. Śraddhāspada Baṅkimbābu balileo nā; svayam Śrīkṛṣṇa balileo hay nā. Bhārati*, Agrahāyana, 1291, p. 347.

31 *Critique of Practical Reason and Other Works on the Theory of Ethics*, Appendix 1889, pp. 361, 362–3. This passage was quoted as comment of a French philosopher on Kant.

> Suppose a person after getting up in the morning swears that he will commit by dusk all kinds of crime under the sun – murder, robbery, and so on. Now, do they [purists] really subscribe to the view that the person in question should be faithful in translating his words – an utterance of even this nature – into action? If they think so then I should have nothing to do with their idea of adherence of truth. I would say, in this case *dharma* or righteousness consists in disregarding the utterance made. Here falsehood becomes truth.

What 'the unconditional command of reason' (to use Kant's expression) is, is very difficult to know in every situation with the required clarity. But truth-telling under the above circumstances is certainly not one of them (*pace* Kant and Tagore[32]). For then we inadvertently turn a moral principle into a moral dogma. And there would be little fundamental difference between a moral dogma and a religious dogma. Remember that Kauśika was trying to keep to his religious principles, as he understood them.

Moral conflict as moral dilemma

Let us now return to the ancient texts we began with to see the contrast with the moderns. We have noticed that in the *Bhagavadgītā* Arjuna faced a serious dilemma when he was torn between two *dharma* principles: the *dharma* of his kṣatriya caste to fight on, and his family *dharma* infused with such admirable moral sentiments as love, devotion and respect for his grandfather Bhīṣma and esteemed teacher Drona. Arjuna himself suggested the third way out – that of complete withdrawal from action – as he said, 'I would rather accept the life of a mendicant' (cf. *bhaikṣyam apīha loke*). But it was more than obvious that it was decidedly too late for such a course of action to be undertaken. At Kṛṣṇa's advice, Arjuna decided to fight, but still, he regretted it many times in the later part of the epic.

Similarly, Yudhiṣṭhira was in a moral dilemma on several occasions. One was when he had to decide between telling a lie (only once in his whole life) and thereby winning the war which he morally deserved to win, and not being untruthful (even for once in his life) and thereby suffering defeat and humiliation by letting Duryodhana win, even though the latter choice would have meant that overall justice would not have been maintained. On the one hand, there was the strong moral principle of telling the truth throughout his life, and on the other, was the equally strong principle of justice – justice for the utter humiliation of innocent Draupadī. Yudhiṣṭhira was torn between the two. At the persuasion of Kṛṣṇa, and with great regret and reluctance, Yudhiṣṭhira decided to tell a lie.

---

32 Tagore changed his view later, in a debate especially over Gandhi's unqualified and unwavering commitment to nonviolence, in principle, while the elements of coercion implicated in what Erikson later called 'militant nonviolence' had deeply worried Tagore as well; but to build an extremely vehement nationalist-patriotic movement on this singled-out principle or presumed, doubtless laudable, cardinal virtue in the tradition was not something that struck Tagore as being really the pursuit of an end-*in*-itself, *for*-itself, and even *by*-itself. It would become a moral dogma [from seminar notes].

Let us take another clear case of moral dilemma in an episode in the *Karṇaparva* of the *Mahābhārata.* Arjuna was faced with a choice between two irreconcilable obligations; promise-keeping and avoidance of fratricide. The incident that led to this is the following. On the very day of final encounter between Karṇa and Arjuna, Yudhiṣṭhira fled the battlefield after being painfully humiliated by Kṛṣṇa in an armed engagement. When Arjuna came to the camp to pay a visit to him and asked what really had happened, Yudhiṣṭhira flared up in anger and told Arjuna that all his boastfulness about being the finest archer in the world was a lot of nonsense, because the war was dragging on. He reminded Arjuna that the latter claimed to be capable of conquering everybody and thus end the war within a few days. In a rage, he not only insulted Arjuna but also slighted the 'Gāṇḍiva bow', the most precious possession of this valiant warrior. The bow was a gift to Arjuna from Agni, the fire-god. He held it so dear to his heart that he had promised to kill anyone who would ever speak ill of 'Gāṇḍiva'. Hence Yudhiṣṭhira's word put Arjuna in a very difficult situation: either he would have to kill his venerated elder brother or break his promise. When his kṣatriya duty (*dharma*) made him choose the first alternative, Kṛṣṇa (his *alter* ego) appeared. On being asked Arjuna explained: he was obliged to commit fratricide in order to fulfil his obligation to keep his promise. Arjuna had full knowledge of the gravity of the crime he was about to commit but like a mistimed Kantian he had already taken a conflict-free decision to meet the kṣatriya obligation of promise-keeping. A quotation from Kant's *Introduction to the Metaphysics of Morals* (1 797) may be relevant here:

> Because ... duty and obligation are in general concepts that express the objective practical necessity of certain actions and because two mutually opposing rules cannot be necessary at the same time, then if it is a duty to act according to one of them, it is not only not a duty but contrary to duty to act according to the other.

For Kant it seems that the objective rules should form a harmonious whole, a system characterized by consistency, much like a system of true beliefs. The moral conflict, which no doubt arises in the minds of moral agents, cannot, therefore, be genuine. It would be at best a confusion, at worst an illusion. It conflates, according to Kant, a genuine duty with a *ground* of that duty. Hence, in a so-called dilemma, one horn is a genuine duty, and the other is merely a ground of duty. There may be conflict between grounds but not between duties. Hence, in Kantian ethics, no agent can be forced to violate his duty. This is at least one of the interpretations of Kantian thought. Hence Arjuna might be said to be anticipating the Kantian model.

Kṛṣṇa, however, was not Kant. When he intercepted and started a discourse with Arjuna, he obviously turned an apparently moral conflict into a genuine moral dilemma. Promise-keeping is, indeed, a strong obligation. Plato is supposed to have described a typical case of dilemma, in which the return of a cache of arms has been promised to a man who, intent on starting mayhem, comes to claim them. Conflict was generated here by two opposing principles, that of promise-keeping and that of benevolence. In fact, promise-keeping is regarded as equivalent to truth-telling. In Sanskrit, promise-keeping is sometimes classed as 'protecting the truth' (*satya-rakṣa*). Hence, both in India and the West, the two obligations are invariably connected. There is no cultural relativism here. In Kantian ethics, truth-telling gets the highest priority. Kṛṣṇa, however, continued to argue that promise-keeping or even truth-telling cannot be an unconditional obligation when it is in conflict with the avoidance of grossly unjust and criminal acts such as patricide or fratricide. Saving an innocent life is also a strong obligation, saving the life of an elder brother would naturally be an equally strong obligation, if not stronger. Hence, in fact, according to Kṛṣṇa two almost equally strong obligation or duties are in conflict here.

How did the tradition look upon such cases? I believe there is strong evidence that it regarded them as genuine dilemmas. Both Arjuna and Yudhiṣṭhira suffered from the moral emotions of guilt and shame for violating the *dharma* principles that they did violate. Both of them held the principles they violated very dear to themselves. Tradition believed that one met moral retribution if one violated any important moral principle. The author of the *Mahābhārata* describes how Yudhiṣṭhira immediately lost the privilege he had enjoyed for upholding the high moral principle of truthfulness throughout his life. Even Arjuna was greatly humiliated toward the end. He lost his prized possession, the invincible Gāṇḍiva bow. When the war was finally over, his famous chariot was reduced to ashes as soon as Kṛṣṇa dismounted. Besides, toward the end (when Kṛṣṇa died), this great hero of the famous battle of Kurukṣetra suffered a crushing defeat and humiliation at the hands of ordinary tribal warriors and robbers, who kidnapped the women of the Yādava clan who were under his protection. When the battle of Kurukṣetra was over, both Arjuna and Yudhiṣṭhira regretted the loss of millions of lives and doubted whether the throne had been worth fighting for. After all, what kind of kingdom was it in which only old people, widows and children were alive? Whatever moral decision the moral agent might have taken in the case of genuine dilemmas, the violation of the conflicting principle was regarded as a violation by the tradition, and hence the talk about retribution seemed justified.

Dharma and Moral Emotions

I wish to regard the above cases as genuine dilemmas for a slightly different reason. I believe that, in the case of a genuine dilemma, the agent has to suffer from certain appropriate moral emotions, such as regret and remorse, guilt and shame, since he cannot rationally justify his preference for one principle and the resultant violation of the other. In the epic stories, both of our moral heroes suffered from such appropriate moral emotions. Regret is not enough; the morally sensitive agent usually feels remorse as well. Both guilt and shame are appropriate feelings for the morally alert agent. The by-now-well-known Rawlsian distinction between guilt and shame may be mentioned here to make a minor point.[33] According to Rawls, guilt invokes the concept of right, while shame appeals to the concept of goodness. Guilt

33 J. Rawls, *A Theory of Justice*, Cambridge: Harvard University Press, 1971.

can be relieved by reparation, it 'permits reconciliation' through forgiveness. Shame invokes aspiration and ideals, that is, certain forms of moral excellence the agent wishes to attain. In the case of our epic characters, they felt both the appropriate guilt and shame, although, as the texts testify, at some times, it was more guilt than shame and at others it was the other way around. For example, when Arjuna had to violate his principle of promise-keeping and refrain from killing his own venerable elder brother, Yudhiṣṭhira, he experienced more a sense of guilt than shame. Hence, when Kṛṣṇa suggested a way for him to relieve himself of the guilt by reparation, Arjuna readily followed his advice. Rāma, in the *Rāmāyaṇa*, also felt more guilt than shame over his controversial acts, such as the abandonment of Sītā. But Yudhiṣṭhira was a different sort of person. After lying to Droṇa, he was overwhelmed with more shame than guilt; after the battle was over his self-shame, contempt and derision knew no bounds. He aspired to a sort of moral excellence and had the same ideals as Dhṛtarāṣṭra, that is, the King of Dharma. But the war was finally won by not very glorious means, and, as Kṛṣṇa made clear to him, it had to be done that way, for there was no other possible alternative. Bhavabhūti's Rāma, however (in his *Uttara-Rāmacarita*),[34] was more like Yudhiṣṭhira, a tragic hero, than the original portrait of him by Vālmīki.

Dharma and its vulnerability

The epic stories presented the *dharma* morality in a novel light. They were dealing with practical problems of everyday life. I claim that sometimes there was more realism in these old epic stories than they are given credit for today. They underlined the two most prominent aspects of *dharma*: the vulnerability of moral virtues and the ever-elusive nature of truth in the moral domain. I shall conclude with another story from the *Mahābhārata*.

On the last day of their exile, the Pāṇḍavas went searching for a deer that had run away along with the two sacrificial sticks stuck to its horns. The ritual is otherwise jeopardized, and *dharma* violated. But they failed in their duty as the deer had vanished. Overcome with thirst in the middle of the forest, each of the brothers was sent by Yudhiṣṭhira to fetch water in a nearby lake; but none returned. Finally Yudhiṣṭhira went and found that all his four brothers were lying dead near the lakeside. As he descended to get some water, a voice spoke: 'Please do not be rash, O Prince. First you must answer my question and then touch the water. Your brothers did not listen and you can see what happened to them. The lake belongs to me.' Utterly surprised, Yudhiṣṭhira asked: 'May I know who you are?' 'I am Yakṣa', was the answer. Yudhiṣṭhira agreed and a question-and-answer session followed. Of the many tricky questions asked by Yakṣa, the most important was: What is the way (to reach a decision about *dharma*)? Yudhiṣṭhira's answer satisfied Yakṣa, who then divulged his identity. Although he appeared in the form of a stork there, he

---

34 Bhavabhūti, *Uttara-Rāmacarita*, trans. P.V. Kane (ed.), Bombay: Nirnay Sagar Press, 1964.

said that he was in fact Dharma, Yudhiṣṭhira's real father, and that he had stolen the sacrificial sticks of the brahmin in the form of a deer in order to teach Yudhiṣṭhira a lesson in *dharma*. This story illustrates the ever-elusive nature of *dharma*: one may fail in spite of everything, so no one should take pride in being a moral hero. Let me comment upon the verse cited by Yudhiṣṭhira in reply to Yakṣa's question. Yudhiṣṭhira said:

> There are different Vedas, even the *dharmaśāstras* vary from one another. There is not a single *muni* [teacher-sage] whose view is not different from that of other teacher. The truth of *dharma* lies hidden in the [dark] cave. But the way [leading to *dharma*] is the one that the *mahājana* had followed.

I have left the crucial term *mahājana* untranslated on purpose. One (comparatively later) meaning of the term is 'a great person', and plurality in such cases is implicit in the grammatically singular expression. Hence the meaning would be: the path taken by great men is the path in matters of *dharma* conflict. If this interpretation is accepted, then it is simply a reference to 'the conduct of the good people' as an authority on, that is, a determining factor of, *dharma*, which was mentioned in the *Manusaṃhitā*. I believe, however, that the second meaning of the term, 'a great number of people', has a wider significance in the context. This may be a statement of a primitive form of a moral theory: the path is that one wherein lies the good for the maximum number of people. It seems to be a primitive proto-utilitarian view, which need not be surprising; for a sort of primitive proto-utilitarianism seems to be implied by the rational side of any ancient (and well-developed) civilization. Besides, the public rituals in classical India used to be prefixed by a benediction ritual-recitation (*maṅgala*), where the following phrase was commonly used:

> *bahujana-sukhāya bahujana-hitāya ca.*
> For the sake of the happiness of many people, and for the sake of the good of many.

Dharma and Pluralism

The more interesting part of the above *Mahābhārata* verse is, however, the pluralistic ideals that it insists upon. For, the demand for rational decision is always greater when pluralism is admitted. Pluralism has several senses, some of them rather specific or technical in nature. In this context, we may take it in one specific sense in order to make some concluding comments. When pluralism is applied to a moral theory, it may offer the counterpoint to a monistic theory like utilitarianism, which, even in some of its modern versions, tries to resolve all moral issues by relying upon one ultimate, uniform criterion: *utility*. A theory that refuses to reduce all judgment of (moral) preference to a quantitative form in a single dimension (so that we can calculate), and that allows for diversity of (moral) goods which are sometimes incommensurable, is pluralistic.

Pluralism raises several important questions. One is: how are we supposed to combine, in our lives, two or three or more conflicting goals, or virtues or principles, which we feel in our bones that we cannot repudiate? Conflict arises because they seem to demand 'incompatible' actions. If the conflict is only apparent (as it sometimes may be), then rational thinking will help resolve the issue. If, however, the conflict is real, we have cases of genuine dilemma, as I have already noted.

Dharma-morality is pluralistic. Hence we must also face the other questions raised by pluralism, which concern rationality in its formal aspects. The allure of utilitarianism is that, among other things, it offers a neat model of maximization of a single homogeneous magnitude, and hence it is hoped that the formal criterion of consistency and completeness may be achievable here. Thus, compared to pluralistic theories, it seems to be the 'rational' moral theory *par excellence*. Pluralism, however, does not necessarily lead to irrationality. Even consistency seems achievable if we recognize the need to find the consistent ordering of priorities in a pluralistic theory. Two offending principles may be put under strict logical scrutiny with regard to a particular situation, so as to discover whether one can be allowed to override the other. The cases of dilemma have already been discussed, where practical wisdom has to bear the occasional burden of moral emotions such as shame or remorse. They might signal the limits to the formal notion of consistency in a moral theory, without necessarily rendering the theory inconsistent. As far as the requirement of completeness is concerned, I believe this may not be necessary in order to keep a pluralistic theory within the bounds of rationality.

Conclusion

Dharma does not have a definitive form. It has an ever-elusive nature that has been well-illustrated in the stories from the *Mahābhārata* and the *Rāmāyaṇa*. It is also open-ended and rational. *Dharma* does not rule, but (as Robert Lingat once put it[35]) it reigns from above. It is a going concern of the society as well as the individual. It demands the best from our practical wisdom. I have tried to lay down the insights of the ancient writers of India with respect to *dharma*. In many ways, we must admit, their formulation of issues are primitive and dated. But the stories they have told sometimes have far-reaching significance and reveal their wisdom in a new light. Today's moral philosophy has become increasingly technical. One needs to talk about the decision-theoretic procedures, the Arrow-Sen impossibility theorem, as well as the Pareto optimality. In this background, exploration of the writings of the ancient Indians may not be relevant. I am, however, interested in cultural history, and I believe the historical understanding of the concept of *dharma* has some relevance today. I believe it is a widely misunderstood concept in the modern study of the history of Indian philosophy. I have tried to clear up part of this misunderstanding. Explanation of the traditional ethos of India has always been somewhat controversial

---

35 Robert Lingat, *The Classical Law of India*, trans. J.D.M. Derrett, Berkeley: University of California Press, 1973.

among the Indianists of today. The sociologists or social anthropologists propagate one way of looking at it. The development economists favour another way of taking it. Both, however, assume that to understand modern India some basic knowledge of classical India is absolutely necessary. My exposition of *dharma* and rationality has been partly aimed at this enterprise. Besides – and last of all – what has often attracted me to such a study is that, although the ancients did not always seem right from our modern point of view, what is surprising is that they also often did get it right. Today they seem to us to have been mistaken in many ways, but that they did sometimes hit upon the right note is worthy of our notice and praise.

Chapter 3

The Myth of the Ethics of *Puruṣārtha* or Humanity's Life-Goals[1]

Daya Krishna

Preamble

Any discussion of traditional Indian thought about human beings and society usually revolves around the notions designated by such terms as *varṇa*, *āśrama* and *puruṣārtha*. It is also generally assumed that the three categories are so intimately related to each other that each cannot be understood without the other. But even amongst these, the notion of *puruṣārtha* is perhaps more fundamental as it defines those ultimate goals of human life which give meaning and significance to it. The usual four-fold classification of the *puruṣārtha*s, it is claimed, encompasses within it all the actual or possible goals that humankind may pursue for itself. Yet, is this true, and do the terms designate in any clear manner the complete set of goals – or what Kant called 'kingdom of ends' – human beings pursue or *ought* to pursue?

Now the relationship between the *puruṣārtha*s, and the number and hierarchy between them, have been the subject of discussion and debate since classical times. One of the best known of these discussions is in the *Mahābhārata* where Yudhiṣṭhira asks all his four brothers as well as Vidura as to which of the *puruṣārtha*s among *dharma* [*ethikōs*], *artha* [livelihood] and *kāma* [*eros*] is the highest, the lowest and intermediate in importance.[2] Arjuna extols *artha* in the sense of production of wealth through agriculture, trade and diverse forms of crafts as the highest of the *puruṣārtha*s. Bhīma, on the other hand, extols *kāma* as the essence of both *dharma* and *artha*, while Nakula and Sahadeva try to support Arjuna's position with some modifications. Vidura tries to give an extensional definition of *dharma* and describes what it consists of. Yudhiṣṭhira , at the end, talks of transcendence of *artha*, *dharma* and *kāma* in *mokṣa* [liberation, freedom], though he is candid enough to admit that he knows nothing about it. He ends by making a statement which hardly offers any clarity on the issue and, in fact, has a fatalistic flavour about it. All in all, it seems

1 A version of this chapter was published as 'The Myth of *Puruṣārthas*', in *Journal of Indian Council of Philosophical Research*, **IV** (1), Autumn, 1986, pp. 1-14, and reprinted in that version in Daya Krishna, *Indian Philosophy: A Counter Perspective*, Delhi: Oxford University Press, 1991, pp. 189-206; revised edn, Delhi: Indian Book Centre, 2006.

2 *The Mahābhārata, Śāntiparva, adhyāya* 161.

a paltry show on the part of the heroes of the great epic on this profound theme which is of such importance to fundamental reflection on human life. Is there then another, more indefeasible approach? That is the question posed and addressed in this chapter.

The goals of life

The usual designation of the *puruṣārthas* is given as *dharma* [morality], *artha* [livelihood], *kāma* [desire-fulfilment] and *mokṣa* [liberation]. There is, of course, the dispute as to whether originally there were only the first three *puruṣārtha*s and that the fourth, i.e. *mokṣa*, was added later on to them. But even if this is admitted, and there seems overwhelming evidence to support the contention, there still remains the question as to what is meant by these terms; and whether – if the Indian tradition is to be believed – they comprehend meaningfully all the goals that human beings pursue or ought to pursue in their lives.

If we forget *dharma* – which is regarded as the distinctive feature of human beings distinguishing them from animals – and concentrate only on *artha* and *kāma* for the present, we would discover that it is not very clear as to what exactly is meant by them. *Kāma*, in the widest sense, may be understood as desire and, by implication, anything that is or can be the object of desire. But then everything will come under the category of *kāma*, since obviously one can and does desire not only *artha* but even *dharma* and *mokṣa*. Such a use of the word *kāma* is not so unwarranted as may seem at first sight. There is the well-known saying in Sanskrit:

> *nāham kāmaye rājyaṃ na svargaṃ na cāpunarbhavam*
> *prāṇināṃ duḥkhataptānāṃ kāmaye duḥkhanāśanam*

Here *apunarbhavam*, that is, *mokṣa*, is expressly mentioned while *dharma* may be supposed to be indirectly implied in the last line. In order to avoid the difficulty, one may restrict the notion of *kāma* to certain forms of desiring or to certain objects of desire or both. Thus, it may be said that the term *kāma* refers only to those desires whose objects are sensuous in nature or where desiring is done in such a way that it necessarily leads to bondage. But this would not only raise the question as to what is meant by bondage, but also whether *svarga* [heavenly-world] which is supposed to be the object *par excellence* of Vedic sacrifices is sensuous or non-sensuous in character. The Vedic injunction in this regard is unambiguous in its formulation. It clearly states '*svargakāmo yajeta*', that is, 'one who desires heaven should perform (the required) sacrifices'. Thus, it is clear that *svarga* is the object of *kāma* for the Vedic seers. Also, as the whole rationale of Vedic authority is supposed to rest on the distinction between *dṛṣṭa* [seen] and *adṛṣṭa phala* [unseen fruit], *svarga* cannot but be treated as *adṛṣṭa* and heaven as non-sensuous in character, that is, as non-apprehensible by the senses. But if so, the restriction on *kāma*, as referring only to those desires whose objects are sensuous in character, would become invalid.

The Vedas, of course, also contain injunctions which promise *dṛṣṭa phala* only, and, as far as I know, none has seriously argued that these parts should be treated as non-authoritative on this ground or as having only lesser or secondary authority. There are, for example, sacrifices prescribed for those who desire to have a son or rainfall or other such worldly things, and the injunction for these has the same form as the injunction for those who desire *svarga*. The text says, for example: '*putrakāmaḥ putreṣṭyā yajeta, vṛṣṭikāmaḥ kārīryā yajeta*'. There is, thus, no essential difference between '*svargakāmaḥ*' and '*putrakāmaḥ*' or '*vṛṣṭikāmaḥ*', even though the latter are the sort of objects which are known to everybody while the former is accepted only on the authority of the Vedas. In fact, the Vedas are charged with containing false injunctions on the ground that these worldly objects of human desire are many a time not obtained in actual practice by the performance of the prescribed *yajñas* or sacrifices. The *Nyāya-Sūtra* 2.1.58, in fact, raises it as an objection on behalf of the *pūrva-pakṣa* [adversary], and tries to reply to it in 2.1.59 by saying that the failure to get the desired result may be due to possible defects in the procedure adopted or the material used or the attitude of the sacrificer itself or all of these together. The strategy adopted by the author of the *Nyāya-Sūtras*, if accepted, would make it impossible in principle to give a counter-example to any causal claim advanced by anybody. This is, of course not the occasion to discuss the *Nyāya-Sūtras* but only to point out the fact that the so-called Vedic authority in that period was supposed to extend as much to the secular desires of human beings as to those which dealt with matters pertaining to life after death. Later, if Śaṅkara's evidence is to be believed, there would be an attempt to disentangle the two, and the Vedic authority confined only to matters which were regarded as strictly non-empirical in character. But if such a distinction were to be seriously insisted upon, a large part of the Vedas would have to be treated as redundant. Not only this, as what they promise in the empirical domain is also attainable through other means which have little to do with sacrifices, their importance for these purposes would only be marginal in character.

But whether *svarga* is treated as transcendentally sensuous or non-sensuous in character, there will remain the problem of characterizing non-sensuous, non-transcendental objects of desire. How shall we characterize, for example, desire for knowledge or understanding? Shall we treat it as a *puruṣārtha* under the category of *kāma* or not? In the Sāṃkhyan framework, as everything, including *manas* [mind] and *buddhi* [intellect], is a part of *Prakṛti* [nature], there should be little difficulty in treating knowledge or understanding as coming under the category of *kāma* as *puruṣārtha*. But what about those who do not accept the Sāṃkhyan position?

The Naiyāyikas, for example, treat *manas* [mind] as a distinct entity which is required to be postulated because of the fact that one does not have two perceptions at the same time, even though different senses are in contact with the same object at the same time.[3] Our task, obviously, is not to go into the details of Nyāya here

3 *Nyāya-Sūtra* 1.1.16 gives this as the reason for postulating *manas*. On the other hand, no specific reason has been given for postulating *buddhi* [intellect], as a separate, independent *prameya* [knowledge-object] in 1.1.15. It only says that the terms *buddhi* [intellect], *upalabdhi*

or to discuss its conceptual structure. What we want to point out is merely the fact that once we grant relative autonomy to the realm of the mind or intellect, then the desires pertaining thereto cannot be treated under *kāma* without transforming the nature of *kāma* itself. But once the term *kāma* is stretched to cover all ends of human seeking, there would remain no distinction between it and the other *puruṣārtha*s. The difference between them could perhaps, then, be drawn on other grounds. *Artha*, for example, could mean instrumentalities such as power or wealth which could be used for the satisfaction of any and every desire. *Dharma* could mean the desire for social and political order without which no desire could be fulfilled. Or alternatively, it could mean any ordering principle which would obviate or adjudicate the conflict between desires, whether of one and the same individual or of different individuals. *Mokṣa* could mean either the desire for freedom in all its senses, or the desire to be *free* of all desires – a second-order desire which itself may take other forms also.

Perhaps, the idea of *niṣkāma karma* [desireless action] is such a second-order desire with respect to all first-order desires. It tries to suggest how desires 'ought' to be desired. But this '*ought*' is a conditional 'ought' as it is formulated in the context of the desire to be free from the consequences of one's actions. If one is prepared to accept the consequences of one's actions, the injunction to undertake *niṣkāma karma* will make no sense. It may be argued that consequences inevitably bind one, and that as no one desires bondage the imperative for *niṣkāma karma* is essentially unconditional. However, it is not clear why all forms of bondage should be treated as intrinsically undesirable or why consequences should inevitably bind one – a point recognized in *bhakti* [devotional] literature where there is nothing wrong in being a servant of the Lord or even in being born again and again, if it is to be in his service or do his work or sing his praises, or be Hers.

Further, if *kāma* means desire, then *niṣkāma* should mean desireless, or a state where desire is absent. But not all desire necessarily leads to action, and if it is the action performed from desire, that is, *sakāma karma* which leads to bondage, then there is no reason to believe that desire or *kāma* by itself would lead to bondage. If 'desire' be re-translated as *icchā*, then *karma* requires not merely *icchā* but also *prayatna* [wishing] and *śarīra* with its *karmendriyas* [body-with-extensional senses]. On the other hand, if *icchā* by itself is supposed to give rise to bondage, then *karma* would become redundant in the situation unless it is argued that *karma* produces bondage of a different kind or in addition to what has already been produced by *icchā* or *kāma* or desire.

[apprehension] and *jñāna* [cognition] are synonyms for each other. It would perhaps have been better if *buddhi* had been postulated to account for non-perceptual knowledge. Also, it is not clear what is the role of *manas* in non-perceptual knowledge or, for that matter, in the context of *karmendriyas* [extensional senses] which, perhaps, may be regarded as relatively more important as far as the *puruṣārthas* are concerned. Of course, the *ātman* [self] itself is supposed to be postulated as that which is required to account for *jñāna* [cognition] besides *icchā* [desire], *dveṣa* [aversion], *prayatna* [wishing], *sukha* [pleasure] *and duḥkha* [pain], according to *Nyāya-Sūtra* 1.1.10. But then, what is the necessity of postulating *buddhi* as a separate *prameya* if *ātman* is already postulated to understand *jñāna*?

This is not the place or the occasion to discuss the whole notion of *niṣkāma karma* or the relationship of *karma* to bondage or liberation. What we are interested in here is to understand the traditional notion of the *puruṣārtha*s, and it is interesting to note in this connection that *karma* [action] does not occur as a *puruṣārtha* at all. Perhaps, it is assumed as a generalized means of attaining all *puruṣārtha*s. But, then, *karma* would become necessary for attaining not only *kāma*, *artha* and *dharma* but also *mokṣa*. This would be unacceptable to at least one major school of Indian philosophy, i.e. Advaita Vedānta, as, according to it, *karma* is inevitably a sign of one's being in *avidyā* [ignorance] and hence in bondage. The *Gītā*, which emphasizes the inescapability of *karma* for all embodied beings, does not seem concerned with the ends which are sought to be achieved through action, but rather with the psychic *attitude* with which the action is undertaken as it is that which, according to it, is the cause of bondage and not action *per se*. But, then, *kāma* would denote not the end for which the action is undertaken, but the attitude with which it is done. The attitude, however, in such a case, cannot be treated as one of the *puruṣārthas* as it is not only not an end of human action but also is naturally present in all human beings, and hence need not be striven for by any special effort on their part.

There is, of course, the problem as to how the word *puruṣārtha* itself is to be understood. Is it to be taken, for example, in a descriptive sense, that is, as describing what human beings actually pursue in their life? Or, is it a prescriptive word which suggests what human beings ought to pursue in order to be worthy of being human? *Artha* and *kāma* as examples of *puruṣārthas* tend to suggest the former, while *dharma* and *mokṣa* lead to the latter interpretation. There does not seem much sense in saying one ought to pursue *artha* or *kāma*, as one naturally pursues them and needs no great exhortation to do so. And if one does not pursue them with great zeal or intensity, one is normally praised and not admonished for not pursuing them, particularly if one is pursuing some other ideal value, say, knowledge or social reform or political freedom or the end of exploitation and repression, or even such a thing as the creation of beautiful objects. I have used these examples consciously as it is difficult to subsume them in any straightforward manner under the categories of *dharma* or *mokṣa*, which are the only other *puruṣārthas* permitted to us by the traditional classification. Perhaps, the best way might be to construe it as being both descriptive and prescriptive, thus reflecting the human condition itself wherein the determination by norms and ideals, and the striving towards them is inbuilt into the condition itself. The Upaniṣadic terms *preyas* and *śreyas* describe well this amalgamation, though they do so by opposing them to each other, treating them as dichotomous opposites rather than as necessary components of the human situation.

However, to bring a prescriptive element into *kāma* and *artha* would not be to bring them under *dharma* or make them subservient to *mokṣa* as, say in tantra it has usually been understood, but rather to say that each human being has to pursue them for the utmost flowering and fulfilment of his being, and if he does not do so because of any reason, it is a deficiency that ought to be rectified as soon as possible. This, however, does not only run counter to the dominant thrust of Indian thought in the field, but also runs against the difficulty that it is not clear what sort of ends are meant by the terms *kāma* and *artha* in the theory of the *puruṣārtha*s, which is supposed to be India's profoundest contribution to thinking about the ends of human life.

The usual response is to interpret *artha* in the sense of *meaning*, as it is only 'meaning' which can be primary or secondary. But, then, *puruṣārtha* would mean that which gives meaning or significance to human life. However, in that case, *dharma* and *mokṣa* would lose that preeminence which normally is attributed to them.

There is another problem with the term *artha* as it occurs in the word *puruṣārtha*. *Artha* itself is a distinctive *puruṣārtha*, and hence could not mean the same as in the compound *puruṣārtha*. Normally, *artha* as a *puruṣārtha* is taken to mean wealth or power or those generalized instrumentalities by which what is desired can be attained. But, in this sense, *dharma* itself would become a part of *artha* as it can be legitimately argued that without the maintenance of *dharma*, or what may be called the normative order, most people will not be able to fulfil their desire with any reasonable expectation of success. The maintenance of social or political order would, then, be only a means for the satisfaction of *kāma* which would be the primary *puruṣārtha* of life. Further, as the distinction between means and ends is always relative and changing with the way one perceives and orders what one seeks, the distinction between *artha* and *kāma* itself would become relative in character. As for *mokṣa*, it is usually supposed to transcend both *dharma* and *kāma* and thus occupies an anomalous position amongst the *puruṣārtha*s, for it is never clear whether this transcendence should be understood as a negation or fulfilment of the other *puruṣārtha*s. The Indian thought on this subject has never been able to make up its mind on either side with the result that confusion has prevailed at the very heart of Indian theorization about the ultimate goal or goals whose seeking renders human existence meaningful. *Mokṣa*, however, conceived, is a desire for release from desire itself, and hence negates the *artha* in the *puruṣārtha* in a radical manner. To use a metaphor from a different context of the use of *artha*, what is being asked for is a language in which there is no reference, except self-reference. Even this residuum is denied in Advaita Vedanta, which argues for the untenability of the very notion of *puruṣārtha* itself. The theory, which argues for the *nitya-siddha* [eternally there] nature of *mokṣa* against the one which treats it as *sādhana-siddha* [discipline-perfected], attests to this.

The essential ambivalence with respect to the relationship between *mokṣa* and the other *puruṣārtha*s is nowhere more evident than in the discussions on its relationship with *dharma*, which is the most clear prescriptive or normative end in this theory of the four *puruṣārtha*s in Indian thought. Is *dharma* necessary for attaining *mokṣa*? The usual answer is that it helps one in getting *svarga* but not *mokṣa*. *Dharma* as well as *adharma* are the causes of bondage and rebirth. For liberation, one has to go beyond both, that is, not only beyond *adharma* but *dharma* also. That is why the author of the *Gītā* has treated the Vedas as the realm of the three *guṇas*, that is, *sattva*, *rajas* and *tamas*, whose heart is *kāma*, and whose injunctions, if followed, lead to *bhoga* and *aiśvarya*. *Mokṣa*, on the other hand is beyond the three *guṇas*,[4]

4 *The Bhagavad Gītā*, II.46.

and hence beyond the world which is constituted by them. But, then, it cannot exactly be called a *puruṣārtha*, or at least, a *puruṣārtha* in the same sense in which the other three are called *puruṣārtha*s. Normally, only that should be designated as a *puruṣārtha* which can be realized, at least to some extent by human effort. But all effort or activity is supposed to be due to the element of *rajas* which is sought to be transcended in *mokṣa*. Perhaps that was one reason why Śaṅkara argued so insistently that *karma* cannot lead to *mokṣa*. In any case, the radical difference between *mokṣa* as a *puruṣārtha* and the other three *puruṣārtha*s has not only to be recognized in any discussion on the subject but also the radical incompatibility between them at least in the direction to which their seeking would lead. The seeking for both *artha* and *kāma* leads one naturally out of oneself and seeks to establish a relationship with objects and persons, though primarily in instrumental terms. It is the pursuit of *dharma* which makes one's consciousness see the other, not as a means to one's own ends, but in terms of one's obligations towards it. Normally, such a sense of obligation arises only for other human beings or even all living beings, but it can be extended beyond these also. *Mokṣa*, however, is a transcendence of that other-centred consciousness from which the sense of obligation arises. In fact, the ontological roots of most conceptions of *mokṣa* in the Indian philosophical traditions either deny the ontological reality of the 'other' or relegate it axiologically to a peripheral position. The Advaita Vedānta radically denies the ultimate reality of the 'other', while the non-Advaitic schools primarily assert the relationship of the self to the Lord, and only secondarily the relationship between oneself and another. Basically, this relationship is mediated through the relationship of each to the Lord and is thus indirect in character. Sāṃkhya does assert the ontological plurality of selves, but they all are like Leibnizian monads, having no interrelationship amongst themselves. The hard-core Nyāya-Vaiśeṣika position denies the very possibility of any conscious relationship between selves in the state of *mokṣa*, as they are not supposed to be conscious in that state.

Amongst the non-Vedic or even anti-Vedic traditions, the Jainas seem to have more or less a Sāṃkhyan conception with little essential relationship between selves which have become free. The Buddhists do not accept the notion of self, but at least they do accept a relationship between the realized and the unrealized persons, and articulate it in their notion of *karuṇā* or *mahākaruṇā* (great compassion). Parallel to this is the notion of the Bodhisattvas who feel their obligation to the suffering humanity to such an extent that they are prepared to forgo entering the state of *nirvāṇa* in order to help others. But even though this is a great advance in the articulation of the relationship between those who have attained liberation and those who have not, it still is an asymmetrical relationship. It is the suffering humanity that needs the Bodhisattvas; the Bodhisattvas have no need of it. The seemingly similar notion of Avatāra in Hindu thought is even more asymmetrical as it is a relationship between God and man. It is only in certain schools of *bhakti* that the relationship becomes a little more symmetrical as God is supposed to need human beings almost as much as human beings need God. But the relationship between human beings, as we have pointed out earlier, becomes basically contingent as it is only as *bhaktas*, that is, as devotees of the Lord that they can have any real relationship with one another.

Tantric thought, on the other hand, does seem to conceive of a necessary relationship with the 'other' without which one cannot be oneself. But then, this 'other' is confined to a member or members of the other sex only, and the relationship is restricted primarily to the sphere of sex. In the Tantric perspective, human beings need only women, and presumably, women only need human beings for self-realization. However, if one reads the texts, it all seems a male affair – at least, at first sight. In fact, if one considers such a ritual as the *kumārī pūjā*, or the worship of the virgin (*kanyākumārī*), it is difficult to see how she is involved as a *sādhikā* or seeker in the process. Rather the whole affair shows a callous disregard for the feelings of the female or the traumatic effect that such a ceremony has on her life.

The self-centric and male-centric character of large parts of Hindu *sādhana* [orthopraxy] need to be explored in greater depth and with greater detachment than has been done until now. One of the possible reasons for this may, perhaps, be the identification of the feminine principle itself with *Prakṛti* and *Māyā* or Nature, which are conceived as non-self – or even antagonistic to self – and as the main cause for the non-realization by the self of its own nature. The roots of the self-centredness of Indian thought, on the other hand, may be said to lie in its ontological, ethical and psychological analysis of the human situation which gradually came to be accepted as unquestioned truth by a large part of the culture over a period of time. The analysis is epitomized in the famous statement of Yājñavalkya, the outstanding philosopher of the Upaniṣadic period, in the *Bṛhadāraṇyaka Upaniṣad* that nothing is desired for itself, but is desired only because it is dear to the self.[5] The illusion referred to here is that any object whatsoever can be dear for itself, the truth being that it is dear only because it subserves the interest of the self. The self in this context is, of course, supposed to be the Self with a capital 'S' and not the little ego or the self with a small 's' which is associated with *ahaṅkāra* [I-sense], *manas* and *buddhi* which are supposed to constitute the *antaḥkaraṇa* ['common-sense'] in some schools of traditional philosophical thought in India and with which the self is usually identified. But such an identification, however inevitable or natural it may seem, is the root of that foundational ignorance which is the cause of all suffering, according to these thinkers. It hardly matters whether the self, so conceived, be with a capital or a small 's' as the centre of all concern, striving, and attention remains something that is not the other but oneself. There is, of course, no 'other' in Advaita Vedānta, but that does not mean that the 'other' is treated as one's own self with a capital 'S' but rather as someone who ought to treat the 'others' as one does oneself, that is, as absolute ontological nullities.

The statement of Yājñavalkya, it should be noted, does not hesitate to use the word '*preyas*' in the context of the *ātman*, that is, the self with a capital 'S', and hence does not seem to subscribe to that radical distinction between *śreyas* and *preyas*

---

5 *Bṛhadāraṇyaka Upaniṣad* II.4.5: *na vā are sarvasya kāmāya sarvaṃ priyaṃ bhavatyātmanastu kāmāya sarvaṃ priyaṃ bhavati.*

which is usually made in this context. Rather it points to a continuity in the concern with *preyas* which, it is contended, cannot be given up in principle as it is the very nature of Being as consciousness to seek it, for it is what it essentially is. The only problem is the illusion with which it is also primordially endowed, that it can achieve it through something other than itself. The difference between *kāma* and *mokṣa*, on this understanding, would consist in the fact that the former is necessarily the result of the illusion that the happiness of the self can be achieved through anything other than itself, while the latter is the giving up of the illusion. But giving up the illusion does not necessarily mean that one is happy or fulfilled or blissful; it only means that one is not dependent on anything else for the achievement of such a state. It may be argued that if it depends completely upon oneself, then what could possibly stand in the way of its non-achievement? Perhaps, it could be the attitude of the self to itself. The famous lines '*ekohaṃ, bahum syām*' suggest some such dissatisfaction at the root of creation itself. The concept of *līlā* [play-time] does not get away from this difficulty as the impulse to play requires as much a dissatisfaction with the previous state as anything else. But if non-dependence on anything else, or even the total absence of all 'other', does not ensure that there shall be no dissatisfaction with the state of one's own being in the sense that one does not want a change in it, then the way is opened for the perception that it is not the 'other' which is the cause of one's bondage but the attitude that one has to the 'other', or perhaps the stance that one takes towards the states of one's own consciousness. This could perhaps provide the clue to the ideal of *kāma karma* adumbrated by the author of the *Gītā*.

The return to the ideal of *niṣkāma karma* does not, however, tell us how to pursue *kāma* or *artha* or even *dharma* in a *niṣkāma* way. The author of the *Bhagavad-Gītā*, it should not be forgotten, is also the author of the *Kāma-Gītā*, if the identity of the two is admitted. The *Kāma-Gītā* is propounded by Vasudeva in the *Aśvamedhikaparva* of the *Mahābhārata* and consists of *ślokas* 11-17 in Canto 13 of the 14th *Parva*. The short *Gītā* concludes not only by making fun of all those who try to destroy *kāma* by stationing themselves in *mokṣa*, but also declares itself to be '*sanātana*', i.e. eternal and '*avadhya*', i.e. indestructible – terms that remind us of the characteristics of Brahman itself.[6]

It may also be noted that the term used in the *Kāma-Gītā* for the state of those who are supposed to be steadfast in *mokṣa* is *mokṣarati*, a term that resonates with what *kāma* stands for in its central meaning in the Indian tradition, that is, sex.

It is, of course, true as Charles Malamoud has argued, that there is always a wider and a narrower meaning of each of these terms, and that the discussion of the *puruṣārtha*s continuously slides between the two. According to him, in 'the sliding from the narrow to the wide meaning, it is always possible to make *dharma*, *artha* or *kāma* into the +1 that encompasses the two other terms in the list, and the *mokṣa*

---

6 *Yo mām prayatate hantum mokṣamāsthāya paṇḍitaḥ/tasya mokṣaratisthasya nṛtyāmi ca hasāmi ca/ avadhyaḥ sarvabhūtānāmahamekaḥ sanātanaḥ* – *The Mahābhārata* 14.13-17.

to boot'.[7] It is not clear, however, whether the statement is supposed to apply to the fourth *puruṣārtha*, that is, *mokṣa* also. *Prima facie*, the term *mokṣa*, does not seem to have a wide or a narrow meaning; it simply has a fairly determinate, specific meaning, even though it may be conceived of differently in different systems of philosophy or even of spiritual *sādhana*. Also, in the usual interpretation, it cannot encompass the other *puruṣārtha*s, specially *artha* and *kāma*, as not only does it transcend them but also negates them. Their functioning as active *puruṣārtha*s in the life of any human being may be taken as a positive sign of the fact that not only *mokṣa* has not yet been achieved, but that it is not even being striven for.

The deeper problem, however, relates to the notions of narrow and wider meanings of the three *puruṣārtha*s. Malamoud has tried to give the narrow and the wider meanings of each of the three *puruṣārtha*s, but it is difficult to agree with his formulations. *Dharma*, for example, in its narrow meaning is, for him, 'the system of observances taught by the Veda and the texts stemming from it'.[8] To the unwary reader, this may seem very specific and definite, but it is nothing of the kind. The texts are so many and prescribe so many conflicting things that the talk of the 'system of observances' is to hide the difficulty, or even the impossibility of determining what one's *dharma* is. If *dharma* in the narrow sense were as clear or an unproblematic as Malamoud seems to make it, the *Mahābhārata* could not have been written. The determination of what *dharma* means is the central enquiry of that great epic, and it is difficult to say whether any definite answer has been given at the end of the epic. Perhaps, the message is that no such simple answer can be given.

On the other hand, it is difficult to see how *dharma* in the wider sense as 'the order of the world and of society' or as 'the point of view allowing perception of the whole as a system organized into a hierarchy',[9] can even be treated as a *puruṣārtha* in the sense that it is something to be achieved or realized by one's actions. An 'order of the world and of society' can obviously not be a *puruṣārtha*, though the achieving of the vision of such an order may perhaps count as one. However, it should be remembered that the achievement of such a vision is the cessation of all activity as to see things *sub specie aternitatis à la* Spinoza – or as revealed in the theophany or cosmic vision presented in the eleventh Canto of the *Bhagavad Gītā* – is to see that everything is what it is, and could not be otherwise. One may, of course, try to order one's own actions in accordance with the vision or to say 'thy will be done' or '*kariṣye vacanaṃ tava*' as Arjuna does in the *Gītā*, but that would be to admit that the cosmic order permits an essential indeterminacy of a certain sort, that is, whether one would act in accordance with the vision or not. Or, rather as most of the time one does not have the vision and I do not know what the so-called cosmic order is, one has to live and act in the context of this essential and almost inalienable ignorance.

---

7 Charles Malamoud, 'On the Rhetoric and Semantics of *Puruṣārtha*', in T.N. Madan (ed.), *Ways of Life: King, Householder, Renouncer: Essays in Honour of Louis Dumont*, New Delhi: Vilas Publishing House, 1982, p. 44.

8 Ibid., p. 44.

9 Ibid., p. 44.

Dharma and *mokṣa*, as *puruṣārtha*s, have difficulties of a different order in the context of their so-called wide or narrow senses than *artha* or *kāma*. But the latter two are not exempt from difficulties, even though they may be of a different order. Malamoud contents himself by saying that '*artha* is a most elastic notion',[10] and seems to think that this absolves him from the responsibility of giving its narrow and wider meanings which he had promised to do earlier. The examples given by him later from the *Arthaśāstra* are themselves not very clear regarding the point that is being made, unless they are taken as illustrative of the elasticity or even the ambiguity of the concept.[11] The *Arthaśāstra*, it may be remembered, is concerned with the *puruṣārtha* of a king, but as everybody cannot be a king what is described therein cannot be regarded as *puruṣārtha* to mean that which is and can be an end for every human being by virtue of the fact that he is a human being. *Artha* in the sense of wealth may be a *puruṣārtha* for everybody, but in the sense of political power it can hardly be regarded as such. But there are no *Śāstras* to tell us how to pursue *artha* as a *puruṣārtha* in the sense of wealth, unless all the diverse methods of cheating the state described in the *Arthaśāstra* are treated as such.

Kāma as a *puruṣārtha*, on the other hand, has perhaps no such problems as whether in the wider sense desire or narrower sense of sexual desire it can be a *puruṣārtha* for everybody. The *Kāmasūtra*, which is a text ostensibly devoted to *kāma* as a *puruṣārtha*, gives both the wider and narrower meanings in *sūtras* 1.2.11 and 1.2.12. The first defines *kāma* as the fitting relationship between each sense and its object which, when in perfect harmony, gives pleasure to the self conjoined with the mind.[12] The second emphasizes the pre-eminence of the sense of touch and the supervening pleasure derived from it that is supposed to be the *kāma, par excellence*.[13] But it seems that the second definition does not carry forward the insight of the first definition. *Kāma* in the narrow sense, the sense in which the *Kāmasūtra* is concerned, may be treated as the paradigmatic case in which not only all the senses find simultaneous fulfilment from their appropriate objects but where the subject is also simultaneously the object. The enjoyer who is also the enjoyed. Malamoud, however, is not using the wider or narrower senses of *kāma* in the sense of the author of *Kāmasūtras* but rather of Bhoja's *Śṛṅgāra-Prakāśa*. Bhoja's attempt to universalize the concept of *śṛṅgāra* is certainly interesting, but it is not clear how it illumines the notion of *puruṣārtha*. Rather, it renders it still more confusing, for it is difficult to see how *rasa* [aesthetic joy] can be a *puruṣārtha*; for if it is to be treated as one, it would not only have to be a *puruṣārtha* alongside other *puruṣārtha*s, but also multiple in its character.

---

10 Ibid., p. 44.

11 Ibid., p. 46.

12 *Śrotratvakcakṣurjihvāghrāṇānāmātmasamyuktena manasādhiṣṭhitānāṃ sveṣu sveṣu viṣayeṣvanukūlyataḥ pravṛttiḥ kāmaḥ* 1/11.

13 *sparśaviśeṣaviṣaviṣayāttvasyābhimānikasukhānuviddhā phalavatyarthapratītiḥ prādhānyātkāmaḥ* 1/12.

Nonetheless, however one may conceive of the wider or narrower senses of the *puruṣārthas*, it hardly helps in solving the problems pointed out; nor does it illuminate the problem of the interrelationships between them. Professor K.J. Shah, in one of the most thoughtful articles on the subject, suggested that the *puruṣārtha*s as goals of human life should be treated as interactional in character, and not as hierarchical. He argued:

> We must realise that *artha* will not be a *puruṣārtha* unless it is in accord with *kāma*, *dharma* and *mokṣa*; and *dharma* will not be *dharma*, unless it too is in accord with *mokṣa*. Equally *mokṣa* will not be *mokṣa* without the content of *dharma*; *dharma* will not be *dharma* without the content of *kāma* and *artha*. The four goals, therefore, constitute one single goal, though in the lives of individuals the elements may get varying emphasis for various reasons.[14]

But if there is only one single goal, then what is it, and what are its relationships with these four goals? Shah was a careful thinker, but, if one reads carefully what he has written, one would find diverse and conflicting pulls in it. One is, for example, surprised to find *artha* omitted when he is talking of *kāma*, and both *artha* and *kāma* omitted when he is talking of *dharma*. Is the omission deliberate or accidental? What has *mokṣa* to do with *kāma* and *artha*? Why has it to relate to them only through the medium of *dharma*? Are *artha* and *kāma* only contents, *dharma* both form and content, and *mokṣa* only pure form, according to Shah? There may be satisfactory answers to these questions but, unless they are given, merely saying that there is only 'one single goal' will not suffice.

However, even if we leave aside the *Mahābhārata* discussion that we began with and touched on again in the context of the *Gītā*, specifically regarding the interrelationship and the hierarchy between the *puruṣārtha*s, the usual traditional answer in terms of the supremacy of *dharma* is not helpful either. And this is for the simple reason that it is not clear what *dharma* is. The four sources usually given by Manu and others for finding what *dharma* is are of little help, as not only do they conflict with each other but there are deep conflicting divisions within each of them. The so-called revealed texts are no less conflicting than the tradition embodied in custom or the behaviour of people generally known as good or one's own inner conscience. The question as to whether they should be treated in a descending or ascending order of importance is irrelevant as none of them by themselves or even all of them together can help in settling any difficult problem of *dharma* except in *ad hoc* or pragmatic manner.

The oft-repeated traditional theory of the *puruṣārtha*s, thus, is of little help in understanding the diversity and complexity of human seeking which makes life so meaningful and worthwhile in diverse ways. The *kāma*-centric and *artha*-centric theories of Freud and Marx are as mistaken as the *dharma*-centric thought of sociologists who try to understand human beings in terms of the roles that they play and society in terms of the norms of those roles and their interactive relationships.

---

14 K.J. Shah in T.N. Madan, 1982.

For all these theories, the independent seeking of any value which is different from these is an illusion, except in an instrumental sense. The ultimately suicidal character of all such theories is self-evident as they do not provide for any independent value to the life of the intellect which they themselves embody. Fortunately for the Indian theory of *puruṣārtha*s, it has postulated the ideal of *mokṣa* which is tangential to all the other *puruṣārtha*s. But it, too, has no place for the independent life of reason as a separate value or for that matter for any other life which is not concerned primarily with *artha*, *dharma*, *kāma* and *mokṣa*. This is a grave deficiency and points to the necessity of building a new theory of the *puruṣārtha*s which would take into account the diverse seekings of human beings and do justice to them.

Chapter 4

The Fires of Strangers: A Levinasian Approach to Vedic Ethics

Laurie L. Patton

> A Brahmin guest enters the house as the fire in all men.
> – *Kaṭha Upaniṣad* 1.7

Images, Ethics, and the Vedic World

The Upaniṣadic author challenges our ethical imaginations: Why is a guest – a stranger in the house – made up of fire? How does the imagery of fire help a Vedic householder behave in the appropriate way toward the one whom he does not know who crosses his threshold? Much of the study of ethical discourse in Hinduism has focused on the question of *dharma*, or moral law – a concept only fully developed in the later Vedic period. This chapter will begin by taking a more phenomenological approach, looking at the question of ethics from the Levinasian standpoint of 'being in the presence of an other.' I will then set the Vedic stage, and introduce basic vocabulary. I will next move on to explore the basic Vedic idea of an 'other'; finally, we will discuss some of the modes of encounter with an other, or stranger – both positive and negative in tone. Overall, I want to add a phenomenological note to the very compelling recent discussions of the Vedic 'other' in early India.[1] I also hope to add a more imagistic note to the idea of Hindu forms of ethics.[2] If Levinas is right in his emphasis on concrete, daily events as the basis of ethics, then Vedic India has much to tell us. This discussion also assumes a 'soft' relativism, in which Vedic forms of ethics might be loosely recognizable and translatable across cultures, but also having their own particular characters and vocabularies which are unique to

1 See Johannes Bronkhorst and Madhav Deshpande (eds), *Aryan and Non-Aryan in South Asia: Evidence, Interpretation, and Ideology*, Cambridge: Harvard University Press, 1999; also Sheldon Pollock, 'Deep Orientalism? Notes on Sanskrit and Power Beyond the Raj,' in *Orientalism and the Postcolonial Predicament*, Carol A. Breckenridge and Peter van der Veer (eds), Philadelphia, University of Pennsylvania Press, 1993, pp. 76-133.

2 For a compelling argument about the use of imagery in ethical thought, see Mark Johnson, *The Body In the Mind: The Bodily Basis of Meaning, Imagination, and Reason*, Chicago: University of Chicago Press, 1987.

the periods and the religious cultures in which they occur. I do not embrace a 'hard' relativism, for I am philosophically committed to the idea of responsible comparison as part of the human scholarly enterprise.[3] I also assume moral complexity at every moment of Vedic history; as in all moments of history, *erasures* of the other exist side by side with *acknowledgments* of the other.

Hindu Ethics and The Relevance of Levinas

Let me begin with short account of the concerns of scholars who have studied Hindu ethics to date. Space will not permit a longer account, but several brief points are worth making about the concerns of each 'moment' of ethical writing in Indological circles. The earliest works, such as Buch's *Principles of Hindu Ethics* (1921), Chartavakar's *Manual of Hindu Ethics* (1925), and Das' *Hindu Ethics* (1927), focus on the larger debate with missionaries about whether morality is central for Hinduism. Other early writers took up the introduction of Sanskrit authors on the topic and 'metaethical' categories, such as Maitra's 'social, psychological, and transcendental ethics' (*Ethics of the Hindus*, 1925). So too, Radhakrishnan in various articles (1911, 1914, 1939) took up the question of ethics to try to combat the stereotypical view of Hindus as world-negating and unconcerned with social uplift. His turn to Sanskrit categories such as *dharma* and *mokṣa*, in turn inspired other writers such as McKenzie (*Hindu Ethics*, 1922) and Hopkins (*Ethics of India*, 1924) to discuss whether these two categories are compatible ones, or whether worldly *dharma* is headed in the opposite ethical direction from otherworldly *mokṣa*. Later, Moore ('Metaphysics and Ethics in Radhakrishnan's Philosophy,' 1952) and Goodwin ('Mysticism and Ethics,' 1956) take Radhakrishnan's initial insight that mysticism and ethics could be related to each other.

Independence brought another kind of need for critical reflection, with a view toward further specifying what a particular Indian vocabulary might look like. Mahadevan ('The Basis of Social, Ethical, and Spiritual Values in Indian Philosophy,' 1951), Saksena ('Moral Philosophy in India,' 1965) and Sen ('Indian Philosophy and Social Ethics,' 1967) introduce sustained reflection on the *puruṣārthas*, life-goals or 'aims of humans.' These included *mokṣa* and *dharma*, but were expanded to include the development of wealth and abundance (*artha*) as well an exploration of the nature of desire (*kāma*). Such an emphasis landed philosophers in explorations of the classical texts of the *Dharmaśāstras*. The notion of *niṣkāma karma*, action without desire, also focused thinkers on the *Gītā* (Moorty, 'A Modern Hindu Approach to Ethics,' 1960; Saksena, 1965; and Raju, 'The Epics and the Ethical Codes,' 1971; Daya Krishna, in this volume). Relatedly, some of these same authors attempted to define *mokṣa* itself as ethical and locatable in social life, rather than other-worldly

3 Here I agree with Roy Perrett's quite elegant and reasonable rejoinder to Arthur Danto's claim (curious, for the late twentieth century) that the moral universe of ancient India is inaccessible to the 'Westerner', whoever she or he might be. See Perrett, *Hindu Ethics*, Honolulu: University of Hawaii Press, 1998, pp. 2-3, 6, 87-93.

and disengaged (Mahadevan, 'Beyond Ethics,' 1950; Nikhilananda, 'Hindu Ethics,' 1952, a and b). In all of these discussions, the law of *karma*, or rule of action and consequences, is considered as an ethical category, and related to the question of caste. Finally, in this post-independence moment the works of Śaṅkara and other authors of Advaita Vedānta are seen as the supreme concept for ethics (Bhattacarya, 'Indian Ethics,' 1953; Nikhilananda 1952 a and b) and Wadia ('Indian Ethics,' 1964). Others, such as Raju ('The Concept of the Spiritual in Indian Thought,' 1954) and Sen (1967) offer *ahiṃsā* as the all-encompassing category, again using classical Indian thought as a basic perspective.

A focus on *contextualization* of Hindu ethical thought within Indian societies characterizes the next phase. The rather long-sweeping *Evolution of Ethical Ideals* (1974) uses the Vedic Sūtra and Epics and Darśana periods, and makes an appeal for Indian thought as 'contextual and reflective.' In his *Dharma in Hindu Ethics* (1977), Austin Creel makes a strong argument for the reintegration of *dharma* into a post-colonial cultural context. This plea for contextual thinking also lends itself well to a re-examination of morality in narrative, particularly in the Epics, where we see Hindery's 'Hindu Ethics in the Rāmāyaṇa' (1976) as well as A.N. Bhattacarya's *Dharma – Adharma and Morality in the Mahābhārata* (1992). Such writers argue that popular classics and plays are as much as *modus vivendi* for ethical thought as were the classical Śāstra documents. Relatedly, in a 1981 review article of recent writing in Hindu ethics, David Miller also complains that Austin Creel's work (and by implication, many others) does not include the rich tradition of lesser-known commentaries in Indian vernaculars as well as Sanskrit. He also points out that more popular life-histories, autobiographies and biographies are excellent sources for ethical theorizing.[4]

At the end of his piece, Miller brings up David Little's and Sumner Twiss' groundbreaking work on the possibility of comparative religious ethics (*Comparative Religious Ethics*, 1978). This volume is nothing less than an attempt to create a common ethical vocabulary across religions. As Little and Twiss argue, each tentative definition of a religious or moral statement must be tested and refined in cross-cultural studies, and then modified and reconstructed once again. The book and related conversations leading up to the book brought into being a series of new, 'issues' oriented writing in Hindu ethics, such as Kana Mitra's 'Human Rights and Hinduism' (1982) as well as the influential volume edited by Coward, Lipner and Young, a series of essays on the specific topics of abortion, euthanasia, and purity (1989).

Perhaps the most elegant and systematic of these recent works is Roy Perrett's *Hindu Ethics* (1998).[5] While Perrett returns to the classical philosophical systems of the *Gītā*, the Yoga Sūtras, and Advaita Vedānta, he does so in a line by line refutation of the various critiques made of Hindu ethics by writers of the 1950s and 1960s.

4 See David Miller, 'Sources of Hindu Ethical Studies: A Critical Review,' in *Journal of Religious Ethics*, 9 (2), 1981, pp. 86-99.

5 Perrett has a chapter in this volume.

He also engages Arthur Danto, an influential Western cultural critic who took it upon himself to engage Hindu mysticism. He shows the plurality of philosophical views of dharma and *mokṣa* and the law of *karma*, all of which should make ethical thinking possible from a cross cultural perspective. Perrett argues to a commitment to traditional Hindu ideals and an openness to Western thought. The same combination of attention to specific, and multiple genres of philosophical thinking is at work in the recent debate (1998) between Ariel Glucklich and Maria Hibbetts (now Heim) on 'Method in Comparative Ethics.' Here, Glucklich and Hibbetts (Heim) debate the dynamics of gift giving (*dāna*) as well as *dharma* in terms of specific genres, such as the Nibandhas and *Dharmaśāstras*.[6]

Finally, mention should be made of Purushottama Bilimoria's work on the moral aspects of Mīmāṃsā, or ritual philosophy, of the 4th century BCE.[7] While Mīmāṃsā derives from a period slightly later than the period I will address here, Bilimoria does acknowledge the clear Mīmāṃsā interest in maintaining Hindu orthodoxy against its critics, specifically Buddhist and Naiyāyika attacks on the exclusive authority of the Veda. Bilimoria emphasizes that this Mīmāṃsaka focus on the authority of the Veda was in fact at the expense of any personal or divine authority, especially in Kumārila's case. For Bilimoria, Mīmāṃsakas are rather Humean skeptics, sprinkled with moral and theological skepticism, as well as ritual determinism. In Bilimoria's reading of Vedic agnosticism, a supreme being independent of the Veda would undermine the efficacy of the Veda itself, and would undermine the autonomy of the moral law (*dharma*). Second, Mīmāṃsakas will go to great lengths to preserve the idea of eternal souls and the kingdom of ends, as essential parts of the efficacy of rituals. They do this because these are crucial elements in preserving the moral autonomy of the Veda. These ideas go a long way toward establishing a basic Hindu ethical system in the context of sacrificial performance.[8]

6 Heim has a chapter in this volume (8).

7 See among many other works, 'Śruti and Apauruṣeya: An Approach to Religious Scriptures and Revelation,' in *Journal of Dharma*, 3(3), 1982, pp. 275-91, 'Hindu Doubts About God: Towards a Mīmāṃsā Deconstruction,' in Roy W. Perett (ed.), *Indian Philosophy A Collection of Readings*, NY and London: Garland Publishing Inc., New York, 2001, pp. 87-106; 'Authorless Voice, Tradition and Authority in the Mīmāṃsā-reflections of crosscultural hermeneutics,' *Nagoya Studies in Indian Culture and Buddhism: Sambhāṣā* 16, 1995, pp. 137-60; '*Autpattika* : The originary signifier-signified relation in Mīmāṃsā and Deconstructive Semiology,' in R.R. Diwedhi (ed.), *Mandan Mishra Felicitation Volume*, Delhi: L.B.S. Rashtriya Sanskrit Vidyapitha and Motilal Banarsidass, 1994, pp. 187-203; 'Liberating Language: Pārthasārathi Miśra on the Sentence and its Meaning,' in Dick van der Meij (ed.), *India and Beyond Aspects of Literature, Meaning, Ritual and Thought, Essays in Honour of Frits Staal*, London/NY: Kegan Paul International in association with Leiden: International Institute for Asian Studies, 1997: pp. 27-49; 'The Idea of Authorless Revelation (*Apauruṣeya*)' in Roy W. Perrett (ed.) *Indian Philosophy of Religion*, Dordrecht: Martinus Nijhoff, 1989, pp. 143-166.

8 Bilimoria has a chapter (7) in this volume on this issue.

Levinas and the Vedas

This short review of moments in ethical writing about Hinduism show that there is a continual movement toward specificity of context and vocabulary in thinking through Hindu ethics. Words and definitions of words continue to matter, and matter more when 'situational ethics' are introduced as methods. Indeed, the trajectory of scholarship suggests that the idea of 'Hindu ethics' is already uncomfortably abstract, and Hindu *dharma* has only fitted awkwardly into the rubric, given its concrete manifestations in epics, poetry, as well as those stubbornly variegated compendia of laws. This is one powerful reason for the tendency in more recent scholarship to more contextualized thinking, to narratives, to folktales and vernaculars. Without such categories, the description of a Hindu ethics can remain dry and somewhat unwieldy.

As Ariel Glucklich has elegantly shown,[9] Hindu *dharma* is better described with reference to phenomenological experience – the languages of emotion and aesthetics and bodily experience. Distinguishing between religious symbols and religious images, he argues that the phenomenology of religion cannot study only religious symbols and ideas, but needs to focus instead on the act of consciousness that brings such symbols to life. While a symbol is something that is by nature, expressive of an object that transcends everything in the world, a living image is not something whose sole nature is to refer, but in fact whose nature is to constitute a mode of being in the world.[10] A living image is something which is generated in the active consciousness of any actor – but in the Vedic case, particularly the ritual actor, and the experience that such an actor brings to his or her understanding of the image. Phenomenology raises images, with their structures and relations, to an equal footing with the structure of metaphysical realities. The same must be true of ethics. Steven M. Parish's *Moral Knowing in a Hindu Sacred City* (1994), makes ethnographic arguments about ethics similar to Glucklich's textual ones about *dharma*: for Parish, moral thinking is a 'felt perception of order in the pattern of life.' Without this phenomenological turn, ethical being and writing risks giving way to a kind of descriptive mechanics.

The Vedic world is usually placed low on the list of sources for Hindu ethics for similar reasons. As compendia of explicit statements about *dharma*, early Vedic texts are woefully inadequate. Even in his impassioned refutation of the usual charge that Vedic Hinduism is amoral, Roderick Hindery (1976, 1980) turns primarily to the Upaniṣads, the identification of *ātman* and Brahman, rather than the earlier Vedic texts of the Saṃhitās or the Gṛhya and Śrauta Sūtras. While I too will deal with the Upaniṣads, their contexts of Vedic sacrificial learning and ritual systems cannot be ignored even as one might 'extract' an ethical principle from them. At best, the hymns to Varuṇa, to be discussed below, are nodded to as 'proto' forms of ethical obligation, but not examined in their own right as kinds of ethical encounter.

---

9 *The Sense of Adharma*, Oxford: Oxford University Press, 1994.

10 Ibid., p. 26. I have made this same argument in my book, *Bringing the Gods to Mind: Mantra and Poetry in Early Indian Sacrifice*, 2004, Chapter One.

But might we not think of the Vedic texts as 'felt perceptions of order in the pattern of life,' as Parish does the Newar city? The poetic and ritual character of many of the Vedic texts might well lend itself to phenomenological analysis. And, as a basis, we might begin by building a complex vocabulary of face-to-face encounter, a move essential to most recent phenomenological ethics. In this way, we are proceeding as Levinas has with the Hebrew Bible,[11] looking at moments – narrative, poetic, and ritual – wherein a sense of being in the presence of another is invoked. In addition, such moments also entail an accounting of one's obligation toward the other, the basis of all ethics for Levinas.

Levinas

As Jill Robbins notes, Levinas places ethics in the 'interlocutionary relation to the other.' For Levinas, ethics is a comportment in which the other, who is strange and indifferent to you, who belongs neither to the order of your interest nor to your affections at the same time matters to you.'[12] It is precisely the strangeness of the other which links that person to you ethically, and provides a relationship. Moreover, for Levinas, the experience of alterity is a prelinguistic, basic form of knowledge which may be the origin of transcendence.[13]

Ethics as daily comportment is quite close to the idea of *dharma*, in its concrete focus on situations and intercaste relationships. It is even closer to the ideas, rules, and behaviours contained in Vedic texts such as the Gṛhya Sūtras, the domestic manuals which regulate the cycles of daily life. To be sure, the sacrificial language of the Vedic texts is not 'daily' in that it is separated off, a geometrically measured sacred sphere, yet it too has much to do with comportment, with what kinds of bodily movements and postures are appropriate, and what kind of speech is the appropriately ethical speech that might order the world.

For Levinas, this comportment is primarily regulated by the face, or the appearance of the face. As he puts it, 'the face is not of the order of the seen, it is not an object, but it is he whose appearing preserves an exteriority which is also an appeal or an imperative given to your responsibility: to encounter a face is straightaway to hear a demand and an order.'[14] In the Vedic world, as we shall note, this encounter takes place mostly in the meeting with the divine, whose face is not seen and yet creates a demand to the sacrificer – a demand based on *ṛta*, or sacred moral order. As Levinas puts it, 'The meaningfulness of the face is the command to responsibility.' Moreover,

11 See 'Revelation in the Jewish Tradition,' and 'The Pact,' in *The Levinas Reader*, 1989, pp. 190-226.

12 'Interview with Francois Poirie,' in *Is it Righteous to Be? Interviews with Emmanuel Levinas*, 2001, p. 48. I will add here that my characterizations of Levinas are geared toward presenting the basics of this thought in a clear and accessible manner – hence my heavy use of Robbins' excellent collection of interviews as well as his own writings. Space prevents me from delving into the intricacies of much of his work.

13 Ibid., pp. 48-49.

14 Ibid.

it is 'the ground of the experience of God and with the infinite.'[15] As we will see below, the Vedic god Agni is frequently defined by his ability to face all beings, to be in their presence and the presence of the sacrificers.

Finally, ethics for Levinas is reorientation toward the concrete. It is an attempt to reconstitute what Husserl called an original *gegenbenheit* ('originary givenness'), the 'concrete circumstances' where a meaning alone can come to mind.[16] To see philosophically (and therefore ethically) that is, without a naive blindness, is to reconstitute ... the concrete situation of appearing. It is to return to the neglected concreteness of its *mise en scene*, which delivers the meaning of the given, and behind its *quiddity*, its mode of being.[17]

Following Levinas, then, we will try to reconstruct the *mise en scene* of Vedic obligation. We do so without the direct translation of positive responsibility that Levinas speaks about when he writes of love. Rather I will describe the experience of strangeness in its objectifying and denigrating aspects as well as its obligation- and relationship-creating aspects. We will explore the Vedic negation of alterity, the 'wish to make the other disappear'[18] as well as the Vedic desire to have the other appear, to cede a place to him. This approach assumes a complex perspective, as all cultural perspectives must be, involving hostile as well as open impulses toward alterity. (Indeed, it is no different than today's complex relationships of alterity.) What we are after is a complex vocabulary that is specifically Vedic, that serves as the ground of ethics in that Vedic world.

The Vedic Period

Setting the Stage in the Vedas: The Ethics of Sacrificial Performance

How might we begin the *mise en scene* of which Levinas writes? I have attempted this sketch elsewhere,[19] and reproduce it here: It is sunrise; a group of men are standing above a rounded fire pit and chanting poetic rhythms. Near the firepit, outside a fenced boundary, the sound of women pounding rice is interspersed with the hymns. Every two or three verses, ending with the sound '*Svaha*', the men pour an amount of ghee from a wooden bowl and the fire flares up, suddenly, as if hungry. Next to the fire pit is a long pole wrapped in yellow, rubbed in an oily substance which makes it glisten in the morning light. In fact, the entire scene is a medley of light: the sunrise, the hungry fire, the golden butter, and the yellow pole. The priests are reciting hymns to Agni, the god of Fire, comparing him to the sun, which is rising now and casting light all around, and also likening him to the colour of the butter being cast into the

15 Op cit., Robbins, 'Being Toward Death,' p. 135.

16 Op cit., Robbins, 'Who Shall not Prophesy,' p. 222.

17 Ibid.

18 Op cit., Robbins, 'The Vocation of the Other', p. 112.

19 'Vedas and Upaniṣads', in Gene Thursby and Sushil Mittal (eds), *The Hindu World*, New York: Routledge, forthcoming.

pit, making a spectacle of sparks and smoke. Later, the rice that the women have pounded will be shaped into balls of rice-offerings, making the arena both a place of offering and a place of eating for the priests and for the community as a whole.

When did this scene occur? It could have occurred in 1500 BCE, the time of the fixing of the Vedic corpus of mantras as we know it, or it could have occurred in Spring, 2000, in Western Maharashtra, in a revival of Vedic sacrifice which attempts to follow the ancient texts exactly. While arguments abound as to its centrality,[20] the Vedic tradition remains a kind of touchstone around which Hindu religious arguments revolve.

This touchstone called the 'Vedas' emerged as a series of practices involving an oral text and a set of sacrifices involving fire. While oral texts and the practice of fire sacrifice probably existed for several centuries, if not millennia, before 1500 BCE, the scholarly consensus is that the Vedic practices emerged as we know them around this time in Western India, and moved Eastward along the Gangetic plain. They were the property of people who called themselves *ārya*, or nobility, and distinguished themselves linguistically from the *dāsa* or enslaved ones, and the *mleccha*, or 'others.' At present much debate exists about the origins of the Aryans themselves.[21] While the debate is still raging, suffice it to say that the Vedic world emerged in a far more complex, gradual way than the earlier, now long-disproved hypothesis of simple violent invasion had suggested.

What distinguished the Aryans from other groups, and the Vedas from other texts? First, the Aryans worked with chariots, horses, and weapons of war, which included iron. Second, their social organization was broadly tribal in nature, and focused on cattle as a form of wealth and status. Third, their method of worship revolved around an elaborate system of sacrifice involving vegetable and animal offerings, in which the power of speech played a central role.

---

20 Many Hindus have criticized the centrality of the Vedas to Hindu identity. Sant Tukarām was clear that the Vedas were not at all central to Hindu identity; rather, he thought that one 'gets tangled up in the Vedas and dies therein.'

21 Much of nineteenth-century British scholarship posited an 'invasion' of an early group, springing from an Indo-European homeland, who migrated through the Caucasus, Iran, and into the Hindu Kush, around 2000-1500 BCE, However, recent archaeological evidence suggests that the story is far more complex and does not involve an invasion at all. Rather, the Aryans might have cohabited and mingled with their counterparts, the inhabitants of the Indus Valley civilization (covering what is now present-day Pakistan and parts of Western India), for several centuries, before the great towns and cities of the Indus Valley civilization fell into decay, around 1700 BCE. Archaeological evidence also suggests that Indus Valley towns and ways of life lasted in smaller scale far beyond that time of the demise of its great cities, and that the Aryans were present in the more central parts of India far earlier than had been previously thought. In light of this picture of ancient developments, some scholars argue that the Indus Valley and the Vedic civilizations were a single civilization. See, for example, the recent book by Edwin Bryant, *The Quest for the Origins of Vedic Culture: The Indo-Aryan Migration Debate*, New York: Oxford, 2001.

This power of speech is where the Vedas, and relatedly, the question of exchange, come clearly into focus. Here is where we encounter the Vedic version of Levinas' 'interlocutionary relation to the other.' The word 'Veda' means knowledge, and four kinds of knowledge are specified as the property of brahmin priests, the hereditary keepers of tradition: the *ṚgVeda*, or knowledge of the verses, the *Sāmaveda*, or knowledge of the chants, the *Yajur Veda*, or knowledge of the ritual directions, and the *Atharva Veda*, or knowledge of the Atharvans, the procedures for everyday life (also called 'magical' formulae). These four divisions reflect a division of labor amongst the priestly elite as to who was to do what, and it meant that knowledge itself was organized around the performance of *yajña*, or sacrifice. For the Vedic Aryans, *yajña* is the central ethical action that was meant to motivate and sustain the entire universe. The Vedas are the words and chants accompanying the actions and served to augment and vitalize the actions into having cosmic power. Without the sacrifice, the sun would not rise in the morning, the cattle could not grow and multiply, the crops would not grow throughout the year, the possibility of long and healthy life for humans, and the worship of the fathers, or ancestors, after death, would not be present. Thus, any form of moral action would take place with an idea of all of these players present on the universal stage.

This knowledge, aside from being a kind of fourfold division of labor of the sacrifice, was also hereditary, and learned entirely orally. The different collections of hymns in the Vedas are called *maṇḍalas*, and are essentially 'family' collections which reflect the idea that this knowledge was passed down father to son, and teacher to student. Moreover, the method of keeping the knowledge oral was the highly advanced science of memorization.[22] The *ṚgVeda* alone consists of some 10,000 verses, and the recitation of such a work involved a mental feat of great magnitude indeed.

Just as the Vedas represented a kind of division of labour, so too the priests' labours are divided into various kinds like any other well organized 'central office' – and the sacrificial arena was the command central of the universe itself. Priests took up their roles at different places within the performance arena, and each form of labour is weighted with a kind of cosmic, mythical significance. The *hotṛ* in charge of the *ṚgVeda*, or poetic formulae; the *adhvaryu* priest, in charge of overseeing the actual movements of all of the sub-priests, and moves all about as a kind of 'master of ceremonies,' the *udgātṛ* priest in charge of the musical elements, a family mythically descended from the Gandharvans, or heavenly musicians. The *brāhmaṇa*

22 The Vedic texts were divided into *saṃhitā-pātha*, or the words combined in euphonic combination (*sandhi*); the *pada-pāṭha*, in which the words are separated and stand on their own; and the *krama-pāṭha*, or syllabic separation which showed the ways in which each syllable was to be memorized and repeated in a regular pattern, and accompanied by bodily movement. To this day, when one attends a performance of a Vedic sacrifice, one sees students sitting near the Vedic fires, learning the *krama-pāṭha* system and moving their heads and hands and wrists in accordance with the rhythm. In the twentieth century, this learning is augmented by books; this was not the case during the Vedic (both early and late) period of early India, from about 1500 to 300 BCE.

priest was in charge of the entire sacrifice, and his role is to sit in silence on a stool at the centre, observing the proceedings and being consulted in moments of ritual error or confusion. Silence in the Veda tends to signify either great insight or great defeat, and of course in this case of the *brāhmaṇa*, insight is indicated. Exchange between priests, then, involves their fulfilling their moral obligations as priests who negotiate both substances and words of the sacrifice. Their functions were to determine the limits of sacrificial action; and of the earliest uses of the term *dharma*, the word so often translated as 'morality,' is 'sacrificial boundary.' (See RV 10.90.16.)

Another, separate ritual role is reserved for the sponsor of the Vedic sacrifice – called the *yajamāna* and his wife, the ones who provide the economic resources for the entire performance. The *yajamāna* holds a special seat during the proceedings, and at various moments at the beginning and the end, performs an inaugurating function. His wife, too, is present at various moments of the sacrifice. At times she is covered with a parasol, and at other she participates in offerings. She represents fertility and a kind of cosmic sexuality, and her public role is to be noted as a major exception to the general role of women during the sacrificial performances.

Many scholars have argued that contest per se is the essence of the Vedic world view: each sacrifice was a kind of brahminical 'potlatch' ceremony in which wealth was displayed, and members of competing Aryan tribes engaged in verbal battles in which the very life of the contestants was at stake.[23] These performances created an escalating scale of violence from which the authors of the more contemplative texts, the Upaniṣads, departed in favour of a more internalized view of sacrifice. Whatever the level of violence was actually and metaphorically present, it is clear that these acts of sacrifice were also bargaining chips for political power in a system of small tribes and tribal alliances, and continued to remain so as the sacrificial system moved into the period of more consolidated kingdoms along the Ganges River.

As one might expect, the Vedic gods are also divided into relative divisions of labour. Agni, the Fire God, and Soma, the god of the sacrificial drink, are the priestly gods who are in charge of transporting the sacrifice to the heavens. With these priestly gods, we see the Vedic world at its most philosophically playful: the texts constantly move between the abstract and the concrete.[24]

The warrior god, Indra, is far more human in his incarnations. His feats include cosmic heroism; he freed the cows from their cave in heaven, and thereby allowed them to roam freely about the world. In so far as cows are also symbolic of light in

---

23 The basic structure of the Vedic sacrifice is that of the Soma sacrifice, the crushing and offering of soma in the morning, mid-day, and evening. Each soma sacrifice consists of several *iṣṭis*, or offerings, of either a vegetable or an animal, and each *iṣṭis* is dedicated to a particular deity and accompanied by mantras that are devoted to that deity. These rites are the skeletal offerings around which the larger procedures, such as the kingly coronation (*rajasūya*), and the horse sacrifice, designed to conquer land (*aśvamedha)*, are built. These larger sacrifices usually involve other, special rites, frequently of a contestual nature.

24 At times Agni is the actual fire, and at others he is clearly the god of fire, and this constant oscillation between the two states is part of the genius of Vedic poetry. Soma, too, is both a deity of eloquence and the sacred drink that is crushed and causes eloquence.

the *RgVeda*, he thereby allows the light to roam freely about the world. He also slays the dragon Vṛtra, whose huge body had dammed up the rivers and stops the waters from flowing. Indra is an appetitive god, and is frequently caught in exploits with sages' wives. The deities of the third class, the agricultural class, are the Aśvins, the twin deities who heal, cause safe childbirth, restore beauty, and prolong life.

Yet the Vedic world is also filled with other deities, identified with but not limited to the natural world. Sūrya, the sun god, is the most prominent of these deities, and is depicted as the deity who rides a chariot across the skies, and whose cyclical journey is identified with the calendrical year.

In addition, the sages (*ṛṣis*) and fathers (*pitṛs*) play an important role in the Vedic cosmos; many would argue that they, rather than the gods, are the real actors in the *yajña*. The *ṛṣis* are said to be present at the original sacrifice that created the world; in this sense they have the same, if not greater, role in creation than the Vedic gods. The fathers, on the other hand, are the receivers of the sacrifice along with the gods. The fathers are seen as the ancestors of the sacrificer who makes the offering; in certain texts they are viewed as the successful sacrificer who has gone on to gain the status of a deity in his next life, by virtue of offering so many sacrifices in his previous one.

The style of these Vedic hymns is frequently enigmatic, built on a set of metaphorical constructions which contain two or more realities. As mentioned above, Agni is both the fire and the fire god, the power of fire itself. Cows frequently represent light, and the free passage of sunlight throughout the world. They also represent wealth and gold. Finally, enigmas can take the shape of explicit paradox, such as 'With the sacrifice the gods sacrificed to the sacrifice,' (RV 10.90.16) in which the poets create a kind of verbal Mobius strip in which nothing can exist independently. Elements of the universe do not engage in a form of linear creation, rather they engage in acts of mutual creation that serve as challenges to the reciter and the hearer in the sacrificial arena.

From the description above, we can see that the ultimate social goods of the Vedic world are the goods of the sacrificial offerings – vegetable, animal, and the verbal mantras composed by the ancient poets. These offerings are exchanged between humans and the gods. In return, the gods will bestow the goods of the natural world, such as sunlight, rains, cattle, and fertile lands. Thus we might say that *moral responsibility consists of appropriate sacrificial performance.* Thus, even poetic words themselves are seen as the most powerful parts of the sacrifice, and therefore are to be used morally and responsibly. As we have seen described above: mutuality occurs on a two-fold level: 1) There is a sense of mutuality between humans and gods; 2) There is also a sense of reciprocity between each of the priestly actors in the sacrifice, each of whom hold a sacred station and whose rank is defined according to sacrificial prowess.

Most importantly for our purposes, such a sacrifice involves face-to-face interaction, both at the actual level of the performance as well as the symbolic language of interaction between humans and gods. We see this in the language of the *sākṣi*, literally the 'fellow-seer,' or 'witness' who is also the companion in the sacrifice.

In his *Nine Talmudic Readings*, Levinas analyzes the Sanhedrin in a similar manner; its semi-circular open space and design is based on the idea of people seeing each other face-to-face.[25] Moreover, Levinas remarks that the Sanhedrin is also seen as the 'navel' of the world, just as the Vedic altar is seen as the 'navel of the world' – where the priests face each other in sacrifice (RV 1.164.34-35).

Moral Engagement: Hymns to Varuṇa as Complex Ethical Sites

Thus, the basics of Vedic ideas of exchange occur within sacrifice. Yet there are subtler, more important explorations which we can get at concerning the imagery of ethics. With this basic *mise en scene* in mind, we turn to examine the idea of moral accountability, turning particularly to the figure of Varuṇa, the god who distributes punishment and makes judgments in the Vedic period. The Vedic hymns to Varuṇa, a mysterious storm god who is also the arbiter of moral exchange, reflect all these themes. They are seen by many as some of the earliest forms of moral reflection known to humankind. In one particular hymn, *ṚgVeda* 5.85, the poet asks forgiveness from his sins from Varuṇa:

1. For the emperor I will sing a splendid, deep prayer, one that will be dear to the famous Varuṇa who struck apart the earth and spread it beneath the sun as the priest who performs the slaughter spreads out the victim's skin.
2. He stretched out the middle realm of space in the trees; he laid victory in swift horses and milk in the dawn cows, intelligence in the hearts and fire in the waters. Varuṇa placed the sun in the sky and Soma on the mountain.
3. Over the two world-halves and the realm of space between them, Varuṇa has poured out the cask, turning its mouth downward. With it, the kind of the whole universe waters the soil as the rain waters the grain.
4. He waters the soil, the earth, and the sky. Whenever Varuṇa wishes for the milk, the mountains dress themselves in cloud and the heroes, brandishing their power, let them loose.
5. I will proclaim the great magic of Varuṇa the famous Asura, who stood up in the middle realm of space and measured apart the earth with the sun as with a measuring-stick.
6. No one has dared this great magic of the most inspired god: that these shimmering torrents, pouring down, do not fill one single ocean with their water.
7. If we have committed an offence against a hospitable friend like Āryaman or a close friend like Mitra, or against one who has always been a comrade, or a brother, or a neighbour – one of our own or a stranger – loosen that offence from us, Varuṇa.

25 'As Old as The World,' in *Nine Talmudic Readings*, p. 72.

8. If we have cheated like gamblers in a game, whether we know it or really do not know it, O god, cast all these offences away, like loosened bonds. Let us be dear to you, Varuṇa.[26]

Varuṇa is depicted as the sacrificial priest 'who struck apart the earth and spread it beneath the sun, as the priest who performs the slaughter spreads out the victim's skin' (Verse 1). Thus, his moral authority comes from his prowess as the cosmic sacrificer. Varuṇa has the power of creation, and of forgiveness: 'If we have committed an offence against a hospitable friend like Āryaman or a close friend like Mitra, or against one who has always been a comrade, or a brother, or a neighbour – one of our own or a stranger, loosen that offence from us, Varuṇa' (Verse 7). Notice here that the category of possibly offended parties includes both gods, with whom humans exist in mutual relationship, and humans – brothers, neighbours, strangers. Such alliances are therefore both sacrificial *and* moral alliances – in fact, as mentioned above, the two are integrally connected. Moreover, the category of persons for whom one is responsible grows wider as the poet begins to think through the problem.

In these hymns, the poet also names unintentional offences, and thus the idea of morality is expanded from personal responsibility to a general fault in the system of moral exchange: 'If we have cheated like gamblers in a game, whether we know it or really do not know it – O God, cast all these offenses away like loosened bonds. Let us be dear to you, Varuṇa' (Verse 9). The moral offence is likened to a bond which must be loosened, and those offences are part of a larger system. So too, Levinas writes of the moral offence toward the other which creates a bond with the other – an inextricable link with him or her whose very nature is mystery and exteriority.[27]

In another hymn (RV 7.86.4), the ethical reflection takes a clearly reflective tone. The hymn takes up a story from RV 7.55, where Vasiṣṭha the sage enters the house of Varuṇa, and when a dog ran at the sage, he put the dog to sleep with several verses. As a punishment for putting the dog to sleep, Varuṇa bound Vasiṣṭha with his own fetters and snares. Vasiṣṭha is trying to praise Varuṇa in the hymn below in order to attain release.

1. The generations have become wise by the power of him who has propped apart the two world-halves even though they are so vast. He has pushed away the dome of the sky to make it high and wide; he has set the sun on its double-journey, and spread out the earth.
2. And I ask my own heart, 'When shall I be close to Varuṇa? Will he enjoy my offering and not be provoked to anger? When shall I see his mercy and rejoice?'
3. I ask myself what that transgression was, Varuṇa, for I wish to understand. I turn to the wise to ask them. The poets have told me the very same thing:

---

26 This follows Doniger's translation, *The Rig Veda*, Harmondsworth: Penguin Press, pp. 211-12.

27 'Time and the Other,' in *The Levinas Reader*, pp. 43-48.

'Varuṇa has been provoked to anger against you.'

4. O Varuṇa, what was the terrible crime for which you wish to destroy your friend who praises you? Proclaim it to me that I may hasten to prostrate myself before you and be free from sin, for you are hard to deceive and are ruled by yourself alone.
5. Free us from the harmful deeds of our fathers, and from those that we have committed with our own bodies. O king, free Vasiṣṭha like a thief who has stolen cattle, like a calf set free from a rope.
6. The mischief was not done by my own free will, Varuṇa; wine, anger, dice, or carelessness led me astray. The older shares in the mistake of the younger. Even sleep does not avert evil.
7. As a slave serves a generous master, so would I serve the furious god and be free from sin. The noble god gave understanding to those who did not understand; being yet wiser, he speeds the clever man to wealth.
8. O Varuṇa, you who are ruled by yourself alone, let this praise lodge in your very heart. Let it go well for us always with your blessings.

In this hymn, the distinction is clearly made between intentional and unintentional, conscious and unconscious harm: In verse 3, the poet asks himself what the transgression was, and then makes the plea, in verse 4: 'O Varuṇa, what was the terrible crime for which you wish to destroy your friend who praises you? Proclaim it to me so that I may hasten to prostrate myself before you and be free from harm, for you are hard to deceive and are ruled by yourself alone' (RV 7.86.4).

In addition to the bond between gods and worshipers, the poet also mentions the relationship between the ancestors and the worshiper, mentioned above. In the next verse of RV 7.86, verse 5, there is a distinction made between those sins which humans have committed with their own bodies, and those committed by 'their fathers.' Any given individual may suffer the consequences of harm done by his or her ancestors, and has a responsibility to care for the ancestors as a result. Thus, the idea of moral accountability extends across generations.

Near the close of the hymn, the poet expresses an even subtler notion of harm – harm caused by forces that interfere with the natural inclination and free will of the person: 'The mischief was not done by my own free will, Varuṇa, wine, anger, dice or carelessness led me astray … Even sleep does not avert evil' (verse 6). Thus, moral accountability is broken by a myriad of causes – intentional, unintentional, ancestral, and outside forces. Levinas, too, writes of the ways in which our relationship with the Other is also always one of failure – a failure to accept one's own diminishment in making space for the other.[28]

In the final verse, this exchange of moral goods is finally spoken of in terms of the exchange of sacrificial goods: 'The noble god gave understanding to those who did not understand – he speeds the clever man to wealth' (verse 7). Here, mantras are insight, and are given to the poet who is close to Varuṇa. So too wealth is a form of

28 Ibid., p. 50.

moral good in the larger cycle of exchange. All of these are returned and offered to Varuṇa in order to be freed from sin, and thus the cycle continues.

As I have mentioned, these hymns tend to be analyzed as 'precursors' to the more 'systematic' ethics of *dharma* that are the traditional focus of twentieth-century writing on Hindu ethics.[29] Yet it is also possible to read this hymn as a struggle with alterity in its own right, to acknowledge both specific and general obligation, and to acknowledge the actual scope of the demand of the other and one's resistance to it.

For instance, the possibility of face-to-face accountability is enjoined in the idea of being close to Varuṇa (7.86.1) and in the idea of 'turning to' the wise and asking what the transgression was (7.86.3). Like Varuṇa's mysterious presence, for Levinas God is, in a sense, 'the other par excellence, the other as other – the absolutely other – and nonetheless my standing with this God depends only on myself.'[30] So too, the Vedic poet searches in his own heart for his own accountability for what he has done (7.86.2).

And yet, the hymns also struggle with the question of being responsible for the state of others. On the one hand, as verses 7.86.5-6 show, the poet wants to be released from the effects of wrong that others might have performed. The harmful deeds of our ancestors are just as binding as ones we commit with our own bodies. The poet is clearly ambivalent about this fact; as Levinas writes also, all human beings must be, as it entails the death of their own imperial, virile, sense of self. However, in the very utterance of the poem, the poet entertains of the possibility that, *no matter what the origin of the wrong*, he himself could still also be responsible. So too, Levinas writes about this state as the condition of being 'the hostage of others': 'I can be responsible for that which I did not do and take upon myself a distress which is not mine.'[31]

The Other Who One Wishes Would Disappear

As hinted at above, Levinas' understanding of our relationship with alterity as the basis for human existence is of course focused on the development of the ethical, the being-for-another.[32] However, he understands this process of becoming-for-another as a complex act, which involves the substitution of the self with the other, and the overcoming of the natural will to virility, the natural fear of the other as a death to one's own imperial desire. Moreover, one begins to understand oneself as *already* a violence in respect to the other.[33] Levinas' stress upon our overcoming our natural

29 Georges Dumezil, *Ouranos-Varuṇa* (Paris, 1934); H. Lommel, 'Die Spaher des Varuṇa und Mitra und das Auge des Konigs,' in *Oriens* 6, 1953, pp. 323-33; H. Luders, *Varuṇa*, Gottingen, 1951, 1959; J. Przyluski, 'Varuṇa, God of the Sea and Sky,' in *Journal of the Royal Asiatic Society*, 1931, pp. 613-22.

30 Levinas, 'Toward the Other,' in *Nine Talmudic Readings*. Translated and with an Introduction by Annette Aronowicz, Bloomington: Indiana University Press, 1990, p. 16.

31 'As Old As the World,' in *Nine Talmudic Readings*, p. 85.

32 'Proximity and the Other,' in *Is it Righteous*, p. 215.

33 Ibid., 'Who Shall Prophesy?' p. 225.

desire 'to declare war against the other'[34] also presumes such an instinct does exist as primary, and it is the human task to acknowledge and overcome it. We can read in the Vedas the same struggle, particularly in the articulation of the *ārya-dāsa* relationship.

Let us turn then to that 'other' which is *not* to be acknowledged – the *anārya*, or *dāsa*. Myths about the *ārya-dāsa* relationship are piecemeal in the *ṚgVeda*. They revolve around celebrating the Aryan warrior god Indra's victories over the *dāsa*s, who are considered dark coloured ones (*kṛṣṇa varṇa*): 'You, Indra, subdued Pipru and powerful Mṛgayyu for Rjisvan, the son of Vidathin, you smote fifty thousand dark ones, you shattered cities, as old age shatters good looks' (RV 4.16.13). Not only are the *dāsa*s considered lesser because darker, but their being conquered actually increases the strength of the conqueror. In one hymn, the ṚgVedic poet says, 'Indra kills *dāsa*s and increases the might of the Aryans' (RV 10.22.8). In this same hymn there are references to the *dāsa* as non-human, or *amanuṣya*, and hence related to the idea of *mleccha*, or those who speak indistinctly.

So too, fire was used as a means of acquiring lands over the dark ones: A hymn to fire suggests this: 'O Fire, due to your fear the dark ones fled; scattered abroad and deserting their possessions, when for Puru, glowing Vaiśvanara, you burn up and tear their cities (RV 7.5.3). Fire also 'Drives out *dāsa*s and brings light to the Aryans' (RV 8.5.6).[35] Relatedly, the *dāsa* seemed enslaved to Indra, or driven out, wandering from place to place. Many hymns refer to the fact that Indra 'binds *dāsa*s one hundred and ten *dāsa*s' and 'leads away *dāsa*s at his will' (RV 5.34.6). So too 'the dark coloured *dāsa*s are driven away by Indra from place to place' (RV 4.47.21).

While these references are important in early Indian imagining about social boundaries, other social boundaries also existed. The *dāsa* is someone who worships the wrong gods, who hoards wealth, who neither conducts Vedic sacrifices nor speaks Sanskrit correctly like the *ārya* (RV 1.32 and 2.12). Moreover, there is also a sense of nobility to the term, connoting dignity and strength. The *ārya* is the one who receives the earth from Indra (4.26) and has superhuman strength.

How might we begin to think phenomenologically about the other in these fragmentary myths about Aryans, and what became of such mythic references over time? We can see that Aryan identity is based on its distinction from the other, darker ones, and exists in relationship to definitions of other peoples. The Aryans' understanding of themselves was based on colour characteristics as well as their prowess in battle and war. Most importantly, the *ārya* had control over sacred language.

Do references such as the ones above imply an ethnicity, or perhaps even more importantly, a race – members of a common biological origin? It is not clear; all we can only glean from the texts is that an *ārya* is someone who is to be respected, who

---

34 Ibid.

35 So, too, fire is used to root out the treasure of another wealthy group, the Pais, whose myth is that they have stored their wealth in a cave, and fire itself has routed it out (RV 6.13.3; RV 7.9.2).

is victorious over the dark ones, and who lays hereditary claim to a higher social status by virtue of language. There is no common consensus as to who these 'dark ones' might be.

Let us look more closely at another word for 'another', or 'other' in the Vedic hymns – the very commonplace *anya*. While it would be tedious and space consuming to examine each example in detail, we can safely say that *anya* can mean 'in one and in another,' as a kind of reciprocity between equals. This idea is implied in the verse 1.95.1:

> Two shapes with two different shades revolve toward their own ends; and each, one and another, nourishes offspring. In one, Hari is the receiver of the oblations; and the other, the shining one is beheld.
> *duve virūpe caratah suarthe anyānyā vatsam upa dhāpayete/*
> *harir anyasyām bhavati svadhāvāñ chukro anyasyāṃ dadṛśe suvarcāḥ//*

Here, one divine being, Hari, is the receiver of the oblations, and the other, the shining one (presumably Agni), is beheld by the worshiper. Here, there are two classes of being, each of which is a god, and therefore both occupying an equal category.

In another hymn (RV 10.117.4), a beggar or *bikṣu*, is the author. The poet speaks about wealth, and about going from 'one man to another, as the wheels of a chariot turn around' (*o hi vartante rathiyeva cakrā anyam-anyam upa tisthante rāyaḥ*). Similarly, in the later verse, the poet/beggar speaks about the need to turn away from a stingy giver: 'let him seek another, more liberal lord' (*pṛṇantam anyam araṇaṃ cid icched*). Here, the meaning is similar to moving between two equal members of a class of society – the word is used not to make a distinction between them, but rather to enumerate them. Similar kinds of meanings occur in a number of other places in these hymns. *Anya* is clearly in keeping with the meanings of 'other' in English, but does not take on the deeper philosophical weight of the 'other' that Levinas places upon it.

There are, however, several uses of the term that clearly imply the other as a potential or actual enemy. Similar to the *ārya/dāsa* distinction, the term *anyaka*, with the nominative suffix, is actually used in a hymn exhorting soldiers to better warfare. It is also used in the sequence of hymns RV 6.59-6.62 by the *ṛṣi* Nabhaka. The verses of the hymns end with the refrain '*na bhanta anyake same*,' or, 'May all our enemies perish.' Here, the idea of other not just as stranger, but hostile stranger, is quite clear.

Perhaps even more telling is the phrase *anya-vrata*, 'he who has chosen another' or 'whose vow is to another.' In RV 10.22.8, the phrase is used about the Dasyus, who are described as *akarma*, not acting in the correct way, and possibly not observing the appropriate rites. In addition, they are *amanuṣaḥ*, not human, or mortal. And more significantly, the Dasyus 'do not know us well' (*abhi no amantur*). Sāyaṇa gives a very intriguing gloss on the prefix *abhi*, here; for him, the prefix means that they 'do not know us face to face.' Thus, the impossibility of face-to-face encounter blocks their acting correctly (the Vedic sense of ethics) and their being human, or mortal. In this sense, they have become enemies because of their lack of face-to-face acknowledgment.

The Ethics of the Everyday: Some Particular Words

What would the hymns reveal if placed in the ethics of daily comportment, as Levinas puts it, or the sense of the search for the concrete? Our expanded notions might give us an expanded sense of inquiry – a sense of what it might be like for a Vedic poet to come face to face with another, in the midst of a sense of obligation, in Levinas' fullest sense. To explore such an idea we might proceed in a way similar to philology, looking at nouns and prepositions in order to glean what Levinas calls the origins of meaning of the face-to-face encounter.[36]

Presence

We might begin with a description of divine presence and face-to-face encounter – through the term '*prati*,' frequently translated as 'in front of' or 'in the presence of.' *Prati* is frequently used of Agni and his multiforms, such as Sūrya, Jātavedas, and so on. An excellent example of Sūrya's multiple presences in RV 1.50.4-5. In verse 4, Agni is described as 'visible to all' (*viśvadarśato*) and the maker of light (*jyotiṣkṛd*). Sāyaṇa, the fourteenth-century Vedic commentator, explains that even the moon and planets are given light by the sun. They are made of water, but reflect the sun's rays and make them luminous like a mirror. So too, writes Sāyaṇa, is the Supreme Spirit (*ātman*) who is helped by all those who wish for *mokṣa*, or liberation from the cycle of existences. The light of the mind that knowledge of *ātman* gives renders all else luminous. Thus, our sense of presence:

> *pratyan devānāṃ viśaḥ; pratyaṅṅ ud eṣi mānuṣān; pratyan viśvaṃ suvar dṛśe*;
> You rise in the presence of the Maruts, in the presence of humankind,
> and so are seen in the presence of the whole of heaven.

The idea here is that the sun is beheld by these Maruts, the heavenly protectors of the god Indra, who are frequently called the people (*viśaḥ*) of the gods, as well as the mortals, and can be seen in the entirety of heaven. The same sense is implied by a later hymn from Book 10 of the *ṚgVeda* (10.88.15-16). Here, in a hymn to Sūrya, the universe is thought of as the two paths for the fathers, gods, and mortals. All of the universe which is between the paternal (presumably, heaven), and the maternal (presumably, earth) goes by means of these two paths. Then, verse 16 goes on: 'The two support [Agni] who is moving, emerges from the head of all things. He is made sacred by songs; he is industrious, quickly moving, shining, and appears in the presence of all beings' (*pratyan viśvā bhūvanāni*).[37]

---

36 Op cit., Levinas, *Of God Who Comes to Mind*, p. 178.

37 See also Agni as praised in RV 2.3.1, by the *Ṛṣi* Gṛtasamada, in a similar fashion.

Additionally, presence can simply be indicated by the copula, to be, plus *pratyan*, such as in RV 10.79.5. Agni here is simply 'present before all beings' (*pratiaṅṅ asi tvam*) Here presence has no object, nor does it have a genitival relationship as in the previous examples. Rather, it has prepositional power in is own right; it means a kind of pure presence. This idea and usage might be similar to what Levinas means when he speaks of presence as a lucidity, a 'watching over being.'[38]

So, too, *pratyan* can mean power over an object, particularly when used with a verb of the same meaning, such as *jagāra*, grasping. Vasukra, Indra's son-in-law, praises the acts of Indra with the phrase, 'The rabbit grasps the sharp claw,' (*pratyañcam jagāra*; RV 10.28.9). So too, in an earlier hymn (19.27.13), Indra is described by the poet as 'seizing with his feet' (*patto jagāra pratyañcam*).

Finally, in RV 10.18, the connotation of the word *prati* and its related forms is to have a hold over something. The hymn is also a hymn to Death, and is sung during the actual rite of a funeral. The hymn contains the simile: 'I have a hold over my voice like the reins hold a horse' (*pratīcim jagrabha vācam aśvan rasanaya yathā*). Earlier in the verse, the poet says, 'They place me at the holding (or 'end,' *pratīcim*) of day, like they place arrows in a quiver' (14 a.b). Here, there is a delightful play on the day 'being held' and the voice 'being held.' Both usages of the term have the sense of binding force. Once again, we might understand the semantic range of the term *prati* as including both being the presence of another, and the 'other' having a binding force over oneself, just as Levinas might.

So the force of the word *prati*, *pratyañc*, and so on, describes a kind of effect, what Levinas might call an 'originary effect.' Grassman[39] gives the word *prati* the connotation of 'response, reply,' as well as in 'front, facing.' This meaning of the word might involve the kind of response of simultaneous vulnerability and power that the other's face calls up in us. Moreover, as many of the hymns discussed above show, the word *prati* can have the sense of being all-pervasive, that which *stands before all beings* as an enlightening force.

In *Of God Who Comes to Mind*, Levinas asks, 'outside all theology,' in what moment the divine word is heard. He posits that 'it is inscribed in the face of the other, in the encounter with the other, a double expression of weakness and demand.[40] The above discussion shows that there is great affinity between the Vedic idea of mantra, as articulated above, and the Levinasian understanding of language. Sacrificial mantra is indeed 'a double expression of weakness and demand' on the part of the poet and the god who might also utter mantras. For the poet, particularly in the strong subjunctives and imperatives throughout the Veda, there is a sense that in uttering words to a god in sacrifice, one is also responsible for feeding him or her. One is literally keeping the god, and therefore the world, alive. So too, the gods are

38 'God and Philosophy,' in *The Levinas Reader*, 1989, p. 170.

39 Hermann Grassman, *Worterbuch zum* Rig Veda *4*, *unveranderert*. 4th edn. Wiesbaden: Otto Harrassowitz, 1964, p. 867.

40 Emmanuel Levinas, *Of God Who Comes to Mind*, 1998; see esp. 'God and Philosophy,' pp. 55-78.

aware of this dynamic and are both givers of divine gifts, abundance, fertility, and sons. However, at the same time gods know that sacrificial words in their own right make gods stronger, able to do the things that human beings need them to do. Note that in one of our previous hymns (RV 10.28.6), Indra also says to the poet that the poet makes him stronger, and that his praise should reach the heavens. So, too, the hymn's last verse tells how sacred utterances nourish bodies (*ye hinvire tanuvaḥ soma ukthaiḥ* RV 10.28.12).

I have treated this exchange value of words in an earlier essay, which attempted to see Vedic language as concrete and parallel to the actual wealth of cattle and gold that might be exchanged in a sacrifice.[41] My point in that essay was not simply to point out the materiality of language, but also to show that language was a value in its own right as a mediational, if not moral, force. In Levinasian terms, this exchange might be spoken of in terms of the 'interlocutionary relation to the other' – the essential feature of ethical language for Levinas.

The Face

Several more semantic features might be helpful to us in exploring these ideas of face-to-face relations. *Mukha* in the RV means 'face' or 'mouth,' wherein the smaller body part of 'mouth' can a times signify the whole visage. It has all the semantic ambiguity that many words for body parts in the Veda do. As Tatyana Elizarenkova has already noted so eloquently,[42] the Vedas frequently possess an initial straightforward meaning, and then a second, metaphorical meaning. She shows this idea with one related word, *murdhan*, 'head,' in which that *murdhan* can mean the actual 'head' of a god (RV 4.2.6), or it can mean the 'head, front, or foremost part,' of the sacrifice (RV 10.88.5).

Mukha in the *ṚgVeda* and *Atharva Veda* texts tends to be best translated as 'mouth,' but the related meaning of 'face' is still implied. For instance, in RV 4.39.6, the purifying deity Dadhikra is invoked in order 'to make our mouth fragrant' (*surabhi na mukhā karat*).[43] In addition, in its metaphorical usage, *mukha* can be the point of an arrow, as it is referred to in the battle hymn 6.75.15 (*atho yasyā ayo mukham*), where its tip is anointed with poison. *Mukha* can also be senses as the mouth of the ladle that pours out clarified butter in the act of offering. (RV 8.43.10: *niṃ sānaṃ juhuvo mukhe*).

In the Gṛhya Sūtras,[44] however, the word *mukha* can take on the primary meaning of the whole face, the visage. In the *Aśvalāyana Gṛhya Sūtra* (AGS 1.20.2, and

41 'Myth and Money: The Exchange of Words and Wealth in Vedic Commentary,' in *Myth and Method*, Charlottesville: University Press of Virginia, 1996, pp. 208-46.

42 Tatyana Elizarenkova, *The Language and Style of the Vedic Ṛṣis*, Albany: State University of New York Press, 1995, p. 38.

43 See also SV 1.358; YV 23.32; AV 20.127.3.

44 See, in addition to these examples, the *Śāṅkhāyana Śrauta Sūtra* 1.12.5.

many other places in the text),[45] the 'face' is an indicator of the ritual (and therefore existential) mode of the sacrificer – how he should face, and whom he should be facing. AGS states that when a pupil takes hold of him, the teacher should sacrifice, sitting to the north of the fire, which his face turned to the east (*prāṅmukha*). The pupil, in contrast, should sit to the east of the fire, with his fact turned toward the West (*pratyāṅmukha*). The student also should recite the Veda on *darbha* grass with his face toward the east (AGS 3.2.2.). In a less sacrificial, and more personal vein, AGS 3.6.8 tells us that the brahmin who has had his life interrupted by a sneeze, an unpleasant sight, or throbbing eye, or a noise, should utter a *mantra* that asks for skill and vigour, and well being in his eyes, face, and ears.[46]

This idea of the 'face' is also invoked in a discussion of the teacher-student relationship in the *The Laws of Manu*. In a description of the right conduct of the *brahmācārya*, or celibate student (2.192-3), the law code enjoins him to harness all of his energies to speech, mind, and senses, he should sit, and with his hands cupped, *looking at his guru's face* [italics mine]. The text then goes on to say: 'His hand should always be bare, his conduct virtuous, and (his body) well-covered; and when he is told, 'Sit down,' he should sit down, facing the guru.[47]

Here, we see a series of modes of encounter in which the face of another, the teacher, becomes the moral regulator of the conduct of the student. Chastity, purity, focus, knowledge, all derive from the posture of the student toward the teacher – the fact of their facing each other. The prepositional usage *adhi mukham* or *prān mukham* 'turning to or turned toward, facing' also gives this connotation.[48]

The Upaniṣadic narratives of the teacher-student relationship also deepens this idea one step further. In the story of Upakośala, and his teacher Satyakāma Jabālā, Satyakāma goes away on a journey and does not teach him. The fires decide to teach him themselves about the nature of Brahman, and as a result, when his teacher returns, the student Upakośala's face is 'glowing like that of a man who knows Brahman' (*Chāndogya Upaniṣad* 4.10-14; See v. 4.14.2 for *mukha*). Here, the use of 'face' is clearly a sign of wisdom, learnedness, and knowledge acquired through both goodness and austerity.

Another fascinating use of face can be found in the *Kauṣītaki Upaniṣad* 3.1, where Indra explains to Pratardana, the warrior, that the ability to perceive Indra is the most beneficial gift for all human beings. As Indra puts it, 'When a man perceives me, nothing that he does ... will make him lose a single hair of his body. And when he has committee a sin, his face does not lose its color.' Indra goes on to explain how he is breath, sight, the vital functions, intelligence, and eventually the Self (*ātman*) (3.2-8). The point here is not absence of moral grounding, but rather

45 Also see AGS 4.7.2, where Brahmins should face north in the śrāddha for the fathers.

46 In AGS 4.7.14, the face is moistened with water in sacrificial vessels in order for a son to be born.

47 Wendy Doniger with Brian K. Smith, *The Laws of Manu*, 1991, pp. 36-37.

48 Monier Williams, Monier, Sir. *A Sanskrit-English Dictionary*, 1963, p. 819.

than one's face remains dignified even in the midst of committing a sin. Presumably, as Indra himself has had to do in his own atonements for the wrong of brahminicide, one would atone for the wrongdoing, but the colour of one's face, one's personhood, would not be lost. This idea is similar to Levinas' notion that in the face-to-face relation, human dignity is already given.[49]

So too, *Śvetaśvatāra Upaniṣad* 2.16.3 refers to the cosmic person whose face is everyone (3.3) and who is the face of everyone (3.11), and who, when born, turns his face in all directions (4.3.0). Hence, like Agni in the RV passages cited above, the face of the cosmic person is the life-giving whole.

The Guest and Inexhaustible Obligation

In addition to the notions of presence and the face discussed above, the word 'guest' (*atithi*) can provide an important understanding of early Indian ideas of the ethics of the stranger, and comportment towards the stranger. *Atithi* occurs in the *ṚgVeda* mostly about Agni, as the invited and most honoured guest at the sacrifice. A common example might be found in RV 8.44.1, where Agni is to be honoured with fuel, awakened as a guest with ghee, and offered oblations. What does Agni as a 'guest' do for the sacrifice? He can act as messenger in front (v.3) , and cause the other gods to sit down at the sacrifice; he can let the ladles come near him in order for the oblations to be received (v. 5) and he can invoke the gods (vv. 5,7). Therefore, one must adore him, kindle him, help him beautify his body, and feed him. All of this adds up to the idea that Agni is like a domestic guest, whom one should treat in a domestically honourable way.

Another, quite compelling, idea of the responsibility one has toward Agni as a domestic guest is RV 1.73.1: He is the giver of food, like the wealth of a father, and like a teacher learned in the Veda, he directs the proceedings, and like a welcome guest, he rests in the sacrificial chamber, and like an officiating priest, he brings prosperity on the house of the worshiper. In other words, Agni plays all the domestic roles that could bring wealth to a household. Verse 2 is especially helpful for us in developing an imagery of encounter with a guest – like the Divine Sun, who knows the truth, Agni preserves through action in all encounters. He is to be cherished because he is unchangeable, and like the self or the soul, is the source of happiness (*ātmeva śevo didhiṣāyiyo bhūt*).[50] This domestic imagery is further reinforced by RV 10.124.3, where Agni speaks after being summoned. He says that he has 'beheld the guest of another family, and has created the manifold dwelling places of sacrifice.' Sāyaṇa thinks that this may be the sun, who is connected with a different, celestial region to be crossed, rather than Agni's earthly realm. Here, then, there are many different 'homes' of sacrifice, and different Agnis who continue to act as different kinds of guests.

---

49 Op cit., Robbins, 'Responsibility and Substitution,' *Is it Righteous*, p. 229.

50 *Atithi* is also a deity, Atithigva, in the RV. It is a name of Divodāsa, and alternately, a name of a figure who helps Indra in battle (RV 1.112.14; 53.8 and so on).

Overall, then, one might characterize Agni is a guest who makes moral demands of the sacrificer, not because of his greediness but because he, as a guest, is also a preserver of the moral order. He is called the guardian of truth for just this reason, and he serves, like the guest who has arrived at the door, as a kind of 'bellwether' for the behaviour of the sacrificer and his willingness to act in a Vedic ethical manner. This is analogous in a certain way to Levinas' idea that the stranger, or other, also makes moral demands on those who receive him. Like our response to Agni as guest, our response to the stranger is the indicator of our own participation in the moral order. Unlike Levinas, however, who does not describe the stranger's obligation to us, the guest-like Agni's role in the making of human flourishing is amply and richly described.

This idea is developed in an intriguing way in later texts within the Vedic tradition. In the fifth century BCE etymological dictionary the *Nirukta* (4.5), *atithi* is the one who goes (*at*) to the houses, or one who goes to the families of houses of other persons on certain dates (*i* + *tithiḥ*). This action of guests is borne out by a reference to this in RV 5.4.5 (also AV 7.73.9). And the commentator Dūrga remarks that a guest will go to a sacrificer's home on full moon days and other days of sacrifice.[51]

In the Upaniṣads, the guest is understood as bringing fire, in an inversion of the simile. In the Vedas, Agni is like a guest, and in the Upaniṣads, a guest is like Agni. In *Taittirīya Upaniṣad*, the guest should be treated like a god, along with one's father and mother and teacher (TU 1.11.3). In *Kaṭha Upaniṣad*, 1.1-18, there is a fascinating tale of Naciketas, whose father Uśan, has given away all of his possessions to a guest. Naciketas asks his father 'To whom will you give me?' And the Father answers, 'I will give you to death!' A narrator goes on to describe all those who have gone before and those who will come after, all going to death. Verse 7 then states:

> A Brahmin guest enters a house as the fire in all men. Bring water, O Vaivasvata, that is how they appease him. Hopes and expectations, fellowship and good will, children and livestock, rites and gifts, all these a Brahmin wrests from the foolish man, in whose house he resides without any food.

Presumably, this passage is describing Naciketas, who has gone to sit in the house of Death as a guest in his own right. Death then goes on to say to Naciketas, the Brahmin, that because Naciketas has stayed in his (Death's) house without any food, he should therefore make three wishes in return (KU 1.9). Naciketas goes on to articulate his wishes, about maintaining long life, learning the secrets of the fire altar, and so on.

Here, the guest Naciketas is one who has a potentially totalizing relationship to the other – he is infinitely demanding of Death, who has no food to give him. Like his father's guest before him, Naciketas uses the rules of hospitality, of facing the other, and turns them back onto Death itself. In a certain way, then, this story might well be about the face that says 'Do not kill me,' in the Levinasian sense. The story implies the other as stranger can make total demands, whereby one must

51 *Nirukta*, p. 58, n.1.

give up one's life. Yet Naciketas then turns guesthood itself into the other side of the demand: As Death's guest, Naciketas asks death to leave him alone, and thus becomes, in a very concrete narrative way, yet another version of the face that says, 'Do not kill me.'

A later Dharmaśāstric text, the *Āpastamba Dharma Sūtra* (ADS), gives rules for the reception of a guest which further concretizes this relationship. ADS 2.6.3-8.5 begins with the phrase similar to the Upaniṣadic one, 'A guest comes blazing like a fire.' A guest is further defined as someone who has devoted himself to the *dharma* and come for no other purpose than to discharge *dharma* (6.5-6). Thus, in the Levinasian sense, the guest (stranger) is only properly a guest when he embodies the morality, the law. The very nature of guest and moral law are intertwined together with each other. The text goes on to specify what should be done if the guest is a brahmin who should wash the guest's feet, how to cook for him, and so on.

The texts goes on to describe the fire as of three kinds – the fire within the guest is the offertorial fire; the fire within the house is the householder's fire; and the fire used for cooking is the southern fire. Thus, like the Upaniṣads, the *Dharma Sūtra* also inverts the earlier metaphor of Agni as guest in the sacrifice, and portrays the guest as fire. In both cases, the potentially all-consuming nature of strangerhood is implied through the imagery of fire – a nature borne out by the example of Naciketas above.

But that is not all. In the *Dharma Sūtra*, the guest has cosmological implications. In ADS 7.16, the various rewards for treating a guest are outlined. For giving shelter for one night, one gains the earthly world; for two nights of shelter, one gains the intermediate world; for three nights of shelter, one gains the heavenly worlds; and for four nights of shelter, one gains the farthermost worlds. The text goes on to say sweepingly that for an unlimited number of nights one wins an unlimited number of worlds (ADS 7.16). Why such cosmological language here? One can interpret this passage, too, as conveying the idea that such a guest-host relationship not only constitutes the moral world, but is the creation of the moral world, as Levinas also sees it. In each of the related passages in the Dharmaśāstric literature, the quality and degree of Vedic learning are the premier criteria for ascertaining the identity of a guest, for such a person embodies morality, and thus is the 'fire common to all men.'[52] Hence, the images of these Dharmaśāstric texts suggest that not only is an obligation toward a guest primordial, but that a sense of obligation toward the guest is indeed inexhaustible, as Levinas would argue.[53]

Some Final Thoughts

There are many obvious ways in which the Levinasian vocabulary simply does not dovetail well with the Vedic world. Among many other incommensurabilities,

52 See *Gautama Dharma Sūtra*, 5.25-45; *Baudhāyana Dharma Sūtra* 2.5.11-20; 3.5-7; 6.35-42; *Vasiṣṭha Dharma Sūtra* 4.5-8; 8.4-8; 11.1-15.

53 'The Vocation of the Other,' in Robbins, p. 112.

Levinas would have us think of the everyday as the ground of the ethical – and the Vedic sacrificial world, with its emphasis on creating a realm 'set apart' appears as the opposite of such a perspective. The focus on who may receive a guest, and how, might also strike Levinas as regulatory and institutional in a way that may not accede fully to the demands of the stranger. The rules for the stranger are of course circumscribed by *varṇāśramadharma*, or sacred duty according to one's station in life. And of course, it should be obvious and go without saying that the Jewish monotheism as a reference point for Levinas is rather different from the henotheism of the Vedic world. We could name many other incommensurables.

However, the point of this chapter is not to delineate a one-to-one correspondence between the two traditions of thought. Nor did Levinas paint a pure, Platonic realm of love for the other, but rather a series of complex ontological moments in which one encounters one's own death in the encounter with another. Indeed, we might read his thought as the description of two simultaneous moments – the experience of one's own imperialism, and the experience of its death as the substitution of the other for the self occurs. Levinas speaks about such complexity, and simultaneity, when he describes moments of everyday compassion in the midst of war; both attitudes toward the other are present.[54] One might also phrase it the other way around, as the Vedic Varuṇa hymns suggest: even in the midst of profound moral accounting there is still the wish that the other disappear.

This chapter has attempted to show some of the detail of such moral complexity: to be an *ārya* implies a moral way of speaking as well as a domination over the dark ones. The *anya/anyaka* or 'other' of the Vedic world can involve both a traditionally defined enemy as well as someone who does not know us, and does not make the effort for face-to-face encounter. So too, we have seen in the Vedic literature that the idea of 'presence' tends to be predominantly wrapped up in the idea of a divine visitor – the god Agni, and the Cosmic Person who 'faces everyone, in all places,' in the Vedic hymns as well as the Upaniṣads.

The overcoming of blood relationship of kinship in the process of becoming-for-another is best expressed in the teacher-student relationship of the Vedic world, where face-to-face interaction constitutes the essence of instruction. Moreover, the infinite obligation to the guest as stranger finds a deeply poignant expression in the imagery of the guest as an all-consuming, demanding fire.

In the ritual of beginning Vedic study in the *Gṛhya Sūtras* (AGS 1.21.1-7), the teacher touches the student's heart and utters a mantra: 'I take your heart into my will, and your mind shall follow after my mind; you will delight in my word with all your energy.' While Levinas locates the ethical moment in a time before speech – the 'saying before speech,' as he puts it – he does acknowledge that some speech can also be a memory of that moment. And this 'saying' in the *Gṛhya Sūtras* seems to be an exquisite example of such language. It is uttered by brahmins in all the alienation and difficulty of a social system of elites, and yet it also carries the possibility of

54 'Zionisms,' in *The Levinas Reader*, p. 278.

carrying the other within oneself. Such a saying is also a clear window into the complex imagery of ethical thought in Vedic India.

Bibliography

Selected Sanskrit Texts and Translations

Āpastamba Dharma Sūtra, ed. U.C. Pandeya, Kashi Sanskrit Series, no. 93, Varanasi: Chowkhamba Sanskrit Series Office, 1969.

Āśvalāyana Gṛhyasūtram, with Sanskrit Commentary of Narayana; English trans., introduction and index by Narendra Nath Sharma; with a foreword by Satya Vrat Shastri, Delhi: Eastern Book Linkers, 1976.

Aśvalāyana Śrauta Sūtra, (English trans.) vols. 1 and 2, Ranade Publications Series no. 2, Poona: Ranade Publications: 1981.

Atharva Veda Saṃhitā, 4 vols, ed. V. Bandhu, Hoshiarpur: Vishveshavaranand Vedic Research Institute, 1960-62.

Atharva Veda Saṃhitā, 2 vols, trans. W.D. Whitney, Harvard Oriental Series, vols 7 and 8, Cambridge: Harvard University Press, 1905.

Chāndogya Upaniṣad, ed. V.P. Limaye and R.D. Vadekar, in *Eighteen Principal Upaniṣads*, Poona: Vaidika Saṃśodhana Maṇḍala, 1958.

Dharmasūtras, The Law Codes of Ancient India (annotated translation of the Dharmaśāstras of Āpastamba, Gautama, Baudhāyana, and Vasiṣṭha), trans. and ed., Patrick Olivelle, Oxford (Oxford's World Classics): Oxford University Press, 1999.

Dūrga Āchārya, Yāska's Nirukta *with Dūrga's Commentary*, 2 vols, ed. H.M.
Bhadkamkar. Bombay Sanskrit and Prakrit Series, nos. 73 and 85, Bombay: Government Central Press, 1918.

Gautama Dharmasūtra, ed. A.F. Stenzler, London: Trubner, 1876; ed. with Haradatta's commentary by N. Talekar, AnSS 61, Poona, 1966; ed. with Maskarin's commentary by L. Srinivasacharya, Government Oriental Library Series, Bibliotheca Sanskrita, 50, Mysore, 1917; ed. with Maskarin's commentary by Veda Mitra, Delhi: Veda Mitra and Sons, 1969, Tr. in Bühler 1879-82.

The Gṛhya Sūtras, trans. Hermann Oldenberg, 2 vols, Sacred Books of the East 29, 30, Reprint of the 1886 edn. Oxford: Oxford University Press; Delhi: Motilal Banarsidass, 1964.

Jaimini, Pūrvamīmāṃsāsūtra, ed. with commentaries of Śabara and Kumārila, 7 vols, AnSS 97, Poona, 1971-81; trans. G. Jha, 3 vols, Gaekwad's Oriental Series, 66,70, 73, Baroda, 1973-74.

The Laws of Manu, trans. Wendy Doniger with Brian K. Smith, Harmondsworth: Penguin Books, 1991.

The Mahābhārata, 19 vols, ed. Viṣṇu S. Sukthankar, Poona: Bhandarkar Oriental Research Institute, 1933-60.

The Mahābhārata, 3 vols, ed. and trans. J.A.B. Van Buitenen, Chicago: University of Chicago Press, 1973-78.

Manu Smṛti, 5 vols, ed. J.H. Dave, Bhāratīya Vidya Series, Bombay: Bhāratīya Vidyā Bhavan, 1972-82.

The Nighaṇṭu and the Nirukta, The Oldest Indian Treatise on Etymology, Philology, and Semantics, Critically Edited From Original Manuscripts and Translated by Lakshman Sarup, London and New York: Oxford University Press, 1920-27.

Pūrva Mīmāṃsā of Jaimini, 2 vols, ed. trans. Mohan Lal Sandal, in *Mīmāṃsā Sūtras of Jaimini*, Delhi: Motilal Banarsidass, 1980.

Ṛgveda with the *Padapāṭha* and the available portions of the *Bhāṣyas* by Skandasvāmin and Udgītha, the *Vyākhyā* by Venṅaṭamādhava and Mudgala's *Vṛtti* based on *Sāyaṇabhāṣya*, ed. Bandhu Vishva in collaboration with Bhīm Dev, Amar Nath, K.S. Ramaswami Sastri, and Pitambar Datta. Hoshiapur: Vishveshvaranand Vedic Research Institute, 1965 (Parts 1 and 7), 1963 (Parts 2 and 3), 1964 (Parts 4-6). Vishveshvaranand Indological Series, nos. 19-25.

The Rig Veda. An Anthology: One Hundred and Eight Hymns, Selected, translated, and annotated Wendy Doniger, Harmondsworth: Penguin Press, 1981.

Śāṅkhāyana Gṛhya Sūtram (Belonging to the Rgveda): The Oldest Treatise on Folklore In Ancient India, ed. S.R. Sehgal; with a foreword by Siddeshwar Varma, New Delhi: The Editor, 1960.

Śāṅkhāyanagṛhyasūtram: Nārāyaṇabhāṣya-Vasudevakṛtasāṅkhayanagṛhyasaṅgraha Hindi-anuvāda-bhūmikā-pariśiṣṭa-saṃvalitam, Sampādako'nuvādakaśca Gangasagararayah, Varanasi: Ratna Pablikesansa, 1995.

Śrauta sūtra of Āsvalāyana, with the commentary of Gārgya Nārāyaṇa, ed. Rāmanārāyana Vidyāratna, Calcutta, Printed at the Baptist mission and Vālmiki Presses, 1874.

Upaniṣads, trans. Patrick Olivelle, Oxford: Oxford University Press, 1996.

The Early Upaniṣads: Annotated Texts and Translation, by Patrick Olivelle, Delhi: Munshiram Manoharlal, 1998.

Selected Secondary Texts

Ahlback, Tore (ed.), *Temenos: Studies in Comparative Religion*, vol. 29, Helsinki: Finnish Society for the Study of Comparative Religion, 1993.

Bernasconi, Robert and Critchley, Simon (eds), *Re-Reading Levinas*, Bloomington: University of Indiana Press, 1991.

Bhattacharya, A.N., *Dharma-Adharma and Morality in the Mahābhārata*, Delhi, India: S.S. Publishers, 1992.

Bhattacarya, Haridas, 'Indian Ethics,' in *The Cultural Heritage of India*, ed. Haridas Bhattacarya, Calcutta: Ramakrishna Mission Institute of Culture, 4 vols, 1953-60. vol. 3, pp. 620-44.

Bilimoria, Purushottama, 'Mīmāṃsā Doubts about God,' in *Philosophy of Religions Reader*, Victoria: Deakin University Press, 1987, pp. 133-46 [see note 7 infra].

______, 'Śruti and Apauruṣeya: An Approach to Religious Scriptures and Revelation,' *Journal of Dharma*, **3** (3), 1982, pp. 275-91.

Böhtlingk, Otto von and Roth, Rudolph von, *Sanskrit – Wörterbuch*, 7 vols in 3, St. Petersburg: Buchdruckerei der Kaiserlichen Akademie der Wissenschaften, 1855-1875.

Bronkhorst, Johannes and Deshpande, Madhav (eds), *Aryan and Non-Aryan in South Asia: Evidence, Interpretation, and Ideology*, Cambridge: Harvard University Press, 1999.

Bryant, Edwin, *The Quest for the Origins of Vedic Culture: The Indo-Aryan Migration Debate*, New York: Oxford University Press, 2001.

Buch, M.A., *Principles of Hindu Ethics*, Baroda: M.A. Buch, 1921.

Chartavakar, G.A., *Manual of Hindu Ethics*, Poona: Oriental Book Agency, 1925.

Coward, Harold, Lipner, Julius and Young, Katherine, *Hindu Ethics: Purity, Abortion, and Euthanasia*, Delhi: Sri Satguru Publications, 1989.

Crawford, Cromwell, *The Evolution of Hindu Ethical Ideals*, Honolulu: The University Press of Hawaii, 1982.

Creel, Austin, *Dharma In Hindu Ethics*, Calcutta: South Asia Books, 1977.

_______, 'Studies of Hindu Ethics: A Bibliographical Introduction,' *Religious Studies Review* 2 (4), 1976, pp. 26-31.

Das, Govinda, *Hindu Ethics: Principles of Hindu Religio-Social Regeneration*, ed. Ganganatha Jha, Madras: G.A. Natesan, 1927.

Dumezil, Georges, *Ouranos-Varuṇa*, Paris, 1934.

Elizarenkova, Tatyana, *The Language and Style of the Vedic Ṛṣis*, Albany: State University of New York Press, 1995, p. 38.

Glucklich, Ariel, 'What's in a List? A Rule of Interpretation for Hindu Dharma Offered in Response to Maria Hibbets,' *Journal of Religious Ethics* 27 (3), 1999, pp. 463-70.

_______, *The Sense of Adharma*, Oxford: Oxford University Press, 1994.

Goodwin, William F., 'Mysticism and Ethics: An Examination of Radhakrishnan (Reply to Schweitzer's Critique of Indian Thought)' in *Ethics* 67 (1), 1956, pp. 25-41.

Grassmann, Hermann, *Wörterbuch zum* Rig Veda *4., unverändert*, 4th edn., Wiesbaden: Otto Harrassowitz, 1964.

Hibbets (now Heim), Maria, 'Saving Them from Yourself: An Inquiry into the South Asian Gift of Fearlessness,' *Journal of Religious Ethics* 27 (3), 1999, pp. 437-62.

_______, 'The Author Replies,' *Journal of Religious Ethics* 27 (3), 1999, pp. 471-76.

Hindery, Roderick, Review of 'Comparative Ethics in Hindu and Buddhist Traditions,' *Journal of Ecumenical Studies* 17, 1980, pp. 699-700.

_______. 'Hindu Ethics in the Rāmāyaṇa.' *The Journal of Religious Ethics*, **4** (2), 1976, pp. 287-322.

Hindery, Sheila, Book Review of *Comparative Ethics in Hindu and Buddhist Traditions* by Roderick Hindery, *Horizons*, 6, 1979, pp. 317-18.

Hopkins, E. Washburn, *Ethics of India*, New Haven, Yale University Press, 1924.

Johnson, Mark, *The Body In the Mind: The Bodily Basis of Meaning, Imagination, and Reason*, Chicago: University of Chicago Press, 1987.

Levinas, Emmanuel, *Is It Righteous to Be? Interviews with Emmanuel Levinas*, ed. Jill Robbins, Stanford, CA: Stanford University Press, 2001.

________, *Of God Who Comes to Mind*, trans. Bettina Bergo, Stanford, CA: Stanford University Press, 1998.

________, *Nine Talmudic Readings*, trans. Annette Aronowicz, Bloomington: Indiana University Press, 1990.

________, *The Levinas Reader*, ed. Sean Hand, Oxford: Blackwell Publishers Inc., 1989.

________, *Otherwise Than Being or Beyond Essence*, trans. Alphonso Lingis, The Hague: Martinus Nijhoff Publishers, 1981.

Little, David and Twiss, Sumner, *Comparative Religious Ethics*, San Francisco: Harper and Row Publishers, 1978.

Lommel, H., 'Die Spaher des Varuṇa und Mitra und das Auge des Konigs,' in *Oriens* **6**, 1953, pp. 323-33.

Luders, Heinrich, *Varuṇa*, Gottingen: Vandenhoeck and Ruprecht, 1951-1959.

Mahadevan, T.M.P., 'The Basis of Social, Ethical, and Spiritual Values in Indian Philosophy,' in *Essays in East-West Philosophy: An Attempt at Philosophical Synthesis*, Charles A. Moore (ed.), Honolulu: University of Hawaii Press, 1951, pp. 317-35.

________, 'Beyond Ethics,' in *Indian Philosophical Congress: Silver Jubilee Commemoration Volume*, Madras and Bangalore: Indian Philosophical Congress, 1950.

Maitra, Susil Kumar, *Ethics of the Hindus*, Calcutta: Calcutta University Press, 1925.

McKenzie, John, *Hindu Ethics: A Historical and Critical Essay*, London: H. Milford, Oxford University Press, 1922.

Miller, David, 'Sources of Hindu Ethical Studies: A Critical Review,' *Journal of Religious Ethics*, 9 (2), 1981, pp. 186-98.

Mitra, Kana, 'Human Rights in Hinduism,' *Journal of the Ecumenical Studies*, 19 (3), 1982, pp. 77-84.

Monier Williams, Monier, Sir., *A Sanskrit-English Dictionary*, Delhi: Motilal Banarsidass, 1963.

Moore, Charles A., 'Metaphysics and Ethics in Radhakrishnan's Philosophy,' in *The Philosophy of Sarvepalli Radhakrishnan*, ed. Paul A. Schilpp, NP: Tudor, 1952, pp. 279-312.

Moorty, J.S.R.L. Narayana, 'A Modern Hindu Approach to Ethics,' in *Religion and Society*, **7,** October 1960, pp. 84-98.

Nayak, G.C., 'Ethical Considerations in Vedānta – A Scientific Approach,' *Journal of Dharma*, 21 (2), 1996, pp. 204-9.

Nikhilananda, Swami, 'Hindu Ethics,' in *Moral Principles of Action*, ed. Ruth Nanda Anshen, New York: Harper, 1952, pp. 616-44.

_______, 'Hindu Ethics,' in *The Upanishads* by Swami Nikhilananada, New York: Harper, vol. 2, pp. 1-34.

O'Neil, L. Thomas, Book Review of *Comparative Ethics in Hindu and Buddhist Traditions* by Roderick Hindery, *Journal of the American Academy of Religion*, **49**, 1981, pp. 729-30.

Parish, Steven M., *Moral Knowing in a Hindu Sacred City: An Exploration of Mind, Emotion, and Self*, New York: Columbia University Press, 1994.

Patton, Laurie L., 'Myth and Money: The Exchange of Words and Wealth in Vedic Commentary,' in *Myth and Method*, Charlottesville: University Press of Virginia, 1996, pp. 208-46.

_______, *Bringing the Gods to Mind: Mantra and Poetry in Early Indian Sacrifice*, California: University of California Press, 2004.

_______, 'Vedas and Upaniṣads,' in Gene Thursby and Sushil Mittal (eds) *The Hindu World*, New York: Routledge, forthcoming.

Perrett, Roy W., *Hindu Ethics: A Philosophical Study*, Honolulu: University of Hawaii Press, 1998.

Przyluski, J., 'Varuṇa, God of the Sea and Sky,' in *Journal of the Royal Asiatic Society*, 1931.

Radhakrishnan, Sarvepalli, 'Mytsticism and Ethics in Hindu Thought,' in Radhakrishnan, *Eastern Religions and Western Thought*, London: Oxford University Press, 1939, pp. 58-114.

_______, 'The Ethics of Vedānta,' in *International Journal of Ethics*, 24 (2), January 1914, pp. 168-83.

_______, 'The Ethics of the Bhagavad Gītā and Kant,' in *International Journal of Ethics*, 21 (4), July 1911, pp. 465-75.

Raju, P.T., 'The Epics and the Ethical Codes,' in his *The Philosophical Traditions of India*, Pittsburgh: University of Pittsburgh Press, 1971, pp. 201-18.

_______, 'The Concept of the Spiritual in Indian Thought,' in *Philosophy East and West*, 4 (3), 1954, pp. 195-213.

Redington, James, Book Review of 'Comparative Ethics in Hindu and Buddhist Traditions,' by Roderick Hindery, *Theological Studies*, 42 (1), 1981, pp. 169-171.

Robbins, Jill, ed. *Is it Righteous to Be? Interviews with Emmanuel Levinas*, Palo Alto, Calif: Standord University Press, 2001.

Saksena, S.K., 'Moral Philosophy in India,' in *Studies in the Cultural History of India*, Guy S. Metraux and Francois Crouzet (eds), UNESCO International Commission for a History of the Scientific and Cultural Development of Mankind; Agra: Shiva Lal Agrawala, 1965.

Sen, Sanat Kumar, 'Indian Philosophy and Social Ethics,' in *Journal of the Indian Academy of Philosophy*, 6, 1967, pp. 63-74.

Sharma, Arvind, 'Hindu Spirituality,' *Cross Currents*, 48 (1), 1998, pp. 83-88.

Sharma, K.L. (ed.), *Social Stratification in India*, New Delhi: Manohar, 1986.

Srinivas, M.N. (ed.), *Caste: Its Twentieth Century Avatar*, New Delhi: Oxford University Press, 1996.

Stone, Martin (ed.), Book Review of *Hindu Ethics: A Philosophical Study* by Roy W. Perrett, *Religious Studies*, 36, 2000, p. 247.

Sutherland, Gail Hinich, 'The Politics of Ahiṃsā,' *Scottish Journal of Religious Studies*, 19 (2), 1998, pp. 185-209.

Wadia, A.R., 'Indian Ethics,' in *Dr. S. Radhakrishnan Souvenir Volume*, ed. B.L. Atreya, Moradabad: Darshana International, 1964, pp. 515-23.

Yogeshananda, Swami, 'The Hindu Mode of Caring,' *Cross Currents*, 36 (4), 1986, pp. 393-97.

Chapter 5

Sāṃkhya-Yoga Ethics

Roy W. Perrett

Ethics is fundamentally concerned with two questions: 'What ought we to do?', and 'Why ought we to do it?'. In seeking to address these questions an ethical theory in turn typically involves two components: a theory of the right and a theory of the good. The first component tells us what we, as agents, should do by way of responding to valuable properties. Consequentialist theories of the right tell us we ought to act so as to *promote* designated values: i.e. the relation between values and agents is an instrumental one. Non-consequentialist theories of the right tell us we ought to act so as to *honour* designated values: i.e. the relation between values and agents is a non-instrumental one in that actions are supposed to exemplify the designated values, even if this means a lesser realization of value overall.[1]

The second component of an ethical theory is its theory of the good. This tells us what is good or valuable. Clearly consequentialism as a theory of the right requires complementing with a theory of the good, for if what we ought to do is promote good consequences then we need to know which consequences are good and to be promoted and which are not. But non-consequentialist theories of the right also require complementing with a theory of the good, for if what we ought to do is honour or exemplify certain values then we need to know what these values are.

The philosophical system of Sāṃkhya-Yoga addresses both of the fundamental questions of ethics: i.e. it tells us what we ought to do and why we ought to do it. It sets out a number of moral precepts and seeks to justify these in terms of a consequentialist theory of the right: acting so will promote certain designated values. Accordingly the system also offers a theory of the good, which tells us what values ought to be promoted. What we may designate as 'Sāṃkhya-Yoga ethics', then, includes all three elements: a set of first-order moral precepts, a consequentialist theory of the right, and a theory of the good.

Strictly speaking Sāṃkhya and Yoga are distinct philosophical systems, two of the six schools (*ṣaddarśana*) of orthodox Hindu philosophy. However, a venerable Indian tradition (dating from early in the Common Era, if not before) views them as sister systems, a complementary pair, with Sāṃkhya articulating the metaphysics and Yoga the practice. Historians of Indian philosophy may well balk at this syncretistic trend and wish to stress important differences between the two schools, and even

1 For this way of drawing the distinction between consequentialism and non-consequentialism see Pettit (1991).

between the views of individual members of the same school. Certainly if we were concerned to trace the historical evolution of the Sāṃkhya and Yoga schools such scholarly qualms would be appropriate.[2] But fortunately for our purposes here it is not necessary to enter too deeply into these matters, for our task is to delineate the logical structure of one part of the developed research programme that came to be called 'Sāṃkhya-Yoga'. Accordingly I shall follow tradition and regard this research programme as roughly a single syncretic school (much as Nyāya-Vaiśeṣika is often regarded).

Metaphysically Sāṃkhya-Yoga is dualistic: it posits just two fundamental categories of reality, *puruṣa* ('spirit', 'self') and *prakṛti* ('nature', 'matter'). Suffering is caused by our confusion of *puruṣa* with *prakṛti* and emancipation follows from correct understanding of the real nature of *puruṣa* and its difference from *prakṛti*. In the Sāṃkhya texts (especially in Iśvarakṛṣṇa's *Sāṃkhyakārikā*) rational arguments are presented for some of the school's major theses.[3] Thus the existence of *puruṣa* is argued for (*Kārikā* XVII) on the grounds that consciousness exists and distinctions in the world are *for* this consciousness, which is itself apart from the world. Moreover there must be a plurality of *puruṣas* because otherwise whatever happens to one consciousness will happen at the same time to every consciousness, which is contrary to the perceived diversity of births, deaths and faculties (XVIII).

Prakṛti, on the other hand, is a unitary material substance that evolves into the world we perceive through our senses. The proximity of *puruṣa* acts as a catalyst in releasing the causal transformation of primordial nature (*mūlaprakṛti*) into the whole of the perceptible world (XX). The order in which *prakṛti* evolves is laid down in the following scheme. First, the pure contentless consciousness of the *puruṣa* becomes focused on the *prakṛti* and out of the delimitation evolves *mahat* or *buddhi* (intellect). The *buddhi* then evolves the ego consciousness (*ahaṃkāra*) which leads to the misidentification of the true self with the ego. From *ahaṃkāra* evolves the *manas* (mind); from *manas* the five sensory organs and the five motor organs; then the five *tanmatras* or subtle elements (sound, touch, form, taste and smell) and the five *bhūtas* or gross elements (ether, air, fire, water and earth). Sāṃkhya thus recognizes in all twenty-four principles (*tattvas*) evolving out of *mūlaprakṛti* in this order. The twenty-fifth (and independent) *tattva* is *puruṣa*. (It is important to note that while Sāṃkhya insists on a dualism of *puruṣa* and *prakṛti*, this is not a Western style mind-body dualism. The active, personal self-consciousness in Sāṃkhya is associated with the material principles of *buddhi*, *ahaṃkāra* and *manas*, i.e. the first evolutes of *prakṛti*.)

---

2 Readers with such concerns may profitably consult the following sources: Larson (1979); Larson and Bhattacharya (1987); Hulin (1978); Woods (1914); Dasgupta (1924), (1930); Eliade (1958); Feuerstein (1974), (1980).

3 For translations of this and other Sāṃkhya texts see Radhakrishnan and Moore (1957), Ch. 12. Larson (1979) includes the Sanskrit text of the *Kārikā* together with an English translation.

The school of Yoga (classically expounded in Patañjali's *Yogasūtra*) broadly accepts this Sāṃkhya ontology.[4] There are some differences, however.[5] The most important is that Yoga (unlike classical Sāṃkhya) is theistic in that it admits the existence of God (*Īśvara*). But *Īśvara* is not an additional ontological principle of the system; rather he is just a special kind of *puruṣa*, one who has never become misidentified with *prakṛti* and hence is particularly effective as a model for those aspiring to release.

Sāṃkhya and Yoga are not only in fundamental agreement on most ontological matters, they are also in agreement on the nature of the *summum bonum*. This is a radical isolation (*kaivalya*) of the true self from ordinary human experience. This release (*mokṣa*, *mukti*) occurs when the *puruṣa* recognizes its real nature as absolutely distinct from *prakṛti*. However, there is a difference of emphasis between Sāṃkhya and Yoga in precisely how this goal is to be achieved. Sāṃkhya seems to recommend a progressive sequence of reflective discriminations (*vijñāna*) that spontaneously lead to liberation. Yoga supplements this formal, rationalistic methodology with a systematic and rigorous meditative praxis. Essentially the Sāṃkhya view of the evolution of the world is utilized by Yoga in a programme for reversing this process in order that the practitioner can increasingly rediscover the original pure consciousness of the *puruṣa* distinct from *prakṛti*.

The Yoga process is constituted by eight stages (hence *astāṅga-yoga*, 'eight-membered Yoga'). It is described in some detail in the *Yogasūtra* (II.28f) and the commentaries thereon. Very briefly, the first four preparatory stages are (1) *yama* and (2) *niyama*, the moral restraints which are necessary for further ascetic practice; (3) *āsana*, the yogic exercises in posture which permit dissociation from bodily distractions; and (4) *prāṇāyāma*, the practice of breath control. These preliminary practices prepare the *yogin* for the next set of meditative practices: (5) *pratyāhāra*, the withdrawal of the senses from their objects; (6) *dhāraṇā*, prolonged concentration of the attention of a single object; (7) *dhyāna*, concentrated meditation where the *yogin*'s consciousness assimilates the object of meditation; and (8) *samādhi*, an enstatic stage where the *yogin* is aware only of his true self and achieves complete release from worldly bondage.

It is the first two stages of this elaborate scheme of mental and physical training that concern us here. For it is the *yama* and *niyama* of Yoga that articulate one of the three elements of Sāṃkhya-Yoga ethics already mentioned: namely the set of first-order moral precepts enjoined by the system. The *Yogasūtra* (II.30) mentions five components of *yama* ('restraints'): non-injury (*ahiṃsā*), truthfulness (*satya*), non-stealing (*asteya*), chastity (*brahmācārya*) and greedlessness (*aparigraha*). These constitute the 'great vow' (*mahāvrata*) and are unconditionally valid (II.31).

4 For translations of this and other Yoga texts see Radhakrishnan and Moore (1957), Ch. 13; Woods (1914). Feuerstein (1979) includes the Sanskrit text of the *Yogasūtra* together with a translation and commentary.

5 For other differences between Īśvarakṛṣṇa's and Patañjali's views see the comparative review in Larson and Bhattacharya (1987), pp. 23-29.

Of these five, *ahiṃsā* (non-injury) is held to be the most fundamental, as Vyāsa's commentary the *Yogabhāṣya* makes clear:

> ...abstinence from injury [*ahiṃsā*] means the abstinence from malice towards all living creates in every way and at all times. And the other abstentions [*yama*] and observances [*niyama*] are rooted in it. Insofar as their aim is the perfection of it, they are taught in order to teach it.[6]

A genuine commitment to non-injury implies a commitment to the other abstentions in the following way. Truthfulness (*satya*) is required because by falsehood we harm other living creatures; non-stealing (*asteya*) is required because theft also causes harm to others; chastity (*brahmācārya*), understood as both refraining from incontinence and checking of interior attachments, is necessary because surrender to passion breeds endlessly increasing cravings and the vain attempt to satisfy these causes injury to oneself and others; greedlessness (*aparigraha*) is enjoined for much the same reasons as non-stealing, but here it is the very attachment to possessions which leads to theft that is to be uprooted by refusing all gifts in order to encourage the cultivation of detachment.

The practice of these restraints leads to the five observances (*niyama*). Whereas the five types of restraint are principally concerned to regulate the yogin's social life, the observances are more concerned with self-discipline. The *niyama* are listed (II.32) as also being of five types: cleanliness (*śauca*), contentment (*saṃtoṣa*), self-castigation (*tapas*), self-study (*svādhyāya*) and devotion to the Lord (*Īśvarapraṇidhāna*). Cleanliness means not only bodily purification, but also ridding oneself of mental impurities; contentment means not to covet more than the means at hand; self-castigation is the bearing of extremes like hunger and thirst, heat and cold etc., in order to attain control of the body; self-study is knowledge of the texts that treat of liberation (*mokṣa*) and repetition of the relevant *mantras*; devotion to the Lord is the offering up of all actions to *Īśvara* in order to foster concentration.

The *yama* and *niyama* together constitute a set of moral precepts, they tell us what we ought to do. As to why we ought to do so, Sāṃkhya-Yoga is frankly consequentialist. Although Sāṃkhya holds the intellectualist view that it is only knowledge (*jñāna*) that can affect liberation, it nevertheless admits the importance of morality (*dharma*) as a purificatory preliminary to the acquisition of such knowledge (*Sāṃkhyakārikā* XLIV). Yoga is even more explicit about this instrumental relation between its moral precepts and liberation. As Patañjali puts it (II.34):

> The unwholesome deliberations [*vitarka*], (such as) harming *et cetera*, [whether] done, caused to be done or approved, [whether] arising from greed, anger or infatuation, [whether] modest, medium or excessive [these find their] unending fruition in nescience and sorrow; thus [the *yogin* should devote himself to] the cultivation of (their) opposites.[7]

---

6 Woods (1914), p. 178.

7 Feuerstein (1979), p. 83.

The *yama* and *niyama* are then recommended as precisely effective in this respect: they neutralize the unwholesome conditions that bind us to suffering.

Yogasūtra II.35-45 spells this out in some detail. Thus non-injury (*ahiṃsā*) prevents the arising of enmity; truthfulness means that whatever the *yogin* pronounces will inevitably come true; non-stealing causes 'all jewels to appear for him' (perhaps meaning that he becomes aware of all valuable things around him); the practice of chastity increases his energy; and greedlessness generates knowledge of the conditions of his births (and hence how to avoid future rebirth). From cleanliness arises 'disgust' (*jugupsā*) with one's own body and hence a protective distance from identification with its desires; from contentment unexcelled joy is gained; the austerities of *tapas* destroy bodily impurities, creating a body possessed of supernormal powers (*siddhi*); self-study establishes contact with the chosen deity, who is helpful to the *yogin*'s work; and devotion to the Lord confers perfection of the transformation of consciousness.

Sāṃkhya-Yoga ethics, then, offers not only a set of first-order moral precepts (the *yama* and *niyama*) but a consequentialist theory of why these actions ought to be performed: they are instrumental for promoting the supreme good, liberation (*mokṣa*). But what is this ultimate value that is to be promoted, i.e. what is the Sāṃkhya-Yoga theory of the good that complements their consequentialist theory of the right? Sāṃkhya-Yoga (like other Hindu schools, and like Buddhism and Jainism too) affirms liberation from the cycle of rebirth (*saṃsāra*) to be the highest good, since all *saṃsāric* existence is characterized by universal suffering (*duḥkha*). Thus the *Sāṃkhyakārikā* begins: 'Because of the torment of the threefold suffering arises the desire to know the means of terminating it (*duḥkhatrayābhighātaj jijñāsā tadabhighātake hetau*). And Patañjali asserts (II.15): 'To the discerning all is but suffering (*duḥkhameva sarvaṃ vivekinaḥ*)'. As we have already seen, the metaphysics of Sāṃkhya-Yoga diagnoses this suffering as caused by a misidentification of the *puruṣa* that is our real nature with *prakṛti*. Correspondingly the Yoga path maps out the route to freedom through a progressive dephenomenalization of the *yogin* until rediscovery of the true self as pure, contentless consciousness is attained. But that liberation is the supreme value has yet to be argued for, and it is to this matter we now need to attend.

We can distinguish two distinct challenges to the Sāṃkhya-Yoga claims about ultimate value. The first is that liberation if negatively conceived, as Sāṃkhya-Yoga does the goal of *kaivalya*, cannot plausibly be the supreme value. The second is that the thesis about the universality of suffering and the primacy of *mokṣa* is unsupported. The former challenge does not reject the idea of liberation as the ultimate goal, but rather rejects Sāṃkhya-Yoga's negative account of that goal. The latter challenge rejects the classical Indian axiom about the equation of worldly existence with suffering and as such undermines the primacy of liberation as a value. Both challenges are to be found in the Indian philosophical literature.

The Sāṃkhya-Yoga ideal is *kaivalya*, isolation of the *puruṣa* from *prakṛti* and all its transformations. At least, this is its eschatological goal (*videhamukti*). Within this life another can be reached: the state of *jīvanmukti* wherein the *puruṣa* continues to be associated with the *buddhi*, but it is a purified *buddhi* such that on attaining separation from the body *kaivalya* is both certain and final (*Sāṃkhyakārikā* LXVII-LXVIII). Although *kaivalya* is an escape from the world of suffering, no positive bliss is associated with it. The self not only has no pain or pleasure in that condition, it is also without knowledge since it lacks the means thereof (i.e. the *buddhi*). Here Sāṃkhya-Yoga is close to Nyāya-Vaiśeṣika, who also claim that the liberated soul enjoys no special happiness over and above the absence of suffering. Against this minimal account of *mokṣa* is ranged the view of Advaita Vedānta and others that liberation is characterized by the soul's enjoyment of a positive bliss over and above the mere cessation of suffering. Part of the disagreement here is over an issue of philosophical psychology: is pleasure nothing but relief from pain or is pain only the negation of pleasure? Also at issue, however, is whether the minimal conception of liberation is sufficient to motivate an agent to seek *mokṣa*.[8] Thus the Advaitin jibe that liberation for Nyāya-Vaiśeṣika is to become like a stone, since it is to become a pure substance devoid of all qualities including consciousness and feeling. Sāṃkhya-Yoga is a little better off here in that in their system sentience is conceived of as the very substance of the self and hence the charge that the liberated self is insentient fails.

However both Nyāya-Vaiśeṣika and Sāṃkhya-Yoga agree that the minimal conception of liberation is sufficient to motivate a rational agent to pursue *mokṣa*. Moreover the agreement for this is one that their orthodox opponents should also be willing to accept, whatever their differences about the metaphysics of *mokṣa*. For given that all life is suffering (*duḥkha*) and that *mokṣa* involves freedom from *duḥkha*, then *mokṣa* is worth pursuing whether or not it brings with it an eternal positive happiness. In other words, since the elimination of suffering is a basic intrinsic value, then the goal of cessation of suffering ought to be pursued for its own sake. And this seems plausible enough, provided that we accept the thesis about the universality of *duḥkha*.

As we have already seen, the *Sāṃkhyakārikā* begins from the ubiquity of the 'threefold suffering'. The commentators explain these as internal (*ādhyātmika*), external or natural (*ādhibhautika*) and cosmic or supernatural (*ādhidaivika*). That is: suffering brought about by factors relating to the internal composition of agents, suffering brought about by the external natural environment, and suffering brought about by cosmic or divine forces. Thus suffering pervades our entire existence. As Aniruddha puts it:

> The body is pain, because it is the place of pain; the senses, objects, perceptions are suffering, because they lead to suffering; pleasure itself is suffering, because it is followed by suffering.[9]

8 For an interesting discussion of this debate, based primarily on Nyāya materials, see Chakrabarti (1983).

9 Eliade (1958), p. 11.

The realization of this leads to a desire to know the means of ending suffering. Ordinary remedies can only be temporary palliatives leaving open the possibility of subsequent pain; what is required are means that are certain and permanent. Yoga concurs with all this. Vyāsa compares the *yogin* to the sensitive eyeball, for even a fine thread of wool fallen on the eyeball causes intense pain (*Yogabhāṣya* II.15). Increasing discernment of the ways things really are means increasing insight into the way the impermanence of things leads inevitably to sufferings. The satisfaction of our present desires cannot prevent future frustrations; indeed any fleeting present satisfactions increase our attachment to our desires and hence the probability of future dissatisfactions.

These views about *duḥkha* Sāṃkhya-Yoga has in common not only with the other schools of orthodox Hindu philosophy, but also with the heterodox schools of Buddhism and Jainism. The first of the Four Noble Truths of Buddhism, for instance, is that 'all is suffering (*sarvam duḥkham*)'. As the Buddha is traditionally held to have put it in the first sermon preached after his enlightenment:

> Birth is painful [*dukkha*], old age is painful, sickness is painful, death is painful, sorrow, lamentation, dejection, and despair are painful. Contact with unpleasant things is painful, not getting what one wishes is painful. In short the five *khandhas* of grasping are painful.[10]

But though these views about the ubiquity of suffering (what Eliade calls 'the equation pain-existence'[11]) and the subsequent commitment to the goal of emancipation from suffering were dominant in India, there were dissenters. These were the Cārvāka or Lokāyata, a short-lived but polemically important group of materialists. Their texts are no longer extant, but according to the reports of their opponents they firmly rejected the majority view about the universality of *duḥkha* and the primacy of the goal of liberation:

> The enjoyment of heaven lies in eating delicious food, keeping company of young women, using fine clothes, perfumes, garlands, sandal paste, etc.
> The pain of hell lies in the troubles that arise from enemies, weapons, diseases; while liberation (*mokṣa*) is death which is the cessation of life-breath. The wise therefore ought not to take pains on account of that [i.e. liberation]; it is only the fool who wears himself out by penances, fasts, etc.[12]

One way to respond to this challenge is to defend the thesis about *duḥkha* as an empirical generalization. This seems to be the tack taken by the Nyāya who argue that while pleasure exists, its nature is always intermingled with pain (though the reverse is not true). In this sense pain is ubiquitous in our experience. But while this

---

10 Radhakrishnan and Moore (1957), p. 274. The parallels between Sāṃkhya, Yoga and Buddhism have generated considerable scholarly debate about lines of influence: for references see Eliade (1958), pp. 37-79, 395-96.

11 Eliade (1958), p. 11.

12 Radhakrishnan and Moore (1957), p. 235.

generalization may have some plausibility, the Cārvāka is unwilling to draw from it the moral he is supposed to:

> The only end of man is enjoyment produced by sensual pleasures. Nor may you say that such cannot be called the end of man as they are always mixed with some kind of pain, because it is our wisdom to enjoy the pure pleasure as far as we can, and to avoid the pain which inevitably accompanies it; ... just as the man who desires rice, takes the rice, straw and all, and having taken as much as he wants, desists.[13]

The Cārvāka reply here indicates the difficulty with treating the doctrine of universal suffering as a straightforward empirical truth. For the ordinary person, while not insensitive to the sorrows of life, generally feels that the transitory pleasures of life are sufficient in their intensity to compensate. Most Indian philosophers and religious thinkers acknowledge this but consider this attitude to be characteristic of the worldling's ignorance, the ignorance (*avidyā*) that keeps us caught in the vicious circle of *saṃsāra*. But then surely '*duḥkha*' cannot be simply a descriptive hedonic term, for otherwise there could be no disputing the claim. 'I find *saṃsāra* enjoyable, hence it is so'. Rather it is an evaluative term to be construed as more objective than a mere subjective feeling.[14] Moreover *duḥkha* is not just to be identified with pain, for pleasure (*sukha*) is widely acknowledged to be included in *duḥkha*.

Although '*duḥkha*' is an evaluative term, empirical observations are relevant to the claim 'Life is *duḥkha*'. Indeed close attention to the world is thought to bring this home as we see how little our flickering joys alleviate the corresponding worries and dissatisfactions. But penetrating to the truth that all life is suffering is not supposed to be an easy task. Thus the Buddha is purported to have said:

> It is difficult to shoot from a distance arrow after arrow through a narrow key hole, and miss not once. It is more difficult to shoot and penetrate with the tip of a hair split a hundred times a piece of hair similarly split. It is still more difficult to penetrate to the fact that 'all this is ill'.[15]

In the Buddhist tradition *duḥkha* is classified as of three kinds.[16] The first is *duḥkha* as physical pain (*duḥkha-duḥkha*); the second is *duḥkha* due to change (*vipariṇāma-duḥkha*) and the third is *duḥkha* through the fact of being conditioned (*saṃsāra-duḥkha*). Obviously, the first is a clear disvalue and presumably is not a truth that is considered difficult to penetrate. The second type of *duḥkha* is a bit more subtle. The point here is that the transitoriness of phenomena is a *duḥkha* because we cannot hold on to the objects of our cravings and this gives rise to a continual frustration which again is an obvious disvalue. In this sense even happy states of experience may be called suffering or *duḥkha*. The third type of suffering is more subtle still.

---

13 Ibid, p. 229.

14 Cf. Matilal (1982) Ch. 1.

15 Conze (1951), p. 45.

16 Cf. *Saṃyutta Nikāya* IV 259; *Abhidharmakośa* 6.II (La Vallee Poussin (1989), pp. 899-900.

It is not just physical pain, nor mental frustration caused by the impermanence of phenomena, but rather the *duḥkha* that is associated with the conditioned nature of phenomena. The idea here seems to be that we want the good life to be resilient, i.e. not hostage to fortune. But the goodness of worldly life is irretrievably fragile since all things are conditioned. Our enjoyment of a present good is inevitably contingent upon innumerable conditions outside of our control; we are the impotent recipients of moral luck.[17] This sense of fragility undermines the goodness of whatever we are fortunate enough to enjoy temporarily, leading in reflective agents to a felt unease.

It is interesting to compare this Buddhist analysis with that of the *Yogabhāṣya*, commenting on Patañjali's claim (II.15) that 'to the discerner all is but *duḥkha*'. Here too *duḥkha* is classified as being of three types: there is the suffering associated with change (*pariṇāma*), with anxiety (*tāpa*), and with habituation (*saṃskāra*). The first suffering is associated with the fact that fulfilment of our desires increases our attachment to them and hence too the subsequent frustration attendant upon their future non-fulfilment. Knowledge of this takes away from our present enjoyment of states of pleasure. The frustration by change of our need for security is associated with the second type of suffering; the anxiety or anguish which is common to all human experience. The third type of suffering is that of habituation, the way in which our desires and the habits they create make for a locus with not only a potential for pleasure, but also an inevitable potential for pain. Insofar as we are conditioned beings, our enjoyment of the good life is fragile. As in Buddhism, it is not that there are no agreeable or pleasurable experiences. Rather the idea is that because of the continual transformation of nature, our experience is permeated with a deep dissatisfaction and anxiety. The radical contingency and fragility of those pleasures we do experience causes the discriminating to experience even these as sorrowful.

It is clear, then, that the claim about the ubiquity of suffering is not simply an empirical generalization, but rather (at least partially) an evaluative thesis. Understood thus as a claim about the deep unsatisfactoriness of ordinary life because of its transiency and fragility it is not so easily dismissed by the Cārvāka taunt about the foolishness of refusing to eat rice because it comes enfolded in husks. Rather the Cārvāka pursuit of desirable things may come to seem (in the Buddhist simile) like licking honey from a razor blade. But still, the Cārvāka will persist, even if ordinary human life is deeply unsatisfactory in this sense, is not the cost of pursuing liberation too high? For if the only way to protect ourselves from suffering is to practice yoga and attain *kaivalya* as Sāṃkhya-Yoga urges, then have we not paid far too much for what we can gain. In the pursuit of immunity from change, fragility and luck we have to give up much of what makes human life worth living.

It is here that the metaphysics of Sāṃkhya-Yoga is invoked. According to their account of reality what we most truly are is rather different from what we ordinarily imagine. *Kaivalya* may not seem a very appealing picture of the good life for human beings, but according to Sāṃkhya-Yoga the ordinary notion of ourselves as human

---

17 On the importance of moral luck see Williams and Nagal (1976). For a treatment of ancient Greek ethics as centred on the problem of moral luck see Nussbaum (1986).

beings is only a shallow misconception of what we really are. Essentially we are *puruṣa* and liberation is the realization of this. Indeed the *Sāṃkhyakārikā* insists that in fact the *puruṣa* is never bound nor released; only *prakṛti* (especially as *buddhi*) transmigrates, is bound and is released (LXII). Liberation costs nothing but our errors about what we are.

This effectively completes our survey of Sāṃkhya-Yoga ethics. We have seen what the first-order moral precepts of Sāṃkhya-Yoga are and how they are justified as right in virtue of their instrumentality in promoting the supreme good of liberation (*mokṣa*). We have also seen how that good is conceived in Sāṃkhya-Yoga as freedom from suffering (*duḥkha*) and how the metaphysics of the system represent liberation as the realization of the true isolation (*kaivalya*) of *puruṣa* from *prakṛti*. These three elements of Sāṃkhya-Yoga ethics (the first-order precepts, the consequentialist theory of the right, and the theory of the good) are thus all present in the system and stand in certain interesting logical relations to each other. One point, however, stands in need of a little clarification, for it may be unclear why the Sāṃkhya-Yoga ethics is consequentialist. After all, do they really say actions are right in virtue of *promoting* the good? Or do they say instead that an agent's duty is to *exemplify* the good? That is: if *mokṣa* is the supreme good, is everyone supposed to *promote* it, or is everyone supposed to *honour* it? But the best way of honouring it may be to pursue one's own liberation in order to exemplify the ultimate good in one's own life, rather than to promote the good of liberation generally. (Among other things, this would undermine the very social structures which support the *yogin*'s efforts.)

This question touches upon an issue debated by the classical Indian philosophers: whether liberation can be achieved by all persons; and if so, whether it can be attained by individuals separately, or only all together.[18] So far as Sāṃkhya-Yoga is concerned universal freedom (*sarvamukti*) is impossible. The *Yogabhāṣya* (IV.33) explains that (i) it would go against the traditional doctrine that *saṃsāra* is endless; and (ii) it would be inconsistent with the doctrine that there are an infinite number of souls. On this view, then, there is an inbuilt metaphysical limitation upon all individuals successfully honouring the value of liberation in their own lives. Thus the right thing to do is to promote that value in consequentialist fashion. In this sense the Sāṃkhya-Yoga theory of the right is indeed a consequentialist one.

References

Chakrabarti, A, 'Is liberation (*mokṣa*) pleasant?', *Philosophy East and West* 33, 1983: 167-82.

Conze, Edward, *Buddhism: its essence and development*. New York: Harper, (1951), 1959.

Dasgupta, Surendranath, *Yoga as philosophy and religion*. Delhi: Motilal Banarsidass, (1924), 1987.

18 Cf. Hiriyanna (1975), Ch. 13.

Dasgupta, Surendranath, *Yoga philosophy in relation to other systems of Indian thought*. Delhi: Motilal Banarsidass, (1930), 1979.

Eliade, Mircea, *Yoga: immortality and freedom*. London: Arkana, (1958), 1989.

Feuerstein, Georg, *The essence of Yoga: a contribution to the psychohistory of Indian civilization*. London: Rider, 1974.

Feuerstein, Georg, *The Yoga-sūtra of Patañjali: a new translation and commentary*. Rochester, Vermont: Inner Traditions International, (1979), 1989.

Feuerstein, Georg, *The philosophy of Classical Yoga*. Manchester: Manchester University Press, 1980.

Hiriyanna, Mysore, *Indian conception of values*. Mysore: Kavyalaya Publishers, 1975.

Hulin, Michel, *Sāṃkhya literature*. Wiesbaden: Otto Harrassowitz, 1978.

La Vallée Poussin, Louis de, *Abhidharmakośabhāṣyam*, trans. Leo M. Pruden. Berkeley: Asian Humanities Press, 1989.

Larson, Gerald J., *Classical Sāṃkhya: an interpretation of its history and meaning*. 2nd rev. edn. Delhi: Motilal Banarsidass, 1979.

Larson, Gerald J. and Bhattacharya, Ram Shankar (eds), *Sāṃkhya: a dualist tradition in Indian philosophy*. Princeton: Princeton University Press, 1987.

Matilal, Bimal Krishna, *Logical and ethical issues of religious belief*. Calcutta: University of Calcutta, 1982.

Nussbaum, Martha C., *The fragility of goodness: luck and ethics in Greek tragedy and philosophy*. Cambridge: Cambridge University Press, 1986.

Pettit, Philip, 'Consequentialism'. In Peter Singer (ed.), *A Companion to Ethics*, Oxford: Basil Blackwell, 1991, pp. 230-40.

Radhakrishnan, Sarvepalli and Moore, Charles A., (eds), *A Sourcebook in Indian Philosophy*. Princeton: Princeton University Press, 1957.

Williams, B.A.O. and Nagel, Thomas (1976). 'Moral Luck'. *Proceedings of the Aristotelian Society Supplementary Volume* 50: 115-51.

Woods, James Haughton, *The Yoga-system of Patañjali*, Delhi: Motilal Banarsidass, (1914), 1988.

Chapter 6

Ethics of Liberation in Patañjali's Yoga

Ian Whicher

I wish to argue that Patañjali's philosophical perspective has, far too often, been looked upon as excessively 'spiritual' or isolationistic to the point of being a world-denying philosophy, indifferent to moral endeavor, neglecting the world of nature and culture, and overlooking the highest potentials for human reality, vitality, and creativity. Contrary to the arguments presented by many scholars, which associate Patañjali's yoga exclusively with extreme asceticism, mortification, denial, and the renunciation and abandonment of 'material existence' (*prakṛti*) in favour of an elevated and isolated 'spiritual state' (*puruṣa*) or disembodied state of spiritual liberation, I suggest that Patañjali's yoga can be seen as a responsible engagement, in various ways, of 'spirit' (*puruṣa* = intrinsic identity as Self, pure consciousness) and 'matter' (*prakṛti* = the source of psychophysical being, which includes mind, body, nature) resulting in a highly developed, transformed, and participatory human nature and identity, an integrated and embodied state of liberated selfhood (*jīvanmukti*).

Patañjali (c. second-third century CE), the great exponent of the authoritative classical yoga school (*darśana*) of Hinduism and the reputed author of the Yoga Sūtra, has often been regarded as calling for the severance of *puruṣa* from *prakṛti*; concepts such as liberation, cessation, detachment/dispassion, and so forth have been interpreted in an explicitly negative light. Max Müller, citing Bhoja Rāja's commentary[1] (eleventh century CE), refers to yoga as 'separation' (*viyoga*).[2] More recently, numerous other scholars[3] have endorsed this interpretation, that is, the

1 *Patañjalayogadarśana* [= *Yoga-sūtras*, YS], with the *Vyāsa-Bhāṣya*[YB] of Vyasa, the *Tattva-Vaiśāradī* [TV] of Vacaspati Miśra and the *Rāja-Mārtaṇḍa* of Bhoja Rāja, ed. Kasinatha Sastri Agase. Poona: Ānandāśrama Sanskrit Series, 47; reference here is to RM I.1, 1904, p. 1. Other texts used: Aranya Swami Hariharananda, *Yoga Philosophy of Patañjali,* trans. P.N. Mukerji. Calcutta: University of Calcutta, 1963. U. Arya, *Yoga-Sūtras of Patañjali with the Exposition of Vyāsa: A Translation and Commentary* - vol. 1: *Samādhi-Pāda*. Honesdale, PA: Himalayan International Institute, 1986; *The Yoga-Sūtras of Patañjali*, ed. and trans. Manilal N. Dvivedi, Adyar: Adyar, Madras: Theosophical Publishing House, 1930.

2 F. Max Müller, *The Six Systems of Indian Philosophy*, London: Longmans Green and Co., 1899, p. 309.

3 See, for example, Mircea Eliade,*Yoga: Immortality and Freedom*, 2nd edn, Bollingen Series no. 56. Princeton: Princeton University Press, 1969. Gaspar M. Koelman, *Patañjala Yoga: From Related Ego to Absolute Self* Poona, India: Papal Anthenaeum, 1970; Georg Feuerstein, *Yoga-Sūtra of Patañjali*, Folkstone, England: Wm. Dawson and Sons, Ltd.

absolute separateness of *puruṣa* and *prakṛti*. In asserting the absolute separation of *puruṣa* and *prakṛti*, scholars and non-scholars alike have tended to disregard the possibility for other (fresh) hermeneutical options, and this radical, dualistic metaphysical closure of sorts surrounding the nature and meaning of Patañjali's yoga has proved detrimental to a fuller understanding of the Yoga Darśana by continuing a tradition based on an isolationistic, one-sided reading (or perhaps misreading) of the Yoga Sūtra and Vyāsa's commentary. Accordingly, the absolute separation of *puruṣa* and *prakṛti* can only be interpreted as a disembodied state implying death to the physical body. To dislodge the sage from bodily existence is to undermine the integrity of the pedagogical context that lends so much credibility or 'weight' to the yoga system. I am not here implying a simple idealization of yoga pedagogy thereby overlooking the need to incorporate a healthy critical approach to the guru-disciple dynamic. Rather, I am suggesting that it need not be assumed that, in yoga, liberation coincides with physical death.[4] This would only allow for a soteriological end state of 'disembodied liberation' (*videhamukti*). What is involved in yoga is the death of the atomistic, egoic identity, the dissolution of the karmic web of *saṃsāra* that generates notions of one being a subject trapped in the *puruṣa* constitution of a particular body-mind.

Not being content with mere theoretical knowledge, yoga is committed to a practical way of life. To this end, Patañjali included in his presentation of yoga an outline of the 'eight-membered' path (*aṣṭāṅga-yoga*)[5] dealing with the physical,

---

1979; Gerald J. Larson and Ram S. Bhattacharya (eds), *Sāṃkhya: A Dualist Tradition in Indian Philosophy*, vol. 4 of *The Encyclopedia of Indian Philosophies*. Princeton: Princeton University Press, 1987. See also Roy Perrett in the preceding chapter.

4 I am here echoing some of the points made by Chapple in his paper entitled, '*Citta-Vṛtti* and Reality in the Yoga Sūtra', in *Sāṃkhya-Yoga: Proceedings of the IASWR Conference, 1981*, Stony Brook, NY, Institute for Advanced Studies in World Religions, 1983, pp. 103-119. See also Chapple and Kelly, *The Yoga Sūtras of Patañjali* , p.5, where the authors state: ' ... *kaivalyam* ... is not a catatonic state nor does it require death'. SK 67 acknowledges that even the 'potter's wheel' continues to turn because of the force of past impressions (*saṃskāras*); but in Yoga, higher dispassion and *asamprajñāta* eventually exhaust all the impressions or karmic residue. Through a continued program of ongoing purification Yoga allows for the possibility of an embodied state of freedom utterly unburdened by the effects of past actions. As such Yoga constitutes an advance over the fatalistic perspective in Sāṃkhya where the 'wheel of *saṃsāra*' continues (after the initial experience of liberating knowledge) until, in the event of separation from the body, *prakṛti* ceases and unending 'isolation' (*kaivalya*) is attained (Sāṃkya-Kārika, [SK] 68). In any case, the yogic state of supracognitive *samādhi* or enstasy goes beyond the liberating knowledge of *viveka* in the Sāṃkhyan system in that the yogin must develop dispassion even toward discriminative discernment itself. For more on an analysis of the notion of liberation in Sāṃkhya and Yoga see C. Chapple's chapter on 'Living Liberation in Sāṃkhya and Yoga', in Andrew O. Fort and Patricia Y. Mumme (eds), *Living Liberation in Hindu Thought*, Albany, State University of New York Press, 1996, pp. 115-134.

5 YS II.29; see the discussion on *aṣṭāṅga-yoga* in chapter 4 of Whicher, *The Integrity of the Yoga Darśana*; Albany, SUNY Press, 1998.

moral, psychological, and spiritual dimensions of the yogin, an integral path that emphasizes organic continuity, balance, and integration in contrast to the discontinuity, imbalance, and disintegration inherent in *saṃyoga*. The idea of cosmic balance and of the mutual support and upholding of the various parts of nature and society is not foreign to yoga thought. Vyāsa deals with the theory of 'nine causes' (*nava kāraṇāni*) or types of causation according to tradition.[6] The ninth type of cause is termed *dhṛti* – meaning 'support' or 'sustenance'. Based on Vyāsa's explanation of *dhṛti* we can see how mutuality and sustenance are understood as essential conditions for the maintenance of the natural and social world. There is an organic interdependence of all living entities wherein all (i.e. the elements, animals, humans, and divine bodies) work together for the 'good' of the whole and for each other.

Far from being exclusively a subjectively oriented and introverted path of withdrawal from life, classical yoga acknowledges the intrinsic value of 'support' and 'sustenance' and the interdependence of all living (embodied) entities, thus upholding organic continuity, balance, and integration within the natural and social world. Having achieved that level of insight (*prajñā*) that is 'truth-bearing' (*ṛtaṃbharā*),[7] the yogin perceives the natural order (*ṛta*) of cosmic existence, 'unites' with, and embodies that order. To fail to see clearly (*adarśana*) is to fall into disorder, disharmony, and conflict with oneself and the world. In effect, to be ensconced in ignorance implies a disunion with the natural order of life and inextricably results in a failure to embody that order. Through yoga one gains proper access to the world and is therefore established in right relationship to the world. Far from being denied or renounced, the world, for the yogin, has become transformed, properly engaged.

We need not read Patañjali as saying that the culmination of all yogic endeavor – *kaivalya* – is a static finality or inactive, isolated, solipsistic state of being. *Kaivalya* can be seen to incorporate an integrated, psychological consciousness along with the autonomy of pure consciousness, yet pure consciousness to which the realm of the *guṇas* (e.g. psychophysical being) is completely attuned and integrated. On the level of individuality, the yogin has found his (her) place in the world at large, 'fitting into the whole'.[8]

In the last chapter of the Yoga Sūtra (*Kaivalya-Pāda*), 'aloneness' (*kaivalya*) is said to ensue upon the attainment of *dharmamegha-samādhi*, the 'cloud of *dharma*' *samādhi*. At this level of practice, the yogin has abandoned any search for (or attachment to) reward or 'profit' from his or her meditational practice; a non-acquisitive attitude (*akusīda*) must take place at the highest level of yogic discipline.[9] Vyāsa emphasizes that the identity of *puruṣa* is not something to be

---

6 YB II.28 (pp. 99-101).

7 YS I.48.

8 See K. Klostermaier, 'Spirituality and Nature', in Krishna Sivaraman, (ed.), *Hindu Spirituality: Vedas Through Vedānta*, London: SCM Press, 1989, pp. 319-337. See note 28 below.

9 YS IV.29 (p. 202): *prasaṃkhyāne'py akusīdasya sarvathā vivekakhyāter dharmameghaḥ samādhiḥ*.

acquired (*upādeya*) or discarded (*heya*).[10] The perspective referred to as 'Patañjala Yoga Darśana' culminates in a permanent state of clear 'seeing' brought about through the discipline of yoga. Yoga thus incorporates both an end state or 'goal' and a process.[11]

Dharmamegha-samādhi presupposes that the yogin has cultivated higher dispassion (*para-vairāgya*) – the means to the enstatic consciousness realized in *asaṃprajñāta-samādhi*.[12] Thus, *dharmamegha-samādhi* is more or less a synonym of *asaṃprajñāta-samādhi* and can even be understood as the consummate phase of the awakening disclosed in enstasy, the final step on the long and arduous yogic journey to authentic identity and 'aloneness'.[13] A permanent identity shift – from the perspective of the human personality to *puruṣa* – takes place. Now free from any dependence on or subordination to knowledge or *vṛtti*, and detached from the world of misidentification (*saṃyoga*), the yogin yet retains the purified gunic powers of

10 YB II.15 (p. 78): *tatra hātuḥ svarūpamupādeyaṃ va heyaṃ vā na bhavitumarhati.* 'Here, the true nature/identity of the one who is liberated cannot be something to be acquired or discarded.'

11 Thus the term *yoga* (like the terms *nirodha* and *samādhi*) is ambiguous in that it means both the process of purification and illumination and the final result of liberation or 'aloneness.' Due to Yoga's traditional praxis-orientation it becomes all too easy to reduce Yoga to a 'means only' approach to well-being and spiritual enlightenment. In the light of its popularity in the Western world today in which technique and practice have been emphasized often to the exclusion of philosophical/theoretical understanding and a proper pedagogical context, there is a great danger in simply reifying practice whereby practice becomes something the ego does for the sake of its own security. Seen here, practice – often then conceived as a superior activity in relation to all other activities – becomes all-important in that through the activity called 'practice' the ego hopes and strives to become 'enlightened'. Practice thus becomes rooted in a future-oriented perspective largely motivated out of a fear of not becoming enlightened; it degenerates into a form of selfishly appropriated activity where 'means' become ends-in-themselves. To be sure, the concern of Yoga is to (re)discover *puruṣa*, to be restored to true identity thus overcoming dissatisfaction, fear and misidentification by uprooting and eradicating the dis-ease of ignorance (*avidyā*). Yet, as Wilhelm Halbfass puts it, true identity 'cannot be really lost, forgotten or newly acquired', for liberation 'is not to be produced or accomplished in a literal sense, but only in a figurative sense'. Halbfass, *Tradition and Reflection: Explorations in Indian Thought*, Albany, NY: State University of New York Press, 1991, pp. 251, 252. Sufficient means for birthing the natural light of the mind are, however, both desirable and necessary in order to prepare the yogin for the necessary identity shift from egoity to *puruṣa*. By acknowledging that 'aloneness' cannot be an acquired state resulting from or caused by yogic methods and techniques, and that *puruṣa* cannot be known (YB III.35), acquired or discarded/lost (YB II.15), Yoga in effect transcends its own result-orientation as well as the categories of means and ends.

12 YB I.18.

13 See Feuerstein, *The Philosophy of Classical Yoga*, Manchester: Manchester University Press, 1980, p. 98.

virtue including illuminating 'knowledge of all'[14] (due to purified *sattva*), nonafflicted activity[15] (due to purified *rajas*), and a stable body-form (due to purified *tamas*).

YS IV.30 declares: 'From that [*dharmamegha-samādhi*] there is the cessation of afflicted action'.[16] Hence the binding influence of the *guṇas* in the form of the afflictions, past actions, and misguided relationships is overcome; what remains is a 'cloud of dharma' which includes an 'eternality of knowledge' free from all impure covering (*āvaraṇa-mala*, YS IV.31) or veiling affliction and where 'little (remains) to be known'.[17] The eternality or endlessness of knowledge is better understood metaphorically rather than literally: It is not knowledge expanded to infinity but implies *puruṣa*-realization which transcends the limitations and particulars of knowledge (*vṛtti*).

The culmination of the yoga system is found when, following from *dharmamegha-samādhi*, the mind and actions are freed from misidentification and affliction and one is no longer deluded/confused with regard to one's true form (*svarūpa*) or intrinsic identity. At this stage of practice the yogin is disconnected (*viyoga*) from all patterns of action motivated by the ego. According to both Vyāsa[18] and the sixteenth-century commentator Vijñāna Bhikṣu,[19] one to whom this high state of purification

14 YS III.49 and III.54.

15 YS IV.7; see also YS IV.30 (n. 16 below).

16 YS IV.30 (p. 202): *tataḥ kleśakarmanivṛttiḥ*. Thus, it may be said that to dwell without defilement in a 'cloud of *dharma*' is the culminating description by Patañjali of what tradition later referred to as living liberation (*jīvanmukti*). To be sure, there is a 'brevity of description' in the *Yoga Sūtra* regarding the state of liberation. Only sparingly, with reservation (one might add, caution) and mostly in metaphorical terms does Patañjali speak about the qualities exhibited by the liberated yogin. Chapple, ('Living Liberation in Sāṃkhya and Yoga', p. 116, see note 4 above) provides three possible reasons for this 'brevity of description' regarding living liberation in the context of the Yoga Sūtra (and Sāṃkhya, i.e. the SK of Īśvara Kṛṣṇa): (1) He states: '(T)he genre in which both texts were written does not allow for the sort of narrative and poetic embellishment found in the epics and Purāṇas.' (2) Perhaps, as Chapple suggests '... a deliberate attempt has been made to guarantee that the recognition of a liberated being remains in the hands of a spiritual preceptor'. What is to be noted here is that the oral and highly personalized lineage tradition within Yoga stresses the authority of the guru which guards against false claims to spiritual attainment on the part of others and thereby 'helps to ensure the authenticity and integrity of the tradition'. (3) A further reason for brevity 'could hinge on the logical contradiction that arises due to the fact that the notion of self is so closely identified with *ahaṃkāra* [the mistaken ego sense or afflicted identity]. It would be an oxymoron for a person to say [']I am liberated.[']' The Self (*puruṣa*) is of course not an object which can be seen by itself thus laying emphasis, as Chapple points out, on the ineffable nature of the liberative state which transcends mind-content, all marks and activity itself.

17 YS IV.31 (p. 203): *tadā sarvāvaraṇamalāpetasya jñānasyā'nantyājjñeyam alpam.*

18 See YB IV.30 (pp. 202-203): *kleśakarmanivṛttau jīvanneva vidvānvimukto bhavati.* 'On cessation of afflicted action, the knower is released while yet living.'

19 YV IV.30 (pp. 123-124). Elsewhere in his *Yoga-Sāra-Saṃgraha* (p. 17) Vijñāna Bhikṣu tells us that the yogin who is 'established in the state of *dharmamegha-samādhi* is called a *jīvanmukta*' (... *dharmameghaḥ samādhiḥ ... asyāmavasthāyāṃ jīvanmukta ityucyate*).

takes place is designated as a *jīvanmukta*: one who is liberated while still alive (i.e. embodied or living liberation).

By transcending the normative conventions and obligations of karmic behaviour, the yogin acts morally not as an extrinsic response and out of obedience to an external moral code of conduct, but as an intrinsic response and as a matter of natural, purified inclination. The stainless luminosity of pure consciousness is revealed as one's fundamental nature. The yogin does not act samsarically (in worldly terms) and ceases to act from the perspective of a delusive sense of self confined within *prakṛti*'s domain. Relinquishing all obsessive or selfish concern with the results of activity, the yogin remains wholly detached from the egoic fruits of action.[20] This does not imply that the yogin loses all orientation for action. Only attachment (and compulsive, inordinate desire), not action itself, sets in motion the law of moral causation (*karma*) by which a person is confined within samsaric (worldly) identity. The yogin is said to be non-attached to either virtue or non-virtue, and is no longer oriented within the egological patterns of thought as in the epistemically distorted condition of *saṃyoga*. This does not mean, as some scholars have misleadingly concluded, that the spiritual adept or yogin is free to commit immoral acts,[21] or that the yogin is motivated by selfish concerns.[22]

Actions must not only be executed in the spirit of unselfishness (i.e. sacrifice) or detachment, they must also be ethically sound, reasonable and justifiable. Moreover, the yogin's spiritual journey – far from being an 'a-moral process'[23] – is a highly moral process! The yogin's commitment to the sattvification of consciousness, including the cultivation of moral virtues such as compassion (*karuṇā*)[24] and nonviolence (*ahiṃsā*),[25] is not an 'a-moral' enterprise, nor is it an expression of indifference, aloofness, or an uncaring attitude to others. Moral disciplines are engaged as a natural outgrowth of intelligent (*sattvic*) self-understanding, insight, and commitment to self-transcendence that takes consciousness out of (*ec-stasis*) its identification with the rigid structure of the monadic ego, thereby reversing the

---

Vijñāna Bhiksu is critical of Vedāntins (i.e. Śaṇkara's Advaita Vedānta school) that, he says, associate the *jīvanmukta* with ignorance (*avidyā-kleśa*) – probably because of the liberated being's continued link with the body – despite Yoga's insistence on the complete overcoming of the afflictions.

20 This is the essence of Kṛṣṇa's teaching in the Bhagavadgītā on *karmayoga*; see, for example, BG IV.20.

21 See R.C. Zaehner, *Our Savage God*, London: Collins, 1974, pp. 97-98.

22 See B.-A. Scharfstein, *Mystical Experience*, Baltimore: Penguin Books, 1974, pp. 131-132.

23 See Feuerstein, *The Yogasūtra of Patañjali*, op cit, p. 81.

24 YS I.33 (p. 38): *maitrīkaruṇāmuditopekṣāṇām sukhaduḥkhapuṇyāpuṇyaviṣayāṇām bhāvanātaś cittaprasādanam*. 'The mind is made pure and clear from the cultivation of friendliness, compassion, happiness and equanimity in conditions or toward objects of joy, sorrow, merit or demerit respectively.'

25 YS II.35.

inveterate tendency of this ego to inflate itself at the expense of its responsibility in relation to others.

Having defined the 'goal' of yoga as 'aloneness' (*kaivalya*), the question must now be asked: What kind of 'aloneness' was Patañjali talking about? 'Aloneness', I suggest, is not the isolation of the seer (*draṣṭṛ, puruṣa*) separate from the seeable (*dṛśya, prakṛti*), as is unfortunately far too often maintained as the goal of yoga, but refers to the 'aloneness' of the power of 'seeing' (YS II.20, 25) in its innate purity and clarity without any epistemological distortion and moral defilement. The cultivation of *nirodha* uproots the compulsive tendency to reify the world and oneself (i.e. that pervading sense of separate ego irrevocably divided from the encompassing world) with an awareness that reveals the transcendent, yet immanent seer (*puruṣa*). Through clear 'seeing' (*dṛśi*) the purpose of yoga is fulfilled, and the yogin, free from all misidentification and impure karmic residue (as in the former contextual sphere of *cittavṛtti*), gains full, immediate access to the world. By accessing the world in such an open and direct manner, in effect 'uniting' (epistemologically) with the world, the yogin ceases to be encumbered by egoism (i.e. *asmitā* and its egoic attitudes and identity patterns), which, enmeshed in conflict and confusion and holding itself as separate from the world, misappropriates the world.

Yoga can be seen to unfold – in *samādhi* – states of epistemic oneness that reveal the non-separation of knower, knowing, and the known (YS I.41) grounding the adept's identity in a nonafflicted mode of action. *Kaivalya* implies a power of 'seeing' in which the dualisms rooted in our egocentric patterns of attachment, aversion, fear, and so forth have been transformed into unselfish ways of being with others.[26] The psychological, ethical, and social implications of this kind of identity transformation are, needless to say, immense. I am suggesting that yoga does not destroy or anesthetize our feelings and emotions thereby encouraging neglect and indifference toward others. On the contrary, the process of 'cessation' (*nirodha*) stabilizes and makes one steadfast toward a life of compassion, discernment, and service informed by a 'seeing' that is able to understand (literally meaning 'to stand among, hence observe') – and is in touch with – the needs of others.

In other words, virtues entailed from other-regarding ethics, care for the other and altruism are not alien to Yoga. Rather, what seems especially significant and relevant for our understanding of yoga ethics is the enhanced capacity generated in yoga for *empathic* identification with the object one seeks to understand. This is no different from the ideal of the *arhant*, *bodhisatva*, the *dalai lamas*, in Buddhist philosophy, which is derived from the self-same resources of the earlier *śrāmaṇic* and gymnostoical (*jina*) traditions. This then is a far cry from the portrayal of the yogin as a socially-disenfranchized, disengaged figure, psychologically and physically removed from the human relational sphere, who in an obstinate and obtrusive fashion severs all ties with the world. Such an image of a wise yogin merely serves to circumscribe our vision of humanity and, if anything else, stifle the spirit by prejudicing a spiritual, abstract (and disembodied) realm over and against nature

26 YS I.33; see n. 24 above.

and our human embodiment. In yoga philosophy 'seeing' is not only a cognitive term but implies purity of mind, that is, it has moral content and value. Nor is 'knowledge' (*jñāna*, *vidyā*) in the yoga tradition to be misconstrued as a 'bloodless' or 'heartless' *gnosis*.

The consequence I derive from the foregoing analysis is therefore that through the necessary transformation of consciousness brought about in *samādhi*, an authentic and fruitful coherence of self-identity, perception, and activity emerges out of the former fragmented consciousness in *saṃyoga*. If Patañjali's perception of the world of forms and differences had been destroyed or discarded, how could he have had such insights into yoga and the intricacies and subtle nuances of the unenlightened state?[27] If through *nirodha* the individual form and the whole world had been cancelled for Patañjali, he would more likely have spent the rest of his days in the inactivity and isolation of transcendent oblivion or as one of Chalmers' zombies rather than present yoga philosophy to others! Far from being handicapped by the exclusion of thinking, perceiving, experiencing, or activity, the liberated yogin actualizes the potential to live a fully integrated life in the world and consciousness. I conclude here that there is no reason why the liberated yogin cannot be portrayed as a vital, creative, thoughtful, empathetic, balanced, happy, and wise person. Having adopted an integrative orientation to life, the enlightened being can endeavor to transform, enrich, and ennoble the world. I am therefore suggesting that there is a rich affective, moral, and cognitive as well as spiritual potential inherent in the realization of *puruṣa*, the 'aloneness' of the power of consciousness/seeing.

Hence it follows that Yoga presupposes the integration of knowledge and activity; there can be no scission between *theoria* and *praxis*. The *Yoga Sūtra* is a philosophical text where *praxis* is deemed to be essential. Without actual practice the theory that informs yoga would have no authentic meaning. Yet without examination and reflection (*theoria*) there would be no meaningful striving for liberation, no 'goal,' as it were, to set one's sight on. In an original, inspiring, and penetrating style, Patañjali bridges metaphysics and ethics, transcendence and immanence, and contributes to the Hindu fold a form of philosophical investigation that, to borrow Taber's descriptive phrase for another context, can properly be called a 'transformative philosophy'. That is to say, it is a philosophical perspective which 'does not stand as an edifice isolated from experience; it exists only insofar as it is realized in experience'.[28]

---

27 Although the historical identity of Patañjali the Yoga master is not known, we are assuming that Patañjali was, as the tradition would have it, an enlightened Yoga adept.

28 John A. Taber, *Transformative Philosophy: A Study of Śaṅkara, Fichte, and Heidegger*, Honolulu: University of Hawai'i Press, 1983, p. 26. See also Purushottama Bilimoria, *Yoga, Meditation, and the Guru – Ethical Implications of Practices in the West.* Delhi: Sterling Publications, 1989; Melbourne: Indra Publishing, 1988.

Conclusion

To conclude, it can be said that *puruṣa* indeed has some precedence over *prakṛti* in Patañjali's system, for *puruṣa* is what is ordinarily 'missing' or concealed in human life and is ultimately the state of consciousness one must awaken to in yoga. The liberated state of 'aloneness' (*kaivalya*) need not denote either an ontological superiority of *puruṣa* or an exclusion of *prakṛti*. *Kaivalya* can be positively construed as an integration of both principles – an integration that, I have argued, is what is most important for yoga. I have proposed that the Yoga Sūtra does not uphold a 'path' of liberation that ultimately renders *puruṣa* and *prakṛti* incapable of 'co-operating' together. Rather, the Yoga Sūtra seeks to 'unite' these two principles without the presence of any defiled understanding, to bring them 'together', properly aligning them in a state of balance, harmony, and a clarity of knowledge in the integrity of being and action.

The purified mind, one that has been transformed through yogic discipline, is certainly no ordinary worldly awareness nor is it eliminated for the sake of pure consciousness. To confuse (as many interpretations of yoga have unfortunately done) the underlining purificatory processes involved in the cessation of ignorance/afflicted identity as being the same thing as (or as necessitating the need for) a radical elimination of our psychophysical being – the *prakṛtic* vehicle through which consciousness discloses itself – is, I suggest, to misunderstand the intent of the Yoga Sūtra itself. There are strong grounds for arguing (as I have done) that through 'cessation' *prakṛti* herself (in the form of the gunic constitutional makeup of the yogin's body-mind) is liberated from the grip of ignorance. Vyāsa explicitly states (YB II.18) that emancipation happens in the mind and does not literally apply to *puruṣa* – which is by definition already free and therefore has no intrinsic need to be released from the fetters of saṃsāric existence.

As well as being one of the seminal texts on yogic technique and transformative/liberative approaches within Asian/Indian philosophy, Patañjali's Yoga Sūtra has to this day remained one of the most influential spiritual guides in Hinduism. People all over the world have been actively practicing some form of yoga influenced by Patañjali's thought, which clearly demonstrates yoga's moral relevance for our times as a discipline that transcends cultural, religious, and philosophical barriers. The universal and universalizing potential of yoga makes it one of India's finest contributions to humanity's struggle for self-definition, moral integrity, and ethico-spiritual renewal.

Chapter 7

Karma's Suffering: A Mīmāṃsā Solution to the Problem of Evil[1]

Purushottama Bilimoria

Preamble

In his article on 'Inherited Responsibility, Karma and original Sin'[2] Peter Forrest made the interesting observation that a person is by definition constituted in relation with other fellow beings, and therefore whatever good or benefit I as an individual derive from the labours of others I share in the responsibility for their exploitation, oppression, whatever. This phenomenon may be called 'group or collective karma'. Through this reasoning, Forrest indicted himself for being, in part at least, responsible for the dispossession and exploitation of the Aborigines of Australia by the British colonists. He draws an analogy between this kind of responsibility and the responsibility of an elderly person for some crime committed in youth, repentance and remorse notwithstanding, whence we judge that restitution should be made. Forrest concludes, 'sharing in the crimes of our ancestors must be like that if it is to be a matter of retributive justice rather than a rhetorical trick intended to ensure distributive justice'. The Law of Karma, he avers, appeals to just such a principle of retributive justice: 'as you sow, thus you shall reap'. This is Forrest's statement on how past wrongs might continue on and affect the lives of individuals. It may not be all about afflicted crimes and misdemeanours; the impersonal law may equally apply to good deeds and virtues and other such 'traces'. Since my actions are actions of various person-like entities of which I, of necessity, form part, my vices, my sorrows, my joys, my virtues are components of the (poorly integrated) character, personality-traits and deeds of these, perhaps long since gone, person-like entities. In Forrest's view, this reconstruction of inheritance and succession of collective action helps set aside rebirth (or reincarnation) as well, thus: 'It is not that I, an individual human being, shall be reincarnated, but rather that a moral person

---

1 The essay from which this chapter is derived was first published in *Sophia* 100th Issue, **34** (1) 1995, pp. 92-119. A number of colleagues read and commented on the paper, and I express my gratitude to them all, especially Bruce Reichenbach, Bruce Langtry, and Patrick Hutchings.

2 *Sophia* **33** (1), 1993, pp. 1-15. For an excellent discussion of the ideal of Karma from various Indian perspectives (Jaina, Hindu, Buddhists) see, Bruce Reichenbach, *Law of Karma: A Philosophical Study*, Honolulu: University of Hawai'i Press, 1991.

of which I am now one of the parts now has other parts in the future.' It is this moral person, comprising a network of karmic heirs and karmic ancestors, 'which reaps as it sows. And I should not complain if the result is suffering for me, for only by being part of that moral person can I be the sort of person who I am.' This is a forceful argument, and sensitively-crafted, at once giving the doctrine of karma a semblance of moral intelligibility, while also appropriating it in a certain creative way. It results in a radical reinterpretation of the doctrine of karma such that one major presupposition underpinning it – *qua* the antecedent and deferred moral responsibility – is vindicated, while the other presupposition (or perhaps even an unwitting consequence according to another scholastic system) – *qua* rebirth/reincarnation – is rejected. The argument is persuasive as it is sound, even though classical Indian theorists may feel moved to object to the hasty dismissal of rebirth or reincarnation on simply these grounds. Leaving the latter disputation aside, however, what of the *truth* of the proposition 'as you sow, thus you shall reap' with its uncanny karmic overtones? And is the involuntary dispersal of the effect of an individual's action over a larger social whole and vice versa an adequate account for retributive justice within the terms of the theory?

I shall not here respond to this argument in any direct way, but draw on what I believe to be a very important insight underscored in Forrest's reconstruction, in an attempt to make further sense of the doctrine of karma, as it is given in traditional understanding, against the challenges of the so-called problem of evil and God's omnipotence. The speculative reconstruction that I venture upon responds to the articulation of these specific challenges towards a viable theodicy.

This preamble is intended also to signal the kind of reflection on the larger problematic that I believe in the end to be more fruitful than one that simply stays with burrowing deep into the etymology and history of the terms or concepts that inscribe the conceptions. So my main concern here will be to inquire into ways in which some Indian or Asian views on karma and suffering can help throw light on – even attempt at a solution of – the so-called problem of evil and God's omnipotence. It might be the case in the end that we may want to consider changing the conceptions, or the framing questions, by looking at some alternatives rather than being bent on demanding a stringent solution to the problem in this respect.

Some definitional issues first. By 'evil' I shall generally mean, alongside gratuitous (superfluous) evil, all three types of evil that Leibniz spoke of: metaphysical (consisting in imperfections of all creatures); physical (applying to disadvantage of intelligent substances); moral (attributed to vicious actions of these substances), or putting it more succinctly, 'Metaphysical evil consists in mere imperfection, physical evil in suffering, and moral evil in sin.'[3] Of course, in recent times, Leibniz's categories of metaphysical and physical evil have been collapsed into natural evil, but 'natural evil' for Leibniz only covered suffering caused by sin. The sense of 'evil' nuanced in the doctrine of karma – if it is at all – is not covered adequately by 'moral evil' nor by 'natural evil' (in Leibniz's terms) as their key referent is

3 Leibniz, *The Theodicy*, trans. by E.M. Huggard, Austin Farrar (ed.), London, 1951, #21 p. 136.

sin, a distinctive Judeo-Christian concept almost entirely absent in Indian thought. The imperfections that come under metaphysical evil, and more significantly, the suffering implicated in physical evil, with the addition of suffering caused by other kinds of perturbations, not least the intentions, false judgements, moral weakness, conscious and unconscious desires, attachments and sheer foolishness and so on, of sentient beings, is what we would like to call (non-reductively or in the broadest possible sense) 'intentional evil' (if we can distinguish this from 'moral evil'), which we take *duḥkha* to correspond to, and this will be the prime focus in connecting evil with the Law of Karma.

Karma (Natural Law of Action)

Now it is often thought that Indian philosophy does not recognize the problem of evil or that Indian thinkers have remained, in Arthur Herman's words, 'strangely silent' about this problem which has bedevilled Western philosophy and theology over the ages.[4] Nietzsche, following Schopenhauer, reinforced this perception when he cited, in his *On the Genealogy of Morals*, Vedānta and Buddhist texts purporting to 'go beyond good and evil'. In other words, the distinction between good and evil was glossed over by the Indians, either because they thought they could transcend evil or because evil, along with the rest of the manifest reality, was an illusion (*māyā*). All misery, suffering, pain, irrational calamities and so on are attributed to an inexplicable mystery which dissimulates once we understand the 'true reality' that hovers behind the world of appearance, etc. The perception of evil is simply the 'filter' through which reality delivers its goods via our intuitions and so on. Given this view, Indian thinkers, it would appear, never felt the need to deal with the problem in quite the same way and provide a justification for evil in the strict terms of what in the West has been called 'theodicy' (*theōs* and *dîke*, God and justice). On the rare occasion, though, there has been some recognition of the elegance of Indian theodicy in attempting to explain suffering and evil, as when John Hick entertains the claim based on the doctrine of karma, although he stops short of Max Weber who adjudged the Indian alternative to be 'the most consistent theodicy every produced by history'.[5]

These various critiques and appraisals however fail to take cognizance of the deeper concerns that underpin certain of the theses associated with the treatment of *duḥkha*, or suffering, as well as with the question of 'creation' or arising of the

---

4 Arthur L. Herman, *The Problem of Evil and Indian Thought*, Delhi: Motilal Banarsidass, 1976. On anthropological treatment, see C.F. Keys and E.V. Daniel (eds), *Karma: An Anthropological Inquiry*, Berkeley: University of California Press, 1993.

5 John Hick, *The Philosophy of Religion*, 3rd edn., Englewood Cliffs, N.J. Prentice-Hall, 1983, chapter. 10; Max Weber, *The Religion of India*, New York: The Free Press, 1958, p. 121; see discussion of both in Roy W. Perrett, 'Karma and the Problem of Suffering', *Sophia*, 24 (1), April 1985, pp. 4-10. On creative element in karma, See Christopher Chapple, *Karma and Creativity*, State University of New York Press, Albany, 1986.

world, in the debate that has raged between Indian philosophers and theologians of a variety of persuasions. Thus part of what I attempt to do here is to bring out some of the concerns and demonstrate how a profound paradox haunts the attempt to resolve the problem, not least because of the difficulties presented by the doctrine of karma. And there is something recognizable as 'a rational theodicy' in the ponderings of philosophers like Śaṅkara, even when their metaphysical picture is impeccably impersonal, where omnipotence and the evaluative rub of descriptive laws, of planetary movements, or of karma for that matter, are not of such major consequence.

The approach to the problem, in the Indian context, usually begins with the existential admission that, as the First Noble Truth of the Buddha has it, there is suffering (*duḥkha*). Suffering is a pervasive fact of human life, indeed of all sentient existence: creatures are born in pain, they suffer pain throughout life and when worn down by age, have their life-breath turned off by the god of death, only to be born again, and so on, in an endless cycle of life and death (*saṃsāra*). But suffering in itself is not necessarily *evil* or equivalent to what in Western theodicies has been called 'evil'. This intentional isomorphism is all but missing. As B.K. Matilal has rightly pointed out, *duḥkha* is 'not always seen as a theoretical or philosophical problem that needs conceptual explanation and argument to avoid or resolve alleged inconsistencies.'[6] Although sometimes it has been taken as a problem in the same manner and discussed extensively. One can, therefore, argue by extension that there would be no suffering had there not been some prior condition that makes suffering, and not, say, unqualified happiness, a real possibility. This precondition, according to the prevailing view at least, must be traceable to a source in ontological evil. By ontological evil one might understand certain imperfections in the very nature of the world or rather of the life-world and the immediate physical environment; contrariwise, the presence and persistence of evil might be accountable in terms of the absence of an omnipotent and benevolent God. Both these interpretations turn on the existential admission of the pervasiveness of suffering or *duḥkha* and its disposition to ontologically link two moments or events, or polarities, that are not ostensibly related.

But why is *duḥkha* being identified so closely with metaphysical evil when earlier on we had introduced the category of intentionality? Why should, say, suffering brought about by plagues and destructive effects of earthquakes and tornadoes be aligned with suffering brought upon by wars and crimes and self-destructive vices which are intentionally (even if unselfconsciously) instigated? One answer, generally favoured in the tradition, is that it is because suffering is not simply viewed as an evil that visits upon an individual in some blind, random and indiscriminate way, but rather that the individual is only such a recipient of suffering as his or her present station and location determines it; the individual, in some sense, more accurately as part of the larger network of complicated relations, past and present, is deemed

6 Bimal Krishna Matilal, *Logical and Ethical Issues of Religious Belief*, University of Calcutta, 1982. p. 28. See also Matilal's discussion (Chapter 2) in this volume.

responsible for the suffering. (In the way, we earlier saw, Forrest making us morally responsible for our ancestors' crimes.) Whatever the remote or originating cause might have been (which to the Buddha is an object of futile speculation), the more immediate cause is located in desire, a blanket term that covers an array of intentional conditioning factors, of which craving (*tṛṣṇa*) would be the central, at least as it is given in the interpretation of the most famous formulae of early Buddhism, namely, the Four Noble Truths.[7] *Suttanipāta* and *Dhammapāda* presuppose the centrality of craving as *kāma* – not karma, not yet anyway. The principle of karma is said to have been introduced by the Vaibhāṣika system to determine *where* and *how* one is reborn.[8] But the prevalence among lay and ascetic communities, influenced by Jaina philosophy, of karma as volition or intentionality (*cetanā*) or, at best activity induced by intention, and therefore serving as a praxis-guiding principle in daily existence cannot be denied. The philosophical appropriation of karma in Buddhist and Hindu-Brahmanical thought, perhaps took a while longer. But what *is* the philosophical understanding of karma and why has it been so important a concept in Indian theodicy?

Karma is indeed a notoriously slippery concept, which can have a multitude of meanings and nuance, depending on the context in which it occurs. The word *karman* is a noun derived from the root *kr.* 'do-, act-, make-, perform-, accomplish-', it may signify a simple action or deed, but it can also imply reference to the causal antecedents as well the consequent effects or results of the action in a seamless temporal or spatial horizon. The doctrine has it that every action leaves behind a residue (*saṃskāra*) in the unconscious. Accumulation of these *saṃskāras* or psychic traces and impressions constellate to generate patterns of habits or latent potential of repetitive dispositions (*vāsanās*). These potentiates take root in the psyche and in due course of time determine or rather moderate the individual's actions, perceptions, and responses to the world around her. Virtuous acts lead to pleasant results – such is the effect of 'good' karma; while unvirtuous acts may lead to unpleasant or painful results – such is the effect of 'bad' karma. The sedimented residual karma (*sañcita*) may 'ripen' presently, i.e. begin to manifest its outcome in the duration of a particular life, in which case it is known as *prārabdha*, or they may be deferred and get liquidated at future time (*ārabdha*). The burden of the unexhausted karma is what helps perpetuate the chain of seamless continuity of an individual's existence (*saṃsāra*), and create conditions for good life, life of suffering, good death or bad

7 *Saṃyutta-nikāya*, LVI, II: 'The Noble Truth of suffering (*duḥkha*) is this: It is this thirst (craving) which produces re-existence and re-becoming, bound up with passionate greed', trans. Walpola Rahula, *What the Buddha Taught*, 2nd edn., New York: Grove Press, 1974.

8 *Suttanipāta*, I.8. Trans. by Rahula (op cit.) Discussion of this attributive view is from Smithhausen, in Ronald Neufeldt (ed.), *Karma and Rebirth: post-classical developments*, Albany, NY: State University of New York Press, 1986, p. 205. On Hindu developments, see Wendy O' Flaherty (ed.), *Karma and Rebirth in Classical Indian Tradition*, Berkeley: University of California Press, 1980; T.G. Kalgathi, 'In the vestibules of Karma', *Sambodhi*, I.i. 1972, pp. 41-62.

birth, and so on. Such are the retributions entailed in the causal network that in itself is an inexorable manifestation of the moral law of nature. It also follows that the empirical agent is deluded when he or she thinks that all their action is freely determined, that free choice is an inescapable human condition, and that ultimate freedom is there for the asking, or privileged in transcendence.

In simpler terms, karma is described as the principle of universal causality resulting from actions. Every meritorious and virtuous deed, and every negative act, leaves its impress or 'trace' on the psyche, which in turn determines the character of the individual as well as her disposition to behave in a certain way or ways. The ethical implication is that whatever good or bad one performs one must reap their results: good deeds lead to happiness, bad deeds lead to suffering. The retributive results are proportionate to the gravity of the act. To guard against an excessively fatalistic reading of the doctrine, one could say that there is no reason why according to this theory some people's greed and avarice could not lead them to enjoy fortune or cause unwanted misfortune to others. Persons who were cheated might never recover their loss in kind, but would nonetheless be owed something by their accomplice, which the inexorable law of karma will take care of in its own inimitable way. What this means is that actions generate their own, intrinsic moral consequences, however well the intentions may be on the part of the performer. Certain acts may violate general or universal principles, such as fair entitlements, deserts, or rights of another (e.g. discriminating on grounds of gender or race). Also, certain acts lead to irreparable and irreversible damage, such that the performer of these acts must bear responsibility for the consequences of the acts, the burden of which must surely pass over to the karmic as much as to the moral sphere (which remain inseparable in Indian metaphysic).

In other words, actions may be rightly judged in respect of rules they violate, or the consequences they lead to, or in respect of the act *qua* act on the premise that certain acts are intrinsically and inherently wrong, bad, or undesirable. The same ethical considerations apply to karma. Telling the truth on the principle that one only ever utters the truth (e.g. through testimony, or disclosure of the flight path to a bandit) in a situation that one knows will lead to the wrongful killing of an otherwise innocent being or victim, will incur the testifier the wrath of karma. The legalistic charges in the court of law may be mitigated against him, as might be the resulting suffering via the merciful intervention of a god or through penitence; but the *moral* burden of the act, as of each and every act, rests squarely on the shoulders of the individual rather than be left as a matter for judgment or adjudication, or pardon, by an external (human or divinely) punitive or be it benign agency. The application of the law may extend beyond the individual person to groups and even nations as well, as the great epic, the *Mahābhārata*, amply illustrates in its long and complex ethical ruminations. (An issue we shall return to again later.)

The ontological implication is that karma may involve one in an endless chain of actions, extending to the afterlife as well. Indeed, the unbroken chain necessitates, despite the falling away of the body at death, rebirth, for the bundle of psychic traces continues, as it were, existence of its own and helps to provide personal identity in the next birth. Although at this point one can rightly raise the objection that the chain of psychic traces only makes for psychological continuity on which identity can, indeed must, be hinged, but that this principle by itself does not lead to any assumptions about the afterlife. Nevertheless, for our purposes here, we shall take the principle in the context of the broader doctrine in question to be fundamentally a metaphysical postulate and as such not amenable to empirical deduction. Thus karma, in as much as karma leads to suffering, is taken to account for ontological evil. Rebirth, as a contingent corollary or entailment, or even as a presupposition of the theory of karma, (the direction of interpretation depends on which system or school one looks at), will not be my concern as such, although I am aware that writers like Arthur Herman have proposed rebirth as the Indian solution to the problem of evil. I will be more concerned to see how the idea of karma *per se* can have implications for the problem of evil and for theodicy at large. There are even some modal possibilities which will be worth considering in passing.

Another question arises here: Is the doctrine of karma fatalistic? Future circumstances issue from past and present choices. But the principle of moral reason tells us that there is a moral reason for past and present choices. Should we say that the moral reason does not completely *determine* present choices, but merely influence them? The problem with this response is that it may leave us with a world which is not fully morally intelligible but only partially so. Should we admit that determinism holds but deny that fatalism follows, as argued also by Western compatibilists? (Some of these issues have been discussed elsewhere.[9]) Let us, for the moment confine ourselves to the moral intelligibility question.

The theory of karma, according to Margaret Chatterjee, affirms at least three considerations: 'the potency of human action to bring about chains of consequences, the assumption that intelligibility includes the demand for justice, and the demand for a causal explanation of events (i.e. the demand that human actions, no less than natural event, be governed by law).'[10] The appeal to moral intelligibility in this and such accounts warrants some discussion, for the dead weight of much (modern) scholarship that largely highlights anthropological impact of the belief in karma, has only helped to obscure the peculiarity of the doctrine, which is firmly grounded in the presupposition that for an action x performed by me or at my instigation (such as, for instance, a sacrifice or *yajña* through an appointed priest), I and no one else is the ultimate beneficiary, or victim, of the act. We want to be provided with a moral rationale for the fundamental features of one's life – such as our general psychological predispositions, our social status, our susceptibility to this or that disease – and in such a way that would render the world *morally* intelligible also. The theory would not be of much value if it simply gave an account of action and

9 P. Bilimoria with P.A.E. Hutchings, 'On disregard for fruits – Kant and the *Gītā*', in P. Bilimoria and P. Fenner (eds), *Religions and Comparative Thought*, Delhi: Indian Books Centre, 1988, pp. 353-368. Arindam Chakrabarti, 'The Dark Mother Flying Kites: Sri Ramakrishna's Metaphysic of Morals', *Sophia*, **33** (3) , 1994, pp. 14-29.

10 Cited by Austin Creel in Neufeldt (ed.) [see note 8 above.] p. 2.

its consequences in those broad terms we are all too familiar with in respect of, say, action theory, psychologism or some versions of cognitive theory. As Daya Krishna puts it, 'The theory of *karma* as elaborated in the Indian tradition ... has to be seen not as a description of facts relating to human action, but as an attempt to render them intelligible in moral terms. This is the basic difference between intelligibility of nature and the intelligibility of the human world. The former may be rendered intelligible by postulating the notion of causality in phenomena, but that alone would not render intelligible the world of men. The latter is constituted by human actions ...'.[11] The solution to this problem in the Indian tradition according to Daya Krishna takes a distinctive turn when from the intuitively self-evident proposition that the world will be a morally unintelligible world if I were to reap the fruit of somebody else's action, or if someone else were to reap the fruit of my actions, it draws the conclusion that in order that the world be morally intelligible, we must live in a 'morally monadic' world. In other words, if 'moral intelligibility' requires that each human being should reap *only* the fruit of his (or her) *own* actions, then no human being, or any other being for that matter, can *really* affect anyone else, however much the appearances may seem to justify the contrary view. Nobody can *really* be the cause of my suffering or happiness, nor can I be the cause of suffering or happiness to anybody else. If I, or anyone else, seem to feel the opposite, that is an *illusion* which is to be rectified by cognitive reflection on the presuppositions involved in the notion of 'moral intelligibility' itself.

Daya Krishna's refreshingly forceful analysis suggests the following. The moral intelligibility requirement is to be identified with the principle of moral reason: there is a moral reason for everything that happens – i.e. everything that happens is morally fitting. (This does not imply that all actions are morally right or virtuous.) The law of karma then becomes a specific way of partially filling this out: good deeds lead to happiness, bad deeds to suffering: moreover good deeds lead to future good deeds, bad deeds to future bad deeds. But still, a number of things remain to be explained. For example, the principle does not say *when* my good deeds and bad deeds will have their effects: maybe later in this life, maybe in a next life, or maybe after a delay of a hundred branching lives somehow still traceable to the present identity (by virtue of moral responsibility or 'debts' stemming from past actions). But the requirement of moral intelligibility declares that there be an answer. Moreover, one can see why it is morally fitting that any present bad deeds have been caused by previous bad deeds. But why is it morally fitting that present bad deeds have, amongst their effects, future bad deeds?

One way to resolve this question is to consider myself as a monadic self in which incessant activity takes place, and so counterfactually no one else's actions can have any effect on me. Alternatively, I may think that I am deceived into believing that the actions are mine, when in fact they are entirely someone else's. Whichever route one takes, action would seem to imply both a psychophysical world of causality and

---

11 Daya Krishna, *Indian Philosophy – A Counter Perspective*, Delhi: Oxford University Press, 1991, p. 177.

some criteria of ascriptional identity as well as an interactive framework to meet the demands of 'moral intelligibility'. This much the theory of karma does presuppose. Here causality is seen in purely moral terms, as regulative (invariant) connectedness towards an end, roughly in the way in which Kant viewed bondage and freedom, and not in strict ontological terms. And in so far as the law of karma pertains to 'moral action' it tries to render the causality that reigns thereon 'morally intelligible'.[12]

But Daya Krishna is insistent that this line of thinking leads to the inevitability of moral monadism. However, I do not believe that 'moral monadism' in the strict sense need be a consequence of this theory, not because it generates the paradox of making morality in the usual sense impossible, but because I do not believe that it is a necessary condition of 'moral intelligibility' that no one else, or the other *qua* alterity, cannot or should not suffer the consequences of someone else's action. Daya Krishna indeed poses the moral of monadism initially – not in the Leibnizian modal world as it might appear to an unsuspecting reader, – but in the context of the performance of a Vedic *yajña*, as we briefly hinted at in an above instance. The Mīmāṃsā commentators on the efficacy of ritual could not countenance anyone else, not even the priest who physically performs the sacrifice while uttering the prescribed *mantras*, benefiting from the performatives which it is the entitlement of the *yajamān* or the high caste host to desire and decree. This monadic predisposition or rather cultural bias became infused with the discourse of karma which earlier on had no direct bearing on the ritualistic tendencies other than the general application of the view that any action is likely to have a remote effect. The bearer of the effect, either in theory or in practical experience, was not confined to the doer or the originator of the action, no more than that the suicide-detonation of a bomb on a passenger-aircraft would likely kill or severely injure or traumatize the bandit and not the others on board. The responsibility passes also onto those ground crew who had failed to detect the explosive device carried in by the bandit posing as a passenger. And how could it be otherwise, morally speaking? For again, as we saw Peter Forrest arguing, it makes perfect moral sense for our generation to feel responsible and therefore suffer for the crimes of our ancestors against the Aborigines. Even so, there is general conformity to the principle that suggests the impossibility of the 'non-perishability of what has been done, and non-receivability of what has not been done'.

But there is yet a problem left outstanding in the karma account, which we will flag and move to its attempted solution in theodicy : why did good and bad deeds come into existence in the first place? Were they the metaphysical inevitable result of the existence of desire? The principle of moral reason assures us that this cannot be the whole story: the existence of good and bad deeds must be morally fitting. But how can this be so? Maybe there was no 'first place': from all eternity there have been good and bad deeds. But merely postulating an infinite regress will not fulfil the demands of the principle of moral reason. We are reminded here of Leibniz's cosmological argument.

12 Ibid., p. 182.

Naturalist Theodicy

I now want to move on to draw out some of the implications of the discussion so far for the problem of theodicy. I will begin with non-theistic schools, where God's existence is not a given. I shall call them a/theological.

The 'a/theological' positions espoused by Buddhists, Jainas and Mīmāṃsakas of India, more or less, rely on the theory of karma to explain the persistence of moral evil (and they each prescribe different routes for escape from this evil condition, which culminates in nirvāṇa, or the attainment of lasting heavenly happiness). Whether one focuses on the cessation of suffering by checking the desire or intention that incites action (as in Buddhism and in Jainism), or by severely curtailing action (as in the ascetic-yogic tradition), or by engaging constantly in religious actions, i.e. rituals, that result in good ends (as in Mīmāṃsā), the consensus is that one does not have to go outside of the human condition to look for the cause and extinction of moral evil. Hence, there is no contradiction that, even in the best of possible worlds, good and evil co-exist, albeit in a dialectical tension. Evil, in this reading, is the limiting case for the good, the *śreyas*, that can be achieved, if one cares to go the root of the problem. The problem of evil is not explained away in this account, but is acknowledged and confronted as a challenge to render sentient life more meaningful and bearable. Indeed, the doctrine of karma on which it turns for its resolution provides a useful metaphor for an alternative perspective on the persistence of suffering, pain, and moral evil. Now this argument also forms the basis of the attack which the a-theologians in India make against those of theistic orientation who want to argue for God's existence and his omnipotence.

Before turning to this counterposition, let us formulate the argument as viewed from the a-theological position in propositional terms:

(a). there is suffering
(b). all suffering has an antecedent cause
(c). there are good deeds
(d). there are bad deeds
(e). suffering results from good and bad deeds, seamlessly
(f). therefore there is karma

The connecting presupposition is provided by moral reason: namely there is a moral reason for everything that happens, i.e. everything that happens is morally fitting. The background postulate is provided by the ideal of *nirvāṇa* (or *mokṣa*), with the consequence that evil is the lower limiting case of the good (not opposed to it), so that (d) becomes a sub-set of (c). Also, under (e) the suggestiveness of a remote or delayed mechanism in operation is rather packed and could be spelled out in a separate premise, but this is intended to be covered by the connecting premise of moral reason, the fitting clause as it were. Taken together, there is, then, no contradiction in affirming these propositions towards a consistent theodicy.

Theistic counter-position

The treatment of *duḥkha*, or pervasive suffering, and the attendant doctrine of karma in the preceding section should make it clear that Indian thinkers did not always advance the notion of an omnipotent and benevolent creator God as being in any way central to their faith, or as an effective explanation of the origin of the universe.[13] However, there have been schools of Indian thought that have put forward such a doctrine and also have formulated sophisticated arguments for the existence of God. We shall not detain ourselves with the details of these arguments[14] – save to note their central thrust and question the coherency of such arguments. An all-transcending Supreme Being is assumed to have the same role as that of a 'creator', although, we must be clear about this at the outset, *creatio ex nihilo* is nowhere a part of this assumption. Rather, most Indian theistic worldviews look upon the creator as the efficient cause after the 'model of the potter'. Nyāya-Vaiśesika has provided the most succinct framework for this view by arguing that God or *Īśvara* creates the world out of pre-existent matter, not unlike the Demiurge in Plato's *Timaeus*. The argument proceeds on the basis of the analogy of the agency involved in the production of an artefact, such as a pot from clay, and the appeal, as I just said, is to causality, since agency is one form of causality. As in the production of a ceramic pot, the clay brought from the river-bank is shaped on a revolving wheel, and the kneading of the clay as well as the motion of the wheel is traced back to some person, namely the potter. The argument is in respect of 'being-an-effect', which is causally linked to an agent. The validity or otherwise of this form of cosmological argument need not detain us,[15] but for the question of evil, to which it yet has to provide an answer. If there is pre-existent matter, in the form of indestructible atoms and so on, and God moves to bring them together in creating the world, where does evil creep in from and how is this consistent with God's omnipotence? For surely, God in his infinite power could have organized the constituents in such a way as to ensure that evil, moral evil that is, that manifests as pain and suffering, does not enter and blemish a product made presumably in the image of his own goodness and compassion? The persistence of evil, so the protagonists argue, seriously undermines the creativity and omnipotence of God.

Śaṅkara echoes similar objections in his *Brahmasūtrabhāṣya* (II.1.34) by arguing that the Lord-God cannot reasonably be ascribed with the cause of the world on the grounds of the contingency of his inequality and cruelty. For, he makes some – e.g. the gods, etc. – experience greatest happiness; others – e.g. beasts and the like – he makes suffer the greatest miseries; while others still – e.g. men etc. – he allows to experience (both these) in moderation. That the Lord should have created the world with such an unequal dispensation argues in His case the presence, as in

13 Matilal, op cit. p. 28.

14 For which see P. Bilimoria, 'Hindu Doubts About God – Towards a Mīmāṃsā Deconstruction', *International Philosophical Quarterly*, December 1990, **30** (4), pp. 481-499.

15 Ibid.

that of ordinary mortal, of love and hatred; and so there arises the contingency of a flat contradiction of the Lord's nature of passionlessness.[16] Then, again, there arises the contingency of compassionless and extreme cruelty – because he brings about visitations of sorrows and encompasses the destruction (at the final dissolution) of the entire creation – (a compassionless cruelty) for which even the most wicked conceive a loathing. Therefore, owing to this contingency of inequality and cruelty, the Lord cannot be the cause.[17]

Śaṅkara will of course refute this objection by bringing in the consideration of karma. But before we move to this particular thesis, I think it is worth recounting this objection in its more polemical form which the Mīmāṃsā has addressed. The objection takes on the form of the paradox of omnipotence that J.L. Mackie has articulated closer to our times (and reflected in the following passage):

> Can an omnipotent being make things which he cannot subsequently control? Or, what is practically equivalent to this, can an omnipotent being make rules which then bind himself?[18]

And here is the Mīmāṃsā version, which (possibly following the Buddhist Nāgārjuna) Kumārila Bhaṭṭa rails against the Nyāya view:

> At a time when all this (earth, water, etc.) did not exist, what could have been the condition of the universe? As for Prajāpati (the creator God) Himself, what could be His position? and what his form? (*Ślokavārttika* (= *SV*), s#44)[19]
>
> Then, again, in what manner do you believe the world to have a beginning in time? (If it be held that it is brought about by a desire on the part of Prajāpati, then) since Prajāpati is (held to be) without a material body, etc. how could He have any desire towards creation? (*SV*, s#45-47)

Evidently, what worries Kumārila is that we cannot have any notion of what the world was like prior to the supposed creation, and how it actually came about. How can we infer anything about that pristine state of affairs? Kumarila considers that in order to create a material and corporeal world, either there has to be some pre-existing substance, or Prajāpati has a material body which is not eternal and out of which he creates or 'emanates' the transient world, as a spider spins a web from its bowels. But why would a perfect and omnipotent God degrade Himself by working through a transient body? Of course, in the Nyāya view He does nothing of the sort: God simply directs the beginningless flux of atoms, dyads, triads, and the 'unseen

16 Ibid.

17 Ibid. See also discussion in P. Bilimoria, 'Hindu-Mīmāṃsā against scriptural evidence on God', in *Sophia*, **26** (1), 1989, pp. 20-31.

18 J.L. Mackie, 'Evil and Omnipotence', *Mind* (1955 vol. LXIV, pp. 200-212); Mackie reconsiders this paradox in his article on 'Omnipotence' in the first volume of *Sophia* 1 (2), July 1962, pp. 13-25.

19 *Ślokavārttika* of Kumārila; detailed texts and references are cited in 'Hindu Doubts about God', see notes 14-15 above.

efficiency' (*adṛṣṭa*), and through his all-extensive desire creates the world; he maintains a continuous relationship with the universe as its preserver, and dissolves the world when conditions require it to be dissolved. The mention or inclusion of 'unseen efficiency' is significant here, to which we shall return shortly.

One could contend, as the earlier Vaiśeṣika school (that developed an ontology taken over by Nyāya), that the unity and functioning of the world could be explained on the basis of the interaction or fusion-effect of the uncreated atoms (substances) and soulful desires. Taken in conjunction with the principle *of adṛṣṭa* or 'unseen efficiency' of *dharma* and *adharma* or merits and demerits, this would effectively rule out the necessity of God, who on this theory is at worst an embarrassment and at best redundant. Discrete *dharma* and *adharma* obviously allude to the pervasive functioning of karma. *Dharma* as the law that governs the functioning of karma is sufficient to account for the impersonal moral component of the universe. But the Nyāya take strong exception to this critique, not least because it panders to distributive justice and is not sufficient to account for retributive justice which, in their view, requires the keen judgement of an uninterestedly detached conscious or personal agency (a disposition that even the effervescent deities of Mīmāṃsā ritualism cannot be entrusted with). The Nyāya turn the argument around to help resolve the contradiction unleashed by the problem of moral evil.

Death of God: The Moral Argument

But let us outline the Mīmāṃsā objection which invokes the problem of evil more fundamentally as we move towards Nyāya's moral rejoinder. The objection is essentially about the characteristic of omnipotence attributed to God, thus: 'Then, again, in the first place, how is it that He should have a desire to create a world which is to be fraught with all sorts of troubles to living beings? For at the time (of the beginning of creation) He has not any guiding agencies, in the shape of virtue (or sin) etc., of the living beings themselves. (*SV* s# 67).

He also considers the suggestion that the Lord might have created the world out of pity. Again, he is puzzled, and wonders for whom God would have pity or compassion on in the absence of beings (prior to creation) (*SV* s#52). Or again, if God were so moved by sheer compassion (for whomever), why did He not create just happy beings or an everlasting happy world? Was he impotent in this respect? Perhaps, as some suggest, God created the world merely for his own amusement or 'play' (*līlā*), as the Vedānta maintains; and this is often the view narrated in folklore and mythology, in the *purāṇas*, *the Bhāgavata*, and so on. Such a God to Kumārila would be an incredibly selfish being, calling upon Himself a good deal of approbium. What a wearisome toil to create a world full of pain and adversity merely for 'sport' or 'amusement', and how can this lead Him to be self-fulfilled and infinitely content? One supposes that here Kumārila is questioning the claim to perfection in God, who nonetheless must resort to an imperfect creation to find lasting fulfilment. Would an artist find self-esteem in his imperfect productions?

The objections basically rehearse the same difficulties as sketched earlier in the passage from Śaṅkara – i.e. how does one explain the overwhelming fact of pain and life of disproportionate adversities or suffering (*duḥkha*), and the cyclical recurrence of death after death (*saṃsāra*). But there is something more happening in this rebuttal which might have escaped us: namely it is addressing yet another postulate which appeals to a moral consideration that Nyāya believes might help preserve the good intentions of God. This actually amounts to a moral argument, namely, the necessity to account for the dispensation of the fruits of actions, which result from people's previous merits and demerits. Unless, the Nyāya argues, there was an all-knowing and intelligent but dispassionate agent, how could we conceive this state of affairs to be possible? The suggestion is that actions create the unseen efficiency (*adṛṣta*), but that in itself is an inert property which continues into the life hereafter. Uddyotkara further suggests that the merit and demerit of the dead people need to be activated by an intelligent agent. Only being activated by an intelligent agent, do the elements (earth, fire, water) up to the realm of ether operate in their respective functions. In other words, there has to be a superintendent being such as God who arranges a person's rebirth and dispenses the appropriate results in the newly-born karmic body. (This is not unlike the moral grounds on which Kant finds himself postulating the dispensatory-transcendental presence of the otherwise empirically-absent God.) So God is supposed to be the comptroller and distributor of justice, reward and punishment, and He creates the world accordingly.[20] The intelligibility spoken of is not only in respect of retributive justice, but frays somewhat into distributive justice as well, for such a merciful God might just decide to make some quick adjustments and tip the scale of justice that would help the hitherto more disadvantaged (or 'wretched') individuals (non-humans entities included) to come up to the level of the more attained and karmically affluent person-entities.

Śaṅkara likewise turns to this reasoning to argue that were the Lord to create this world, with all its inequalities, without regard to any such consideration, then he would be guilty of the dual faults of inequality and cruelty. But that is not how he functions. He creates the world along with its inequalities *after* having shown due consideration. What is that to which he shows due consideration? Answer: It is to the merit and demerit. This looks to be circular; nonetheless Śaṅkara opines: the inequality, etc. in the creatures is due to no fault of God Himself. God is the common cause, like rain that constitutes the common cause for the production of a variety of crops, like rice, barley, etc., and the actions, karma, appertaining to the various souls serve as the special causes for the same (II.i.34). And so, he concludes, the Lord is not compromised in his power and transcendental status for dispensing rewards and punishments in due consideration of the specific actions of beings, etc. as is said in the *Bhagavadgītā*.

Of course, Śaṅkara is aware that the argument presupposes the prior existence of karma, i.e. prior even to the creation of the world. What evidence do we have that there is such a repository or dormant bank of karma, the unseen effectuality, in

20 Matilal, op cit., p. 29.

which each bundle is stamped with its distinct individual identity? Why could it not be the case that traces of karma simply dissipate at death and mingle with fire and air as the body burns on the pyre? (The Australian Aborigines seem to have a view of the unseen force that has the function of accounting for the individual's suffering and pleasures as he or she moves through life on earth, but this force, in this view, terminates with death and has no effect beyond that.)

Is it highly speculative of Śaṅkara and Vedānta generally to suppose that (a) karma continues beyond this life; (b) that even after the dissolution of the universe, karma somehow remains intact. We remarked earlier on (a), but Śaṅkara has a reply to (b) which, though not at all empirical, helps him to retain a consistent metaphysical narrative. He remarks that if the kind of differentiation which karma generates were absent at the beginning, we would be compelled to posit the *first* creation as being free from all inequalities. But Vedānta is categorically of the view that this transmigratory-creation (*saṃsāra*) is beginningless, just as the world is without a beginning, and between karma and inequality there is an endless chain of cause-effect relation – as with seed and its sprout – hence, here is no contradiction in the good Lord's creativity and omnipotence (I.II.35).

But what is interesting in both the Nyāya and the Vedānta arguments we have just considered is that neither thinks that 'God's alleged omnipotence is incompatible with His dependence upon other factors in creation.' It is probably allowed that he could have done otherwise or chose not to. Or, it may be argued that omnipotence is compatible with acting according to a rule or law. (Even) God in his creation abides by the law of *Karma* and *avidyā* (or ignorance). This amounts to saying that God's omnipotence is bound by ethico-causal and logical laws. Therefore, contrary to the general belief that the solution of the problem of evil, according to Vedānta, lies in the assertion that evil (and the world) is an illusion, it is clear from the above that both Vedānta and [Nyāya]-Vaiśeṣika are prepared to accept that God's omnipotence is limited or even that God does not actually create this world and human souls, out of nothing.'[21]

The apparent resemblance to the (Western) compatibilist theories notwithstanding, Mackie's classic paradox haunts the attempted solution in another way. Let us suppose God in creating the world – whether he did so a finite time ago or from all eternity – co-operated with other factors which he did not create, such as atoms of matter. Let us also suppose that God is constrained by the law of karma, two questions remain: (i) Could God have ensured that there were no bad deeds, and if not, why not? (ii) Why is it morally fitting that the history of the universe contain any bad deeds at all? The response from the Indian side, although unsatisfactory, would be that, yes, God could have ensured that there were no bad deeds, but in his infinite wisdom he let (so to speak) the dice roll; and secondly, that a universe equal to God's own supreme identity is not conceivable for that would be no universe at all as we know and experience it. (The latter is not unlike Leibniz's principle that God would not create two indiscernibly identical things.) Thus, God created the best of all

21 Ibid., p 30.

possible worlds, in the maximal moral sense, and his omniscience, though perhaps not his omnipotence, is not compromised in any way. This is not incompatible with the Middle Knowledge position. (The Buddhists likewise were anguished more about the charges against the omniscience of the Enlightened Buddha than about his omnipotence; this particular disentanglement of omnipotence from omniscience in Indian thought is worth noting, but not an issue that can be gone into here.)

We are now in a position to formulate the Indian theist's argument as follows (borrowing and modifying the Plantinga-Langtry schema):

(a) There exists a perfectly good God
(b) There are 10^{13} turps of evil in the world
(c) All the evil in the world is moral (i.e. ontological) evil due to the prior karma of sentient beings, defeasibly and seamlessly so.

The connecting supposition is provided by the pre-existent moral law of nature, i.e. *karma*, along with the auxiliary hypothesis of *adṛṣta* the 'unseen efficiency', as God is said to operate in full knowledge of what each being's residual merit and demerit accounts are, but the mechanism for the retributive operations are left entirely or autonomously to the law of karma.

The Indian theist would argue that he has successfully clarified and reconciled the premises that inform his belief; that rather than denying God's perfect nature (and thereby explaining away his existence), he has made God's creation supervene on another independent principle. Since God is not held morally responsible for creating an imperfect world out of nothing (which he claims not to have) and since he does not create human souls as agents endowed with absolute freedom, the erstwhile problem of evil does not present logical difficulty of the kind that has beleaguered many a theodicy.

We cannot, however, leave this disputation without giving the final word to the Mīmāṃsā, who has grave doubts about the virtue and propriety of appropriating the law of karma to, as it were, save 'the face of God' against the threat posed by the ubiquitous problem of evil. I will simply state two objections the Mīmāṃsā makes to the Moral Argument. While agreeing with the Nyāya and Vedānta that in the absence of actions of human beings there would be *no unseen efficiency (adṛṣta)*, and hence no result or fruits, the Mīmāṃsā repeats the question, why would God, who is supposed to be impartial to all creatures, act in such a way as to bring about disproportionate fruits? Why would a kind and loving God allow such an iniquitous situation? If *dharma* (merits and demerits) were absolutely under His control, why should there be persistent pain (in the world)? The question implies another question: does he not have a plan to help the souls work through their karma and bring this deplorable situation to a speedy end?

If, on the one hand, the activity of the world were to be dependent upon (i.e. regulated by) these (*dharma*, etc.), then this would entail accepting something else (i.e. an agency other than God's desire). But this would also deprive God of His independence. If on the other hand we accept God's will or desire, this would undermine the law of karma; that notwithstanding, God's will still must have a cause (if it is to activate *dharma-adharma*). In that case, we might as well accept the *adṛṣṭa* as the cause of everything and the law of karma as the autonomous regulating-dispensatory agency functioning independently of any personal agent. Otherwise, as Hume would put it later on in a similar dispute, since there is so much pain and suffering, which is not good or morally desirable, we have to assume either two world-powers, one working for the good and the other evil, or else a single morally neutral creator.

Underscoring the case for the independent operation of karma, Kumārila asks, is it so inconceivable that people's own actions could directly bring about results? Is not the law of karma a sufficient postulate to explain the process of dispensation? And if the law of karma is inexorable, then what is the place and necessity of God? Or, alternatively, if God is so powerful, can He not annul that law? Moreover, if there were some end absolutely essential to be achieved, could not God achieve this without needing to create the world, a world which he then so brutally destroys?

Here I cannot but help noting a poignant observation made by Bruce Langtry in the context of the present discussion:[22] The view which dispenses with God can usefully be compared with the neo-Platonist view, defended by John Leslie. According to Leslie, the universe exists because it is morally required, or fitting, that it exist. Moral requirements of themselves have causal efficacy. We need not suppose that there exists an omnipotent personal agent to recognize what is morally required and bring it about. If we do continue to use the word 'God' we should do so in a new sense: the word does not denote a *being* but rather the causal power possessed by moral principles. Leslie's view encounters an obvious objection: it is logically impossible that an abstract principle should possess causal power.

As we have noted, even the Indian theist has no difficulty in accepting that abstract principles have causal power (otherwise the 'Big Bang' theory would have to be discounted also). His only difficulty with this view is that it lacks a morally causative force, and that even if the Mīmāṃsā argument were to be admitted, it still lacks a justly retributive force (as distinct from an indiscriminate distributive compulsion). Hence it is that some Nyāya writers would happily embrace a middle position by suggesting that God merely creates the auxiliary causes by which justice is dispensed in the world. The world comes about as a result of the merits and demerits, the good and bad action of human beings; it assumes a continuous creation in which actions of people have as much part as any grand design for the world. This, again, looks uncannily close to Mackie's proposition of Omnipotence (which, of course, he rejects for its incoherency), which does not do away with the paradox of omnipotence but helps to transmute the severity of the objection. Or it comes close to the position Terence Penelhum has defended, namely, that in so far as there is any evil in the world, it is a derivative part of God's design for a purposeful world. God puts in place certain contrary and contradictory processes so that the tension leads

22 Private communication.

to more creative, rather than simply destructive, outcomes. In this way, the desired *telos* is fulfilled.

Of course, as we noticed a little earlier, Śaṅkara would have little difficulty with one part of this suggestion, namely, that the world too can be credited with having come about as a result of the merits and demerits of human souls. God is simply a demiurge and like the good architect helps to facilitate the process. But he is still needed for at least this task and for the purposes of overseeing a just and fair retribution process, in the long run at least. Does such a functionary need to be omnipotent and even good? Omnipotent in the derivative sense, or the second-order Omnipotence, will not suffice, for this is not a coherent proposition, and omnipotent in the strong sense is ruled out by the theory.

This indeed is the impasse, and discussions within the tradition do not seem to move much past this point as the paradox is too obvious to all the participants in the debate. The resolution beyond this logical hurdle often depends on tearing down the road of faith, or deferring to the pronouncements of scriptures, or simply reinscripting a root (*mūla*) metaphysical proposition, such as 'Brahman is All' – i.e. recourse to an impersonal transcendental principle (much like the faceless *Nothingness*) of which even Anselm's supposed fool would not be seduced into asking : 'Why, if you are all loving and caring, you have created a world full of evil?' Or one may turn to a benevolent deity, *Īśvara*, or *Saguṇa* Brahman (the One with a personal face), as the second-order Omnipotence, who too depends on the law of karma to provide moral regulative order to the world. But such a God cannot be said to compete with first-order Truth, and so falls short of the full explanatory power to allow the argument to go through.

In conclusion, I am left with the following question: Is karma a convenient fiction, as some believe it to be, or perhaps a heuristic device, which even if it does not resolve the problem of evil, becomes a morally helpful principle for guiding human action, i.e. an instrument towards stimulating effort at good action (increasing pleasure and joy) and avoiding bad action (decreasing pain and suffering)? Could this be the Indian discovery of Consequentialism, without the hard-headedness of classical utilitarianism? It appears also to have a therapeutic value and serves as a good metaphor adduced to account for suffering of all kinds, gratuitous evil included. At least, now speaking anthropologically, that seems to have been the basis of its appeal not least in much of Asia, now in pockets of the modern West too. But as a philosophical enigma, I must admit, it can only be seen as a project that needs much more in terms of explication, clarification, and debate before its intelligibility as a moral principle is made fully transparent.

The other major problem with it is that 'the doctrine of karma contains within it an inescapable core of *evaluation*, and it is the received wisdom of Western culture', as Penelhum notes, 'that no evaluative elements belong to the understanding of the way the natural world is structured'. We don't expect the law of gravitation to yield to judgments of good and bad. The doctrine might be confusing descriptive with prescriptive laws, that is, it is too legalistic or legislative, and indeed even fatalistic or deterministic, when the real challenge that faces us is – using an existentialist phrase – our throwness in freedom. But to dismiss the doctrine of karma as fatalistic, (*pace* Penelhum), seems equally confused, since it is of the essence of the doctrine to maintain that our future circumstances issue from past and present choices, though not in a strict deterministic sense either. One has to appreciate that the doctrine is a logical consequence of an understanding of the universal order as an intrinsically retributive one. Otherwise, the world of human actions would appear to be morally unintelligible. That there might be something flawed in this understanding and perception is quite another matter, and even further difficulties arise when one begins to reconcile various other beliefs with this, such as the Hindu conception of the self and the transcendent, personal God vis-à-vis the impersonal absolute, rebirth or afterlife, and so on. This is exactly where certain fundamental weaknesses become apparent, which – as I have tried to show – run deep into the attempted solution to the challenges of theodicy. But for all this, as Weber too was moved to comment, it is a rather elegant theodicy, or a/theodicy.

Chapter 8

Dāna as a Moral Category

Maria Heim

Indian systems of learning have extensively theorized the gift (*dāna*) as a means of investigating moral practices and virtues. The Sanskrit word *dāna*, translated as gift, generosity, gift-giving, alms, and hospitality, describes a key religious practice of making merit as well as a central social value of hospitality widely affirmed in South Asian religions. *Dāna* attracted considerable interest in premodern traditions of Indic thought among *Dharmaśāstra*, Jain, and Buddhist scholars. In these traditions, *dāna* was treated as part of a branch of knowledge called *ācāra*, that is, the systematic investigation of moral and religious custom or practice.

In contrast to the prolific theoretical attention to the gift in South Asian traditions, it has not been until recently that modern western philosophers have begun to explore the rich ethical possibilities of the gift (although it was a category of moral reflection by ancient philosophers from the western traditions, perhaps most notably by Seneca). In modern western circles, the topic of the gift has been taken up mostly by anthropologists, stimulated by Marcel Mauss's classic 1925 essay on the gift which demonstrated the usefulness of analyzing the gift as a basic category of culture. More recently philosophers and scholars from other disciplines are reexamining Mauss and his assumptions about gift exchange, and what they suggest about human nature, sociality, and ethics.[1] Examination of premodern discourses on *dāna* can fruitfully join these larger conversations to further moral inquiry on several fronts.

Specifically, medieval Sanskrit and Pali discourses on the gift draw our notice to the face-to-face hospitality encounter. They locate in the gift relationship a locus for considering ethical questions concerning motivation: should gifts be given freely without return, or are they based on reciprocity and obligation? What are the dispositions that should accompany gift giving? What is the moral response of the recipient? Does gratitude play an essential role in the gift relationship? The South Asian gift theorists considered here also draw our attention to the formal properties of the gift, to etiquette and ritual, and how they structure moral agency in gift giving. They also consider ways in which the gift is an index and marker of status, constituting and reaffirming idealized hierarchy and difference.

1 Several volumes from different disciplines that explore the ethics of the gift have recently come to press (Komter, 1996; Coles, 1997; Schrift, 1997; Starobinsky, 1997; Derrida, 1992, 1995, 1997, 2000; Vandevelde, 2000).

When the Indic authors conceive of *dāna* as a distinctive category of moral and religious practice that warrants systematic treatment, they put it forth as an object of second-order reflection. The gift is a site for formulating moral reflection in a context-sensitive manner and provides a way of analyzing moral values within a certain well-defined sphere of human activity. This contextual approach proceeds by analysis of particular encounters and relationships to consider the ethics of a face-to-face morality. A context-sensitive[2] approach to morality has both benefits and limitations. Among its limitations is that moral reflection on the gift is not likely to yield a comprehensive or categorical philosophical system that covers every aspect of the moral life. The qualities of a generous donor may not alone exhaust the range of virtues a moral agent should have. Nor is the study of the gift or other situated moral practices likely to generate universal principles or moral laws true for all times and all places.

However, studying the ways in which Indic traditions have theorized particular moral practices and situated moral agency can lead to insights that might slip by a quest for categorical principles. Certain reflections on the gift encounter are concerned with those responses of moral agents which are, by their very nature, unmediated by impartial and universal moral laws. Their focus is on the virtues and dispositions that prompt moral response between persons in a face-to-face encounter.

Bernard Williams has argued that there are some encounters among moral agents that should not be mediated by a quest for general principles, but instead are conceived as responses that virtuous agents automatically make when confronted with a certain type of situation or person. He invites us to consider the case of a man in a situation in which he can save only one of two drowning victims, one of whom is a beloved spouse and the other a stranger. Surely no one would condemn the man for saving his wife over the stranger. But Williams argues in addition that if the man were to attempt to seek out a general moral principle by which to motivate or justify his partiality, other than simply recognizing that it is his wife and jumping in to save her, then he has constructed 'one thought too many.'[3] Some types of moral situations describe relations of partiality and immediacy in which attempting to construct general principles may, in fact, be inappropriate.

The *dāna* theories similarly focus on relationships of partiality and the moral agency of responsiveness in certain highly specified contexts. The discourses on the gift discussed in this essay analyze the dispositions of a generous donor, the qualities of an appropriate recipient, and the ways in which the ritual etiquette of the gift gives rise to ideal moral response. They delineate a particular domain of moral space – the face-to-face relationship between giver and recipient – as a source for ethical reflection.

---

2 See A.K. Ramanujan (1989) on this Indic preference for context-sensitive moral deliberation, and Charles Hallisey (1996, 1997) on ethical particularlism. Hallisey describes a refusal in some forms of Theravada moral discourse to generalize across particular cases and to generate universal or generally applicable moral principles.

3 Williams, 1981, pp. 17-18.

South Asian Discourses on the Gift

South Asian theorists investigated the topic of the gift in a variety of genres. The most systematic indigenous gift theory from premodern South Asia traditions is the *Dharmaśāstra dānanibandha* literature. These are books on gift giving, starting in the eleventh century CE with Lakṣmīdhara's *Dānakāṇḍa*, that take the form of compendia or anthologies of material from earlier sources. Some of these books are quite extensive – Hemadri's thirteenth-century *nibandha* on *dāna* extends well over a thousand pages in the printed edition. Another important book on *dāna* is Ballalasena's *Sea of Giving* (*Dānasāgara*, 1168 C.E.) which aims to provide an exhaustive account of the rules and values of *dāna* in over seven hundred pages.[4] The medieval commentaries, the *Mitākṣarā* and Apararka's commentary on *Yājñavalkyasmṛti* also treat *dāna* in considerable detail.

These medieval *nibandhas* and commentaries systematize and analyze the rules associated with gift giving. To be sure, various rules and practices of *dāna*, especially the offering of gifts to brahmans, were also discussed in the classic *Dharmaśāstra* works, such as *Manusmṛti, Yājñavalkyasmṛti*, and in the Śānti and Anuśāsana *parvans* of the *Mahābhārata*. It is in the medieval period, however, that the topic of *dāna* comes to be treated systematically as a category of sustained analysis with entire books devoted to it. The *nibandhas* draw from earlier *purāṇas* and *śāstras* to describe the moral and religious requirements of the donor and the recipient, to prescribe the correct etiquette and procedure of giving, and to classify all the various types of gifts. Their commentaries, as well as their choices of organization, inclusion, and omission, provide a theoretical analysis of the essential values of gift giving. This extensive body of material presents us with premodern inquiry into one of South Asia's most central social and religious practices.

Dāna is a virtue and practice that was widely shared across religious systems in premodern South Asia. It was discussed at length by Buddhists and Jains as well as Hindus, and is a major translocal cultural idiom that attracted the interest of religious thinkers quite broadly. In Jainism, the articulation of ideals concerning gift giving occupies a substantial portion of the extensive medieval *śrāvakācāra* literature, that is, the books and commentaries concerned with the correct moral and religious behaviour of the laity.[5] Similarly, Theravāda Buddhists also developed books devoted to articulating the ethical conduct of lay people, which also treat *dāna*

---

4 Other *nibandhas* on *dāna* include the *Dānaratnakara* of Candeśvara (c. 1300–1370), the *Dānaratna* or *Dānavivekoddyota* of Madanasimha (c. 1425), the *Dānasāra* of Dalapati (c. 1500), the *Dānakriyākaumudī* of Govindānanda (c. 1500), the *Dānamayūkha* of Bhaṭṭa Nīlakaṇṭha (c. 1625), and the *Dānaprakāśa* of Mitra Miśra (c. 1625). For a complete listing of the *dāna* treatises see 'Note D' of K.V. Rangaswami Aiyangar's 'Introduction,' *Dānakāṇḍa*, Baroda: Gaekwad's Oriental Series 91.

5 The Jain *śrāvakācāra* literature is extensive. Hemacandra's *Yoga-śāstra* and *Svopajñavṛtti* treats *dāna* carefully, as does Devendrasūri's *Śrāddhadinakṛtya*, and Siddhasena Gaṇin's commentary on the *Tattvārtha Sūtra*, among others. There is also a small book devoted to *dāna* called the *Dānādiprakaraṇa*, and the narrative collection, the *Dānāṣṭakakathā*.

systematically.[6] Like the *Dharmaśāstra nibandha* authors the Jains and Buddhists set forth *dāna* as an object of sustained analysis and reflection.

In a less systematic way but no less prolifically, *dāna* has also been explored in narrative literature. Stories of great gifts occur in the epics and *purāṇas* as well as collections of narratives in both Sanskrit and the vernaculars. Buddhist and Jain story collections investigate the ambiguities and moral conundrums associated with gift giving. Such ambiguities are perhaps most pointedly explored in the well-known *jātaka* story of Prince Vessantara, who gave away his wife and children to attain perfect spiritual awakening. Although not considered here, the narrative literatures from all of these traditions sometimes affirm and sometimes challenge the conclusions of the systematic gift discourses in critical ways.

South Asian Gift Theories

A generous donor

Perhaps more than anything else the term *dāna* invokes the paradigm of the householder at the door offering alms to the monk, nun, or brahman. *Dāna* defines the chief religious practice of the religious laity in these traditions as well as one of the primary interactions between lay people and the religious elite. One of the most intriguing aspects of the ideal *dāna* is its lack of reciprocity. Gifts from lay people to brahmans, monks, or nuns are one-way transactions, and no return, even in the form of gratitude, is expected. This particularly Indic lack of balanced reciprocity in gift giving arrangements, a feature noticed by Mauss and puzzled over by many anthropologists since, places unreciprocated *dāna* against the widely posited 'moral norm of reciprocity' that some scholars have considered a basic principle of social life.[7] This feature suggests that *dāna* was not regarded as a means for strengthening social ties through mutual and balanced exchange, and that ideally *dāna* is not motivated by reciprocity.

The lack of gratitude in the *dāna* relationship is also striking. While gratitude (*kṛtajña*, literally, 'knowing what was done') is extolled elsewhere in these traditions, it does not figure in *dāna* theory. In contrast, the Roman philosopher Seneca framed much of his treatise on the gift in terms of gratitude. Seneca does not hold, like Mauss, that all gifts should be reciprocated, but he does insist that gratitude is the natural response to benefits. For Seneca, the gift relation secures the bonds of human fellowship that are violated and disrupted by ingratitude: 'there is nothing that so effectually disrupts and destroys the harmony of the human race as this vice.'[8] As

---

6 The Pali *Saddhammopāyana*, the *Sāratthasamuccaya*, the *Suttasangahaṭṭhakathā*, and the *Upāsakajanālaṅkāra* all treat *dāna* in the context of describing the morality of the householder.

7 See Gouldner, 1960.

8 Seneca, 1958, p. 241.

with Mauss, a sense of social obligation that expresses balance and harmony is the key feature of the gift relation; gift giving is properly an exchange of some sort.

Another striking feature of *dāna* ideology is its emphasis on giving to worthy recipients (*supātra*). Indeed, the entire ethical structure of religious giving depends upon the social and religious superiority of the recipient. Gifts should be given to worthy ones, in particular highly esteemed brahmans or monastics. It is considered far more meritorious to give to the religious elite out of esteem, than to give to the poor and needy out of pity. The medieval theorists considered here preferred to conceive of *dāna* less as charity (in the modern sense of giving to the needy) than as a means of offering tribute, an act of veneration or homage to the recipient.

These two distinctive features – the lack of mutuality and the giving to superiors – raise questions of motivation. What prompts a lay person to give gifts? The *Dharmaśāstra nibandhas* extend much energy on this issue, analyzing at length the different kinds of gifts that articulate the various motivations, attitudes, and dispositions of the giver. They describe two possible causes of *dāna*: esteem (*śraddhā*) and devotion (*bhakti*),[9] and six motivational grounds for *dāna*: one gives out of Dharma, [self-]interest, passion, shame, happiness, and fear.[10] The Dharmaśāstra *nibandhas* speak of the best gift of all being a *dharmadāna*, defined as 'that which is given constantly to worthy recipients without regard to any ends, only with the thought of giving up.'[11]

The Jains provide varying lists of the donor's virtues. The Śvetāmbara commentator Siddhasenagaṇin says that the giver should lack ill will toward the recipient, lack sorrow at parting with the gift, lack contempt (or condescension) for the recipient, be joyful while anticipating, giving, and remembering the gift, have good intentions, disregard worldly fruits, lack deception and lack motive.[12] The Digambaras formulated a standard list of seven qualities of a donor: esteem (*śraddhā*), devotion, contentment, zeal, discrimination, disinterestedness, and forbearance or patience.[13]

The Pali Buddhist sources extol the virtues of the donor in a variety of ways. One list describes the five gifts of a good person: such a person gives with esteem (*saddhā*), with due honor, in a timely fashion, with a mind that holds nothing back,

---

9 These are the two *hetu* of *dāna* (*Dānasāgara*, p. 28, verse 3; Cf. *Dānakhaṇḍa*, p. 14 and *Dānakāṇḍa*, p. 5).

10 *Dharmam arthañ ca kāmañ ca vrīḍāharṣabhayāni ca / adhiṣṭhānāni dānānāṃ ṣaḍ etāni pracakṣate* (*Dānasāgara*, p. 28, verse 4; Cf. *Dānakhaṇḍa*, p. 14 and *Dānakāṇḍa*, pp. 5-6).

11 *pātrebhyo dīyate nityam anapekṣya prayojanam / kevalam tyāgabuddhyā yad dharmadānaṃ tad ucyate* (*Dānasāgara*, p. 28, verse 5; Cf. *Dānakhaṇḍa*, p. 14 and *Dānakāṇḍa*, p. 5).

12 *dātṛviśeṣaḥ pratigrahītaryanasūyā tyāge 'viṣāadaḥ aparibhāvita ditsato dadato dattvataś ca prītiyogāḥ kuśalābhisandhitā dṛṣṭaphalānapekṣitā nirupadhatvam anidānatvam iti* (Siddhasenagaṇin's commentary on the *Tattvārtha Sūtra*, p. 120).

13 Williams, 1963, p. 153.

and without reducing the gift.[14] Another list says that a good person gives with due honor, intentionally, with his own hand, does not give leftovers, and gives whenever a guest approaches.[15]

One disposition that occurs regularly in the *dāna* texts in all three traditions to describe the appropriate qualities of the donor is *śraddhā* (*saddhā* in Pali), and it would not be overstating the case to say that language of *śraddhā* thoroughly pervades medieval *dāna* theory. The *Dharmaśāstra* writers emphasize *śraddhā* by treating it as a special topic of analysis in their compendia.[16] Though often translated as 'faith' or 'confidence,' *śraddhā* seems to have a different and more specialized meaning in the context of *dāna*.

The *Dharmaśāstra* definition of *dāna* involves giving in terms of *śraddhā*: '*dāna* is the presenting of wealth with *śraddhā* when a worthy recipient has arrived.'[17] *Śraddhā* is defined as 'when someone is full of good will and is cheerful, and so on, at the sight of recipients and is welcoming and unbegrudging (*anasūyā*).'[18] Ballālasena says that *śraddhā* means the lack of spite, *anasūyā*, where spite is defined as 'uncovering faults where there is virtue.'[19] The *dāna nibandhas* all state that one should give out of high regard for a respected recipient, with a pleased mind and without ill will.[20] A donor should give unquestioningly, cheerfully, and without

14 *Pañc'imāni bhikkhave sappurisadānāni. Katamāni pañca? Saddhāya dānam deti, sakkaccaṃ dānaṃ deti, kālena dānaṃ deti, anaggahitacitto dānaṃ deti, attānañ ca parañ ca anupahacca dānaṃ deti* (*Upāsakajanālaṅkāra*, pp. 295-96; *Suttasangahaṭṭhakathā*, p. 11).

15 *Pañc'imāni bhikkhave, sappurisadānāni. Katamāni pañca? Sakkaccaṃ deti, cittīkatvā deti, sahatthā deti, anapaviddhaṃ deti, āgamanadiṭṭhiko deti* (*Upāsakajanālaṅkāra*, p. 295 from A.iii.172).

16 *Dānasāgara*, pp. 32-33; *Dānakhaṇḍa*, pp. 84-87.

17 *arthānām udite pātre śraddhāya pratipādanam / dānaṃ ity abhinirdiṣṭaṃ vyākhyānaṃ tasya vakṣyate* (*Dānasāgara*, p. 28, verse 1; *Dānakāṇḍa*, p. 5 has *pratipāditam* for *pratipādanam*).

18 *saumukhyādyabhisamprītir arthināṃ darśane yadā / satkṛtiś cānasūyā ca tadā śraddheti kīrtyate* (*Dānasāgara*, p. 29, verse 15; *Dānakāṇḍa*, p. 6; *Dānakhaṇḍa*. p. 15). Compare with *Mitākṣarā* (on Yāj. 203) which glosses *dāna* as 'purified by *śraddhā* (*śraddhāpūtam*)' as 'made pure by *anasūyā*.'

19 *asuyā ca guṇe doṣāviṣkāraḥ* (*Dānasāgara*, p. 30). Hacker (1963) and Köhler (1973) have also noted the frequency of the gloss *anasūyā*, lack of spite or envy, for *śraddhā* in the context of *dāna*. Köhler argues that *śraddhā* in the context of hospitality relations indicates giving with delight (Spendefreudigkeit) and that the emphasis on *anasūyā* entails 'not being envious of the privileges of other men and not mentioning the faults of other men' (Köhler, 1973, pp. 59-60). Jamison argues that *śraddhā* suggests the 'unquestioning hospitality' owed to a guest (Jamison, 1996, p. 178).

20 *dānadharmaṃ niṣeveta nityam aistipaurttikam / parituṣṭena bhāvena pātram āsādya śaktitaḥ // yat kiñcid api dātavyaṃ yācitenānasūyāya / utpatsyate hi tat pātram yattārayati sarvaśaḥ // yena yena tu bhāvena yad yad dānaṃ prayacchati / tat tat tenaiva bhāvena prāpnoti pratipūjitaḥ // dānaṃ hi bahumānād yo guṇavadbhyaḥ prayacchati / sa tu pretya dhanaṃ labdhvā putrapautraiḥ sahāśnute* (*Dānasāgara*, p. 33; *Dānakāṇḍa*, pp. 10-11; *Dānakhaṇḍa*, p. 17).

looking for weaknesses in the recipient. The donor should never give with contempt toward the recipient.[21] A Jain author agrees: 'great people should accept the virtues and ignore the faults as geese drink the milk and leave the water; for this is the nature of those who are pure.'[22] Such a mind is not tainted with evil thoughts and is generous and charitable.[23]

The singular importance attached to esteem in Indic gift theory suggests that discriminating admiration is a key feature of South Asian moral thinking worth further investigation. *Śraddhā* describes an impulse of uncritical receptivity and responsiveness to the recipient. The emphasis on pleasure, delight and welcoming in the sentiment suggests that giving is ideally done in a manner that exceeds obligation and duty, and issues from a spontaneous sense of good will. It is a curious blend of discernment and recognition (in order to identify a worthy recipient), while at the same time it is a generous response unmediated by 'one thought too many.' Additionally, since the response of *śraddhā* is connected to recognition of the excellence of the other, it also brings one face-to-face with one's difference from the other in a posture of deference. In some Theravāda sources this difference is rendered explicit by passages with link *śraddhā* (Pali, *saddhā*) with shame.[24] The giver becomes aware of difference and his or her own unworthiness in the gift encounter.

That esteem is at the heart of gift giving explains why reciprocity and gratitude do not figure in the morality of *dāna*. *Dāna* depicts a particular human relationship that is to be free of the gnaw of obligation and return. If esteem is the principal sentiment in giving, then the gift is *not* conceived in terms of mutuality and balance in human relations, for esteem is unidirectional and hierarchical. Esteem cannot be returned without its changing into something else, such as mutual regard. Seneca would be puzzled by *dāna* ideology. On the one hand, he too values esteem in gift

---

21 *nāvajñayā pradātavyaṃ kiñcid vā kenacit kvacit / avajñayā tu yad dattaṃ dātus tad doṣam āvahet* (*Dānakāṇḍa*, p. 19). Cf. the Jain author Siddhasenagaṇin, who also emphasizes the importance of not having contempt (*anādara*) in the context of *śraddhā* (p. 120).

22 *tasmān mahānto guṇam ādadantāṃ doṣānaśeṣān api santyajantu / gṛhṇanti dugdhaṃ jalam utsṛjanti hamsāḥ svabhāvaḥ sa nijaḥ śucīnām* (*Dānādiprakaraṇa*, p. 32, verse 17). In Sanskrit poetry geese are said to have the ability to separate milk from water.

23 It is interesting to note, as W.C. Smith has done, the compatibilities of Christian notions of charity and Indic notions of giving with *śraddhā*. To be related to a person in the older use of charity is to 'recognize that person as of high intrinsic worth, and to treat him or her as of high worth. (Latin *caritas* is from *carus*, valued, cherished, dear in the sense of high-priced, literally precious)' (Smith, 1979, p. 231). Charity has since come to mean, more narrowly, acts of donation to the poor, but may preserve some of this original sense of recognizing high worth in that the Christian value of seeing intrinsic worth in the poor, regarded to be in the image of Christ, is still present. We still speak of being 'charitable' or 'generous' toward someone in the sense of seeing virtues where there may actually be faults. Giving *dāna* with *śraddhā*, then, may be something like charity in the older sense of the term: recognizing only good qualities of the person, one is moved to generosity.

24 *saddhā hiriyaṃ kusalañca dānaṃ / dhammā ete sapurisānuyātā / etaṃ hi maggam diviyaṃ vadanti / etena gacchati devalokan* (A.iv.236).

giving: 'a gift is not a benefit if the best part of it is lacking – the fact that it was given out of esteem.'[25] On the other hand, throughout his treatise Seneca inveighs against ingratitude: 'not to return gratitude for benefits is a disgrace, and the whole world counts it as such.'[26] Yet what would it mean to be *grateful* for the esteem others confer upon one? Gratitude suggests an element of dependence, a reversal of rank, from which esteem, as gratuitous regard and deference, steers clear.

A worthy recipient

Since the most meritorious type of giving is motivated by esteem toward the recipient, the Indic writers devote considerable attention to identifying a worthy recipient and the qualities that make a recipient admirable. Esteem requires recognition and discernment of moral qualities. For the *Dharmaśāstra* authors, brahmans are the best recipients, but even among them one can discern different kinds of brahmans on the basis of their moral qualities. According to the *Dānasāgara's* discussion of brahmans:

> A proper recipient is recognized by three (characteristics): his conduct, which is known by living near him, his purity, which is found to be in accordance to well-established convention [or, by his livelihood], and his wisdom which is known by conversation ... Proper conduct is thirteen-fold: one is pious, devoted to the manes and gods, even and gentle, not harming others, lacking ill-will, soft and not harsh, friendly and of pleasant speech, grateful, one in whom refuge may be taken, and tranquil.[27]

Such descriptions do two things: they define the category 'brahman' as first and foremost a moral category, and they encourage morality in recipients. Brahmans are regarded as entitled to their social status because of their moral attributes and religious piety. Here we see the *dāna* relationship as a means of regulating conduct – material support depends, in part, on moral and religious practice.

The medieval authors insisted that the most fruitful gifts flow upwards to the religious elite, that is, monks, nuns, and brahmans, which makes *dāna* problematic from the standpoint of altruism. In the logic considered here, gifts to the poor and wretched – offered out of compassion or pity rather than esteem – are not as meritorious.[28] A basic principle behind religious gifts, as has been articulated by Jean Filliozat, is that in Indic ethics the 'good or evil resulting from an action is

---

25 Seneca, 1958, p. 49.

26 Seneca, 1958, p. 127.

27 *śīlaṃ saṃvasatā jñeyaṃ śaucaṃ sadvyavahārataḥ / prajñā saṃkathayājñeyā tribhiḥ pātraṃ parīkṣyate // śīlañ ca hārītenoktaṃ / tathā ca hārītaḥ – brahmaṇyatā devapitṛbhaktatā samatā saumyatā aparopatāpitā anasūyatā mṛdutā apāruṣyaṃ maitratā priyavāditā kṛtajñatā śaraṇyatā praśāntiś ceti trayodaśavidhaṃ śīlam* (*Dānasāgara*, pp. 15-16).

28 Some Mahāyāna Buddhist treatises on lay conduct which treat *dāna* take exception to this preference for a worthy recipient, and instead praise indiscriminate giving and giving out of compassion. See Heng-ching, 1991; Chappell, 1996; Tokuno, 1995.

proportional to the dignity of the object to which it is directed.'[29] Both the capacity to feel esteem on the part of the donor and the merit made from the gift are dependent upon the moral worth of the recipient. Virtue and dignity, not need, are the primary considerations in choosing a recipient.

Although South Asian religious thinkers extol compassion at length in other discourses, as attested in some of the other essays in this volume, considerations of compassion toward the needy do not figure prominently in the *dāna* theory considered here.[30] The *nibandha* writers, though mostly silent about giving to the needy, quote from the *Mahābhārata* that 'the lame, the blind, the deaf, the mute, and the diseased should be maintained, but should not be given formal gifts.'[31] The trouble with the needy is that their moral status is perceived as dubious or unclear, at least within the terms of a karmic framework; karmic justice affirms and supports hierarchy and human difference. Ballālasena says that one should give 'to those whose livelihood is dancing, acting, or begging, out of pity,' but does not use the term *dāna* to describe such giving.[32] Pity is a different sort of disposition than esteem in that it entails looking down upon rather than up to the recipient; pity humiliates its recipient. Perhaps this may be why the texts in some instances say that *dāna* to the unworthy is fruitless – akin to 'seeds fallen on saline soil, milk into a broken pot, and pouring sacrificial offerings into ashes'[33] – or even demeritorious.[34] The Jain texts clearly differentiate between gifts of pity and gifts of esteem, and insist that pity is completely inappropriate when giving to monks and nuns.[35] Gifts should be given to the worthy out of discrimination and discernment by one recognizing moral virtue. Gifts given indiscriminately are not praiseworthy.

---

29 Filliozat, 1991, p. 240.

30 Mahāyāna Buddhist discourses on *dāna*, in contrast, often configure giving as altruistic and compassionate action, evidenced most clearly in the Bodhisattva's cultivation of the perfections (*paramitā*). In Theravāda Buddhism there is also admiration for the Bodhisattva's giving to the lowly in the context of the perfections, but in discourses about ordinary lay obligations of *dāna*, gifts of esteem are more meritorious than gifts of compassion.

31 *paḍgavandhabadhirā mūkā vyādhinopahatāś ca ye / bharttavyāste mahārāja na tu deyaḥ na deyaḥ pratigrahaḥ* (*Dānasāgara*, p. 28; *Dānakāṇḍa*, p. 48; *Dānakhaṇḍa*, p. 40).

32 *kṛpayā naṭanartakayācakavatteṣu dadyāt* (*Dānasāgara*, p. 28).

33 *ūṣare patitaṃ bījaṃ bhinnabhāṇḍe ca dohanam bhasmany api hutaṃ dravyaṃ tadvad dānam asādhuṣu* (*Dānasāgara*, p. 24, verse 1; *Dānakāṇḍa*, p. 45). Cf. the Jain author Somadeva: 'The wise say that where the Three Jewels are lacking, [gifts] sown on a non-recipient are in vain, like [seeds] on saline soil' (*yatra ratnatrayaṃ nāsti tad apātraṃ vidur vudhāḥ / uptaṃ tatra vṛthā sarvam ūṣarāyāṃ kṣitāv iva* [*Upāsakādhyāyana*, p. 301, verse 799]).

34 *ye ca dharmādapetebhyaḥ prayacchanty alpamedhasaḥ / śataṃ varṣāṇị te pretya purīsaṃ bhuñjate janāḥ* (*Dānasāgara*, p. 28). In this verse, unworthy recipients are those who have fallen from Dharma, and giving to them results in the giver eating feces for a hundred years after death.

35 The *Śrāddhadinakṛtya* of Devendrasūri vigorously condemns giving out of pity to monks, since pity is connected here to contempt (vol. I, p. 134).

The emphasis on giving to admirable superiors rather than the needy suggests that these *dāna* theories entail what we might call an 'ethics of esteem' rather than an ethics of altruism. Esteem is the moral value of recognizing excellence in the other and responding to it with a reaction that is at once delighted and obliged, spontaneous and automatic.

Correct procedure

The *dāna* theorists were interested in how the presence of certain others can have an effect on moral agency in a face-to-face encounter. *Dāna* brings one into immediate contact with esteemed others, which itself is regarded as morally transformative. Ballālasena says that

> Whenever knowledgeable brahmans, who are pious, austere, intent upon truth and restraint, who practice meditation, and whose senses are conquered, approach, they purify *on sight*. What more when there is association [with them]! Upon giving to them, and upon their enjoyment [of the gift], one goes to the highest realm![36]

Seeing, associating with, and giving to a worthy person are morally enhancing. Giving describes an immediate connection to admired others that is purifying and meritorious.

The formal properties of the face-to-face gift encounter attracted considerable interest. In addition to describing a particular moral act and the relationship between moral agents, the *Dharmaśāstra* writers also scrutinized the ritually prescribed formalities of gift giving (*dānavidhi*). The *vidhi* refers to both the ritual behaviour itself and also the rules or injunctions governing the procedure – in other words, the 'etiquette' of the gift. The attention to etiquette and form in the South Asian sources depicts a moral aesthetics of reverence toward religious and social superiors.

With some exceptions modern western ethics has not often considered codes of ritual etiquette as providing serious sources of moral reflection.[37] Ritual might even be seen as antithetical to morality insofar as it involves rote following of rules rather than making free moral choices. Nonetheless, there may be some instances in which codes of ritual etiquette overlap with codes of morality: both can be concerned with external form and rule-governed behaviour, and both involve considerations of other-regard. In the Indic sources, identifying affinities between etiquette and morality can help us reconfigure the role of ritual in the moral life. In particular, more attention to the ways in which formalized external behaviour can be seen to

---

36 *vidyāvantaś ca ye viprāḥ suvratāś ca tapasvinaḥ / satyasaṃyamasaṃyuktā dhyānavṛttā jitendriyāḥ / punanti darśanaṃ prāptāh kiṃ punaḥ saṅgatiṃ gatāḥ / teṣām dattvā ca bhuktvā ca prāpnuyuḥ paramāṃ gatim //* (*Dānasāgara*, p. 17, verse 20).

37 A notable exception is Sarah Buss (1999).

yield internal disposition suggests that etiquette need not be entirely alien from the study of ethics.[38]

The South Asian gift theorists saw external form as cultivating disposition and character, and thus subjected the regulation of the etiquette of the gift to scrutiny and detailed prescription. For example, a Theravāda Buddhist text instructs that when giving a good person performs various acts of hospitality including venerating the recipients and the gift itself, inviting the worthy recipients to sit down on an appointed and well-swept seat, and providing them with plentiful and nourishing food without defects.[39] The rules and ritual prescriptions in hospitality discourse often seem aimed at creating moral virtue rather than presupposing it. By following the correct rules of hospitality, especially repeatedly, one becomes generous and reverent to esteemed others. The ritual activity of worship reinforces the various noble attitudes and dispositions that are so integral to an ethics of esteem. Ceremonial acts of deference, such as humbling oneself by jumping up to wash the feet of the guest, mark difference and generate humility and esteem toward one's religious superiors.

In his discussion of *dānavidhi*, a medieval Jain author, Siddhasenagaṇin, stipulates that the donor should be cognizant of the place, the time, and the worthiness or the recipient in accordance with the scripture. With a mind full of love and joy and with the body 'covered in a cloak of horripilation' he should rise at once to offer a seat, worship the guest, rub his feet, honor him, and concentrate his mind on this one particular act. These actions are the 'means' (*upāya*) by which the donor, 'endowed with the qualities of *śraddhā*, energy, zeal, forbearance, discipline and non-attachment (to the thing given), is transformed in this way [to say]: 'I give.'[40] Here is an explicit description of the effect of external ritual gesture on internal virtue, where the actions of hospitality and worship, including the prescribed horripilation, are the 'means' that 'transform' the giver into one willing to make a gift.

As Siddhasenagaṇin sees it, the ritual etiquette of hospitality involves a transformation of the donor so that he reaches a voluntary desire to say, 'I give.' Ritual means produce the desired intention, dispositions, and affective responses. The curious tension between ritualism and morality, where formalized rule-governed

38 Talal Asad (1993) has helped us to see an alliance between ritual and morality in certain forms of religious ethics. His study of medieval Christian monastics shows how ritualized monastic discipline was intended to produce moral agency, in particular, to cultivate the moral virtue of voluntary obedience.

39 *sakkaccāti sakkaritvā deyyadhamme ca dakkhineyyesu ca gāravam uppādetva deti. tatha uttaṇḍūladidosasamantāgatāhāraṃ adatvā paṇītam majavantaṃ katvā dento deyyadhammaṃ sakkaroti nāma. yatha vā tatha vā anisīdāpetvā nisīdanaṭṭhānaṃ sammajjitvā āsanāni paññāpetvā dakkhiṇeyyapuggalaṃ vicinitvā tatha nisīdāpetvā dānam dento puggalām sakkaroti nāma* (*Suttasangahaṭṭhakathā*, p. 11).

40 *deśakālapuruṣāvasthāḥ samprekṣyāgamānusāriṇā ragapramodanirbhareṇa cetasā romāñcakañcukopagūḍhavapuṣā va 'bhyuthānāsanapradānavandanacaraṇa-pra mārjanasatkārapūrvakaṃ samādhāyaikāgryam ity ādir upāyaḥ / ātmeti dātā śraddhāśakt isattvakṣamāvinayavitṛṣṇatāguṇasampanno dadāmīty evaṃ pariṇataḥ* (Siddhasenagaṇin's commentary on the *Tattvārthasūtra*, p. 117).

behaviour may not seem to allow for the free will on which moral action is said to depend, is resolved here. The ritual act of giving does not replace the element of voluntarism; rather it creates a subject who wants to give. The gift can be both rule-bound behaviour and spontaneous, freely-bestowed generosity. Ritualized behaviour stimulates the development of virtuous disposition, and, in an intriguing way, formalized behaviour becomes a mechanism for generating spontaneous response.

The nature of the gift object

The Indic authors were also quite occupied by describing what constitutes an appropriate gift. Indeed, the bulk of the *nibandhas* is given over to classifying and describing the correct sorts of gifts, from the magnificent *mahādānas* of kings, to humble gifts of food and clothing of ordinary people. Generally, the texts endorse giving munificently, yet do not exclude those of modest means but good intentions. Although the texts often employ the standard phrase 'according to one's means' (*yathāśakti*) to suggest that the amount and substance of the gift should be appropriate to the economic position of the donor, the quality and quantity of the gift are by no means irrelevant. Gift objects mark the prestige and status of both the recipient and the donor, and underscore the hierarchical nature of the relationship. The extensive analyses and typologies of the different types of gifts in the *dāna* literatures track moral and cultural values by classifying and ranking material culture and persons. Worshipping a brahman with fine substances rather than mediocre ones imposes certain identities on both the donor and the recipient. The donor projects his or her religious, political, and class status by the gift, and identifies and displays the worthiness of the recipient. The materiality of the gift becomes the very currency of social status.

While coding material life and prescribing proper and appropriate gifts, generosity also embraces a range of social and moral concerns that are not so tangible. Widely extolled types of *dāna* are the gift of fearlessness (*abhayadāna*) in which one refrains from harm to others and offers amnesty to the persecuted, the gift of health (*ārogyadāna*), the *Dharmaśāstra* gift of knowledge (*vidyādāna*), and the gift of the teaching (*dharmadāna*) in both Jainism and Buddhism. Describing the values of education, health and safety in the idiom of generosity broadens the moral reach of *dāna* ideals. The gift of fearlessness, often construed as refraining from harming someone, is philosophically interesting in that it aligns generosity and nonviolence; curbing one's propensity to wreak harm on others is a freely-bestowed gift to them, rather than a social obligation entailed by a right or a social contract.[41]

41 See my article Hibbets, 1999.

Ethics, Social Difference and Hierarchy

The emphasis on esteem in *dāna* theory challenges assumptions of both Seneca and Mauss that gift giving is a matter of exchange and social balance, forged either through material or symbolic return. This position offers a means to critique and reexamine basic assumptions in western philosophical and anthropological discourse regarding human sociality. Moreover, these Indic discourses on *dāna* challenge not only western theoretical material on the gift, but also recent ethnographic evidence on gift relations in contemporary India.

Those familiar with recent anthropological studies of South Asian gift practices may find the ethics of esteem surprising since what is most often noticed about gift practices in contemporary India is considerable ambiguity about the status of recipients. The fieldwork studies of both Jonathan Parry (1986, 1989, 1994) and Gloria Raheja (1989) in particular have shown that, Brahmanical ideology notwithstanding, brahmans, *qua* recipients, have dubious moral and social status in places in modern India. Both studies posit a structural relationship of inequality of power and status between the donor and the recipient, and suggest that the gift conveys a kind of 'poison' or 'inauspiciousness' that is transferred to the obliged (and often despised) recipient. Although there are important differences between their studies, relevant here is a feature they share which differs so markedly from the ethics of esteem: it appears that the donor claims power and prestige in giving to a moral inferior rather than expressing and conferring admiration on a moral superior.

The insights of contemporary ethnography are very useful for exposing gaps between practice and theory, between contemporary fieldwork and premodern textual sources, and between actual and ideal. But the differences here also reveal items of particularly philosophical importance. Both Parry and Raheja see imbalance and dependency as obstacles to the moral life rather than resources for it. The structural hierarchies and imbalances asserted by the gift relationship result not in esteem but in contempt.

The dispositions and virtues described in the premodern South Asian gift discourses, in contrast, promote esteem, recognition, and difference as necessary components of a moral life. They pose the question of how we can understand moral thinking that takes place within – and itself configures – a stratified and hierarchical social order. Unlike much post-Enlightenment western thinking, in which moral philosophy presumes human equality and sameness as basic prerequisites for justice and moral action, these medieval discourses make no such assumption – human beings are socially, religiously, and morally differentiated from one another. What is meant by esteem is not the generalized respect one should have for all persons; philosophers sometimes distinguish between respect and esteem in that respect is owed to everyone in virtue of being a human being, whereas esteem is reserved only for those who earn or are entitled to a special regard.[42] An ethic based on esteem assumes and renders explicit difference, hierarchy, and special classes of persons who are admired apart from others. It is concerned not with sameness or mutuality between moral agents, but is rather attentive to human difference and asymmetrical relationships. The attention the medieval theorists give to well-mannered, aesthetically pleasing, face-to-face encounters of other-regard offers a concrete place to begin to investigate how moral thinking might work within a hierarchical and stratified social order.

The ethics and aesthetics of esteem challenge the view of a universally applicable principle of reciprocity. In some ways, the grip that this view continues to have on anthropologists, economists, philosophers, and other scholars may be the result of distinctively modern and western notions of bounded and autonomous individuals. Where human beings are conceived to be autonomous agents interacting with one another on rational principles of mutual exchange, reciprocal gift giving practices are regarded as the norm. Marcel Mauss began a western moral discourse that assigns privileged moral and aesthetic value to the mutual obligations to give, to receive, and to give back – a balanced, rational, and harmonious vision of human sociality. In contrast, in societies where reciprocity is not in evidence, either in practice or theory, the situation may come to be regarded as one of domination and exploitation. Religious ideologies that articulate ideals of esteem, partiality, and nonreciprocity may then be represented as primarily discourses of power and hegemony. In this view, the ethics of esteem either masks a deeper and unacknowledged reciprocity or debt, or is simply religious rhetoric subverting the natural or ideal relations of human beings. Brahmanical and monastic discourses exalting recipients of gifts may be seen as countering the ambiguities of their dependency with elitist ideology.

It is crucial to consider the role of power and status in creating social ideologies, and to acknowledge that elite South Asian gift ideologies, like any other ideology of the gift, may perhaps never be entirely isolated from power, status, and economic interest. There is no question that our sources were composed by elite authors whose interests lay in mystifying and exalting hierarchies and economic arrangements that no doubt benefited chiefly themselves. At the same time, if we assume at the outset that power and economic interest exhaust the range of concerns and motivations of the South Asian authors, then we preempt their capacity to critically reflect upon their own social practices. This may be too high a price to pay.

Perhaps no one has taught us more about the role of power in the history of ideas than Michel Foucault. At the same time, Foucault insists upon making a place for a domain of reflection, what he calls 'thought,' that is not determined by ideas or mentalities. For Foucault, 'thought is freedom in relation to what one does, the

42 Charles Taylor (1991, p. 46) suggests a similar distinction between honor and dignity, where honor is intrinsically linked to inequalities, and dignity to modern ideas of a notion of the dignity of human beings in a universalist or egalitarian sense. Honor is tied to recognition, and dignity to identity.

motion by which one detaches oneself from it, establishes it as an object, and reflects upon it as a problem.'[43] He insists here that human thinking is not entirely and exhaustively conditioned by relations of power. If we deny the capacity of human beings to distance themselves from their own actions to reflect critically upon moral practices, we efface a critical and valuable dimension of human experience and freedom.

Thus it would be preemptive to dismiss the *Dharmaśāstra* (or any other South Asian discourse of the gift), as only apologetic rhetoric that reflects Brahmanical interests and the domination of an unjust status quo. It may be the case that the gift relation is particularly vulnerable to exploitation and corruption, and it may be as well that esteem is easily converted to its opposite. At the same time, esteem's fragility or scarcity in the world suggests part of its moral value. In premodern Indic discourses the features of the examined moral and religious life, at least in the context of certain gift relations, include reverence, recognition, and esteem as valued moral virtues. Indeed, a significant part of what it may mean to *be* moral or religious in some South Asian moral theories is to esteem certain types of others. The gift is first and foremost, in the view of the South Asian gift theorists considered here, a moment of generous response of seeking to admire the merits and look past the faults of others.

These considerations can help us refine the differences between prestige and esteem. While prestige is claimed for oneself, esteem must be conferred by others. The gift's chief feature, rightly understood, is something that can only occur between persons in an encounter between self and other that is properly described as a moral relation. The gift theorists were theorizing a moral agency that occurs in the presence of the admired other, and is, in an important way, conditioned by the other.

The historical breadth and endurance of these *dāna* ideologies are significant. Despite important differences in other matters of religion, philosophy, and ethics in the three religious traditions considered here – *Dharmaśāstra*, Theravāda Buddhism, and Jainism – they share a good deal on their conceptions of the ideal gift. We find in *dāna* a comparative category that can lead to refining our appreciation of the shared cultural presumptions as well as the differences between the major religious and intellectual traditions from India. Moreover, the medieval discourses on the gift, which themselves are codifications of earlier material from each tradition, give voice to longstanding elite cultural values in South Asian religious history. The translocal and transreligious moral aesthetics of hierarchical modes of respect enduring for centuries, even millennia, in the Indian cultural sphere suggest that the notable challenges that *dāna* theory poses to western thinking on the gift are not minor aberrations, but are of widespread intellectual and cultural significance.

43 Foucault, 1994, p. 117.

Selected References

Pali and Sanskrit Sources listed by title

Caturvargacintāmaṇi of Hemādri. vol. I *Dānakhaṇḍa*, ed. Paṇḍita Bharatacandra Śiromaṇi, Calcutta: Bibliotheca Indica, 1873.

Dānādiprakaraṇa of Sūrācārya, ed. Amrutlal M. Bhojak and Nagin J. Shah. Ahmedabad: L.D. Institute of Indology, 1982.

Dānakriyākaumudī of Govindānanda, ed. Paṇḍita Kamala Kṛṣṇa Smṛtibhuṣana, Calcutta: Baptist Mission Press, 1903.

Dānamayūkha of Nīlakaṇṭha Bhaṭṭa, ed. Paṇḍita Ratna Gopāla Bhaṭṭa. Benares: Vidyā Vilāsa Press, 1909.

Dānasāgara of Ballālasena, ed. Bhabatosh Bhaṭṭacharya, Calcutta: Bibliotheca Indica, 1956.

Dānāṣṭakakathā: Recueil Jaina de huit histories sur le don, ed. and trans. into the French by Nalini Balbir, Paris, 1982.

Le Dasavatthuppakaraṇa, ed. and trans. into the French by Jacqueline ver Eecke. Publications de l'Ecole Francaise d'Extreme-Orient, vol. 58, Paris: Ecole Francaise d'Extreme Orient, 1976.

Kṛtyakalpataru of Bhaṭṭa Lakṣmīdhara, vol. 5, *Dānakāṇḍa*, ed. K.V. Rangaswami Aiyangar, Baroda, 1941.

Manusmṛti, trans. Georg Bühler, *The Laws of Manu*, Sacred Books of the East 25, New York: Dover Books, 1969 [1886].

Saddhammopāyana, ed. R. Morris, JPTS, vol. II, 1887, pp. 35-98.

Saddhammopāyana, trans. by A.A. Hazlewood, JTPS, vol. 12, 1988, pp. 65-168.

Sāratthasamuccaya nama Caturbhanavaraṭṭhakathā, ed. Upasena. N.p.: Sucaritodaya, 1903.

Sārasaṅgaha, ed. Genjun H. Sasaki, London: Pali Text Society, 1992.

Sīhalavatthuppakaraṇa, ed. and trans. Jacqueline Ver Eecke, Paris: Ecole Francaise d'Extreme-Orient, 1980.

Śrāddhadinakṛtya with *Svopajñavṛtti* of Devendrasūri, Bombay: Jinasasana Aradhana Trasta, 1988.

Suttasaṅgahaṭṭhakathā, ed. Baddegama Piyaratana, Simon Hewavitarne Bequest, vol. 25. Colombo: Tripitaka Publication Press, 1929.

Tattvārthasūtra of Umāsvāmin and commentary of Siddhasenagaṇin, Devacandra Lalābhāi Jaina Pustakoddhara, no. 76, Bombay. 1930.

Upāsakādhyāyana. ed. and trans. A.F.R. Hoernle, Calcutta, 1890.

Upāsakajanālaṅkāra, ed. H. Saddhatissa. London: Pali Text Society, 1965.

Yājñavalkyasmṛti with the commentary of Aparārka. vol. 1. Pune: Ānandāśrama-samskṛtagrathāvaliya, no. 46, 1903-1904.

Yājñavalkyasmṛti with the commentary of Vijñāneśvara called the *Mitākṣarā*, ed. Shivrāma Janārdan Shāstrī Gore, Bombay: Ganpat Krishnaji's Press, 1887.

______, trans. by Śriśa Chandra Vidyārṇava, Allahabad: The Indian Press, 1918.

Yogaśāstra of Hemacandra with *Svopajñavṛtti*. ed. Muni Jambuvijaya. Bombay: Jain Sāhitya Vikās Maṇḍal, 1977-86.

Secondary Literature

Aiyangar, K.V. Rangaswami, 'Introduction,' to *Kṛtyakalpataru* of Bhaṭṭa Lakṣmīdhara, vol. 5. *Dānakāṇda*, 1-129. Baroda: Gaekwad's Oriental Series 91, 1941.

Appadurai, Arjun, 'Gratitude as a Social Mode in South India,' in John Carman and Frederick Streng (eds), *Spoken and Unspoken Thanks: Some Comparative Soundings*, Cambridge: Center for the Study of World Religions, Harvard University, 1989.

Asad, Talal, *Genealogies of Religion: Discipline and Reasons of Power in Christianity and Islam*, Baltimore: Johns Hopkins University Press, 1993.

Balbir, Nalini, 'The Micro-genre of *Dāna*-stories in Jaina Literature: Problems of Interrelation and Diffusion.' *Indological Taurinensia*, XI, 1983, pp. 145-161.

Benveniste, Emile, *Indo-European Language and Society*, trans. Elizabeth Palmer. London: Faber and Faber Limited, 1973.

Bhaṭṭacharya, Bhabatosh, 'Introduction,' to *Dānasāgara of Ballalāsena*, Calcutta: Bibliotheca Indica, 1956.

Buss, Sarah, 'Appearing Respectful: The Moral Significance of Manners,' *Ethics*, **109**, 1999. pp. 795-826.

Camenisch, Paul F., 'Gift and Gratitude in Ethics,' *Journal of Religious Ethics*, **9**(1), 1981, pp. 1-34.

Chappell, David W., 'Searching for a Mahāyāna Social Ethic,' *Journal of Religious Ethics*, 24 (2), 1996, pp. 351-375.

Coles, Romand, *Rethinking Generosity: Critical Theory and the Politics of Caritas*, Ithaca: Cornell University Press, 1997.

Cone, Margaret and Gombrich, Richard F., *The Perfect Generosity of Prince Vessantara*, Oxford: Clarendon Press, 1977.

Davis, Donald R., *Religion, Law, and Gifts in Medieval India: An Analysis and Partial Translation of the Dānakāṇḍa of Lakṣmīdharabhaṭṭa*, Unpublished Masters Thesis. University of Texas at Austin, 1995.

Derrida, Jacques, *Given Time: I. Counterfeit Money*, trans. Peggy Kamuf, Chicago: University of Chicago Press, 1992.

______, *The Gift of Death*. trans. David Willis, Chicago: University of Chicago Press, 1995.

______, *Adieu à Emmanuel Levinas*, Paris: Editions Galilee, 1997.

______, *Of Hospitality*, trans. Rachel Bowlby, Stanford: Stanford University Press, 2000.

Dhammapala, Gatare, 'Towards the Definition of *Saddhā* and *Bhakti*.' *Buddhist Studies in Honour of Hammalava Saddhatissa*, Sri Lanka, 1984.

Endo, Toshiichi, *Dāna: The Development of its Concept and Practice*, Colombo: Gunasena, 1987.

Filliozat, Jean, *Religion, Philosophy, Yoga*, Delhi: Motilal Banarsidass, 1991.

Foucault, Michel, *Ethics: Subjectivity and Truth*, ed. Paul Rabinow, trans. Robert Hurley et al., New York: The New Press, 1994.

Gouldner, Alvin, 'The Norm of Reciprocity: A Preliminary Statement.' *American Sociological Review*, **25** (2), 1994, pp. 162-178.

Gregory, C.A., 'The Poison in Raheja's Gift: A Review Article,' *Social Analysis*, 32, 1992, pp. 95-110.

Hacker, Paul, '*Śraddhā*,' WZKSO 3, 1963, pp. 151-189.

Hara, M., 'Note on two Sanskrit Religious Terms: *Bhakti* and *Śraddhā*,' IIJ, **7**, 1964, pp. 124-145.

Hallisey, Charles, 'Ethical Particularism in Theravada Buddhism.' *Journal of Buddhist Ethics*, 3, 1996.

______, 'A Response to Kevin Schilbrack,' *Journal of Buddhist Ethics*, **4**, 1997.

Heesterman, J C., *The Inner Conflict of Tradition: Essays in Indian Ritual, Kingship and Society*, 1985, Chicago: University of Chicago Press.

Heim, Maria, *Theories of the Gift in South Asia: Hindu, Buddhist, and Jain Reflections on Dāna*, New York: Routledge, 2004.

Hibbets, Maria, 'Saving them from yourself: An Inquiry into the South Asian Gift of Fearlessness,' *Journal of Religious Ethics*, 27.3, 1999, pp. 437-463.

Jamison, Stephanie W., *Sacrificed Wife, Sacrificer's Wife: Women, Ritual, and Hospitality in Ancient India*, New York: Oxford University Press, 1996.

Kane, P.V., *History of Dharmaśāstra*. vol.1, 2. Poona: Bhandarkar Oriental Research Institute, [1941] 1962.

Köhler, Hans-Werbin, *Śrad-dhā- in der Vedischen und Altbuddhistischen Literatur*, Wiesbaden: Franz Steiner Verlag, 1973.

Komter, Aafke E. (ed.), *The Gift: An Interdisciplinary Perspective*, Amsterdam: Amsterdam University Press, 1996.

Laidlaw, James, *Riches and Renunciation: Religion, Economy, and Society Among the Jains* Oxford: Clarendon Press, 1985.

______, 'The Uses and Abuses of Theology: Comments on Jonathan Parry's *Death in Banaras*,' *South Asian Research*, 16 (1), 1996, pp. 31-44.

Leach, E.R., '*The Gift*, by Marcel Mauss' [Book Review], *Man*. (n.s.), 1955, 55, p. 30.

Levi-Strauss, Claude, 'The Principle of Reciprocity,' in Aafke Komter (ed.), *The Gift: An Interdisciplinary Perspective*, Amsterdam: University of Amsterdam, (1949). 1996.

Ludowyk-Gyomroi, Edith, 'The Valuation of *Saddhā* in Early Buddhist Texts,' *University of Ceylon Review*. V (2), 1947, pp. 32-49.

Malinowski, Bronislaw, 'The Principle of Give and Take,' in Aafke Komter (ed.), *The Gift: An Interdisciplinary Perspective*, University of Amsterdam, (1922), 1996.

Mauss, Marcel, *The Gift: The Form and Reason for Exchange in Archaic Societies*, trans. W.D. Halls, London: W.W. Norton (Paris, 1925), 1990.

Michaels, Axel, 'Gift and Return Gift: Greeting and Return Greeting in India, On a Consequential Footnote by Marcel Mauss,' *Numen* 44, 1997, pp. 242-269.

Nath, Vijay, *Dāna: Gift System in Ancient India (c. 600 BC – c. AD. 300): A Socio-Economic Perspective*, Delhi, 1987.

Parry, Jonathan, 'The Gift, the Indian Gift, and the "Indian Gift".' *Man*, 21 (3) 1986, pp. 453-473.

______, 'On the Moral Perils of Exchange,' in Jonathan Parry and Maurice Bloch (eds), *Money and the Morality of Exchange*, Cambridge: Cambridge University Press, 1989.

______, *Death in Banaras*, Cambridge: Cambridge University Press, 1994.

Raheja, Gloria Goodwin, *The Poison in the Gift: Ritual, Prestation, and the Dominant Caste in a North Indian Village*, Chicago: University of Chicago Press, 1988.

Ramanujan, A.K., 'Is there an Indian Way of Thinking? An Informal Essay.' *Contributions to Indian Sociology*, 23 (1), 1989, pp. 41-58.

Saddhatissa, H., 'The *Saddhā* Concept in Buddhism,' *The Eastern Buddhist*, XI (2) 1978, pp. 137-142.

Schrift, Alan D. (ed.), *The Logic of the Gift: Toward an Ethic of Generosity*, New York: Routledge, 1997.

Seneca, Lucius Annaeus, *On Benefits*, trans. John Basore, Cambridge: Harvard University Press, 1958.

Shih Heng-ching, trans. *The Sūtra on Upāsaka Precepts*, Berkeley: Bukkhyo Dendo Kyokai, 1991.

Smith, Wilfred Cantwell, 'A Hindu Contribution,' in *Faith and Belief*. Princeton: Princeton University Press, 1979.

Starobinski, Jean, *Largesse*, trans. Jean Marie Todd, Chicago: Chicago University Press, 1997 (1994).

Taylor, Charles, *The Ethics of Authenticity*, Cambridge: Harvard University Press, 1991.

Tokuno, Kyoko, 'The Book Resolving Doubts Concerning the Semblance Dharma,' in Donald S. Lopez (ed.), *Buddhism in Practice*. Princeton: Princeton University Press, 1995.

Trautmann, Thomas, *Dravidian Kinship*, Cambridge: Cambridge University Press, 1981.

van der Veen, Klaas W., 'The Brahmin, the Individual and the Poisonous Gift,' in van den Hoek, et al. (eds), *Ritual, State, and History in South Asia: Essays in Honour of J.C. Heesterman*, Leiden: E.J. Brill, 1992, pp. 695-716.

Vandevelde, Antoon (ed.), *Gifts and Interests*, Leuven, Belgium: Peeters, 2000.

Williams, Bernard, 'Persons, Character and Morality,' in *Moral Luck*, Cambridge: Cambridge University Press, 1981.

Introduction to Part B

Buddhist and Jaina Approaches to Ethical Decision Making

This section of essays examines the Buddhist and Jaina approaches to making ethical decisions. These traditions arose from India, but unlike the more dominant Hindu system, Buddhism and Jainism remain mute on various theological positions. In the absence of a Creator (or Supremely Transcendent Being) who might promulgate moral or natural law, or implant principles in the soul or within the intellect, philosophers in the East much before their counterparts in the West (barring perhaps the Stoics) looked at various other kinds of possible sources – in the corresponding will, intuition, reason, or in the supposed ethical properties in the real world – to ground their ethics. For instance, rather than positing that the existence of the world owes itself to a common deity or an array of various gods and goddesses, these traditions assert the primacy of universal causation, stating that one's relationship with the world is not created by a god, but arises due to the accumulation of *karma* over countless rebirths. This has rendered Buddhists and Jainas quintessential voluntarists. One exists in one's present state due to one's past actions (*karma*). In the present, one can either repeat behaviours conditioned by the past, or, through an act of will, seek to purify oneself. One takes up ethical behaviours because of the negative consequences that can and will arise because of impure activities.

Buddhism and Jainism emphasize personal vows. Though the precepts of each faith can be found in various iterations (lists of five, lists of ten, and so forth), both systems agree on four primary observances: nonviolence, not stealing, not lying, and sexual restraint. By not causing harm, one helps to lessen the potential to harm for oneself. By not stealing, one does not incur the wrath of others and learns contentment. By not lying, one becomes trusted and honoured by others. Through sexual restraint, the mind becomes pacified and can regard others with greater respect and empathy. This emphasis on personal improvement, though seemingly self-centred, in fact promotes activities and attitudes that uphold the common good.

Ethics within Buddhism and Jainism emerge from within. Due to a perception of the consequences of one's actions, a practicing Buddhist or Jaina strives to enter a disciplined life. For the Buddhist, this arises when one perceives the (first) Noble Truth: all is suffering (*sarvam duḥkham*). Through this acknowledgement of the frail and evanescent nature of reality, the Buddhist seeks to understand the root causes of his or her suffering. This leads to a path of introspection and self-correction. For the Jaina, the path to the moral life begins with a moment of awakening (*saṃyak dṛṣṭi*) wherein one sees the all-pervasiveness of life forms and seeks to promote the protection of life (*jīva*). This compassion helps release some of a person's bondage (*bandha*) and advances one along a fourteen-fold path of spiritual ascent (*guṇasthānas*) leading ultimately to the Siddha Loka, a goal not unlike the goal of achieving Buddha-Nature. Psychologically, the adaptation of an ethical lifestyle in both Buddhism and Jainism, arises from a maturation of one's point of view. Rather than seeking to gain pleasure for oneself, one seeks to fully and deeply understand oneself. In the process of self-understanding, one develops concern for others.

Although it appears that Buddhist and Jaina ethics are grounded in self-understanding and psychology, there are nevertheless complexities bordering on the metaphysical and epistemological that need to be recognized. There are departures from the usual approach that treats ethics as an elaborate enumeration of the psychological mechanism that at once accounts for the experience and identity of the person in the absence of belief in a substantial self. The extensive and all-inclusive categorization of the constituents of consciousness or mental phenomena are also the 'stuff' of ethical reflections and corrective dispositions. But this splendid marriage of phenomenology and ethics is given another twist in the Abhidhamma (Skt. Abhidharma). While more usually the mental dispositions that are conducive to a moral life are subsumed under the *dhammas* – in the form of affectations, emotions, other-regarding virtues and so on – Abhidhamma has the *dhammas* do the work of providing the foundations of ethical 'form of life' as 'facts' did for Wittgenstein of the Vienna Circle phase. Abhidhamma retains an external ontology while also searching for the basis of ethical judgment within the individual. In a curious way this recalls (or foreshadows) the 'ought from is' solution, but it also lays itself open to the charge of naturalistic fallacy (*pace* G.E. Moore). But the realm of 'facts' for the Abhidhamma are as much within as they are without: all the constituents are of the same stuff, whether of mental phenomena or in the ontic spread of the world. That is the way it is. Hence, *ought* follows from the *is*, first encountered in the mental world within. And so the Moorean objection of the endless attempt to define moral properties as, say, the 'good' does not have quite the force, for the 'good', as indeed all value, is related to the conduct and appropriate responses an individual makes to external situations in consonance with the co-dependent ordering of mental life within. The approach may be characterized as a 'rational' activity, although it would seem a better description would be 'rational intuition' (of the sort the Stoics developed extensively with reference to a similarly schematized internal constitution of the elements of the self).

The chapters in this section highlight these basic principles through both generalized and specific examples. Quite often, even within India, religiously oriented people can be derided for being solipsistic and aloof. At the same time, Buddhism has been dismissed by some philosophers and theologians as being non-theistic and hence not worthy of consideration. This section of the volume provides a correction to these mistaken attitudes. From the beginning, Jainas and Buddhists alike have worked at building a gentler society. The Jainas have worked most famously in the area of animal protection. The Buddhists have similarly taken up various causes throughout Asian history, such as the releasing of animals, that reflect a keen adherence to the precept of nonviolence. While speaking from the vantage of individual liberation, both groups emphasize the primacy of duties over rights. In Jaina subcultures and in the Buddhist societies of South East Asia, accountability to one's community dominates the cultural ethos. Sallie King and Nancy McCagney give several examples of this in the contemporary Buddhist world, in their respective chapters in Volume II. King explains how contemporary Buddhist leaders such as Sulak Sivaraksa and Ariyaratna have brought positive change through the innovative implementation of Buddhist precepts in Thailand and Sri Lanka, respectively. These living examples of the enactment and engagement of these principles underscore the relevance of Buddhist ethics for the modern world.

Some further reflections on Jaina Ethics and its modern developments

As noted already, one of the lesser known ethical traditions of India is that of the Jainas. Jainism is both a philosophical system and a way of life in its own right. It was founded around 500 BCE by Vardhamāna Mahāvīra, an ascetic and unorthodox teacher thought to be a contemporary of the Buddha, to whom he is often compared. Jainism was least inclined towards metaphysical speculations and was decidedly non-theistic, rejecting as is the case with Buddhism a 'supremely personal God' (but not gods, albeit of a less-than-divine status). It was often charged that Jainas concerned themselves far too much with individual morality, with its heavy orientation towards monastic life. Internal disputes over this issue gave way to two distinct Jaina groupings, the Digambaras ('non-clad') and Śvetāmbaras ('white-clad'); the latter shifting toward a more pragmatic approach to lay life in contrast to the strictly austere life embraced by the former.

The source of Jaina teachings was apparently identified by Mahāvīra himself with a much older ascetic group of 'great teachers' (Tīrthankaras) called Nirgranthas. These teachings were codified and systematized in canonical texts known as *Nigaṇṭha pavayana*, most of which are no longer extant. The basic philosophic belief of the Jainas is that every entity in the world has *jīva* or a sentient principle, whose distinguishing feature is consciousness along with vital energy and a happy disposition. The idea is that consciousness is continuous and nothing in the universe is without some degree of sentiency at varying levels of conscious and apparently unconscious existence, from its more developed form in adult human beings to invisible embryonic modes at 'lower' animal and plant levels. (Sentience is not determined merely by pain-pleasure responses.) Each and every *jīva*, more or less atomically configured, however, subsists in a contingent relation to the quantity of *karma*, which is described as a 'nonconscious immaterial' *matter* of the most subtle form that determines the relative nature of the being. Activity, of both volitional and non-volitional kinds, induces *karma* and by association conditions the development of the sentient principle, resulting in the eventual death and re-embodiment of that particular 'soul'. If *karma* can be prevented and exhausted the bondage could be broken, the cyclical process arrested, and the sentient principle could grow to its fullest possible realisation – a belief Jainism shares with much of Hindu and Buddhist thought.[a]

The ethical implications of this 'spiritual' worldview is that the individual has to pursue a disciplinary life of renunciation, which in turn entails a mode of life, *dharma*, conducive to this pursuit, individually as well as collectively. A monastic community (*saṅgha*) is the preferred model, though a social life that aims to maximize this principle in a secular environment is acceptable. The life of a monk, particularly of an *arhant*, a philosopher-ascetic, who through his stoic practices has attained something of a quiescent state, may well be equipped to serve as the normative for the laypeople who also have equal claim to attaining that glorious final liberation (*mokṣa*) which is the end-goal of Jaina life. Thus the duties of the laypeople in civil life are ideally derived, in part, from those observed by the monk in a monastic *saṅgha*. But an over-emphasis on this stoical source of morality, it will be observed, would *a fortiori* rule out the possibility of an autonomous social ethics, for as with Hindu Yoga, self-culture and personal 'salvation' and soteriological concerns would take priority over all else. But paradoxically, this end is not attainable without the annihilation of all self-interests and self-centred desires and inclinations. The sentient principle in that state is both disinterested and inactive. So perhaps the idealized monastic disciplinary matrix serves as a check upon and sets limits to lay or social ethics, *ceteris paribus*

The ethical life of the Jaina becomes almost synonymous with the observance of a list of vows and austerities, and abstention from useless and untoward activities. The practical manual of Jaina ethics defines right conduct in terms of the observance of vows of restraints progressively geared toward the complete renunciation of the ascetic. This is their axiological scheme. There are five such 'vows', namely, *ahiṃsā*, *satya*, *asteya*, *brahmācārya* and *aparigraha*, which we shall describe briefly.

Ahiṃsā, generally rendered as 'nonviolence', is perhaps the most fundamental concept of Jaina ethics and it refers to the noninjury or nonharming of sentient beings. With its broad understanding of sentiency, Jaina ethics inevitably reflects, as Albert Schweitzer put it, an uncompromising 'reverence for all life'. The restraints comprise dietary habits, such as nonconsumption of meat, alcohol, and foods of certain kinds, and ruling against the abuse, subjugation, exploitation, ill-treatment, tormenting, discarding and slaying of 'all breathing, existing, living, sentient creatures'. There are prohibitions against injurious treatment of animals, such as beating, mutilating, branding, overloading and depravation of food and space. Meat-eating is strictly prohibited on the grounds that this requires the killing of animals.

These concerns make the Jainas among the earliest protagonists of 'animal liberation' and they excelled the Hindus and Buddhists on this moral stance and in their propagation of vegetarianism. Furthermore, Jainas were so sensitive to intentionally and accidentally killing living matter that they would strain water to separate the animalculae in it, brush ants and insects from the path, and wear masks over the mouth to prevent minute '*nigodhas*' (microbe-like entities) from being inhaled. The logical extreme of this ethic would be to curtail all movement and starve oneself (to death), as indeed some Jaina monks did, a sure antidote to hedonism and eudaemonism!

One important qualification however has to be noted here. While the vow of *ahiṃsā* may appear to have been practiced on altruistic grounds, the concern here is as much with the motive of avoiding injury or harm to oneself, which could occur through any number of actions, not just in acts that lead to the suffering of others. Thus if one told lies this could be harmful to oneself for it hinders the development of one's *jīva* or 'soul'. Thus a Jaina monk will maintain silence where telling a lie to the bandit could well save the life of his innocent prey. A layperson however may be inclined to place the interest of the victim above his own minimally threatened interest. This rather negatively articulated virtue has not been without some appeal and influence on the wider Indian ethical tradition, and as we shall see shortly Gandhi was sufficiently inspired to work it into a positive active principle.

The other vows pertain to being truthful (*satya*); not appropriating what is not one's own (*asteya*); exercising sexual continence (*brahmācārya*), which legitimizes the institution of marriage for the laity; and non-possessiveness (*aparigraha*), which encourages disinterested dealings in daily life. Fasting, giving alms, forgiveness, compassion and kindness toward others are some of the positive virtues that are encouraged. It could be said that the question of 'rights' and interests of others are not raised, except superficially under *ahiṃsā*, for the ultimate justification for all ethical practices is that they should raise the moral stature of the practitioner, not necessarily of the victim. One even pardons another for this reason. In the stark absence of other beings, a lonesome Jaina might not accumulate much meritorious *karma*! Sometimes monks appeal to adverse social consequences to explain the evils of the non-observance of vows, but such prudential and utilitarian considerations are merely expedient rationalizations rather than their justification.

It has been claimed by some modern writers that virtues such as *ahiṃsā* have intrinsic value and that their justification lies not in their being derived from tested empirical statements, which they clearly are not, but from experience which is self-evident. What is 'right' is in harmony with this experience. *Ahiṃsā*, for example, is an experience related to the occurrence of pain and suffering among living beings and is universalized for others from one's own experience of pain. Again, the fact-value distinction is not adhered to.

One senses that Jaina ethics strive to be autonomous, it is preeminently non-natural and normative, and it admits the possibility of objective values, of which *ahiṃsā* seems to be its most significant and distinctive contribution.

Influence of Jaina and Buddhist Ethic of noninjury on Gandhi

A discussion of Gandhian ethics might also be seen as belonging here because it flows with the foregoing narrative (Epic and Jaina in particular), it echoes many of the elements of Buddhist ethics, it is discussed in the chapters in this section, for example, on Jaina ecological ethics, Buddhist ethical theory and democracy, animal ecology etc., and it is representative of by now what is taken to be rather classical style of thinking on ethic of action. But since Gandhi is seminal also to modernist critiques in Indian ethics we have decided to append this discussion at the end of the Introduction to Part C.

Christopher Key Chapple, with P. Bilimoria

Chapter 9

Purgation and Virtue in Jainism: Toward an Ecological Ethic

Christopher Key Chapple

Jainism

The Jaina religious tradition poses numerous philosophical challenges in ways not encountered in other systems of thought. Simultaneously, Jainas posit a metaphysical and physical approach to reality that defies categories found elsewhere. As LeValley has noted, 'Jain scriptures emphasize nonviolence and toleration of multiple viewpoints. Jains today emphasize those same two points.'[1] However, to fully understand the application of nonviolence and toleration in Jainism, we need to look at two key aspects of the Jaina philosophical view: the purgation of karma and the insistence on cultivating a virtuous life. The purgation of karma underscores the physical aspects of Jaina thought, due to the perception that karma has a material presence. The physicality of karma has resulted in a marked cosmological emphasis within Jainism. The cultivation of virtue, particularly through the practice of nonviolence, demonstrates the link between the metaphysical and the ethical in Jainism. From this combination, the Jainas posit a living universe that must be protected, and a worldview that, as we will see, accords well with some aspects of contemporary ecological and cosmological investigations.

Jaina Cosmology

Jainism has been traced to Pārśvanātha, a teacher who most likely flourished around 2800 years ago. A few hundred years after his death, Vardhamāna Mahāvīra, also known as the Jina, a contemporary of the Buddha, codified the tradition, laying the foundation for the religion that is now practiced by several million people in India, both laypeople and monastics. In the *Ācārāṅga Sūtra*, a text recorded within a couple hundred years after his death, Mahāvīra outlines the following basic principles and practices. He taught that the soul is uncreated and eternal, that it has been clouded with the dust of karma since beginningless time, and through the application of a rigorous moral code one can purge one's karma and attain a state of liberation or *kevala*. Mahāvīra very much affirmed the existence and importance of the physical

1 LeValley, 'Naked Philosopher-Ascetics', 2000, p. 146.

world and asserted that one's relationship to the world reflected and determined one's moral status. Understanding of and respect for life in its myriad forms held the key to one's liberation. Mahāvīra arrived at his definition of life through direct observation:

> Thoroughly knowing the earth-bodies and water-bodies, and fire-bodies and wind-bodies, the lichens, seeds, and sprouts, he comprehended that they are, if narrowly inspected, imbued with life. (*Ācārāṅga Sūtra* I.8.I.11-12)

The earliest known Jaina text, cited above, lists in detail different forms of life and advocates various techniques for their protection. The text states that 'All breathing, existing, living, sentient creatures should not be slain, nor treated with violence, nor abused, nor tormented, nor driven away. This is the pure, unchangeable, eternal law' (I.4.1). The *Ācārāṅga Sūtra* mentions how to avoid harm not only to animals, but also to plants, by not touching them, and to the bodies that dwell in the earth: the water, the fire, and the air. For instance, Jaina monks and nuns must not stamp upon the earth, swim in water, light or extinguish fires, or thrash one's arms in the air.

This respect for life developed into a series of comprehensive treatises on the nature of karma. The later philosophical tradition, as articulated in Umāsvāti's *Tattvārtha Sūtra* (ca. 100 C.E.), states that the universe is brimming with souls weighted by karmic material (*dravya*), many of which hold the potential for freeing themselves from all karmic residue and attaining spiritual liberation (*kevala*). These souls constantly change and take new shape due to the fettering presence of karma, described as sticky and colourful. By first accepting this view of reality and then carefully abiding by the five major vows (nonviolence, truthfulness, not stealing, sexual restraint, and nonpossession), the Jaina aspirant moves toward the ultimate goal of untrammeled spirituality. At the pinnacle of this achievement, all karmas disperse and the perfected one (*siddha*) dwells eternally in omniscient (*sarvajña*) solitude (*kevala*).

Umāsvāti explains how careful action will help ensure one's rebirth in a higher realm. Violent action might thrust one down into one of seven infernal regions or hells; auspicious action might elevate one to one of the eight heavenly regions. The highest spiritual action can only be undertaken in the middle realm, Earth or Jambūdvīpa, by human beings. If effective, one's meditation and careful observance of nonviolence might release one into a state of perfection, the Siddha Loka, where one dwells eternally experiencing energy, consciousness, and bliss, while retaining one's sense of individuality, symbolically represented by ascent to the summit of one's own mountain peak. Human beings who have successfully led a religious life achieve this through the release of all karmic bondage. One cannot attain this state from the heavenly or hellish realms; only through a human birth lived well according to spiritual precepts can this final abode be gained. In spatial orientation and its theory of moral consequences, it seems to evoke Dante's system of hell, purgatory, and heaven. Depending on one's actions, one earns a berth in one of the three domains.

The Jainas were careful to observe and describe the many life forms that they hoped to spare in order to advance on the spiritual ladder. They categorized them according to the number of senses they possess. Earth bodies, plants, and micro-organisms (*nigodha*) are said to possess the sense of touch. Earthworms and mollusks are said to add taste to touch. Crawling insects add the sense of smell. Moths, bees, and flies add sight. Jainas place animals that can hear and those that can hear and think, including reptiles, birds, and mammals into the highest realm. Śānti Sūri, a Jaina writer of the eleventh century, summarizes this assessment of different life forms in the *Jīva Vicāra Prakaraṇam*, a text of fifty verses. He makes clear that all forms of life, from clods of earth to human beings, have life, breath, bodily strength, and the sense of touch.[2] Hence, all must be protected.

According to the *Tattvārtha Sūtra*, 8,400,000 different species of life forms exist. These beings are part of a beginningless round of birth, life, death, and rebirth. Each living being houses a life force or *jīva* that occupies and enlivens the host environment. When the body dies, the *jīva* seeks out a new site depending upon the proclivities of karma generated and accrued during the previous lifetime. Depending upon one's actions, one can either ascend to a heavenly realm, and take rebirth as a human or animal or elemental or microbial form, or descend into one of the hells, as a suffering human being or a particular animal, depending upon the offense committed.

Śānti Sūri's *Jīva Vicāra Prakaraṇam* lists types of life in the earthly realm, their frequency of appearance, and cites an approximate lifespan for each. For instance, he states that hardened rock can survive as a distinct life form for 22,000 years; water-bodied souls for 7,000 years; wind bodies for 3,000 years; trees for 10,000 years, and fire for three days and three nights (*JVP* 34). Each of these forms demonstrates four characteristics: life, breath, bodily strength, and the sense of touch. Moving from the descriptions of elements to descriptions of plants, he lists various plant genres, with precise detail given for plants with fragrance, hard fruits, soft fruits, bulbous roots, thorns, smooth leaves, creepers, and so forth.

He then describes that two-sensed beings, ones that possess touch and taste, such as conches, cowries, gandolo worms, leeches, earthworms, timber worms, intestinal worms, red water insects, white wood ants, among others are said to live twelve years (*JVP* 15). Three-sensed beings live for 49 days and include centipedes, bedbugs, lice, black ants, white ants, crab-lice, and various other kinds of insects (*JVP* 16, 17). These beings add the sense of smelling. Four-sensed beings, which add the sense of sight, live for six months (*JVP* 35) and include scorpions, cattle-bugs, drones, bees, locusts, flies, gnats, mosquitoes, moths, spiders, and grasshoppers (*JVP* 18). At the top of this continuum reside the five-sensed beings, which add the sense of hearing and can be grouped into those who are deemed mindless and those who are considered to be sentient. This last group includes the denizens of hell, gods, and humans. Various life spans are cited for five-sensed beings, which Śānti Sūri describes in great detail. Examples are land-going, aquatic, sky-moving, and so forth.

---

2 Śānti Sūri, *Jīva Vicāra Prakaraṇam* (*JVP*), 1950, p. 163.

The detailed lists by Śānti Sūri and his later commentators present a comprehensive overview of life forms as seen through the prism of Jainism. In order to ascend along the path to the Siddha Loka, one had to know and respect each of the earth's several life forms. By carefully observing harmlessness to the greatest degree possible, one purges oneself of the negative karmas that cause repeated rebirth within the lower realms of the cosmos.

Food, Sustenance, and the End of Life

The eating of food poses a particular dilemma within the Jaina tradition. Jainism values all forms of life, including one's own human form. It also recognizes that all life feeds on other forms of life and that the sacrifice of life is essential to ensure the continuance of life. However, whereas as some animals exert no measure of control or reserve in seeking out food, such as tigers and birds of prey, Jainas seeks to moderate and control the human appetite, developing an elaborate system of cataloging food types and advocating avoidance of certain foods that are deemed particularly suffused with life. To begin, no Jaina is allowed to consume food that contains more than one sense. One-sensed food includes vegetables, fruits, and fluids, including milk and milk products. However, even within the hierarchy of vegetables, one finds distinctions. Root foods are generally rejected, such as carrots, because of the violence involved with pulling a carrot from the ground. Many Jainas eschew eggplants and figs because of the numerous seeds they contain. Many reject honey because of the many micro-oganisms housed therein. The style and time of eating takes on additional significance. In traditional Jaina villages, people generally do not eat after dark, to avoid ingesting unseen insects. A Jaina will also take care to eat all the food on the plate, to avoid the burgeoning of bacteria that might meet an inauspicious fate as the remains are cast into the garbage.

In addition to being careful about the foods one consumes, the Jainas also promote a rhythm of abstinence from food. One antidote to the unavoidable violence that eating entails is to schedule periodic fasts on a weekly or semi-weekly basis, culminating in the Paruyshan festival in late August or early September, in which many individuals seek to take no food for seven days and seven nights. These fasts are said to diminish the hold of karma on the body and spirit, preparing the practitioner for advanced levels (*guṇasthāna*) of spiritual attainment. All Jainas participate freely in these fasts, whether monks, nuns, or laypeople. They are said to help guarantee a smooth passage into one's next birth, presumably back into a family that practices nonviolence.

When life reaches its natural decline, and when death has been deemed imminent by a competent medical authority, a Jaina might request to embark on the ultimate act of nonviolence through fasting, specifically the *sallekhanā* or *santhāra* fast. This fast, described in the medieval texts, emulates the passing of Pārśvanātha and Mahāvīra, who at the end of their very full lives, gradually renounced all food, then all water, and then finally died, consciously moving into their permanent abode in the Siddha Loka.[3] For an ordinary Jaina monk or layperson, it would hopefully guarantee an improved next birth.

Jaina Cosmology: A Universe Permeated with Life

Jainism provides one of India's most thorough attempts to encapsulate a comprehensive worldview or cosmology that integrates the place of the human person within the continuum of the universe. From one's own birth, to the recognition of and respect for other life forms, to one's gradual transition into preparing for one's next birth, Jainism attempts to explain the place of the human being in a great continuous reality. It emphasizes hierarchy and vitality within its vision of the cosmos. Jainism identifies two primary categories of reality: living and nonliving. Living reality or *jīva* is broadly defined as dynamism and suffuses what in pre-contemporary physics would be considered inert. Each *jīva* is said to contain consciousness, energy, and bliss. Earth, water, fire, air bodies, which comprise material objects such as wood or umbrellas or drops of water or flickers of flame or gusts of wind all contain *jīva* or individual bodies of life force. The category of nonliving 'things' includes properties such as the flow of time and space and the binding of matter known as karma or *dravya* onto the *jīva*. The nature of this karma determines the course of one's embodiment and experience. Negative karma causes a downward movement both in this birth and in future birth. Positive karma releases the negative, binding qualities of karma and allows for an ascent to higher realms, either as a more morally pure human being or as a god or goddess. Ultimately, the Jaina path of purification through its many strict ethical precepts may culminate in joining the realm of the perfected ones, the *siddhas*. These liberated souls have released themselves from all karma and dwell in a state of eternal consciousness, energy, omniscience, and bliss.

In this cosmological system, one's station in life can be understood in terms of one's degree of effort in following ethically correct patterns of life as taught by the Jaina Tīrthankaras or spiritual leaders. The world of nature cannot be separated from the moral order; even a clod of earth exists as earth because it has earned its particular niche in the wider system of life processes. A human's experience includes prior births of various animals, micro-organisms, elemental entities, and perhaps gods and goddesses. To see and recognize and understand the world is to acknowledge one's past and potential future. Though the Jaina insistence on the uniqueness of each individual soul does not lend itself to an ultimate vision of interconnected monism, it nonetheless lays the foundation for seeing all beings other than oneself with an empathetic eye. In past or future births, one could have been or could become a life form similar to any of those that surround one in the vast unlimited cosmos.

3 See contemporary accounts of this practice in Christopher Chapple, *Nonviolence to Animals, Earth, and Self in Asian Traditions*, 1993 and S. Settar, *Pursuing Death*, 1990.

The Story of Contemporary Cosmology and Jainism

The contemporary story of the universe as told by physicists and cosmologists is complex and varied, requiring an understanding of higher mathematics and a reliance on sophisticated instruments such as electron microscopes and telescopes that penetrate deep into distant galaxies. Though many interpreters of science such as Stephen Hawking and Carl Sagan have summarized the various theories about the origins and structure of the universe, few have attempted to create a world of meaning from this raw data. Brian Swimme, however, has attempted to make sense of the insights of modern physics and examine the implications of this newly discovered world order for human behaviour. In this section, one aspect of his interpretation will be summarized, and then discussed in light of Jainism and the larger context of environmental ethics.

In their observations of the behaviour of matter and energy, planets and galaxies, Einstein and Hubble calculated that the world flared forth some 15 billion years ago. From that time and point of origin, all things blasted forth away from one another. The stuff of stars and elements continue to move apart from one another and, over the course of 15 billion years, as yet uncounted galaxies spin forth and continue to move outward. Because of this initial momentum, everything retains a part of this original being. And because everything continues to move from that point of origin, everything that contains a bit of that point of origin is at the centre of everything else that is moving forth. And because everything is moving forth and everything originated from that original flaring moment, everything is the centre of the universe and yet is moving from everything else.

Furthermore, the space that separates all these discrete masses of atomic materiality continues to generate evanescent particulate matter that constantly emerges and then dissolves. Even empty space is not empty but carries what Swimme describes as the 'all-nourishing abyss.' As he describes it,

> The usual process is for particles to erupt in pairs that will quickly annihilate each other. Electrons and positrons, protons and anti-protons, all of these are flaring forth, and as quickly vanishing again. Such creative and destructive activity takes place everywhere and at all times throughout the universe.
>
> The ground of the universe then is an empty fullness, a fecund nothingness. Even though this discovery may be difficult if not impossible to visualize, we can nevertheless speak a deeper truth regarding the ground state of the universe. First of all it is not inert. The base of the universe is not a dead, bottom-of-the-barrel thing. The base of the universe seethes with creativity, so much so that physicists refer to the universe's ground state as 'space-time foam'.[4]

This account of the materiality abounds in mystery, unpredictability, and dynamism. The ground for the manifested world lies hidden in forces like the *yin* and *yang*

4 Brian Swimme, *The Hidden Heart of the Cosmos: Humanity and the New Story*, 1996, p. 93.

of Chinese philosophy that constantly vacillate between presence and absence. Furthermore, like the Jaina system of transmutation of life forms, this primal energy constantly seeks new expression.

Both the story of contemporary cosmology and that of Jainism allow for awe and respect for materiality. According to Swimme, our deadened view of the material has led to the blight of consumerism, where ultimate meaning in life is mistakenly sought in the accumulation of things. This has resulted in lives of loneliness, depression, and alienation. He writes:

> Consumerism is based on the assumption that the universe is a collection of dead objects. It is for this reason that depression is a regular feature in every consumer society. When humans find themselves surrounded by nothing but objects, the response is always loneliness....[5]

For Swimme, the remedy for this angst can be found in a rediscovery of awe through appreciation of the intricacy and beauty of the material world, from the complexity of the meadow to the splendid grandeur of the Milky Way. Swimme writes that:

> Each person *lives* in the center of the cosmos. Science is one of the careful and detailed methods by which the human mind came to grasp the fact of the universe's beginning, but the actual origin and birthplace is not a scientific idea; the actual origin of the universe is where you live your life. The center of the cosmos refers to that place where the great birth of the universe happened at the beginning of time, but it also refers to the upwelling of the universe as river, as star, as raven, as you, the universe surging into existence anew.[6]

In this vision of the human place within the cosmos, each individual, each context holds ultimate meaning in its immediacy and its ongoing participation in the process of co-creation. As centres of creativity, all beings, all particles, play an important, integral role in the greater scheme of things. While retaining a unique and unencroachable perspective, each point of life holds a commonality with all others due to their shared moment of origin 15 billion years ago.

In some ways, this vitalistic account of creation and reality bears similarities with the Jaina tradition, as well as notable differences. The fundamental disagreement would lie in the premise that the world began in the single moment of the Big Bang or Flaring Forth. Jainism, like Buddhism, asserts the eternality of the universe and rejects the notion of an initial creation moment. However, just as Swimme contends that the consumerist obsession with dead objects leads to depression, in Jainism, the abuse and manipulation of materiality leads to a thickening of one's karmic bondage, guaranteeing a lower existence in this and future lives. Swimme suggests that the things of the world should be regarded as a celebration of the originary moment of creation, that people turn their attention to the beauty and mystery of creation as an antidote to the trivialization of life brought about by advertisements and accumulations. Jainism similarly asserts that things share a commonality in their

---

5 Ibid., p. 33.
6 Ibid., p. 112.

aliveness, which must be acknowledged and protected. Through respect for life in all its forms, including micro-organisms and the elements, one can ascend to a higher state of spiritual sensitivity.

Traditional Jaina cosmology and contemporary scientific accounts of the workings of the universe hold implications for the development of ecological theory. Both systems place value on the natural order. Both systems hold the potential to evoke the affective dimension of human responsiveness. Both systems develop an ethical view that calls for greater awareness of one's immediate ecological context. Swimme's system offers a prophetic critique of unbridled consumerism and its consequent trivialization and deadening of the material world. Jainism develops a specific code of behaviour that seeks to respect the life force in its various forms including its material manifestations.

Jainism and Social Engagement

Thomas Berry and Brian Swimme propose a new story based on scientific explanations regarding the origin and nature of the universe. Though this story holds distinct differences from that of the Jaina cosmological tradition, both systems seek to sacralize all aspects of worldly existence. By seeing all that surrounds us as suffused with life and worthy of worship, Jainism and the new cosmology offer stories that decentralize and universalize ethics, taking away overly anthropocentric concerns, and bring into vivid relief the urgency of respecting life in its various elemental, vegetative, and animal forms. The new cosmology and the story of the universe in the Jaina tradition promote a sense of immediacy and need for caring for all life forms. Berry and Swimme call for a renewed, spiritual commitment to environmental activism. As we look at Jaina history, we see a similar call to social engagement and activism.

The Jainas were quite assertive in making their minority religious views known in areas of India where they gained ascendancy. Though Jainism began in northeast India, many Jaina migrated to central and south India starting in around 300 B.C.E., establishing the Digambara sect, which advocates total nudity for its most senior monks. Others moved west, and became known as the Śvetāmbaras, named after the signature white robes worn by their monks and nuns. Many of the southern kingdoms of Karnataka offered protection and patronage to the Jainas, who won several concessions regarding public laws designed to encourage vegetarianism and discourage hunting (Saletore). Jainism exerted profound influence throughout this region from 100 to 1300 C.E. In the northern kingdoms of Gujarat, they experienced a golden era when Kumārapala (r. 1143-75) converted to Jainism. He encouraged the extensive building of temples, and under the tutelage of the Jaina teacher Hemacandra (1089-1172) became vegetarian.[7] He enacted legislation that reflected Jaina religious precepts regarding the sanctity of all life. In the north central area

---

7 John Cort, *Open Boundaries: Jain Communities and Cultures in Indian History*, 1998, p. 100.

of India, Jincandrasūri II (1541-1613), the fourth and last of the Dadagurus of the Śvetāmbara Khartar Gacch of Jaina monks, traveled to Lahore in 1591 where he greatly influenced the Mughal Emperor Akbar the Great. Akbar protected Jaina places of pilgrimage and ordered noninterference with Jaina ceremonies. Most remarkably, he forbade the slaughter of animals for one week each year.[8] The Jainas tirelessly campaigned against animal sacrifice, which is now illegal in most states of India. Mahatma Gandhi, the most well-known leader of modern India, was deeply influenced by the Jaina commitment to nonviolence and adapted it in his campaign for India's political independence from Britain. In the twentieth century, Acharya Tulsi, leader of the Terāpanthi sect of the Śvetāmbara Jainas, advanced a public campaign to promote vows such as avoidance of war and pollution.[9] Jainas remain active in their campaigns for animal protection in India, and continue to support shelters (*pinjrapoles*) for ill or neglected animals.

At first glance, the Jaina tradition might seem to be inherently ecologically-friendly. It emphasizes nonviolence. It values all forms of life. It requires its adherents to engage only in certain types of livelihood, presumably based on the principle of *ahiṃsā*. Jainism's earth-friendly attitudes have been celebrated in Dr. L.M. Singhvi's *Jaina Declaration on Nature*, in Dr. Michael Tobias' video *Ahimsa* and its companion volume, *Life Force*, in my own book *Nonviolence to Animals, Earth, and Self in Asian Traditions*, in the proceedings of the Ladnun conference on Ecology and Jainism and the Harvard Conference on Jainism and Ecology, as well as other materials. However, if we look at both the ultimate intention of the Jaina faith as well as the actual consequences of some Jaina businesses, we might detect a need for the sort of in-depth critical analysis and reflection that Thomas Berry has suggested might be needed. For instance, Jainas have long avoided using animal products in their many businesses. Lists of green-friendly materials could be developed by Jainas to be used in manufacturing processes. The Jaina programs of environmental education could be expanded to prepare future leaders to be more familiar with environmental issues. Jainas could actively support air pollution reduction initiatives by making certain that their own automobiles in India conform to legal standards.

In some respects, however, environmental activism, at best could earn a secondary place in the practice of the Jaina faith. The observance of *ahiṃsā* must be regarded as ancillary to the goal of final liberation or *kevala*. Ultimate meaning is not found in the perfection of nonviolent (in this case eco-friendly) behaviour but in the extirpation of all fettering karma. Although the resultant lifestyle for monks and nuns resembles or approximates an environmentally-friendly ideal, its pursuit focuses on personal, spiritual advancement, not on a holistic vision of the interrelatedness of life. In terms of the lifestyle of the Jaina layperson, certain practices such as vegetarianism,

---

8 Lawrence A. Babb, *Absent Lord: Ascetics and Kings in a Jain Ritual Culture*, 1996, p. 124.

9 See Christopher Chapple, *Nonviolence to Animals, Earth, and Self in Asian Traditions*, 1993.

periodic fasting, and eschewal of militarism might be seen as eco-friendly. However, some professions adopted by the Jainas due to their religious commitment to harm only one-sensed beings might in fact be environmentally disastrous, such as strip-mining for granite or marble, unless habitat restoration accompanies the mining process. Likewise, how many Jaina industries contribute to air pollution or forest destruction or result in water pollution?

As Thomas Berry has noted, the task of ecological repair requires the networking of the political, economic, business, education scientific, as well as the religious communities. Jainism, given its ethic of nonviolence and its deep involvement with the governmental structures of India and the business community worldwide, is well equipped to initiate the process. But in order for any of this work to be effective, it must proceed from a story. The story of the human superiority over nature has been told throughout the world, even by the Jainas who seek to rise above nature. And this story has been realized, as seen in the success of consumer culture worldwide. Native habitats continue to be destroyed as industrialization expands. As this happens, entire species of animals, insects, and plants disappear, never to return. Yet humans proliferate, taking up more space worldwide with their houses and condominiums and farmland, encroaching on and destroying the wild, isolating humans within fabricated landscapes that separate the human from the pulse of non-human life. A shift in consciousness must take place that values life in its myriad forms. The cosmological views of Jainism, the insights of contemporary science, and the growing perception of the beauty and fragility of the natural order all can contribute to this essential shift.

Bibliography and References

Babb, Lawrence A., *Absent Lord: Ascetics and Kings in a Jain Ritual Culture*, Berkeley: University of California Press, 1996.

Berry, Thomas, *The Dream of the Earth*, San Francisco: Sierra Club Books, 1988.

Berry, Thomas, 'Religion in the Ecozoic Era,' Plenary Address presented at the American Academy of Religion, Washington, DC, 1993.

Chapple, Christopher Key, *Nonviolence to Animals, Earth, and Self in Asian Traditions*, Albany: State University of New York Press, 1993.

________, 'Jainism and Nonviolence,' in Daniel L. Smith-Christopher (ed.), *Subverting Hatred: The Challenge of Nonviolence in Religious Traditions*, Cambridge, Massachusetts: Boston Research Center for the 21st Century, 1998.

________, 'The Living Cosmos of Jainism: A Traditional Science Grounded in Environmental Ethics,' *Daedalus*, Fall 2001, 120 (4), pp. 207-224.

Chapple, Christopher Key (ed.), *Jainism and Ecology: Nonviolence in the Web of Life*, Cambridge, Massachusetts: Center for the Study of World Religions, Harvard Divinity School, distributed by Harvard University Press, 2002.

Cort, John (ed.), *Open Boundaries: Jain Communities and Cultures in Indian History*, Albany: State University of New York Press, 1998.

Dundas, Paul, *The Jains*, London: Routledge, 1992.

Jaina Sūtras: Part I. The Ācārāṅga Sūtra. The Kalpa Sūtra, trans. Hermann Jacobi, New York: Dover, 1968 [1st edn, 1884].

Jaini, Padmanabh S., *The Jaina Path of Purification*, Berkeley: University of California Press, 1989.

________, *Gender and Salvation*, Berkeley: University of California Press, 1993.

________, 'Fear of Food: Jaina Attitudes on Eating,' *Collected Papers on Jaina Studies*, Delhi: Motilal Banarsidass, 2000, pp. 281-296.

LeValley, Paul, 'Naked Philosopher-Ascetics: Some Observations on the Shramana Religious Spectrum,' *Sophia*, **39** (2), Oct-Nov 2000, pp. 143-159.

Matthews, Clifford N., Tucker, Mary Evelyn and Hefner, Philip, *What Science and Religion Tell Us About the Story of the Universe and Our Place in it*, Chicago: Open Court, 2002; Christopher Key Chapple chapter on 'Jainism and Ecology,' pp. 283-292.

Saletore, Bhaskar Anand, *Medieval Jainism*, Bombay: Karnatak Publishing House, 1938.

Settar, S., *Pursuing Death*, Dharwad: Institute of Indian Art History, Karnatak University, 1990.

Singhvi, L.M., *The Jaina Declaration on Nature.*

Śānti Sūri, *Jīva Vicāra Prakaraṇam (JVP) along with Pathaka Ratnakara's Commentary*, ed. Muni Ratna-Prabha Vijaya, trans. Jayant P. Thaker, Madras: Jain Mission Society, 1950.

Swimme, Brian, *The Hidden Heart of the Cosmos: Humanity and the New Story*, Maryknoll, New York: Orbis Books, 1996.

________, *The Universe is a Green Dragon: A Cosmic Creation Story*, Santa Fe: Bear & Co., 1984.

________ and Berry, Thomas, *The Universe Story: From the Primordial Flaring Forth to the Ecozoic Era, A Celebration of the Unfolding of the Cosmos*, San Francisco: HarperSanFrancisco, 1992.

Tobias, Michael, *Ahimsa*, Los Angeles: JMT Productions, Public Broadcasting Corporation, 1989.

________, *Life Force: The World of Jainism.* Berkeley: Asian Humanities Press, 1991.

Umāsvāti, *That Which Is (Tattvārtha Sūtra): A Classic Jain Manual for Understanding the True Nature of Reality*, trans. Nathmal Tatia. San Francisco: HarperCollins, 1994.

Chapter 10

Buddhist Ethical Theory

Padmasiri de Silva

Ethics is generally divided into metaethics and normative ethics. 'The term "metaethics" implies that we are not taking part in the practice of ethics itself, but rather reflecting on the practice, as if from a different level from which we can view it as a whole, and see what is going on, when people are, say, arguing about rights and wrongs of eating meat.'[1] Normative ethics on the other hand seeks to directly influence actions. When we condemn people for breaking promises, the killing of animals, and stealing, and thus make judgments about right and wrong actions, there is a kind of activity, which we describe as making *normative* judgments. When moral philosophers raise basic issues about the nature of such moral judgments, whether they are based on facts or logical reasoning, subjective or objective and so on, they are engaging in metaethical reflections. Thus in metaethics we are asking basic questions about ethics, rather than participating in the process of reasoning and making decisions about good and bad and right and wrong. As normative ethics has an impact on our day-to-day decisions which have moral implications, as well as the larger conceptions of a good life that guide us, it is necessary that we understand the nature of such judgments and the theoretical perspectives in which they are rooted.

Now, in Buddhist ethics there is a very close link between ethics and the broader philosophy of leading a meaningful life. The Buddha accepted the relative objectivity of moral judgments, and espoused a middle position between relativism and any foundationalist view regarding the relationship between facts and values. By its very nature Buddhist ethics is *practical ethics*, though some of the issues that are considered in contemporary Practical Ethics discourse may not have been live concerns during the time of the Buddha. In the way that the Buddha accepted a relative objectivity for moral values they were also considered as relevant within a contextual and pragmatic framework. The Buddha also found that 'facts' were relevant for grounding values, though there was no logical entailment. Thus while intellectual and critical concerns about ethical pursuits were encouraged by the Buddha, they were not thought to constitute an end as such but merely regarded as a means to morally enhancing life that would tend towards the liberation from suffering. Thus in general there is no attempt to move ethical inquiries towards excessive metaethical reflections regarding facts and values and similar issues.

---

1 Peter Singer (ed.), *Ethics*, Oxford, Oxford University Press, 1994, p. 10.

Our inquiry into Buddhist ethics is concerned to develop a preliminary framework accommodating both the Western and Buddhist traditions of ethics. While we will see that Buddhist perspectives on environmental ethics are close to a concern with issues in practical ethics, now we will attempt to look at the framework of normative ethics in the Western and Buddhist theories of ethics. One of the metaethical issues relevant for this study to which some reference will be made in the next chapter is the relationship between facts and moral values.

Three ethical traditions have developed around three classic works in the history of Western moral philosophy – Aristotle' s *Nicomachean Ethics*, Kant's *Fundamental Principles of the Metaphysics of Morals* and John Stuart Mill's *Utilitarianism.* In a sense, they have given different answers to the same problem, but in another sense, they have also been dealing with different sorts of problems.[2] As there has been prolonged controversy between the followers of Kant, the deontological tradition, and the followers of Mill, the teleological-cum-consequentialists, it would be best to begin with a brief look at these traditions. In the way that Aristotle's work is a treatise in the art of moral education, Kant's work is a work on the moral law, influenced by the Hebrew moralists, Roman Stoics and the ecclesiastical puritan jurists who preceded Kant. His task was to draw the moral principle, not from the diverse and variable characteristics of human beings, but from the impersonal and invariant principles of rational beings. These principles are necessarily and universally true, *a priori* by nature. Mill was an economist concerned with the production and distribution of economic goods. From a very narrow point of view, the more wealth is produced in a system, the better it is for the people in that society. As money is merely of instrumental value, it was necessary to have some conception of intrinsic good to convert this economic model into an acceptable moral system. Instead of saying that actions are good in terms of their contribution to the GNP, Mill claimed that happiness or pleasure is the good. Thus administrators have the task of formulating rules and certain principles for the production of greater happiness all round. As the term 'utility' had more 'economic flavour', this was the term that generated the nomenclature of 'utilitarianism'. Kant's ethics emphasizes the logical priority of duties and is referred to as 'deontological' ethics, whereas for Mill the duties are derived from the goals of life, and thus came to be called 'teleological'. (Their difference in practical terms has been illustrated with examples in the General Introduction to this volume.)

The dialogue and the debates between these two groups of moral philosophers could take quite sophisticated turns and there could be positions of compromise and hybrids where one attempts to combine the best of both worlds. The development of rule utilitarianism and motive utilitarianism, as well as attempts to bring values into Kantian thinking, are examples of different meeting grounds. Emphasis on 'ends', 'consequences', 'rules', 'duties' and 'rights' are terms that are found in just about every moral system, both in the Western and Eastern traditions of moral philosophy,

2 Joel Feinberg, 'Three Classical Theories', in Henry West (ed.), *Moral Philosophy: Classic Contexts and Contemporary Problems*, Eucino: Dickensen Publishers, 1977, p. 10.

and doubtless in other cultures. Also, when a discourse on duties and rights enters an Eastern system, such as the Confucian or the Buddhist moral traditions, it acquires the flavour of a local variant, such as the rule of 'righteousness' or the 'wheel of righteousness'. In these systems, it loses the Kantian texture and is expressed, for instance, as the wheel of righteousness or the reciprocal duties and obligations of the householder, as in the Buddhist tradition. Sometimes in this process the dichotomies and dilemmas found in the Western systems are diffused or these different theoretical strands work together in a more holistic system. While the teleological-consequential axis is very clearly found in Buddhism, there is a limited strand of thinking that offers some similarity to utilitarianism – for instance, working for the good and the welfare of the many, as advice to both the kings and the monks.

Consequentialism is not synonymous with utilitarianism, and this is very much so in the Buddhist context also. Though the general concept of working for the welfare of the many is an idea that Buddhism and utilitarianism may share, Buddhism does not employ any hedonistic calculus as in classical utilitarianism. Buddhism also accepts a more integrated notion of motive, intention, consequence and foresight. For instance, in the practice of giving (*dāna*) food, money or clothes to a beggar, the volition before the act, during the act, and after the act of generosity (*cāga*) are all important. Also, the merit that one gains varies according to the motive of the person who gives, the character and spiritual qualities of the recipient, and the nature of the gift. In Buddhism, there is an important emphasis on the value of an act of giving based on wisdom, generosity and compassion. If these qualities are lacking, there are deficiencies. Thus one discerns a qualitative dimension to the act of giving or, on a larger scale, working for the welfare of other people. Also, according to the kammic (karmic) laws, one discerns the possibility of benefits of an act of generosity in a future birth or as an act that will enhance one's quest for enlightenment. Basically, giving is an antidote for egoism and greed. Metaphors of a consequentialist flavour abound in the discourses of the Buddha: If you sow seeds in a fertile and well-watered field, there will be bountiful yield; giving alms to the virtuous also yields great results.[3]

In fact, it would be wise to use the term 'Buddhist consequentialism', to indicate how Buddhism integrates the logic of the concept of consequentialism into Buddhist moral discourse. Thus Buddhism has certain strands of an ethic of duties and obligations, without following the Kantian legalistic and *a priori* strain; it also has a clear teleological-consequential axis, without necessarily being a utilitarian one. Buddhism would yet offer also an ethic of virtues and vices. Again it is not exclusively Aristotelian, as there are certain metaphysical differences between the two systems.

There are further elements in the ethics of Buddhism that go beyond both the Kantian and the utilitarian approaches. There is a need then for an alternative framework for morality, which will not emphasize only obligation, consistency and rationality as in Kant, but also emotions, particularly the moral emotions. Schopenhauer's

3 *Aṅguttara Nikāya* (*A*), IV.238.

work, *On the Basis of Morality* (1965), as interpreted by Lawrence Blum, offers an additional strand of contemporary moral thought, beside those perspectives offered by deontology, teleological consequentialism and the Aristotelian ethics of virtues and vices. In spite of the fact that, as Blum says, Schopenhauer displays an extremist criticism of Kant – his close association with Vedānta accounting for some differences from Buddhism, and the atmosphere of pessimism which sometimes pervades his writings – he did open a window for the entry of Buddhist thinking in the Western traditions of moral philosophy.[4]

When one looks at the discourses of the Buddha, these discourses abound in advice given to monks and laypersons on matters pertaining to ethics. Though the Buddha did not present a well-knit treatise on ethics as such, the material can be put together to develop a Buddhist perspective on ethics (as a number of scholars have attempted to do over time). But the framework in which a philosophically rigorous Buddhist ethics is to be charted involves certain elements which are not found in the Western ethical systems that we have outlined above. The acceptance of *kamma* as the law of moral causation, the belief in survival after death, the Buddhist soteriological ideal of *nibbāna* (Skt, *nirvāṇa*) as a liberation from the wheel of existence, and the (metaphysical) law of dependent origination etc., lend a special kind of texture and hermeneutics to the Buddhist concepts of consequentialism, teleology and duties and rights. Thus for instance it may be necessary to use the term 'Buddhist consequentialism' and to emphasize the specific nature of the Buddhist ethic of duties and obligations. In the same way, Buddhist altruism in the form of the four divine states is rooted in meditative states of absorption, which makes it different, in certain ways, from altruism in the Western tradition. Thus we have to be aware of this 'framework' or background of presuppositions, apart from the differing historical and sociological contexts, when we attempt to describe Buddhist ethics in terms of Western ethical concepts. There is a need to go beyond the two dominant moral philosophies in the West at this time; as I observed once before: 'Though the popular opposition in ethics has been that between the deontological ethics of Kant and the teleological consequentialism of Utilitarianism ... there is room for a third alternative which emphasizes the altruistic emotions grounded in a direct concern for and wellbeing of others'.[5]

---

4 Also see Padmasiri de Silva, 'Theoretical Perspectives on Emotions in Buddhism', in Joel Marks and Roger T. Ames (eds), *Emotions in Asian Thought*. Albany: SUNY Press, 1995; Lawrence A. Blum, *Moral Perception and Particularity*. Cambridge: Cambridge University Press, 1994.

5 Padmasiri de Silva, *Twin Peaks: Compassion and Insight*. Singapore: Buddhist Research Society. 1992: pp. 166-7; see also de Silva, Padmasiri 1998, *Environmental philosophy and ethics in Buddhism*, London: Macmillan, and New York: St Martin's Press, 1998; 'Buddhist Ethics', in P. Singer, (ed.), *A Companion to Ethics*, Oxford: Blackwell, 1991.

The Moral Assessments of Actions In Buddhism

First, some attempt will be made here to delineate the theoretical structure of Buddhist ethics, and then explore the question of whether Buddhism could contribute to the current search for an ethics which goes beyond both the deontological ethics of Kant and the teleological consequentialism of utilitarianism.

Buddhist ethics is based on the ultimate good, the liberation from suffering, the state of *nibbāna*. The nature of right and wrong in terms of this ideal good has been described in broad outline in terms of the eightfold path. But it would be necessary to look closely at the kind of criteria used for the moral assessment of actions. The crucial concept that illuminates the Buddhist consequential-teleological axis is the notion of *kamma* in Pali, and *karma* in Sanskrit. The term refers to volitional actions and their concomitant mental factors causing rebirth and shaping our destinies for the future. The Buddha's succinct statement, '*cetanāham bhikkhave kammam vadāmi*' is often translated as 'I call the motive the deed'. It means that volitional activity by body, speech and mind generates kammic consequences. It is more like a concept that holds together the motivational roots like greed, hatred and delusion, intention and motive (for example, to kill an animal), the activities of body, speech and mind making the killing of the animal, and the different types of consequences which follow from it. The teleology can be understood in terms of the ideals we consciously adopt in terms of a better birth, and the liberation from suffering.

The term 'Buddhist consequentialism' indicates that items like the motivational roots (*mūla*), motive (*cetanā*), the volitional activity and the consequences are linked closely in terms of the ideal of a good rebirth or the complete cessation from suffering. There is no need to isolate them, except when in detailed analysis one wishes to look more closely at the motive or the different types of consequences. Also, intended consequences, unintended consequences and actual consequences need to be understood in terms of this conceptual structure of the notion of *kamma*. In a very deep sense, the practice of mindfulness may help us to commit ourselves to some kind of foresight and vision about the future. An authentic follower of the Buddha would be concerned about the consequences of the actions on others, on themselves and society, as well as on future generations and on the non-human world, as a good environmentalist would do. The concept of *kamma* is a kind of 'thick concept'.

The fact that the Buddha lays down a deeper layer of 'conditions' for the emergence of *kamma* indicates the close link between the psychology of Buddhism and the ethics of Buddhism. Greed, hatred and delusion are conditions for the emergence of kammic activity. The unwholesome actions conditioned by these three conditions, such as killing, stealing, illicit sexual relations, uttering falsehood, slandering, rude speech and foolish talk, have bad consequences. In terms of consequences in a next birth, it is said that he who indulges in these unhealthy activities may encounter, for instance, disease and poverty, whereas if he practices wholesome activities he will be rewarded with wealth and health.[6] It is also said that some kammic consequences will ripen during one's lifetime, others in the next birth and still others in subsequent births.[7] There is a strange duality about performing good actions like giving charity to the poor and helping needy people with the intention of getting a good birth, as this will provide fuel for a longer journey in *saṃsāra* (the wheel of existence). If one is committed to the ideal of complete liberation from suffering (*nibbāna*), doing of good actions will be for the primary aim of the eradication of greed, hatred and illusion. Thus good actions will develop the sort of character (*saṇkhāra*) that will be greatly oriented towards liberation, rather than towards reaping material benefits in another life. There is nothing wrong in opting for benefits in the next life, which would also provide a sound basis for leading a good life. But it is not oriented towards liberation, with any sense of urgency. To use a graphic metaphor of the Buddha, such a person does not feel that 'his turban is on fire'. Such a person will have the ideal of *nibbāna* before her but not work towards this ideal with a sense of urgency. This difference is also seen in a more clear light in the distinctive types of advice given by the Buddha to monks and the laymen. But again, there were laymen who attained high states of perfection and others who were diligently working towards this ideal.

These two types of orientations may be conceptualized in terms of two metaphors, the 'craftsmanship model' and the 'judicial model'. If a person helps a needy persons by giving them food and clothing, several consequences follow from this act. There is a psychological law that if you do a good act and continue to act in this manner you tend to develop such dispositions (*saṇkhāra*) or a character. Thus what is most characteristic of a good action is the tendency to repeat such actions. What is worse about a bad action is also the tendency to repeat such actions. The character building aspect is what one may describe by the metaphor of the craftsmanship model. The tendency to see one's actions in terms of rewards and punishments is what may be called the judicial model. In fact, there are two sets of Pali words, which are of great interest in this context. *Puñña*, which is rendered as merit, and *pāpa*, demerit. They refer basically to good and bad as the returns that you get in lives to come as rewards and losses. *Kusala* and *akusala*, though sometimes used to cover merit and demerit in the above mentioned sense, are exclusively used for *nibbāna*-oriented actions. It is also of interest to note that Horner has translated the word *kusala* as 'skilful' and *akusala* as 'unskilful', reminding us of Aristotle's claim that a good man is like a good carpenter because the skills manifest themselves in the most natural way as if it were second nature.[8] When a perfect one (*arahant*) performs good actions, those good actions flow in the most natural and spontaneous way and they do not accumulate any karma good or bad. The perfect one presents the very paradigm of actions described as *kusala.* They do not generate kammic consequences. The concept of the *arahant* implies that the perfect one is not capable of actions which are described by the term *akusala.* It is a misunderstanding to think that a perfect one

6 *A*, III.40; *M*, 135.

7 *A*, III.98.

8 *M*, I.

is beyond good and evil. A perfect one, as seen visibly in the life of the Buddha, was capable of a richness of virtues, with a tremendous variety and refinement.

Though he could discern humanity in very impersonal terms, that is, in terms of the law of dependent origination, and in terms of the five constituents that go to make the individual, he was yet capable of understanding the logic of character, the shades of good and evil in their multiplicity, among those who came to him with problems. The Buddha's mission after enlightenment was to work for the wellbeing and happiness of the many, out of compassion and for the benefit of all. This is also a message that he conveyed to the monks. He admonished the rulers to govern according to the principles of a wheel-turning monarch (*cakkavatti*). Buddha's compassion has on many occasions been extended beyond humans to all living beings. In this kind of ethic he recommended for the householders we discern the outlines for the development of a social ethics for the benefit of the many, a theme to be taken up in the chapter on Buddhist environmental ethics.

Utilitarianism

If Buddhist ethics is understood in terms of the teleological-consequentialist axis as described above, to what extent does it resemble utilitarianism? As mentioned above, there is a certain strand of utilitarian ethics which offers some similarities. There are a number of differences, some of them brought out when utilitarianism is placed in a historical continuum. But at a certain point, comparisons become difficult, as they are looking at different types of problems and answers in the human predicament. Consequentialism is the ethical theory that moral assessment of actions has to be based on consequences, and to do this one has to have a goal or *summum bonum* which is of intrinsic value. But the concept of ultimate value is important. As there are clear differences between the ultimate ideal of Buddhism and that of utilitarianism, some of the similarities are 'formal' similarities, in that they favour a consequentialist-teleological frame, rather than a deontological frame. The concept of the ultimate liberation from suffering is alien to utilitarianism or for that matter to other dominant Western theories of ethics. It is at the level of social ethics that an intelligible dialogue with utilitarianism is possible. Even Buddhist environmentalism has to be very much explored as a social ethics. As very clearly stated by John Lachs, Mill's contribution to social ethics has to be placed against the background of the kind of social and economic evils of the era of industrialization, when England went through a painful transition: 'there was no social mechanism in place for the rational distribution of this bounty. Private and class interests narrowly conceived stood in the way of improving the living conditions of all. While there was substantial sentiment for the liberalization of society and for the elimination of blatant cruelty and injustice, the wheels of reform turned slowly'.[9] Mill considered utilitarianism as an answer to these social and political issues, and Lachs says that in

9 John Lachs, 'Mill, J.S.', in Robert J. Cavalier and J. Gouinlock (eds), *Ethics in the History of Western Philosophy*, London: MacMillan, 1989, p. 247.

some of his 'sanguine moments' Mill considered the greatest moralists and religious reformers as utilitarians, broadly concerned with the welfare of the multitude, and not any sectional groups. The Buddha was also concerned with the oppressions of caste, the evils of animal sacrifice, starvation and poverty, as well as the perennial riddles of life and death. Mill also 'respected variety in motivations *too* much *to* believe that they could all be reduced *to* a single, simple one'.[10] But searching for a method for making decisions he ended up with what has been called a hedonistic calculus. Though Mill made considerable attempts to refine his notions of pleasure and pain and prove that this went far beyond a doctrine worthy for the swine, there have been critical issues which have emerged, all along the history of contemporary utilitarianism, regarding the method of decision making, the semantics of hedonism, as well their ethical implications. The philosophy and economics of utilitarianism have of course been refined over the years, by others like Sidgwick, and more recently by Richard Brandt, Amartya Sen and Derek Parfit. Briefly, we shall sum up some of the standard criticisms of utilitarianism.

Consider the dilemma of the surgeon, whether he should let the patient suffering from a brain tumour die in order that he may save the life of two other patients who needed heart and brain operations. At this point, on issues of justice, the hedonistic calculus is put to strain, and utilitarians have to search for other explanations, or fall back on saving the patient with the brain tumour by including a modifying rule, as a constraint. If we take another example like capital punishment, can we justify it on the ground that this will deter others from committing crimes? A Buddhist may not justify capital punishment but would back the case for reforming the criminal. But the doctrine of *kamma* brings a new dimension to the issue, as an individual will anyway reap the harvest for his deeds, here or in a next life. Also, the consequences of actions and policies in the social sphere will have an element of uncertainty. The Buddhist is expected to look at the actions in terms of the individual psyche, the genesis in unwholesome roots and motives, and their expression in speech and action. Thus there is a difference of focus in the Buddhist assessment of moral action. Though the Buddha was concerned with the overall social impact of the actions on individuals and the ethics that should guide the kings in framing social policies, he emphasized the transformation of the individual instead of searching for a moral calculus for society. The Buddha also focused on smaller social units like the family as the focus of economic and moral uplift. In general the emphasis was not always on 'what should I do?', but 'what sort of person should I be?'. Thus individuals who develop the right kind of character would respond to particular situations in the most natural way, by taking the context into account. Moral freedom for the Buddhist would involve a more reflective turn of mind than merely the ability to vary choices. Both in the area of interpersonal relations among humans, as well as our attitudes to the non-human world, Buddhism does not use a kind of interpersonal measuring technique but responds in terms of the more emotionally binding pathways of compassion and kindness. Sharper distinctions in the moral sphere like those between benevolence

10 Ibid., p. 248.

and kindness, kindness and compassion, compassion and sympathetic joy are hard to catch through an impersonal calculus. Utilitarian philosophy, specially as represented in the work of Mill, emerged in a certain historical context and, to be fair to that philosophy, it has to function within that framework. The Buddhist framework is somewhat different, in spite of the formal resemblances to utilitarianism in upholding a moral theory with a teleological-consequentialist axis.

In spite of all these restrictions, the utilitarian emphasis on sound social policy and welfare are important, and if they are not obsessed with the maximization of the utility principle, Buddhist social ethics may have some common concerns with utilitarian social policies, and especially so in the area of environmental ethics. With the intrusion of cost-benefit analysis and the invasion of commercial values into environmentalism, utilitarianism needs to do a more critical appraisal of its methodology for social welfare.

Deontology

Contemporary deontologists say that the more important aspects of our lives ought to be guided by moral rules. These rules should not be broken, because it is wrong to violate them independent of their assessment in terms of consequences. The nature of the deontological claim may be described in the words of Fried: 'It is part of the idea that lying or murder are wrong, not just bad, that these things you must not do no matter what. They are not negatives that enter into a calculus to be outweighed by the good you might do or the greater harm you might avoid'.[11] Such a view is described as deontological, originating from the Greek word '*deon*', meaning duty. It is contrasted with '*telos*', meaning goal. In the history of moral thought in the West, it was Immanuel Kant who first developed the notion of 'Duty for Duty's sake'. Kant rejected maxims of a non-universalizable nature and said that all rational agents should follow a categorical imperative based on a universal law of reason. A later variant of the ethics of duty is W.D. Ross's notion of *prima facie* duties, which was an attempt to reduce the extremism of the Kantian position. He says that we have a *prima facie* duty to help others, another to keep our promises, another to repay past acts of kindness and so on. He does not try to weave all this into any logical system.

In all these theories, in spite of variations, there 'is an emphasis on duties, rules which should not be broken, promises which should be kept'. In contrast to the consequentialist maximization of happiness, deontologists would defend the rights of an innocent victim, and focus on the principle of justice, rather than the happiness of the many.

There are no deontological facets in Buddhism in the strong sense of the word, like an impersonal categorical imperative. Richard E. Gombrich, examining 'The Duty of a Buddhist According to the Pāli Scriptures', observes that the only strong sense in which one could speak of a central obligation or duty of a Buddhist is in

11 C. Fried, *Rights and Wrong*, Cambridge, Mass., Harvard University Press, 1978, p. 9.

relation to attainment of liberation from suffering, embodied in the phrase *katam karaniyam*, 'what had to be done is done'. But then there is no flavour of a categorical imperative in that sense, it is some sort of self-imposed duty.[12] The important point about this context is that the resolution to end suffering emerges out of an empirical and experiential context and is not *a priori*. It is not an external voice or command. It is something which emerges from the understanding of the nature of things as they are *yathā bhūtaṃ pajāňāti*. Leaving out this context, what is found in the Buddhist texts is a group of precepts, rules, reciprocal duties and obligations.

If one looks at the five precepts, to which reference has already been made, they appear more like ground conditions that facilitate the development of morality and social harmony, as well as providing a congenial soil for the germination of the practices of concentration and development of wisdom. They have a strong pragmatic texture in them. The rules for the monks have even been modified depending on context. Also, these rules, both for the monk and laymen, are the guidelines for a full-blooded and finely nuanced moral culture to emerge. Thus the rules and precepts in Buddhism bring constraints into the practice of morality, delineate surroundings in which the ethics has to be practiced and provide the soil in which the practice of mindfulness and concentration takes root. These foundations in the practices of morality, if persistently practiced, will get transformed into a finer form. In the perfect *arahant* the ideal moral qualities have become second nature, spontaneous and natural.

Duties and obligation emerge in a pragmatic social context bringing the Buddhist community of monks, laymen and families together. The kings are also expected to be guided by duties to rule in the light of the principles of righteousness, impartiality and equity. We have already made a reference to the reciprocal duties and obligations found in the *Sigālavādasutta.* A wife should be ministered to by her husband in five ways: by being courteous to her, by not despising her, by being faithful to her, by handing over authority to her and by providing her with necessary adornments; the wife should minister to her husband in five ways: by ordering the household well, by hospitality to their relatives, by fidelity, by taking care of his wealth and by her industry.

A child who has once been supported by parents has to support them when the need arises, perform duties which were incumbent on the parents, keep to the traditions of the family and be worthy of his heritage. Parents are expected to restrain the children from vice, train them to a profession, contract for them a suitable marriage and, in due time, hand over the inheritance.

The pupils have certain duties by their teachers: rising from their seat and greeting them, waiting upon them, displaying enthusiasm to learn, being of service to them, acquiring the essence of their teaching. The teachers are expected to make sure that they have given the students a good training, that they have seen that the students have duly understood their teaching, that they have given them a complete

12 Richard F. Gombrich, 'The Duty of a Buddhist According to the Pāli Scriptures', in Wendy Doniger et al. (eds) *The Concept of Duty in South Asia.* New Delhi: Vikas, 1978.

grounding of the varied skills of every art, and that they speak well of them to others and that they have seen to their safety.

Duties that employers have to their employees are described as the following: to assign work according to their strength, give them food and wages, look after them when they are sick, share rare delicacies with them, grant hours off from work to relax. The employees reciprocate by rising before them, retiring after them, being content with what is given to them, doing their work well and speaking well of their employers.

The reciprocal relations between friends and companions are described in the following manner: a person should display towards a friend generosity, courtesy and benevolence, treat him or her well and keep to promises. The friend thus ministered to in turn should reciprocate such conduct by protecting in return his or her companion when they are careless and off their guard, looking after their property, offering a refuge in danger, not letting them down in their troubles, and by showing consideration for their family.

The householder is expected to be friendly to ascetics and brahmanas in act, speech and thought, to keep his house open to them and to supply their temporal needs. The ascetics and brahmanas should admonish householders to refrain from doing evil, to direct their mind towards the good, to show compassion towards them, to teach them what they have not heard, to correct any wrong conceptions they have received, and to reveal the path towards heaven.

These detailed reciprocal duties and obligations centring on the family give us some insight into the way that the Buddha interpreted duties and obligations. These duties do not betray any strong deontological perspective, as they rest on the notion of reciprocity. This is a soft blending of the ethics of care and the ethics of rights. The notion of reciprocity both in relation to society and nature is a basic theme in the development of a Buddhist environmental ethics. We may construct a homily to nature bringing in animals, trees and the ecosystem, thus providing the ground for an environmental ethics. Reciprocity is a concept that goes beyond both domination and subordination and emphasizes the notion of interconnectedness.

We have shown elsewhere the implications of these perspectives for duties and obligation and the Buddhist understanding of the logic of the concepts of equality and rights. The morality of rights differs from the morality of responsibility; it emphasizes separation rather than connection.[13] When reading through the *Sigālavādasutta* homily and grasping the moral texture that lies beneath it, someone familiar with the work of Carol Gilligan may discover a kindred voice in her work *In a Different Voice*:[14]

13 Padmasiri de Silva, 'The Concept of Equality in the Theravada Buddhist Tradition', in R. Siriwardena, (ed.), *Equality and the Religious Traditions of Asia*, London: Frances Pinter. 1987.

14 Carol Gilligan, *In a Different Voice*, Cambridge: Harvard University Press, 1982, pp. 164-5.

> The morality of rights is predicated on equality and centred on the understanding of fairness, while the ethic of responsibility relies on the concept of equity, the recognition of differences in need. While the ethic of rights is a manifestation of equal respect, balancing the claims of other and self, the ethic of responsibility rests on an understanding that gives rise to compassion and care.

The other contexts where the Buddha refers to duties are the duties of the monk to spread the *dhamma* (Skt. *Dharma*) for the welfare of the many and for the king to govern according to the principles of the dhamma. Kingship was the established institution of the time, and it was the king who was in charge of the political and economic administration of the country. The Buddha was attempting to humanize the institution of kingship and give it moral stature. The notion that the king should govern with the approval and consent of the people was the axiom to be followed. A significant phrase used to describe the king was *mahāsammāta*: the king was so entitled as he has been selected by the people. He was also expected to govern according to the principles of the dhamma and to ensure that the moral and cosmic order of the universe was reflected in the way that he governed. He was referred to as a wheel-turning universal monarch.

A Way Beyond Conflicting Theories In Ethics

> The difficulty is to achieve some kind of integrity in human life without either overwhelming its personal core with a pervasive impartiality or bulldozing the impersonal standpoint in the name of what one must personally do. ... The discovery of an alternative that we can live by I take to be the task of ethical theory.[15]

There is a healthy feature emerging in the contemporary traditions of moral philosophy, and in saying this, we refer to the fact that some of the most celebrated philosophers of our time are having a second look at the dichotomies through which they have charted their philosophical reflections. The words from Nagel's paper perhaps reflect his declared drift towards anti-reductionism. The recent attempt by Peter Singer (in a project undertaken with Leslie Cannold and Helga Kuhse[16]), to reflect on the critics of impartialism is again a most welcome response to generate a much-needed dialogue with the critics of impartialism. Both the Kantian heritage and the utilitarian heritage have during recent times been together labelled as 'impartialism'. In spite of the fact that a philosopher like R.M. Hare has blended utilitarian perspectives with Kantianism, the spectre of abstract impartialism has been the target of criticism.

Lawrence A. Blum, in his book, *Moral Perception and Particularity*, presents a critique of moral philosophies 'that have been too focused on rational principle, on

15 Thomas Nagel, *Other Minds*. New York: Oxford University Press, 1995, p. 171.

16 Peter Singer, Leslie Cannold and Helga Kuhse, 'William Godwin and the Defence of the Impartialist Ethics', *Utilitas*, vol. 7(1), May, 1995.

impartiality, on universality and generality, on rules and codes of ethics'.[17] Blum, inspired by the work of Iris Murdoch, emphasizes the need for a moral philosophy rooted in the psychological dimensions of moral life. He lays special emphasis on the psychology of emotions, motivation, judgment and perception. This is a theme not so long back also developed by Owen Flanagan as 'psychological realism' in ethics.[18] A moral theory has to have a conception of a moral agent that takes into account the richness, variety and complexity of moral experience as well as its subtlety. A schematic and abstract presentation of moral philosophy is bound to sacrifice its rich contextualism. Murdoch's own words in criticizing the rule-obedience model describe Blum's point well. She says that though recent British philosophy has been dominated by the rule-obedience model, 'very different models are in fact held by morally sensitive people – by those, for instance, who see moral endeavour as the realizing of a pattern of life or the following out of a pilgrimage'.[19] According to her, what is important is not merely the ability to vary choices and answer the question, 'What shall I do?', but also to raise the question, 'What does my life add up for'. Apart from the emphasis on psychological realism and the critique of the rule-obedience model, the central question is the question raised by Singer regarding the conflict between partialism and impartialism. Partialists claim that impartialists' theories cannot account for our personal relationships, like those with children, parents, friends and spouses. When close personal relationships are threatened it is claimed that our actions must be guided by impersonal standards. Sometimes when moral concern for strangers conflicts with moral concern for those whom we love, we often think that the latter deserve consideration.

The Singer, Cannold and Kuhse paper presents a good response to the problem: 'Our feelings for our spouses, children, lovers or close friends have their roots deep in our human nature. We have evolved as mammals living in small and relatively stable groups. This means that we are concerned to protect our kin, and liable to form long lasting reciprocal relationships ... any successful rules for everyday life should build on these aspects of our nature'.[20] They conclude by saying that the conflict between partialism and impartialism is real, and the only tenable position is to recognize both. Lafollette's study on personal relationships also recognizes that tension, and he says that we can neither develop moral knowledge nor empathy for an impartial morality, unless we experience intimate relationships, for personal relations empower us to develop an impartial morality.[21]

---

17 Blum, op cit, p. 3.

18 Owen Flanagan, *Varieties of Moral Personality*, Cambridge, Mass: Harvard University Press, 1991.

19 Iris Murdoch, *The Sovereignty of Good*, London: Routledge and Kegan Paul, 1970, p. 35.

20 Peter Singer, Cannold and Kuhse, op cit, p. 17.

21 Hugh Lafollette, 'Personal Relationships', in P. Singer, *A Companion to Ethics*, 1991.

A Buddhist Response to Moral Dichotomies

Some of the moral dilemmas of our times emerge because of the tensions between competing moral perspectives. The Buddhist options of two facets of morality for the monks does help Buddhism to diffuse some of the tensions that emerge out of special relationships in the family and a more generalized benevolence directed to larger humanity. In the *Sigālavādasutta* discourse the Buddha outlines in detail the spirit of caring and fellow feeling .which ought to pervade relationships in the family. But in the life of renunciation advocated for the monks there is an attempt to move away from that network of relationships. We do of course know that after the attaining of enlightenment, the Buddha spent 45 years in actively guiding the thousands of people whom he met. This included preaching to Siddhartha's wife and child, who also finally attained states of perfection. As Joel Kupperman very clearly points out, unlike the utilitarians, some of the Buddhist recluses carried their altruism to its logical conclusion, by a commitment to work for the larger humanity like the Buddha. There is no comparable literature on 'saintliness' in utilitarianism.[22]

Lafollette's point that personal relationships empower us to expand into more impersonal or generalized forms of caring and compassion is also important. The Buddha takes a mother's love for a child as the paradigmatic expression of compassion. While we see in the Buddha the most profound expression of universal compassion, at the same time, he was sensitive to the tremendous variety of people who came to listen to him. The Buddha selected particular persons from the audience for a sermon, and then made it relevant to others. He understood specific individual ailments and suggested corresponding remedies. The Buddha had a flexibility to move from particular individuals to larger groups, and come back to individuals again. The sermons were highly focused, with specific anecdotes, but also carried a broad and general message.

Also, the term 'impartiality' has different facets of meaning. One meaning of being impartial is that one has to be fair in making a judgment, and weighing the evidence. Impartial judgments do not necessarily imply aloofness or indifference to particular individuals. As Eamon Callan says, 'Impartiality is not the implacable enemy of the virtues of intimacy but often an indispensable ally to their role in the good life.'[23] Callan also points out that the suppression of bias does not always mean the suppression of all emotion.

Impersonality

The term 'impersonality' needs to be understood independent of the term 'impartiality', for they cannot *always* be used as synonyms. In the Buddhist context,

---

22 See Joel J. Kupperman, 'Emotions of Altruism: East and West', in *Emotions in Asian Thought*, 1995, op cit.

23 Eamon Callan, 'Impartiality and Virtue', in *The Journal of Value Inquiry.* **28,** 1994, p. 409.

the question has to be raised as to how Buddhism blends agent-centred projects with the quest for liberation, which in its final form has gone beyond any person-oriented predicates. There are two important strands of the meaning of the term:[24]

1. An ethical theory which requires the dissociating of preferences and desires from individuals, and the agglomerating of them (Utilitarianism).
2. An ethical theory which recommends to individuals the restructuring of their motivational economies with the aim of transcending personal craving and desires (Buddhism).

Expanding on this very important distinction, Flanagan makes an insightful observation:

> But truly living according to the tenets of Buddhism or any other very impartial, impersonal (in the second sense), or detached form requires an extremely complex and disciplined kind of character, possibly richer and more complex than that required to live as a liberal individualist.[25]

Flanagan recognizes that those who follow the Buddhist path aspire to realize an impersonal reality, the ideal of attaining *nibbāna.* He also recognizes that the Buddhist analysis of the nature of personality is made in terms of impersonal constituents. But yet he says that to realize this impersonal ideal of *nibbāna* a great deal of individual commitment, effort, and a very rich form of discipline is necessary. Even the Buddha accepts that 'right view' (*sammā diṭṭhi*), with which a Buddhist makes gradual progress on the path, is an individual point of view which gets refined and refined as one proceeds on the path. Flanagan's point is that being an agent aspiring with a project towards liberation from suffering, a point of view, is a precondition for making progress towards its final realization: 'Indeed, as I have stressed, being a person, an agent capable of having a point of view and certain desires and projects, is a necessary condition for successfully realizing the project of being a Buddhist'.[26] Thus a Buddhist too requires an agent-oriented perspective to reach a more impersonal goal. As was mentioned earlier, the right view is a preliminary starting point, and it will remain as a personal point of view of an agent till it gradually becomes progressively refined and moves towards a more impersonal point of view. The Buddha's celebrated metaphor of the raft emphasizes that one should use this standpoint as an aid to explore experientially the realities that one encounters on the path but not intellectually to cling to it. A second point which needs emphasis is that out of the three facets of egoism, craving (*taṇhā*), wrong views and 'I-conceit' (*māna*), the 'I conceit' is transcended *only* in the last phase of liberation. A subtler residue of the subjective and personal point of view is carried through, till it is transcended at the final stage. The term *ahaṅkāramamakāra mānānusaya* may be

24 Owen Flanagan, op cit, p. 75.

25 Ibid., p. 78.

26 Ibid,. p. 78.

translated as, 'latent tendencies to the conceits of "I-making" and "mine-making"'. They are inbuilt tendencies which emerge without deliberation and awareness but yet are intentional. Even the perfected ones do perform 'intentional activity', activity that is purposive, but these actions have no trace of *upādāna* (clinging) and thus do not generate *kamma.* In the *Saṃyutta Nikāya*, the five aggregates (*khandas*) are associated with intention (*cetanā*) independent of clinging).[27] The perfected one is free from 'clinging to the five aggregates'. Being an 'individual' with biological needs, the *arahant* would engage in activities like eating food without the psychological and the dispositional residue, verbally described as 'I am taking food'. Our thinking on the concerns about 'subjectivity' and the 'personal view' falls in line with the interpretation that the *arahant* remains an 'individual' as distinct from other individuals, but is not a somebody or a 'self'.[28] Thus if we look at the possible conditions for a minimalist conception for the personal point of view, its application to the perfected one would be different from the others who are at varying levels of development. But Flanagan's main contention is that the Buddhist path calls for rich and complex patterns of personal discipline to reach the goal. This would be one of the most significant ways in which we bring a personal and impersonal viewpoint together, in the context of Buddhism.

Going through Derek Parfit's tangled web of arguments on personal and impersonal viewpoints, we discovered a refreshing insight. He says that on his interpretation (which he unfortunately describes as a 'reductionist view'), the unity of each life is not automatically ensured as in the 'nonreductionist view'. It is something we can influence and generate, as the unity found in our lives is a 'matter of degree'. Parfit argues:

> We may want our lives to have greater unity, in the way that an artist may want to create a unified work. And we can *give* our lives greater unity, in ways that express or fulfil our particular values and beliefs. Since the reductionist view gives more importance to how we choose to live, and to what distinguishes different people, this is a second way in which it is *more* personal.[29]

Our final point is that people *do not* in actual life, often, summon a deductive calculus of moral logic to guide their lives. To reach even the most sublime impersonal 'truths' (as in the Buddhist quest), or to act in accordance with the most desirable moral rules (as with Kant and the utilitarians), people struggle with the emotions and desires that obstruct them and generate and cultivate the most ennobling sentiments and attitudes. In the words of Parfit, the struggle is to live creatively, like producing a work of art. This would be the most auspicious way of concluding a chapter on Buddhist ethics, intended to provide a background to Buddhist contributions to environmentalism, as 'a way of life'.

---

27 *S.* 5, III.60.

28 Thero Nanavira, *Clearing the path*, Colombo: Path Press, 1984.

29 Derek Parfit, *Persons and Reasons*, Oxford: Clarendon Press 1984, p. 446.

References

Translations of the discourses of the Buddha

Aṅguttara Nikāya (*A*), trans. Thera Nyanaponika and Bhikkhu Bodhi, *Numerical discourses of the Buddha*, an anthology of *suttas* from the *Aṅguttara Nikāya*, New York: Rowman and Littlefield.

Aṅguttara Nikāya, II. Morris and II. Iiardy (eds), vols 1–5, London: Pali Text Society, 1885–1900.

Gradual sayings, F.L Woodward, (trans. vols 1, 2, 5) and trans. E.H. Hare, (vols III–IV), London: Pali Text Society, 1932–36.

Majjhima Nikāya (*M*), R. Chalmers Trekner and C.A.F. Rhys Davids, vols 1–4, Pali Text Society, London. *Middle length sayings*, trans. I.B. Horner, London: Pali Text Society, 1954–59.

Bhikkhu Ñanamoli and Bhikkhu Bodhi, *Middle length discourses of the Buddha*, translation of the *Majjhima Nikāya*, Kandy: Buddhist Publication Society, 1995.

Saṃyutta Nikāya, (*S*) trans. Bhikkhu Bodhi, *The connected discourses of the Buddha*,

vols 1–2, Boston: Wisdom Publishers, 2000.

Pali Texts

Atthasalini (*Expositor*), trans. Rhys Davids, London: Pali Text Society, 1920–21.

Dīgha Nikāya, Rhys Davids and J.E. Carpenter (eds), vols I–III, London: Pali Text Society, 1890–1911.

Dhammapada S. Sumangala (ed.), London: Pali Text Society, 1897.

Jātaka Stories, E.B. Cowell (ed.), vols 1–6, London: Pali Text Society, 1895–1905.

Suttanipāta, D. Anderson, D. Smith and H. Smith (eds), London: Pali Text Society, 1948.

Vinaya Piṭaka, H. Oldenberg (ed.), vols 1–5, London: Pali Text Society, 1879–83.

The Book of Discipline, trans. I.B. Horner, London: Pali Text Society, 1938–66.

Sigālavādasutta in the *Digha Nīkāya*, vol. I, London: Pali Text Society, 1890-1911.

Chapter 11

Are there 'Human Rights' in Buddhism?[1]

Damien Keown

In the autumn of 1993 the Parliament of the World's Religions met in Chicago to determine whether a consensus on basic moral teachings could be found among the religions of the world. The meeting was attended by representatives of the major world religions as well as ethnic and other minority groups. Representatives of many Buddhist schools, including Theravāda, Mahāyāna, Vajrayāna, and Zen were present and the main closing address was given by the Dalai Lama in Grant Park on 4 September.

One of the major fruits of this interfaith convention was a document known as the Declaration toward a Global Ethic.[2] The Global Ethic sets out the fundamental moral principles to which it is thought all religions subscribe. Many of these principles concern human rights, and the Global Ethic sees the universal recognition of human rights and dignity by the religions of the world as the cornerstone of a 'new global order.'

A related aim of the Global Ethic was to provide 'the basis for an extensive process of discussion and acceptance which we hope will be sparked off in all religions.'[3] The present chapter is a contribution to this process from a Buddhist perspective. Its aims are limited to an exploration of some of the basic issues that must be addressed if a Buddhist philosophy of human rights is to develop. I say 'develop' because Buddhism seems to lack such a philosophy at present. Buddhism is a latecomer to the cause of human rights, and for most of its history has been preoccupied with other concerns. It might be suggested, in defence of Buddhism, that concern for human rights is a post-religious phenomenon which has more to do with secular ideologies and power-politics than religion, and it is therefore

1 First published in the *Journal of Buddhist Ethics*, 2, 1995, pp. 3-27, and reprinted in Damien V. Keown, Charles S. Prebish and Wayne R. Husted (eds), *Buddhism and Human Rights*, London: Curzon Press, 1998. The permission of Curzon Press to republish in the present collection is gratefully acknowledged. This edition contains minor modifications and formatting changes.

2 The text of the Declaration, along with commentaries and supplementary information is available in Hans Küng and Karl-Josef Kuschel (eds), *A Global Ethic. The Declaration of the Parliament of the World's Religions*, London: SCM Press, 1993.

3 Ibid., Küng and Kuschel (eds), (1993), p. 8.

unreasonable to accuse Buddhism of neglect in this area.[4] I will suggest below that such an understanding of human rights is mistaken, but leaving the specific issue of human rights to one side there is no doubt that Buddhism lags far behind religions such as Christianity and Islam in developing the framework for a social gospel within which questions of this kind can be addressed. For such an intellectually dynamic tradition Buddhism is a lightweight in moral and political philosophy. A fig-leaf of a kind may be found in the suggestion that since much Buddhist literature remains untranslated there may be hidden treasures in these areas awaiting discovery. Such appeals to the unknown, however, lack credibility. For one thing, it would be curious if only texts on these subjects had been lost to history while literature on all manner of other topics abounds. Nor can it be a coincidence that these subjects are absent from the traditional monastic curricula. The absence of a discipline of philosophical ethics in Indian culture as a whole makes it much more likely that Buddhism simply invested little time in questions of these kinds.[5]

Political events in the course of this century, however, have forced the issue of human rights to the top of the agenda.[6] The Chinese invasion of Tibet, the bitter ethnic conflict in Sri Lanka, and the experience of military dictatorship in countries such as Burma have all provided contemporary Buddhism with first-hand experience of the issues at stake. Another development which has done much to focus attention on social and political themes is the emergence of 'socially engaged Buddhism,' a movement whose very name implies a critique of the more traditional (presumably 'disengaged') forms of Buddhism. Leading Asian and Western Buddhists now routinely express their concern about social injustice in the Western vocabulary of human rights. What I wish to consider here is how appropriate this language is for Buddhism, and what grounds there are for supposing that Buddhism is committed to the cause of 'human rights' or has any clear understanding of what the concept means. Given the lack of intellectual effort down the centuries in articulating, promoting and defending rights of the kind which the world (and especially the West) is now called upon to secure for oppressed groups like the Tibetans, the more cynical might suggest that this late conversion to the cause is born more of self-interest than a deep and long-standing commitment to social justice. In calling for respect for human rights today, then, is Buddhism simply riding on the coat-tails of the West or is there, after all, a commitment to human rights in Buddhist teachings?

My theme in this paper may be summed up as the conceptual and doctrinal basis for human rights in Buddhism. I am concerned with the intellectual bridgework which

---

4 For a range of cultural and ideological perspectives on human rights see Adamantia Pollis and Peter Schwab, *Human Rights: Cultural and Ideological Perspectives*, New York: Praeger, 1979.

5 On the absence of ethics in Hinduism see Austin B. Creel, *Dharma in Hindu Ethics*, Calcutta: Firma KLM, 1977, p. 20ff.

6 In spite of its contemporary importance, however, little appears to have been written on the subject from a specifically Buddhist perspective. The only monograph on the subject appears to be L.P.N. Perera, *Buddhism and Human Rights. A Buddhist Commentary on the Universal Declaration of Human Rights*, Colombo: Karunaratne and Sons, 1991.

must be put in place if expressions of concern about human rights are to be linked to Buddhist doctrine. There are many aspects to this problem, but three related issues will be considered here: the concept of rights, the concept of human rights, and the question of how human rights are to be grounded in Buddhist doctrine. I ask first if the concept of 'rights' is intelligible in Buddhism. To answer this question it will be necessary to gain some understanding of the origin of the notion in the West. Next I ask whether the Buddhist concept of human rights (if such a thing exists) is the same as the Western understanding. Finally I consider in what specific area of Buddhist teachings a doctrine of human rights might be grounded.[7] Since the discussion is essentially theoretical, detailed reference will not be made to particular Buddhist cultures or schools, to specific human rights 'abuses,' or to the human rights 'record' of particular regimes.[8]

Before turning to these issues a preliminary point must be made about Buddhism itself. In speaking of 'Buddhism' I should make clear that I am writing with reference to an abstraction which might be termed 'classical' Buddhism. This abstraction is neither the same as nor different from Buddhism in any historical or cultural context. It is not meant to represent the views of any sect and is broad enough to include both Theravāda and Mahāyāna schools. The justification for this fiction lies in the belief that whatever concept of human rights we regard Buddhism as holding must be one that is universal in form. The essence of any doctrine of human rights is its unrestricted scope, and it would be as strange to have distinct 'Theravāda,' 'Tibetan' and 'Zen' doctrines of human rights as it would be to have 'Catholic,' 'Protestant' and 'Eastern Orthodox' ones. To insist on the priority of cultural and historical circumstances would be tantamount to denying the validity of human rights as a concept.

Rights

The concept of a 'right' has a long intellectual history in the West, and the contemporary notion of a right as an exercisable power vested in or held by an individual has its antecedents in a more impersonal understanding of what is objectively true or right. Etymologically, the English word 'right' is derived from the Latin *rectus* meaning straight. *Rectus*, in turn, can be traced to the Greek *orektos* which means stretched out or upright. As Richard Dagger notes, 'The pattern ... is for the notion of straightness

7 On the analogous question of whether there is an 'African' doctrine of human rights see Rhoda Howard, 'Is there an African concept of human rights?' in R.J. Vincent (ed.), *Foreign Policy and Human Rights*, Cambridge: Cambridge University Press, 1986, pp. 11-32.

8 For information on these empirical questions see Charles Humana, *World Human Rights Guide*, Oxford: Oxford University Press, 1992; James C. Hsiung, *Human Rights in East Asia: A Cultural Perspective*, New York: Paragon House, 1985; K.M. de Silva et al. (eds), *Ethnic Conflict in Buddhist Societies: Sri Lanka, Thailand and Burma*, Boulder, Co: Westview Press, 1988. Also *Human Rights in Developing Countries*, *Yearbook 1993*, Copenhagen: Nordic Human Rights Publications, 1993.

to be extended from the physical realm to the moral – from *rectus* to rectitude, as it were.'[9] In other words, the property of a physical object, namely that of being right, straight or upright, is applied metaphorically in a moral context. Dagger suggests:

> By analogy with the physical sense, the primary moral sense of 'right' was a standard or measure for conduct. Something was right – morally straight or true – if it met the standard of rectitude, or rightness ...

Once the idea of 'rightness' had been transferred to the moral domain, the next development was to view it as denoting a personal entitlement of some kind. Dagger continues:

> From here the next step was to recognize that actions taken 'with right' or 'by right' are taken *as a matter of right*. The transition is from the belief that I may do something because it is right, in other words, to the belief that I may do something because I *have a right* to do it ... Thus the concept of rights joins the concept of *the right*.[10]

The metaphorical moral usage of terms such as 'right,' 'straight' and 'upright' (in opposition to 'crooked,' 'twisted' and 'bent') readily suggests itself to the mind. The rationale for the transition from the moral use of 'right' to the notion of a right as a personal entitlement, however, is less obvious. Indeed, this development which took place in the West during the late middle ages, and which has been described as the 'watershed'[11] in the history of 'right,' may be a phenomenon which is culturally unique. The evolution of the concept in this direction occurs sometime between Aquinas in the thirteenth century and the jurists Suarez and Grotius in the seventeenth. The modern usage appears clearly in Hobbes, writing in the middle of the seventeenth century, and the idea of a right as a personal power occupies centre stage in political theory from this time on.

As part of this evolution in the concept of a right the notion of 'natural rights' comes to prominence toward the end of the seventeenth century, notably in the writings of John Locke. The belief that there are natural rights flows from the recognition of human equality, one of the great ideals of the Age of Revolution. Natural rights are inalienable: they are not conferred by any judicial or political process nor can they be removed by these or other means. These natural rights of the seventeenth and eighteenth centuries are the forerunner of the contemporary notion of human rights.

Two questions might be asked concerning the evolution of the doctrine of natural rights in the West. First, why did it take so long for the concept of natural rights to appear? The answer seems to lie in the fact that for much of Western history 'rights'

---

9 Richard Dagger, 'Rights,' in Terence Ball et al. (eds), *Political Innovation and Conceptual Change*, Cambridge: Cambridge University Press, 1989, pp. 292-308. I am indebted to Dagger's excellent paper throughout this section.

10 Dagger (1989), p. 294. Original emphasis.

11 J.M. Finnis, *Natural Law and Natural Rights*, Oxford: Clarendon Press, 1980, p. 206.

were closely tied to social status, and were essentially a function of position or role in society. A hierarchical social structure, such as was predominant in Roman and medieval society, is antithetical to the notion of natural rights. In these circumstances a person's duties and responsibilities are determined fundamentally by the office they hold (lord, citizen, slave), offices which are to a large extent hereditary. It was only when the hierarchical model was challenged and replaced by an egalitarian one that the idea of natural rights began to gain ground.

Thc sccond and morc important qucstion for our prcscnt purposcs is: Docs the part played by the unique cultural matrix of social political and intellectual developments in the Enlightenment mean that human rights are essentially a function of the historical process? This conclusion need not follow, for while it may be said that in the seventeenth and eighteenth centuries the notion of natural rights was 'an idea whose time had come,' the idea itself was not entirely new. The influence of Christian doctrine can be seen in several respects,[12] such as the belief (ultimately derived from Judaism) of a 'universal moral law rooted in the righteousness of God.'[13] Since human beings are created in the image of God and loved by him as individuals each is worthy of dignity and respect. Furthermore, since each is a member of the human community under God, all other memberships (tribe, state, nation) are secondary.[14] Apart from Christianity, ideas about the just treatment of individuals on the basis of their common humanity are found in a secular context in Stoicism and the writings of Cicero and Seneca.[15] The philosophical justification for a doctrine of human rights has thus always been available, although the ground

12 Max Stackhouse lists five in *Creeds, Society, and Human Rights*, Grand Rapids, Michigan: William B. Eerdmans Publishing Company, pp. 435ff. David Little shows the dependency of the modern Western secular and liberal ideology on Christian theology by tracing the historical connection between the Christian concept of conscience and the intellectual framework within which the American doctrines of liberty and religious freedom emerged in the eighteenth century in the writings of Thomas Jefferson and James Madison. He suggests that this Western framework applies relatively unproblematically to Buddhism and Islam, and notes in general: 'Thus, current human rights formulations, along with the important notions that underlie them, are by no means necessarily irrelevant to cultures outside the West.' See David Little, John Kelsay and Abdulaziz Sachedina (eds), *Human Rights and the Conflict of Cultures*, Columbia, SC: University of South Carolina Press, p. 31. For perspectives on human rights from the world's religions see Leroy S. Rouner, *Human Rights and the World's Religions*, Notre Dame: University of Notre Dame Press, 1988; and Arlene Swidler (ed.), *Human Rights in Religious Traditions*, New York: Pilgrims Press, 1982. A commentary on the *Universal Declaration* from the perspective of Buddhism, Hinduism, Christianity and Islam may be found in L.H.H. Perera (ed.), *Human Rights and Religions in Sri Lanka. A Commentary on the Universal Declaration of Human Rights*, published by the Colombo: Sri Lanka Foundation, 1988. The Buddhist commentary by Perera was republished separately in 1991 (see note 5 above).

13 Stackhouse (1984), p. 35.

14 Stackhouse (1984), p. 36.

15 For a survey see R.W. Carlyle and A.J. Carlyle, *A History of Medieval Political Theory in the West*, Edinburgh: Blackwood and Sons, 1950.

in which this seed might flourish – a particular combination of social, political and intellectual developments – has not.

So much for historical background. What of contemporary theories of rights? The concept of a right has been analyzed in a number of ways, as evidenced by the extensive interdisciplinary literature on the subject spanning diverse fields such as politics, law, philosophy and history. Within this discourse of rights there is no single definition of a right which commands universal assent. For our present purposes, however, a basic understanding of the concept will suffice. We noted above that a right is something personal to an individual: it may be thought of as something an individual 'has'.[16] What the holder of a right has is a benefit or entitlement of some kind, and at the most general level this is an entitlement to justice. This entitlement may be analyzed into two main forms for which there are corresponding rights: rights which take the form of a claim (claim-rights), and rights which take the form of a liberty (liberty-rights).[17] A claim-right is the benefit which A enjoys to impose upon B a positive or negative requirement. A liberty-right is the benefit which A enjoys of being immune from any such requirement being imposed by B.[18] This basic understanding of a right may be summed up in the following working definition: *a right is a benefit which confers upon its holder either a claim or a liberty*.

One important feature of any right is that it provides a particular perspective on justice, in that the right-holder always stands in the position of beneficiary. This subjective aspect of the entitlement, which, as we have seen, appeared early in the history of the concept, remains crucial to the modern understanding of a right. This is brought out in the following definition by Finnis:

> In short, the modern vocabulary and grammar of rights is a many-faceted instrument for reporting and asserting the requirements or other implications of a relationship of justice *from the point of view of the person(s) who benefit(s)* from that relationship. It provides a way of talking about 'what is just' from a special angle: the viewpoint of the 'other(s)' to whom something (including, *inter alia*, freedom of choice) is owed or due, and who would be wronged if denied that something.[19]

The above brief review of the Western concept of a right was required as a preliminary to an assessment of its relevance to Buddhism. We are now in a position to ask whether the concept of a right is found in Buddhism. If it is, then talk of *human rights*

16 Finnis (1980), p. 208.

17 The most influential modern analysis of rights is that by Wesley Hohfeld, *Fundamental Legal Conceptions*, New Haven: Yale University Press, 1964.

18 Finnis (1980), pp. 199-205.

19 Finnis (1980), p. 205, original emphasis.

in Buddhism seems legitimate.[20] If it is not, there is a danger of anachronistically foisting onto the tradition a concept which is the product of an alien culture.[21]

Buddhism and Rights

We took our cue for the discussion of rights in the West from etymology, and perhaps we can glean something further from this source. Above it was noted that the English word 'right' is derived from the Latin rectus meaning straight. Both 'right' and *rectus* themselves, however, have a more remote ancestor in the Sanskrit *ṛju* (straight or upright). The equivalent form in Pāli is *uju* (or *ujju*) meaning 'straight, direct; straightforward, honest, upright.'[22] It would therefore appear that both the objective sense ('straight') and the metaphorical moral sense ('rectitude') of the word 'right' referred to earlier occur in Buddhist as well as Western languages. Despite a common Indo-European etymology, however, there is no word in Sanskrit or Pāli which conveys the idea of a 'right' or 'rights,' understood as a subjective entitlement.[23]

Does this mean that the concept of rights is alien to Buddhist thought? Not necessarily. Alan Gewirth has pointed out that cultures may possess the concept of rights without having a vocabulary which expresses it. He suggests that it is 'important to distinguish between having or using a concept and the clear or explicit recognition and elucidation of it ... Thus persons might have and use the concept of a right without explicitly having a single word for it.'[24] Gewirth claims that the concept of rights can be found in feudal thought, Roman law, Greek philosophy, the Old Testament, and in primitive societies. In connection with the last Finnis points out that anthropological studies of African tribal regimes of law have shown that the English terms 'right' and 'duty' are usually covered by a single word derived from the form normally translated as 'ought.' He suggests that the best English translation

---

20 Perera's discussion of Buddhism and human rights does not address these questions, and seems to assume that the concept of rights and human rights as understood in the *Universal Declaration* are directly applicable to canonical Buddhism.

21 For the view that moral values are determined by culture, as maintained by many anthropologists, see John Ladd (ed.), *Ethical Relativism*, Lanham: University Press of America, 1983. The defensibility of a specific cultural custom (female circumcision) from a human rights perspective is discussed by Stephen A. James, 'Reconciling International Human Rights and Cultural Relativism: the case of female circumcision,' *Bioethics* 8, 1994, pp. 1-26.

22 *Pāli Text Society Pāli-English Dictionary*, *uju* and *ujju*.

23 On the concept of rights in Hinduism and the meaning of *adhikāra*, see Purushottama Bilimoria, 'Is "*Adhikāra*" good enough for "rights"?' *Asian Philosophy*, IV (1), Winter 1993, pp. 3-13; also Creel (1977), p. 19. In Buddhist languages the notion of rights may be distributed among a variety of terms, as perhaps, in Latin among the words *auctoritas*, *potestas*, *dominium*, *iurisdictio*, *proprietas*, *libertas and ius* (Dagger 1989, p. 291).

24 Quoted in Dagger (1989), p. 286.

in these cases is 'due' because 'due' looks 'both ways along a juridical relationship, both to what one is due to do, and to what is due to one.'[25]

It seems, then, that the concept of a right may exist where a word for it does not. Could this be the case in Buddhism? In Buddhism what is due in any situation is determined by reference to the universal moral law, or Dharma. Dharma determines what is right and just in all contexts and from all perspectives. With respect to social justice the Rev. Vajiragnana explains:

> Each one of us has a role to play in sustaining and promoting social justice and orderliness. The Buddha explained very clearly these roles as reciprocal duties existing between parents and children; teachers and pupils; husband and wife; friends, relatives and neighbours; employer and employee; clergy and laity ... No one has been left out. The duties explained here are reciprocal and are considered as sacred duties, for – if observed – they can create a just, peaceful and harmonious society.[26]

From this it would seem that Dharma determines not just 'what one is due to do' but also 'what is due to one.' Thus through A's performance of his Dharmic duty B receives that which is his 'due' or, we might say, that to which he is 'entitled' in (under, through) Dharma. Since Dharma determines, for example, the duties of husbands and the duties of wives,[27] it follows that the duties of one correspond to the entitlements or 'rights' of the other. If the husband has a duty to support his wife, the wife has a 'right' to support from her husband. If the wife has a duty to look after her husband's property, the husband has a 'right' to the safe-keeping of his property by his wife. If under Dharma it is the duty of a king (or political authority) to dispense justice impartially, then subjects (citizens) may be said to have a 'right' to just and impartial treatment before the law.

Should it be concluded, then, that the notion of a right is present in classical Buddhism? The answer depends on the criteria adopted for 'having' a concept. Dagger sets out the options:

> If one is willing to look primarily for the idea or the notion, however it may be expressed, then one can confidently say that the concept of rights is virtually as old as civilization itself.

On the other hand:

> If one insists that the form of expression is crucial ... so that a concept cannot be said to exist unless there is a word or phrase that distinguishes it from other concepts, then one would have to say that the concept of rights has its origin in the middle ages.[28]

---

25 Finnis (1980), p. 209.

26 Ven Vajiragnana, 'Justice in Buddhism,' *Vesak Sirisara* (unpaginated version from the Electronic Buddhist Archive, 1992).

27 See, for example, the *Sigālavādasutta.*

28 Dagger (1989), p. 297.

I think our conclusion should be that the concept of rights is implicit in classical Buddhism in the normative understanding of what is 'due' among and between individuals. Under Dharma, husbands and wives, kings and subjects, teachers and students, all have reciprocal obligations which can be analyzed into rights and duties. We must qualify this conclusion, however, by noting that the requirements of Dharma are almost always expressed in the form of duties rather than rights. In other words, Dharma states what is due in the form 'A husband should support his wife' as opposed to 'Wives have a right to be maintained by their husbands.' Until rights as personal entitlements are recognized as a discrete but integral part of what is due under Dharma, the modern concept of rights cannot be said to be present. In this respect, however, Buddhism is far from unique, and a similar comment could be made about many other cultures and civilizations. Finnis points out with respect to Roman law:

> [I]t is salutary to bear in mind that the modern emphasis on the powers of the right-holder, and the consequent systematic bifurcation between 'right' ... and 'duty,' is something that sophisticated lawyers were able to do without for the whole life of classical Roman law.[29]

He also suggests, rightly I think, that 'there is no cause to take sides as between the older and the newer usages, as ways of expressing the implications of justice in a given context.'[30] A right is a useful concept which provides a particular perspective on justice. Its correlative, duty, provides another. These may be thought of as separate windows onto the common good which is justice or, in the context of Buddhism, Dharma. It would therefore be going too far to claim that the notion of rights is 'alien' to Buddhism or that Buddhism denies that individuals have 'rights.' In sum it might be said that in classical Buddhism the notion of rights is present in embryonic form although not yet born into history.

Whether anything like the Western concept of rights has, or would, appear in the course of the historical evolution of Buddhism is a question for specialists in the various Buddhist cultures to ponder. In many respects the omens for this development were never good. Buddhism originated in a caste society, and the Asian societies where it has flourished have for the most part been hierarchically structured. MacIntyre, citing Gewirth, mentions that the concept of a right lacks any means of expression in Japanese 'even as late as the mid-nineteenth century.'[31] The preconditions for the emergence of the concept of rights would seem to be

---

29 Finnis (1980), p. 209.

30 Finnis (1980), p. 210.

31 Alasdair MacIntyre, *After Virtue. A Study in Moral Theory*, London: Duckworth, 1981, p. 69. Cf. Theodore de Bary on the Chinese neologisms which have been coined to express these concepts: 'Neo-Confucianism and Human Rights,' Leroy S. Rouner (ed.), in *Human Rights and the World's Religions*, Notre Dame: University of Notre Dame Press, 1988, p. 183. And in the same volume, Julia Ching, 'Human Rights: A Valid Chinese Concept?', in Leroy S. Rouner (ed.), (ibid.).

egalitarianism and democracy, neither of which have been notable features of Asian polity before the modern era. On the other hand, a justification for the rejection of hierarchical social structures is not hard to find in Buddhism – one need look only at the Buddha's critique of caste.[32] Buddhism also holds, in the doctrine of no-self, that all individuals are equal in the most profound sense.[33] Like the Christian doctrine that all men are created equal before God this would appear to be fertile ground for a doctrine of natural rights. What seems to have been lacking in both faiths, but perhaps more so in Buddhism, was the will to incarnate this theoretical vision of man in the flesh of social institutions.

Human Rights

In the preceding section attention was focused on the concept of a right. Here we consider what it means to characterize certain rights as human rights,[34] and pursue further the discussion initiated in the preceding section as to whether Western notions of human rights are compatible with Buddhism.[35]

The point has already been made that what are today called human rights were originally spoken of as 'natural' rights, in other words, rights which flow from human nature. In the seventeenth century philosophers and statesmen began to define these rights and enshrine them in early constitutions such as the 'Fundamental Orders of Connecticut' as early as 1639. Documents of this kind inspired the publication of other declarations, charters and manifestos in a tradition which has continued into modern times. As an example of a modern charter of human rights we may take The Universal Declaration of Human Rights proclaimed by the General Assembly of the

32 The institution of caste is criticized in numerous early discourses, notably the *Sonadaṇḍasutta*.

33 Michael Carrithers suggests that the Buddhist concept of the 'self' (which he relates to Mauss's concept of the 'moi') is one which is easily transportable across cultural frontiers. This enhances the prospects for a Buddhist doctrine of universal human rights. See 'An alternative social history of the self,' in M. Carrithers, S. Collins and S. Lukes (eds), *The category of the person. Anthropology, philosophy, history*, Cambridge: Cambridge University Press, 1995, pp. 234-256.

34 Useful discussions of the philosophical basis of human rights may be found in Jack Donnelly, *The Concept of Human Rights*, London and Sydney: Croom Helm, 1985; and James W. Nickel, *Making Sense of Human Rights*, Berkeley: University of California Press, 1987.

35 On how far the Western concept of human rights is relevant or applicable to other cultures see Raimon Panikkar, 'Is the Notion of Human Rights a Western Concept?' *Diogenes*, 120, 1982, pp. 75-102; Fernando R. Teson, 'International Human Rights and Cultural Relativism,' *Virginia Journal of International Law*, 25, 1985, pp. 869-898; Yogesh K.Tyagi 'Third World Response to Human Rights,' *Indian Journal of International Law*, 21, 1981, pp.119-140.

A.J.M. Milne, *Human Rights and Human Diversity*, London: Macmillan, 1986; C.E. Welch and V. Leary, *Asian Perspectives on Human Rights*, Boulder, Co: Westview Press, 1990.

United Nations in December 1948. Since its promulgation this thirty-article code has been used as a model for many subsequent human rights charters.

What is the Buddhist position with respect to declarations of this kind? It may be useful to begin by asking whether Buddhism would endorse the Universal Declaration on Human Rights. The repeated calls by the Dalai Lama for respect for human rights give some reason to think that it would. The signing of the Global Ethic by many Buddhists also suggests that Buddhism has no reservations about subscribing to charters or manifestos which seek to secure universal human rights. Moreover, there seems to be nothing in any of the thirty articles to which Buddhism would take exception. Perera's commentary on each of the thirty articles of the Universal Declaration shows them to be in harmony with early Buddhist teachings both in letter and in spirit. In his Foreword to the commentary Ananda Gurugé writes:

> Professor Perera demonstrates that every single Article of the Universal Declaration of Human Rights – even the labour rights to fair wages, leisure and welfare – has been adumbrated, cogently upheld and meaningfully incorporated in an overall view of life and society by the Buddha.[36]

But how are these rights to be justified with reference to Buddhist teachings? In asking this question I am not seeking justification by reference to textual passages which seem to support the rights claimed. There are many passages in the Pāli Canon, as Perera has ably demonstrated, which support the view that early Buddhist teachings were in harmony with the spirit of the Declaration. The justification required at this point has more to do with the philosophical presuppositions underlying these passages and the overall Buddhist vision of individual and social good.

The various declarations on human rights themselves rarely offer a justification for the rights they proclaim. MacIntyre observes dryly how 'In the United Nations declaration on human rights of 1949 [sic] what has since become the normal UN practice of not giving good reasons for any assertion whatsoever is followed with great rigor.'[37] A gesture toward justification is sometimes made in recital clauses by reference to the 'inherent dignity ... of all members of the human family' or some similar form of words. The Global Ethic, which provides a fuller statement than most, echoes the Universal Declaration in its call for 'the full realization of the intrinsic dignity of the human person'.[38] It states: 'We make a commitment to respect life and dignity, individuality and diversity, so that every person is treated humanely.' This is amplified as follows:

> This means that every human being without distinction of age, sex, race, skin, color, physical or mental ability, language, religion, political view, or national or social origin

36 Perera (1991), p. xi.
37 MacIntyre (1981), p. 69.
38 *A Global Ethic*, p. 14.

> possesses an inalienable and *untouchable dignity*. And everyone, the individual as well as the state, is therefore obliged to honor this dignity and protect it.[39]

Elsewhere, as part of his dialogue with world religions, Küng makes a constructive suggestion on this point to which students of Buddhism might do well to pay heed:

> Should not Buddhist thinkers, as they critically assess their own and alien traditions, make a more direct effort to establish an anthropology centered around *human dignity* (which the Buddha himself deeply respected)? Buddhists are fully aware that man can be adequately understood only as conditioned in every way, as a relational being within the totality of life and the cosmos. But should they not reflect more earnestly, especially in an ethical vein, on the problems of the unique, inviolable, noninterchangeable human self, with its roots in the past and its future destiny?[40]

It is by no means apparent, however, how human dignity is to be grounded in Buddhist doctrine. The very words 'human dignity' sound as alien in a Buddhist context as talk of rights. One looks in vain to the four noble truths for any explicit reference to human dignity, and doctrines such as no-self and impermanence may even be thought to undermine it. If human dignity is the basis of human rights Buddhism would seem to be in some difficulty when it comes to providing a justification for them. The theistic religions, on the other hand, seem much better equipped to provide an account of human dignity. Christians, Muslims and Jews typically refer to the ultimate source of human dignity as divine. Article one (paragraph 1700) of the most recent Catechism of the Catholic Church, for instance, states: 'The dignity of the human person is rooted in his creation in the image and likeness of God.' Buddhism, clearly, would not wish to make such a claim. Küng notes how leading Buddhists at the Parliament of the World's Religions felt called upon to protest at calls for 'a unity of religions under God,' and at references to 'God the Almighty' and 'God the Creator' in invocations during the proceedings. He suggests, however, that these differences are reconcilable since the Buddhist concepts of 'Nirvana, Shunyata and Dharmakaya ... fulfill analogous functions to the concept of God' and can be regarded by Christians as 'parallel terms for the Absolute.'[41]

It may or may not be the case that Mahāyāna schools recognize a transcendent reality which resembles the Christian concept of God as the Absolute, and there are those better qualified than myself to address such a question. Here I will make only three brief points about the problems which arise in regarding these things as the source of human dignity. The first is that since these concepts are understood differently by the main Mahāyāna schools they are unlikely to provide the common ground that is required as a foundation for human rights. The second is that it is difficult to see how any of these things can be the source of human dignity in the way

---

39 *A Global Ethic*, p. 23, original emphasis.

40 Hans Küng, Josef Van Ess, Heinrich Von Stietencron and Heinz Bechert, *Christianity and the World Religions*, 2nd edn. London: SCM Press, 1986, p. 383f., original emphasis.

41 *A Global Ethic*, p. 62f.

that God can, since no school of Buddhism believes that human beings are created by them. The third point is that even if some metaphysical ground of the above kind can be identified in Mahāyāna Buddhism it still leaves the problem of how human dignity is to be grounded where Theravada Buddhism is concerned. For the Theravāda, Nirvāṇa is not a transcendent Absolute, nor do the concepts of 'Shunyata and Dharmakaya' have anything like the meaning or significance they attain later. No grounding for human rights can be truly satisfactory, I would suggest, unless it unambiguously forms part of the core teachings of classical Buddhism as a whole.

One suggestion as to how human rights can be grounded in Buddhist doctrine has been made by Kenneth Inada. In a discussion of 'The Buddhist Perspective on Human Rights,' Inada suggests 'there is an intimate and vital relationship of the Buddhist norm or Dhamma with that of human rights.'[42] He explains the relationship as follows:

> Human rights is indeed an important issue, but the Buddhist position is that it is ancillary to the larger or more basic issue of human nature. It can be asserted that the Buddhist sees the concept of human rights as a legal extension of human nature. It is a crystallization, indeed a formalization, of the mutual respect and concern of all persons, stemming from human nature. Thus, human nature is the ultimate source, the basis from which all other attributes or characteristics are to be delineated. They all have their respective *raison d'être* in it. They are reflections and even byproducts of it. The reason for assigning human nature the basic position is very simple. It is to give human relations a firm grounding in the truly existential nature of things: that is, the concrete and dynamic relational nature of persons in contact with each other, that which [sic] avoids being caught up in rhetorical or legalistic tangles.[43]

Few would disagree with the proposition that human rights are grounded in human nature. Toward the end of the extract, however, Inada seems to move away from his initial suggestion that human nature is the 'ultimate source' of human rights toward the view that the ultimate ground is the 'dynamic relational nature of persons in contact with each other.' In other words, it is in the interrelatedness of persons rather than in the persons themselves that the justification for human rights is to be found. This is confirmed a little later:

> Consequently, the Buddhist concern is focused on the experiential process of each individual, a process technically known as relational origination (*paticca-samuppāda*). It is the great doctrine of Buddhism, perhaps the greatest doctrine expounded by the historical Buddha. It means that, in any life-process, the arising of an experiential event is a total, relational affair.[44]

42 Kenneth K. Inada, 'The Buddhist Perspective on Human Rights,' Arlene Swidler (ed.), in *Human Rights in Religious Traditions*, New York: Pilgrims Press, 1982, pp. 66-76, p. 71.

43 Inada (1982), p. 70 (paragraphs joined).

44 Ibid.

How is the link between dependent-origination and human rights to be forged? The argument reaches its conclusion in the following passage:

> Like a storm which consumes everything in its wake, an experience in terms of relational origination involves everything within its purview. Hence, the involvement of elements and, in our case, human beings as entities should not be in terms of mere relationship but rather a creative relationship which originates from the individual locus of existence. In other words, each individual is responsible for the actualization of an 'extensive concern' for everything that lies in his or her path of experience. So, we may say that the sum total of the 'extensive concerns' can be referred to as a mutually constituted existential realm, and it thereby becomes a fact that there will be mutual respect of fellow beings. It is on this basis that we can speak of the rights of individuals. These rights are actually extensions of human qualities such as security, liberty, and life.[45]

In simple language, the argument seems to be as follows. Human beings, like everything else, are part of the relational process described in the doctrine of dependent-origination; since no one exists independently we should look out for one another; looking out for one another means respecting each other's rights; examples of the rights we should respect are security, liberty and life.[46]

Although I have described this as an 'argument' it is little more than a series of assertions. Working backwards, it is difficult to know what sense to give the concluding sentence: 'These rights are actually extensions of human qualities such as security, liberty and life.' It is unclear what is meant by 'human qualities' here. In what sense is security a 'human quality' (perhaps a 'need')? Why is life described as a 'quality' of a human being? Even granted that these things are 'human qualities,' what does it mean to say that rights are extensions of 'human qualities'? In the first extract quoted above, Inada suggests that 'the Buddhist sees the concept of human rights as a legal extension of human nature.' What is left unexplained, however, is how human nature (or 'human qualities') become legal rights. Do all 'human qualities' extend into rights or only some? If so, which and why? Finally, if 'human qualities' are what give rise to rights, why invoke the doctrine of dependent-origination?

---

45 Inada (1982), p. 70f.

46 An earlier attempt to ground Buddhist ethics in dependent-origination can be found in Joanna Rogers Macy, 'Dependent Co-Arising: The Distinctiveness of Buddhist Ethics,' *Journal of Religious Ethics*, 7, 1989, pp. 38-52. Macy offers the Sarvodaya Shramadana, a self-help movement in Sri Lanka, as 'A notable example of the ethics of *paticca-samuppāda*,' but, like Inada, fails to explain how a moral imperative arises out of this doctrine. Also drawn to the seemingly magnetic doctrines of no-self and dependent-origination is Taitetsu Unno, whose 1988 article, supposedly about rights, is taken up almost entirely in providing a Pure Land perspective on these two doctrines ('Personal Rights and Contemporary Buddhism,' in Leroy S. Rouner (ed.), *Human Rights in the World's Religions*, 1988, pp. 129-147).While these doctrines offer a congenial metaphysical backdrop for Buddhist ethics, they cannot provide a *moral* ground for rights. Ian Harris (1994) expresses doubts that dependent-origination can provide a satisfactory basis for Buddhist ecology ('Causation and Telos: The Problem of Buddhist Environmental Ethics,' *Journal of Buddhist Ethics*, 1, 1994, pp. 45-56).

The derivation of human rights from the doctrine of dependent-origination is a conjuring trick. From the premise that we live in 'a mutually constituted existential realm' (we all live together) it has 'thereby become a fact' that there will be 'mutual respect of fellow beings.' In the twinkling of an eye, values have appeared from facts like a rabbit out of a hat. However, the fact that human beings live in relationship with one another is not a moral argument about *how they ought to behave*. By itself it offers no reason why a person should not routinely abuse the rights of others. Inada's suggestion that human rights can be grounded in the doctrine of dependent-origination turns out to be little more than a recommendation that people should be nice to one another on the ground that we are 'all in this together.'[47]

The approach adopted by Perera is rather different. Perera's main concern is to demonstrate that the articles of the Universal Declaration are adumbrated in early Buddhist teachings, rather than explore their philosophical foundations. He acknowledges that 'Buddhism credits the human personality with a dignity and moral responsibility'[48] but does not explain fully whence this arises or how it provides a foundation for human rights. In a number of places he suggests certain possibilities regarding the source of human dignity, not all of which seem to be compatible. At one point he defines 'the ethical assumption on which the Buddhist concept of human rights is founded' as the 'fundamental consideration that all life has a desire to safeguard itself and to make itself comfortable and happy.'[49]

Basing rights on desires, however, is problematic. One reason is that certain people, for example those who seek to end their lives through suicide, seem to lack the desire in question. Nor is it difficult to conceive of a justification for human rights abuses along the lines that the victims 'no longer cared what happened to them.' If they themselves had no interest in their future, whose rights would have been violated? A deeper problem is that the mere existence of desires establishes nothing from a moral point of view. Desires are many and varied and can be met in manifold ways. Moral questions arise both at the level of whether a desire *should* be met and *how* it should be met. The identification of a desire may be a starting point for moral reflection, but it is certainly not its end.[50]

On the preceding page Perera suggests an alternative foundation for human rights, one which links it to human dignity. He writes: 'Buddhism posits, as Jean Jacques Rousseau did much later, that the essence of human dignity lies in the assumption of man's responsibility for his own governance.'[51] No Buddhist sources are cited in

---

47 In a second essay on the subject Inada gives much less emphasis to dependent-origination and seems to want to ground human rights in compassion. See 'A Buddhist Response to the Nature of Human Rights,' Claude E. Welch Jr. and Virginia A. Leary (eds), in *Asian Perspectives on Human Rights*, Boulder, Co: Westview Press, 1990, pp. 91-103.

48 Perera (1991), p. 28 (cf p. 88).

49 Perera (1991), p. 29.

50 A further problem, although I believe it is ultimately a pseudo-problem, is that Buddhism sees desire as the cause of suffering. Desire would therefore seem an unlikely foundation for human rights.

51 Perera (1991), p. 28.

support of this claim, and I believe it is unlikely that Buddhism would wish to link human dignity quite so closely to politics. Perhaps if this suggestion were developed a little further it would make reference to underlying human capacities such as reason and autonomy which enable individuals to constitute themselves into orderly societies, and then point to these as the underlying source of human dignity. While political institutions may be produced through the exercise of distinctively human capacities, however, it is unlikely that Buddhism would locate 'the essence of human dignity' in their creation. According to the *Aggaññasutta*, the evolution of political societies is the consequence of depravity and decline, which makes them a dubious testament to human dignity.

Where, then, should the foundations for a Buddhist doctrine of human rights be sought? The proper ground for a doctrine of human rights, I suggest, lies elsewhere than in the doctrine of dependent-origination, as suggested by Inada, or in either the desire for self-preservation or the acceptance of responsibility for self-government, as proposed by Perera. Perera, in fact, comes closest to what in my view is the true source of human rights in Buddhism in his commentary on Article 1.[52] In discussing the first sentence of the Article ('All human beings are born free and equal in dignity and rights') he comments that 'Buddhahood itself is within the reach of all human beings ... and if all could attain Buddhahood what greater equality in dignity and rights can there be?' To focus attention upon the goal, I believe, is more promising than any of the other approaches considered thus far. Perera seems to grasp its significance in a remark toward the end of his commentary on Article 1. He writes:

> It is from the point of view of its goal that Buddhism evaluates all action. Hence Buddhist thought is in accord with this and other Articles in the Universal Declaration of Human Rights to the extent to which they facilitate the advancement of human beings toward the Buddhist goal.[53]

I believe the above statement provides the key to understanding human rights from a Buddhist perspective. What is missing in Perera's commentary, however, is the explicit linkage between the goal and human dignity, and it is this which I will now try to establish. What I will suggest in general is that the source of human dignity should be sought not in the analysis of the human condition provided by the first and second noble truths but in the evaluation of human good provided by the third and fourth. Human rights cannot be derived from any factual non-evaluative analysis of human nature, whether in terms of its psycho-physical constitution (the five 'aggregates' which lack a self), its biological nature (needs, urges, drives), or the deep structure of interdependency (*paticca-samuppāda*). Instead the most promising approach will be one which locates human rights and dignity within a comprehensive account of human goodness, and which sees basic rights and freedoms as integrally related to

52 Article 1: 'All human beings are born free and equal in dignity and rights. They are endowed with reason and conscience and should act toward one another in a spirit of brotherhood.'

53 Perera (1991), p. 24.

human flourishing and self-realization.[54] This is because the source of human dignity in Buddhism lies nowhere else than in the literally infinite capacity of human nature for participation in goodness.[55]

The connection between human rights and human good can be illustrated by asking what the various declarations on human rights seek to secure. Documents which speak of human rights commonly announce a list of specific rights and freedoms and proclaim them to be inviolable. The rights proclaimed by the Universal Declaration include the right to life, liberty, security of person, equality before the law, privacy, marriage and protection of family life, social security, participation in government, work, protection against unemployment, rest and leisure, a minimum standard of living, and enjoyment of the arts. The exercise of these rights is subject only to such general limitations as are necessary to secure due recognition and respect for the rights and freedoms of others and the requirements of morality, public order and general welfare (Article 29.2). Otherwise, the rights are expressed in categorical forms such as 'Everyone has ...' and 'No one shall ...'. For example, Article 3: 'Everyone has the right to life, liberty and security of person.' And Article 4: 'No one shall be held in slavery or servitude; slavery and the slave trade shall be prohibited in all their forms.' The document thus understands the rights it proclaims as both 'universal' and exceptionless. Using the terminology introduced earlier it can be seen that some of these rights are claim rights while others are liberty rights. Article 2 confirms this when it speaks of an entitlement to both the '*rights* and *freedoms* set forth in this Declaration.'[56]

What do these rights and freedoms amount to? It might be said that they map the parameters of human 'good-in-community.' In other words, these rights and freedoms are what is required if human beings are to lead fulfilled lives in society. Article 29.1 recognizes this when it observes 'Everyone has duties to the community *in which alone the free and full development of his personality is possible*.'[57] In the absence of human rights the scope for human development and fulfilment through social interaction is drastically reduced. The rights specified define and facilitate aspects of human fulfilment. The right to life is clearly fundamental since it is the condition for the enjoyment of all other rights and freedoms. The right to 'liberty and security of person' (Article 3) is also basic to any understanding of human good. Without these minimum conditions the scope and opportunity for human fulfilment would be intolerably restricted. The same would apply in the case of slavery (Article 4), torture (Article 5), and the denial of rights before the law (Article 6). It can also be seen that many of the detailed rights identified are actually derived from more fundamental ones. Article 3, for example, 'No one shall be held in slavery,' is clearly

54 A discussion of human nature and human good in Buddhism will be found in part one of my *Buddhism & Bioethics*, London: Macmillan, 1995.

55 A more familiar way of making the same point in Buddhist terminology would be to say that all beings are potential Buddhas or possess the 'Buddha-nature.'

56 Emphasis added.

57 Emphasis added.

implied in Article 2, 'Everyone has the right to ... liberty.' It might thus be said that many of the thirty articles articulate the practical implications of a relatively small number of fundamental rights and freedoms which are the basis of the common good.

It may be noted that the Universal Declaration itself and modern charters like it do not offer a comprehensive vision of human good. This is not intended as a criticism, for the purpose of such charters is to secure only what might be termed the 'minimum conditions' for human flourishing in a pluralistic milieu. The task of articulating a comprehensive vision of what is ultimately valuable in human life and how it is to be attained falls to the competing theories of human good found in religions, philosophies and ideologies. Buddhism provides one view of human nature and its fulfilment, Christianity another, secular philosophies a third. To pursue any of these different paths, however, requires the substructure known as 'human rights,' a complex of fundamental rights and liberties which are the preconditions for the realization of the particular opportunities made available by the competing ideologies.

If the aim of human rights declarations is understood in the way outlined above then human rights is fundamentally a moral issue. Where there is no right to life, liberty and security of person, and where torture is routine, the opportunities for the realization of human good are greatly reduced. Freedom of religion (Article 18), for example, is vital to the Buddhist vision of individual and social good, and the consequences of the loss of these rights are all too obvious in Tibet. Human rights is thus an area in which religions have a legitimate and vital stake, and there is every reason why it would be proper for Buddhism both to endorse the Universal Declaration and call upon others to respect and implement it.[58]

If religions have a legitimate stake in human rights, we might expect to find many of the rights and liberties spelled out in human rights charters present in either an express or implied form in their moral teachings. These typically include, as in the case of the Five Precepts of Buddhism, commandments or precepts forbidding the immoral treatment of others in such ways as by killing, stealing, and lying. These evils are prohibited because it is immediately apparent that they are antithetical to human flourishing-in-community. The rationale for these prohibitions, I suggest, coincides to a large extent with that of the various human rights manifestos.[59] These

58 In the view of Perera: 'From the religious angle, it is possible to state that in this Declaration lie enshrined certain values and norms emphasized by the major religions of the world. Though not directly expressed, the basic principles of the Declaration are supported and reinforced by these religious traditions, and among them the contribution of the Buddhist tradition, to say the least, is quite outstanding' (1991, p. xiii). Though not wishing to deny that the early teachings support the principles of the Declaration, I do not agree that the contribution of the Buddhist *tradition* to the cause of human rights is in any way 'outstanding.'

59 In certain areas (such as the prohibition on alcohol and matters of sexual morality) the precepts go beyond the more limited aims of human rights charters. This is because Buddhism provides a *particular* vision of human good and also defines the practices required for its fulfilment.

manifestos, indeed, may be regarded as a translation of religious precepts into the language of rights. The process of casuistry can be seen at work in both. Just as a limited number of moral precepts can be expanded to meet the needs of different social situations (many of the extensive Vinaya rules, for example, have their source in a handful of moral precepts),[60] so the many articles in human rights charters are extrapolated from a comparatively small number of basic rights and freedoms.

It must be admitted there are grounds for skepticism toward the parallel which has just been suggested since it cannot be denied that the Buddhist precepts look and sound very different from contemporary declarations on human rights. The Buddhist precepts make no reference to 'rights' at all, and are couched instead in the form of undertakings.[61] Let us examine what these undertakings involve. On the basis of our earlier analysis it would seem that 'taking the precepts' in Buddhism is actually the formal acknowledgement of a subsisting duty, a duty which arises from Dharma. The person who takes the precepts is saying in effect 'I hereby recognize my Dharmic duty not to do x, y, and z.' Since duties have their correlative in rights, however, rights must also be implicit in the good the precepts seek to promote. We saw earlier that rights provide a way of talking about what is just and unjust from a special angle. We noted further that a person who has right has a benefit, a benefit which can be described as either a claim or a liberty. In the context of the precepts, then, the right-holder is the one who suffers from the breach of Dharmic duty when the precepts are broken. In the case of the first precept this would be the person who was unjustly killed. The right the victim has may therefore be defined as a negative claim-right upon the aggressor, namely the right not to be killed. In simple terms we might say that the victim has a right to life which the aggressor has a duty to respect.

That the translation between precepts and rights is accurate, and that the agreement between the two formulations is more than superficial or accidental, is supported by the authenticity with which the Dalai Lama was able to affirm the Global Ethic. Kuschel comments as follows:

> The reason why the Dalai Lama's speech was so convincing, and indeed seized people's hearts, so that it was often interrupted by spontaneous applause, was that this man simply wanted to be an *authentic Buddhist*. His plea for mutual respect, dialogue and collaboration, for understanding between peoples and respect for creation, was not an adaptation to Christian or Western values, but came from the depths of his own Buddhist spirituality.[62]

60 Damien Keown, *The Nature of Buddhist Ethics*, London: Macmillan, 1992, p. 33.

61 Sometimes a contrast is drawn between the 'voluntary' nature of the Buddhist precepts and the 'commandments' of Christianity. While the format of the Buddhist precepts is certainly more appealing to liberal tastes, the distinction has little real meaning. The precepts apply whether or not they are formally 'undertaken,' and are commandments in all but name.

62 Küng and Kuschel (eds), (1993), p. 104, original emphasis.

Further evidence of the linkage between the Buddhist precepts and social justice is found in the Theravada tradition. Writing on the theme of 'Justice in Buddhism' Vajiragnana states:

> Man is responsible for society. It is he who makes it good or bad through his own actions. Buddhism, therefore, advocates a five-fold disciplinary code for man's training in order to maintain justice in society ... These five ... precepts are extremely important fundamental principles for promoting and perpetuating human welfare, peace and justice.[63]

I suggest, then, that the apparent differences between the moral teachings of Buddhism and human rights charters is one of form rather than substance. Human rights can be extrapolated from Buddhist moral teachings in the manner described above using the logic of moral relationships to illumine what is due under Dharma. A direct translation of the first four precepts yields a right to life, a right not to have one's property stolen, a right to fidelity in marriage, and a right not to be lied to. Many other human rights, such as the rights to liberty and security can either be deduced from or are extant within the general corpus of Buddhist moral teachings. A right not to be held in slavery, for example, is implicit in the canonical prohibition on trade in living beings.[64] These rights are the extrapolation of what is due under Dharma; they have not been 'imported' into Buddhism but were always implicitly present.

If modern conceptions of human rights and Buddhist moral teachings are related in the way I have suggested, certain conclusions follow for our understanding of the Buddhist precepts. If there are universal and exceptionless rights, as human rights charters affirm, there must be universal and exceptionless duties. If human rights such as a 'right to life' (by which I understand a right not to have one's life taken unjustly) are exceptionless, there must also be an exceptionless duty to abstain from unjustly depriving a human being of life. The First Precept in Buddhism, therefore, should be understood as an exceptionless duty or moral absolute.

Is this reverse translation, from absolute human rights to absolute moral duties, supported by textual sources? There is every reason to think that it is. Such an understanding of the precept is clearly evident in classical Buddhism, which tirelessly reiterates the principle of the sanctity of life found in the pan-Indian teachings on non-harming (*ahiṃsā*), and which gives no reason to suppose that its moral precepts are to be understood as anything other than exceptionless norms. If, on the other hand, it is thought that the precepts are not to be understood as moral absolutes, then it is difficult to see what justification there can be for Buddhists to hold that there are universal and exceptionless human rights. It would be inconsistent to affirm the latter but deny the former.

The above account of human rights in Buddhism has been given entirely within the context of an understanding of human good which has its apex in nirvana-in-this-life. Reference to the transcendent dimension of human good and its ground

---

63 Vajiragnana (1992).

64 A.iii.208.

has been avoided for several reasons. The first is that no reference need be made to transcendent realities in order to ground human rights. That this is so can be seen from the absence of any reference to such realities in contemporary human rights charters, and the fact that many atheists are vigorous defenders of human rights. Where Buddhism is concerned, the vision of human good set out in the third and fourth noble truths provides the necessary basis for a doctrine of human rights. Human rights turn out in essence to be what justice requires if human good is to be fulfilled. The second reason for avoiding reference to transcendent realities is that my aim has been to suggest a basis for human rights acceptable to classical Buddhism as a whole. Since all schools of Buddhism affirm the third and fourth noble truths and the vision of human good they proclaim, the required common ground for a pan-Buddhist doctrine of human rights is present.

The above should not be read as a denial that there can be a transcendent ground for human rights in Buddhism. Because the transcendent dimension of human good is left obscure in Buddhist teachings, however, the transcendent ground for human rights is also obscure. In terms of the account given here, the transcendent ground for human rights would be post-mortem nirvana, not in the sense of an absolute reality (as suggested by Küng) but as the universalization of human good on a transcendent plane. The twin axes of human good are knowledge (*prajñā*) and moral concern (*karuṇā*), and on the graph defined by these axes can be plotted the soteriological coordinates of any individual. Through participation in these twin categories of good, human nature progressively transcends its limitations and becomes saturated with nirvāṇic goodness. Eventually, in post-mortem nirvāṇa, this goodness attains a magnitude which can no longer be charted. If a transcendent ground for human rights is desired, this is where it should be sought.

To sum up: it is legitimate to speak of both rights and human rights in Buddhism. Modern doctrines of human rights are in harmony with the moral values of classical Buddhism in that they are an explication of what is 'due' under Dharma. The modern idea of human rights has a distinctive cultural origin, but its underlying preoccupation with human good makes it at bottom a moral issue in which Buddhism and other religions have a legitimate stake. The Global Ethic endorses the view that the principles it sets forth on human rights are neither new nor 'Western' when it states: 'We affirm that a common set of core values is found in the teachings of the religions, and that these form the basis of a global ethic.'[65]

A final thought. Above I have spoken only of human rights, and in the context of Buddhism this perspective may be unduly narrow in that it seems to preclude the universe of sentient non-human beings from any entitlement to rights. Buddhists may feel, therefore, that it is less prejudicial in discussions of this kind to revert to the older terminology of 'natural' rights. Whether or not animals have rights, and whether these are the same rights as human beings, is a matter which requires separate discussion. If human rights flow from human nature, as suggested, it may be that rights of different kinds flow from natures of different kinds. Such would seem

65 Küng and Kuschel (eds), (1993), p. 14.

to be the understanding of classical Buddhism as set out in its hierarchical scheme of the different realms of rebirth.

Chapter 12

Buddhism and Democracy[1]

Jay L. Garfield

What is the relationship between Buddhism and liberal democracy? Are they compatible frameworks or social values, which can somehow be joined to one another to gain a consistent whole? Or are they instead antagonistic, forcing those who would be Buddhist democrats into an uncomfortable choice between individually attractive but jointly unsatisfiable values? Or do they operate at entirely different levels of discourse so that questions regarding their relationship simply do not arise?

The question is important for several reasons: first, we indeed have in Buddhism and in liberal democratic theory two *prima facie* plausible frameworks for value, and their independent plausibility leads immediately to the question of their compatibility. Second, each framework has staked a claim to a central role in the global quest for human rights and justice, and indeed partisans of each have used the other in defence of their respective frameworks. Third, the Tibetan government in exile has formulated a national charter explicitly grounded in a Buddhist view of moral and social life and espousing a liberal democratic social ideology. It would be nice to know whether that vision is coherent. Fourth, the perennial debate between proponents of the universality of the liberal vision and those suggesting that liberalism is incompatible with 'Asian values' might move forward if it turned out that at least one major Asian tradition is compatible with liberal democracy, or on the other hand that there is a fundamental incompatibility between these two systems.

In this chapter I argue that not only are Buddhism and liberal democracy compatible, but that they are complementary in a deep sense: democracy, I argue, is strengthened by values drawn from Buddhist moral and social theory, and Buddhist moral and social theory gains concrete institutional and procedural specificity when it is articulated through the framework of liberal democratic theory.

The terms *Buddhist* and *liberal democracy* are each, to be sure, vague, and I will be painting them throughout this chapter with a broad brush, as it were. Nonetheless, I will explain how I understand these terms for present purposes. My conception of liberal democracy is that of the social contract tradition, and more particularly that of Locke, Kant, and Rawls. Its central tenets regarding the distinction between public and private and the centrality of individual rights are articulated in Mill's *On Liberty*,

1 I thank Anna Alomes, the Ven Geshe Ngawang Samten, Jeffrey Wallen, and Mark Siderits for comments on earlier drafts and for helpful conversations on this topic. This chapter was first published in my *Empty Words* (2002) reprinted by permission Oxford University Press, Inc.

in Rawls's *A Theory of Justice*, and are enshrined in the United States Constitution. To be sure, these texts do not speak on all issues with a single voice, but they indicate a clear and coherent vision of the nature of justice, of the primacy of fundamental individual rights in justice, and of the primacy also of justice over any particular conception of the good. They also indicate a need for a just society to tolerate a plurality of conceptions of the good and of the responsibility of government to its populace.

The Buddhism I have in mind is the Mahāyāna tradition of moral theory, comprising and extending the Pāli tradition of morality as expressed in the eight-fold path by the addition of the Bodhisattva ideal and the six perfections as providing an analysis of human moral perfection. More specifically, I have in mind that tradition as it is understood and expounded in medieval India and Tibet by such figures as Āryadeva, Śāntideva, and Tsong khapa. But I will also draw on insights from contemporary scholars and activists in the so-called 'Engaged Buddhist' movement, whose work is in the spirit of this tradition. Again, this tradition is not homogenous, but the conceptual space it marks out is coherent enough for present purposes. It is not so much an exercise in exegesis as it is in deploying the insights I find in these traditions. Indeed, given the contemporary context of the problematic with which I am concerned, it will often be the case that the implications I draw from the Buddhist tradition would not have been considered by classical scholars.

The Division of Theoretical Labour

I first note that in a strictly formal sense, Buddhism and democracy are mutually independent. Buddhism neither precludes nor entails liberal democracy; liberal democracy neither precludes nor entails Buddhism. Buddhism – and by this term I understand the doctrine presented in the *suttas* of the Pāli canon and developed in the Indian Mahāyāna *śāstras* insofar as this doctrine can be relatively uncontroversially identified – is generally silent about social institutions and forms of government. In the first instance it is a doctrine about the good life for the individual and about the values, practices, traits of character, states of mind, and view of reality that conduce to the liberation of the individual from suffering. Though this is elaborated in the Mahāyāna into an altruistic doctrine, Buddhist theory for the most part remains resolutely a theory about individual life and practice.

There are two classes of exceptions to this generalization, one of which will turn out to be important for our project. First, there is the *Vinaya-piṭaka*, devoted in good measure to the elaboration of the social and administrative structures for the Buddhist *saṅgha*, or monastic community. While this might appear to be the right place to begin an inquiry into the relationship between Buddhism and democracy inasmuch as the *Vinaya-piṭaka* comprises the most explicitly sociopolitical of all Buddhist scriptures, here we find discussion of the method of choice of leaders of the assembly, of the method for decking community membership, of resolving disputes, and so on. But there are compelling reasons for *not* starting here as well: the *Vinaya* is a code formulated explicitly and solely for the government of a voluntary, celibate, ideologically homogenous monastic community. Liberal democracy gets its very point from the presumption of heterogeneity, and from the need to adjudicate disputes and to formulate institutions and policies in circumstances where the option of removal from the community is not present. If Buddhism and liberal democracy are to be joined or compared, it must be on this more secular terrain.

This brings us to the second body of literature, considerably smaller in size: the corpus of Buddhist advice to rulers, of which Nāgārjuna's 'Letter to a Friend' and *Ratnāvali* are the best examples. Here we find direct advice grounded in Buddhist moral values regarding the ruling of a state. And from this literature two general salient points emerge (as well as a number of more specific points with which we will be concerned later): first, Buddhism has *nothing* to say about the appropriate *form* of government. Nāgārjuna's letters are addressed to *king*. But in these letters we find neither a conservative royalist defence of monarchy nor a revolutionary tract calling for a democratic order. Nāgārjuna is silent about these matters, focusing instead on the goods the state must deliver: hospitals, roadside resthouses, good water supply, care for animals, schools, and so on. Buddhism emerges in these texts as a theory about the good, silent about procedures, except for the general implicit proviso that only procedures capable of facilitating the pursuit of that good are legitimate. But with respect to the good, Buddhism has a lot to say: the goal of any social order, on a Buddhist view, is the maximization of happiness, the minimization of suffering, the provision for the least advantaged and the cultivation of traits of character such as compassion, patience, generosity and wisdom. If a monarchy can do this, fine. If a democracy can accomplish that, fine, too.

Liberal democratic theory – that is, the democratic theory of the social contract tradition as handed down from Locke through Jefferson to Mill to Rawls – is, by contrast, relatively silent about the good, not quite articulate and specific about social institutions and procedures. Indeed, liberal democracy – while to be sure embodying some specific values relative to social good, values that I will discuss later in this chapter – is self-consciously minimalist with respect to such commitments. This, indeed, is one of its strengths, and part of the genius of the liberal democratic tradition is the insight that procedures themselves can be legitimized independently of many nonprocedural values and that legitimate procedures can legitimate both institutions and conceptions of the good.

Now, the contrast between Buddhism and liberalism on this score can easily be overstated, and it is important to be careful here. It is neither true that Buddhism is devoid of procedural ideas nor that liberalism is bereft of specific values or conceptions of the good life or the good social order. Each tradition embodies commitments of both types, and indeed it would be a conceptual impossibility for a moral framework to be either entirely substantive or entirely procedural in content. Procedures reflect substantive values and vice versa. And indeed these values at the extremes must be mutually constraining. This is evident, for example, in constitutional protections of some values against ready change, however democratic the procedure.

The contrast, however, is real, and can be properly emphasized in two ways: first, the respective orders of legitimation for the two traditions are *toto genere* distinct. Liberal democratic theory legitimates its goods on procedural grounds; Buddhism legitimates any procedures on the grounds that they produce appropriate goods. Second, and related, procedures of particular kinds are constitutive of liberal democracy, whereas commitments to particular social goods are constitutive of Buddhist societies in a very deep way whereas liberal democratic societies may differ widely (or one may change wildly over time) with respect to some particular vision of the good (say free education, universal health care, or a minimum wage) and remain recognizably democratic, any society that abandoned election, open access to offices, or transparency of the judicial process would ipso facto no longer count as a liberal democracy. There is, however, also a sense in which a specific conception of the good is built into most Western liberal democracies beyond the necessary implication of some minimal conception of the good by the procedural commitments and by the initial presuppositions of the contractual situation: most liberals – whether they acknowledge it or not – tacitly supplement democratic principles with a heavy dose of Judeo-Christian values, including the presumption of human dominion over the earth, of the sanctity of individual property, of the primacy of individuals over collectives, of the legitimacy of violence in the service of a legitimate cause, among others, which are called upon [sometimes in suitably secularized language, sometimes in the original] in policymaking or in the adjudication of institutions to fill in the gaps left by liberal theory. A Tibetan student once asked in a class of Locke's political philosophy, 'Do you have to be a Christian to take this theory of property and natural rights seriously?' Maybe.

Similarly, while some Buddhist societies might be monarchies and others democratic, or the same one might change its form of government over time and remain recognizably Buddhist, any society that abandoned commitment to non-violence, to maintaining the welfare of the least advantaged, to providing health care and education to all its citizens, and to facilitating spiritual practice for those who aspire thereto would cease to be recognizably Buddhist.

For these reasons we can treat Buddhism and liberal democracy as diametrically opposed on one issue, namely, the direction of legitimation as between procedure and conception of the good. But this does not entail that they are therefore incapable of fusion. Legitimation, after all, might not in the end have a foundational structure: it might well be that procedures and conceptions of the good are mutually reinforcing. In fact this is a picture we will suggest. But these observations suggest more by way of a strategy for social and political philosophy a division of theoretical labour: a Buddhist democratic theory needs, after all, a theory both of the good and of the political institutions capable of and appropriate to realizing that good. Why not, then, turn to Buddhism for the former task, and liberal democratic theory for the latter? I propose to do just that, allowing each body of theory to do what it does best, with the hope that we will end up with a consistent set of institutions and social objectives that lend normative support to each other. As we shall see, however, it will not be enough simply to spell out independently the demands and content of each theory and to join them by the word *and*. To show their deep theoretical connection and affinity, I will turn to the explicitly Buddhist notion of *upāya* – of skilful-means – as a mediating concept.

Buddhist ideals for a society

From the fundamentals of Buddhist moral theory as articulated in the *sūtras* and *śāstras* we can distil several specific components of a theory of social good: first, social institutions should aim at maximizing happiness and minimizing suffering for all members of society. In particular, given Buddhist egalitarian concerns and given the content of compassion, social institutions should aim at equity in distribution and opportunity and especially at the minimization of suffering for the least advantaged.

The Buddhist doctrine of the *pañcaśīla*, or five ethical precepts for laypersons, adds to the Buddhist conception of social institutions and conceptions of the good: these precepts enjoin refraining from killing, stealing, lying, sexual misconduct, and intoxication. Put together and viewed in a social context, they together constitute advice against violent arid actions likely to sow discord, and favour openness and integrity.[2] These more general values can inform the development of social institutions. If we were to read them too narrowly and apply them crudely as instruments of social policy, it might seem that they require not only the criminalization of homicide, theft, and perjury, but also the prohibition of alcohol and a strict code of sexual conduct. But this would be far too narrow a reading and in any case would fail to see the values that underlie this moral code and their relevance to social theory.

What do killing, theft, intoxication, sexual misconduct, and lying have in common that they should be brought together as *the* five things any person is admonished to forswear? Just this: all are either directly violent or are seeds of violence. The fundamental value thus reflected in this code is non-violence and the obvious application to social philosophy is that political institutions and policies should themselves be non-violent and directed primarily to the eradication of violence in society. Spelling out the content of this prescription is, of course, not a trivial task and must remain outside the scope of this chapter. But the sense of the fundamental value should be clear.

Buddhist moral literature distinguishes a number of important human virtues or perfections of character. Given that we are asking from Buddhism a conception of social good, and given that for Buddhism society can only be seen instrumentally as a mechanism for ensuring the good of individuals, it follows that social institutions

---

2 Violence, from a Buddhist perspective, can be directed either outward, towards others, or towards oneself. Though here I am emphasizing the former, given my concern for social policy in this essay, in most canonical literature, concerned as such literature is for individual spiritual development, the emphasis is on the latter. In that context, these five proscriptions are most explicitly linked by their tendency to inflame passion and hence to impede spiritual progress. This, too, is a form of violence in speech and action.

should, from a Buddhist perspective, encourage, develop, and foster these virtues A brief list of these would include prominently generosity, patience, wisdom, moderation, and non-attachment. Buddhist moral theory can best be characterized as a concern with certain *vastus* – areas of importance in conduct, traits of character, and ranges of behaviour on which one should focus in worrying about one's moral development – and not as a set of imperatives or specific prescriptions. Now since Buddhist literature is so sparse when it comes to very specific advice on social institutions or policies, I – simply spelling out the way that Buddhist and democratic theory can be joined – will allow myself to be even more reserved. That is, I will not venture here a specific set of recommendations for how political arrangements might encourage, develop, and fluster these virtues. But I can say a few things to indicate the direction that such an account might take.

Social structures and institutions that reflect ideals build consensus regarding the probity of those ideals. Protection of the freedom of speech, for instance, not only reflects the view that speech should be free but encourages that value in those who dwell in societies with such policies. Generous social programmes and programmes conducive to equity will not only reflect but encourage values such as generosity and moderation. Policies creating shared public goods and enabling their enjoyment without the amassing of private wealth will generate non-attachment The facilitation of education will encourage the development of wisdom. Public disarmament will conduce to private non-violence and so forth.

Moreover, since the Buddhist ideals I here take seriously include those of the Mahāyāna, Buddhist social institutions and political arrangements should presume and cultivate a sense of responsibility for others. This requirement would most obviously find expression in the requirement for extensive health and welfare services as the primary brief of government but would extend to the establishment of service agencies involving substantial numbers of citizens, perhaps involving a civil service force in which all or most would serve at some time.

The Formal Promise of Liberal Democracy

We have seen that Buddhism provides a rich positive conception of social goods and of the values a political system ought to reflect and encourage. What does liberal democratic theory bring to the table? A lot, of course: it demands a respect or a basic set of universal human rights, prominently including the right to vote for those who will hold significant government offices; the right to free speech and expression broadly conceived; the right to free religious expression and against the imposition of religious beliefs or practices; freedom from torture or unwarranted imprisonment or restriction of movement; the right to informational privacy and allied rights. All of these can be summed up as the right to participate without fetter in an open public sphere, and to be free from unwarranted interference in the private sphere.

To continue in the same vein, liberal democracy requires that institutions preserve and reflect the equal liberty of the citizens of the state and the rule of law and that all offices be open and all processes transparent. That is, special privileges or restrictions on citizens should result from fair allocation procedures; positions of authority should in principle be open to any citizen, and their occupants should be fairly chosen; all political and legal processes should be open to scrutiny and assessment, be fair, and have consensual support.

Also, pluralism is fundamental to the liberalism of any liberal democracy. Aside from the minimal set of values adumbrated above (perhaps plus or minus a few), liberalism is committed to impartiality among conceptions of the good and to providing each citizen with the liberty to pursue his or her own conception of the good, so long as that commitment does not trammel the rights of others. A consequence of this is that a liberal democracy will be committed to allowing the flourishing of a number of ideologically and axiologically distinct communities as part of a body politic, without either assisting or hampering in special ways any of these in its independent activities.

This brief outline of the central commitments of these two frameworks reinforces the sense that while they are not directly contradictory to one another, there is no obvious point of intersection between the two. If we were to leave the analysis at this point, it might then seem that while a Buddhist democratic theory is not impossible, it would at least have a peculiar accidental relation to, and would in no way be conceptually motivated either by Buddhism or by liberal democracy. I now turn to a construct from within Buddhism that, I argue, provides the necessary link, that motivates specifically attempts to forge Buddhist democratic theory.

Upāya as a Conceptual Bridge

An important and insufficiently noticed conceptual construct in Buddhist theory is that of *upāya*, or skilful means. From a Buddhist perspective, skill is necessary to cultivate because enlightenment is difficult to achieve and to facilitate, and because the Buddhist virtues – and this is true both of individual and social virtues – require not simply intention, but success. It is not enough to form a desire, even a sincere desire, to be generous. Without the successful completion of generous acts, generosity is not realized. Even an act motivated by generosity, if it does not succeed in benefiting its target, fails, on a Buddhist analysis, to be a fully generous act. The road to hell, one night say, is paved with good intentions; the road to Buddhahood, with good realizations. This is not, of course, to say that such an act is thereby vicious, or bereft of moral worth, but only to recognize that complete virtue requires more than just good intention. (The parallels to Aristotle's argument for the need for practical wisdom in moral life are intriguing here. But a full comparison would take us far afield.) What goes for generosity goes as well, *mutatis mutandis* for patience, wisdom, effort, concentration, compassion and the rest. The injunction to any virtue is always, in Buddhism, *ipso facto* an injunction to cultivate the *upāya* necessary for its realization.

Moral skill is necessary for the expression and development of Buddhist virtues and for the attainment of the good as seen from the Buddhist standpoint. But the other side of this coin is that such skills are therefore valued not for their own sake, but rather simply as *means* to goods that are antecedently regarded as valuable (and these, too, instrumentally valuable , and in particular because they conduce to enlightenment). And any skill or method that conduces to Buddhist virtues or goods is, simply in virtue of that fact, worthy of cultivation. This is not to say that other considerations might not weigh against the use of any particular means: Buddhism is resolutely multivariate and non-absolute in its assessment of actions and institutions and admits an indefinite range of moral quality between the irredeemably wicked and the morally perfect, depending on the complex admixture of motives and consequences involved. The centrality of this category of instrumental good, however, allows for a distinctively Buddhist justification and interpretation of democracy.

The route to such a justification and interpretation should be clear: given the conception of the collective, social good to which we have seen Buddhism is committed, if it turns out that liberal democracy is the best means to achieve those goods, it follows straightforwardly from Buddhist principles and from the theory of *upāya* that liberal democracy is the preferred Buddhist social framework. Moreover, considerations of *upāya* would then determine the precise shape of those democratic institutions and the social ends towards which they are to be directed. From this standpoint the intuition with which I began this discussion reappears: that democratic theory could provide the institutional and procedural framework for a social order whose conception of the good is rooted in Buddhism as potentially vindicated through this mediating concept. The important question to ask, then, is this: Is liberal democracy plausibly construed as the best means for realizing the social goods Buddhism seeks? It is to this question I now turn.

The Empirical Argument from Efficacy

The argument at this point becomes empirical, if only in the broadest sense of that term. For if *upāya* is what counts, the question regarding whether Buddhism permits or even demands a liberal democratic political order boils down to the question, 'Does liberal democracy represent the best method for maximizing happiness or minimizing suffering, for realizing equity, for achieving non-violence, and or cultivating virtues such as patience, generosity, wisdom, and commitment to others?' If it does, we are home free. If not, perhaps we should be seeking a different sociopolitical order.

If this is the question, the answer appears to be too easy. A quick glance around the world's nation states reveals that on any reasonable index of social utility the world's liberal democracies lead their more totalitarian rivals. This is so whether we look at straightforward economic indicators such as median income, percentage of population living in poverty, equity or distribution, and the like, basic welfare indicators such as access to medical care, housing, nutrition, or schooling, or softer indicators such as level of social unrest or satisfaction with government. There is no doubt that on hierarchizing the world's nations on these parameters the liberal democracies rise to the top. Neither can doubt exist about the empirical evidence that liberal democracy tends to reduce suffering and engender happiness.

What about the violence/non-violence dimension? Here is one striking fact: in the last two-hundred years, one democratic country has never waged war against another. Democracy, one might say, as Kant argued, is the best inoculation against war. At the level of personal violence, the story is more equivocal. There are indeed some notably violent democracies (such as the United States) and some notably peaceful autocracies (Singapore). But these exceptions aside, the trend still evidently favours democracies even at this level.

We have seen that the Buddhist conception of the social good also includes an account of the virtues to be encouraged, cultivated and supported by a social order. This is a harder desideratum with respect to which to make the requisite empirical claim. There may be good plausibility arguments on both sides, and there are no obvious data, whether rigorous or intuitive, to which to appeal. I can at least say that on this dimension liberal democracy is no worse, as far as I know, than its alternatives.

This brief empirical argument is hardly conclusive. It is at best a good motivator. I have not appealed to any hard data. Nor would the generalizations I defend based on these intuitive characteristics lack exceptions. Nonetheless, I feel confident in saying that empirical considerations at least favour the hypothesis that liberal democracy is most likely the best political means for achieving the kind of society that Buddhist moral theory recommends. I turn now to some more theoretical considerations to suggest that the central feature of liberal democracy, the articulation and protection of fundamental human rights, is the best way to promote a Buddhist conception of the good, and hence that such a framework is indicated from the standpoint of *upāya*.

The Argument for the Importance of Rights as a Facilitator

As we have seen, a straightforwardly empirical argument or liberal democracy as the best means to realize Buddhist social ideals is, while a bit tendentious, a good motivator. But in the absence of compelling empirical evidence either way, I turn to a more theoretical argument, asking whether there is good reason to believe that respect for the fundamental set of human rights and the correlative political institutions recognized in the liberal democratic tradition provides greater promise as a vehicle for the development of a society conforming to Buddhist ideals than do its competitors. The answer to this more forward-looking question is more strongly positive.

Asking this question also gives us additional theoretical leverage. For by focusing on the more abstract connections between Buddhist and democratic ethics and politics, we can get some insight into the ways in which the two bodies of theory might mutually inform each other and into how a Buddhist democracy might actually look. That is, at the same time that we examine the degree to which these two systems are consistent or even axiologically complementary we can determine the exact nature of that complementarity.

What are *rights* good for? From the standpoint of classical liberal theory, an important class of personal rights, which we might call 'privacy rights', can be understood as constructing protective barriers against the intrusion of other individuals and state power into our private lives. Examples include rights to free speech and association; to freedom of religious expression; freedom against unwarranted search and seizure, and so on. First and foremost, these rights protect their bearers against gratuitous harms, whether inflicted by other individuals or by government and, equally important, create a space in the private sphere in which an individual or group can pursue and cultivate the good as they see it. Without a framework of such basic personal privacy rights, no one can be secure to pursue any particular vision of the good. Now, as I argued above, Buddhism is nothing if not a view about the good. It follows that if the protection of privacy rights is ipso facto a protection of the realization of such views, liberal democracy's commitment to such rights enables a Buddhist life, at least for individuals. But at this level of analysis, all that we are really saying is that the individual rights enshrined by liberal democracy provide protection for any set of values an individual might wish to pursue, and not that there is any special relationship between democracy and Buddhism. We can, however, go further.

One important core value in Buddhist social morality is the minimization of the suffering of the disadvantaged. How can a social order best realize this value? One obvious answer is this: enshrine a fundamental civil right to a minimal standard of living and minimal access to such basic goods as medical care. Now, to be sure, these goods themselves can be provided by even the most totalitarian regime. But the only way to guarantee them effectively is to establish them as fundamental rights within a political order and the institution of rights itself has its home only in the context of a liberal political order. The best way to realize this particular value, a core of the Buddhist conception of the good, is therefore to embed these specific rights in a liberal social order.

Similarly, we can ask what the best route is to the achievement of non-violence in social institutions. I noted above that in general, democracy is an excellent guarantee against the settling of major internal disputes through organized physical violence, such as civil war. That empirical argument counts of a lot. But violence comes in other more implicit forms, such as institutional racism, oppression, coercive political and economic structures, and the like. Each of these forms necessarily rests on a foundation of either explicit or constantly threatened violence for its maintenance. Liberal democracy is therefore the best way imaginable to combat these, both because of its universal enfranchisement and because of its respect for fundamental rights to reduce and to eliminate the degree of violence present in a society. Many of the forms of institutional violence I have examined consist directly in the violation of recognized rights or the failure to recognize rights enshrined in liberal democratic institutions. Essential features of such political orders such as universal enfranchisement and the openness of political processes combine with principles generally acknowledged by citizens and enshrined in law concerning access to education and basic social welfare codes to dramatically reduce the level of such institutional violence in all liberal democratic societies, when this is compared with totalitarian neighbours. Liberal democratic societies also cultivate a greater sense of mutual responsibility than do their totalitarian counterparts, simply because they offer their citizens a genuine voice and chance to participate in civic affairs. The sense of membership in a common venture this engenders cannot be underestimated, and the consequence is an increased commitment to the common good – after all, it is a good in which every citizen has a voice in determining.

Openness of government institutions has two other benefits that support Buddhist values: inasmuch as Buddhism is concerned first and foremost with soteriology and with the religious practices that support liberation, it has an interest in political regimes that permit the free exercise of religion and of course the privacy, and hence the protection of religious practice is a hallmark of liberal democratic theory and societies. But this openness also limits the possibilities for corruption and hence alleviates the suffering that corruption inevitably produces.

Now all of this is subject to innumerable objections to the contrary. There are many examples both of liberal democratic societies that fail to live up to these ideals or that fail, despite living up to them, to deliver all of the goods I have enumerated. And there are certainly plenty of examples of illiberal societies that do deliver at least some of these goods. I need not however, in order to make the case for liberal democracy as *upāya*, show that there is a clear line between liberal democratic societies and all others, with Buddhist goods realized in their entirety for all citizens on the one side and denied to all on the other. To claim that this is possible would be foolish. All that is necessary is to show that overall the social structures advanced by liberal democracy represent the best means to achieve the ends recommended by Buddhism. And this I have endeavoured to do.

What Liberal Democracy Can Offer to Buddhism

Can Buddhism gain anything from attention to liberal democratic theory? I think so. It is a striking feature of Buddhist literature, as I noted previously, that despite the tremendous importance of the structure of a society and its institutions, including predominantly its political structures, in determining the conditions of human life and the possibilities for the attainment of both temporal and spiritual goods, there is very little – really nothing – in the Buddhist philosophical tradition by way of social or political theory. This must be regarded as a serious lacuna in a philosophical system that aims at characterizing the nature of suffering and of its elimination for a being who is ineliminably social.

On the other hand, as also noted, Buddhism demands of its practitioners the development of *upāya*, and this must include social and political *upāya*. If what I have said about the conceptual and empirical relationships between the Buddhist conception of the good and the deliverances of democracy is valid, liberal democratic theory might simply be the obvious body of theory with which to fill this gap. The Mahāyāna canon prides itself on its perpetual openness to new texts. Perhaps it is time to make space in canonical collections of such mahapanditas as Locke, Rousseau, Mill, Jefferson, Dewey, Rawls, and Habermas. And indeed in the democratization of the Tibetan exile government and in the discussions of Buddhist democratic institutions within that community, I see the beginnings of this process.

What Buddhism Can Offer to Liberal Democracy

But the benefits of intercultural fusion philosophy do not flow in one direction only. Liberal democratic theory and those formulating policy in liberal democratic societies can also benefit from an injection of Buddhist ideas. Again, attention to the development of Buddhist democratic institutions in the Tibetan exile community can be instructive – and not only, I emphasize, to Buddhists or members of Buddhist societies, but to secular theorists and policymakers.

There is a curious tension at the base of liberal democracy. When I examine the strategies by means of which it is legitimated – and I have in mind those of Hobbes, Locke, Rousseau, and Rawls – there is an essential appeal to practical reason in the following sense: it is argued that for arbitrarily chosen citizens, described in abstraction from their particular fortunes within society, it is rational to choose liberal democracy precisely because it offers the best chance for achieving personal happiness, or at least the best chance for avoiding the worst suffering. This is, of course, captured with the greatest clarity in Rawls's account of the original position and of the deliberations of the parties.

On the other hand, while liberal democracy offers this prospect precisely because it promises a government and set of social institutions that will not obstruct individual efforts to realize the good, it is deliberately minimalist in its promise to provide particular social goods, leaving such decisions either to contingent political processes or to individual enterprise. The reason for this is straightforward: democratic theory is resolutely both individualistic and pluralistic. The individualistic side leads to an emphasis on a broad zone of privacy and little positive social intervention for good or ill into the lives of individuals, the pluralism leads to a hesitancy to propose any but the most general and formal social goods as the objects of state action for fear that any more determinate commitment to a particular vision of the good will run roughshod over the rights and aspirations of those who do not share that vision.

But given the logic of legitimation that underlies this political framework, any enhancement of the basic stock of goods delivered to its citizens by a liberal democratic society would be chosen by initial contracting parties, so long as those goods are not parochial in nature – so long as they benefit the society generally and, as Rawls puts it, benefit the least advantaged, and hence protect citizens' vital interest in not falling too far in terms of total utility. That is, not only would a basic minimum of primary social goods be demanded by any rational contracting parties, but any rational parties would insist that as much as possible should be available to as many as possible, and that avoidable poverty be avoided.

At this point Buddhism has something to contribute to the framework. First, the Buddhist goal of eliminating suffering enjoins a strong social welfare policy. That is, it enjoins the provision of basic education, health care, and a decent minimum standard of living for all citizens. Contracting parties who take this injunction seriously – who recognize both the universality of susceptibility to suffering and the possibility of its remediation – would think only briefly before rejecting an unbridled free market, for instance, and would insist on liberal social welfare programmes. This is already an enrichment of the minimal conception of the good in most liberal theory.

But we can go farther. On any plausible contractarian story of the legitimation of and limits of government power, the parties to the initial contract know the general facts about human nature, though they may not know their specific circumstances, preferences, or positions. Knowledge of these general facts enables them to imagine the likely effects of any social order they contemplate establishing. Now it is overwhelmingly plausible that the set of virtues endorsed by Buddhist theory – patience, wisdom, non-violence, generosity, and so on – in fact, when broadly realized, yield happier, more stable societies. Social institutions can be designed to encourage, reward, and foster these values or to discourage them. Parties to a social contract cognizant of these facts can be expected to agree to institutions that foster rather than discourage them. Again, this represents a substantial enrichment over a more value-neutral liberal framework.

We would therefore expect to find in a Buddhist democracy not armies but social service corps; not private health insurance schemes but a strong social welfare and health care system; egalitarian access to education; and significant incentives to do charitable work. Institutions like this would take over incentives to competition, to the concentration of wealth, and to the development of power differentials this substantive account of good stands in contrast to an emphasis on economic growth and the encouragement of private gain. But none of this is in any way incompatible with the democratic ideals of equality before the law, of participation in a public discourse, of open office and of a broad range of personal freedoms. In fact it is, one would argue, central to enabling these freedoms to make a real difference in the quality of human life. There is also no reason to think that Buddhist moral theory is unique in its ability to contribute a positive conception of the good to liberal democracy. Other substantive value systems may do as well. I only argue that it can make a contribution, and one that liberal democratic theory is in a position to reciprocate.

Conclusion

I hence conclude that while Buddhist values have typically been overlooked as valid considerations in the legitimation and design of social institutions in democratic theory and practice, this is both unnecessary and unjustified. A democratic society that draws on these principles in its social order and institutions has a greater prospect for success, and providing its citizenry with good lives and in fact greater claim to moral legitimacy than one that is neutral with respect to these principles. Buddhist democracy is thus not only not oxymoronic but is better democracy even when judged on the terms that the liberal tradition itself chooses, and better Buddhism when judged on the terms that Buddhism itself chooses, for moral evaluation. I conclude that these systems are – far from being antithetical – complementary, and that each is more compelling when adjoined to the other.

Chapter 13

Buddhist Reductionism and the Structure of Buddhist Ethics

Mark Siderits

Buddhism teaches that there is no self, and that the person is not ultimately real. Buddhists also hold that the highest good for humans, *nirvāṇa*, is a state that is attained through abandoning belief in a self. And it is claimed as well that those who enter this state will naturally devote themselves to helping others overcome suffering. But how are these claims related? Is it, for instance, that having ceased to believe that I have an enduring self, I shall cease to have concern for my future, and so shall enter into a state of unsullied enjoyment of the pure present? And is the enlightened person's selfless devotion to the welfare of others supposed to be a simple consequence of their knowing themselves to be devoid of self? Is it that without belief in a self, egoism naturally turns into altruism? While such readings of the Buddhist tradition are not unknown, they are highly problematic. Still there are, I think, deep and important connections between Buddhist Reductionism and such basic claims of Buddhist ethics as that *nirvāṇa* represents the *summum bonum*, and that the enlightened person will be motivated to promote the welfare of all. To see what those connections are, it is crucial to be clear about just what Buddhist Reductionism does and does not say about the nature of our existence. For here, I think, we will find the key to understanding the structure of Buddhist ethics.

I shall proceed as follows. First I shall explain what I take Buddhist Reductionism to be.[1] Then I shall explore what this might tell us about the nature of the liberated state. This will involve looking briefly at how the cessation of suffering might be thought to result from coming to know that there is no self and that persons are only conventionally real. Then I shall take a rather longer and more systematic look at the claim that knowledge of the truth of Reductionism leads one to work for the benefit of all. Then I shall conclude with a few words concerning what I take the overall structure of Buddhist ethics to be. But first a word of caution is necessary concerning my project. What I shall be presenting might best be construed as a rational reconstruction of the Buddhist tradition. Classical Buddhist philosophers do not use precisely the terms I shall use to characterize their positions. Nor do they

---

1 I follow the useful convention, first introduced by Derek Parfit in *Reasons and Persons*, Oxford: Clarendon Press, 1984, of employing the capitalized 'Reductionism' to indicate a reductionist view of persons.

make precisely the same conceptual connections I shall draw in trying to exhibit the logic of their overall view. It is, I believe, possible to defend my reconstruction through a systematic examination of the classical Buddhist philosophical literature. But I shall do shamefully little of that here. I want instead to sketch the picture that I think makes best sense of all the details I here pass over.

I

To be a reductionist about a certain kind of thing is to hold that the existence of a thing of that kind just consists in the existence of certain other sorts of entities, entities that are thought to be in some sense more basic or fundamental. To be a reductionist about clouds, for instance, is to hold that a cloud is really nothing more than a very large number of liquid water molecules suspended in the air in close proximity to one another. To be a reductionist about persons (a Reductionist) is thus to hold that the existence of a person just consists in the existence of a large number of psychophysical elements: body parts, feelings, perceptions, desires, etc. But of course not just any collection of psychophysical elements will count as a person (any more than just any collection of liquid water molecules will count as a cloud). They must be related to one another in certain characteristic ways. Moreover, persons are things that endure for some time, while most of the psychophysical elements are relatively ephemeral. The continued existence of a person must then be said to consist in a causal series of sets of suitably arranged psychophysical elements: these body parts only exist for a while but cause similar successor parts to arise; this feeling only exists for a while but causes a successor desire, etc. Buddhist Reductionists hold, then, that the existence of a person just consists in the occurrence of a causal series of psychophysical elements.

Reductionists hold generally that the reducing entities are in some sense more basic or fundamental than the things that are reduced. Buddhist Reductionists put this point, as it concerns persons, by using the Buddhist distinction between conventional truth and ultimate truth. They claim that while it is conventionally true that there are persons, this claim is neither ultimately true nor ultimately false. It is, on the other hand, both conventionally and ultimately true that psychophysical elements exist and enter into causal relations with one another. This is because a statement can be ultimately true only if it neither asserts nor presupposes the existence of mere conceptual fictions.[2] The stock example of a conceptual fiction is a chariot. We all

2 The second disjunct explains why no assertion about persons can be ultimately false. The difficulty is that to give a truth value to a statement about a whole is to presuppose that things of that nature could exist. The notion of the ultimate truth is based on the idea that these are all mere conceptual fictions. We may see this idea at work in various Buddhist assertions to the effect that none of the following four alternatives hold: P, not-P, both P and not-P, neither P nor not-P. It is claimed, for instance, that the enlightened person may not be said to exist after death, not exist after death, etc. None of these alternatives can hold, since each involves the false presupposition that persons exist.

agree that the parts that make up a chariot are real. But is there, in addition to the parts, an extra entity, the whole? Buddhist Reductionists say 'No'. They point out that when the parts are arranged in one particular way (the 'assembled chariot' way) we tend to judge that there is a single entity there. But when the same parts are arranged in a different way (the 'strewn across the battlefield' way), we judge instead that there is not one thing but many. This difference is clearly mediated by the fact that in the first case we use the convenient designator 'chariot', while in the second case we have no one word for the set of parts. But why do we have a single word in the first case and not in the second? Clearly because of facts about our interests and practices. The common-sense intuition that chariots are real represents no more than a projection onto the world of our own subjective needs and cognitive limitations.[3]

A person, like a chariot, is a whole made of a large number of parts, namely all the psychophysical elements in the causal series. Hence persons are conceptual fictions, things that we believe to exist only because of our employment of a convenient designator. It follows that no statement about persons can be ultimately true (or ultimately false), but many statements about persons are conventionally true. This point may be put by saying that while persons are ultimately unreal (i.e. are mere conceptual fictions), they are conventionally real. What are ultimately real are just the psychophysical elements; when these enter into causal relations of the right sorts, we may use the convenient designator 'person' as a shorthand device for referring to them. But the ultimate truth is thoroughly impersonal. Only the individual elements themselves may be said to exist, not the complexes into which they enter. We might be tempted to believe that among these elements there is some one special entity that is the essence of the person, the true 'me'. But this is ruled out by various arguments for non-self, such as the famous argument from impermanence.[4] Such words as 'I' do not ultimately refer to any one part of the causal series of psychophysical elements (since there is no self), nor do they refer to the causal series as a whole (since such wholes are mere conceptual fictions). Statements using such words cannot be ultimately true (or false), they can at best only be conventionally true.

The Buddhist claim that statements about persons can be conventionally true (i.e. that persons are conventionally real) is what marks off the distinction between the Buddhist Reductionist and the Eliminativist. Both Reductionists and Eliminativists deny what Non-Reductionists affirm: that persons are ultimately real. Non-Reductionists typically believe that the true person (the true referent of 'I') is a self, some one special part of the psychophysical complex that constitutes its enduring core or essence. Reductionists and Eliminativists deny that there is any such entity.

3 Buddhist Reductionists developed powerful arguments for the conclusion that partite entities like chariots are ultimately unreal. Their arguments generally rely on showing that a whole can be said to be neither identical with nor distinct from its parts. Modern formulations of Reductionism make use instead of *sorites* arguments. I explore both means of defending Reductionism, and also explore the wide variety of objections that have been raised to the view, in my *Empty Persons*, Aldershot: Ashgate, 2004.

4 To be found, for instance, in *Saṃyutta Nikāya*. III.66f.

They must, however, somehow explain the fact that people commonly think of themselves as persons who endure over time, and who have various relations, such as ownership and control, toward the empirically given psychophysical elements. This they do by claiming that belief in the existence of persons is the result of a sort of folk or common-sense theory of personhood. Just as we were socialized to think of the chariot as some one thing that serves our transportation needs, so we have been socialized to think of a causal series of psychophysical elements as one thing with its own distinctive set of properties. Reductionists and Eliminativists agree that this folk theory is ultimately false. Where they disagree is over whether it serves any useful purpose, and so should be deemed conventionally true. Eliminativists claim that our belief in persons is like our ancestors' belief in disease-causing demons. Reductionists claim instead that it is like our belief in clouds and chariots: not ultimately true, but still useful for purposes of everyday transactions.

According to the folk theory of personhood, persons have the following crucial features: they endure at least a lifetime; they bear desert over time; they take up such future-directed attitudes as anticipation and dread; and they take up such past-directed attitudes as remorse. Since Buddhist Reductionists deny there are any such things as persons, why would they think it useful that a causal series of psychophysical elements adopt the theory that it is an entity of such a sort? To answer this question, it helps to consider what actually occurs as a child is socialized into our personhood practices. The child must learn to identify with and appropriate the states of its past and its future; this is not something that small children do spontaneously. And because small children do not do this naturally, they are more likely to act imprudently if left to their own devices. That is, it is more likely that there will be behaviour directed at immediate gratification that also results in greater long-term pain in the future of that causal series. Consider the case of getting the child to brush their teeth. Only if the present set of psychophysical elements identifies with and appropriates those future elements that potentially contain the pain of tooth decay will the present set see a reason for undergoing the present mild discomfort of tooth-brushing in order to prevent the far greater future pain of tooth decay. What this helps us see is that inculcating the practices associated with our personhood theory is a way of attempting to minimize overall suffering.

This point bears repeating. We consider ourselves to be persons only because that practice helps minimize suffering by, among other things, preventing us from acting in grossly imprudent ways. It is sometimes claimed that by virtue of their having a so-called survival instinct, all animals possess a special interest in their own futures. But this is simply wrong. What all animals are likely to possess is a tendency to engage in certain actions that promote their future well-being in the animal's normal environment. Natural selection explains how this comes to be. And in non-human animals this does not involve the organism's identifying with and appropriating its future states. With adult humans it is different. Our ability to promote our long-term interests does depend crucially on such identification and appropriation. But this is because we were socialized to do so. We learnt to become persons – to feel such person-involving attitudes as anticipation and dread toward our future states, and to take the interests of that future being as one's own. And, the Buddhist Reductionist adds, it is better all things considered that we did so.

The Eliminativist disagrees. While Eliminativists need not have any particular replacement theory in mind when they advocate supplanting a prevalent folk theory, they typically do. For instance, Eliminativists speaking about disease-causing demons will point to the success of the microbial infection theory of disease as grounds for rejecting the belief in demons. Likewise, it is not necessary that Eliminativists say what they wish to replace our theory of personhood with, provided they can demonstrate the incoherence of the theory. But Eliminativists typically advocate either punctualism (the view that we should only identify with what are now considered person-stages), or else a sort of world-soul view according to which we should identify with the totality of causal series of psychophysical elements. According to punctualism (which is the more common form of Eliminativist theory), we last only as long as all the important members of a set of psychophysical elements continue to exist and interact in the relevant ways. Depending on which elements are considered essential, this may mean we exist for as little as a moment to perhaps as much as a few days. But in any event, such p-persons (as we may call them) will be far more ephemeral than persons. This will give rise to considerable difficulties in the imprudence department. But the punctualist will respond that at least p-persons have the advantage of being ultimately real.

The Buddhist Reductionist disagrees with this last claim. A p-person is no more real than a chariot (all of whose parts also typically exist simultaneously). Thus the theory that we are p-persons could not be ultimately true (or ultimately false either). This theory could at best be true conventionally. And for it to be true conventionally, it would have to be the case that adopting this theory better satisfies our interests than the alternatives. Its adoption would have to result in less overall suffering than would ensue from adopting any of the other theories we might use to gather together sets of psychophysical elements. This is likely to be false. The theory that we are persons is likely to be better at minimizing suffering. More suffering will probably be averted if each set of psychophysical elements is disposed to choose actions based on its assessment of how they will affect the welfare of successor sets in that causal series.[5] The Buddhist Reductionist will have similar things to say about the proposal that we should think of ourselves as some one overarching entity, the world-soul. They will deny that such an entity is ultimately real, and they will be skeptical concerning the claim that such a belief could better maximize welfare than the belief that we are persons.

A Buddhist Reductionist holds that persons are conventionally real. It is thus rational for each of us to consider ourselves as entities that endure, that carry desert,

5 A condensed version of this debate between Reductionism and Eliminativism is to be found in *The Questions of King Miliñda*, II.2. The considerations that are there said to tell in favour of Reductionism (i.e. in favour of considering persons to be conventionally real) include not only the avoidance of gross imprudence, but also the effectiveness of the criminal law at deterring others and reforming criminals.

and that entertain the appropriate future- and past-directed attitudes, including, crucially, interest in our own future welfare. This is so not because we actually are persons, but rather because the adoption of such beliefs and attitudes by what is ultimately real (a complex of psychophysical elements) leads to less overall suffering than would occur under any alternative theory. But this is not to say that the personhood theory is maximally optimific. There is, in fact, a significant net increase in overall suffering that comes about when we take too seriously the idea that we are persons. Thinking of myself as a person typically leads to the belief that my life has meaning, value, and purpose. But the fact of impermanence, once its implications are fully appreciated, undermines my efforts to sustain the sense that my life has value in the long run. This gives rise to frustration, alienation and despair – in short, to existential suffering. The suffering that is discussed in Buddhism's four noble truths is precisely this existential suffering. And the middle path that is said to lead to its cessation is Reductionism. Reductionism is said to be a middle path because it avoids the two extremes of Non-Reductionism and Eliminativism. Like Non-Reductionism, Buddhist Reductionism counsels that we consider ourselves to be persons. Like Eliminativism, it also counsels that we not consider persons to be ultimately real. The middle path consists in knowing that our taking ourselves to be persons is merely a useful way of achieving the maximization of welfare. Thus I should not 'take it personally' when it turns out that the life of the person who is me cannot have ultimate significance. This is how to render the personhood theory optimific: if we make it transparent to those who adopt it, we can reap the gains of preventing gross imprudence and other non-optimizing behaviour, and at the same time avoid the existential suffering that comes from taking it too seriously.

II

To attain enlightenment, and thus enter into the state of *nirvāṇa*, is to come to know the truth of Reductionism, both in theory (through mastery of the theories and arguments of Buddhist philosophy), and as concretely embodied in one's own case (through meditation). This should tell us something about the character of life in *nirvāṇa*. This is a life that is devoid of existential suffering. But such release from suffering is not achieved by 'living wholly in the moment'. The enlightened person has as much reason as the rest of us to floss their teeth. Failure to floss can lead to gum disease, which is painful and should thus be prevented, since pain is a bad thing. What the enlightened person knows, however, and we do not, is that this reason has nothing whatever to do with the identity of the future person with gum disease. We commonly think our reason to floss has to do with the fact that that future person will be me, that I am preventing my own future pain. The enlightened person knows this is false. Our reason has simply to do with the fact that this present action can prevent that future pain. It so happens that each of us is quite commonly in a position to prevent future pain in one particular causal series. That is why it was useful that we learn to think of that causal series as a person, me. That is why it was useful that we learn to identify with and appropriate future states in that causal series. Because that turns out to be a very efficient way of preventing a great deal of future pain. But this means that my reason to prevent what I think of as my future pain does not derive from the fact that it is mine; it stems from the fact that it is pain, which is bad, and the fact that I am usually better situated than others to prevent it. Adopting the personhood theory is a maximizing strategy.

The life of the enlightened person will be devoid of existential suffering. It will not, however, be devoid of all pain. Even those who brush and floss regularly do sometimes get cavities and gum disease, which can be quite painful. *Nirvāṇa* is not a cure for tooth decay. To say this is not, however, to say that enlightenment has no effect whatever on ordinary pain. There was once an ad campaign that promised that a certain product was a cure for 'the heartbreak of psoriasis'. That promise was probably false. But there is a sense in which enlightenment might be said to be such a cure. This is not to say that attaining enlightenment is likely to diminish the pain and irritation resulting from this skin condition. That outcome seems improbable. But that is not what the ad copy meant by 'the heartbreak of psoriasis'. What was meant by that phrase is the sense of indignity and personal violation that sufferers from this chronic condition often feel. Indeed a great deal of ordinary pain is attended by feelings of anxiety concerning what this state says about me and my future – about who I am and where I am going. It is in this way that ordinary pain can be transformed into something quite like existential suffering. And since the enlightened person knows that there is ultimately no 'me' for whom this condition represents an indignity or a violation, it follows that this common accompaniment of ordinary pain will be absent from the life of the enlightened person. The enlightened psoriasis sufferer will do what they can to ease the pain and prevent future flare-ups. But they will not suffer from the heartbreak of psoriasis.

III

The enlightened person will also strive to help others overcome suffering. This claim is more heavily emphasized in the Mahāyāna tradition, but it is to be found in Abhidharma teachings as well.[6] This obligation to exercise altruism is said to follow from two simple facts: the fact that pain is bad, and the fact that the badness of pain is not affected by where it happens to occur.[7] But the simplicity of these facts is deceptive, for they need to be understood in a Reductionist way. Otherwise the obligation to exercise compassion would not follow. Consider the fact that pain is

6 See, e.g. *Visuddhimagga* IX.40-87 for a Theravādin discussion of the virtue of compassion or loving-kindness.

7 This argument is most clearly formulated at *Bodhicaryāvatāra* 8.101-103, 8.97-8. For a very different reading and assessment of this argument see Paul Williams, *Altruism and Reality*, Surrey: Curzon, 1998. Williams and I discuss our differences in an exchange in *Philosophy East and West*, 50, 2000, pp. 412-59.

bad. We would, of course, all agree. We know that persons only choose pain when they believe it will lead to greater pleasure. But when we agree that pain itself is bad, what we are agreeing to is probably not simply that pain is bad. What we are agreeing to is that pain is bad *for the person whose pain it is*. Consider too the second fact, that the badness of pain does not depend on where it happens. Suppose that you and I were suffering from equally intense lower back pain, which endured the same amount of time and had equally adverse consequences for our lives. Now we might agree that in that case your pain and mine were just as bad, that the mere difference in spatial location did not make for a difference in badness. But by this we would probably mean that your pain is as bad for you as my pain is for me. That is, we would agree that you have just as strong a reason to remove your pain as I have to remove mine. The upshot is that when we put together these two facts, the badness of pain and the irrelevance of spatial location, we do not get the conclusion that we each have an obligation to help others overcome suffering. All we get is that each of us has an equal reason to prevent our own equally bad pains. No one doubts that, but that is not equivalent to a reason for altruism.

What happens, though, when we adopt Reductionism? What the first fact then amounts to is the claim that the occurrence of pain is bad even when it is not thought of as belonging to someone. Buddhist Reductionists put this as, 'There is suffering but none who suffer'.[8] Do we still agree that pain is bad, even though there is no one who feels pain? Is it, in other words, ultimately true that pain is bad? Does it make sense to say that pain is impersonally bad? To say that it does is to say something like the following. Take those psychophysical elements that make up what is called MS, and suppose that among those elements is a feeling of pain, and a consciousness that registers that pain. Now suppose I recognize that there is no 'me' who has that pain, that the sense of there being a subject of this pain just comes from our using the convenient designator 'I' to gather together things like these psychophysical elements. Even so, according to this thesis, as a result of the occurrence of the apprehension of this pain there will be the desire to make it cease, and that desire is not the result of any mistake or ignorance on my part. This pain is impersonally bad – its badness is still there even when we remove all false beliefs about a self.

Now this is the sort of thing that can supposedly be confirmed through the careful introspective observation that skill in meditation is said to facilitate. And what is disclosed in this process is, we are told, that it is of the nature of pain itself to be painful, i.e. to hurt. But perhaps we can each confirm this in our own experience of pain, just by asking ourselves what the experience is like before there is any thought of what this pain means and what needs to be done about it. What we seem to find when we do this is that the experience is such as to bring about a desire to

---

8 Buddhaghośa quotes a verse to this effect in *Visuddhimagga* XVI. Note that to say this is not to say that pains somehow float about in the air. Pain sensations have specific spatio-temporal locations, and their causal histories are typically confined to just one causal series of psychophysical elements. This is the ultimate truth about pains which serves as the basis of the conventional truth that pains are states of persons.

make it cease. In this respect it is quite unlike seeing a warning light flashing on the dashboard of one's car. One need not know what a pain means or what it portends to want to make it cease. It hurts, and that is enough. Pain is impersonally, intrinsically bad.

Consider now the second fact, that location is irrelevant to the badness of pain. Construed as a Reductionist thesis, this becomes the claim that the reason there is to prevent any given pain holds for all agents, and not just for the agent whose pain it is. Now this thesis mentions agents and the reasons that they have. So the thesis cannot be ultimately true. But the Buddhist Reductionist claims it is conventionally true, and that indeed it follows from the fact that the first thesis (that pain is impersonally bad) is ultimately true. For consider the fact that I have a reason to prevent my own future pain. This reason, we have seen, cannot derive from the fact that that pain will occur to me. If Reductionism is true, things are just the other way around: that pain is 'mine' because this 'I' has been socially constructed in such a way as to acknowledge a reason to prevent that pain. And this in turn is so because pain should be prevented, and the constituents of this causal series are well positioned to prevent that pain. My reason to prevent my future pain stems from the impersonal badness of pain, plus an accident of location. This tells us that once there are things on the scene that are of a sort to have reasons, the reasons they have will extend to the prevention of all preventable pain. I have just as much of a reason to prevent another's pain as I have to prevent my own. If the badness of pain means it should be prevented, and pain is impersonally bad, then the reason that each of us has to prevent pain extends to all pain regardless of where it occurs.

Of course most people believe otherwise. They might think it would be very nice if everyone believed they had just as much of a reason to care about the welfare of others as they do to care about their own welfare and that of their nearest and dearest. But they do not think that rationality requires this of us. Indeed they believe that the requirements of rationality and those of morality can often conflict: while morality might demand that I help the stranger in a desperate plight when doing so will cost me little, I am not rationally required to do so unless this somehow enhances my welfare. Now the Buddhist Reductionist will say that this picture of the rational person depends on ignoring a crucial fact, that pain is impersonally bad. Given that fact, rationality demands that we be equally concerned with the welfare of all. But the Buddhist can do something else too: they can explain the source of the intuition that my reason to prevent pain only extends to the pain of me and mine.

Recall that according to Buddhist Reductionism, the person is merely a convenient fiction. Why is it useful that we bundle together all the psychophysical elements making up a causal series? Because I am often in a position where, by doing something now, I can prevent pain in the future of this series. This happens far more often than it happens that something I can do now will prevent pain in another causal series. So getting the present elements in a series to identify with the past and future elements of that series – getting them to think of themselves as a person – is a cognitively cheap way of preventing a great deal of pain that might otherwise occur. It is when we take this convenient fiction too seriously that we end up thinking we each have some special relationship to the future events in that particular series. We forget that the purpose behind the convention was just to prevent as much overall pain as possible. Not your pain, or my pain, but pain – because pain is impersonally bad. We forget that 'person' was just a handy device that, with some care and reflection, we can improve upon.

IV

It will be clear that I see Buddhist ethics as consequentialist in character. This characterization will no doubt be controversial in some quarters, so perhaps I should say something in its defence. It is sometimes claimed that Buddhist ethics should be viewed as a species of virtue ethics, like Aristotelian ethics.[9] It is true that much Buddhist ethical teaching comes in the form of injunctions to cultivate this or that virtue. But the Aristotelian model simply will not work here. The difficulty is that Aristotle's account of the virtues is derived from an account of human flourishing, which is in turn grounded in a thick theory of human nature. (This would appear to hold for the Confucian form of virtue ethics as well.) And Buddhist Reductionism is incompatible with any theory of human nature that is robust enough to serve as the basis of an account of human flourishing. For such a theory must make some substantive claim about a human essence: the virtues are here identified as dispositions toward those activities that promote human flourishing by best realizing the human essence. And Buddhist Reductionists explicitly deny that persons have an essence. To believe in a human essence is, they claim, to believe in a self.

We might do better to think of Buddhist ethics as a form of aretaic consequentialism. In a prescriptive ethics of this variety, one is enjoined to develop a character of a certain sort, but the justification of this injunction rests finally in the claim that these traits are conducive to the cessation of suffering. Such a structure would appear to be required of a Reductionist if they are to succeed in explicating the good in strictly impersonal terms. Here the good consists in the least amount of pain (including existential suffering), impersonally construed; and the virtues are those habits of character that have been found to be conducive to the good. Aretaic consequentialism might, like rule consequentialism, be considered a kind of indirect consequentialism, by contrast with the more direct act consequentialism. Act consequentialism is thus seen as the purer form of consequentialist theory: right action is identified for each specific situation by looking to what the theory tells us is the good. But, the indirect consequentialist claims, agents cannot always be counted on to correctly identify what the theory tells us is the right action on a case-by-case basis. Because of the various cognitive limitations that agents are prone to, the best overall outcome is achieved by introducing shortcuts: rules, according to rule consequentialism; virtues, according to aretaic consequentialism. Such shortcuts may result in an indirect consequentialist theory being strongly self-effacing. Thus a rule utilitarian might hold that the best

---

9 See, e.g. Damien Keown, *The Nature of Buddhist Ethics*, London: Macmillan, 1992, pp. 193-227.

way to maximize utility is for people to believe that the actions prescribed by certain moral rules are intrinsically good (for instance, by holding a deontological moral theory). Likewise an aretaic consequentialist might hold that the best way to bring about the consequences that their theory holds to be intrinsically good is for people to come to think of certain traits of character as having intrinsic value.

On some formulations of indirect consequentialism, moreover, it is recognized that some fine-tuning is possible. Because a list of virtues or rules represents a shortcut, it is to be expected that there will be individual cases where practicing those virtues or acting in accordance with those rules does not realize the good. The theory might then acknowledge this fact by allowing that individuals with the appropriate cognitive skills may sometimes bypass the shortcut: in cases where the virtuous conflicts with the good (as identified by act-consequentialist procedures), they may choose the good.[10] There is, of course, a danger here. One of the chief cognitive limitations that alternative forms of indirect consequentialism are designed to correct for is the tendency of agents to over-estimate their ability to discern the good. Thus if there is to be a bypass to the shortcut, extreme care must be taken to ensure that it is only open to the genuinely qualified.

I submit that this is the overall structure we find in Buddhist ethics. Consider, for instance, the fact that the Buddha is said to have taught the existence of a self on several occasions. (The Buddhist distinction between the two truths grew out of commentators' attempts to reconcile this fact with the teaching of non-self.) We are told that this came about in the following way. Those whom the Buddha was addressing on these occasions were unaware of the facts of karma and rebirth, and for that reason were not properly diligent in conforming their actions to the demands of common-sense morality. Knowing this, the Buddha taught them that one's self is reborn in accordance with the kind of moral character one had in this life: those with a virtuous character earn a pleasant rebirth, those with a vicious character earn a pain-filled rebirth. Of course rebirth does not involve the continued existence of a self, but the Buddha presumably believed that these individuals were not yet able to comprehend the Reductionist account of rebirth. And, we are to understand, the Buddha also perceived that belief in a system of karmic reward and punishment would make them more likely to cultivate the virtues of common-sense morality. Now in this case he is appealing to their hedonistic motivational structure, which is supposedly incompatible with attaining *nirvāṇa*: a life devoted to the pursuit of sensual pleasure tends to reinforce one's tendencies toward attachment and clinging, thus prolonging one's career in *saṃsāra*. But he reasons as follows. Were they to persist in their vice, then given the laws of karma, they would earn painful rebirths, from which entry onto the path to *nirvāṇa* is extremely unlikely. Virtuous conduct here, on the other hand, would earn them a more favourable rebirth, from which

10 All this is nicely expressed by Mill in Chapter 2 of *Utilitarianism*: '[M]ankind must by this time have acquired positive beliefs as to the effects of some actions on their happiness; and the beliefs which have thus come down are the rules of morality for the multitude, and for the philosopher until he has succeeded in finding better.'

entry onto the path is more likely. Moreover, and more importantly, the practice of the conventional moral virtues itself tends to cultivate qualities that are thought to be crucial to attaining the cessation of suffering. To develop the habit of truth-telling, for instance, is to become more attuned to ways in which we often distort the facts out of purely selfish motives. Such heightened sensitivity can make us better at discerning the Reductionist truth about ourselves. And it is this discernment, Buddhists hold, that ultimately effects the cessation of suffering. Here we see the sort of self-effacement of theory that is characteristic of indirect consequentialism. Given the cognitive limitations of this audience, the good is best realized by instilling in them a disposition to practice the virtues of common-sense morality. To the very different audience of committed practitioners who have embarked on the path to *nirvāṇa*, on the other hand, it is explained that such virtues are of merely instrumental value. For the genuinely discerning, there is a bypass provided to this particular shortcut.

We see the same pattern extended a step further in Mahāyāna discussions of the career of the *bodhisattva*. There can be a strongly antinomian cast to this career, as we see for instance in the case of Vimalakīrti, an enlightened person who nonetheless has a wife and children, engages in a profitable business, and consorts with gamblers, drinkers, and prostitutes. While we are assured of the purity of his motives in all this, still these are activities and pursuits forbidden those who aspire to enlightenment. Why is Vimalakīrti held up as a moral exemplar when he engages in activities that would be deemed vicious by the standards provided for those on the path? Presumably because, being an enlightened person, he has attained the sort of understanding that makes shortcut rules of thumb unnecessary.

For another instance of self-effacement, consider the Buddhist solution to the so-called paradox of liberation. Buddhism, in common with other theories of emancipation in the Indian tradition, claims that liberation from *saṃsāra* requires that one cease acting out of selfish desire. It is also held that liberation from *saṃsāra* represents the *summum bonum* for persons. But this appears to mean that any action one takes to attain the cessation of suffering will be motivated by selfish desire, namely desire for the highest good for persons. Hence liberation turns out to be unattainable. The Buddhist resolution of this apparent paradox also follows the general Indian pattern. Certain traits of character are identified as virtues, and their cultivation is enjoined on the grounds that they have intrinsic value. But these traits, it turns out, are such that habituation in them tends to undermine selfish desire. This is obviously true in the case of such virtues as generosity and loving kindness. But it is true as well of the virtue of wisdom, insofar as the content of the wisdom that is here extolled is just the Reductionist insight that ultimately there is no 'me' whose interests might be benefited by actions. Virtue may not be its own reward, but the belief that it is may be instrumental in attaining liberation.

These, then, are the chief reasons I believe we should think of Buddhist ethics as a kind of aretaic consequentialism. That Buddhist ethics must take a consequentialist form follows, I think, from its being grounded in Reductionism. The hypothesis that it is an indirect consequentialism fits with a number of facts about the tradition, such as its tendency toward self-effacement. And given the prominent role that virtues play in Buddhist ethical teachings, aretaic consequentialism seems the best choice among kinds of indirect consequentialism.

Chapter 14

Animal Ethics and Ecology in Classical India – Reflections on a Moral Tradition[1]

M.K. Sridhar and Purushottama Bilimoria

Ahiṃsā paramo dharmaḥ
Nonviolence is the highest form of dharma

Absence of injury of any sort towards all beings at all times is non-injury (*ahiṃsā*)
—*Patañjali*

A problem in species ethics

Here is a problem for practical reason. Two contradictory courses of action may follow from roughly the same attitude or sentiment, namely, the *love of animals*. Thus:

(a) This animal is beautiful, it has tender silky skin, a soulful pair of eyes, and graceful movement, really quite healthy, I love this animal, and so will the gods
→ let us pick then this one for the ordained sacrifice; pleaseth it be to the god who receives its soul!
(b) This animal is beautiful, it has tender silky skin, a soulful pair of eyes, and graceful movement. Really quite more healthy; I love this animal, so do members of my [extended] family
→ let us take care of her and not abandon this cute darling again, etc.

This is the kind of ethical tension, reminiscent of Kant's moral antinomies, that we wish to explore in the attitude and conduct towards animals in India, particularly

1 Dr M.K. Sridhar is grateful to Prof. B.V. Subbarayappa for permission to use material from an earlier essay prepared for vol. IV of B.V. Subbarayappa (ed.), *Medicine and Life Sciences in India, Volume IV part 2 of History of Science, Philosophy and Culture in India Civilization*, General Editor: D.P. Chattopadhaya, Centre for Studies in Civilizations, New Delhi entitled 'Animal Science and Tradition', published by ICPR, New Delhi April 2001; P. Bilimoria refers to in acknowledging his own previous articles, web publications and other citations in the notes and the bibliography. Primary sources are at the end of this chapter.

among textual reasoners in the classical, meaning ancient and medieval, periods, with their reverberations – in the sense of retrieval *or* reversal – in contemporary India. Apart from 'mining the conceptual resources' (*pace* Callicott[2]), we shall draw out some distinctive ecological attitudes and moral ramifications thereof, from a range of texts in the tradition that sanction or have recorded for posterity one or the other of the two propositions suggested above. Diversity of views, interlocking differences and variations to the central doctrines will be dealt with within the encompass of the general thrust of the argument, which is that, the tradition and sages – if not also the ordinary folks and law-makers – gradually came to see the contradictions in their often instrumentalist or otherwise minimalist if not ambivalent dispositions towards the animal species. And they moved to reflect upon, reconsider and/or reform the same, and dismantle the foreclosure in which animals, and much of natural biosphere, constituted a substratum of utility for the flourishing of human beings and gods (the personhood, *pauruṣeya*, agencies on this side of creation). It did not happen in as short a time as it takes to move a court injunction or legislature in modern democratic or highly litigious, or militant, societies. There might have been other motivations too, for instance, the convergence of an assiduous quest for human self-realization or enlightenment and certain self-fulfilling, or redeeming, moral precepts that strengthened the pathway on the one hand, and the burgeoning urban social environment in which the fear of the wildly 'brutish' forces of nature had also diminished. Other traditional societies, such as those of the Australian Aboriginal people and the Native Indians of North America, also lived in close relationship with the natural world in an attitude of mutual respect, reciprocity and caring for the land and all things that make the earth their natural habitat.[3]

The animal ethics of Jainas and Buddhists (taken together for the time being) present an interesting case in this regard. The approach we take here will begin with a historical survey of some seminal texts and move towards a more discursive treatment of the problematic, particularly in the contemporary Indian context (which is properly the subject of the aligned chapter in Volume II). But we are conscious that a resort to classical texts in the interest of working up an argument for animal ethics will have its own constraints, and could even result in a simplistic generalization, no less than in forays made in similar ways by Indologists and ecologists, cosmologists and cosmogonists, working from ancient texts in their quest to retrieve some bygone insights or a non-existent golden age, and so on – a process that has been dubbed by a recent scholar as 'Romanticization'.[4] Such romanticization would be anathema

---

2 J. Baird Callicott, *Earth Insights: A Survey of Ecological Ethics from the Mediterranean Basic to the Australian Outback*, Berkeley: University of California Press, 1994, cited in 'Series Foreward' to *Hinduism and Ecology The Intersection of Earth, Sky, and Water*, Christopher Key Chapple and Mary Evelyn Tucker (eds), Camb, MA: Harvard University Press with Center for the Study of World Religions, 2000, p. xxi and n.10.

3 Callicott, ibid.

4 Laurie Patton, 'Nature Romanticism and Sacrifice in Ṛgvedic Interpretations', *Hinduism and Ecology*, 2000, p. 40 (note 2 above).

to the proper task of the ethical inquiry, anywhere. One has to be mindful of such tendencies and the timely reminder against its (ecological) slippages also.

Nevertheless, there stand basically two grounds for taking environmental ethics in the Indian and cross-cultural traditions seriously, to whit: issues in environmentalism or *ecology* are basically ethical in kind; and *ethics*, as a discipline, offers a helpful framework or theoretical 'paradigm' for reflection on these issues. Of course, the question of whether there is an adequately developed *ethics* as moral philosophy *per se*, in the Indian tradition is a moot question which has been the guiding and 'limit question' of this volume; and it is a claim continued to be viewed with suspicion even by those who venture away from such large projects on 'Indian ethics' to write shorter commentaries on Hindu ethics.

- 'Environment' refers to the *external* conditions or surroundings of organisms, including inanimate systems;
- 'ecology' signifies the *relationships* between organisms and their external conditions, including sentient and non-sentient systems.

Animals and Ecology in the Pre-Vedic age

It is generally believed (barring some dissenting Indicists) that the Indus valley people (as far back as 10,000 BCE) domesticated several herbivorous wild animals. They trained those animals for use in agriculture, travel and hunting. Their settlements were on river banks, amidst dense jungles and forests and hence they maintained a close relationship with the natural environment. They superimposed a supernatural force on every aspect of nature and worshipped the same. The five great elements (*pañcabhūtas*) such as earth, air, water, fire and ether became the objects of worship. The trees and animals were objects of adoration and they treated them as the manifestation of a higher order of being(s). Observable phenomena such as the rising and setting of the sun, moon and the stars, the rains, the wind and its power, symbolized divinities of a sort, but their presence nevertheless was not in the skies, rather, these were part of the natural environment.

Animals and Ecology in the Vedic textual reasoning

The *ṚgVeda* (*RV*) praises the sun, moon, dawn, *Indra* (the might of rain) as the gods of the heavens, wind (*Vāyu*) as the gods of the firmament and earth (*Pṛthvi*) and fire (*Agni*) as the gods of the terrestrial regions. Trees and rivers are also invoked for the well being of the individuals. One hymn praises the rivers thus:[5]

> May the rivers Sarasvatī, Sarayū, and Sindhū come to our sacrifices for protecting us. They who are radiant, motherly and inspirers, give us ghee-like sweet waters.

5 *RV* X.64.9.

In another hymn the sage praises the wind thus:

> The Vāyu who prevents ailments is also the giver of medicines. May he give us longevity.

This 'personification of natural forces' thematic has broader religious implications, which is not our concern here, suffice it to note that the dynamic and vital picture that emerges from such a *dārśanic* outlook augurs for a more naturalistic and less positivistic attitude towards nature than might otherwise be the case. The exaggerations may in the long run serve a heuristic purpose and even create antinomies or counterfactuals within the established injunctions ('If you desire A, do sacrifice B'; but suppose B leads to C which violates A, then A is false and the consequent, B, cannot be true, or is true regardless of A.). Likewise for the emphasis on the 'supra-natural' qualia and earthy symbolism of animals which checks the too-often humanly assumed prelapsarian stewardship over the rest of nature, as in the patriarchal Biblical vision down to Francis Bacon: that God had created nature so that it may serve Man.

Hence it is that the cow occupies a pride of place in several hymns of the *ṚgVeda*. The cow, its variegated species, and their habitat are described in the texts in glamorous details. The sages considered the cow as the personification of motherhood, fertility and liberty. The cow was compared to the goddesses such as *Pṛśni*, *Aditi* and *Uṣas*. Rain was regarded as nothing other than the milk pouring from the udder of a cow. It is not surprising therefore that in the early Vedic period, the cow was killed for sacrifice as the main offering (*havis*), because it was seen to have such a resemblance; and this earthly 'good' might well be sufficient to please the gods who would, for their part of the bargain, return rain and calves a plenty.[6] A peculiar type of cow called *vaśa* was used in sacrificial rites and offered as an oblation to the gods.[7] The cow, like the horse, was also given in sacrifices as 'gift' (*dakṣiṇā*). The cow, owing to her apparent intelligence, patience and acquiescence was adjudged as among the best sacrificial animal (*yajnīya paśu*).

Nevertheless, the Ṛgvedic people regarded animals as an integral part of their agrarian and pastoral culture. Their predominant god, *Indra*, was a culture-hero who was invoked for the protection of cows. During the Ṛgvedic period, various animal cults such as theriolatry and ophiolatry had emerged. The deification of animals, apart from the sacrificial theology, probably also indicated a gesture towards animistic beliefs among the indigenous and non-Aryan groups in the region.

Notice also that the sacrifice, when it was undertaken, always occurred in and through the medium of fire, the intermediary god between the earth and the heavens, not unlike Hermes, the purveyor of messages from earth to heaven, gods to (human)kind. Laurie Patton in an interesting study of Ṛgvedic ritual sacrifice, with and without animals, notes that the sacrificial fire is the 'most essential part of the ritual' that doubles up 'as [an] agent of purification, which protected against evil

6 *RV* I.16.114.10.

7 *RV* X.169.3; II.7.5; X.91.14.

spirits'. The fulgurating flame is also an earthly representation of the sun's energy around which the main players in the sacrificial process circumambulate, as might also the animal to be offered, or around it as it stands by the pit doused with ghee and sandalwood. But Patton follows up this description with a poignant observation, to whit:

> In sum, as many Vedic hymns and later ritual texts … indicate, sacrifice of an animal into the fire was part of the ecological balance in the ancient Vedic world; the killing and distribution of the animal was part of a larger understanding of human harmony with natural forces.[8]

She points to the interdependence of cosmological functions (broadly encompassing ecological functions as well) and sacrificial functions:

> The gods are given food and return it through their natural bounty; thus, the ecology of sacrificial food production and consumption is the central, guiding metaphor for the survival of earthly and celestial worlds.[9]

The wider implication of these insights are captured in this surmise:

> To be sure, it is an ecological commonplace to claim that, as inherent processes in nature, decay and violence are necessary for nourishment, and that creativity requires a movement between life and death. However, in our ecological readings of the ancient world we rarely incorporate these insights and cautions from ancient sacrificial processes into our ecological sensibilities of the twentieth and twenty-first centuries.[10]

The lessons to be derived here are that, historically, the killing of animals and their distribution otherwise was part of a larger hermeneutic of the harmony of the human life-world with the natural forces; and, for the nonce, what it might mean to re-disperse the natural world in the process of rejuvenation, and what it might mean to hasten the processes of life and death; and how the troupes of harmony with nature *and* sacrifice could well converge[11] in short, a kind of redistributive justice in the context of the natural environment.

* * *

Antinomianism of fuzzy ṛṣis

However, the antinomian tension alluded to at the beginning of the essay, caught up, it would seem, with the Vedic *ṛṣis* (seers), in respect of this somewhat 'fishy' or fuzzy moral reasoning. And so although the sacrificial spirit so described continued

8 Patton, *op cit*., p. 43.
9 Ibid.
10 Ibid.
11 Ibid.

to inform later Vedic texts, the proclivity towards focusing on the subaltern species as the sacrificial *havis* changed over the course of time as other implements and matter became available with the growth of agrarian productivity, which were in turn utilized to achieve the same ends. Thus the seers are heard speaking of the cow as a frail animal, to be properly guarded and used with care. The priests decreed against ruthless killing of the cow even in the sacrificial process. Instead, the cow is requested to smell the vessel (*droṇakalaśa*) containing *soma* juice – symbolically representing a purification rite. A goat is requested to safeguard the sacrificial materials and precincts of the altar in general. The tortoise is also praised in several hymns. According to a seer of the *Yajur Veda* (*YV*) the animal surveys the bricks employed in the *agnicayana* (fire) sacrifice, wherein fire is both the medium and symbolically 'martyr' of the sacrifice. The animal is walked in to 'guard' the bricks piled up on the sacrificial altar from possible infiltration of vagrant micro-amoebic and departed (*bhūtaka*) creatures, and so on. The four-legged animal certainly stands promoted in the hierarchy of the species sphere.

Animals in *Yajur Veda* were also considered to be the representatives of the hosts (requesting the rite) to approach, at the commencement, the celestial gods and to, as it were, speak on behalf of the terrestrial sacrifice. Hence there are in *Yajur Veda*, a number of sacrificial formulae which are offered as prayers to the chosen animals such as cow, horse, ewe, goat, tortoise, female frog, and others.[12] The horse is requested to smell the share of *Bṛhaspati*, which may be symbolic of cleansing the region and portions of food.

A single hymn is devoted for the female frog (*mandūki*) in the context of *agnicayana* (fire) sacrifice. In one of the rituals, the frog is tied to a bamboo stick and it is waved over the altar to dispense any evil omens. The female frog is chosen because the bamboo stick is feminine in gender. This symbolically represents the purifying quality of the frog in waters. Insects hovering around the sacrificial place were symbolically removed by waving the sacred *darbha* grass. A priest of *Yajur Veda* requests the sacrificer and his assistants to bring several species of animals into the sacrificial hall. The animals are tied to the sacrificial posts, while several specific hymns are chanted for each animal and then they are set free.

---

12 *YV* IX.8-9; XI.15A. Chattopadhyaya informs us that there was a wide prevalence of the killing of the horned cattle-like cows, bulls, buffaloes etc., at sacrifices. The horses besides being used for chariot races and warfare, were sacrificed at the time of the *aśvamedha* sacrifices. The Brahmins did partake of, indeed, were encouraged to, the meat (beef) as remnant of the food offered up to the gods. This practice may have continued for some centuries and was likely common among other castes and sub-caste groups, without access to the sacrificial 'purifying' rites. But it does not lessen the fact that the habit was possibly something carried over from the arid nomadic life-style of as yet non-pastoralized and urbanized Aryan people, given that similar practices continued in regions far to the east where religious-sacrificial tendencies, linguistically linked to the Ṛgvedic, were also in prevalence. These are however matters also of considerable speculation.

The *Atharva Veda* (*AV*) gives a detailed list of the available fauna and flora. It praises the earth in one of the hymns termed as *pṛthvi-sūkta* thus:[13]

> People are born from you and function with you. You support people and the animals. The trees and plants firmly stand on you. The sea, the rivers and other water reservoirs are found on you. The forest animals roam on you. The birds of various kinds fly over you. The hills and mountains with verdant forests stand on you. The rice and barley grow on you. The rich deposits of gold and other animals are found on you. The autumn, winter and rainy seasons enrich on you. The cool breeze moves on you, thus spreading the fragrant pollen grains and gently moving the trees. O Pṛthvi!! You are my mother and I am your son.

The *Atharva Veda* also praises water which the sage says has the capacity to nourish the animate and inanimate beings, cleansing of the body and for curing a plethora of diseases.[14] Fire, personified as a representative of all deities in rituals, is invoked in several hymns.[15] The wind, as an important component of nature and as a life-supporting system, is praised in several hymns.[16] These descriptions of the five basic elements reveal the emotional attachment of the Atharvans to the nature and their reverential attitude towards the building-blocks, as it were, of the natural world and for the immeasurable help received from their proper workings by people.

The *Atharva Veda* offers a series of charms to overcome an attack of worms, snakes and evil birds. The sages recognized several types of deadly worms such as *kururu*, *algandu*, *calūna*, *avaskara*, *vyadhvara* and others. Several hymns extolling a cow, an ox, and a horse are described in the text. The cows were treated as the benefactors of human beings, as they yielded milk, milk produce and good calves.[17] The bull was praised as the husband of cows and the father of the calves. The sages exhorted the people to give away bulls as 'gifts' as they would then obtain cows, progeny and strength. Needless to say, since the practice of animal sacrifice had not been completely done away with, the priest of the *Atharva Veda* would offer a white sheep, goat and cow at some select sacrifices.[18]

The Atharvans were conscious of the cleanliness of the food to be eaten. They would request *Agni*, the lord of fire, to destroy those insects and bacteria which enter into the sacrificial hall, and inhere in the food that is not cooked, half cooked, over cooked, or present in milk, cream and food grains. The rising sun, and the sages *Atharvana*, *Kaśyapa* and *Kaṇva* were requested to destroy the insects and bacteria present in waters. Mention is also made of the *ajaśringī* and *brāhmī* plants which have the capacity to destroy those harmful bacteria.[19] Afraid of both venomous

13 *AV* XII.1.
14 *AV* III.17.1-9; III.15.1-5.
15 Ibid., II.13.1-3; V.27.1.
16 Ibid., IV.27.2-4.
17 Ibid., IV.21.1-7; VII.73.7-11A.
18 Ibid., IX.9.I.20, II.29.1-8, IV.14.1-9; X.9.1-27.
19 Ibid., II.3.2-5; V.29.1-2, 6-7; II.32.2; IV.1-11.

and non-venomous snakes, they offered prayers to them. They were aware of the uncontrolled menace of the rodents and hence requested the *Aśvin* gods to ward them off, and even pleaded to the pests and harmful worms to quietly leave their agricultural fields.[20] They were aware of the medicinal effects of the conch shell and the capacity of its resounding sound when blown for driving away the worms or bacteria.

The Atharvan sages had a more specific knowledge about the nature and behaviour of animals compared to Ṛgvedin seers, it seems. They were more realistic and down-to-earth, and therefore less 'sacralizing' in the sense of patronizing from the gods-eyes' view of the subaltern species, at least in comparison to the people of the Ṛgvedic era.

We will now move on to the latter period, that of the *Purāṇas*, which is more properly the medieval period in the Indian context.

Ecology in the *Purāṇas*

Purāṇa literally means lore or legends and mythologized stories of the past, of former times (even 'ancient' times). There is here invariably a supplement weaved into the narrative of collective hopes, desires, and fantasies, thus stretching history towards the shared moral and spiritual – and its counter-positive in the secular – agonies, fractured and synthetic relations, and teleology in the broader economy of culture. This genre of literary productions then generally deals with the lives, dilemmas, trepidations, inter-relations, moral (in)exactitudes and exploits of the emperors, kings, heroes, deities and folks alike, of a particular period in the subcontinent, that perhaps parallels, temporally, the 'dark-ages' of Europe. In India this period witnessed an explosion of a highly literate and manifestly religious and even politically concerned culture. There are around eighteen recognized *Purāṇas*, whose authorship is attributed to sage *Vedavyāsa*, though there is no historical evidence of this. These texts occupy a distinct position in the sacred and secular literatures of India.

Although the texts treat of the larger issues as indicated above, there are within its ecological tracts frequent references to animals and the environment associated with them. Cosmologically, the *Purāṇas* advocated the unity of all sentient (*cetanā*) and non-sentient (*acetanā*) beings. The *Viṣṇu Purāṇa* informs us that gods, men, animals, reptiles and birds are but the various forms of the creator Brahmā since these have emerged from his limbs.[21] The treatise also gives details regarding the origin of animals, their primordial place and leadership in the creation process. There are also efforts to enumerate the kinds and numbers of animal species that abound. For instance, the *Nārada Purāṇa* mentions 68 species of animals, the *Vāmana Purāṇa* of 137 animals, and *Garuda Purāṇa* speaks of 300 animals. Of course, by modern day archeological, zoological and veterinarian wisdom these figures are palpably far

---

20 *AV* VI.50.1-2.

21 *Viṣṇu Purāṇa*, 15.46.

off the mark; but recall that the purāṇic inquiry was not 'scientific' in our modern sense of the term and that the discourse on animals was part of their more immediate agrarian and pastoral culture. The sages of the *purāṇic* ages envisioned that human beings ought to co-habit in harmony with nature without being destructive of any part thereof. Hence Krishna calls the fellow cowherds to offer devotion to hills, forests and cows over and above performing Vedic rites to Indra, who (like our present-day weatherman) fails to send them rain anyway.[22] *Bhāgavata* and *Varāha Purāṇas* lavish praise upon the trees, which they say have the capacity to relieve the fatigue of the travellers, and also provide resting places to the flocks of migratory birds, and medicines for the sick.[23]

Although the period over which the *Purāṇa*s seem to have been composed extends across several centuries, there is nonetheless continuity of certain thoughts and ideals in all these texts. On the moral-ecological side, they request the people to lead a life of righteousness and not to bring about any kind of environmental pollution. The *Bhāgavata Purāṇa* hails the rivers as the 'veins' of the Cosmic Person and the trees as the 'hairs' of his body, the ocean his 'waist', the air as his 'breath', hills, dales and mountains as his skeletal 'bones'.[24] The Cosmic Person (*Puruṣa*) of Ṛgvedic fame is thoroughly naturalized and denuded of the ritual-social utility for which this particular image seems to have been sculptured. The Purāṇic people were exhorted to consider trees and animals as their adopted sons and daughters, and further instructed people to nourish them. An injunction is issued in a verse typifying the *Purāṇic* wisdom: 'One should treat animals such as deer, camel, ass, monkey, snake, bird, flies and the like as their own children.' Hence the *Agni* and *Matsya Purāṇas* implore people to look after plants and animals by giving them good nourishment.[25] The *Brahmavaivarta Purāṇa* and *Bhaviṣya Purāṇa* urge that a progeny may bring joy or happiness to the parents but a tree always gives joy to the people and hence there is greater merit in protecting the trees: 'One tree is equal to ten sons' is the sort of trope that has echoed down the tradition from around this period.[26]

It is interesting that such a future-regarding comparison is made long back in the *Purāṇas* that by its very name is about the times (and yet to be): namely, *bhaviṣya* (the 'future' conjuncted with *purāṇa*, 'the past', would be an apt signifier for a Benjaminian space walking backward into the future). And so the argument by the best inference goes a fair way towards supporting an ecological perspectivism that is not confined contingently to the interests and needs of the current generation, much less of the terrestrially past or the celestially departed, but factors in the predictable

22 *Skānda Purāṇa*, I.20.

23 *Bhāgavata Purāṇa*, X.22.32-35/*Varāha Purāṇa* XVI.41-42.

24 *Bhāgavata Purāṇa*, X.3321; X.32.

25 *Matsya Purāṇa*, Ch 35.

26 *Bhaviṣya* , *Madhyamaparva*, see *Hinduism and Ecology* p. 109, See Vasudha Narayam, 'One tree Is Equal to Ten Sons: Hindu Responses to the Problems of Ecology, Population, and Consumption'. *Journal of the American Academy of Religion* **65** (2) 2, January 1997, pp. 291-332.

depletion of resources exacerbated by the excesses (e.g. exponential) growth of the population burdensomely on Mother Earth, which more than likely will prove detrimental, if not catastrophic, to the needs and interests of the future generations (*bhaviṣyaloka*), to which they have equal entitlement. This is not only a mark of good ecology but decent philosophy also.

Rituals associated with animals

However, it was not good news all the way down the hierarchy especially for the subaltern species. Several animals were involved in rituals and sacrifices. Cow, bull, goat and other domesticated animals figure in the rituals connected with the departed manes (*pitrudevatā*).

The *Matsya Purāṇa* enjoins that a bull should be released at Gaya and a tawny cow should be gifted away in order to satisfy the departed ancestors. It mentions that the gifting of a black bull is equal to the performance of an *aśvamedha* (royal horse) sacrifice. The flesh of the rhinoceros was offered to the manes and they could survive for twelve years on its flesh and the bones of a rhinoceros had the power to ward off evil.[27] The she-goat was also considered as an important animal. *Kūrma Purāṇa* explains that prior to the sacrifice, the place should be strewn with sesame seeds and goats should tread all over the place so that the pollution and haunting of evil spirits could be warded off from the site.

The *Agni Purāṇa* explains that some elephants are conducive to prosperity if sprinkled with holy and purificatory waters. The elephants should be stationed in an array in the shape of a crocodile or shark on the outskirts of the city. Various gods and goddesses such as *Viṣṇu*, *Lakṣmī*, *Skānda*, *Ananta*, *Śiva*, *Indra*, *Aśvin*, *Rudra* and others have to be worshipped along with their respective weapons. Then the astrologer should mount upon the selected tusker and whisper in the ear thus. 'You have been chosen as an elephant of victory (*śrīgaja*) by the king. You are the chief among the herd of elephants. You have to safeguard the king in the war, on the march, and also in the home country.' Later the king mounts that sanctified tusker in an auspicious moment and proceeds for the conquest.

Various vows (*vrata*) connected with the beasts are mentioned in the *Purāṇas*. For instance, a person performing the vow of Heroism (*vīravrata*) should give the gift of an animal made in gold for securing higher benefits. He attains the domain of *Śiva* having gifted a gold lion. If one gifts the golden deer, then, he would attain the virtue akin to that of a horse sacrifice.[28]

A king, on the other hand, for the protection and other distributive boons or omens on behalf of the citizens, was enjoined to kill wild beasts. The animal was slaughtered when a man of reverence arrived at a festival,[29] but those hunters should not kill a beast that was sleeping, having sexual intercourse, feeding a calf, or one

27 *Skānda Purāṇa, Prabhāsā Khānda.* Ch 205.

28 *Matsya Purāṇa* 100.28; ibid., 35.

29 *Brahmānda Purāṇa* (*Br. Pu*) II.4.650-57.

which was drinking water.[30] The same *Purāṇa* also enlists eight types of animal killers such as one who enjoys killing, one who allows it, accomplishes it, one who sells the beast , one who purchases it, the actual killer, one who carries it, and one who causes it to be killed; and based on the gravity of such animal killings, they should be punished.

Expiation ceremonies

As the animals were elevated to the state of demi-gods, and some continued to be associated with evil spirits, there was a taboo on both counts against keeping or rearing animals as pets. *Manu Smṛti* says that if a celibate committed sexual indiscretion, he was called by the name *avakīrna* and as a remorse he had to cover his body with the hide of an ass.[31] *Brahma Purāṇa* says that *Indra* took the form of a cat and fled after seducing *Ahalyā*.[32] Thus keeping a cat in the house invited censure and such a person was treated as a person of abject birth according to *Liṅga Purāṇa. Viṣṇu Purāṇa* informs us that a person keeping a cat, rooster, dog, pig, or bird will, upon death, descend into hell or the nether regions.[33] According to S.A. Dange, this taboo was indicative specifically of the *vaiṣṇava* attitude towards the keeping of animals as pets, while other folks, and in particular people tilling the land with the help of animals, were not affected by the theological sanctions.[34]

A number of *Purāṇas* suggests several types of expiation rites in connection with riding on carts driven by forbidden animals. For example, if a person mounts a cart drawn by camels or donkeys, he will accrue demerit. He may regain his purity only at the end of three nights after performing prescribed purificatory rituals. In fact, he should enter the lake in the nude and stay half-immersed in the water for three nights. If a person touches a dog accidentally or if some dog bites him, then he should drink milk for three days to counter the demerit and the sting.[35] It is said that a Brahmin who sells his daughter, land, cow, or son is cast into hell forever.[36] A Brahmin who sells a horse was akin to a murderer.[37] Certain castes were then not to part with their animals, and certain castes were not permitted to be in too close an association with animals. There are obviously sociological complexities in the structure, functioning, and distribution of labour encumbent upon such a society that relied so heavily on the 'technology' or agricultural prowess of animals that belie any straightforward moral judgments we might feel justified in making from

30 *Skānda Purāṇa* (*Sk Pu*) VI.10-12.
31 *Manu Smṛti*, XI.118.122.
32 *Br. Pu.*, 87.52.
33 *Vi. Pu.*, II.6.19.
34 Dange, op cit.
35 *Kūrma Purāṇa*, II.33.58; II.33.42.
36 *Brahma Purāṇa*, 150.9; 165.11-12.
37 *Brahma Vaivarta Purāṇa*, I.58.98.

this distance in the post-industrial era, where indeed the technology of International Harvester and the abattoir remain dominant.

Purāṇic reasoning on animal health-care

Early Indians took great care in keeping the animal environment clean. *Garuda Purāṇa* prescribes the following medicinal herbs for keeping the elephants healthy: myrobalans (Terminalia chebula), *hārītaki* (Chewbulix myrobalan) and *brahati*. These should be dried, powdered and mixed together with black rock salt, and fed to the elephants. Pastes of several medicinal herbs are recommended for curing several ailments of elephants.

Further, the *Purāṇa* says that leaves of turpentine, margosa, guggula, mustard, ghee, sesame, should be tied to the neck of a horse to ward off worms hovering around and infesting the animal's body.[38]

Agni Purāṇa informs us that if a horse is suffering from abdominal pains, it should be administered with an insertion of Basri oil through a tube or an incision should be made in the veins of the abdomen to allow controlled bleeding. Further, a paste prepared from garlic, rock salt, buttermilk and gruel oil should be applied. Curds, Margosa leaves should be used for curing the wounds of horses. Generally, a purificatory ritual (*aśva śānti*) was done for the welfare of the horses.

This was done on the bright half of the month of *āśvayuja* (September-October). The gods to be worshipped were the *Aśvins* and *Varuṇa*, to whom barley and ghee were offered. Several animals such as roosters, monkey, cow with her calf, and goats were kept in stables for the welfare of the horses.[39]

When any tank was dug for the sake of a ritual, a fish, a crocodile, a non- poisonous snake called *dundubha* made out of gold, a frog and fish made out of copper, and a porpoise made out of iron should be placed on a plate and thrown into the water. As all these were aquatic animals, the early Indians thought that one would harm them or their environment while digging a tank and hence, as an act of expiation, this was performed by the people concerned. This cautious attitude of the *purāṇic* people reflects their views on eco-balance or biodiversity.

The authors of the *Purāṇas* decried and prohibited the killing of animals either for game or for food as this would upset the eco-balance of nature. This taboo clearly presupposes that there was killing of animals in ancient India. Several edicts proscribe a brahmin killing a frog, ichneumon, monkey, some birds, crane, peacock, hawk, crow and others. He should perform various expiation rites and donate gifts to ward off the sins resulting from such animal killings. He could also cleanse himself by worshipping a cow.[40] *Garuda Purāṇa* prescribes the release of five black bulls and white calf for two years for killing an elephant.[41] *Kūrma Purāṇa* states that the

---

38 *Garuda Purāṇa* (*Ga. Pu*), 201.35-39.

39 *Matsya Purāṇa*, 216.21-22.

40 *Kūrma Purāṇa*, III.32.50-54.

41 *Ga. Pu.*, I.105.34.

theft of an elephant, a horse, a cow and a bull should be viewed as a great sin and such thieves would be driven to a perpetual hell.[42] The *Garuda Purāṇa* records that even the worst sinner can be released from those demerit points if he sights a bear or worships a cow.[43]

The *Arthaśāstra* treatises on polity

Kauṭilya (Kauṭalya, or Cāṇakya) is believed to have lived and written the *Arthaśāstra* around 321-296 BC, or perhaps even later. The *Arthaśāstra* is a comprehensive treatise on statecraft that gives cohesion to the political thinking of Kauṭilya's predecessors. Mostly instructional, and bereft of solid arguments or theoretical depth of the kind one finds in, say, Adam Smith, nevertheless certain of his important teachings were appropriated by the *Dharmaśāstras*. On closer reading, Kauṭilya is concerned to guarantee the welfare and well-being of citizens, which is not exclusive, in his discourse on polity, of animals and the terrestrial environment.[44] Kauṭilya described laws restricting urban location of major caste-groups, the duties of kings, ministers, caste-groups and mixed communities alike. Conscious of the diversity from ancient days of the Indian regions, Kauṭilya allows for a degree of flexibility in matters of law and justice. So he could find himself changing rules and governance from previously accepted patterns in ways that could affect the forest and animal kingdom as well. Even the king could no longer consider himself to be above *dharma*, the impersonal rule and codes of transcendental ethics symbolized in the rod.

Although not so relevant perhaps in the context of the present discussion, it may be noted in passing that Kauṭilya is credited with having been among the first to set down codes of law, as distinct from listing desirable prescriptions and customary rules, regardless of their moral or philosophical merits. These all appear to be practical human concerns in the interests, predominantly if not solely, of political economy, and it would be difficult to infer a systematic environmental ethics from this discourse on polity, which at times appears to border on the excesses of a Machiavellian statecraft. But even amidst his grander concern of enframing the legal and administrative structure of the royal administration (*rājadharma*) checked by a secular legislature (council of ministers informed about custom and normative practices), and strategic diplomacy among neighbouring territories, Kauṭilya found a space for his concern over animals. These concerns, however, were primarily subsumed under the management and protective tasks assigned to three departments that specialized in the instrumentalities of the natural resources and

42 *Kūrma Purāṇa*, III.108.22-23.

43 *Ga. Pu.*, I.214.50.

44 See P. Bilimoria, 'Kauṭilya', in *Routledge Encyclopedia of Philosophy*, London/NY: Routledge, 1999-2000, pp. 220-222; see also Introduction to Part A (*supra*) under *Adhikāra*.

urban development: namely, agriculture (*sītādhyakṣa*), forest produce (*kuyādhyakṣa*) and mineral mines (*ākarādhyakṣa*).[45]

There are definite injunctions against deforestation, over-tilling and recurrent use of arable fields, and other human interventions that lead to the depletion of natural resources. Maintaining forests (for agri-benefit, but also as demarcation lines between urban and rural, farming and rustic, forest-protectors and border rangers), as well as the diversity and proper management of space, elemental material and natural resources are instructive stories that contemporary scholars have come away with in their quests to link modern ecological concerns with ancient wisdom.[46] The *Arthaśāstra* shows a remarkable understanding of the intricate implications of space in geographical and secular urban-reconfiguration terms, and there is deep knowledge of the diversity and variety of fauna, plant varieties, animal life, and naturally occurring minerals etc., as well as the appropriate 'sciences' (metallurgy, animal husbandry, game-keeping, irrigation, public works, etc.). In all, the first principle seemed to be a more tolerant attitude towards the 'dark' regions and threatening inhabitants of the forest, before any official moves are made to reach out for the beneficial resources. In other words, Kauṭilya underscored respect for nature.

Since animals were part of the equation of 'respect for nature = human benefit by its guarded exploitation', certain rules were deemed necessary for animal welfare as well. For instance, Kauṭilya emphasized that a cowherd should always take care of the old and diseased cows. In the same way, a horse incapacitated for work, war, travel, or suffering from disease or old age should receive food for maintenance.[47]

Consistent with his policies on statecraft (*rājanīti*) and the 'rule of the rod' (*daṇḍanīti*), Kauṭilya prescribed various types of punishments for violators of animal welfare or their proper care. For instance, a person killing a cow or a calf or one who incites another to kill or steal a cow is meted out the severest of punishment. One who changes the cow for the royal cattle should pay a very huge fine. Even a person, milking for the second time during the day out of greed, should be warned and if he persists punished. Other kinds of cruelty against animals, bestiality, and people engaging in violent animal games, using live animals for improper exhibitionism

45 Helpful discussion in Mary McGee, 'State Responsibility for Environmental Management: Perspectives from Hindu Texts on Polity', *Hinduism and Ecology* (q.v.) pp. 59-101, p. 64ff. McGee cites Indian scholars who suggest that external trade and warfare during Mauryan rule augmented land management and expansion of technology, but that the landscape was only being just freed from the primeval forest-pastoral enclaves since the diffused Aryan occupation into private landholdings and production of commodities. But this also brought about a conscious and deliberative policy of managing dependency on the earth and her natural resources. Ibid., pp. 64-65.

46 Again, Mary McGee acknowledges the biologist David Lee's concerns about the vanishing bio-diversity and this sent her back to the ancient texts such *Arthaśāstras* and *Dharmaśāstras*, ibid., pp. 76-77.

47 Kauṭilīya *Arthaśāstra* (=*Ka. Ar.*), II.30-48.

and art were not spared either. A person causing a bull of one herd to be hurled by another bull, was to pay a heavy fine.[48]

A horse keeper who fails to look after the horse, or transgresses the proper laws, should be punished by halving his daily or monthly wages. One should not ride those horses kept either for some religious rites or by the physician. The violator of this rule was fined with twelve *paṇas*. Veterinary doctors who showed dereliction or negligence in their duty, such as failure to treat a diseased animal, or contributed to the plight of the suffering and sick animal by administering wrong medicine, were penalized with double the cost of the treatment. In the case that the diseased animal or the animal in the care of an animal keeper dies accidentally, they had to pay the actual price of the animal.[49] An elephant rider who drives his elephant to the land of others for grazing, or leads it to a thicket of trees without the permission of the forest superintendent, was fined very heavily.

Kauṭilya emphasized great care for animals, their habitat and for conservation of the environment. For instance, if a person killed a herd of cattle even by accident, or set fire to green pastures, a field, a thrashing floor, a house or a stable of forest produce meant for animals, he was to be executed.[50]

R.P. Kangle is of the opinion that the corporal punishments mentioned here represent a rather primitive stage in thinking on penal laws, and that they came to be gradually replaced by corresponding monetary fines in the *Arthaśāstra* and *Dharmaśāstras*.[51]

Animals and the concept of non-violence (*ahiṃsā*)

The common ethos emerging through the reflections of *Purāṇas*, *Arthaśāstras*, and the epics appears to be this: It is part of the *dharma* of the *rājanīti* that the king and his ministries maximize protection and maintenance of people and the resources of the kingdom, or all that belongs to the earth (*bhauma*). The prosperity of the land translates into the benefit of the people. 'In other words, the common good of the kingdom – its social, economic, political, and ecological welfare – was rooted in the *dharma* of the king.'[52]

The treatises on ethics and religion (*Dharmasūtras* and *Smṛtis*), the two epics (*Rāmāyaṇa* and *Mahābhārata*), and ancient lores (*Purāṇa*) emphasized the fourfold values of life which could be practiced in two ways, i.e. an active life in this world

48 *Ka. Ar.* II.29.1-48.

49 Ibid., II.30.45-48.

50 Ibid., IV.11.8.

51 *The Kauṭilīya Arthaśāstra*, ed. and trans. R.P. Kangle, Delhi: Motilal Banarsidass, 3 vols, 1986, 1988, 1992, Part III.

52 McGee, op cit, p. 62.

(*pravṛtti*) and renunciation of the world (*nivṛtti*).[53] The virtues of the second tradition perhaps led to the development of non-injury (*ahiṃsā*) in Hinduism.

Saral Jhingran contends that the early Indian way of life was not particularly given to the ideal of non-violence, whereas it was one of the main doctrines of Buddhism and Jainism. The ancient thinkers made great efforts in reconciling the two traditions by arguing that all types of violence, beginning with the minutest injury, were acts of demerit, except when performed for the purpose of specific Vedic rituals.[54]

A more compassionate leaning paved the way for a more successful development of non-violent sacrifices in which pulses, cereals, ghee were substituted for animals in the sacrificial fire.[55] The *Mahābhārata* declared non-injury as the highest duty to be performed by an individual.[56] But this has to be balanced with its predilection towards war, which has been a source of moral dilemma and emotional conflict for the players in the epic.[57] Saral Jhingran further opines that it was only with the development of the theistic devotional tradition (*bhakti*) that the ideal of non-violence was fully reinforced into the Hindu system.[58] But there has too often been a hasty obfuscation between non-injury and non-violence: they are categorically distinct, though not separable; yet the former does not entail the latter. (The conditional counterfactual being: If I follow the precept of non-injury, then I practice non-violence; but the latter is false for in a combat battle I could kill another, the animals that come in the way notwithstanding.) The Hindu concept of *dharma*, as enunciated in the text of *Dharmaśāstras*, encompassed non-injury as among the highest duty and virtue which should be practiced by all human beings. It is interesting to note that while the authors of the *Dharmaśāstras* condemned violence, they did not rule out its use in social and political situations.[59] In fact, some might want to argue that violence was a structural ingredient of governance and political economy of the state, which was in turn in the hands of the upper castes. To an extent violence was accepted as a part of life unless it threatened the stability and fabric of social order. As explained in the earlier paragraphs, Kauṭilya was to an extent liberal in the treatment of the subject of punishments for various forms of crimes and sins. He prescribed severe punishments, including capital punishment for the offenders from lower castes, but refrained from underwriting comparable retributive measures or deterrence against the privileged and self-exclusive Brahmin caste.

---

53 For discussion see works of Greg Bailey and T.S. Rukmani, 'Literary Fundations for an Ecological Aesthetic: *Dharma*, Ayurveda, the Arts, and *Abhijñānaśākuntalam*,' in *Hinduism and Ecology*, q.v. pp. 101-126.

54 *Manusmṛti*, V.22 ff 31, 39, 44; Saral Jhingran, *Aspects of Hindu Morality*, Delhi: Motilal Banarsidass, 1999, pp. 18-19.

55 *MBh* Śāntiparvan. *P.* CCLV.24 ff; CCLVII.4 ff; CCLXI.19; CCLXIV.17.

56 Ibid., Śāntiparvan. CCXXXVII.17 ff.; CCLXIV.19 ff. *Anu Parvan* CXVI.72; CXVII.37-39.

57 See Matilal's chapter in this volume.

58 Saral Jhingran, op cit, pp. 18-19.

59 *Manusmṛti*, VIII.345-346.

A better way to approach the quandary that arises out of this telling recognition is to begin with the suggestion that one of the cardinal duties and values to be developed in the *dharma* tradition (in the shadow of the proto-yogic descendants, and Jainism and Buddhism) was that of *general non-injury*. The most refined expression of this value is represented in the great epic of the *Mahābhārata* (circa 100 BCE to 200CE). Much moral development proceeds through organizing and placing constraints on the otherwise presupposed liberties of human life. Of chief concern is the impact that one's action, pursuits and conduct might have on the other. In this regard, non-injury is prescribed unequivocally.[60]

The *Bhagavadgītā* – which in the context of the epic *Mahābhārata*, has been much discussed already in this volume – provides quasi-philosophical grounding for the values extolled in the *Mahābhārata* and is more decisive in its ethical pronouncements. It is for this reason that the *Gītā* (for short) has had a profound impact on modern Hindu-Indian thought and is drawn upon obliquely in Western ethical and ecological deliberations as well.[61] Two most commented upon verses in this context are the following:

> The one whose self is disciplined by yoga.
> Sees the self abiding in every being
> And sees every being in the self;
> He sees the same in all beings.

---

60 See Philip Lutgendorf, 'City, Forest, and Cosmos: Ecological Perspective from the Sanskrit Epics', in *Hinduism and Ecology*, pp. 269-289; Vasudha Narayan, 'Water, Wood, and Wisdom: Ecological Perspectives from the Hindu Traditions', *Daedalus*, **120** (4), Fall 2001; P. Bilimoria, 'Indian Religious Traditions', in *Spirit of the Environment*, edited by Joy Palmer and David E. Cooper, London and NY: Routledge, 1998, pp. 2-14..

61 Gandhi, 1962; Naess, 1989, p. 194; Jacobsen, 1996, pp. 231-233; although, Lance Nelson acknowledges that powerful ecological 'resources' can be culled from various passages in the *Gītā*, bordering even on the universalist Buddhist empathetic outlook on all creatures and spheres of the cosmos, in addition to its platitude towards the virtue of non-injury and the worrying asceticism of detachment. However, Nelson argues that 'this will not take us very far unless we first undertake certain more demanding tasks'. His worries are the underlying worldview, the hierarchical dualism of *ātman/dharma* (divine) and *prakṛti/māyai* (nature), the attitude towards the beguiling attraction of natural things in the world, and the self-serving valuation of *ahiṃsā* , where compassion for other is secondary. It makes for a 'static social vision'. See Lance E. Nelson, 'Reading the *Bhagavdgītā* from an Ecological Perspective', in *Hinduism and Ecology*, pp. 127-153. Gerald Larson has voiced similar reservations about relying on Indian philosophical texts for ecological perspectives and programmatic, which can only be systemic. Gerald J. Larson, 'Conceptual Resources in South Asia for "Environmental Ethics"', in *Nature in Asian Traditions of Thought: Essays in Environmental Philosophy*, J. Baird Callicott and Roger T. Ames (eds), Albany, NY: State University of New York Press, 1989, pp. 267-277. But contemporary philosophizing is also a creative process, and it is a pity that philosophers on India are not as daring in their art as, say, Martha Nussbaum who derives heavily from ancient (Stoic and Hellenistic) sources but is also critical and creative in what she builds upon the erstwhile insights.

When one sees pleasures and pain of others
To be equal to one's own, O *Arjuna*,
He is considered the highest yogin.[62]

Several commentators, including *Śaṅkara*, have observed that the feeling of pain is universalized so as to derive a principle of empathy and non-injury. *Śaṅkara* characteristically commented that one who sees that what is painful and pleasant to himself is painful and pleasant to all creatures, will cause no living beings pain, and that he who is non-injurious is the foremost of yogins.[63] Self-realization in the *Gītā* takes due cognizance of the moral principle of *lokasaṃgraha*, the well-being of all peoples. The world of living things is brought together in a process governed by moral cause-effect relationships and it makes it imperative for each being within it to respect the autonomy, the interests and destiny of the other, and ultimately to find a way out of the cyclic implications of this process.[64]

The *Mahābhārata* initially regarded *ahiṃsā* as a special virtue for Brahmins and monks only, whereas fighting wars, proceeding for conquests, awarding the punishments, protection of the weak and the timid, and munificence were the primary duties of warriors. In fact, Yudhiṣṭhira was informed time and again by the sages that non-injury, friendliness towards all the animate and inanimate creatures of the world were the duties of the Brahmins and not that of the warriors.[65] The story of *Dharmavyādha* in the epic reveals that for the people belonging to the *vaiśya* (merchant class) and *śūdra* (lower castes), injury and non-injury did not interfere with their regular duties of everyday life.[66] The historic case of Arjuna's renunciation of the weapons at the coal-front of the battlefield and Krishna's argument in persuading Arjuna to perform his duties as a warrior, although it is a fratricidal war, is a case in point. Thus for the layman, it appears as though Krishna is motivating Arjuna for a wholesale massacre of innocent and innocuous warriors, but in reality, Arjuna was performing his bounden duty as a warrior.[67]

The ancient Hindu law-givers were chiefly interested in social organization and hence emphasized the duties to be performed by people belonging to various classes. Thus Manu gives ten characteristics of *dharma*. *Ahiṃsā* was also one among them.[68] Gautama of the Nyāya tradition, reviewing on the Hindu concept of universal morality, added kindness towards one and all (*dayā sarva bhutheṣu*). Yājñavalkya went to the extent of saying that non-injury to all the beings for all times was a part

62 The *Bhagavadgītā*, VI.29-32; A.T. de Nicolas, *Avatāra, The Humanization of Philosophy Through the Bhagavadgītā*, Stony Brook, NY: Nicolas Hay, 1976, p. 110.

63 *Śaṅkara* (Bhg. Commentary, 1972), pp. 198-99; Bilimoria and Hutchings, 1988, p. 36.

64 P. Bilimoria, op cit, pp. 17-18.

65 *Mbh*, Āraṇyaparvan CLXXVII.16ff; ccvi 11-13.

66 *Mbh*, Āraṇyaparvan, ch. CIC, especially 1-3.

67 See chapters in first part of the volume, especially Matilal, Mohanty, Daya Krishna, and the Introductory discussion to that section.

68 *Manusmṛti*, X.63.

of the dharma of *ahiṃsā*.[69] Saral Jhingran comments that this inclusion of non-injury and seeking the good of the creatures in philosophical literature provides some saving grace to this otherwise unimaginative and confusing list of moral duties or virtues given by the ancient law-makers.[70] Thus the concept of *ahiṃsā* slowly came to be consolidated into the Hindu mainstream, propelled to a large measure by its advocacy in Jainism and Buddhism.[71]

However, to deepen reflection on these traces within the Brāhmaṇic-Hindu tradition, a link needs to be made between the sudden, or gradual, acceptance of non-injury – as evidenced in the growing practice of vegetarianism among caste Hindus – and Jain and Buddhist eco-moralism of non-injury/non-violence. We begin with the observation that, while the word *ahiṃsā* does not appear in Vedas or *Brāhmaṇa*s, *hiṃsā* does, but its counter-positive had not yet been thought of, for the Vedic aficionado might have believed that killing was the same in all (possible) worlds and its benefits from the sacrificial offering of the victim animal was the same in all worlds. (In fact, without the *apūrva*, smoky potency, deposited in the other (possible) or transcendental world there would be no effects instantiated in this world.) The word *ahiṃsā* finds its first mention in the *Chāndogya Upaniṣhad*.[72] Some scholars are of the opinion that this might have been a concession to the growing influence of the Jain tradition on the Brāhmaṇic religions. The culture of the *śramaṇa*s (ascetic, with their parallel in the Hellenic Gymnosophists)[73] among the Jainas might have percolated into the Brāhmaṇic texts. The world *śramaṇa* appears in the texts of the *Brāhmaṇas* where it denotes a religious order other than Vedic (or Vedic affirming, i.e. *āstika*) tradition, especially that which is protected and marked by extreme austerities. Obviously the *śramaṇa* path of Buddhism and Jainism are suggested here. *Vṛṣabhadeva*, the first *Tīrthanakara* of Jainas is mentioned in both the *Viṣṇu* and *Bhāgavata Purāṇas*. Some scholars researching on the seals and figurines of the Indus valley civilization infer that some of the human postures bear resemblance to the later Jain statues. The bull, the symbol associated with *Vṛṣabhadeva*, is quite common among the Mohenjo-Daro artifacts.

A Theoretic pause

We pause at this juncture, to make the following reflection. We have attempted to understand the classical and medieval Brāhmaṇic-Hindu attitudes towards animal ecology in a context that exceeds the religious injunctions and practices they inherited from antiquity. But we still are moved to ask: Whether, even if in religious practice

69 *Yājñ.Smṛti*, I.122.

70 Saral Jhingran, op. cit. p. 176.

71 Preceding chapters in Part II of the volume have dealt with these traditions in this context amply.

72 *Ch. Up.*, III.17.4.

73 See Paul LeValley, 'Naked Philosopher-Ascetics: some observations on the shramāṇa religious spectrum', *Sophia*, **39**(2), 2000, pp. 143-159.

and scriptural sources, there was failure to prohibit outright abuse of animals and also to observe the cherished principles of non-injury and non-violence towards animals, the moral intuition *as a philosophical and rational insight* is not lacking or annihilated, as time and again these intuitions are appealed to. It is, we claim, these *intuitions* and not the edicts of Manu and such religious patriarchs that form the horizon against which wider ecological and cosmological perspectives, and the entailed practices, are garnered. Crossing over and looking for a parallel in non-Indian traditions, one could draw attention to the Judaic tradition. In an interesting article by Andrea Weisberger on 'Animal Rights within Judaism',[74] we find the following astute observation, which is worth citing in full as its comparative value is instructive:

> It seems undeniable that the views of the Jewish religious tradition have impacted our consciousness of the treatment of animals, even though Christianity (for the most part) has repudiated the ancient injunctions against mistreating animals. What is at issue is whether or not the moral code embedded within the religious tradition is independently justifiable, on 'rational' grounds, and utilized as the foundation for the religious code. Clearly, the traditional Christian attitude toward animals has been questioned and revised. Has religious consciousness contributed to this? Or, has it always been a matter for our moral intuitions, which have been overridden for a time by perceived religious dogma? Or, is what we call a moral code, morality, or a moral intuition today and for the past 2,000 years, a product of a Western tradition based in large part on the Christian world view? Is the idea we have of what constitutes "rationality," that seeming foundation of moral inquiry in the West, itself rationally derived, or derived from a Christian religious perspective? Is not the tradition of Descartes, which led him to view rationality as distinct from bodily existence, an existence that mere animals solely possess so that they might be tortured without pangs of conscience, the same tradition that allowed Kant to equate the rational with the moral so that following a moral code requires rationality, rendering sensibility of no consequence, and sensible creatures outside the realm of moral concern? So long as what we view as "rationality" is made the criterion for a moral code, non-humans will be precluded from our moral concern. Is, then, what the West considers to be ethics religiously based? Is contemporary ethical discourse dependent upon a view of humanity which severs reason from even the most common sense, a sensibility which

---

74 A.M. Weisberger, 'Animal Rights within Judaism; the Nature of the relationship between Religion and Ethics', *Sophia*, **42**(1), May 2003, pp. 77-83. See also, B.J. Gibbons, *Spirituality and the Occult, from the Renaissance to the Modern Age*, London/New York: Routledge, 2002. Chapter 5, where early Christian and patristic attitudes towards animals and meat-eating are discussed, particularly in the writings of Paracelsus, John Gerard, Samuel Pondage et al. For a defence of Christian reservations on a *sui generis* animal ethics, see Brian Scarlett, 'God and Animal Pain', *Sophia*, vol. **42**(1), May 2003, pp. 61-76, which is a reply to Peter Harrison, 'God and Animal Minds: A Response to Lynch, in *Sophia*, **35**(2), Sept-Oct 1996, pp. 67-78; and the work that tops it all is *Animal Theology* by Andrew Linzey, Illinois: University of Illinois Press,1995; other works by Linzey include, *After Noah*; *Animals and the Liberation of Theology*, and *Animal Gospel*, for which see wesbite with other interesting additions from Christian and Jewish animal liberation theologians http://www.yiffle.com/spirituality/animaltheology/.

must lay inert and valueless because of a theological desire to devalue flesh of any sort, even our own? Is the valuing of the "rational" over the "passional" a product of dogma? If so, what then can be used as a standard for determining moral conduct?

We shall return to the comparative theoretic discussion once more when examining Gandhian and modern-day South-North Asian approaches to the ecological challenges in the chapter on contemporary Indian ecology in Volume II. Meanwhile, we shall continue to explore the challenging question posed here in the animal-cum-ecological moral forays of Jainas and Buddhists, and modern-day sensibilities.

The rational concept of non-injury in Jainism

Jainism made a powerful impact on Hinduism with its pristine virtue of *ahiṃsā*. It was already built into the metaphysical theology of the Śramaṇas.[75] The Jaina ontology, comprising the soul (*jīva*), matter (*ajīva*, *attam* or *jada*), space (*ākāśa*), motion (*dharma*), inertia (*adharma*) and time (*kāla*) revolves around *ahiṃsā*. Life is the result of the interaction of the fundamental forms of energy, namely, soul and matter; the same energy that vibrates in human life vibrates in all life forms. This marks the principle of sentience. The capacity to feel pain (and enjoy pleasure) is in proportion to the number of the senses and development of the complex of subtle bodily functions (sensory organs, nervous systems, neural receptors, brain formation). From this is derived the principle of 'respect for all life'.

If there is resemblance here to a modern-day utilitarian case for the moral relevance of animals based on the consideration from sentience, then Peter Singer was a Jaina in one of his past lives (or so said a Jaina monk when the central thesis of 'Animal Liberation' was explained to him, which he mused was thought up first by the Jainas themselves centuries back in the form of *paśumokṣa* or *jīvāpavarga*). However, the Jainas would not draw the line between a shrimp (arthropod) and an oyster (a mollusc) in the same way that Singer would, for even the minuscule pulsating two-cell amoeba is considered to have a modicum of sentience; and plants, air, and water are classified under 'one-sense' bio-neurology. But of course this does not necessarily entail that all species have the same interests and equal moral standing and worth; indeed they do not. That the religiously ordained moral practices or virtues might inculcate equal respect and exercise of non-injury towards all life forms, regardless of their status in the bio-evolutionary scale, does not mitigate the philosophical insight of possible variance in interests. Prudence would have the better of a Jaina practitioner intent on achieving freedom from the bondage of matter and the attractions of the world. Here one has to look at Jaina soteriology.

The basic Jaina belief is that the soul progresses through a dynamic interaction with karmic particles. It is always in the process of acquiring and shedding these karmic particles. The first step in this purification process is the shunning of vices

75 On Śramaṇas and possible historical linkages with Gymnosophists and the teachings of Stoicism, see LeValley, note 73 (above).

such as injury (*hiṃsā*), falsehood (*asatya*), theft (*asteya*), incontinence (*maithuna*), and possessiveness (*parigraha*).

The *Tīrthankaras* (fortmakers or pathfinders) in their analysis of the consequences of causing injury to another life form suggest that it is the presence of 'evil' thoughts, feelings or attitudes that are more harmful than the material or physical effects, such as pain or the feeling of displeasure and suffering experienced by the subject. It does not necessarily depend on the act of *killing*, but on the intention and inner disposition of the individual, for it is the latter *saṃskāra*, 'moral traces' that one carries with one and which feeds into other of the person's 'evil' traits: 2+2=5. While for practical purposes, and as part of the normative order, the injunctions, codes and precepts are directed towards caution and deterrence against causing physical injury, on the theory that a socially disproved behaviour is easier to restrain than the private thoughts and emotions, intentions, of the citizen. Hence the Jaina teachers and exemplary monks prescribed the universal virtue of non-injury towards all the beings of the world and suggested that the people do not interfere with the state of nature. They exhorted that an interference with nature could be deemed an injurious act, which in its stronger form would be violence. Hence the *ahiṃsā* principle incorporated within itself this natural balance of harmony and co-existence of the sentient and the non-sentient beings. Logically, the Jaina principle of rejecting something has the latent meaning of accepting its opposite. Thus in following *ahiṃsā*, the negations prescribed have a more positive attitude associated with them. Avoiding injury is complemented with a feeling of respect and concern for the interest of others, humans, gods, and animals alike.

Non-injury or *ahiṃsā* was one among the five cardinal principles or precepts, perhaps lifelong resolutions (*pañca mahāvratas*), to be followed by every devout Jain. Injury and in its stronger form, violence, was strictly prohibited in the woes or precepts. Although the Brāhmaṇic tradition later on had come to recognize *ahiṃsā* as a great moral virtue, but to an extent did not forbid *hiṃsā* in the context of sacred rituals, it was Jainism that strictly forbade *hiṃsā* in any form and any domain. Jains in order to cultivate this special virtue go to the extent of not cooking meals or burning light after sunset as they would attract worms leading to inadvertent killing of them. In fact the Jaina monks of this country walk by brushing the path with a smooth brush in their hands so that no worms or insects should come under their feet. Jaina followers refrain from cooking or consuming meat and are strict vegetarians, eating only grains, legumes, vegetables, fruits, nuts, and seeds. They would avoid killing any life form when plucking the plant, and avoid plants that grow beneath the ground as uprooting them would disturb or injure earthworms and insects.

Further, *ahiṃsā* was understood and practiced in Jainism in a very broad way. Violence or injury caused to any living being in any form was considered *hiṃsā*. *Ahiṃsā* was practiced in all three aspects of thought, word and deed. The Jaina philosophers went to the extent of saying that speaking ill will against someone in thought or speaking harsh words to anyone is a clear example of *hiṃsā* which is almost akin to inflicting bodily injury to a person. Jaina tenets explain that forcing somebody to do something against her will or checking one's freedom, causing injury by negligence (*pramāda*), was considered violence. Practising *ahiṃsā* was considered to be like that of penance (*tapas*) in a broad way, *ahiṃsā* comprised love and compassion for all the living beings of the world.

To sum up this part of the discussion, recent scholars have gallantly extolled the virtues of non-injury or *ahiṃsā*, in part because the Jaina ethic of non-injury is as much part of a regime of internal discipline as it is of external conduct or behaviour towards others. They also tend to endorse the operative cosmology of the Jainas as 'perhaps [being] the most sympathetic to an ecological worldview', even while recognizing that the basic teleology of the Śrāmaṇic tradition is aimed towards transcendence of the self from the constricting human conditions of desire and attachment.[76] The second point to note is that the Jaina ethic of non-injury and a compassionate regard for others (insects, micro-amoebic entities, animals, human beings, gods, and spirits) finds its support on prudential grounds, for doing harm to other beings will result in more negative karma for oneself! Thus the ultimate justification for all ethical practices is that they should raise the moral stature of the practitioner; if derivatively, perhaps unavoidably given the interconnectedness of all *jīvās*, it raises the moral profile of the community (in the broadest biotic sense), then this is all the more reason for persisting with it.

Some writers, however, would argue that such virtues as *ahiṃsā* have intrinsic value and that their justification lies in their being derived, not from objective facts (such as 'all life has sanctity'), but from some experience that is self-evident. What is 'right' is in harmony with this experience. *Ahiṃsā*, in their view, is an experience related to the occurrence of pain and suffering among living beings and is universalized for others from one's own experience of pain. *Ahiṃsā* stands as the 'good' to which other values tend.[77]

Hence it follows that if there is to be a clearer articulation of Jaina environmental ethics it too would strive to be autonomous and normative, admitting the possibility of objective value, of which *ahiṃsā* would seem to be the most significant and distinctive feature.[78]

Buddhist reasoning on non-violence

It can be argued that the Buddhist view of *ahiṃsā* begins to cross the line between general non-injury and non-violence, even though the blur was not entirely removed. After Buddhism it becomes more realistic to speak of non-violence rather than the

76 Chapple, C.K., *Nonviolence to Animals, Earth, and Self in Asian Thought*, Albany: State University of New York Press, 1993, pp. 9-18.

77 Songani, K.C., 'Jaina ethics and the meta-ethical trends' in P.M. Marathe (ed). *Studies in Jainism*, Poona: Indican Philosophical Quarterly Publications no., 7:237-47, 1984, p. 243; Bilimoria, 'Indian Ethics', 1991, p. 53 (see General Introduction).

78 P. Bilimoria, 'Environmental Ethics of Indian Religious Traditions', *The Living Water Project*. www.deakin.edu.au/~pbilmo.

perfunctory preceptive disposition towards general and specific non-injury as this continues in the Jain tradition (to which we will return shortly). Hence we shall render *ahiṃsā* interchangeably as non-injury and non-violence, which seems more appropriate. The point to be emphasized here is that the moral principle of *ahiṃsā* or non-violence to which the Buddha gave exceeding prominence in Buddhist praxis, was to prevail irrespective of the status of the sentient being. Its emphasis though, it may be remarked, was weighed more in the interest of the spiritual progress of the human being than a blanket concern for the welfare of the creature or being at issue.[79] In the Buddha's collected sermons there are compassionate calls to show due care and loving kindness towards all sentient creatures; and where once upon a time Hindu gods would have been present, birds and animals bear witness to the Buddha's testimony, and they also become dialogic partners in the ensuing discourses. Hence 'The Buddha Among the Birds', which is part of the 550 stories from the *Jātaka* tradition that narrates Buddha's life among animals, and there are stories that recall Buddha's experiences *as* animal in his former births.

It would seem that the Buddha was re-evaluating the human-cosmos relationship that had been prevalent in the Indic civilization since the arrival in India of the Vedic Aryans with their proclivity towards sacrifice, exploitation of four-footed animals for agriculture and warfare, and subservience to a de-aesthetized Brāhmaṇic pan-naturalism with its ingrained fear of the forces of nature, indeed nature itself. The Buddha succeeded in shifting the perception from one of the islands or 'deities' made out of fearful warring nature-forces withholding agri-and-urban growth to the elegance of rolling mountains, streams, loving animals, and benign disposition of nature as it is.

One of the insights of Gotama that is nowadays seen as embedding a key to the growth of Buddhist ecological consciousness over the course of two millennia and across the Asian regions it impacted upon, is that of dependent arising (*pratītya-samutpāda*): 'on the arising of this, that arises'. The causal principle of interdependence registers an ecological vision that, as a recent scholar aptly put it: 'integrates all aspects of the ecosphere – particular individuals and general species – in terms of the principle of mutual codependence'.[80] The relational model undermines the sovereignty and presumed autonomy of the self over and against other beings and creatures (animals or plants). The ideals of *dharma* and virtues developed in accordance with this insight have been topics of intense reflection and debates among Buddhist schools, but they have also been arduously implemented at different historical junctures, such as by Emperor *Aśoka* after his conversion to

---

79 P. Bilimoria , 'Buddha', in Joy A. Palmer (ed.), *Fifty Key Thinkers on the Environment*, London/NY: Routledge, 2001, pp. 1-7; see also Padmasiri de Silva and other chapters on Buddhism in this volume and the next.

80 *Ariyapariyesana Sūtra, Majjhima Nikāya*, cited in Donald K. Swearer, 'Buddhism and Ecology: Challenge and Promise', *Earth Ethics*, Fall 1998, pp. 19-22, p. 21 (text in single quote also Swearer's own description).

Buddhism, who institutionalized care and welfare towards animals, has the following edict poignantly records for us:

> Here no animal is to be killed for sacrifice...
> Formerly in the Beloved of the God's kitchen several hundred thousand animals were killed daily for food; but now at the time of writing only three are killed – two peacocks and a deer, though the deer not regularly. Even these three animals will not be killed in future.
> ... the Beloved of the Gods has provided medicines for man and beast...
> *medicinal plants* ... [Roots and fruits have also been sent where they did not grow and have been planted along the roads for use of man and beasts].[81]

The verses demonstrate that rights and protection of certain liberties of animals have been recognized in Buddhism. Another side of the causal principle of interdependence is the consequent or karmic continuum, which suggests that every action conditions a being's personal history of suffering, the cessation thereof and subsequent liberation from the karmic continuum: 'on the cessation of this, that ceases'. From the particularity of individual suffering (karmic action-effect), the Buddha was able to generalize to humankind, the animal world and natural environment, themselves as distinctive manifestations of the cumulative effect of karmic conditioning. He eschewed any hierarchical dominance of one order of being over the other. A social and ecological ethic, *dharma* (in Pali, *dhamma*) based on undoing the cyclical and all-devouring chain of karmic effects or conditionings was the primary goal of the Buddha. His ardent followers developed the teachings for their application in several different directions. This is borne out in the Buddha's expectation that monks and lay Buddhists alike ought to strive always for the 'welfare of the many', 'the happiness of the many', 'compassion for the world'.[82] It must, however, be said that the Buddha's teachings, unlike some developments, did not separate out a uni-dimensional emphasis on environmental ethics from an ontology and ethics of spiritual transformation or sacred making *dharma* of the human and natural world's beings alike. It has been argued that ontological notions such as Buddha-nature or Dharma-nature provide a basis for unifying all existent entities in a common sacred universe, even though the tradition has come to privilege human life vis-à-vis spiritual realization.[83] In other words, Buddhism underscores the inherent moral worth and 'considerability', in principle at least, of all beings towards which there are certain mutual and reciprocal obligations. We might not ordinarily consider, for instance, the humble gurgling stream as having any particular obligation towards human beings, but the small schools of fish might be very appreciative of the sustenance and safer ecosystem that the cool water provides for them.

---

81 De Bary, *Sources of Indian Tradition*, vol. I revised edn. A.T. Embree, New York: Columbia University Press, 1988, pp. 144-145.

82 *Middle Length Sayings*, cited in Padmasiri de Silva, *Environmental Philosophy and Ethics in Buddhism*, NY: St Martin's Press; London: Macmillan Press, 1998, p. 31.

83 Ibid.

While the Buddha may have realized the diversity and interconnectedness of the bio-community, his worldview was neither entirely naturalistic nor biocentric as Buddhism in its different forms has sometimes become. In this context while the relevance and role of the environment is recognized in the ecology of individual movement towards the end-goal of *nirvāṇa*, the blurring of autonomous boundaries and the particularity necessary for grounding an ethic on duties towards others, rights and positive legal protection of minority and endangered species, weakens the enfranchisement and empowering strength needed for a balanced ethic of poly-ecoism. The Buddha's refusal to prescribe unqualified vegetarianism, it is often argued, and his own physical death allegedly enhanced by taking a little bad pork offered to him, are indicative of such a weak link in the Buddha's otherwise noble and promising prolegomenon for all future environmental ethics.[84] Nevertheless, the Buddha's plea of compassion for all life forms in their mutual interdependency and the aestheticization of nature that undergirds his wisdom-teachings, paved the way for a radical transformation of attitudes towards nature and its eco-communities in regions and countries to which Buddhism travelled.

The moral practice of showing respect and responsible predation to all nature became a way of life for Buddhists in India and in lands far apart. Even though the Buddhist anti-metaphysical thrust outside of the subcontinent continued the influential Indian Buddhist doctrine of the absence of self-nature or intrinsic existence of properties and substances alike, proclaiming thus the 'emptiness' of all

84 On the question of consuming flesh of animals, the Buddha appeared to have held a rather ambivalent position; some say he took the middle path, meaning that practical considerations went towards moderating the extremes of idleness on the one hand and impractical or idealistic tendency on the other. The material on the disputes the Buddha and later his followers had with other hard-nosed protagonists of *ahiṃsā* and non-eating of flesh is too extensive to go into here. All that needs to be said is that the view favoured by the Buddhists was, very generally, that if an individual is not directly responsible for the killing of an animal, then he is justified in eating its flesh. The argument turns on the motive or intentionality of the partaker, in consonance with the Buddhist theory of karma. Namely, if you were not aware of the animal when it was alive and it was not your intention to kill the animal; moreover, you did not possess the means of killing it, nor did you carry out the act that lead to its death, then you are not responsible for its death and you accrue no bad karma (demerit). This means that you could front up at the butcher's shop and without asking any questions buy whatever meat you might fancy and take it home for the sizzling oven. This also means that since the butcher was not expecting you, neither he nor you can say that the animal was killed for you in particular, for someone else could just as well have come by the butcher's shop before you (or after you) and bought the same meat; it follows therefore that you cannot be held responsible by guilt of association. For a rebutal of its unsound moral logic, see P. Bilimoria, 'Of suffering and Sentience: The Case of Animals (revised)', in H. Odera Oruka (ed.), *Philosophy, Humanity and Ecology Philosophy of Nature and Environmental Ethics*, African Centre for Technology Studies, Kenya, Nairobi, 1994, pp. 329-344; on a humorous counterargument on 'me-eat' see, Arindam Chakrabarti 'Meat and Morality in the Mahābhārata', *Studies in Humanities and Social Sciences*, 1996, III(2), pp. 259-68.

things, its moral framework paradoxically gained strength from this standpoint, on three counts, as follows.

(i) Moral properties such as those of the good, compassion, and loving kindness or respect, by no means absolute, have solid presence (contingently supervenient on 'emptiness'), inasmuch as human interaction and communication or ethical life generally presuppose these properties.
(ii) A pluralistic ontology that has fair regard for members within it without privileging any particular species easily gets translated into a non-anthropocentric respect for biodiversity.
(iii) The religious-soteriological 'end' requires certain self-motivated ethical practices and norms, including restraint on desires, meditation on the limits of the ego-self, altruism based on the moral properties of reverence and deep (but not condescending) compassion for all living and non-sentient beings. In other words, the normative constructs for monks, nuns, lay people, farmers and nomads too, underscore benign concern for the environment.

Summing up this discussion and bringing together some of the positive insights bequeathed by the Buddha, it can be said that transcending the human-centric (ego-bounded) perspective is one of the great strengths here of the interdependent or interconnected vision of all things within the natural-human-social matrix. As de Silva puts it: 'The Buddhist environmental philosophy may be described as a shift from an egocentric stance towards an ecocentric orientation.'[85] Key ontological and moral concepts that help ground Buddha's ecological thinking comprise:

- *Pratītya-samutpāda*, interdependent conditioning
- *karma* (*kamma*), the law of moral causation
- *duḥkha* (*dukka*), unsatisfactoriness
- *dharma* (*dhamma*), reciprocity of obligations or rights within the bounds of duties
- *śīla* (*sīla*), cultivation of virtues, disciplines, and the overcoming of vices – among the virtues highlighted are: restraint, simplicity, loving-kindness, compassion, equanimity, patience, wisdom, non-injury, and generosity.

These concepts are predicated to the general principle of *consequentialism* (the gravity and impact of agency in one's actions judged by their consequences), moderated by *teleology* (a larger purpose or particularity of ends towards which each species strives even in the apparent absence of agency – hence the mountain having its own silent *telos*), and *deontology* (*dhamma* for *dhamma*'s sake, intended as a check against excessive altruism, unmitigated utilitarianism, and ritualized narcissism or a 'grand narrative' teleology). In the present day we find such sentiments echoed in post-(classical) utilitarian thinking, particularly in the works of Holmes Rolston

85 *Vinaya Piṭaka*, discussed by Padmasiri de Silva, op. cit., p. 23.

III, Warwick Fox, Freya Mathews[86], Val Plumwood, Larry Johnson, Sylvan and Forrest, Vandana Shiva, Anil Agarwal, Paul Taylor, Robin Attfield, Peter Singer, Tom Regan, Thomas Berry, David E. Cooper, and Christopher Chapple, among others. Some of these writers will be discussed a little more extensively in the next volume. Meanwhile, as Paul Taylor could well articulate, mantra-like, this assuring perspective: 'To accept the biocentric outlook and regard ourselves and the world from its perspective is to see the whole natural domain of living things and their environment as an order of interconnected objects and events. The interactions among species-populations and between those populations and the physical environments comprise a tightly-knit web.'[87]

However, all too often Western writers are oblivious to the fact that 3,000 years of ecological thinking in the Orient or the East, that over time, and especially with the European discovery of and Orientalist fascination with the antiquarian texts and cultures of India and China, have percolated through and formed effectively the 'background knowledge' to the advances in research programmes made in the West – but perhaps for the sharper analytical/theoretical articulations[88] – compelled by the tensions and contradictions within post-industrial-capitalist, post-Cold War, and post-Judeo-Christian *lebenswelt.*

Contemporary Developments and Case Studies

Water Management

There has been a long tradition of water harvesting throughout India, but the system and practice has been in disarray over the last two hundred years. The range of techniques included canals for tributary diversion of stream water, small and large tanks (from temple holy tanks to huge summer catchments), and bunds or embankments, wells and reservoirs – to collect every possible source of water. A system of measured distribution of water across villages, determined in terms of prioritized needs of the sharing communities, functioned in a decentralized and locally-administered form. Large-scale damming of rivers and run-off groundwater was discouraged, except if it helped to moisten the soil for summer planting or storage in smaller tanks. So a Narmada and the Yangtse Three Gorges Dam Projects would have been inconceivable. Thus in the event that the annual rainfall fails in some years, there would be sufficient water in reserve for rationing across the

86 Even as I edit this, hot-off-the-press her second book in the area, lands on my desk, viz., Freya Mathews, *Reinhabiting Reality Towards a Recovery of Culture*, Albany: SUNY Press, 2005; Sydney: University of New South Wales Press, 2005. Freya echoes, again, some of the concerns being canvassed here, though there isn't time here to do justice to her work as it requires much closer reading, for another occasion.

87 Paul Taylor, *Respect for Nature, A Theory of Environmental Ethics*, New Jersey: University of Princeton Press, 1986, p. 21.

88 This is taken up in Volume II of *Indian Ethics*.

inhabitants of the region, and channelled across to other regions if the demand there was negotiably greater.

During the colonial period this varied system of harvesting water was all but destroyed, and further debilitated by a series of droughts, failed monsoons, invented famines, and the current side-effects, one supposes, from the greenhouse syndrome. The British did much to disrupt the water-traditions. As late as 1820 Col. Thomas Munro in Madras could be full of praise for the astonishingly efficient system of tanks and locally-constructed catchment structures. But the British deployed their own 'scientific' experts and set about re-organizing the agro-ecological system, and also distribution of land and water, in ways that they thought would maximize production, following the utilitarian edicts of John Stuart Mill.

Apart from the erstwhile problem of land-tenure or land-lordism (under a zamindar system), an alien concept of territorial and produce rights, and an oppressive revenue collecting system, these changes effectively wiped out traditional patterns of small-scale irrigation and water-care, replacing them with large dams and canals, and concomitant bureaucratic control – not unlike the hydraulic system that prevailed under the emperors in China.

In the decades after Independence (in 1947), successive Indian governments have not made any effort to revisit the traditional methods, but instead invested in mega-irrigation and damming running groundwater with the primary intent of generating hydro-electricity, influenced by the arcane technological dreams of Western countries, especially the Soviet Union. Other changes in several parts of India have further eroded the traditional water management system. Overall, community self-management has declined as bureaucratic intervention in village affairs increased from the centre and from politicians. Only a few could afford the tube-wells sunk under licence from the state government's water boards. Agarwal's concluding paragraph is telling: A decentralized 'system of water management demands a community-based system of natural resources management. Most laws that govern India's land, water and forests are the same today as those formulated by the British. The Indian government tries to deal with twenty-first-century problems of environment management with the ninetenth-century legislation and (gilded) bureaucracies of colonial ruler…or will they democratize its control and leave its management to rural communities?'[89]

Southern states were also centres of traditional water harvesting systems. The Vijayanagar empire, a powerful Hindu kingdom around the thirteenth to fourteenth century, had extended its ingenious technological skills in the area of water

89 Anil Agarwal and Sunita Narain, 'Decline and Revival of Traditional Water Harvesting Systems in India', *The Ecologist*, **27**(3), May/June 1997; Nirmala Sengupta, 'Irrigation: Traditional vs Modern', *Economic and Political Weekly*, **20**, (45-47), 1985, pp. 1919-38. Earlier in the twentieth century a Premier of the colonies of Australia, Sir Alfred Deakin (also a theosophist by temperament), visited India and Ceylon to study its extensive irrigation system and to bring back the wisdom of the technology for the more arid conditions of the Australian agricultural landscape.

containment to southern regions of Andhra Pradesh and northwestern Karnataka,[90] where they had built reservoirs, tanks and embankments to collect monsoon flows, which would then flow out through small channels, seepage, moisture, and wooden rotating pumps to the agricultural lands and villages around. This system lay in ruins for centuries, and is only just being repaired and revived by local authorities, inspired no doubt by the projects. In the next volume, which further treats developments of animal ethics and ecology in the twentieth century, beginning with Gandhi, we shall briefly return to this discussion to show how this traditional practice is being revived and how this ecology of water is being utilized with great results for human beings and the environment alike.

Bibliography and References (Primary)

Vedas

Atharva Veda with the commentary of Sāyaṇa, trans. by Whitney, William Dwight, (1905) Massachusetts: Cambridge University Press, reprinted Delhi: Motilal Banarsidass. 1962, 1971, 1984.

Rigveda, in *The Hymns of the Ṛgveda*, trans. R.T.H. Griffiths. Delhi: Motilal Banarsidass, 1973. *Rig Veda Saṃhitā with Sāyaṇa's Commentary*, vols 1-9, ed. Manmathanatha Dutt, Calcutta : Society for the Resuscitation of Indian Literature, 1968.

Yajur Veda, vols I-III, ed. with Kannada trans, Rameshwara Avadhani, Shankarapuram, Bangalore: Jyothi Samskrita Pratisthanam, 1990-99.

The Rig Veda, An Anthology, ed. W.D. O'Flaherty, London/NY: Penguin Books, 1983.

Mantramañjarī The Vedic Experience, An Anthology, compiled, trans. by Raimundo Panikkar *et al.*, London: Darton, Longman and Todd, London, 1977.

Upaniṣads

The Principal Upaniṣads, ed. and trans. S. Radhakrishnan, New York: The Humanities Press, 1974.

Upaniṣads, ed. and trans. with Introduction, Patrick Olivella, NY: Oxford University Press, 1996.

Smṛti

The *Bhagavadgītā* in the *Mahābhārata*, ed. and trans. J.A.B. van Buitenen, Chicago: University of Chicago Press, 1985.

Caraka-Saṃhitā, trans. P. Ray and H.N. Gupta, Delhi: National Institute, 1965.

90 See note 78 above.

Jaini, Padmanabh, *The Jaina Path of Purification*, Delhi:Motilal Banarsidass, 1979.
Kane, P.V., *A History of Dharmaśāstra: Ancient and Medieval Religious and Civil Law in India*, vols I-V. Poona: Bhandarkar Oriental Institute, 1969.
Kauṭilīya Arthaśāstra, Parts I-IV, trans R.P. Kangle, New Delhi: Motilal Banarsidass, 1992.
Mahābhārata, Critical edition, General editor V.S. Suktankar, Bhandarkar Oriental Research Institute, Poona, 1933-69.
Manusmriti with Kullūkabhaṭṭa commentary, English introduction by S.C. Banerji, ed. J.L. Shastri, Delhi: Motilal Banarsidass, 1972-74.
The Manusmṛti, ed. Satya Bhushan Yogi, Delhi: Motilal Banarsidass, 1975.
Rāmāyaṇa of *Vālmīki*, trans. Hari Prasad Shastri, 3 vols, London, 1962.

Purāṇas

J.L. Shastri, General Editor, *Ancient Indian Tradition and Mythology* Delhi: Motilal Banarsidass, multi-volume and compilation of assorted editions, translations, earlier or recent; some new translations by Board of Scholars, 1978-1987: comprising:

- *Agnipurāṇa*, vols 27-30 , trans. N. Gangadharan, Part I, 1984; Part II, 1985, Part III, 1986, Part IV, 1987.
- *Agni Purāṇa*, Poona: Ananda Sanskrit Series, 41, 1957, trans: Manmatha Nath Dutt, Calcutta, 1901. Reprint: New Delhi: The Cosmo Print & Publications, 1985.
- *Bhāgavata Purāṇa with the commentary of Śrīdhara*, trans. J.M. Sanyal (Bombay, 1832), 1984; *Bhāgavatapurāṇa*, trans, ed. J.L. Sastri, 4 vols, New Delhi: Motilal Banarsidass, 1978.
- *Brahma Purāṇa*, vols 35-36, Parts I-IV, ed. J.L. Shastri and G.P. Bhatt, New Delhi: Motilal Banarsidass, 1985-1988.
- *Garuda Purāṇa*, Parts I-III, ed. J.L. Shastri and G.P. Bhatt, New Delhi, Motilal Banarsidass, 1978-1980.
- *Gautamī Māhātmya*, ed, G.P. Bhatt, New Delhi, Motilal Banarsidass, 1986.
- *Kūrma Purāṇa*, vols 27-30, trans. Ganesh Vasudev Tagare, Part I (1981) and II 1982.
- *Liṅga Purāṇa*, Parts I-II, ed. J.L. Shastri, New Delhi: Motilal Banarsidass, 1983.
- *Matsya Purāṇa*, ed. Nag Sharan Singh, Delhi: Nag Publishers, 1990.
- *Skānda Purāṇa*, vols 49-54, in J.L. Shastri, 1984.
- *Varāha Purāṇa*, trans. Iyer S. Venkatesubramonia, vol. I, 1983, vol. II, 1985.
- *Varuṇa Purāṇa*, trans. Anand Swarup Gupta, Varanasi: Chowkamba Sanskrit Series, 1986.
- *Viṣṇu Purāṇa*, trans. Manmatha Nath Dutt, H.C. Dass, Calcutta: Elysium Press.
- *Vāyu Purāṇa*, vols 37-38.

Saṃyutta-nikāya, Suttanipāta, Bodhi, Bhikkhu, *The connected discourses of the Buddha*, vols 1 and 2, translation of the *Samyutta Nikāya*, Wisdom Publishers, 2000.

Śaṅkara, *The Bhagavad Gītā* with the Commentary of *Śrī Śaṅkarāchārya*, trans. A.M. Sastry, Madras: Samata Books, 1972.

Introduction to Part C

Reflections on Moral Ideals and Modernity; Gandhi and Nonviolence

Part I

As has been argued in our General Introduction, ethical valuations and judgments shift over time. The notion of sacrifice so important in Vedic culture, where it is seen as a cosmic responsibility necessary for upholding the universe, does not have quite the same resonance today. Likewise, most people in our time would regard *satī* as an illegitimate extension of uxorial loyalty. Alasdair MacIntyre and Bernard Williams among others have demonstrated the historicity of ethical concepts.[1] MacIntyre, for example, compares three lists of virtues, that of Aristotle, that of Jesus in the Sermon on the Mount, and that of Ben Franklin, and shows that what are virtues to one are often vices to the others. Thus, the grandeur and magnanimity valourized by Aristotle as the marks of an Athenian gentleman do not sit easily with the meekness and humility that Jesus prizes, and both Aristotle and Jesus would have disapproved of the virtues of thrift and parsimony so emphasized by Franklin at the dawn of the modern capitalist era. In a similar vein, Bernard Williams argues that impersonal rules of action and the stress on moral obligation are characteristically modern Western preoccupations, not shared, for example, by the early Greeks for whom notions of personal integrity involving the moral emotions and community-based responsibility are more dominant.

This historical variability should not surprise us. The judgments of what a society considers good and correspondingly judgments about right and wrong and what is obligatory vary according to time, context, and circumstance. Questions of historicity come into special focus when dealing with moral traditions. Tradition, as its etymology suggests, is something that is carried forward in time. By its very nature, therefore, a tradition is open-ended and subject to continual interpretation and evaluation as to what is living and what is dead in it when examined in new contexts. If a tradition has nothing in it that can outlast the context of its articulation, it either dies or gets transformed into something different.

The chapters in this section deal in different ways with the tension between tradition and modernity. Modernity, of course, is not just contemporaneity, but

1 Alasdair MacIntyre, *After Virtue*, Notre Dame: University of Notre Dame Press, 1981 and Bernard Williams, *Ethics and the Limits of Philosophy*, Cambridge, Mass.: Harvard University Press, 1985.

signifies a difference of world-views shaped by developments in science, technology, and social and economic organization. Western modernity has meant, thanks to these developments, rationalization in the Weberian sense — that is, the differentiation of different spheres of life — the rise of capitalism, liberal democracy, and the nation state. These features are themselves of a particular social and institutional history, spanning the scientific and political revolutions of the sixteenth and seventeenth centuries and the Enlightenment and the French and American Revolutions of the eighteenth century. The questions that explicitly or implicitly concern some of the thinkers dealt with in this section like Max Weber, Gandhi, and Sri Aurobindo were the normative universality of Western modernity, and whether modernization signified westernization. Weber certainly thought so, and his study of Hindu ethics, examined here by Pratap Bhanu Mehta, was, at least in part, motivated by a developmental logic similar to Hegel's pointing to the inevitability of the processes of rationalization, the 'disenchantment of the world,' and the 'iron cage' of modernity.

Gandhi and Sri Aurobindo by contrast strongly resisted the equation of modernization and westernization. Much as Gandhi admired aspects of Western modernity — its scientific temper, its pragmatism, efficient organization, and civil liberties, for example — he considered it a fundamentally violent and destructive form of life. One could argue, as I try to in my chapter, that Gandhi offered an alternative and non-Western form of modernity, that embodied a different set of values and ideals, which blended what he considered to be the best of both Indian tradition and modernity. It is a mistake to regard Gandhi as a staunch traditionalist as he often is described. This characterization overlooks the fact that Gandhi was quite critical of many aspects of Hindu tradition, from caste and untouchability to its seeming lack of concern for questions of social and economic justice. By the same token, modernity for Gandhi did not imply the wholesale rejection of tradition. This tension between tradition and modernity is evident, for example, in the evolution of Gandhi's views about technology. From the wholesale rejection of modern technology that is prominent in *Hind Swaraj* (1909), we see him moving toward an approbation of what is nowadays called 'appropriate technology,' that is, technology adapted to human scale and to the needs and resources of a particular people. Hence his fascination with the sewing machine.

Sri Aurobindo was educated at Cambridge in the Western intellectual tradition and discovered his own tradition and its riches only on his return to India. In his mature thought one finds an interesting fusion of a version of *Advaita Vedānta* given an evolutionary turn with a philosophy of history that sees the world as fully real. Like Hegel's Absolute, Aurobindo's *Brahman* manifests itself in progressively evolving shapes of reality, which include evolving forms of human consciousness. The motor of this evolution is not, however, as in Hegel's case a historical dialectic, but rather different forms of spiritual consciousness which have earthly instantiations. Aurobindo like Gandhi rejects the materialism and reductive naturalism of the West; although unlike Gandhi he espouses a philosophy of history delineating emergent forms of historical consciousness.

In an interesting essay, 'Indian Thought: Between Tradition and Modernity,' J. N. Mohanty argues that public, though non-academic philosophers like Tagore, Gandhi, and Sri Aurobindo have managed a synthesis of the traditional and the modern while remaining deeply rooted in tradition. In Gandhi's case this traditionalism embraces the world of the *Gītā*, his own eclectic version of *Vedānta*, and the devotional ideas of medieval Hindu saints. In Aurobindo, as just pointed out, the primary influence is that of the religious philosophy of the Vedas and the Upaniṣads. Tagore too, while being remarkably open to Western thought, remained deeply rooted in Upaniṣadic mysticism. And yet in spite of the traditionalism of all three thinkers, their influence on modern India and the world at large has been considerable. By contrast, Mohanty complains, 'The Indian philosopher finds himself between two worlds — not at home in either — and more often than not lacking expertise and first-rate scholarship in either.[2] However harsh this statement may sound — and Mohanty goes on elsewhere in the essay to make a few exceptions — there is a measure of truth to it. Indian academic philosophy, again with some notable exceptions that include Mohanty himself, has languished, at least relative to philosophy in other parts of the world. This is especially true of the field of ethics. With the exception of Gandhi — and he is not strictly speaking a philosopher — there is hardly an Indian moral (in contrast to spiritual) philosopher who has attracted widespread attention either in India or elsewhere. And while there have been attempts to treat Indian moral philosophy systematically, many of them for the most part have been descriptive accounts of the moral ideas scattered over the tradition without much analysis or conceptual rigor.[3] This volume represents one of the first attempts to look rigorously at some of the ethical ideas articulated over the years in the Indian tradition.

This lacuna of rigorous moral philosophy in the broader field of Indian philosophy has been remarked on by many thinkers, most recently by Bimal Matilal.[4] It may be instructive to probe a little deeper to diagnose this deficiency. It has nothing to do with the purportedly other-worldly character of Indian thought *à la* Albert Schweitzer, or with any lack of concern with the right ordering of society, for these matters are dealt with extensively in the non-philosophical literature. It is rather that early on in the tradition the umbrella notion of *dharma* (itself the successor of the concept of *ṛta*) with its vast semantic spread was developed and all human values and norms got referred back to that concept. There is, I suppose, in Greek ethics a parallel with the Platonic notion of the Good, but already with Aristotle's *Nichomachean Ethics* we get a concerted effort to pick out the distinctively moral,

---

2 J.N. Mohanty, 'Indian Thought: Between Tradition and Modernity' in *Explorations in Philosophy: Indian Philosophy,* edited by Bina Gupta, Delhi: Oxford University Press, 2001, p. 59.

3 See such books as Saral Jhinran, *Aspects of Hindu Morality*, Delhi: Motilal Banarsidass, 1989; Surama Dasgupta, *Development of Moral Philosophy in India*, Delhi: Munshiram Manoharlal Publishers, 1961; I. C. Sharma, *Ethical Philosophies of India*, New York: Harper & Row, 1965.

4 See the quote from Matilal, 'Moral Dilemmas: Insights from Indian Ethics,' mentioned in our General Introduction and his chapter (2) in this volume.

in contrast to the eidetic and mystical, meanings of the term. This, it seems to me, did not happen in the Indian tradition, where the notion of *dharma* was allowed to remain deliberately vague. *Dharma* provides an overall framework for a system of norms, rules, and mores, the specific contents of which are determined by context as, for example, in the *varnāśrama dharmas* contained in the *Manusmṛti*. The broad imperative it enjoins on moral agents is the duty to preserve and sustain the organic unity of being, the intrinsic harmony of the cosmos. With this convergence of both moral and cosmological ideas, the primary category is not that of moral principle but of a primordial order that is neither exclusively moral nor exclusively cosmological but both together at once. It is difficult to see how the ethical can be deduced from the cosmological. Human beings are part of a larger order in which they participate by attempting to find their place in the scheme of things, but no specifically ethical norm or rule can be deduced from such a vague idea. In actual fact, duties and rights were specified in accordance with both caste considerations and one's psycho-social stage in life (the *āśramas*). Each of these had *dharmas* attached to them by social convention rather than by some justified moral rule.

As Mohanty quite rightly points out, '…none of these stages in any sense is a reflection of man's place in the universe; at most it is the picture of an ideal journey through life on one's way toward *mokṣa* or freedom from *karma*-rebirth, toward the Highest Good. This account, which contains the account of *dharma*, does not itself reflect some deeper-lying functional place in the universe, although as closely connected with the idea of *varṇa* or caste, the doctrine of *dharma* connects with an individual's place in society, and as connected with the rebirth-*mokṣa* structure, it points beyond society in two directions: one determining the 'rationality' of social (world) and of individual deserts, the other pointing beyond the social toward attainment of a place above the social, a free, spiritual individuality.'[5] Between the sociological schema and the soteriological goal, the specific moral notion seems to get swallowed up.

It is obvious that this is a holistic and hierarchical model of life and the world, where duties, roles, and functions are stressed within an overarching order of right. Social and moral ideals like freedom, justice, and equality are relativized to this larger order. In such a closed and hierarchically structured society, the assignment of duties and functions is carried out through the power relations of ritual status or social authority and not through independent moral or legal justification. It is obvious that such a tradition meets with difficulties when it attempts to negotiate the demands of a democratic, open, and pluralistic society, that is, when it encounters modernity.

In a similar spirit, while Rajendra Prasad evokes ideas about social justice scattered across the literature and attempts to bring modern concepts of equality and distributive justice to bear on them, one would be hard pressed to find in the Indian tradition any systematic reflection about justice along the lines of, say, John Rawls's

5 J.N. Mohanty, *Classical Indian Philosophy*, Lanham, Maryland: Rowman & Littlefield, 2000, p. 108.

Theory of Justice. This is partly because in the organic model of society prevalent in traditional India, ideas of compassion, hospitality, sensitivity to the distress of others and a whole host of personal and social virtues gets emphasized. What does not get stressed is the notion of rights which individuals can enjoy *qua* individuals. Rawls's theory draws on the legal and juridical notion of rights articulated by Hobbes and Locke and attempts on that foundation to come up with principles of impartial deliberation about the fair allocation of rights and responsibilities, what he calls the 'basic structure of society.' His notion of the 'veil of ignorance,' for example, is meant to reflect and buttress the basic principle of such deliberation: namely, that each person should take into account the dignity and needs of others as free and equal human beings. Louis Dumont is not the only person to point out that the idea of social equality, as against that of equality before God, does not really get developed in India.[6] Nor for that matter does the idea of moral equality in the Kantian sense, where each person is considered an end in himself and thus deserving of respect. The various inequities inherent in the caste system militate against such ideas of equality. It is obvious from what I have written that I agree with Matilal and others that there is indeed a lacuna in the tradition of Indian philosophy with respect to moral philosophy.

That lacuna is precisely what motivated the present two volumes and this section in particular. One will find here a vast array of topics covered from the theodical account of Hindu ethics suggested by Max Weber, through historical accounts of the ethics of Gandhi and Aurobindo and of cultural rights in British India to contemporary concerns of environmental ethics, religious tolerance, and social justice.

What I want to stress in conclusion is that the lacunae which I have pointed out do not have so much to do with the lack of ethical theories as such. I agree with the late Bernard Williams that ethical theories that attempt to fit the many varieties of moral action and motivation into a single framework are misguided. Unlike science or mathematics the attempt to legitimize and ground our moral beliefs and practices via fundamental principles is not likely to be fruitful. It is thanks to the work of scholars like Williams and Alasdar MacIntyre that contemporary Western ethical discussion has returned to a more descriptive Aristotelian account of the virtues and character, analyzed in terms of what Williams calls 'thick concepts,' that is, concepts in which elements of description and evaluation are seamlessly interwoven.[7] This interweaving gives us a way to ignore or bypass the rigid distinction between fact and value that has bedeviled so much abstract ethical theorizing. From that perspective the descriptive accounts of *dharma* and other ethical ideas found in the Indian literature fare better, provided they are analyzed with rigour and imagination, as the authors represented in this section attempt to do.

Joseph Prabhu

---

6 See his *Homo Hierarchichus: The Caste System and its Implications*, Chicago: University of Chicago Press, 1980; and his *Essays on Individualism: Modern Ideology in Anthropological Perspective*, Chicago: University of Chicago Press, 1986.

7 See Bernard Williams, *Ethics and the Limits of Philosophy*, op. cit.

Part II

Gandhi's reconciliation of truth and non-injury

The ideas of M.K. Gandhi, or Mahatma Gandhi as he is popularly known, are all but forgotten in India; and yet Gandhi more than most in recent times struggled to advance Indian ethics beyond the pale of its apparently diminishing relevance in a modern, civilizing and progressive world. Perhaps Gandhi does not present himself as much of a theoretician. But his genius lay in his practical wisdom, particularly in his ability to take an idea from a traditional practice or context (e.g. *sat*, 'true to being', or religious fasting) and applying that with vivacity to disparate contemporary issues or situations, whether on dietary matters or in an act of civil obedience. For this he would attract criticism from both traditionalists and modernists alike.

Gandhi is, of course, rightly famous for his hand in bringing down the two century-old British *Rāj* or sovereignty in India, precipitating a spate of anti-colonial movements across the globe. Thus he stood hard against one kind of oppression, and one form of exploitation, though he was also pained by other consequences of its manifestations. But what is more significant is the *way* or means by which he was able to achieve this feat and how this ties in with the particular ethics he gave voice to. That in the process he also ends up questioning many of the traditional (Hindu) values and customary practices, as well as a host of modern (Western) values, though perhaps not overturning them, is also significant. So he was happy to switch his grounds for vegetarianism from customary habit to ethical consideration for animals.

But Gandhi was a curious mix of the radical and the conservative. For example, he took up the cause of civil rights in South Africa, but his struggle did not extend much beyond the rights for the Indian community. Still, he set an example of 'civil resistance' which some Black leaders, and their Christian sympathizers of the time, followed. Returning to India, Gandhi was much anguished by the injustices of the caste, class and religious divisions that had taken deep root in Indian society. He became a champion of the cause of the 'untouchables', whom he gave the name Harijan ('People of the Lord', nowadays better known as 'Dalits'), rallying against the prejudices and 'the evils of the caste system'. It looked as though Gandhi was set to have the entire *varṇa* structure dismantled.

In the long run, however, Gandhi defended the *varṇa* qua class system, on the grounds that it was (i) different from the proliferate caste system; ii) a sensible scheme for the division of labour; and iii) it was a law of human nature, and hence part of *dharma*. What he did not find agreeable was the inordinate rights and privileges that one class, especially the brahmin, abrogated to itself over the other classes. Equality, he thought, is not an issue in the design, but it becomes a problem when the structure gets tilted vertically[8] The enigma of *dharma* oddly places constraints

---

8 M.K. Gandhi, *My Varnashrama Dharma*, Bombay: Bharatiya Vidya Bhavan, Bombay, 1965, p. 80.

on the otherwise splendid idea of civil and human rights that Gandhi awakened to rather early in his career; but it also helped him to forge a principle of human action which itself has buttressed the struggle for rights of one kind or another in different quarters. That principle is nonviolent action or *ahiṃsā.*

Gandhi initially adopted a form of non-cooperation, which was echoed in the works of Tolstoy, Henry Thoreau and reinforced by his Quaker friends in South Africa. It underpinned the idea of 'non-resistance', meaning the renunciation of all opposition by force, when faced with evil, injustices and oppression. Gandhi called this 'passive resistance' even as he modified his strategy, and coined a new term, *satyāgraha*, which, he said, better reflected the Indian basis of this technique. What this implies is that Gandhi, no longer content with simply 'turning the other cheek' or just withholding taxes, obligations, or advocating 'go slow', sought a method by which to bring the adversary to (a) confront the situation and, as it were, meet eye-to-eye on the issue in dispute, and b) redress the evil or wrong without coercing or inflicting injury or violence onto the other party.

In developing this method, what Gandhi does, in effect, is to combine three cardinal notions that had long currency in Hindu, Jaina and Buddhist ethics.. And these notions or concepts are, *satya, ahiṃsā,* and *tapasya.*

The last of these came up in our discussion of the practice of austerities (*tapas*), aligned with asceticism and Jaina practical ethics. For Gandhi, this concept provides a setting for the cultivation of courage, fortitude, stamina and, most importantly, disinterestedness (here invoking the *Gītā*), necessary for the successful deployment of the ensuing technique. While *satya*, as we saw, has to do with 'truth', but truth in the three senses of being truthful, the truth of knowledge and the truth of being or reality. Its original sense is of course derived from *sat*, which means the 'IS' of existence, the really existent truth; whether this is identified with Non-being, Brahman, *Nirvāṇa*, or God is a matter for philosophy to determine. For Gandhi *Truth* is God, by which he meant we should continue to strive for truth beyond all human conception.

On a practical level, *satya* means *truth as action*, or *satyāgraha*, which suggests the idea of 'seizing' or 'holding firmly to a good cause'; thus *satyāgraha* is a categorical attitude or 'force' to which one holds firmly, grasps and hangs in there until truth triumphs in the situation. And this truth-force, he argues, must meet the needs of the social being, or of society at large beyond the individual's selfish end.[9]

Now, there is in the idea of *satyāgraha* all the connotations of a *force*, or exertion, of pushing oneself, or doggedly putting one's foot down, and so on. The force could be a subtly coercive one, or an overtly injurious or violent one, and this is where Gandhi found the Jaina precept of *ahiṃsā* or 'not causing injury or harm to another being' to be most instructive. Of course, we should not overlook the Buddhist emphasis on just the same precept. Gandhi acknowledges as much and uses this negative precept to qualify *satyāgraha* so that no hurt or harm should arise. But

---

9 Gandhi, *Harijan*, 1939, in *The Selected Works of Mahatma Gandhi*, Ahmedabad, Navajivan Publishing House, 1968, vol VI, pp. 171f.

he does more: Gandhi transforms *ahiṃsā* into a dynamic condition for a stratagem that does not stop until the goal of the action is achieved. In other words, far from a passive 'do not' injunction, *ahiṃsā*, when intertwined with *satyāgraha*, becomes a positive mode of action that raises the *intent* of this injunction to a much higher ethical level: it seeks to bring about what is *right* in the situation at hand. Further, the interests of the other is not compromised, for the activist would rather suffer injury or violence on herself than have it inflicted on the other, and compassion or 'love' as Gandhi calls it, as well as utter humanity or humility must accompany the act. And this Gandhi believes can be universalized to form a principle of disinterested non-violent action.

This principle is then put to use in social and political action, in civil disobedience movements, in non-violent freedom and rights struggles, some of which have achieved remarkable results. One can argue as to whether the application of this principle in some instances will or will not entail coercion, and whether this would nullify the principle; or whether the inadvertent violence unleashed in the process defeats the purpose all together. The consensus of those who have been influenced by this principle, such as Martin Luther King, Jr., in leading the struggle for Black Rights in North America, is that the purpose is never defeated. This will perhaps go down as a most significant development in Indian ethics in the 20th century.

Purushottama Bilimoria

Chapter 15

Hindu Theory of Tolerance

Bhikhu Parekh

Hindus place high value on moral and cultural pluralism, and claim not only to tolerate but also to respect and cherish different ways of thought and life. Although their historical record is good and in some respects better than that of most other societies, it has its dark passages and is not as honourable as they imagine. In this chapter I critically examine the philosophical foundations of Hindu pluralism, showing how they foster both tolerance and intolerance, contain an internal tension, and need to be revised. Since the term 'Hindu' is a subject of dispute, I begin with a brief discussion of what I take it to mean and refer to. I then analyze the logical structure of the Hindu theory and practice of tolerance and assess its strengths and weaknesses.

Grounds of Tolerance

The term 'Hindu' originally referred to the people living to the East of the river Indus, and included the different communities that lived there. It was largely a geographical expression and had no cultural or religious content.

Over several centuries these communities interacted, fought, and imposed or borrowed each other's gods, goddesses, beliefs, rituals, and practices, leading to considerable fusion and convergence at several levels.[1] They also threw up great cultural and religious leaders, who sought to systematize the vast array of Hindu beliefs and practices, introduced several new ideas of their own, and propagated and popularized them. As a result of both these processes, Hindus began to share a broad structure of beliefs and practices, which either replaced or accommodated the existing ones. The emerging consensus was not uniformly shared by all Hindus. Different groups accepted different parts of it and integrated these into their traditional ways of thought and life in different ways.[2]

This broadly but loosely and unevenly shared body of beliefs and practices provided a common vocabulary and basis of interaction between different communities, paved the way for yet greater convergence, and over time gave rise to a recognizably Hindu identity with a more or less all India reach. Since the civilizational heritage was large

1 John Keay, *India: A History*, London: HarperCollins, 2000, pp. 57-8.

2 For a good discussion, see Romila Thapar, *A History of India* (London: Penguin Books, 1990), vol. 1, chs 2 and 3.

and eclectic, different Hindus could and did make different choices of rituals, gods, goddesses, etc., but they were all alike participants in a common civilization and just as Hindu as the next man or woman. The Hindu identity was therefore inherently plural. Since new gods, goddesses, rituals, gurus and religious texts kept appearing, and since the Hindus had no organized church or a similar central institution to monitor and screen out some of them, the content and boundaries of their civilization were never fixed. Their identity was also therefore porous and open.

The emergence of a common civilizational identity gave the term 'Hindu' a new meaning. Hitherto the term had only a geographical meaning, and referred to all those who lived on Indian soil. It now referred to people participating in and owing allegiance to a common civilization. Not all Hindus in the territorial sense were Hindus in the civilizational sense. Although the tribal communities could not altogether escape the influence of Hindu civilization, the influence in many cases was rather shallow, raising the hitherto unresolved question whether they should count as Hindus. Even the civilizational sense of the term was not without its difficulties. Since it encompassed religious, social, and other areas of life, the question remained whether those should count as Hindus who shared its religion but not its social ideas and structure, or did the opposite, or were atheists. While the debate between the territorial, civilizational, social, religious and ethnic definitions of the Hindu remains unresolved, and has been given a dangerous twist in recent years by the Sangh Parivar, most Hindus tend to opt for the capacious civilizational self-definition. Anyone whose basic beliefs, practices and way of life are derived from the Hindu civilization and who defines himself as one is a Hindu.

In the light of our discussion the term 'Hinduism' is deeply misleading and even meaningless. Hinduism refers to a religion, whereas what Hindus share in common is a civilization of which religion is a part. Hinduism implies that all Hindus share or are expected to share a common body of beliefs and practices, and that is clearly not the case. No single belief is common to all Hindus, some of whom are even atheists. Although Hindus subscribe to the caste system, it is not constitutive of Hindu identity. It is a late development in the history of Hindu society; Hindu renunciates have no caste; and even if the caste system were to disappear altogether, as it is increasingly doing, Hindus would not cease to be Hindus.

Several general beliefs are central to Hindu identity and have played and continue to play an important part in Hindu thought and practice.[3] Although not all Hindus share them, most do.

First, *primacy of conduct*. For Hindus, the ethical quality of life rather than a body of beliefs is at the heart of religion, and matters most. Beliefs are not important in themselves but only insofar as they affect one's ability to lead the good life. Hindus take a largely pragmatic view of beliefs and stress their moral effects rather

3 For an accessible account of classical Hindu religious thought, see R.C. Zaehner, *Hinduism*, New York: Oxford University Press, 1966. For an equally accessible account of modern Hindu thought, see Glyn Richards (ed.), *A Source-Book of Modern Hinduism*, Surrey: Curzon, 1985.

than cognitive validity. A Hindu therefore enjoys a considerable freedom of religious belief, and may promiscuously combine those drawn from different Hindu sects and even non-Hindu religions so long as they lead to a good life.

Second, *a dhārmic view of morality*. The ethically acceptable life is one lived according to *dharma* or a set of moral principles and duties. *Dharma* is divided into two types: *sādharaṇadharma* or universally binding principles or duties such as telling the truth, non-injury to other living beings, non-stealing, purity, freedom from envy, and control of passions, and *varṇāśramadharma* or the duties pertaining to one's caste and stage in life. The former *dharma* is moral in nature, the latter social. Each caste has its own appropriate moral life, which is binding on its members.

Third, *individual uniqueness*. For Hindus, every human being is the ultimate architect of his life and must work out his salvation himself. Salvation is not a gift or an act of grace, but a personal achievement based on one's *karma* or deeds. While sharing the *ātman* (soul) with others, each individual has a distinct self consisting of a unique set of psychological and moral dispositions (*svabhāva*), which is a product of his *karma* in his previous life and which he can and should improve upon in this one. Every human being goes through a cycle of births in the course of a journey all his own, and builds up a distinct personality or self. Although they all have the same destination, namely liberation from the cycle of rebirth, their paths and requirements vary.

Fourth, *religious pluralism*. The ultimate reality, called *Brahman*, *Īśvara*, God, Allāh, or anything else, is infinite and cannot by definition be grasped in its totality by the finite human mind. Human beings are also socially situated and have different individual hopes, fears, temperaments and needs, and necessarily conceive the ultimate reality from their particular standpoints. All religions therefore grasp some aspects of it and miss out others. Like the blind men trying to imagine the size and shape of the elephant on the basis of one particular part of it, each both partially correct and mistaken, different religions represent different and inherently partial visions of the ultimate reality and contain both truth and error.[4] Even though God reveals himself in history, He reveals Himself differently to different societies and epochs depending on their needs. Although the basic moral principles of all religions are the same, the emphasis placed on them and the revealed aspects and attributes of the divine are different. Divine self-revelation is a continuous process, and even as God revealed Himself on different occasions in the past, He will continue to do so in the future. No religion therefore provides or can provide the final and definitive knowledge of God.

For Hindus, religions are so many different ways of understanding and realizing God. As one of the Vedic maxims asserts, 'Truth or Reality is one, though sages call it by different names'.[5] In the *Bhagvadgītā*, Krishna says that 'whoever comes to me through whatever route, I reach out to him', and that 'all paths in the end lead

4 This is an influential and frequently invoked metaphor in Hindu thought. It seems to be Jaina in origin.

5 *Ekam sat viprā bahudhā vadanti.*

to me'.[6] Although they define them differently, all religions centre on a vision of transcendence, a deep yearning for release from the mortal world, purity of the soul, prayer for guidance, ethical conduct, and so on. If sincerely followed, they all lead to salvation. This raises the question whether some religions may not be wholly misguided or unworthy of respect. The Hindu response is ambiguous. Some rule out this possibility. Some others hold that every religion has a self-correcting mechanism and that a wholly misguided one is bound eventually to collapse under the weight of its errors and false promises. Most, however, admit the possibility of a false or misguided religion, and argue that a religion that violates *sādharaṇadharma* or universal moral values, and enjoins murder, deception, lying, and so on is inherently suspect. In their view certain values are so central to any conception of the good life that they set limits to what constitutes a religion or one worthy of respect.

Religious pluralism is interpreted by Hindu thinkers in two related ways. Some take it to mean that since each religion is sufficient for salvific purposes and is generally best suited to its adherents, they may, even perhaps should, stick to it. Others argue that since no religion is perfect, its adherents may freely borrow what they find attractive in others. In either case Hindus see no need for conversion or abandoning one's religion in favour of another. Conversion makes sense only if one's religion is wholly false, and that is not the case, or if it disallows borrowing from another, which is not the case with the Hindus. Hindus therefore strongly disapprove of one of them converting to, or being induced to convert to, another religion. And they have themselves no interest in converting the followers of other religions. They argue that other religions should follow their lead and allow their followers the freedom to borrow freely what they like in another religion, rather than confront them with the extreme choices of either feeling trapped within their religion or rejecting it altogether.

These four beliefs form the basis of the Hindu theory and practice of tolerance. Since religion is concerned with the quality of life and not subscription to particular dogmas, Hindus argue that all theological disputes and quarrels about religious beliefs are pointless.[7] The *dhārmic* view of morality implies that different individuals should lead different forms of life depending on their caste, psychological make up, etc., and that inducing or coercing them to do otherwise both violates their moral integrity and damages their well-being. The principle of individual uniqueness implies that no religion suits all equally, that the idea of a single universal religion is fundamentally flawed, that each religion should allow its adherents sufficient freedom to adopt its doctrines and practices to their unique spiritual needs, and that we should encourage not only tolerance *of* other religions but also *in* each of them. Finally, religious pluralism implies that since all religions lead to the same

6 *Gītā*, IV.11; IX.22.

7 Al-Biruni, an eleventh-century traveller to India, commented on the Hindus: 'On the whole there is very little disputing about theological topics among themselves…; they will never stake their soul and body or their property on religious controversy.' Cited in Zaehner (op cit), p. 4.

destination, mean much to their members, and contain both truth and error, they deserve equal respect. For Hindus mere toleration is not enough. Toleration implies disapproval of other religions accompanied by a willingness to put up with them. It is doubly mistaken because it uses one's own religion to judge others and refuses to engage in a dialogue with and learn from them.

Since the four central Hindu beliefs justify tolerance on different but closely related grounds, they rule out intolerance for related but different reasons. The centrality of moral conduct means that intolerance is pointless and a waste of energy. The *dhārmic* view of life makes it immoral. The principle of uniqueness renders it both useless and immoral, the former because no individual can benefit from a religion unsuited to him, the latter because it violates his moral and spiritual integrity. Since no religion is perfect and absolutely superior to another, religious pluralism undermines the very basis or rationale of intolerance.

Critical Assessment

The Hindu theory of tolerance approaches the question of tolerance from an angle very different to that of most of its European counterparts, and has its obvious strengths and limitations. Although it does not reduce religion to morality, it takes the latter to be central to religion. Since religious beliefs have only an instrumental value, quarrels about them are unnecessary. If an individual can lead the good life by holding one set of beliefs rather than another, he is left free to subscribe to them. This partly explains why the Hindu religious tradition has generally been able to live with vast and deep doctrinal differences and avoid sectarian quarrels. Since it expects each individual and social group to lead their own appropriate way of life, it places pluralism at the centre of morality, and avoids the all too familiar monistic disputes about which way of life is the best and can be imposed on others. Its tolerance, further, is not based on epistemological scepticism in a way that Locke's and Bayle's is. It does not hold that we do not know the truth about the ultimate reality but rather that different individuals, sects and religions capture different aspects of it, and that none can claim to be in possession of the whole truth. Such epistemological pluralism breeds humility and creates a climate of mutual respect and dialogue. The principle of individual uniqueness places stringent limits on what can be done to an individual. Her salvation is her responsibility, her spiritual and psychological needs are different from those of others, and she must work out her salvation at her own pace and in her own way. Any form of coercion is therefore not only immoral but also bound to fail. This partly explains why Hindu sects did not generally compete for followers, and even when they did, they left each individual fully free to decide for himself.

While the Hindu theory of tolerance has these and other strengths, which at least partly explain the considerable toleration of the Hindu society, it also has its weaknesses, which partly account for the Hindu society's intolerance and periods of interreligious violence. Its weaknesses arise from the twofold fact that the grounds on which it rests are not all mutually consistent, and that each of them is not as unproblematic and benign as its advocates suggest.

While the Hindu theory allows considerable freedom in matters of belief, it tends to be intolerant in relation to the way individuals lead their lives. Hindus are expected to follow the *dharma* of their caste on pain of social ostracism and, under traditional Hindu kingdoms, legal sanctions. As the *Gītā* says, 'it is better to die doing one's *dharma* than to adopt that of another'.[8] This does not mean that individuals can never get out of their castes. They can and, contrary to the orientalist myth, have done so for centuries. One can renounce the world and render oneself casteless; groups of individuals can set up a caste of their own and decide upon its *dharma*; or isolated individuals or whole castes can raise their status by emulating the rituals and practices of higher castes. Since the first involves renouncing the social world altogether, few are either inclined that way or prepared to pay the price. The second is not much help in the long run because the new caste imposes its own *dharma*. The third mode of escape has more or less the same outcome, for the *dharma* of the higher caste exercises the same constraints as those of one's own. It is therefore hardly surprising that despite some degree of social mobility, most Hindus remain trapped within the castes of their birth.

The combination of extensive freedom of religious belief and social conformity creates a paradox which the Hindu theory of tolerance is unable to resolve. The Hindu may hold whatever beliefs he likes as long as he observes his caste duties. This raises the question whether he may adopt beliefs that involve rejecting the caste system altogether while remaining a Hindu. The Hindu theory has three answers. It either restricts his freedom of beliefs, or allows him to hold egalitarian beliefs on condition that he does not act on them, or it allows him to live by these beliefs. The first undermines or at least severely limits its claim to tolerance; the second creates a hiatus between beliefs and practices and violates the individual's moral integrity; the third is too costly because an isolated individual who leaves his caste is cut off from his community and has nowhere to go. Even if the whole caste embraces egalitarian beliefs as has happened sometimes, it has little practical value because the higher castes, against whom the equality is asserted, rarely concede the claim.

The Hindu theory of tolerance also suffers from what Max Weber calls 'absolute relativization' and obsession with hierarchy.[9] It is closely bound up with an extensive system of moral and cultural pluralism. For Hindus difference is the central feature of human life as well as its organizing principle. Every society is different; within each, castes and social groups are all different; and ultimately all individuals too are unique and different. Since they are all different in their nature and modes of being, different forms of life are appropriate to them. As we saw, every caste and stage of life has its own appropriate *dharma*. Every society too has its distinct traditions and ethos, and hence only a particular way of life is appropriate to it. The pluralism is also extended

8 *svadharme nidhanaṃ śreyaḥ paradharmo bhayāvahaḥ*. *Gītā* III.35.

9 See H.H. Gerth and C. Wright Mills (eds), *From Max Weber*, New York: Oxford University Press, 1948, pp. 149f.

to different spheres of life, such as the political, the economic, the religious, and the artistic. Each of them has its appropriate logic, none can be reduced to another, and their imperatives cannot all be harmonized. Statecraft, for example, is concerned to maintain order, safeguard national territory, promote national prosperity, and so on, and involves a kind of morality that is irrelevant to and even unacceptable in personal or social life. In all these and other cases, differences are relativized, tied to particular individuals, groups and spheres of life, and domesticated within an inviolable framework.

This form of pluralism has its virtues. Since it places individuals at the centre of a way of life and judges the latter in terms of what suits them, it rules out the very idea of an objectively best or only truly human way of life to which all can be required to conform. It encourages respect for the integrity of different ways of life and nurtures a pluralistic ethos. Hindu pluralism also alerts us to the fact that we often have to follow different even contradictory principles in different areas of life, and that we must accept and learn to live with the inherent ambiguities and incoherences of human life. There is no single overall rational order in life; rather the latter is made up of and sustained by overlapping, competing and conflicting forms of order in different spheres. Human choices are therefore inescapable, and they are necessarily contingent. Hindu religious texts and especially the epics explore in great detail the tensions that this creates, the inevitable dissonance and ambivalence of life, and the disasters that strike individuals and societies when they avoid choices or expect a non-existent overall rational and moral order to underwrite them.[10]

Relativized pluralism, however, also has its problems. Since every sphere and way of life is separated and invested with its own appropriate logic and morality, it becomes difficult to take an overall view of society and order the latter according to a wider vision of the good life. This may partly explain why utopian thought, a bold and imaginative reconstruction of society inspired by a will to change the world, is largely absent in Hindu thought. Relativized pluralism also freezes society. Different individuals lead different ways of life because these are appropriate to their temperament, moral capacities, stage of life or position in society. While this protects them against others' interferences and ensures their freedom and autonomy, it also severely restricts their choices, discourages them from changing or revolting against their society, and leads to the toleration of often intolerable constraints and practices.

Although the pluralism underpinning the Hindu theory of tolerance is relativized, it is not at all relativist in nature. This is so because it is accompanied by certain general principles which allow it to grade different forms of life and establish a hierarchy among them. The fact that different ways of life are appropriate for different individuals and social groups and deserve equal respect does not mean that they are equally good objectively or attain equal moral and spiritual excellence.

---

10 For a sensitive discussion of Weber, see Pratap Bhanu Mehta, 'The Ethical Irrationality of the World: Weber and Hindu Ethics', *Critical Horizons*, **2**(2), 2001 and chapter 17 in this volume. *Contra* Matilal in his chapter.

A *śūdra*'s way of life is as worthy *for him* as a Brahmin's is *for him*. However that does not detract from the fact that the latter attains higher excellence and is morally superior. Although a thoroughly bad Brahmin's life is inferior to that of the best *śūdra* because the latter attains at least some excellence whereas the former attains none, a good Brahmin's life is superior to that of a good *śūdra*. The same hierarchy applies to human activities. Pursuit of wealth is an autonomous and worthy activity, but military activity, statecraft and governing a country are higher in worth; and philosophical and religious activities are the highest and most worthy. The caste hierarchy is based on the hierarchy of human activities, those castes being higher who traditionally engage in higher activities.

The hierarchical principle extends to forms of religious life as well. Although they are all equally legitimate, they are not all equally worthy. As the *Gītā* says, those of inferior intelligence (*alpamedhasān*) who worship inferior gods receive inferior spiritual rewards.[11] Those who discharge their *dharma* conscientiously but remain attached to the fruits of their actions do accumulate spiritual merit, but only enough to get them a better birth in the next life and not a permanent release from the cycle of births or *mokṣa*. Again, though there are different wayṣ to attain *mokṣa* such as *jñānayoga*, *karmayoga* and *bhaktiyoga*, the first is generally considered the highest and the most reliable.

Thanks to the hierarchical gradation of human activities, ways of life, etc., Hindu pluralism grants them equal validity but not equal worth, and hence equal respect but not equal esteem. The objectively higher or worthier forms of life are deemed to be beyond the reach of those lacking the requisite capacity. For the latter lower ways of life alone are appropriate and, since these fulfil them and help them realize their potential, they should be respected. The principle of individual uniqueness and the *dhārmic* view of life do, of course, ensure that the worthy ways of life are not imposed on others, but they do not undermine the hierarchy of worth. Hindu pluralism thus remains inegalitarian and is eviscerated of its radical potential. Whenever it has challenged the hierarchy as in the case of the popular *bhakti* movement or more recently and powerfully under the leadership of Gandhi, and asserted either the equal worth of all human activities and ways of life or the equal capacity of all to lead the highest ways of life, it has provoked strong opposition.

As we saw, Hindus hold that religions represent so many different ways of understanding and realizing God, that they all contain both truth and error, that none is perfect, and that they all deserve equal respect.[12] This religious pluralism is an important part of Hindu ways of thought and life, and explains the considerable

---

11 *Gītā*, VII.23; XI.25; III.25 and 26.

12 The Hindu pluralist tradition has had many powerful advocates, the more recent and the most influential being Swami Vivekananda and Mahatma Gandhi. For Vivekananda, pluralism represents India's 'greatest religious contribution' to the world. It has been the 'backbone of our national existence' and has made India 'the glorious land of religious toleration'. *Collected Works*, Calcutta: Advaita Ashram, 1989, vol. III, pp. 186f. God's book is 'not finished' and there is 'a continuous revelation'; ibid., vol. II, p. 372. Stressing the value of dialogue and rejecting conversion, he says, each individual 'must assimilate the spirit of

tolerance Hindus have shown over the centuries to other religions. Religious persecution is relatively rare in Indian history. Jews, who were persecuted or discriminated against in many parts of the world, have lived in India in peace since at least the eleventh century, and have enjoyed official patronage and financial support and even a self-governing district of their own in the Hindu kingdom of Cochin.[13] Christians, Muslims and Zoroastrians began to arrive in India from the fifth, ninth and tenth centuries respectively. They were invariably well received and given full freedom of religious belief and practice. Hindus have interacted with these and other religious communities, borrowed some of their beliefs and practices, and respected their prophets. In some parts of India, several Hindu communities have both Hindu and non-Hindu customs for different spheres of life, and see nothing wrong in describing themselves as both Hindu and Muslim ('Muslim Hindus') or Hindu and Christian ('Christian Hindus'). In the 1911 census, over 200,000 Indians identified themselves as 'Mohammedan Hindus'. Mole-Salam Girasia Rajputs traditionally had two names for every member of the community, one Hindu and one Muslim. Some Hindu temples have shrines of both a Hindu god or goddess and a Muslim saint. The Hindus widely worship Sai Baba, who was a Muslim saint. India perhaps is one of the very few countries in which new movements have constantly sprung up seeking to bring together followers of different religions, synthesizing their doctrines, and creating new syncretic religions based on old ones.

While Hindu religious pluralism has its obvious strengths, it also has its limitations arising largely out of the way in which it is grounded. Hindus are convinced that pluralism is a true doctrine. For them no religion can exhaust the plenitude of the infinite, all religions contain important insights, and being spiritually unique different individuals have different religious and spiritual needs. In their view their religion recognizes and respects these fundamental truths, and was indeed the first to discover them. By contrast other religions ignore these truths. They claim perfection and refuse to extend equal respect to others. They also insist on credal conformity, and deny their adherents the freedom to redefine their central doctrines to suit their needs and to borrow from other religions. In this important respect Hindus think that other religions are deeply mistaken. Since religious pluralism is true, a pluralist religion is deemed to be superior to the monist. While some Hindus insist that their religion is therefore the best and absolutely superior to others, most argue that it is superior in this respect but not in others where other religions have advantages over it. Some are more egalitarian than it (Islam) or more committed to the service of fellow-humans (Christianity). In either case many Hindu thinkers use their religious

---

others and yet preserve his individuality and grow according to his own law of growth'. vol. I, p. 22.

13 The Rāja of Kadungalore gave Joseph Rabban and his descendents the district of Arhuvanam, the title of a 'prince', and the right to collect taxes and enjoy all the decorations, trappings and privileges of his office. The relevant copper plates survive in the Cochin synagogue. Some scholars trace them to the eleventh century. The oral tradition among the Cochin Jews traces them to the fourth.

pluralism to judge and grade other religions, and turn it into a new principle of hierarchy. The more pluralist a religion, that is, the more it accepts others as its equal and the more it cherishes its internal diversity, the higher it is taken to be. Here as elsewhere, the principle of hierarchy distorts and emasculates the egalitarian thrust of the Hindu pluralist insights.

Hindus have great difficulty making sense of and coming to terms with perfection-claiming and exclusive religions, which strike them as self-righteous, arrogant and even blasphemous. While they are prepared peacefully to coexist with them as they have done over the centuries even when they had the power to discourage or suppress them, they are implacably hostile to those that proselytize and engage in missionary activities. In their view such religions are not content to claim perfection and take a dim view of other religions; they actively seek to destroy the latter by mocking, ridiculing and attacking them and weaning away their followers.[14]

Hindu hostility to them has philosophical, moral and political roots. Philosophically they simply cannot understand how any religion can ever be justified in claiming to offer the final, exhaustive and definitive knowledge of the infinite and wanting to rid the world of all its rivals. Morally Hindus argue that religions that would not tolerate others do not themselves deserve to be tolerated. Their argument is broadly similar to the liberal argument about not tolerating the intolerant. Politically Hindus think that since they do not themselves proselytize, allowing others to do so puts them at a disadvantage. More importantly, since their lower castes have often been all too willing to embrace egalitarian religions, the motive of self-preservation also plays a part.

Historically speaking Hindus encountered proselytizing religions at three different periods in their history, and each provoked much resentment and, when Hindus had the power, considerable intolerance. The rise of Buddhism was the first of these. Buddhism was a reaction against the beliefs, practices and rituals of the Brāhmaṇic orthodoxy, and unlike Jainism it was concerned not just to exist alongside but to challenge it and win over its followers. Not surprisingly, it provoked a strong opposition and even some disorder, particularly when it received royal support from Aśoka. This is why Aśoka's edicts had to urge his subjects to 'hear one another's principles', to 'honour another man's sect', and not to fight in the name of religion.[15] Once the Hindu kings replaced Aśoka's Maurya dynasty, Hindu leaders took advantage of the royal patronage, harassed the Buddhists, and even destroyed some of their monasteries.

Islam provoked a similar opposition, but this time Hindus were in no position to retaliate. There were occasional acts of disorder when Muslim rulers and soldiers encouraged proselytization. Over time they learned to leave the Hindus alone, and some of them even sought to build interreligious bridges. The British learned from the

---

14 In a recent attack on missionaries by the followers of Vishva Hindu Parishad, the symbol of an axe demolishing a cross had a caption, which read: 'Father, do not forgive them for they know what they do'. Quoted in *Seminar*, May, 2002, p. 24.

15 See Thapar, vol. I, p. 87; Keay, pp. 88f.

Muslim experience, and for decades banned Christian missionary activity. When the latter resumed, it was relatively low key, enjoyed no official patronage, and largely relied on voluntary conversions. Even then the Hindus remained deeply uneasy about the missionaries, bitterly complained against their activities, and occasionally resorted to force to drive them away. Even someone as deeply sympathetic to Christianity as Mahatma Gandhi repeatedly added his voice to the protest.

Hindu pluralism then takes a low view of perfection-claiming, and is actively antipathetic to and even intolerant of proselytizing religions. This raises the question whether the pluralism is philosophically well-founded and represents, as the Hindus claim, a fundamental self-evident truth about religion. The Hindu pluralism asserts that all religions are basically concerned with the same thing, have the same goal, worship the same God, take the same view of salvation, eventually lead to it, and so on. This is too simplistic and even reductionist, and ignores the deep differences between religions. Different religions entertain not only different conceptions but also different concepts of God, and some even dispense with the concept altogether. *Brahman*, the qualityless cosmic consciousness of the Advaitins and free of all human emotions including love and mercy, has little in common with the quasi-anthropomorphic conceptions of God common to Hindu dualists and the three Semitic religions, and the latter again differ greatly in their conceptualizations of God. The Buddhists are agnostics, and the Jainas atheists. Different religions, again, differ greatly in the way they relate God and the universe, define human life and destiny, imagine salvation, and the paths to it. The dominant Hindu idea of *mokṣa* has little in common with the popular Hindu and the Christian and Islamic views of it or even the Buddhist notion of *nirvāṇa*. The Hindu, Buddhist and Jain views of salvation have little room for the idea of divine grace which plays such an important part in Christian thought. Although all religions do share some moral principles in common, they differ in several others, and define and prioritize the former very differently. Given these and other deep differences, it makes little sense to say that all religions are so many different paths to an identical destination and equally valid.

Hindu pluralism also holds that no religion is perfect, free from error, or the last word on the divine will. Many religions especially Christianity and Islam deny this. They claim not only to be the final and definitive divine self-revelations, but also to have a moral and religious duty to propagate their truths and save the rest of humankind from eternal damnation. It is not easy to show how their claims can be refuted.[16] It would not do to say that no religion is or can be perfect, etc., for they would rejoin that they do not accept this view, that God has told them otherwise, and that they are not based on fallible human conceptualizations as Hindus imagine but on God's own self-revelation. If pressed, some of their followers might concede that their religion is not free from errors, but would insist that these do not touch their central truths or that they contain less errors and imperfections than other religions.

---

16 See Stuart Elkman, 'Religious Plurality and Swami Vivekananda', and Wilhelm Halfbass's response in Eli Franco and Kevin Preisendanz (eds), *Beyond Orientalism* Amsterdam: Rodopi, 1997.

They would also question the Hindu objections to proselytization, arguing that it is an act of love and that it would be grossly immoral of them not to do all they can to bring their salvific truths to the attention of outsiders. They would agree that they should not use force, but would insist that they should do everything short of it to encourage conversions.

Hindu thinkers are not without an answer. They could rejoin that the claim that a particular religion represents the fullest revelation of the divine will is ultimately based on faith and has no validity for outsiders. Since such claims are also made by others, even the most devout followers should temper their claim with a measure of self-doubt or at least humility and open-mindedness. Hindu thinkers could also argue that those making perfectionist and exclusivist claims cannot explain why God reveals himself differently to different religions and whether we should not more plausibly take this to imply religious pluralism. In their view a close study of religions shows that each has insights missing or underdeveloped in others, and that each may therefore rightly claim superiority in those respects. Since no religion can therefore claim absolute or even relative overall superiority over others, each should accept others as equal partners in a mutually beneficial dialogue. As for proselytization, Hindu thinkers would argue that while all religions may, indeed should, bring their central truths to the attention of others, they should leave it to the latter to respond to them as they please, and should not seek to influence their judgment by fears, inducements, and subtle forms of coercion.

Missionary religions would challenge these arguments, and Hindu pluralists would rejoin with an appropriate response.[17] The debate is inherently inconclusive for there is no way of refuting transcendentally accredited missionary claims by empirical evidence or rational arguments. On balance religious pluralism has more to be said for it, though on the same grounds as those central to Hindu thought. Religions are profoundly different and incommensurable. They are not all paths to the same destination, nor all equally valid. However it is precisely because they are different and incommensurable that their claim to absolute superiority over others not only cannot be established in a noncircular manner but is also logically incoherent. Furthermore since they are different, each can profit from a dialogue with others as is shown by the historical evidence relating to such limited interreligious dialogues as have taken place. And obviously there can be no dialogue without mutual respect and conversational equality. Such a pluralist attitude also has the further advantage of avoiding spiritual and physical violence, and encouraging each religion to take a relaxed and liberal attitude to internal dissent and disagreement and interreligious borrowing.

To conclude, the Hindu theory of tolerance contains both profound insights and serious errors. It is right to stress the moral rather than the credal aspect of religion, and to make the ethical quality of life rather than doctrinal beliefs the centre of

17 For a valuable discussion, see Joseph Prabhu (ed.), *The Intercultural challenges of Raimon Panikkar*, New York: Orbis Books, 1996. The editor's introduction and chapters. 2, 4 and 14 are particularly interesting.

religious life, but wrong to separate the two so neatly. It is right to stress individual uniqueness, but wrong to account for it in terms of the quasi-deterministic doctrine of *karma*. Its *dhārmic* view of life is deeply problematic because it leads to a static and hierarchical view of moral and social life and domesticates differences by segregating and relativizing them. Although the relativization of a way of life or *dharma* is agent-sensitive, judges the latter in terms of its relevance to individuals constituted in certain ways, and possesses these and other virtues, it becomes deeply problematic when it is absolutized, static and defined by outsiders rather than the agent himself. Hindu religious pluralism is persuasive, but it is best defended by grounding it not in a reductionist and homogenizing account of religions but in a full recognition of their irreducible diversity and mutually stimulating differences. In short, the Hindu theory of moral, cultural and religious pluralism needs to be purged of hierarchy, absolute and static relativization and reductionism if it is to respect diversity and realize its liberating potential. There is as yet no sign that this task is being undertaken with the requisite degree of seriousness. Modern India has rightly chosen to reject social hierarchy in favour of a plural and egalitarian society. Unless the Hindu theory is radically revised along the lines I have suggested, its hierarchically structured resources for tolerance would prove grossly inadequate to the new reality, and we would continue to witness dark periods of intolerance and brutality of the kind that recently scarred Gujarat.[18]

18 For a further discussion, see my 'Making sense of Gujarat', *Seminar*, May, 2000.

Chapter 16

Action Oriented Morality in Hinduism

Christopher Key Chapple

In discussing the Hindu tradition of morality, one is automatically confronted with an interesting problematic. Hinduism is a rich tapestry of many traditions: some theistic, others not; some life-affirming, others ascetic. In this chapter, I will attempt to survey some of the ethical vectors of Indian tradition as can best be reconstructed from textual and historical evidence, and then show how these themes have come to be understood in the modern era.

Most discussion of Hindu thought begins with the *ṚgVeda* and appropriately so: an often-used litmus test to ascertain whether a school of thought is authentically Hindu is whether it refers to the Vedas, even if in negative terms, as in the case of *Sāṃkhya Kārikā*. However, several cornerstone ideas of Hinduism do not have their origins in the Vedas, at least in any systemic fashion. These largely absent elements include notions of karma, rebirth, yoga and nonviolence, which in the later tradition became pivotal in the development of Hindu ethics, particularly as known to the West through the work of Ramakrishna, Mahatma Gandhi and others. These apparently have their origins in the so-called Śrāmaṇic traditions of India, which, according to some scholars predate the Brāhmaṇical traditions and perhaps are attributable to the civilizations of Mohenjodaro and Harappa.[1] In order to understand social ethics in the later traditions, it is important to have a sense of these underpinnings of the broader Indian world view.

Karma and Rebirth

These twin notions are perhaps the most widely known and least understood hallmarks of Indian (and with the expansion of Buddhism, Pan-Asian) traditions. Teachings on karma establish ethical norms; stories of rebirth offer cosmological explanations. As we will see, the former teaches responsibility of one's actions, the latter attributes a perdurance or continuity to action that goes beyond the

1 See Padmanabh S. Jaini, *The Jaina Path of Purification*, 1979, p. 33 and Richard Lannoy, *The Speaking Tree: A Study of Indian Culture and Society*, 1974, p. 10. This view is rejected by Hans-Peter Schmidt, 'The Origin of Ahiṃsā', in *Mèlanges d'indianisme: A là memoire de Louis Renou*, 1968, pp. 625-655 and Doris Srivivasan, 'The So-Called Proto-Śiva Seal from Mohen-Daro: An Iconological Assessment,' *Archives in Asian Art*, 29, 1975-76, pp. 47-58.

boundaries of finite biography. The word karma, as I have explained elsewhere[2] means action. Derivative and additional terms have not come to be seen as identical with the concept karma, such as *saṃskāra*, which refers to the imprint or residue left by a particular action, and *vāsanā*, which seems to refer to indwelling habit patterns. Whether one considers these individually or collectively, one common strand is evident: our actions have repercussions beyond our individual experiences. Action in the present moment plants a seed (*bīja*). This seed can lie dormant for an undetermined period of time; its arising at a later time may prompt occurrences that stem from a forgotten time, but nonetheless provide retribution or reward for an earlier action. In virtually all Indian traditions, karma takes two forms: afflicted (*kliṣṭa*) and unafflicted (*akliṣṭa*). The former causes repeated suffering; the latter allows one to be liberated from repeated sufferings and frustrations (*duḥkha*) of the past. In either case, responsibility for one's actions lies within oneself; as proclaimed in the *Yogāvasiṣṭha*, it is indeed possible to overcome the negative influences of the past through concerted action in the present: 'There are some men who, due to their afflicted desire, have incapacitated themselves to such an extent that they cannot squeeze their fingers together sufficiently enough to hold water, without scattering several drops. On the other hand, there are some who, by efficacious actions, take on the responsibility of seas, mountains, cities and islands, as well as families, for whom even the earth itself would not be too much…Without a doubt, the fault of the past is appeased by the attributes of the present. The aim of this is the destruction of yesterday's faults by today's attributes' (11.4.20; 11.5.12). When viewed existentially, the 'karma' teaching is clearly a call for responsible action within the present moment, aimed at casting off affliction and suffering. The means to achieve this, as discussed below, are ethical in nature and thus also minimize the suffering of others.

In addition to providing a rationale for the performance of moral action, the doctrine of karma also supplied a view of the life process rooted in continuity. Rather than seeing death as finality, early Indian thinkers viewed death as an intermediary stage, with a life (*jīva*) returning through the force of past impressions into a new life form to create yet more activities. This early vision of conservation of energy made it virtually inconceivable that our lives are discrete and relatively insignificant. In both the Jaina and Buddhist traditions, all life forms are tremendously ancient, existing since 'beginingless time'. For the Jains, this means that all life has at one point or another been born within the family of every other life form. The Laṅkāvatāra Sūtra, a Mahāyāna Buddhist text, similarly states that 'in the long course of *saṃsāra*, there is not one among living beings with form who has not been mother, father, brother, sister, son or daughter or some other relative. Being connected with the process of taking birth, one is kin to all wild and domestic animals, birds and beings born from the womb.' The late Brāhmaṇical Hindu tradition, as we will see below, uses a more 'personalistic' approach to the rebirth story. In all three instances, however, a vision

2 Christopher Chapple, *Karma and Creativity*, 1986.

of life is offered that goes beyond one's fixed, apparent biography, placing one's experience as an individual within a much broader continuum.

Yoga

The taking of repeated births is referred to as *saṃsāra*, an aimless, afflicted wandering through one of five or six different realms.[3] The uniqueness of human life is that it provides sufficient incentive in the form of suffering to desire to transcend repeated existence, as well as sufficient time in order to cultivate unafflicted, meditative action that can counteract the deleterious effects of prior action. Throughout Indian traditions, the forms of Yoga were developed for the purpose of putting an end to repeated involvement in the *saṃsāra* or *punarjanma* process. Yoga postures are seemingly depicted in the seals uncovered at Mohenjodaro and Harappa, and it appears to have been common to the Śrāmaṇic groups that gave rise to the Jaina and Buddhist traditions. The *ṚgVeda*, in fact, refers to bearded figures that place themselves outside of societal norms.[4] Later Hindu texts such as the *Śvetaśvatāra Upaniṣad*, the *Bhagavad Gītā*, and the much later *Yoga Sūtra* of Patañjali clearly demonstrate that certain aspects of the Śrāmaṇic tradition had become part of the Hindu tradition.

Whether in its Jain, Buddhist, or Hinduized forms, the goal of Yoga is to bring about a cessation (*nirodha*) of those thought propensities that lead to continued afflicted behaviour. The theological and cosmological bases for the practice of Yoga are diverse. For the Jains, there are said to be millions upon millions of individual, eternal life forms (*jīvas*) that must disentangle themselves from the sticky effects of karma (said to have a physical reality) in order to attain a state of eternal, splendid aloneness (*kevala*), wherein one sees and knows all things yet remain unsullied. For the Buddhists, there is no discussion of individual selves. Reference is made only to the suffering (*duḥkha*), impermanence (*anitya*) and lack of abiding nature (*anātmā*) of things. For the Upaniṣadic Vedāntin, for the one of purified consciousness, all reality is seen as not different from Brāhmaṇ. For the Sāṃkhyan Yogi, life is seen to be composed of unconscious, repeated activity (*prakṛti*) and a mode of disaffected witnessing (*puruṣa*), with the goal being to establish oneself in the latter form, allowing the realm of activity to dissipate itself. Within this variegated theo-cosmological salad, we find a host of seemingly unreconcilable presuppositions; a plurality of identities, no identity, divine identification, and sublime detachment that mirrors divinized status.[5] Yet despite this ideological disharmony (well-recognized and widely debated amongst the respective schools), on the level of praxis there is

3 These 'destinies' vary according to tradition. The Buddhists, for instance, posit six: human, animals, hell beings, titans, gods, demons.

4 *ṚgVeda* X.136.

5 See *Yoga Sūtra* I.23-29 and II.4 for a description of *īśvara praṇidhāna* where one aspires to assume the consciousness of the unfettered deity.

an apparent agreement. All the schools of Indian thought emphasize moral action as an integral part of the path to liberation.

Nonviolence

Nonviolence or *ahiṃsā* is at the core of Indian morality from the aspect of the renouncer traditions. Within Jainism, renunciation was honed to a fine science out of a concern to avoid all forms of violence. Any form of agitated activity was said to impair one's innate consciousness, bliss and energy. In order to free one of this harmful, obscuring stuff, all acts of violence were to be eschewed. Furthermore, all things, including what in non-Jaina eyes are deemed inanimate, were in fact said to possess life force (*jīva*); by impairing the consciousness, energy and bliss of rocks and grass as well as air, water, and fire bodies through acts of violence, karma adheres to one's own *jīva*, preventing the ascent to pure aloneness. Consequently, the Jainas took great care to provide a moral map of the universe, outlining a hierarchy of life forms and then prescribing practice to minimize violence to them.[6]

In order to clarify how life is to be protected, the Jainas outlined four types of violence: intentional, non-intentional, related to profession, and performed out of self-defence. It is hoped that no violence whatsoever need to be committed, and to assist in this endeavour, five specific practices are listed: restraint of mind, control of tongue, carefulness on roads, removing things from roads, and eating in daylight. The first requires that one examine all thoughts to make certain that harm is not intended. The second demands attention to speech. The third and fourth have given rise to communities of Jaina practitioners who always walk with a broom to remove insects from their path, and to a ban on long-distance travel. The last rule was applicable in pre-technological society, when poor illumination in Indian households made it impossible to detect forms of life which may have fallen into one's food. Food consumed by a Jaina must be vegetarian: all Jainas whether monastic or leading a secular life, are expected to subsist on only one-sense beings, hence limiting their diet to vegetables and milk products. Additionally, certain professions are deemed acceptable for the lay community. These include government and farming, which are the least acceptable due to their potential for causing harm; writing, arts and crafts, which are considered slightly less violent; and finally commerce, which is considered the least violent profession of all, provided that the goods traded are not obtained by violent means.

For those who choose the life of a monk or a nun, progressively more stringent limitations designed to minimize violence are imposed. For instance, at an advanced stage of monkhood, one is not allowed to dig in the earth, to avoid hurting the earth; nor to swim or bathe, in order to protect the water; not extinguish fires or light a match, to preserve fire; not to fan oneself, to prevent harm to the air, not to walk on or touch greenery thus cultivating nonviolence to plants. Hence, all areas of life are

6 See Jagmanderlal Jaini, *Outlines of Jainism*, 1916, pp. 7-66.

considered; no act for the serious Jain can be performed without respect given to the vow of *ahiṃsā*.

The Buddhists also advocated respect for life. Their opposition against the Hindu practice of animal sacrifice is illustrated as follows in an allegory found in *Jātaka Tale* 18: 'Once upon a time, a goat was led to a temple and was about to be sacrificed by the presiding Brahmin. Suddenly, that goat let out a laugh and then uttered a moaning cry. The Brahmin, startled by this odd behaviour, asked the goat what was happening. The goat responded as follows: "Sir, I have just remembered the history of what has led up to this event. The reasons I have laughed is that I realized this is the last of 500 births I have suffered as a goat; in my next life I will return again as a human. The reason I have cried out of compassion for you, you see, 500 births ago I was a Brahmin, leading a goat to the sacrifice. After killing the goat, I was condemned to 500 births as a goat. If you kill me, you will suffer the same fate." The Brahmin, visibly shaken; immediately freed the goat, who trotted away. A few minutes later, lightning struck the goat and he was free to become again human. The Brahmin likewise was spared, due to the goat's compassionate intervention.'[7]

Throughout Buddhist history, events have occurred which affirm reverence for life. The emperor Aśoka, who in the third century BC united much of India, converted to Buddhism and established several laws which required kind treatment to animals, in reflection of the Buddhist observance of noninjury to living beings. These include the restriction of meat consumption, the curtailing or hunting, and the establishment of hospitals and roadside watering stations for animals.[8]

Hence, from ancient times in India, there has been an indigenous concern for respecting life. The purpose of this is to minimize one's involvement in the world, with the ultimate intention of using techniques of Yoga to extricate oneself from the cycle of accumulating karma and repeated births.

The Vedic and Brāhmaṇical world views

The entry of Indo-European peoples into the Indian sub-continent brought with it new cultural sensibilities, new gods, and a new social structure. As opposed to the more sedentary peoples of the Indus Valley cities (which apparently were in decline even at the start of the Aryan incursion), the newcomers were wanderers, eventually spreading their lore and language throughout India.

For the first thousand years they were primarily based in the northwest quadrant of India; archeological evidence points to an eastward (and ultimately southward) movement taking place in approximately 500 BC.[9] The goals and activities of these Vedic peoples stand in marked distinction from the glimpses we have seen of the renouncers. The Vedas celebrate full enjoyment of life, including the use of

---

7 Retold from H.T. Francis and E.J. Thomas, *Jātaka Tales*, Selected and Edited with Introduction and Notes, 1916, pp. 20-22.

8 See Amulyachandra Sen, *Aśoka's Edicts*, 1956.

9 See Hyla S. Converse, 'Hinduism,' 1988, pp. 63-64.

inebriating substances such as soma and the consumption of beef. The many gods spoken of in the Vedas have direct parallels with European counterparts and similarly are invoked for purposes of live conquest, knowledge, medicine, magic and more. Additionally, similar to the social structure found in ancient Europe and Persia, a self-conscious sociology was introduced and then adapted to the Indian context. These two aspects of Hinduism will be discussed briefly as providing an alternative model for moral action in India.

The Vedic World View

Max Müller, the noted German Indologist, has referred to the Vedic system as henotheism or kathenotheism[10] in which a deity appropriate to one's immediate needs of success in war, the deity Indra would become the deity to whom sacrifices are presented in order to invoke the power he symbolizes. In modern times this practice is continued, for instance, in the innovation of the goddess Lakṣmī to enhance one's wealth and of the goddess Sarasvatī to increase one's knowledge. Combining the multiple deity structure with an existential interpretation of W. Norman Brown's cosmogonies analysis of the *ṚgVeda*[11], Antonio T. deNicolas has reconstructed a FDIC philosophical methodology. Out of an undifferentiated chaos (*asat*), symbolized by the dragon Vṛta, structure (*sat*) arises. Sacrifice (*yajña*) within this context then allows for a full vision (*dhīḥ*) and flow (*ṛta*) that proceeds from the power involved in the sacrifice. This then gives way to the chaos, and desire once more yields a new sacrificial context. The phenomenological and scientific terminology employed by deNicolas intentionally brings forth worlds that are seen not as competing but as complementary.[12] Although this process as presented in the *ṚgVeda* seemed widely accessible to members of society, the establishment of the Vedic peoples throughout India results in specialization: one group of the Aryan folk came to control this artificial technology and reserved for themselves exclusive access to power, contributing to the full development of a fully stratified caste system.

Caste and Hindu Dharma

The earliest record we have of the caste system in India comes from *ṚgVeda* X.90, wherein the cosmic person, as symbol for the totality of society,[13] is divided into four

10 Max Müller, *The Six Systems of Indian Philosophy*, 1988.

11 See Norman W. Brown, 'The Creation Myth of the ṚgVeda,' *Journal of the American Oriental Society* **62**, 1942, pp. 85-98.

12 Antonio T. deNicolas, *Meditations Through the Ṛg-Veda: Four Dimensional Man*, New York: Nicolas Hays, 1976.

13 Marriott and Inden refer to this Vedic figure as Code Man. Because he carries all the castes within his body (*Brahmāṇas* are in the mouth, *kṣatriyas* his arms, *vaiśyas* his thighs, *śūdras* his feet [*ṚgVeda* X.90], he is seen as symbolizing the underlying unity of Hindu

transactional arenas, corresponding to the various tasks required for the operation of the world. At the top, associated with the head and speech, is the domain of the Brahmin, the teacher and priest. This caste commands the greatest respect and, as specialists in Vedic ritual, Brahmins are essential for the performance of world-maintaining sacrifice. The next group, the kṣatriyas, are identified with the arms and serve as warriors and politicians. The vaiśyas or merchants are associated with the thighs, the workers or *śūdras* with the feet. The use of the human body, which itself is organismic totality, underscores the reciprocity of this social relationship. Without the feet, the head would become disembodied, deprived of food, and incapacitated. Without the protective arms of the warrior, the merchant would be unable to apply his trade. Rather than communicating a closed system wherein one group remains pure of the other, this image betokens a conscious recognition of interdependence amongst groups. The whole is impossible without its parts. Standing alone, the person seen as cosmos could be interpreted as providing a basis for the development of respectful, transactional society wherein each person knowingly and happily contributes through the performance of his or her particular role. This ideal is lauded in the *Bhagavad Gītā* and the recent sociological analyses of Dumont, Mckim Marriott, Ron Inden and others likewise highlight the benefits of this structure.

However, the caste system met an interesting marriage partner in the form of the indigenous rebirth doctrine. The Śramaṇas, as we have seen, had come to view all life as continuous, with humans being the highest birth attainable. With the Brāhmaṇical system, by contrast, humankind itself became hierarchized with some persons being regarded as less than human and others as useful merely in a menial sense. Only the highest three castes were deemed worthy of education and twice-born status, due to their superior action in past lives. This system proved very effective for social regulation. With the threat of a lower human or animal birth if one strays from one's dharma, there is a little incentive to go awry.[14]As Norvin Hein noted, this thorough and convincing cosmology contributed greatly to keeping Hindus in village India satisfied with their lot.[15]

As true incentive for moral action, the caste system perhaps leaves much to be desired. In the analysis of Dumont, it might be argued that moral action is only possible for those who have renounced social order. Persons within the caste structure do not possess the ego-identity associated with the West European or American model of the individual, and derive their meaning only in terms of their group relationships, i.e. their role in the family and the role their caste plays in the village.[16] Certainly, from both the modern natural law and indigenous nonviolence perspectives, the fatalism and docility and servitude bred by the caste system seem repugnant. Gandhi sought

---

social transactions. See Mckim Marriott and Ronald B. Inden, 'Caste Systems,' *Encyclopedia Britannica*, 15th edn, Macropaedia III, 1974, p. 983.

14 See Ariel Glucklich, 'Theories of Karma in the *Dharmaśāstra*,' 1984.

15 Comments made during presentation at the IASWR Conference on Nonviolence, Stony Brook, New York, 1984.

16 P.T. Raju, *Structural Depths of Indian Thought*, 1986, p. xvi.

to rectify the abuses of this system, with some success and historians of religion have recently criticized similar abuses in East Asia.[17] However, it is important to keep in mind that the renunciation morality has continued to coexist and in some ways has altered the caste system from within, primarily as it has influenced epic literature and sensibility.

Amalgamation of traditions: Liberation as universal paradigm

Within the Indian context we have two independent moral universes, which hold distinct ultimates. For the renouncer tradition, non-involvement with the ways of the world is idea. Transcendence is achieved by ceasing activities and even thought itself (*citta-vṛtti-nirodha*). The person at the highest state stands alone, with an individuality and identity separate from socially sanctioned structures. Conversely, the Brāhmaṇical model views the world in terms of interrelating, complementary components, not different from oneself. The pursuit and fulfilment of desire is seen as a celebration of life that is to be appreciated and encouraged.

Yet aspects of each system can be detected in the other. Both contain and express reciprocal relationships. The renouncer is dependent upon the education provided by his or her society in order to learn of the significance of renunciation. Without the context, nothing can be given up, because nothing has been held. Likewise, the structure of the caste system has been developed within a context that consistently has offered an alternative: dropping out. Ironically, renunciation is probably the most ancient of Indian traditions. The twice-born consciously takes on a new identity at the time of initiation which then at a later stage is consciously renounced.

The dynamic tension between conformity and release has long been a theme in Indian literature and philosophy. As various historians have noted, *mokṣa* or liberation became an officially sanctioned goal promoted by the Brahmin caste, who themselves were encouraged to renounce the village life at the end of their careers, searching out higher meaning in an ashram context. But what began in India from time immemorial and then was appropriated (along with nonviolence and vegetarianism) by the Brahmin caste eventually percolated throughout society. The great epic figures of Rāma, Yudhiṣṭhira, and Arjuna, all of them warriors, flirt with renunciation, return to their *dharma*, and then indeed renounce. The renouncer ideal of detachment becomes universalized in traditions of war and love[18] and spreads with Buddhism throughout Asia.

As Madeline Biardeau has written, 'the *purāṇas*…opened the mind to the idea of accessibility of *mokṣa* to all.' Citing various passages from the later sections of the *Mahābhārata*, she observes that this new, liberalized conception of liberation, 'gave every *svadharma* (one's own societal duty) religious content and an access to

17 See Lee Siegel, *Fires of Love, Waters and Peace: Passion and Renunciation in Indian Culture*, 1983.

18 Madelaine Biardeau, 'The Salvation of the King in the *Mahābhārata*,' pp. 77, 96-97, 1982.

ultimate salvation. The Brāhmaṇic model was not lost sight of, but was generalized so as to fit all other categories of Hindu society, including *śūdras*, women and all impure castes. Once the kṣatriya gained access to salvation through his specific and impure activities, the generalization became easy. Every sort of impurity could be sacralized and turned into *svadharma*. Nothing was outside the realm of ultimate values, though at the same time the status of the Brahmins remains unimpaired.'[19] This infusion resulted in a heightened sense of moral responsibility. One is obligated to perform one's dharma not merely because of the admonitions of the village Brahmin, but because such actions indeed hold the world itself together. The *puruṣa* that in Sāṃkhya is the pinnacle of detached, liberated consciousness is also the silent omnipresent figure that encompasses and is identical with all the things of the universe: the renouncer image of aloofness is amalgamated with the Brāhmaṇical universal form. To see the stoppage of the world-generating process is in fact to see the world as it truly is.

For many this was a call to action, and continues to be so. In the Yogāvasiṣṭha, a late Gupta text combining aspects of renouncer, idealistic Buddhism with socially active Hindu forms, it is said that by overcoming impurities that cloud the mind one gains the strength to be creative in the world. Several hundred years later, the symmetry of Ramakrishna and Vivekananda is similarly poignant, Ramakrishna stands as the renouncer par excellence of colonial and post-colonial India: he left behind his family, he served at a temple of questionable lineage, specialized in reverie, and very little else. Yet he inspired a movement that transformed India and was felt world-wide through the very concrete work exerted by Vivekananda toward the cultivating of Hinduism through the establishment of schools, missions, and hospitals.

Another instance of action oriented morality is found in the life and work of Mahatma Gandhi. Gandhi used the renouncer techniques of fasting, scrupulous nonviolence, and chastity to achieve a very this-world goal: the liberation of India from the colonial domination of Britain. His efforts may be interpreted as sacrifice (*yajña*) in the Vedic sense wherein his own well-publicized protests served to focus the attention of the world on India's predicament. Though many have criticized his technique as an abuse of solemn religious practices, in a certain sense Gandhi continues a long tradition of action-oriented morality wherein the leader of *dharmarāja* comes to symbolize and enact the highest values. By using nonviolence as his primary focus, Gandhi comes to symbolize and enact the highest values. By using nonviolence as his primary focus, Gandhi identified with the most ancient religious practices in India, a practice that cuts across ideological borders. His articulation of *ahiṃsā* as a blueprint for society updates the practice in terms of economic theory. I must confess that I do not draw a sharp distinction between economics and ethics. Economics that hurt the moral well-being of an individual or a nation are immoral and therefore sinful. True, economics stands for social justice, it promotes the good of all equally including the weakest, and is indispensable for decent life. Strictly speaking, no

19 M.K. Gandhi, *My Socialism*, 1959, pp. 33-35.

activity and no industry is possible without a certain amount of violence. What we have to do is to minimize it to the greatest extent possible. Indeed the very word nonviolence, a negative word, means that it is an effort to abandon the violence that is inevitable in life. Therefore, whoever believes in *Ahiṃsā* will engage himself in occupations that involve the least possible violence.[20]

Gandhi's economic ideal focused on the model of independently operating villages, 'My idea of village *swaraj* is that it is a complete republic, independent of its neighbours for its own vital wants, and yet inter-dependent for many others in which dependence is a necessity. Thus, every village's first concern will be to grow its own food crops and cotton for its clothes. My economic creed is a complete taboo in respect to all foreign commodities whose importation is likely to prove harmful to our indigenous interests. This means that we may not in any circumstances import a commodity that can be adequately supplied from our country.'[21] Village intimacy is seen as a place where the accountability for one's actions is automatically regulated by one's direct involvement with all aspects of the economic process. In this model, which in a certain sense also resembles Confucian ideals, identity is gained through relationships with others, minimizing occasions for antagonism. Reflective of the Vedic world as well, one's own prosperity is also beneficial for the group: success is part of the rhythm and flow (*ṛta*) of life.

Both the Ramakrishna-Vivekananda Mission and the social agenda of Gandhi share concern for action-oriented morality. Both follow a traditional model well-established in Hindu tradition that combines concern for absolute truth (*paramārtha*) with action in the world of relativity (*samvṛtti*). By anchoring the intention of one's activity in the changeless, one gains a sense of detachment that further empowers one in the realm of change. In the third chapter of the *Bhagavad Gītā*, Krishna urges Arjuna to continue to engage in action, but to do so free from attachment:

> Know that action originates from Brahman, and Brahman springs from the imperishable. Therefore, the all pervading Brahman is eternally established in sacrifice. Here on earth he who does not follow the wheel thus set in motion is evil in nature; by indulging in the sense, he lives in vain, O Pārtha. He who delights in Self alone, who is satisfied with the Self, who is content in the Self, for him no work remains to be done, he is not dependent upon mortal creatures for any object. Therefore, always perform without attachment the work that should be done. By doing work without attachment, man attains the Supreme.[22]

Krishna specifically calls for the perfection of oneself accompanied by benevolent action performed for others, invoking the famous king Janaka, who in earlier times is said to have presided over a perfect kingdom as *dharmarāja*: Through the path of action alone, men like Janaka and others reached perfection. You should perform action also with the intention of guiding people in the right direction. Whatever

20 M.K. Gandhi, *The Village Reconstruction*, 1996, p. 30.

21 B. Srinivasan Murthy Tr., *The Bhagavad Gītā* (*Bhg*), 1985, III.15-19.

22 Ibid., *Bhg*, III.21-22.

a great man does, others will copy. The people will follow whatever standard he sets.[23]

Moral action is attained when it is done in a spirit free from egotism and attachment:

> As the unwise act with attachment to their work, O Bharata, so should a wise man act without attachment for the good of the world. Let no wise man create confusion in the minds of the ignorant who are attached to (selfish) action. He should, rather, inspire others to act by his disciplined performance of actions. All kinds of actions are done by the modes of nature but he whose mind is confused by egotism things, "I am the doer." He who knows the true distinction between the soul and the modes of nature and their works, O-mighty-armed, realizes that it is the modes which operate upon the modes, and he does not get attached.

Hence, the *Bhagavad Gītā's* model of karma yoga makes any action a viable conduit for the enactment of higher knowledge.

In conclusion, we have seen that two primary ethical values have contributed to the Hindu moral universe. On the one hand, renunciation of involvement with the world, stemming from the ancient *śramaṇas* and enacted today in the lives of Hindu *sādhus*, Jaina *munis*, and Buddhist monks throughout Asia, serves as a positive reminder of the impermanence of things in the world. On the other hand, activity in the world, performed in the spirit of sacrifice, is held also to be sacred, from the time of the Vedas and *Dharmaśāstras* up to the work of Vivekananda and Gandhi. The two seemingly competing models have come to complete one another in such a way that action itself can be seen as a path of liberation.

* * *

Bibliography and References

Biardeau, Madeleine, 'The Salvation of the Kind in the *Mahābhārata*,' in T.N. Madan (ed.), *Way of Life: King, Householder, Renouncer: Essays in Honour of Louis Dumont*, New Dehli: Vikas, 1982, pp. 77, 96-97.

Brown, Norman S.,'The Creation Myth of the Ṛg Veda', *Journal of the American Oriental Society*, New Haven, 1942, 62, pp. 85-98.

Chapple, Christopher Key, *Karma and Creativity*, Albany, NY: SUNY Press, 1986.

Converse, Hyla S., 'Hinduism,' in Bush et al. (eds), *The Religious World: Communities of Faith*, New York: Macmillan, 1988.

deNicolas, Antonio T., *Meditations Through the Ṛg-Veda: Four Dimensional Man*, New York: Nicolas Hays, 1976.

Francis, H.T. and Thomas, E.J., *Jātaka: Tales Selected and Edited with Introduction and Notes*, Cambridge: Cambridge University Press, 1916, pp. 7-66.

---

23 Ibid., *Bhg*, III.25-28.

Gandhi, M.K., *My Socialism*, Ahmedabad: Navajivan Publishing House, 1959.

Gandhi, M.K. *The Village Reconstruction*, Bombay: Bharatiya Cidya Bhavan, 1966.

Glucklich, Ariel, 'Theories of Karma in the *Dharmaśāstra*,' doctoral dissertation, Harvard University, 1984.

Jaini, Jagmanderlal, *Outlines of Jainism*, Cambridge: Cambridge University Press, 1916.

Jaini, Padmanabh S., *The Jaina Path of Purification*, Berkeley: University of California Press, 1979.

Lannoy, Richard, *The Speaking Tree: A Study of Indian Culture and Society*, London: Oxford University Press, 1974.

Marriott, Mckim and Inden, Ronald B. 'Caste Systems,' *Encyclopedia Britannica*, 15th edn., Macropaedia (1974), III, p. 983; Louis Dumont, 1980 (1966).

Müller, Max, *The Six Systems of Indian Philosophy*, London: Longmans, 1988.

Raju, P.T. *Structural Depths of Indian Thought*. Albany, NY: State University of New York Press, 1986, p. xvi.

Schmidt, Hans-Peter, 'The Origin of Ahiṃsā', in Louis Renou (ed.), *Mèlanges d'Indianisme à la memoire de Louis Renou*, Paris: Publications de l'Institute de civilization Indienne, 1968, pp. 625-655.

Sen, Amulyachandra, *Asoka's Edicts*, Calcutta: The Institute of Indology, 1956.

Siegel, Lee, *Fires of Love, Waters and Peace: Passion and Renunciation in Indian Culture*, Honolulu: University of Hawaii Press, 1983.

Srinivasan Murthy, B. Tr., *The Bhagavad Gītā* (*Bhg*), Long Beach, CA: Long Beach Publications, 1985, III.15-19.

Srivivasan, Doris, 'The So-Called Proto-Śiva Seal from Mohen-Daro: An Iconological Assessment,' *Archives in Asian Art*, 29, 1975-76, pp. 47-58..

Chapter 17

The Ethical Irrationality of the World: Weber and Hindu Ethics

Pratap Bhanu Mehta

Max Weber is a daunting figure for anyone interested in the project of comparative political theory or comparative ethics. It is now abundantly clear that Max Weber was not doing merely comparative sociology but comparative ethics as well. He was read, much too easily, as a forerunner of American style modernization theory rather than an heir to Schopenhauer and Nietzsche, whose engagements with the ethical rationality of the world haunt Weber's pages. Thanks to the work of Henis, Tenbruck, Scaff and Goldman, some of these mischaracterizations of Weber's corpus have been cleared up and it is not my intention to talk about Weber's larger project.[1] But the insights generated by recent attention to Weber's ethical interests have yet to be fully extended to our reading of his work on the religions of India and China which are still read primarily through old lenses. The revolution in Weber scholarship brought about by Wilhelm Tenbruck's claim that theodicy was central to Weber's enterprise has not yet been fully explored in this context. Tenbruck argued that,

> rationalization in all its historical fragility was born from the compulsion of an inherent logic, which was situated in the irresistible drive towards the rationalization of religious ideas. (Religion's) specific problematic, is at root what Weber termed the problem of theodicy. The stages of religious advance are the more and more articulated conceptions of this problem and its solution.[2]

Tenbruck was right in emphasizing the centrality of theodicy to the process of rationalization. But the development of this insight has been limited in two respects. First theodicy was central not only to Weber's *sociological* enterprise; Weber's work also represents an *ethical* response to the perceived failures of all attempts at a theodicy. In his forays into comparative religion Weber is interested not only in the range of theodicies on offer, or the different forms of rationalization produced

1 For works that emphasize Weber's ethical orientation and in particular the problem of 'personality', see Wilhelm Hennis, *Max Weber: Essays in Reconstruction*, trans. Keith Tribe. London: Allen and Unwin, 1988; Wilhelm Tenbruck, 'The Problem of Thematic Unity in the Works of Max Weber', *British Journal of Sociology*, XXI (3) 1988; Harvey Goldman, *Max Weber and Thomas Mann*, Berkeley: University of California Press, 1988.

2 Tenbruck, 'The Problem of Thematic Unity,' p. 334.

by different theodicies. He is equally interested in the ways in which theodicies – attempt to render the world ethically rational – break down in different ways and the responses generated by that breakdown. The cross-cultural question Weber is interested in is not simply why the Occident generated capitalism and others didn't. Rather, it is how the fundamental facts of the ethical irrationality of the world are reckoned with in different contexts. It is, in other words, the same dialogue he is having with Kant, Nietzsche and Schopenhauer. Second – and equally important for our context, Tenbruck was wrong in assuming, as many Weber commentators still do, that only in the West did theodicy lead to disenchantment. It is indeed Weber's central claim that each culture produces its own distinctive forms of disenchantment and to that extent we are all in the same boat.

In this chapter I attempt to do two things: First, I argue that Weber's account of *dharma* is far more subtle than is usually recognized. Weber's reconstruction of Indian ethics highlights the inner conflicts of that tradition rather than disguising them. Second, and substantively more importantly, I argue that according to Weber, the axiology of Indian ethics corresponds to his own axiology to a considerable degree. Both Indian ethics and Weber are axiologically committed to a value pluralism that leaves our fundamental ethical conflicts unresolved. While Weber's response to the fact that our fundamental ethical conflicts cannot be resolved is different from Indian ethics, the parallels between Indian ethics and his own merit some attention. I suggest that his articulation of our existential predicament comes through a deep engagement with Indian ethical theory, and that both carry significant implications for ethics in general. As a caveat, I would remind readers that this paper deals only with particular aspects of Weber's treatment of Hindu ethics.

Weber's presupposition about the East

Weber's writings on India and China provide a hermeneutical challenge at many levels.[3] First of all, there is the simple fact that these are amongst the notoriously worst translated of Weber's writings and the layers of misinterpretation that dog his other work are compounded many times over. Second, these writings are, in my view, more exploratory and tentative than commentators have acknowledged. It is true that Weber will often pose some pointed questions or assimilate the mass of data to a few central schema, but Weber's own analysis and insights overflow any grid he might have attempted to impose upon them. Third, and perhaps most importantly for those interested in comparative ethics, Weber's writings often display an interesting double hermeneutical dialogue between his own philosophical inheritance and the materials he is examining, interpreting one in the light of the other. As we shall see below, two examples will illustrate this point perfectly. Take on the one hand his reading of Buddhism, which is clearly mediated through Schopenhauerian

3 In this essay I will concentrate only on Max Weber, *The Religion of India: The Sociology of Hinduism and Buddhism*, trans. H.H. Gerth and Don Martindale, Glencoe: Free Press, 1958, hereafter referred to as *ROI.*

categories; on the other hand one of the central terms in his description of modernity *Eigengesetzlichkeit*, owes something to his attempts to translate and understand the import of the Sanskrit term *svadharma*. There is, in these attempts, something as close to a fusion of horizons, to use Gadamer's phrase as we are likely to witness in comparative ethics.

The greatest strength of *The Religions of India* is the way in which Weber decentres our understanding of the character of ethical thinking in India. By decentring I mean that Weber emphasizes the following features of Indian ethical theory. Rather than looking for the essence of the central Indian ethical concept of *dharma*, he emphasizes its manifold functions and tensions. First, he repeatedly emphasizes that there is no source of ethical injunctions that can be taken to be uniquely authoritative. Second, that the order of *dharma* is not a closed system whose different components can be rendered into a harmonious whole without seriously abridging the tradition; the different poles of its constituent tensions cannot be wholly reconciled. Third, Weber gives a subtle account of the relationship between intellectual ideas and the particular properties that the social system of any society exhibits. There has been a good deal of Hegelian residue in much of the writing on Indology, which assumes that the real is rational, which assumes that there must be a close fit between intellectual conceptualizations of social structure in a society and the social structure itself. Weber is sensitive to the fact that not all the possible range of legitimations that a society may be able to imagine translate equally into social practices. For instance, despite Weber's recognition of the appalling centrality of caste as a social practice in India, he recognizes that it does not exhaust or even wholly determine the possible range of Indian ethical thinking. Indeed Weber's methodology opens up a range of even subtler questions: why do a whole series of seemingly opposed intellectual tendencies and ethical orientations: ritualism and ethical rationalism; other worldly and inner worldly asceticism; expediency and duty, all end up sustaining, or at least not opposing the institution of caste? If the legitimation of caste seems over determined in the Indian case, as it often appears, Weber prompts us think a lot harder about why this is the case. It will not do to trot out over-determined structuralist explanations as are still fashionable.[4] In this chapter I will not go into a full discussion of Weber's interpretation of caste as a sociological reality.[5] But I want to indicate enough to show how Weber managed to pull off the rare feat of both treating caste as a central institution, without suggesting that all ethical thinking had to be mediated through it. And in the process of doing so I want to bring to light some of the inner contradictions of the tradition that Weber managed to highlight. The reader encounters a general difficulty in reading Weber's writings on India because of the fact that Weber has a keen eye for the paradoxes, contradictions and ironies of Indian ethical thinking and those looking

4 As is done in Bruce Sullivan, *Classifying the Universe*, Oxford: Oxford University Press, 1994.

5 For treatment of caste and its implications, imbroglios, in modern-day secular India, see Pratap Bhanu Mehta, *The Burden of Democracy*, New Delhi: Penguin, 2003.

for the essence of Indian society will often be led astray. Occasionally Weber himself writes as if the heterogeneity of the Indian tradition could be made sense of within a single schema, or a privileged centre of interpretation, but his own analyses are usually the best warnings against such temptations. I think it is more fruitful to read Weber as articulating a whole series of tensions than run through what he takes to be Hindu tradition and it is important not to minimize the poles of these tensions.

Weber, like so many commentators on India, is struck both by the versatility of caste and its simultaneous immutability.[6] Caste society can be joined as a group, there is even room for internal mobility of groups, and one can renounce it as an individual but the system itself endures. As Heesterman pointed out, caste was given stability by the fact that caste is linked to two tendencies that, at first sight seem opposed. On the one hand caste society is, for Weber, traditionalist and anti-rational. It is manifested through ritual observances and magico-religious practices. On the other hand it manages to legitimize itself through the ethical rationalism of karma theodicy which 'explains' consistently why an individual is in a particular social location.[7] The paradox here is that the theodicy that underpins the social structure is ethically rational. But the actions through which the social structure expresses and reproduces itself are thoroughly traditionalist and anti-rational. This is one instance where ethical rationalism serves to justify and underpin behavioural traditionalism. In many ways this conjunction of rationalism and traditionalism is a particularly good example of the way in which Weber is so good at pointing out how rationalism has its roots in, and is often sustained by, its very opposite.

Weber argues, in a familiar kind of way, that the caste system allowed the separation of political and priestly power which allowed the development of politics as an 'autonomous' realm. This differentiation of functions is then extended into a general claim about caste: there are only *dharma*s or duties that are specific to each caste (*svadharma*).[8] Weber's formulation of this extreme ascription is illustrated in terms of a band of robbers (*thuggies*) who could, in the Indian setting, have their own *svadharma*.[9] Weber seems to think that the principle of specialization had been carried such an extreme that some injunctions might constitute a *svadharma* simply because they derive from a profession that exists. This description of the scope of permissible *svadharmas* is extreme and is belied by the fact that elsewhere Weber himself says that there is a universal prohibition on stealing (so much for the robbers!).[10] Besides it is impossible to imagine that any social order could sanction a sphere of action based simply on the internal norms of that sphere, especially if

---

6 *ROI*, pp. 29 ff.

7 J.C. Heesterman, *The Inner Conflict of Tradition*, Chicago: Chicago University Press, 1985.

8 *ROI*, p. 144.

9 *From Max Weber*, trans. H.H. Gerth and C. Wright Mills, New York: Oxford University Press, 1948, p. 123.

10 It is interesting to compare the difficulties of the notion of *svadharma* with the conception of practical identity that Christine Korsgaard has so powerfully formulated in *The Sources of Normativity*, Cambridge: Cambridge University Press, 1997. As G.A. Cohen's

the premises of that sphere of action are socially dysfunctional. But Weber's general point is, I think, a challenging one. What really does integrate the caste order? What is the comprehensive order of which *svadharmas* are merely complementary aspects? Is there an overriding *dharma* that can integrate the duties of various groups into a harmonious and complementary whole. Most of the writing on caste, including by Indians themselves, have always assumed that the caste system is an organically integrated whole, with each of its constituent parts fitting one another. Certainly, the self presentation of the caste system in some Indian texts lends credence to this view. Yet, as Weber notices, in most Indian texts, the heterogeneity of castes, and the varying injunctions drawn from them, subvert an integrative principle. The answer to the question – what conception of *dharma* integrates the caste order – remains rather obscure in Indian ethics and most of the theoretical work on caste barely seems to articulate one. One could even make a stronger point: Weber's suspicion that the proliferation of *svadharmas* threatens any integrative economy that caste might possess is historically and textually better founded than the claims of those who criticize him for not articulating the principles of integration. To take one example, not mentioned by Weber, and only slightly less dramatic than his example of robbers: the caste of *veśyās* (courtesans or royal prostitutes). The problem of what caste they belong to was posed within the system. Texts such as the *Arthaśāstra* give explicit direction on the proper regulation of their profession. Vijñāneshwara's commentary on *Yājñavalkyasmṛti* simply declares them to be a fifth caste.[11] Clearly, the basic system of classification that underlies the caste system is unable to contain the proliferation of specialized duties; and it is hard to imagine a single moral economy being capable of integrating into a whole, functions as distant from the obligations of householders as those of courtesans.

The difficulty of articulating an integrative conception of *dharma* is evident throughout Weber's text, but I submit that we see this as a more accurate reflection of the traditions he was writing about, than a lack in his understanding. One can see this most clearly in his discussions of '*dharma*.' It has often been pointed out that Weber's own analysis of *dharma* is not entirely clear. This is because on the one hand he associates *dharma* with caste duties most closely. Hence *dharma* for Weber is compartmentalized: a series of specializations that elaborate the ethical injunctions that arise from membership in a particular professional group. There was thus according to Weber, no universal ethic, 'but only a status and professionally differentiated *dharma* according to caste.'[12] Yet, on the other hand, he acknowledges some features of a universal ethic. These take three forms: first, there are virtues, like forbearance, patience, freedom from envy, purity, tranquillity, correct life, freedom from desire, and freedom from covetousness, which could be designated as universal.

---

sharp response points out, even a *mafiosi* has a practical identity in Korsgaard's sense and so any attempt to articulate the necessary and sufficient conditions of morality must fail.

11 See Daya Krishna, 'The Varṇāshrama syndrome of Indian Sociology', in *Contributions to Indian Sociology*, 19 (2), 1985.

12 *ROI*, pp. 142-144.

Second, five maxims of conduct that could be understood as commandments for all castes: non-injury, truth telling, refrain from stealing, pure living and control of passions. In passing Weber also mentions ritual prohibitions like the forbidding of the killing of cows.

Why Weber minimizes the import of the *dharma* that transcends *svadharma* is something of a puzzle. Dieter Conrad, who first pointed this out, argued that Weber had simply confused the 'is' and the 'ought' in his understanding of *svadharma*.[13] The term could be used as a descriptive reference as well as a normative one, so that one can speak of the *svadharma* of a band of thieves as meaning something like: 'it is their nature to be such' rather than as an indication of an ethical approval of their activities. Given Weber's own resolute insistence upon this distinction, I find this explanation to be inadequate. I think Weber downplays the 'universalist' features of *dharma*, at the expense of *svadharma* for a couple of reasons. First, as a sociological phenomenon Weber was probably not incorrect in thinking that greater weight was placed on *svadharma*, rather than duties in general. His point about the priority of *svadharma* over *dharma* in general is more a comment on the social system than on the availability of certain concepts. Second, he came to argue that although the precepts of *dharma* might be general in the sense of being applicable to all castes, they were far from absolute.[14] This is because, paradoxically speaking, the theodicial structure of the world, as I shall argue below, precluded the efficacy of absolute precepts. This was not only Weber's own outlook, he ultimately found it in his engagement with Indian thought as well.

But despite his downplaying the tensions between *svadharma* and *dharma* in general, Weber deserves some credit for intimating that the order of *dharma* might be open and conflictual rather than closed and settled. As one investigates further the inner conflicts only increase. There is for example the tension between ritual and expediency. Weber argues that expediency obtained in all profane areas of life, which enabled Hinduism to 'do justice in their own terms to the informing spirit of the most varied spheres of life and knowledge, promoting the development of special sciences.'[15] The difficulty in ascertaining what Weber means here is that the scope of the sacred and the profane is never clearly delineated. On the one hand, there is in this claim, a clear sense that ritualistic prohibitions did not exhaust the field of human actions; on the other, it is not clear what the scope of the profane is. What restrictions does ritual place on expediency? This is the line of questioning that those most suspicious of Weber's explanation of economic traditionalism in India

13 Dieter Conrad, 'Max Weber's Concept of Hindu *Dharma* as a Paradigm,' in Detlef Kantowsky (ed.), *Recent Research on Max Weber's Studies of Hinduism*, Munich: Verlag, 1986, pp. 169-193. Hereafter referred to as Conrad, 'Max Weber'.

14 Conrad speaks of general and absolute character of the precepts as if they were one and the same thing. Precepts can be general without being absolute and it seems that Weber thought that the tradition itself disavowed the absoluteness of precepts.

15 *ROI*, p. 152.

most assiduously pursue. Here I merely want to suggest that Weber leaves himself open to this line of thought.

Weber has some difficulty in dealing with the question: In Indian traditions what precisely is the balance between ritual, duties of one's station (*svadharma*) and those moral imperatives that might be thought of as being more universal. Sociologically speaking, he has very little doubt about the pre-eminence of ritual. The distinctions of caste are, amongst other things, marked most strictly by ritual; to be found wanting in the performance of rituals is to risk losing social identity almost entirely and ritual seems to function as the axis of social legitimation. But it is an advantage of his methodology that he treats them as, at least in principle, discrete elements rather than trying to mediate them through one single grid as most of the writing on the subject has done. Weber does not take for granted, as so much anthropology since him has done, that the ritual axes of purity and pollution can be easily mapped on to a set of distinctions derived from the functions of different castes in the division of labour. Nor further still does the set of ritual duties exhaust the range of injunctions an individual has to live under.

But here two dilemmas arise. I have already mentioned the possible conflict between the *dharmic* injunctions of one's caste and other *dharmic* injunctions. The second dilemma is what precisely is the relationship between the performance of caste duties and salvation? Weber is prescient in seeing the tension between the mundane order of caste and the quest for salvation. That is, the performance of caste duties in this life can hold out the promise of a better caste position in the next, but that is not quite the same thing as the real prize: salvation. Indeed while the mundane order is not without this soteriological significance to the extent that one's position in it can be improved, the very things that sustain it, the cycle of birth and rebirth, pose unanswerable questions about the existential *meaning* of this cycle. Weber is prescient in seeing that the caste order, rather than being an answer to the question – what is the significance of the world and my place in it – is again paradoxically only the beginning of the question. The tension between the order of ritual and salvation persists and according to Weber, is not successfully mediated by *dharmic* commandments. The very meaningfulness of *dharmic* injunctions is put into question. How exactly was ritual supposed to lead to salvation? What is its value to the individual? Weber insists that the soteriological value of a social institution such as caste remains a matter of doubt within the tradition. The doctrine of karma, while functioning as a theodicial explanation of the distribution of reward and suffering within the world, only works to heighten existential angst. Like Calvinism, Weber's second exemplar of an ethically rational theodicy, the doctrine of karma produces its own form of psychological dread. In *deus absconditus* (Calvinism), the anxiety generated by the doctrine of predestination leads to an inner worldly asceticism that expresses the desire to look for a sign of grace. Karma theodicy produces an eternal dread because the possibility of repeating a cycle, like the prospect of immortality, *ad infinitum* could, if fully contemplated, produce considerable dread. Weber's own words are worth quoting:

> However certain and ambiguous this ethically rational world order might present itself, the individual, once he raised the question of the 'meaning' of his life in this compensatory mechanism could experience it as dreadful.... It is important to realize that it was not primarily the dread of ever new life on earth which is after all so beautiful. Rather it was the dread of the ever new and ineluctable death. Ever and ever again the soul was enmeshed in the business of living and the heart enchained to things and above all dear ones. Ever again it must be ceaselessly torn from them through rebirth to be entangled in unknown relations to face the same fate. Such repeated death was truly dreadful. One can hardly fail to feel this and to be moved by the pathos when reading between the lines of the inscriptions the preaching of the Buddha and other redeemers.[16]

This is a remarkable passage for many reasons. Once again we see the classic Weberian manoeuvre that draws out the psychological and existential implications of a metaphysical doctrine. Second, the theodicy of karma, in the very process of making moral sense of the world renders it senseless to us. Third, the full pathos of this senselessness is premised on the thought that it is *individuals* who experience this. This seems fairly obvious; but the decades of anthropological denial of the existence of individuals other than the renouncer should make us attend to this description. If society is the enactment of the law of the dead, as it is in structuralist descriptions like Louis Dumont's, then neither individual agency nor individual angst can be accommodated except perhaps at the upper reaches where the Brahmin's other ascetic self creates an Archimedean point through a renunciation of the world in order to comment on it. The escape from the circularity of structured structures, which are structuring structures, becomes possible only for the renouncer. Weber is able to see in a way that Dumont is not that the existential weight of the social system could bear heavily upon anyone who cared to contemplate it. The loneliness that karma theodicy produces is a kind of inner loneliness akin to that which the Calvinist experiences: both are experiences that dread the thought of ruptured relations with other. For the Calvinist, the loneliness is produced by the fact that we do not know who is dammed and who is saved; for the believers in karma it is produced by the fact that all relations have to be torn asunder.

Weber is able to see again, in ways we have ignored, that the connection between the order of ritual and caste on the one hand, and salvation on the other, is at best tenuous. Since Brāhmaṇism derives its ideological hegemony from ritual functions, the less these are connected to salvation, the more problematic that hegemony becomes. But Brāhmaṇism survives this doubt about the ultimate soteriological significance of the mundane order of caste and ritual, by endowing these mundane institutions with a more limited but, in some senses this-worldly benefits.

What is interesting to note is that on Weber's reading the earthly institution that is endowed with such significance is the institution of the householder rather than caste. The order of the householder procures, through the rites of ancestor worship

16 *ROI*, pp. 158 ff; See Bilimoria's chapter in Part A for criticisms of similar Orientalists' interpretations of the erstwhile doctrine, and how better to make sense of it in terms of modern a/theodicies.

and care for progeny, a this-worldly holiness. Its rewards are this-worldly: a better birth for forebears and descendants; but otherwise it seems to have little in common with other-worldly personal holiness that the world renouncer possesses.

This abbreviated discussion of the relation between caste and salvation is of some significance. Sociologically, the holy other-worldly seeking, managed to break through the confines of ritual and ancestor worship. It allowed individual virtuosos to overcome the limitations imposed by the duties and piety to the family that remained central in China. Axiologically, it opened the way for the relativization of holy paths according to the intent and personal charisma of the holy seeker. The laity, can, by participating in ritual, better their condition and that of their ancestors; but those endowed with a greater charisma of gnosis can escape the world of ephemeral things. Weber has some acute descriptions of the form that this gnosis can take. If Weber's axiological hunches are correct standard ways of doing the history of Indian ethics that try to come up with an ideal type construction of the 'goals of man,' and the means to achieve those is operating on a limited horizon, the goals turn out to be too plural and heterogeneous to be simply ordered. And it must also make more problematic any claim to the effect that Hinduism can be reduced to *varnāśrama dharma* (duties of caste). The inner conflicts of tradition run through individuals rather than between them. While Weber had no doubts about the pervasiveness and strength of the institution of caste, he is not tempted to explain this by its simple soteriological significance. Quite the contrary, he gives the impression that the tradition itself had some difficulty in explaining the significance of caste. The tension between the social claims of caste, and the ultimate goals of liberation remains. The recognition of this tension paves the way to an understanding of caste that is less moored to over-determined religious constructions, and is more squarely placed within the rough and tumble of the operations of power and the more mundane modes of legitimation that sustain it. And it constantly emphasizes that *dharma*, far from being an integrative ethical principle is constantly at odds with itself.

Weber on the structure of Indian religious society

For Weber the problem that our ultimate religious interests and the structure of society could not be easily reconciled is to be found in his acute reading of the *Bhagavad-Gītā* (or *Bhagwad Gītā*, as he renders it). As is familiar, the central dilemma in this text involves the heroic figure of Arjuna, who as a Kshatriya, is obliged to engage in battle with his cousins despite serious misgivings about the violent consequences that will accrue from his duties. The advice Arjuna gets from lord Krishna, is that Arjuna need not shrink from obligations of his caste *dharma*, even though acting seems to bind him to the ephemeral and material world. Krishna's solution is that while action in the world is inevitable, attachment to the fruits of one's action can be avoided, and this is what Arjuna should strive for. By cultivating a disposition of detachment towards the fruit of one's actions one can escape the effects of one's own karmas and achieve salvation. This is what Weber has described as a means of bridging the tension between the injunctions of the social system and the striving for salvation.[17] What Krishna ends up proposing is a theory of inner worldly flight, which allowed for action to be undertaken in accordance with one's caste duty in a manner compatible with the aims of salvation. It was not so much that the *Bhagavad-Gītā* provided a religious sanction to the caste system itself as that it provided no reason to question it.

Weber's reading of the *Mahābhārata* is significant for two other reasons that take us to the heart of Weber's larger ethical enterprise. He is not the first to note that the world depicted in the *Mahābhārata* is not governed by a single ethically rational order. Rather than being an ethically consistent theodicy, the text functions almost as an anti-theodicy where a genuine solution to the problem of the distribution of reward and suffering is not to be found. The text is replete with a belief in fate and an arbitrary play of chance with men that can hardly be reconciled with the ethical rationality of karma doctrine. Indeed the course of the world appears to be in the text impenetrably enigmatic, governed by a game of dice whose rules are known to be deceptive, and all values and ideals are successively subverted by experience. In it the central character Yudhiṣṭhira – the son of *dharma* and its very embodiment – ends up cursing *dharma* itself and the only resolution in face of this irrationality and blameless misfortune seems to be an anti theodicy reminiscent of Job. Weber explains this internal tension of the epic by historicizing it.[18] The references to fate and the irrationality of the world are reminiscent of a warrior ethic where the reign of chance governs, on which is superimposed a rationalized soteriology of intellectuals. Whatever the merits of this speculation – and my own sense of the internal unity of the text makes this implausible – Weber is right to notice that the order of the world subverts itself in a way that is deeply problematic for ethical action. The consequences of one's actions seem paradoxical and fraught with unintended consequences; ideals turn out to be self-defeating; every ethical theory turns out to be subverted by the disclosures of time. This might provide a clue to the fact that just as renunciation breaks open the caste order, the structure of the world in the *Mahābhārata* puts the harmony of *dharma*, the premise that the world is a rationally ordered whole, governed by a divine providence, where each individual performing the duties of their station will lead to a just distribution of rewards, all into question. What do ethical injunctions mean in such circumstances. If the world will not pick up my actions in the right way; if *dharma* becomes the source of disorder rather than its upholder, what will sustain the cogency of ethical action?

To illustrate this let me pick an example from the *Mahābhārata* itself which will make the conflict of '*dharma*' and the world clearer, in what many Indian commentators regard as the 'spiritual heart of the text,' namely, the episode where Yudhiṣṭhira is put to the test by a Yakṣa (who turns out to be his own heavenly father).[19]

---

17 *ROI*, p. 177.

18 *ROI*, p. 181.

19 The episode is also discussed in the chapter by Bimal Matilal in this volume, but with a slightly different emphasis; Matilal also discusses Weber and his treatment of *dharma*.

Halfway through the text he is asked the question, 'What is the highest *dharma* in the world?' Yudhiṣṭhira replies: the highest *dharma* is non-injury (*ānṛśaṃsya*). There is no doubt from the text that this is a truly sincere and profound formulation of *dharmic* value and Yudhiṣṭhira's character is meant to embody this. Yudhiṣṭhira is endowed with non-injury and compassion. Yet we know that Yudhiṣthira is also a significant actor in the drama of destruction that the text unfolds. He fights, kills, and however reluctantly, stakes claims to a kingdom and his actions are part of the complex that leads to general devastation. There is a real disjuncture between his values and the consequences of his action and at the end of the text he perceives a shocking lack of correlation between his moral stance and the structure of the world. Given what we know about the story the proclamation of *ānṛśaṃsya* or *ahiṃsā* (non-injury) as the highest *dharma* seems almost ironic. Yet it is not ironic in the sense of being insincere; it is ironic only in the sense that the relationship between ethics and the world is no longer clear. What would the injunction to non-injury mean, in a world actively hostile to that moral intention? There is not only no guarantee that the world will take up our moral actions in the way we intend them, there is positive evidence that the world will not. The rational ethical imperatives of the world find themselves in complete tension with the irrationalities of the world. The world seems constantly off balance, spiralling out of control and not responsive to the effects of ethical action. The existential drama of the *Mahābhārata* is that the structure of the world does not correspond to our ethical intentions; it constantly subverts them. It is the tension between the structure of the world and the course of moral action that makes a harmonized ethics almost impossible At least this part of the conclusions of the *Mahābhārata* harmonized with Weber's own sense of the ethical irrationality of the world.[20] It is difficult to shake off the feeling that Weber's critique of a pure ethic of conviction, which takes its orientation in the world from absolute moral injunctions, stems from a profound sense that the world cannot be made to conform to our intentions, and that any ethical theory that does not recognize this is bound either to subvert itself or end up in fanaticism. The *Mahābhārata* gives Weber another example of an *Eigengesetzlichkeit* text amply articulating this fact.[21]

The engagement with Hindu texts also provides Weber with a term that becomes crucial for his interpretation of modernity: the idea often translated as lawful autonomy. Weber had characterized the modern condition using the term polytheism to denote the predicaments faced by individuals who have to deal with the demands of different values which are incommensurable and incapable of being ordered in a rational way. The world no longer appears to be a unified whole. Each of the particular spheres – religion, art, politics, the economy – requires a particular kind of conduct that cannot be made consistent with the imperatives of other spheres; each sphere has its own lawful autonomy and mode of acting and there is no higher rationality that can be invoked to overcome the contradictions that develop between the demands of

20 *ROI*, pp. 181-183.

21 For Weber's critique of the 'ethics of conviction', see 'Politics as a Vocation', in *From Max Weber*, pp. 120 ff.

autonomous spheres. This is why Weber embraces a kind of existentialist position by insisting, that in the final analysis, all our choices of action are contingent. They are contingent in the sense that there is no inner necessity or transcendental grounding for one choice over another. But two points are clear: that Weber formulates his insights into the predicament of modernity by drawing upon, at least in an analogical way, the understandings of a quite different tradition. Thanks to the labours of Dieter Conrad, it is clear that one of Weber's central terms of art for describing modernity (*Eigengesetzlickeit*), was evolved in active engagement with his reading of Hindu ethics and his attempts to translate the concept of *svadharma*. The significance of *Eigengesetzlickeit* had been obscured for English readers of Weber by inconsistency in translation, where at least six different words or phrases were used for the same term. While none of these phrases was inaccurate they concealed the fact that Weber had coined a new term to express the central idea of the 'lawful autonomy' of spheres. It is now widely agreed that the first extensive use of this term occurs in the second essay on Hinduism 'The Orthodox and Heterodox Salvation Doctrines'. His use of the term here mirrors his use of the term made more famous in his 'Intermediate Reflections' and the essential import in both cases is the same. As Conrad writes:

> ...the very first use of the term seems to have been made in the section on *Dharma*. It makes its appearance right at the beginning of the opening passage. The priestly power had to recognize that the world of politics followed its own laws (*andere Eigengesetzlickeit*). This textual finding makes it seem no far fetched assumption that Weber coined the term in connection with his interpretation of *dharma*. It has been shown that the whole theme of that elaboration is the principle of *svadharma*, carried even to the point of exaggeration. What seems to have struck Weber is the independent normative rationalization of various spheres of action – an early paradigm for the modern cultural differentiation into various spheres regulated by their own rationality.[22]

It is perhaps not an accident that in 'Politics as a Vocation', when discussing the tension between religion and politics, Weber again mentions the Indian example to underscore both points central to his interpretation of modernity: that different occupations were subject to their own 'immanent and autonomous laws' and that politics, being centrally connected with violence was forever in tension with any kind of ethical absolutism. And in this passage he again uses the term '*Eigengesetzlickeiten.*'[23]

It is difficult not to see in Weber's summary of the ethic of the *Bhagavad Gītā*, something of a reflection of Weber's own views on ethical thinking; I also happen to think that Weber's interpretation is mostly on target. Let me quote his summary in full:

> Indian 'tolerance' rests upon this absolute relativizing of all ethical and soteriological commandments. They are organically relativized not only according to caste membership, but also according to the goal or end sought by the individual. It is no more a matter of

22 Conrad, 'Max Weber', p. 179.

23 See *From Max Weber*, p. 123.

> negative tolerance but (1) of positive – relative and graded – appreciation of quite contrary maxims of action; (2) *of the recognition of the lawful and ethical autonomy and the equal and independent value of the various spheres of life*, which had to result from their equal devaluation as soon as ultimate questions of salvation were at stake.

This characterization of Indian ethical thinking is replete with classic Weberian themes: the relativizing of all ethical commandments; the lawful autonomy of different spheres of action; the lack of a unifying ethical principle that could render the world whole. What Weber himself could not subscribe to was the 'organic' character of society that this produced. In the Indian case, the lawful autonomy of spheres was both an axiological thesis and a sociological one and the axiology and sociology coincide. An axiological thesis about the plurality of values, each with their own lawful autonomy and irreconcilable commitments, was the normative correlate for a social structure, where each caste, in some sense, represented a different value. Nor could Weber concur with the thought that from the point of view of salvation all these realms stood roughly at the same plane: they did not contribute to it. This is because for Weber, there was no such thing as salvation, and he found ignoble the withdrawal from the world that the quest for salvation produced.

Chapter 18

Social Injustice, Retribution and Revenge: A Normative Analysis of the Contemporary Social Scene[1]

Rajendra Prasad

Justice as Criterial

Social Justice is Distributive Justice

Even if there is some difference between the two concepts, in this chapter I will be using the terms for them interchangeably. The term 'social justice' has the advantage of being emotively more provocative than 'distributive justice'. The latter, on the other hand, appears to be dull and dry. But it has the advantage over the former, like some other non-emotive, or emotively emaciated, terms for being more precise, or matter of fact, as Hume would put it.

The question of social or distributive justice arises when something is to be distributed among a group of people by an agency that has the authority and responsibility to do the distribution. The distributing agency could be an individual, e.g. the king of a monarchical state; a group of people, e.g. the syndicate of a university; or the representative of a group of people, e.g. the prime minister of a democratic state. But the conceptual and substantive problems which the exercise of distributive justice is likely to give rise to and for which it must have some solution, if the exercise is to be successfully done, are likely to remain, by and large, unchanged, whatever be the nature of the distributing agency. Even if all of them are not, at least those with which I shall deal, it seems to me, are.

Justice is a criterial concept. This means that giving *X* to *A* would be just if and only if *A* fulfils the criterion or criteria which entitles him to have a justifiable claim on *X*. This would also mean that not giving it to him, or giving it to *B* who does not fulfil the criterion (or criteria), would be unjust. The criterion, thus, exercises a restrictive as well as a facilitative function. It prohibits or disallows the distributor

---

1 A shortened and modified version of this essay was published as 'Social Injustice, Retribution and Revenge: An Examination of the Indian Experiment,' in P.K. Mahapatra (ed.), *Social Justice: Philosophical Perspectives*, New Delhi: D.K. Printworld Ltd., and Bhubaneshwar, USA in *Philosophy*, Utkal University, 1999, pp. 14-55.

of *X* from giving it to someone who does not satisfy it, and facilitates his task of deciding whom to give it to. It thus sanctions or justifies his giving, or not giving, it to a person. This in no way means that the distribution of justice, where a criterion is available, is an extremely easy affair. It becomes a difficult affair, for example, when it is not clear whether or not a subject fulfils the relevant criterion, or which one, or ones, fulfil it better than some other, or others. All this generally happens when the available criterion is not sufficiently precise or discriminative, or when the situation in which it is to be applied is very greatly complicated, or unusually different from earlier situations. In such cases the applier may not feel sure as to whether it should. or should not, be applied, and if it should be, whether it should be applied as it is, or in a modified form. In the latter case, he may not know in which way it should be modified.

But in spite of such difficulties, dispensation of justice cannot be done without some criterion (or criteria). The criterion used in a case must be relevant to it, and, by and large, our commonsense, normal intuitions about the relevance of a criterion are right, or right enough to enable us to proceed in a just manner. For example, to make fatness of the neck of an individual, which makes his neck's fitting into the hangman's noose, a criterion for putting him to death by hanging, is, our intuitions would say, absolutely wrong. That is why Bhartendu calls the king who used this criterion senseless (*caupata*) and the city in which it was done lawless (*andherapura*).[2]

The above is too obviously an example of an irrelevant criterion. But it very clearly is a good example of a criterion which our normal intuitions would reject. In moral matters, and so also in matters pertaining to the dispensation of justice, our normal intuitions play the role of a touchstone. That is why when a theory of justice offers a criterion for being a rightful deserver of a benefit or burden, which goes against our normal intuitions, our reaction is that there is something wrong with the theory, or that the theory needs to explain or justify its counter-intuitive stand.

We generally talk of distributive or social justice when what is to be distributed is a benefit, i.e. something preferred, desired, wanted, needed, etc., by those who believe they have a claim on it. But this does not have to be the case. Justice, or injustice, may be done in distributing even a burden, i.e. in distributing something unwanted, avoided, despised by, or even hurtful to, the recipients. The distribution of public land among the landless could be done justly or unjustly, and so can the imposition of a collective fine on the residents of a village for their allegedly demolishing a police station. Therefore, when I speak of distributive justice, I have in mind both the distribution of benefits and of burdens, though I may not always mention both of them.

---

2 In a Hindi dramatic satire, *andherpura nagarī caupata rājā; take sera bhājī, take sera khājā*, Bharatendu Harischandra portrays the administration by the king of a city which ordains that if the neck of the criminal to be hanged is so thin that it slips out of the noose of the hangman's rope, anyone else whose neck is fat enough to fit into the noose, be hanged and the thin-necked criminal be let off. The result is that, instead of the real criminal, who is thin-necked, a fat-necked young recluse is hanged.

Goods to be distributed may not be sufficient in the sense that there may not be enough of them to be given, or given in equal quantity, to each one of the claimants. Strict adherence to the criterion of just distribution then would help the distributor to eliminate those whose claims are not tenable, or are comparatively weaker than to the claims of some others, though both the groups, in some way, satisfy the criterion, i.e. possesses the qualifying property or properties which ordinarily make the distribution of the concerned goods to them just or justified, and the act of distribution *an act of justice*. I would call such a property a justice-making, or simply, a justifying, property. When, in a distributive act, a justifying property is ignored, or a non-justifying property is invoked, injustice is committed. Drona invokes a candidate's possession of the property of being a prince (*rājaputra*) as the justifying property for his being admitted in his school. Since Ekalavya did not have it, he was not admitted. But the property invoked is not a justifying property. Therefore, Drona's non-acceptance of Ekalavya is an act of (social) injustice.[3] And so is his act of admitting his own son, Aśvathāmā, in it though he too is not a prince.

Reference to a justifying property is equally important even when the goods to be distributed are available, or can be made available, in abundance. Suppose the chief minister of a state decides to give a job to every unemployed engineering graduate, and has the resources to create as many jobs as are needed. Suppose, further, that he assigns the job of supervising the generation of electricity to a chemical engineer and that of supervising the construction of a highway to an aeronautical engineer. He has given a job to each one of the claimants. But he has ignored the relevant justifying properties the possession of which by the job-claiming engineers has to be taken into account in deciding which specific job has to be given to which engineer, keeping in view his area of specialization. He has done, therefore, an injustice to both, the chemical and the aeronautical engineers, the injustice of giving each one of them the jobs which should not have been given to him; or, to put it a little differently, of not giving to him the job which should have been given to him. It would be another matter if both of them, since they were unemployed, are extremely happy, and. instead of calling the chief minister's act an act of injustice, extol him as an apostle of social justice. But it is obvious that such acts would be acts of societal injustice, i.e. injustice to society because they would ultimately lead to the impoverishment of the society's, or the country's, resources.

Maybe the chief minister had no criterion, or, justifying property, in mind in distributing the jobs. Still, the way he did it was unjust. A distributive exercise which uses no criterion, as well as one which uses a wrong one, e.g. the size of an individual's neck in deciding whether he should be put to the gallows or let off, would, in all likelihood, result in injustice, and if it sometimes does not, that would be only by a fluke or accident. Therefore, in the dispensation of justice the desirability of using, and being clear about, the relevant justifying property or properties for making the distributive process just can never be brushed aside, or taken in a casual manner. The justifying property must really justify the distribution, and in deciding whether

3 *The Mahābhārata*, vol. I, Saṃbhava Parva, Ghorakhapur: Gita Press, pp. 397-402.

or not it does, our normal intuitions about justice are extremely helpful. They may not be so important in the dispensation of legal justice because in it the legal system provides in a codified manner the set of justifying properties. But even here when the codification is not adequately clear, and sometimes it is not, the judiciary has to take the help of relevant normal intuitions about justice. The latter are generally moral intuitions, and rightly so because what is morally fair should also be (made) legally fair but the legally fair need not always be.

Social Justice and Retribution

The concept of social justice definitely, and perhaps that of justice per se, involves a sense of retribution from which follows a sense of pride or self-dignity in the recipient of the benefit justly given to him.

What I deserve to get, what I have a right to, or claim on, I ought to get, or, must get, simply because, in a timeless or moral, sense, it is *mine* though it may not at the moment be in my possession. The agency which is involved in making it available to me, therefore, ought to, or must, make it available to me. If it does, it would be doing only justice, or social justice, to me, and not an act of favour, or charity; it would only be giving to me what is mine, and not a gift or alms. Therefore, in receiving or accepting it, I do not have to compromise my self-respect. Rather, I should have a sense of pride, self-dignity, or elevated satisfaction, for having got what I ought to have. This means I would not be doing anything wrong, rather I would be doing something commendable, courageous, or heroic, if I fight to get it in case it is withheld from, or denied to, me. One who withholds it from, or denies it to, me, does an act of gross injustice.

Such feelings can become very strong. Sometimes they do in a natural way because of some gross injustices having been really perpetrated for a very long period of time on an individual, or a group, by another individual or group. Sometimes they do because of having been pumped up by some interested persons, say, politicians holding an ideology of a certain type, or hoping to get, in the coming general election, the votes of the allegedly wronged people by posing to be the protectors of their rights.

Such feelings in an individual, or group, become generally strong when the concerned individual, or group, *believes* that a gross injustice, or a set of gross injustices, has been perpetrated on it by another individual, or group, for a very long period of time. For the feelings to rise high it does not matter whether the belief is or is not true; only the belief must be there. In the case of a false belief, however, sometimes rational persuasion by a Gandhi or a Jai Prakash Narayan, may succeed in convincing the alleged victim that no injustice has really been done to him and thereby in calming him down. But this is a very difficult job and becomes more difficult when a large group, say, a caste-group, or a religious group, of people hold the (false) belief. But this also is true that rational persuasion by a neutral person, or a group of persons, is the only peaceful way of assuaging the strong feelings by showing untenability of the belief or beliefs concerned.

The belief that a gross injustice has been done retributively causes, in the believing individual or group, the urge to get the injustice undone. This urge makes the believers agitational, sometimes in a natural way and sometimes because of having been whipped up by some interested individual or group. In certain conditions, such an agitation is very likely to become violent because the agitators think they have a retributive justification to use violence to get back what has been denied to them. Their thinking proceeds in some such way: We deserve to have *X*, but it has been denied to us. The existing social machinery is not sincerely trying to restore it to us. Therefore, even if we use violence to get it back, we would be doing nothing wrong, not even if we destroy this social set-up.

Retribution and Revenge

A natural ally of the feeling of retribution is the feeling of revenge. *A* has taken *X* from me; therefore I must take it back, and even if I hurt him in the process, nothing wrong would be done by me. He would deserve the hurt because of what he has already done to me. Retribution and revenge do not have to go together; they are only likely to go together. The retributive agent sometimes, and generally when he becomes revengeful, forgets that the feeling of revenge very often overshoots its target and then it takes away a small or large part, of *moral* merit of retribution. Draupadī's insulting Karṇa[4] by not allowing him to compete in her *svayaṃvara* on account of his (allegedly) low parentage, gives to Karṇa the retributive right to make Draupadī give him the respect he deserves and repent for her misbehaviour. But his feeling of revenge overshoots the retributive target when, in the game of dice, he calls her a whore,[5] for which he himself later repents. A large part of the moral merit of his retributive right to get undone the injustice she has done to him is destroyed by his own act of injustice, or immorality, committed through his revengeful act of calling her a 'whore'.

The conceptual line which separates retribution from revenge is very thin, and very often it is either not noticed, or unwittingly crossed over, without letting one realize that thereby he has entered a different kind of territory, that from the moral he has passed into an amoral or immoral territory: 'That *A* has deprived me of what, in a timeless, moral, sense, is mine – my land, social status, opportunity for advancement, etc. – retributively implies that I have a moral right to recover, or get restored, what he has taken away, or damaged.' This is what retributive morality, retribution within the bounds of morality, means. That *A* has deprived me of *X* does not imply that I have a moral right to take away from *A* what in a timeless, moral, sense belongs to him, i.e. to do him an injustice in return. That Draupadī does an injustice to Karṇa does not (retributively) imply that he has a moral right to do an injustice to her. It is

4 *The Mahābhārata*, vol. I, Svayṃavara Parva, p. 540.

5 Ibid., Dyūtaparva, p. 902.

a moral truth that nothing can give one, or imply that he has, a moral right to do an immorality which an act of injustice obviously is.

The revengeful person does not clearly see what retribution really implies and what it does not. Partly because of his conceptual dim-sightedness and partly because of his disturbed emotional state he thinks that retribution implies, or justifies, revenge, or is indistinguishable from it. But the fact of the matter, as mentioned above, is that retribution only justifies the restoration of the moral balance disturbed by an immorality, or a set of immoralities. It does not justify the commission of a counter-immorality for the simple reason that nothing can. To think that it does is a gross error, conceptual as well as moral. But so many people, philosophers and non-philosophers alike, very often commit it. It is committed by all those who define the doctrine of retribution as justifying taking an eye for an eye, a tooth for a tooth.

Revenge as Contingently Moral

The motivation behind a retributive action is moral; it is an urge to get a moral wrong, an injustice, undone in a morally right or permissible manner. When a landless labourer, with the help of the village *pañcāyat*, legal machinery, social persuasion, or even use of violence when no other means is available, or other means fail, gets back his plot of land which had been wrongly grabbed by someone else, he gets an injustice undone. If he is a retributionist, after getting back the lost plot of land, he would become satisfied. He would not like to hurt the land-grabber further. A retributive act, or system aims at restoring the disturbed moral order. The injustice of his plot having been grabbed had disturbed the moral order which has now been restored with the return of the plot to him. It could also have been restored, if anything else equivalent to the plot, would have been given to him by the grabber himself, or as a result of a governmental decision. There is a form of theism according to which God is the greatest retributivist who administers the world in such a manner that everyone gets in return for what he does, what he is entitled to; and so does the law of karma according to the classical Indian world-view.

On the other hand, the motivation behind a revengeful act is merely the satisfaction of a grudge, no matter whether the grudge is justified or not. Since the grudge does not have to be a moral grudge, a revengeful action has no moral boundaries. It is contingently, and not necessarily, moral in the sense that it does not have to operate within the bounds of morality. It may be moral, immoral, or non-moral. The revengeful landless labourer may collect a group of other landless labourers and kill all members of the family some ancestor or ancestors of which had grabbed the land. As enacted in the Hindi movie *Umraon Jaan*, a revengeful criminal, after being released from the prison, kidnaps the baby daughter of the person who had given true evidence against him in the court on the basis of which he was convicted. He then sells her to a manageress of a brothel, who forces her, when she attains her youth, to lead the life of a whore, and the circumstances so contrive that the young lady ends her life by drowning herself in the Ganges. Here the kidnapper does not get anything back. He only gets the satisfaction of having hurt the man who had given evidence against him which involved no immorality. He only satisfies his urge to avenge.

But very often the distinction between retribution and revenge is forgotten, or not clearly recognized; and a revengeful act is taken to be retributive and therefore justified. For example, the labourers may think that they have acted retributivelv and therefore justifiably in killing innocent members of the family because some ancestor or ancestors of it had, according to their belief, taken possession of the land by means of fraudulent legal devices. But they would be mistaken because retributive morality justifies only such an action which is at least morally permissible, and not any immorality like the one they have done. The aim of retribution is to restore moral order, to set moral imbalance right. Killing innocent persons would upset, and not restore, moral balance. It would be an act of revenge and not of retribution. Perhaps only a feeling of revenge can push a person, or a group, to commit such a gruesome act.

It is also possible that a retributive measure may be mistaken for being a revengeful one. Suppose members of the caste *B* are not allowed to enter a Hindu temple, and they are agitating against it. The management of the temple realizes that by so far not allowing entry to them, it has done great social injustice. To compensate for this moral lapse it makes the rule that the members of *B* will henceforth not only be allowed but be given preference over others in entering the temple. This would be a retributive, compensatory, moral step. But the members of *B* may mistakenly think that they have avenged their injustice on the so-far favoured castes and even the latter may make the error of thinking that they have been. But the fact of the matter is that no caste has avenged or been avenged. Rather, a moral lapse, or injustice, an immoral social practice, has been rectified by a supererogatory, or retributive step, perhaps in an over-enthusiastic manner.

To avenge on someone for something he has done is, in some sense, to hurt or humiliate him, to make him feel small. The avenger himself, on the other hand, when he successfully avenges, feels, in some sense, great, or more powerful than the person avenged on. All this happens no matter what is the moral quality of the revengeful action and of the action of the person avenged on for which he is avenged on. Therefore, it is very likely that the person avenged on, if he can, or when he can, would take a retaliative action against the avenger. In this way, the process of revenge and reactive revenge is likely to continue and to keep the social or moral order more or less disturbed. On the other hand, if the wronged person takes retributive action against the wrongdoer, keeping himself well within the bounds of morality, the situation is likely to be much better. For example, if the landless labourer gets his lost land recovered through his own, or through society's, morally permissible efforts, the person from whom it is taken back may feel a sense of loss. But then there is a reason available to the person whose land it really is, and to any observer, which can be used to convince him that he has not really lost anything. We can tell him that what has been taken away from him is not really his; it really belongs to the person to whom it has gone. Therefore, in taking it away from him, nothing of his has been taken away; or in losing it, he has not lost anything which is his. If all this is done in a proper setting and if the social surrounding is amicable, it is very likely that he would get convinced and would not feel any animosity with the recipient of the land, or with one who has helped him in regaining it. He may, rather, feel a sense of relief or satisfaction, indistinguishable from a sense of purification, a sense that a wrong has been righted. If such things happen, they would certainly strengthen the moral order, the moral fabric of the social order.

From Revenge to Retribution: The Philosopher's Way

Both the retributive and the revengeful propensities are natural to man. But social planning has to aim at strengthening the former and weakening the latter. How this can be done is a very important question in practical or applied ethics, the area to which the administration of social justice belongs. There cannot be a simple answer to it. I would only say that a number of things are necessary to achieve even the modicum of success in this venture. Some of them are the following: good education, formal and informal, morally motivated and politically unbiased methods of publicity about the wrongs done to some sections of the society and right methods of compensating for them and of stopping their recurrence, meaningful and effective encouragement for retributive correction and discouragement for revengeful attempts, exemplary behaviour from the makers and implementers of social policies, non-political methods for diagnosing and correcting social injustices, etc. Explaining even a single one of them would require me to explain the others, and that cannot be done in this work. I would content myself only with saying a few things about the philosopher's role in this matter.

We may not approve of Hegel's attempt at building a grand philosophical system, but we can never ignore or minimize the importance of his saying that philosophy is a thinking consideration of things. It can influence human beings only, or primarily, by working on their thinking. There is no doubt that it works on human thinking. The conceptual distinction between retributive and revengeful action, and the likely after-effects of each one of them, as I have explained in some of the foregoing pages, when properly understood and acknowledged, can go a long way to strengthen the propensity for one and weaken the propensity for the other.

One who acknowledges the distinction between the two, i.e. acknowledges that retribution works within the bounds of morality and revenge tends to ignore them, would have in his acknowledgement itself a very good reason for not letting the retributive effort be superseded by a revengeful one. And, if he is a rationally mature person, then, because he would have a reason against becoming revengeful, it is very likely that he would not become revengeful. Secondly, a society's acknowledgement of and respect for the distinction, would facilitate its task of keeping the propensity of revenge in some of its members under appropriate control without subduing, or curbing, their retributive propensity of not tolerating injustices done to them, i.e. without dampening their moral heroism.

The Gandhian struggle for India's Independence is a very good example of a retributive, as against a revengeful, one: a struggle to take back what the British Government had taken away, but not to avenge the injustice by trying to take away anything from the latter which belonged to them. This is very clear from the fact that Gandhi (unlike Subhaschandra Bose) never agreed to side with Hitler in his war against the British. A revengeful Gandhi would have readily done the latter. Even Nehru exhibited the non-revengeful spirit of India by agreeing, after India's becoming independent, to be a member of the British Commonwealth instead of joining a block hostile to the British.

The philosopher, therefore, can contribute to the individual's and societal efforts for the promotion of social justice, or the removal of social injustice, by doing well his own job, his *svadharma*, the job he is equipped to do. That is, by diagnosing accurately the conceptual distinction between revenge and retribution, stating it clearly, cogently and comprehensively, and making it available to thinking people in an easily intelligible vernacular. He can improve the chances of his conceptualization becoming action-guiding and persuasive by highlighting the differences between the likely consequences of revengeful and retributive actions and policies. Examples of such actions and policies he can easily find in the history of humankind, and if he does not, or does not want to spend time in digging into history, he can hypothesize cases and draw an impressive picture of the consequences each one is likely to yield and their likely fallout for the social or moral order, for the targeted personal or social welfare for which such actions and policies are allegedly adopted.

All this is neither unimportant nor easy. It is not unimportant because people who confuse revenge with retribution and therefore consider revenge justified are available galore. Because of the unclarity of the distinction between the two, politicians find it easier to call cruelties inflicted on innocent people, done out of revenge, retributive actions justified because of past injustices done by the victims' forefathers. To be convinced that it is not easy to catch the distinction correctly one has only to try his hand.

Duryodhana thought that he was acting retributively in humiliating Draupadī when he tried to get her de-robed and to make her sit on his thighs, because she had humiliated him by saying that being a son of a blind man he also behaved like a blind man. So did Kṛṣṇa[6] when he advised Bhīma to strike his *gadā* at Duryodhana's thigh-joints, the areas prohibited by the rules of *gadā* warfare. He thought, and also made Bhīma to think, that doing so was retributively justified because of Duryodhana's having earlier humiliated Draupadī. One has only to do an unbiased conceptual analysis to correctly ascertain whether what Duryodhana, Kṛṣṇa or Bhīma, did, was really retributive or revengeful.

6 Ibid., Gadāparva, pp. 4295-98.

The Indian Social Scene

Imbalance of Social Well-being

The present-day Indian society is in a state of moral imbalance. By this I do not mean the oft-repeated saying that there is a collapse of values in all, or almost all, spheres of Indian life. The general collapse of values is not irrelevant to the specific kind of imbalance I have in mind. But I would almost exclusively concentrate on a particular kind of social or societal imbalance which is basically a moral imbalance. The imbalance I have in mind is, to put it in a way not too precise, an imbalance of well-being. A large section of the society has been, for a pretty long time, denied opportunities of growth and advancement leading to the general ill-being of its members. They have become economically poor, academically backward or uneducated, socially disrespected or neglected, etc., etc. Some of them were, until recently, considered untouchable.

To cause the ill-being of any section of the society is to commit immorality. Such things as poverty, ignorance, low mental development, etc., caused by some social practices or policies, and not by the lapses of the individuals or groups suffering from them, are moral, and therefore social, evils. It is important to emphasize, or even overemphasize, this truth because the implications of calling them moral evils are much more far-reaching than those of calling them just evils. Take ignorance, for example. If the resultant ignorance of any section of the society is a moral evil, then it becomes the moral duty of the government and the capable people of the country to get it removed. Ignorance can be removed by proper education and therefore proper education ought to be provided. The concerned agencies, if they do not make honest efforts in this direction, would, then, be not only negligent or incompetent but morally condemnable. Moral condemnation is the vilest that can be slung at any individual, group, or even political party.

To characterize this sort of moral evil, more precisely, to deprive a section of the society of adequate opportunities for developing their abilities, or ameliorating their living conditions, is an act of social injustice. Independent India has adopted a societal or political measure on a large scale to stop fresh occurrences of such injustices, and compensate for the past ones. I shall try to examine it in the light of the theoretical framework presented in the earlier sections.

The Hindu society is basically a caste-constituted society. By this I mean that the broadest or proximate groups or sections into which it can be divided are castes or caste-groups. Every Hindu by birth belongs to some caste. The oft-repeated assertion that in classical India an individual's caste was determined by his capabilities is only a red herring. This assertion is not provable. Rather, it would never have been true because it is not possible to determine anyone's caste on the basis of his abilities. Whatever might have been the case, at a very early stage of Indian history even in classical India, castes had become birth-determined. Moreover, today castes are birth-determined, and it is the social injustices suffered by, and facing some modern, birth-determined, caste-Indians, I am talking about here. (For a detailed critical discussion of classical Indian social order, see chapter 7 of my *A Conceptual-Analytic Study of Classical Indian Philosophy of Morals*, PHISPE, New Delhi. To be published by December 2006.)

Caste, Concession and Conversion

The non-Hindu sections of the Indian society are not, in the sense in which the Hindus are, caste constituted. Among the non-Hindus, Muslims, Christians, Buddhists, Jainas, and Sikhas in principle, are casteless groups because neither one of them admits of caste distinctions or divisions. In this respect they are more rational or equalitarian than Hinduism. This means that anyone who is a Muslim, a Christian, or a Buddhist et al, by birth or conversion, cannot claim to be of this or that caste. Consequently a Hindu, after becoming converted to any one of these religions cannot retain his pre-conversion caste. He must lose it, or give it up, otherwise he would not be a genuine convert. No one can have two religions. A man of one religion may have sympathy for, or even appreciation of, some aspects of another, but he cannot be a member of two religious groups, an adherent of two religious faiths. This means that a Hindu of caste *B*, after his conversion to, say, Christianity, ceases to be a member of caste *B*. Suppose, sometime after his conversion, the government passes a legislation to give some concessions to those members of caste *B* whose annual income is less than a certain amount, say *M*. Suppose further that the annual income of the convert, before and after his conversion, is less than *M*. But since he is no longer a *B*, he cannot claim the concessions. Concessions are, *ex hypothesi*, available only to him who is both a *B* and an earner of annual income less than *M*. The convert's annual income is less than *M* no doubt but he is not a *B*, and therefore is not covered by the legislation. He would have been covered had it also been applicable to Christians with annual income less than *M*, or to all Indians with annual income less than *M*, irrespective of their castes, or religions.

Therefore, when a converted non-Hindu claims to have a concession, available to a person of a certain caste, on the ground that in his pre-conversion period he belonged to that caste, it means that his conversion is not complete or genuine, or that the caste-system, through this move of his, has entered, or is entering, into the religion he has been converted to, or that he is unscrupulous, with no regard for his new religion, disposed to do anything for his selfish gain.

Let us limit the discussion to the Hindu sector of the society. If individuals or groups, who have suffered social injustices, were classified in some non-caste manner, then the entire gamut of the Indian society could have been uniformly covered by concessional or ameliorative measures. But the policy-makers found it easier to classify them in caste-terms. It was true that members of some castes were denied social justice *because* they belonged to those castes. Even if anyone of them improved his living condition and obtained some respectable job, he was not given the social status a person of equivalent rank but belonging to a so-called upper, or privileged, caste enjoyed. The caste of a person, thus, did become, in a large number of cases, the cause of his ill-being. Therefore, in a good number of cases the caste of a person was taken to be the indicator of the fact that social injustices had been done to him. It was not, thus, completely unreasonable to classify socially injusticed people into some caste-groups. The prospect of reaping a rich electoral harvest, by exploiting caste-feelings of the voting public, was also very clearly seen by the policy-makers and they were keen to tap it to the fullest extent. All this happened because behind such moves political motivation was always very strong. Some would even say that it was stronger than the alleged ethical motivation of preventing the privileged castes from doing further injustices, and of compensating for those already done, to the exploited, unprivileged or underprivileged, i.e. de-privileged, castes.

The Compensatory Measure in Operation: Revenge and Retribution

In order to make the discussion more accessible and manageable, I shall take up a particular area of social life, simplify it as much as possible, without, of course, making it look unrealistic, and then examine the Indian attempt to restore social justice relevant to that area. My objective would be to highlight some of the problems it is likely to give rise to and to suggest some ways of destroying, or curtailing, their power to disturb social harmony. Perhaps they cannot be completely eliminated, but it would mean a lot if their fire-power is reasonably reduced. Some such problems, it seems to me, have already arisen. That they have begun to disturb the social and moral order, or are not letting us have the kind of social-moral order the restoration of social justice is expected to usher in, is apparent to any neutral observer of the Indian social scene.

The area I want to limit myself to is that of education. Take a caste, which I would call *U*, most of whose members are uneducated, or very poorly educated. Generations of them have been socially neglected, disrespected, and denied facilities for good education. They have neither the economic resources to meet the cost of good education, nor the proper atmosphere in their families to motivate and help their children to do well in their schools which now have been made available to them. Therefore, their children very seldom secure good grades in their examinations. Since very high grades are required of a student to be admitted in a professional college, say, a medical one, none of these children is likely to receive medical education. And, all this is so, they feel and many others as well do, because generations of their caste members have been subjected to social injustices. The Indian experiment, to ameliorate this situation, is to provide to some of these children admission in a medical college in a concessional manner, by reducing the admission requirements for them in such a manner that at least a few of them would meet them. As the number of seats are limited, it so happens that some children of the caste *P*, an advanced one, with much better grades, are denied admission even if their economic and family background are not better than those of the concessionally admitted *U*-caste students. This is possible because some members of *P* may not be economically or familially better than some members of *U*, even though, as a caste, *P* is much more advanced or privileged than *U*.

Let us now imagine some of the possible ways in which the *U*-student and the *P*-student may react in the situation outlined above. The former may think in some such way:

> 'Generations of *P* have done social injustices to generations of my people. In giving me a seat in the medical college the government has not really given any concession to my caste. Rather, because of the power democracy has given to it, it has, in effect, snatched some seats from *P*, and thereby has avenged at least some of the injustices.' The *P*-student may also think that a revenge has been taken on his caste by *U* and the members of his caste have not been able to resist because of their weaker position in the country's politics. He may even blame some leaders of his caste to have betrayed his (and their) for fulfilling some of their personal political ambitions.

This kind of thinking may then lead to what generally happens when some people think to have avenged on, or to have been avenged on by, some others. The avengers may feel victorious, or become arrogant, and the avenged-on may start preparing for a direct or indirect reactive revenge. For example, it may happen that when he completes his education, the *U*-student becomes the boss of the *P*-student. The latter may then try to satisfy his propensity of revenge by not giving him the respect and courtesy he deserves in virtue of his official status. Sometimes the reactions of either party could be very strong and even violent. But whether they are mild or strong, concealed or open, the revenge-interpretation of the Indian move, of restoring social justice by the method of granting concessions to the undeveloped or under-developed sections of the society, would always be inimical to the protection or establishment of social harmony. Therefore, by means of proper dissemination of information about the relevant facts of social history and value-based education, attempts must be made to reduce, as much as circumstances permit, the possibility and appeal of the revenge interpretation. One step in this direction would be to get it replaced or countered by what I call the retributive interpretation. Suppose the *U*-student takes the Indian experiment as a retributive one: He thinks he has got the concession as a moral recompense for past injustices, the provision of concession as a moral mechanism for correcting social imbalance in the society.

To think in this way is to have a retributive, a moral, attitude towards the mechanism of concession, i.e. towards its provision and its consequences for him as well as for others like him, i.e. for the people of his caste and of some other castes. For anyone, to adopt a moral attitude is to have a care or concern for the welfare of others. Therefore, he would have some care or concern for others if he adopts the above-mentioned moral attitude. This means he would have a concern for the welfare of even those who would be deprived of admission to a medical college though they are, in merit, equal to, or better than, him. It is very likely, therefore, that instead of celebrating the consequential deprivation of admission to the latter, as he would have done had his attitude been one of revenge, he would then feel sorry for them. His reaction to his admission would be something like this: I have got what I ought to have got and thereby an injustice done to me and my caste has been compensated for. But this has caused an injustice to someone else; it has adversely affected his welfare This means that though my admission, being a case of giving me a moral compensation is a moral good, it has involved an immorality by adversely affecting someone else's welfare This is inevitable because the provision of the concession is the only way available to the society for correcting the social or moral imbalance. This sort of immorality is, therefore permissible or condonable, *but nothing more than that*. Since it is an immorality, it should not continue forever. The society must work for ushering in a social order in which resorting to such immoralities becomes uncalled for. This would mean, in this particular case, ushering in a social order in which (a) every, or almost every, candidate deserving admission in a medical college gets admitted, and, (b) the question of depriving any deserving one of admission in order to accommodate some undeserving, or not equally deserving one, on some non-academic ground, does not arise.

The stage mentioned above is not easy to reach, and it may even look utopian. But it is extremely desirable to be utopian these days because, in the name of what is called grass-roots realism, Indian politicians have almost completely eroded all values from an average Indian's picture of the good life. Not only the members of the weaker section, but every Indian, should aim at reaching this stage, though its description might vary a little in the case of others. Gandhi has made a remark somewhere that one should never wish to get something for nothing. But unfortunately the reverse seems to have captured the mind of Indians. One can very easily find a person, to whichever sphere of life he turns his eyes, gloating over having got something for nothing. It is this idea, ensconced in Gandhi's remark which I have tried to emphasize with the example of the stage I have talked about.

It is true that concessions are given to a person not simply because he belongs to a certain caste. Economic considerations are also taken into account and those belonging to the creamy layer are not entitled to them. But it is also true (a) that the majority of the members of certain castes, being below the poverty line, or socially backward, are entitled to them, (b) that there is some unclarity about how thick the cream in the creamy layer should be to make one belonging to it disentitled and therefore there exists the possibility of its different quantitative characterizations, and (c) that politicians make frequent references to castes in talking about concessions. The facts (a), (b) and (c) make it highly plausible for the beneficiary of a concession to believe that he has got the benefit because of his caste and for the consequential sufferer who has been deprived of it to believe that he has suffered the loss because of his caste. It is very likely, then, that both of them attach undue importance to their castes and develop casteist biases, the caste of politics. If this unfortunate thing happens on a large scale, it is very likely to cause social imbalance and disharmony, just the opposite of what the provision of concessions is intended to achieve. Minimizing, to the utmost possible extent, reference to castes in such matters alone can retrieve the situation. This does not seem to be possible in the near future because of the way Indian politics has been shaping itself in the last few decades. But it has to be done if the Indian society is to survive in a viable manner.

Well-designed Education as a Prophylactic to the Mechanism of Concession

It seems to me that the existing situation can be improved a lot if care is taken to adapt the quality and format of education given to *U*-students to their needs and capabilities. A fully-fledged programme of the relevant kind of education cannot be outlined here. I would rest satisfied with simply making some general suggestions.

It is said that because of centuries of exploitation, social neglect and injustices meted out to them, the will of a *U*- student to learn and rise in life has been terribly weakened. He has lost his self-confidence, his faith in his own individuality. Therefore, even if he is now given the chance to educate himself, he cannot do as well as a *P*-student can; the former's score would very seldom be comparable to that of the latter, etc., etc. Therefore, if he intends to join a medical college, the requirements of admission have to be very much relaxed to accommodate him. I am not questioning all this. I want to reiterate, as I have already made the point, that his concessional admission, even his concessional appointment as a doctor and promotion, etc., may not restore in him his self-confidence, his faith in his own capabilities, in his own individuality. Even if in some cases they do, they would not do so as effectively as improving his merit would. Therefore, I suggest an adaptation of the existing system of education in such a manner that when he is drilled through it, the chances of getting his merit improved become much brighter. More specifically, I suggest that syllabes taught to him be staggered in such a manner that he has to carry a lighter load than that of an average *P*-student, and consequently the number of years of schooling required for him has to be greater than that required for the latter. After a *U*-child is given some general schooling, a diagnostic test may be held to judge his aptitudes and abilities. If the average index of his performance is found to be much lower than that of a *P*-student of his age, in the coming classes a lighter load may be given to him so that he can perform better. In this way, he would take a little longer, say, twelve years, instead of ten years, to complete his secondary education. But his loss of two years would be very well compensated for by the resulting enrichment of his capabilities. It will boost up his self-image if he becomes able to get, because of his merit, what he is given nowadays because of some concession granted to him.

Concluding Overview

Social justice consists in giving to an individual, or letting him have, what he deserves to have in virtue of his being what he is. Social injustice is the denial of social justice. The victim of social injustice has to be compensated for the injustice done to him. The mode of compensation would depend on the nature of the commodity he deserved to have and which has been denied to him. Making the compensation may cause some suffering to someone else who may be the agent himself who has done the injustice, or to another person related directly or indirectly, immediately or remotely, to the latter. But it is also possible that no link is establishable between the agent, an individual, or a group, who has done some injustice or injustices, to some member or members of the *U*-caste and the individual, or group, belonging to the *P*-caste, who are to suffer, or be deprived of something, as the result of some concession granted to the victims of the injustice or injustices. This may happen because of the complexity of the case, or of the situation in which the alleged injustice was done. An unusually long gap of time between the injustice done and the compensation made may also be responsible for it.

The beneficiary of the compensation may have towards the compensation or its consequential sufferer an attitude of revenge or one of retribution. The same is the case with the attitudes the consequential sufferer may have towards the suffering caused to him, towards the beneficiary, or towards the agencies who have made the compensation available to the beneficiary. The attitude of revenge is very likely to cause immediately, or a little later, social, or societal, imbalance, whereas that of retributivity is not. Since the latter is a moral attitude, one who has it would have some care for the welfare of others. Therefore, it can generate some sympathy for the sufferer of the compensation in the mind of the beneficiary of the compensation. In a similar way, it can generate some understanding, even sympathy, in the mind of the sufferer for the beneficiary.

The Indian experiment of providing compensation to some members of some castes to whom social injustices have been done is, in principle, morally right if the motivation behind it is to restore social balance which has been disturbed by social injustices done to the latter. But the way it has been talked about, propagated, or championed, gives rise to the impression that it has been done to avenge on the wrong-doers, or, to put it realistically, on their distant descendents because the majority of the former are dead and gone. It is, therefore, very likely that the beneficiary thinks that his wrong-doers are avenged on for their misdeeds, and he who suffers in consequence thinks that he is being avenged on for something some of his ancestors have allegedly done. An attitude of revenge, or a revenge-interpretation of a situation, is extremely prone to generate a reactive attitude of counter-revenge in the other side, which may take revenge on the beneficiary in a direct or indirect manner, sooner or later, when he is in a position to do so. All this will obviously disturb social balance and harmony. To ward off this eventuality it is necessary that a social or moral climate is created in which both the beneficiary of compensation and its consequential sufferer have towards the provision of concessions or compensation the attitude of moral retribution. This would mean that both the beneficiary of a concession and the consequential sufferer need to be motivated to think that the former's benefiting from a concession is a moral compensation for some past immorality done to him or his predecessors, and the consequential suffering or deprivation caused to the latter is due to the peculiar nature of the Indian societal situation, due specifically, for example, to the paucity of resources, extreme poverty of the members of certain castes, etc. If such a climate of understanding is created, each one of them would have some sympathy for the other and both would admit that social affairs should be managed in such a manner that, as early as possible, the Indian society becomes so harmonious or cohesive that the benefit of one member of it does not become a burden on some other member.

A concession granted to an unprivileged, or underprivileged, person in the present set-up, means giving something to him by lowering, and more often than not, lowering very greatly, the qualifications which are normally required of a person from the privileged class to be eligible for making a claim to it. This practice is likely to generate in the recipient of the concession a feeling of inferiority which may get in the way of his developing into an elegant, self-respecting, individual. On the other hand, if it generates in him a feeling of pride, or of being a favoured person, allowed to have something with a merit much lower than that of some others to whom it has been denied, it would hamper his growth as a cohesive and cooperative individual. It has been suggested that, to ward off such possibilities, the concession-needing individuals should be given a kind of education specially designed for them, say, by extending the time-span and making provision for a reduced load of work required, so that when they come out of it they become able to stand on equal, or almost equal, footing with claimants from privileged classes. A suitable scheme for developing their skill and abilities can be made and implemented even for the present beneficiaries of concessions who are already holding some responsible ranks in some public or private concerns, or in some professional areas.

The ultimate objective of restoring social justice in the social order, by compensating for past injustices by means of granting to the victims a set of concessions, should be not merely to remove their economic hardships by giving them jobs or opportunities by lowering the criteria of entitlement. It should rather aim at helping them develop into individuals who are self-respecting, socially cohesive, and promotive of the constructive goals of the nation. One may say, in an objecting tone: But this should be the aim of education for all individuals. Everyone should develop into such beings. This is true, and I am emphasizing it because it is true. Ultimately, or in principle, all Indian citizens should form a single stream. The two streams, one of citizens entitled to concessions and the other of the remaining ones not entitled to them, must not run separately for ever, or for a long time. The sooner they merge into one, the sooner the number of concession-needing individuals becomes nil or negligible, the better for the country even if not so for the politician.

As I have argued, it is an ethical, or a meta-ethical truth that a social injustice has to be compensated for, since the concept of being compensated for is retributively contained in that of social injustice. And, depending upon the nature of certain empirical factors pertaining to the case concerned, the compensation may sometimes be done by doing something more than the corresponding act of social justice. For example, the Board of Trustees of a temple may not only allow, hitherto disallowed members of the scheduled castes to enter the temple, but also appoint one of their members its chief priest when the existing practice required is that the chief priest be a *brāhmaṇa*. The primary purpose of all such moves is to raise the social, or rather, overall, status of the members of the *U*-castes, and thereby to improve their style of life.

Equipping the members of the *U*-class with a sound value-structure is as *bona fide* a part of the programme of restoring social justice to them as is the provision of certain types of concessions in education, health-care, housing, jobs, etc. Their behavioural and thinking patterns have to be suitably changed along with making available to them, in a dignified manner, certain facilities which had been until recently denied to them and are not yet being fully utilized by them.

This was Gandhi's objective in all that he did and intended to do to improve the status of the down-trodden. He did not intend that they were helped to shine better by using some cosmetics donated by the society or governments. Rather, he struggled to help them have all that was needed to enable them to clean themselves of the dross, by their own efforts, that had accumulated on them because of the social injustices done to them and therby let the human gold in them shine in its own natural light.

He obviously tried to get all this done retributively because his method was to persuade the upper castes to realise that some benefits had to be given to backward castes because they deserved them and they were unjustly deprived of them till then. In a similar way, his struggle for India's freedom was retributive because their freedom was the moral right of Indians. What made it obviously retributive was its being *satyāgraha*, one which allowed only truthful, i.e. morally right, means and was to be conducted in accordance with the moral principle of non-violence (*ahiṃsā*) which did not permit any injury to British rulers against whom it was directed. The British response to it was a clear example of a revengeful move because its sole motivation was to suppress the struggle for justice by using even immoral means.

It would not matter here if Gandhi's struggle were called one for political freedom, and therefore for political justice. Political injustice is a species of social justice being an injustice caused by one sector of the international community, human society, to another. Therefore political justice is only a species of social justice.

Chapter 19

Gandhi, Empire, and a Culture of Peace

Joseph Prabhu

In a survey conducted by *Time* magazine in late 1999 about whom its world-wide readership considered the most significant person of the twentieth century, Gandhi came in a close second behind Albert Einstein. The choice seems appropriate; Einstein undoubtedly revolutionized our ideas of the physical world, whereas Gandhi can be said to have revolutionized our ideas about the moral-political world. Not only did he succeed in winning political independence for India from the British with scarcely a shot being fired; more significantly, he has served as the inspiration for a series of nonviolent freedom struggles from the Civil Rights Movement in the US to independence campaigns in places as disparate and as distant as South Africa, Eastern Europe, the Philippines, and the former Soviet Union. Einstein himself paid homage to him fulsomely: 'Generations to come will scarcely believe that such a one as this ever in flesh and blood walked upon the earth.'

What is the nature and scope of that moral revolution? At a first approximation one would have to say that Gandhi's contribution lies in the demonstration through his life and writings of the power of nonviolence. And yet at a theoretical level there is nothing new about the precept of nonviolence. From the Sermon on the Mount to the teachings of many religions and philosophies, the idea that one should have good will toward one's fellow men and women, including one's enemies, and the concomitant notion that one should respond to evil with good have been widely proclaimed, even if rarely practiced. Gandhi himself said that the idea of nonviolence is 'as old as the hills.' What is new in Gandhi is the broadening and the deepening of the idea beyond the private sphere to social and political realms. As Martin Luther King, Jr. once asserted, it was from Gandhi that he learnt that the power of the love ethic of Jesus was not merely confined to the personal sphere, but was as applicable to political thought and action. Gandhi has often been described as a saint among politicians and a politician among saints, and that peculiar synthesis of religion and politics that he achieved will be examined later in this essay for both its positive and negative consequences.

One can think of others in history with a religio-political message from Socrates and Confucius to Mohammed to Swami Vivekananda. And yet Gandhi was neither a sage nor a prophet. One studies him not so much for any deep or startling original spiritual or political insight as for the integrity and the integrative power of his life. As he said on more than one occasion, 'My life is my message.' If one looks at the details of the life, its priorities, the values it embodied, and the ideals it tried to achieve, one might be both surprised and struck by the fact that most of Gandhi's time in South Africa and in India was spent not in direct political activity, but in his *ashrams* trying to establish and sustain model communities. This accounts in part for the otherwise bewildering range of topics covered in the more than ninety volumes of his collected writings – everything from tooth care to theology, hygiene to mysticism. It is clear when one looks carefully at his life that his priorities lay in realizing through these model communities a more comprehensive vision of nonviolence, which overstepped the boundaries of conventional political activity. It is this vision that I am calling his 'culture of peace.'

There are at least two different kinds of violence: First, there is overt violence, which can take sundry forms from riots and revolutions at the social level to harmful words and actions at the personal. This is the violence that one cannot help but notice because it is so visible and manifest. But secondly, there is a more subtle and less apparent form of violence, that following Johan Galtung, I shall call 'structural violence.'[1] This is the violence contained in unjust institutions and practices that may be legal but which nonetheless oppress or exploit people. Corresponding to these forms of violence, we may for analytical purposes distinguish between two aspects of nonviolence in Gandhi's thought and practice, one which tries to meet and diffuse overt violence and the other which attempts to overcome structural violence by offering a holistic way of life that is peaceful and harmonious. This way of life may be likened to the Buddha's fourth Noble Truth. Whereas the first three truths diagnose the nature of our suffering and seek its causes, the fourth, also known as the Eight-Fold Path, goes further and prescribes a way of life that in its integrity prevents existential suffering from arising in the first place. It is, in other words, a philosophy of health rather than of sickness. Much of the 'constructive program' that Gandhi outlined for a healthy society was his antidote to the violence and the sickness that he perceived in modern industrial society.

Twentieth-century imperialism was for Gandhi one of these sicknesses, a logical consequence of the greed and voraciousness of the modern industrial system. Unlike other analysts of imperialism, he located its roots not in notions of national glory or of civilizing missions, but in the economic imperatives of the system driven as it was by ever-increasing production and the desire for markets. Gandhi's struggle against the British Empire was not just against the political domination that it imposed but more broadly against the materialistic – and for him violent – lifestyle it represented.

Gandhi was not a philosopher in the conventional sense of the term, that is, someone who thinks in terms of abstract concepts about the nature of the world and the self. He was primarily a man of action, a *karma yogi*. Nonetheless, a coherent philosophy can be constructed out of his multifarious sayings and writings. That is what I shall attempt primarily in the areas of his social and economic thought. I shall focus on the following: (1) his critique of modernity issued from the viewpoint of

---

1 Johan Galtung, *Peace by Peaceful Means: Peace and Conflict, Development and Civilization*, London: Sage Publications, 1996.

(2) his fundamental ethical ideas, his notions of truth [*satya*], nonviolence [*ahiṃsā*], and truth-force [*satyāgraha*]; (3) his economic philosophy and the constructive social program he outlines for a more peaceful and harmonious existence; and (4) the relevance of his thought to the recent resurgence of imperialism. [This essay was written in May-June 2003.] Needless-to-say, this is an interpretive exercise, which like all such exercises allows for criticism and alternative interpretations; but I hope to show that this particular interpretation is at the very least quite plausible.

Gandhi's Critique of Modernity

In November 1909, on his return by ship from London to South Africa, after an unsuccessful lobbying mission, Gandhi had what commentators described as a 'profound experience of illumination,' comparable to Rousseau's on the road to Vincennes. Many of the ideas, thought and feelings that had accumulated over the previous twenty years ripened and came to a head. In ten days on board the ship *Kildoan Castle*, he produced 275 manuscript pages written as such a harrowing pace that when his right hand got tired, he plodded on with his left. Years later, looking back at the experience, Gandhi wrote, 'Just as one cannot help speaking out when one's heart is full, so also I had been unable to restrain myself from writing the book since my heart was full.' The book that Gandhi produced with such a sense of urgency and mission was *Hind Swaraj*, or *Indian Home Rule* as the book came to be known in English. As Anthony Parel in his new edition of this text remarks, *Hind Swaraj* is Gandhi's seminal work. It was through this that he hoped, as he put it 'to use the British race' for transmitting his 'mighty message of *ahiṃsā* to the rest of the world. It was to this text that he returned throughout his career as if to the source of his inspiration.' [2]

The context within which Gandhi wrote *Hind Swaraj* sheds light on his intentions in writing the book. While in London he met a number of Indian intellectuals, including V.D. Savarkar, one of whose supporters, Nathuram Godse, would later assassinate Gandhi. These intellectuals Gandhi found were all enamored with modern Western civilization even while they decried colonialism. Gandhi pointed out to them the contradiction in their position, namely, that colonialism itself was a logical consequence of modern civilization insofar as its economic engine drove it to seek sources of cheap labor and raw materials and markets for its expanding industrial production. Furthermore, Gandhi disagreed with Savarkar and others about the means by which freedom should be attained: they favoured violence and terrorist tactics and indeed one of Savarkar's friends, Madan Lal Dhingra, had in July 1909 assassinated the political aide-de-camp to Lord Morley, the Secretary of State for India. For Gandhi such nationalist violence was connected with the instability of the modern West and was both impractical and undesirable: impractical because the British were vastly better armed, and undesirable because in taking up arms India

2 Anthony Parel (ed.), *Gandhi: Hind Swaraj and Other Writings*, Cambridge: Cambridge University Press, 1997, pp. xiv-xv.

would be adopting the worst features of Western civilization. 'To arm India on a large scale is to Europeanize it. Then her condition will be just as pitiable as that of Europe…whom do you suppose to free by assassination? The millions of India do not desire it. Those who are intoxicated by the wretched modern civilization think these things.'[3]

The stimulus of these encounters with Indian anarchists together of course with Gandhi's own experience of British culture both during his student days in London and in South Africa from 1893 onwards provided the occasion for him to collect his thoughts and reflect systematically about the course of Western modernity, after having spent nearly twenty years in the West. He had certain advantages in this enterprise. As one belonging to a colonized country and to an oppressed minority in South Africa, he was able to discern the darker face of modern civilization. Furthermore, as one who brought to this encounter with the West the values of a quite different civilization, he was able to see the West through Indian eyes and uncover its hidden impulses, drives, and contradictions. There is, of course, some irony in the critique of *Hind Swaraj*. When Gandhi first came to England, he himself was quite enamored with British culture. In light of Winston Churchill's later sneer about 'that half-naked fakir,' it is amusing to read about Gandhi's sartorial adventures – his Saville Row suits – and his attempts at trying to become a British gentleman. Longer acquaintance with the culture and deeper reflection allowed him to see through the surface glamour, and while he always maintained a deep respect for certain aspects of Western civilization – its scientific temper, its energy and spirit of enterprise, organization skill and civil liberties, for example – he began increasingly to see it as materialistic, soulless, and fundamentally violent toward both nature and human life.

In *Hind Swaraj*, for example, Gandhi comes out with a long list of evils spawned by the modern industrial system. He ties together his critique of the economic system with that of its technological underpinning, the larger phenomenon of industrialism, a self-propelling process creating larger and larger industries to satisfy the insatiable demand for cheap consumer goods and profits. Since it has a built-in momentum of its own, it renders men largely powerless and passive and hence represents a modern and insidious form of slavery, the more dangerous because of its meretricious charms, which are greedily seized. It mistakes material comfort for progress, constant motion for purposeful movement, restlessness for vitality and dynamism, speed for efficiency, and consumerism for an improved quality of life. From Gandhi's point of view the Western path of modernization is a fundamentally alienating and unstable one. It is materialistic, exploitative of nature and human beings, unrestrained and lacking a sense of direction and moral purpose.

It is this industrial momentum that Gandhi identifies as the primary source of imperial ambition. Unlike some of his contemporaries like Bankim Chatterjee or Aurobindo Ghose, Gandhi does not identify the root causes of modern imperialism in exaggerated notions of national glory but rather in the mode of social production.

3 Op. cit., p. 77.

It is this drive for ever-increased production designed to meet the needs of ever-expanding consumption and the ruthless competition that accompanies the process that impels the system to seek colonial possession which can be economically exploited as a source both of raw materials and of markets.

> They [the English] hold whatever dominions for the sake of their commerce. Their army and their navy are intended to protect it....the English entered India for the purposes of trade...They wish to convert the whole world into a vast market for their goods...They will leave no stone unturned to reach that goal.[4]

Gandhi's argument here is applied to the social and technological process of industrialism rather than to a specific economic form of such a process, such as capitalism. From Gandhi's viewpoint both modern capitalism and socialism are characterized by the industrial system which he sees as alienating and exploitative. The mere socialization of industry will not fundamentally alter or mitigate such exploitation.

> Pandit Nehru wants industrialization because he thinks that if it is socialized it would be free from the evils of capitalism. My own view is that evils are inherent in industrialism and no amount of socialization can eradicate them.[5]

Even though the analysis of industrialism and imperialism is couched in economic terms, the fundamental source of their evils is seen in moral terms and is placed in modern materialism. Gandhi assays an ethical critique of modern economics and technology which we will consider more fully in section 3. For our present purposes, we get a better idea of Gandhi's position when we see his alternative, and essentially moral, definition of civilization. 'Civilization is that mode of conduct, which points out to man the path of duty. Performance of duty and observance of morality are convertible terms. To observe morality is to attain mastery over our mind and our passions. So doing we know ourselves. Civilization means good conduct.'[6] Gandhi's idea of civilization is essentially a *dharmic* one, where *dharma* connotes a fixed position of duty and right, that which gives cohesion to and holds together all of life [*lokasaṃgraha*]. From this may be derived the idea of mutual responsibility and reciprocity. Just as one is upheld by the natural and human orders of life in terms of sustenance and nurture, both physical and cultural, so also one has the obligation to sustain and enhance these orders of existence.

By contrast, modern Western civilization driven by the imperatives of industrialism, according to Gandhi, sees human beings primarily as consumers driven by greed and self indulgence, propensities which the market both encourages and exploits. Thus,

---

4 Op. cit., p. 41.

5 M.K. Gandhi, *The Collected Works of Mahatma Gandhi*, 100 volumes, New Delhi: Publications Division, vol. 73, pp. 29-30, (hereafter CWMG); quoted in Partha Chaterjee, *Nationalist Thought and the Colonial World: A Derivative Discourse?* Delhi: Oxford University Press, 1986, p. 88.

6 Parel, op. cit., p. 67.

any idea of self-rule and self-control on the one hand and responsibility and concern for one's fellow humans and for nature on the other, is vitiated by the relentless pursuit of material satisfaction. Lost in the process is the sense of moral restraint and direction provided by ethical living. It is the lineaments of that ethical living, both personal and social, that we will now spell out by analyzing some of Gandhi's key moral concepts.

Gandhi's Moral Universe

Gandhi is a moralist through and through and yet it is difficult to write philosophically about his ethics. This is because Gandhi is fundamentally concerned with practice rather than with theory or abstract thought, and such philosophy as he used was meant to reveal its 'truth' in the crucible of experience. Hence the subtitle of his *Autobiography* – 'the story of my experiments in truth.' The experiments refer to the fact that the truth of concepts, values, and ideals is fulfilled only in practice. Prior to that practical fulfilment they remain spectral and abstract. Furthermore, Gandhi's ethics are inextricably tied up with his religion, which itself is unconventional. Though an avowed Hindu, he was a Hindu in a philosophical rather than a sectarian sense, and there was much Hindu ritual and practice that he subjected to critique. In accordance with this religio-philosophical ideal, his religion could be described as the life of the self attempting to realize itself as Self, and thus achieving *mokṣa* or spiritual liberation. But *karma yogi* that he was, Self-realization had to be expressed through work in the world and the details of daily life rather than through renunciation of the world. Gandhi's own ethics have a decidedly spiritual cast, but because he takes pains to express them in a neutral philosophical manner, he intends them to have general validity. Thus, when he switches from affirming that God is Truth to saying that Truth is God, his rationale is that the latter is a more general statement which has resonance even for unbelievers:

> God is Truth, but God is many other things also. That is why I prefer to say that Truth is God…you may simply worship what you find to be the truth for Truth is known relatively. Only remember that Truth is one of the many qualities that we name. It is the living embodiment of God, it is the only Life and I identify Truth with fullest life and that is how it becomes a concrete thing for God is His whole creation, the whole Existence, and service of all that exists.[7]

This statement is a testament to Gandhi's innate sense of tolerance and inclusiveness in that he believes that his ideals of truth and nonviolence are accessible even to those who do not share his religious metaphysics. It is a feature of some moral statements that they can be differently interpreted and justified and yet be shown to have validity at different levels of understanding. Thus, the precept of honesty can be justified on the grounds of prudence ('honesty is the best policy'), or of promoting

---

7 CWMG, vol. 68, p. 81.

trust and social harmony in society (utilitarian), safeguarding one's own integrity and righteousness before the law (Kant), as duty owed to others as autonomous moral agents (Kant and some versions of Christianity), as a cosmic obligation (a *dharmic* justification), to mention only some possibilities. Likewise, people may agree on certain human rights, even though they ground those rights quite differently. In a similar spirit, Gandhi wanted his teaching of nonviolence to have the widest possible adherence. But if one wants to understand his own particular justification and interpretation of his ethical ideas, we cannot escape the religious metaphysics that serves as their ground and presupposition. James Hart captures this well when he writes:

> When the Vedāntic tradition holds that each self as Self is profoundly and irreducibly nonobjectifiable, it moves in the direction of holding that the truth of things and other selves has a form of causality other than that of material objects. The fundamental sense of oneself and the other which the commitment to Truth awakens is the incommensurability of selves with material, unselved, unbesouled objects. *Ahiṃsā* is the practice of a kind of transcendental reduction because it preserves this most basic truth. And being awakened to this most basic Truth, the truth about selves and meanings, is what provides the central importance of *ahiṃsā*.[8]

With these prefatory remarks I shall briefly analyze and comment on some of Gandhi's key ethical concepts.

Truth

Truth for Gandhi is not merely, or even primarily, the property of statements, though Gandhi does not deny the importance of factual truth or the correspondence between propositions and states of affairs in the world that either confirm or refute them. Rather, his multifaceted notion of truth emphasizes ontological, moral, and existential aspects. Ontologically, *satya* is derived from *Sat*, the self-existent essence, both the Is and the Ought of reality. It was this derivation that led Gandhi often to say, 'Nothing exists in reality except Truth, everything else is illusion.' Beyond the illusory temporal flux of phenomena lies the eternal Truth, what Gandhi also called Absolute Truth. We humans with our finite capacities can have access however only to relative truth, an assertion Gandhi uses to justify epistemological humility and tolerance. All our perceptions of truth are inevitably partial and therefore claims of cognitive absoluteness are both unwarranted and dangerous.

While the ontological aspect of truth points to a more objective notion, the moral and existential aspects move in the direction of a more subjective, almost Kierkegaardian, notion of truth as subjectivity, the deeply personal intuition of truth which can be experienced only through action. Raghavan Iyer brings out the duality between the subjective and objective aspects of truth:

---

8 James Hart, 'Recent Works in Gandhi Studies,' in *Philosophy East and West*, 44 (1), January 1994, p. 156.

> Gandhi could not regard truth either as solely the object of reason or as simply the product of human decision. For him…truth is nothing less than the splendor of reality and cannot be gained without an understanding of the Eternal Law of Nature, but when it is perceived and seized it must be acted upon. In this sense truth must be both discovered and created, found and enacted…In this activist view of truth…it is not enough for thought to be based upon truth; the life of the thinker must express it, must represent it visibly in his actions.[9]

As already intimated, this idea of truth for Gandhi found its fullest expression in the field of politics, which in accordance with his moral outlook he regarded as the arena for doing good on the largest possible scale. The idea that Gandhi used to encapsulate this moral conception of politics was *satyāgraha.* This was conceived as a practical experiment to introduce truth and nonviolence into the political field. Gandhi adopted this idea early in his political career when he chose *satyāgraha* as the name for his resistance movement against the repressive South African government. Explaining his decision, Gandhi wrote, 'Truth [*satya*] implies love and firmness [*āgraha*] and therefore serves as a synonym for force. I thus began to call the Indian movement *satyāgraha*, that is to say, the force which is born of truth and love of nonviolence.'[10] The forceful and activist character of *satyāgraha* should correct a common misperception; namely that it denotes a passivity of resistance, a mere turning of the other cheek. Although Gandhi insisted that violence be met with love and understanding, the nonviolent means chosen should not obscure the powerful end – that of establishing justice and truth. In fact, he is on record as saying that if the choice were between the passive acceptance of injustice and violent resistance to it, he would choose the latter. He was convinced, however, that nonviolent resistance was superior to both alternatives.

Satyāgraha begins with reasoning with one's opponent or adversary in an attempt to arrive at a just solution, recognizing that no party has a monopoly on the truth, or is wholly in the right. The purpose, therefore, is to work out a rational compromise that will be agreeable to both sides. It is only when such processes of reasoning, persuasion, and compromise have been tried and have proved unsuccessful that one adopts the direct action techniques of *satyāgraha. Satyāgraha* involves performing actions such as noncooperation (strikes, boycotts, lockouts, fasts); civil disobedience (nonpayment of taxes, disregard of specific laws or injunctions); publicizing one's cause through marches, rallies, picketing, and other forms of peaceful protest; and constructive programs (low-cost housing, education, health facilities, cooperative banks for the poor). A big part of such nonviolent resistance is *tapas* or the willingness to suffer for one's cause. As Thomas Pantham puts it, 'It is the assumption of *satyāgraha* that when reasoning fails to move the head, the argument of suffering by the *saatyāgrahis* helps move the heart of the oppressor or opponent. Self-suffering,

---

9 Raghavan Iyer, *The Moral and Political Thought of Mahatma Gandhi*, Oxford: Oxford University Press, 1973, p. 154.

10 M. Gandhi, *Satyāgraha in South Africa*, Madras: S. Ganesa, 1938, p. 172.

moreover, is the truth-serving alternative to the truth-denying method of inflicting violence on others.'[11]

Contained in this idea of *satyāgraha* is the question of means and ends, which for Gandhi are two sides of the same coin. Gandhi disagrees strongly with the conventional political idea that the ends justify the means. To the contrary, he held that immoral means taint and distort potentially good ends and to that extent he placed at least as much, if not more, emphasis on the means, which he described as ends in actions. 'The means may be likened to a seed, the end to a tree; and there is just the same inviolable connection between the means and the end as there is between the seed and the tree.'[12]

The forceful and activist character of *satyāgraha* leads naturally to the idea of nonviolence. Gandhi is obviously invoking the Jaina precept of *ahiṃsā*, or not causing deliberate injury or harm to any being, but Gandhi takes the precept far beyond its merely negative formulation to mean the largest love, the greatest charity. 'If I am a follower of *ahiṃsā*, I must love my enemy or a stranger as I would love my wrong-doing father or son. This *ahiṃsā* necessarily includes truth and fearlessness.'[13]

Ahiṃsā then is the deployment of moral force to persuade one's opponent or adversary. It differs from violence in that it respects the autonomy and dignity of the other, whereas violence does not. It differs from violence in the perpetual willingness to dialog and negotiate with the other and, as far as is consistent with rightness, to come to a compromise. Given that one's grasp of the truth is at best partial, it is imperative to see and appreciate the truth in the position of the other and to try and achieve a higher or dialectical reconciliation of conflicting ends. This negotiated compromise has the opposite effect of violence, which involves vanquishing and putting down one's opponent that inevitably sets up a cycle of resentment, ill will, and further violence.

Of course, Gandhi was not so naïve as to think that such moral persuasion would come about easily. He was all too aware that people who exercise power over others are not likely to give it up without some pressure being exerted. All the means of *satyāgraha* mentioned above should then be adopted as a way of morally coercing one's opponent to negotiate. It is true that coercion is being exerted, but it is a coercion that still respects the moral agency and dignity of the other, not least by the willingness to undergo self-suffering.

The strategy presupposes that the opponent does have a minimal openness to such moral appeal, a trait that Gandhi was willing to grant to most people. However, he also recognized that there are madmen and tyrants, rapists and aggressors who would not fall within that category. In those extreme cases Gandhi was willing to use physical force for the purpose of self defence, as, for example, when he sanctioned

11 Thomas Pantham, 'Habermas's Practical Discourse and Gandhi's *Satyāgraha*,' in *Political Discourse: Exploration in Indian and Western Thought*, Bhikhu Parekh and Thomas Pantham (eds), New Delhi: Sage Publications, 1987, pp. 292-310.

12 CWMG, vol. 10, p. 431.

13 Letter in *Modern Review*, October 1916, quoted in Iyer, op. cit., p. 180.

the use of military force to drive back the Pakistani Army in what he considered to be the invasion of Kashmir in 1948. Less satisfactory was his response to Martin Buber, when the latter skeptically asked Gandhi whether he thought that the Jews should use *satyāgraha* against Hitler.[14]

The three concepts I have discussed, *satya*, *satyāgraha*, and *ahiṃsā* might give us some idea of the texture of Gandhi's ethical thought. As mentioned earlier, the ideas of truth and nonviolence are certainly to be found in the Jain, Buddhist, and Hindu traditions, but there is a big difference between Gandhi's conceptualization of these ideas and traditional ones. The high standards of moral and spiritual discipline that Gandhi invokes were traditionally part of the *sādhana* of monks and saints, but decidedly not of people in political life. To the contrary, political thinkers like Manu and Kauṭilya sanctioned the use of physical force both for self-defence and for purposes of political order. Gandhi by contrast considerably softens the traditional dualism between religion and politics. Instead, he attempts to forge a non-dual relationship between the two, where religion seen as reverence for and service to Life necessarily leads to politics, the arena for the greatest potential public service; and where politics in turn is saved from power mongering and the conflict of factional interests by the moral purification involved in religion at its best. It is very important to distinguish Gandhi's highly moral notions of both religion and politics from the ideological conceptions of them all too common in our time. Certainly the rise of religious fundamentalism and right-wing religious groups would make any peace-loving person nervous about the marriage of religion and politics. It should be clear, however, from what I have written that the moral checks and balances that Gandhi exercised over religion and politics purified both domains and offered the world a far different and more noble conception of them that we have yet to measure up to.

But it was not just to the realm of politics that Gandhi wanted ethical and religious ideas extended. In line with his insistence that justice is the basis of peace, Gandhi believed that economic arrangements were crucial for the cause of nonviolence. Imperialism was the usurping not just of political but also of economic sovereignty and in his economics of *swadeshi*, Gandhi offered ideas of relevance not merely to India's independence struggle, but more generally for a just and peaceful economic patterning of society. It is to a consideration of those economic ideas that I now move.

Gandhi's Economic Philosophy

Given Gandhi's philosophical anthropology, which sees human beings as primarily moral and spiritual beings, his economic philosophy and its implied critique of modern economics follow. There are at least three interrelated points at which

14 Martin Buber and J.L. Magnes, *Two Letters to Gandhi*, Jerusalem: Rubin Mass, April 1939, cited in Dennis Dalton, *Mahatma Gandhi: Nonviolent Power in Action*, New York: Columbia University Press, 1993, p. 228. See also Gandhi's exchanges with other Jews, which Dalton discusses on pp. 134-138.

Gandhi criticizes modern western economics. First, it has an exclusively materialistic character in that it equates material satisfaction with human welfare. Seeing human beings primarily as consumers, the modern economic system operates through encouraging an endless multiplication of wants, well in excess of needs. In doing so, it encourages greed and envy, which in turn breed competitiveness, dishonesty and violence. Gandhi's economic prescriptions go in the opposite direction. 'There is enough in the world for everyone's need, but not for everyone's greed.' With his *dharmic* notion of mutual responsibility, Gandhi emphasizes not the multiplication of wants but their voluntary restriction, frugality in lifestyle and economy in our use of resources. Granted that some material comfort is a condition of spiritual welfare, it nonetheless ought to be seen as a means to an end and not an end in itself.

Second, self-interest is both the cause and the consequence of the economic individualism of market capitalism. Indeed, the notions of preference, choice and maximization which are the core concepts of modern micro-economics all operate on the unquestioned assumption that what should be maximized is the set of preferences of the individual economic actor. If materialism deals with the anthropological side of the economic system, self-interest concerns its ethical aspect, although it is obvious that the two are closely related. Gandhi's notion of *dharma* and soul-force again point in a radically different direction toward mutual care and concern. It is axiomatic for Gandhi that we are our brother's (and sister's) keeper. If that is so, then what has to be maximized is not individual satisfaction, but the common good and it is via the common good that individuals ought to seek their well-being. Instead of the atomistic idea of the self that exists prior to and independently of social relations, Gandhi as a communitarian holds an organic conception of the self, where parts and the whole are essentially connected.

Third, as far as the social organization of production is concerned, Gandhi is critical of both unregulated market capitalism and bureaucratic socialism. The first he feels inevitably leads to a social Darwinism in the economic sphere with cutthroat competition and a Hobbesian war of all against all. The 'fittest' that survive do not necessarily go in for socially useful production or promote the social good. Furthermore, such laissez-faire capitalism ineluctably results in gross inequalities of income, wealth and power, so that any kind of democratic accountability is circumvented and abuses of various sorts flourish unchecked. As far as bureaucratic socialism is concerned, in Gandhi's judgment, that leads to a different kind of harm, with the concentration of power now in the hands of state bureaucrats. In addition, centralized planning is notoriously insensitive to the needs and condition of the people, especially those residing in villages. Gandhi' own ideas here go in the direction of decentralization, with each village trying as far as possible to achieve self-sufficiency and then organizing regional markets and cooperatives. These ideas have been in the vanguard of contemporary movements in localized and regional production from 'local exchange and trading systems' (LETS) to 'community supported agriculture' (CSA).

Gandhi's best known scheme to employ and feed the unemployed millions was through homespun cloth (*khadi*) produced by the spinning wheel, which Gandhi wanted to make the foundation of village – and by extension – national economic life. He described it as a symbol of self-help, freedom from domination and non-violent economic self-sufficiency. He was quite aware that from one set of criteria commonly adopted in economic calculation, *khadi* was both 'inefficient,' insofar as power-driven spindles could do the work more quickly, and more costly in terms of the amount of labor that had to be employed relative to labor- and time-saving machines. But in talking of his 'socialism of the spinning wheel,' Gandhi responded to these criticisms thus: '*Khadi* serves the masses, mill cloth is intended to serve the classes. *Khadi* serves labor, mill cloth exploits it.' Its main purpose, he said, was 'to harness every single idle minute of our millions for common productive work.'[15] Appropriate technology and economics required that one see what resources were in abundance and what in relative scarcity and within those parameters that one maximize the social good. While, from a narrowly economic point of view, textile mills might prove cheaper, from a broader social perspective Gandhi believed that the social costs of unemployment in terms of dehumanization and the loss of self-respect should figure more prominently.

In short, Gandhi's economic and industrial policy strongly rejected the imitation of western models so beloved not only by so-called 'experts' from the West, but also by Indian educated elites, models stressing development from 'on top': frantic urbanization, heavily capital-intensive industrialization, mass production, centralized development planning, or unregulated market capitalism and, finally, sophisticated technology. By contrast Gandhi's scheme was one of a grass-roots development strategy 'from below': village economics, self-sufficiency, stabilization, and enhancement of a traditional peasant way of life by way of labor-intensive manufacture and handicrafts, decentralized decision making, even if this drastically reduced the pace of urban and industrial growth.

Within this framework, Gandhi's general philosophy of work becomes clearer:

1. Everyone has a right to work and society has the obligation to provide work, even if it means a reduction in gross national product (GNP), or some other quantitative measure of economic performance. Gandhi was more concerned with 'production by the masses than mass production,' more interested in improving the quality of life of ordinary people than in enriching a select few.
2. All work enjoys equal dignity, be it a lawyer's or a barber's; each person has the duty to contribute to the common-weal according to his or her capacities.
3. The good of the individual is contained in the good of all, given his organic view of the self.
4. Manual labor should be an essential component of each person's work; the purported superiority of intellectual to physical work is a false one. Each individual should strive for self-sufficiency and self-reliance by taking care

15 Glyn Richards, *The Philosophy of Gandhi*, New Jersey: Barnes and Noble Books, 1982, p. 119.

of his manual chores. For this reason, he recommended that the Congress Party, which was leading India's national struggle against the British, should make the wearing of *khadi* a condition of membership and felt that it should also advocate the practice of spinning for all as a symbol of political self-determination and of spiritual protest against the depredations of industrial civilization.

5. There is a special grace to the work of the peasant and craftsman, both because they provide essential food and clothing and also because they stay close to the land and to the rhythms of nature.

All these principles Gandhi adopted from his reading of Tolstoy, Ruskin and Thoreau, but he added to them another one which he took from the *Bhagavad Gītā*, the single most important scripture for him, namely the principle of *naiṣkarmyakarma* or detachment in, but not from, work: 'To action alone has thou a right, but not to the fruits thereof.' No work is good unless it is purged of attachment for extrinsic gain or advantage. By contrast, that action is right that is done for its own sake and not as a means to some further end.

The Indian philosopher and economist, J.C. Kumarappa, in his important book *The Economy of Permanence* sums up the Gandhian philosophy of work:

> If the nature of the work is properly appreciated and applied, it will stand in the same relation to the higher faculties as food is to the physical body. It nourishes and enlivens the higher man and urges him to produce the best he is capable of. It directs his free will along the proper course and disciplines the animal in him into progressive channels. It furnishes an excellent background for man to display his scale of values and develop his personality.[16]

Gandhi's attitude toward work is therefore quite opposed to modern economic ideology. From the standpoint of the individual employer, work figures as an item of cost in the wage bill and should therefore be reduced to a minimum, if not eliminated by, for example, automation. From the standpoint of a professional economist looking at employment in macro-economic terms, the chief criteria are inflation on the one hand, and the GNP on the other, the volume of goods produced in a given span of time. Gandhi's economics, to adopt Schumacher's famous phrase, was an 'economics as if people mattered.' Unemployment does not just deprive a person of an income, or reduce her contribution to GNP; it does something far more serious from Gandhi's perspective: it dehumanizes and degrades a person by depriving her of the opportunity to discipline herself in creative and self-affirming work.

---

16 J.C. Kumarappa, *The Economy of Permanence*, Kashi: Sarva-Seva Sangh Publications, (4th edn), 1958, p. 32.

Gandhi vs. Empire

This chapter is entitled 'Gandhi, Empire, and a Culture of Peace.' I have in the previous sections outlined the key ideas – ethical, religious, political, and economic – underlying what I have called Gandhi's culture of peace. In this final section I should like to spell out how strongly his ideas militate against imperialism. Like violence, imperialism also comes in at least two different forms, overt and tacit. Overt imperialism is the one we are more familiar with, when a state effectively controls the sovereignty of another political society or group of people either by force or by economic and social domination. Such empires have existed throughout history from the Persian and Roman empires of antiquity to the emerging American empire as it attempts to establish hegemony in the Middle East. Whatever rationales are offered for imperial rule – establishing law and order, responding to internal pleas, preventing ethnic and religious strife, for example – it is clear from independence struggles that self determination and political freedom are as widely accepted today as the sentiment against slavery. Hence the horror that people around the world felt and continue to feel at the US invasion and occupation of Iraq.

But imperialism also exists at levels that do not get quite the same attention. Such is the case, I would argue, with the economic imperialism exercised by global corporation, especially over poor countries in the South. Two hundred corporations have twice the Gross Domestic Product of four-fifths of humanity. Here are some other figures that indicate the inequalities of income, wealth, and human well-being brought about by corporate-driven globalization. While the world's population has doubled during the past thirty-nine years from three to six billion people, the real world product (i.e. the inflation-adjusted sum of all gross domestic products or GDP) has quadrupled in the same period, so that real per capita world product is now roughly twice what it was in 1960. But a significantly large proportion of humankind is not participating in this economic prosperity. At the bottom of the economic scale, in the poorest quarter or quintile, conditions continue to be desperate: 1.3 billion people, that is 22 per cent of the world's population, live below the international poverty line, which means that they have a daily income of roughly 1.5 dollars in terms of current purchasing power. As a consequence of such severe poverty, 841 million (14 per cent of the world's population) are malnourished today, 880 million (15 per cent) are without access to safe drinking water, 1 billion (17 per cent) are without adequate shelter, 1.3 billion (22 per cent) are without access to any kind of health care, 2 billion (33 per cent) are without electricity, and 2.6 billion (43 per cent) are without access to sanitation. What is even worse, a quarter of all children between 5-14, 250 million in all, are compelled to work, often under cruel conditions, in occupations ranging from mining and factory work to textile production and prostitution. Such poverty is, of course, nothing new. What is new, however, is the increasing inequality between rich and poor produced by economic globalization.

Incomes in the top quintile of the world's population are as much as 220 times higher than in the bottom quintile at current market exchange rates.[17]

In such a situation Gandhi's thought and ideas, always vital, acquire a new urgency and relevance. If imperialism connotes control of the economic and political sovereignty of another country, Gandhi stands for autonomy and self-determination. If imperialism points to rule over others, Gandhi points to *swaraj* and self-rule. If imperialism implies domination by force or economic pressure or both, Gandhi emphasizes nonviolence and truth. If imperialism involves corporate control and centralization, Gandhi champions local self sufficiency and decentralization. It is not surprising therefore that people engaged in struggles for self-determination all over the world are turning once again to Gandhi for inspiration.

Short Bibliography

The literature on and about Gandhi is massive. The following references are divided into two sections: the first, Gandhi's own writings and the second, books about Gandhi.

The most important primary sources on Gandhi are the following:

Gandhi, Mohandas K., *An Autobiography: The Story of my Experiments with Truth*, Boston: Beacon Press, 1993.

______, *The Collected Works of Mahatma Gandhi*, 100 vols, New Delhi: Publication Division, Ministry of Information and Broadcasting, 1958-1994.

______, *Constructive Programme: Its Meaning and Place*, Ahmedabad: Navajivan, 1941.

______, *Non-Violent Resistance (Satyāgraha)*, New York: Schocken Books, 1985.

______, *Satyāgraha in South Africa*, Madras: S. Ganesha, 1938.

Iyer, Raghavan (ed.), *The Moral and Political Writings of Mahatma Gandhi*, Oxford: Clarendon Press, vols 1 and 2, 1986, and vol. 3, 1987.

Parel, Anthony J. (ed.), *Gandhi: Hind Swaraj and Other Writings*, Cambridge: Cambridge University Press, 1997.

A few secondary sources include the following:

Bondurant, Joan V., *The Conquest of Violence*, Berkeley: University of California Press, 1967.

Brown, Judith M., *Gandhi: Prisoner of Hope*, New Haven: Yale University Press, 1989.

Chatterjee, Margaret, *Gandhi's Religious Thought*, Notre Dame: University of Notre Dame Press, 1983.

17 Thomas Pogge, 'On International Redistribution,' unpublished paper based on the annual reports of the United Nations Development Program's *Human Development Reports*. Also see Thomas Pogge, *World Poverty and Human Rights*, Cambridge: Polity Press, 2002.

Dalton, Dennis, *Mahatma Gandhi: Nonviolent Power in Action*, New York: Columbia University Press, 1993.

Erikson, Erik, *Gandhi's Truth: On the Origins of Militant Nonviolence*, New York: Norton, 1969.

Hardiman, David, *Gandhi: In His Time and Ours*, New Delhi: Permanent Black, 2003.

Iyer, Raghavan, *The Moral and Political Thought of Mahatma Gandhi*, Oxford: Clarendon Press, 1973.

Parekh, Bhikhu, *Gandhi's Political Philosophy*, Notre Dame: University of Notre Dame Press, 1989.

Terchek, Ronald J., *Gandhi: Struggling for Autonomy*, Lanham and New York: Rowman and Littlefield, 1998.

Chapter 20

Ethical Skepticism in the Philosophy of Sri Aurobindo

Stephen Phillips

A revolutionary's other calling

Sri Aurobindo Ghose (1872-1950), a yogin and spiritual teacher as well as a nationalist politician of prominence, wrote widely. With a career that began as a speechwriter and journalist, Aurobindo became a philosopher and poet after varied efforts as newspaper editor and polemicist urging the end of British rule. In his forties, he dropped out of politics to give, by his own account, his entire attention to yoga. As a philosopher, Aurobindo advocates a mystical *summum bonum* along the lines of the classical schools of Yoga and Vedānta. But he adds a rather original cosmology, claiming sensitivity to science. He puts forth a metaphysics best classified as a modern Vedāntic theism or neo-Vedānta.

Aurobindo's ethical teaching is not, however, what one might expect from a modern guru in the neo-Vedāntic mold. He does not subscribe to a divine command theory. He recognizes no scripture or 'śāstra' as valid. Moreover, Aurobindo is no deontologist, no upholder of general duties, except in a slim sense that I shall try to explain. Nor does he endorse a teleological ethics, although it would be legitimate to say that, according to him, actions and practices do, for certain people at certain times, derive their worth in relation to a supreme good. This would be mystical experience of the One, Brahman, and spiritual transformation by Brahman's 'Shakti,' bringing about a spiritual life. And while it is possible to read Aurobindo as a hedonist – pleasure as a form of *ānanda*, Brahman's nature as 'bliss,' motivating in various forms all action – his hedonism is strictly a psychological thesis, not an ethical theory. Aurobindo expressly denies an ethics of general utility, despite his psychological hedonism. He argues that pleasure, to include the bliss of mystical experience, typically trumps morality in life and action, moral injunctions being social and practical expediencies.

Other than championing a duty to self, which is questionably a *moral* duty, Aurobindo finds no moral principle or criterion that would apply to all situations or that should be universally endorsed. Moral standards are makeshift, liable to abandonment or modification with changing circumstances. Moral standards have no deeply binding psychological pull or force, and a will or motivation to follow a moral principle is, for Aurobindo, only one among many psychological pulls, not essential to a self or person. With respect to the relation of ethical norms and the development of a person's spirituality, the upshot of his sometimes circuitous discussion is debunking and skeptical.

To be sure, Aurobindo endorses positive values, principally values of self-development which include ethical traits. The Western tradition of virtue ethics and the Buddhist ideal of the Bodhisattva are precursors. Aurobindo's message is in fact hopeful in the extreme, claiming that we have supernormal capacities. Like the Bodhisattva who is beautiful and has the six 'perfections,' *pāramitā*, ranging from charity to wisdom, the perfected individual is held up as an ideal for us all to aim at by Aurobindo. He affirms the Indian tradition of *siddhi*-seeking often derided by high-brow philosophers. In the folk traditions of India, superior powers and character traits (*siddhi*) have commonly been attributed to accomplished yogins. Note that these include ethical virtues, extraordinary degrees of compassion, fair-mindedness, and so on, traits that are endorsed by Aurobindo along with special abilities. Spirituality would normally include, according to him, such characteristics as 'truth, fearlessness, purity, love, compassion, benevolence, absence of the will to hurt,' and other ethical virtues.[1] This is an important part of Aurobindo's teaching to which we shall return after looking at his skepticism.

Synthesizing yoga with ethics

In this second portion of the chapter, I shall try to imitate the style of a classical commentary on a text of exegetical interest. I shall elucidate three or four pages of an important book of Aurobindo's, *The Synthesis of Yoga*, from a chapter entitled 'Standards of Conduct and Spiritual Freedom.'[2] In the third and final section, I shall relocate Aurobindo's views both within classical Indian spirituality and, with caveats, within virtue ethics as the area of moral philosophy with which his ideas have their nearest affinity. I shall also identify one or two key issues for evaluating his views.

Like Aurobindo's major work of metaphysics, *The Life Divine*, the *Synthesis*, as the book will be called here, was published from 1914 to 1921 in a monthly journal co-founded by Aurobindo in Pondicherry (i.e. in French India where he was safe from British harassment, being perceived as still a leader of the independence movement). The larger portion of the text, about three quarters of the fifth edition which I shall quote, dates to that first publication, with only minor revisions made by Aurobindo subsequently. But our chapter, 'Standards of Conduct and Spiritual Freedom,' was revised along with the entirety of Part One (out of four Parts) and expanded during the 1940s, the last decade of Aurobindo's life. A second, revised edition of *Synthesis* was published in 1948. Other editions followed posthumously

1 Sri Aurobindo Ghose, *The Synthesis of Yoga*, 5th edn, Pondicherry: Sri Aurobindo Ashram Trust, 1973, p. 540.

2 Ibid., pp. 190-93.

with minor emendations. The point is that our chapter presents Aurobindo's most mature thought.

Compared especially to nationalist exhortatory (not to say inflammatory) speeches Aurobindo made forty years earlier in high Victorian rhetoric, it is striking how profoundly skeptical he shows himself regarding ethical values and rules. Let us begin with what is for his part a summary statement.

> ... there is, above society's external law and man's moral law and beyond them, though feebly and ignorantly aimed at by something within them, a larger truth of a vast unbound consciousness, a law divine towards which both these blind and gross formulations are progressive faltering steps that try to escape from the natural law of the animal to a more exalted light or universal rule.[3]

Efforts to transcend a self-interested animal nature are credited as progressive in a particular cosmological light. That is, Aurobindo sees Brahman – the Absolute, the One, the Divine – as self-manifesting, i.e. creating out of itself, a universe in which spiritual development is a secret *telos*. By 'society's external law,' Aurobindo means to suggest that survival demands individuals to restrain or moderate natural desires to live in rough harmony with others in communities. This constitutes an enforced progress for the individual. To observe a moral law would be a step further away from the animal in human nature, behaviour arising along with a mental will and an intellectualization of desire. By this he means not only a mental weighting of desires but also assimilation of desire to the mental mode, a sublimation or transformation. Thus he apparently sees moral philosophy as superior to, and potentially reformatory of, societal practices based merely on co-operative exigencies. He sees effort to lead a moral life as normally helping a person or soul shape itself in a spiritual direction. However, 'the natural law of the animal' is not to be taken as having negative connotation in the passage above. The animal in us, our baser drives and desires, are not to be neglected but spiritualized. That is, they are to be assimilated by, or integrated into, not a mental but a spiritual element in our psychology. Aurobindo's teaching is world-affirmative, that is to say, life-affirmative, though not by a moral standard. (Here he echoes William Blake.) The problem with following a moral law is that it is insufficiently transformative, failing both to bring out valuable life possibilities and to transform the animal in us in the really right ways.

To continue with the passage from *Synthesis*, any genuine law of human interaction would have to be:

> ... a law and truth that discovers the perfect movement, harmony, rhythm of a great spiritualized collective life and determines perfectly our relations with each being and all beings in Nature's varied oneness.[4]

3 Ibid., p. 190.
4 Ibid., p. 191.

Societal and moral laws are not the divine 'law' to which a spiritual individual would be attuned. For Aurobindo, Brahman is real and accessible in life. The Divine interacts with the developing yogin, and the interrelations are complex and specific to a vast variability of our individual and collective natures. These natures, we learn in *The Life Divine*, the metaphysical treatise, are not predetermined: souls make themselves in part, says Aurobindo, echoing both Romantics and existentialists. We are the history of our choices, or of the ways we have allowed our talents and desires to flourish, as well as self-determinations of Brahman, Aurobindo tries to show in hundreds of pages of abstract argument.

The ethicist may think there is a single moral law because he or she vaguely intuits the fact of a single Divine being, whose nature as infinite 'Sachchidananda' (Aurobindo's anglicization), 'Existence-Consciousness-Bliss,' grounds all being and real possibility. But anyone, presumably even Aurobindo himself, would err, inevitably, in trying to state what is too complex for statement.

> The ethical idealist tries to discover this supreme law in his own moral data, in the inferior powers and factors that belong to the mental and ethical formula. And to sustain and organise them he selects a fundamental principle of conduct essentially unsound and constructed by the intellect, utility, hedonism, reason, intuitive conscience or any other generalised standard. All such efforts are foredoomed to failure. Our inner nature is the progressive expression of the eternal Spirit and too complex a power to be tied down by a single dominant mental or moral principle.[5]

Allegiance to a monolithic moral standard is liable, Aurobindo suggests, to block spiritual progress. That each of us is in the process of developing spirituality, expressing Brahman uniquely, is a truth that overrides the generalized statements of the moralist. The exception not only always looms large but fits somehow a larger pattern.

Presumably, Aurobindo does not mean that certain types of action, such as murder, are not right or wrong. One senses a minimalist or libertarian morality centred on a principle of not harming others just beneath the surface of his statements. However, politically he was no pacificist, urging, for example, unlike Gandhi, full co-operation of Indians in the British war effort against Nazi Germany. To have a morality, as in the phrase, 'Christian morality,' would be to have a life-orientation governed by the mental element in our psychology, a life-orientation governed too much by beliefs and rules, he suggests. He says explicitly that moral systemization, by which he means not philosophic effort to find a set of coherent rules but rather application of a set of rules in all areas of life, cannot succeed. No system can succeed in the sense of actually dominating life and desire, nor in the sense of being adequate to the richness of life. There is too much diversity.

The later religions endeavor to fix the type of a supreme truth of conduct, erect a system and declare God's law through the mouth of Avatar or prophet. These systems, more powerful and dynamic than the dry ethical idea, are yet for the most part no

5 Ibid., p. 191.

more than idealistic glorifications of the moral principle sanctified by religious emotion and the label of a superhuman origin. Some, like the extreme Christian ethic, are rejected by Nature because they insist unworkably on an impracticable absolute rule. Others prove in the end to be evolutionary compromises and become obsolete in the march of Time. The true divine law, unlike these mental counterfeits, cannot be a system of rigid ethical determinations that press into their cast-iron moulds all our life-movements.[6]

By 'the moral principle,' Aurobindo means whatever standard is most prominent in a given society, utility in Victorian society and the Raj, for instance. Most of the remainder of the passage is clear. By 'later religions,' Aurobindo probably means Christianity and Islam, though perhaps also modern Hinduism. Again, he stresses a variability and unregulability of life, which is seen as a self-expression of spirit.

In the Indian context, the most distinctive feature of Aurobindo's spiritual vision is its emphasis on life. Though some would say yoga practice is 'religious,' Aurobindo seems to see the religious differently. Note in the next passage the ironic tone of the expression, *sanātana dharma*, which translates 'eternal duty' or 'eternal sacred law' and is sometimes used as shorthand for the Hindu web of belief.

The older religions erected their rule of the wise, their dicta of Manu or Confucius, a complex *śāstra* in which they attempted to combine the social rule and moral law with the declaration of certain eternal principles of our highest nature in some kind of uniting amalgam. All three were treated on the same ground as equally the expression of everlasting verities, *sanātana dharma*. But two of the elements are evolutionary and valid for a time, mental constructions, human readings of the will of the Eternal; the third, attached and subdued to certain social and moral formulas, had to share the fortunes of its form. Either the *śāstra* grows obsolete and has to be progressively changed or finally cast away or else it stands as a rigid barrier to the self-development of the individual and the race. The *śāstra* erects a collective and external standard; it ignores the inner nature of the individual, the indeterminable elements of a secret spiritual force within him. But the nature of the individual will not be ignored; its demand is inexorable.[7]

Such iconoclasm is surprising in Aurobindo not only in virtue of his yoga teaching but also his Vedānta, his endorsement of the teaching of the Upaniṣads. However, he gives new, individualist spin to the Vedāntic view of a *summum bonum*. Spiritual individuals, reincarnating psychic beings, differ in many ways in the fineness of their growth or development. The individual etchings of their personalities differ, as do their talents and sensibility and consciousness. Thus no single '*śāstra*,' no single set of rules, can be adequate to the routes of spirituality.

An individual may be refined spiritually in a particular way without being particularly virtuous, Aurobindo seems to say. Krishna (as portrayed in the *Purāṇas* and later literature) is mischievous, stealing butter and committing adultery. Of course, Aurobindo interprets Krishna's acts symbolically: God's adultery with the

---

6 Ibid., pp. 191-92.

7 Ibid., p. 192.

soul. But he does not let us miss the grit in the images. In personal letters to disciples and confidants, the guru rarely endorses conventional wisdom or conventional values. This is not to say that the yoga or 'spiritual discipline' he laid out for a group of followers was not a tough regimen. Generally speaking, celibacy, to cite a telling example, seems to have been advised. Nor does Aurobindo think of Krishna's 'sins' as possibly immoral, even on the most literal reading, in the sense of hurting anyone. Krishna brings people to bliss. Aurobindo thinks of the Avatar as full of love and compassion, and of his mischief-making as delightful. (Krishna is very beautiful and plays beautifully the flute.) Again, the talk of love-making is metaphoric, or, if taken literally, would, by a disciple of Aurobindo's, be understood as premised on a yogin's celibacy, a precondition for dalliance with God. Still, the 'sinners' among Aurobindo's followers were thought of, as I understand things, simply as insufficiently skilled along certain dimensions of life, and that only, and might be, despite the failings, considered quite proficient yogins or yoginis nonetheless.

One must keep in mind the distinction between (a) prudential considerations that Aurobindo lays out for his disciples, i.e. for people committed to following his yoga, considerations that are often phrased in prescriptive language, and (b) his, let us say, theoretical ethics, the theme of his philosophy that we should be suspicious of prescriptions. Aurobindo's use of 'should' and similar terms is normally prudential and premised on an individual's desire and choice to follow a yogic path.

Within a wider context, or considering the wider audience that *Synthesis* was apparently meant to address, we should say that Aurobindo's chief message is that human consciousness is much more than mentality, which is in fact only its instrument, an instrument potentially out of control in 'living ethically.' This is a dominant theme. 'Life before mind' is the *mantra*.

Dominant too is the claim that modern Westerners (now perhaps Easterners too) tend to be overly mental, refusing to rely on non-mental modes of awareness and closing themselves off from a spiritual life – a refrain sounded didactically in almost all of Aurobindo's books. The anti-intellectual Indian mystic is, of course, highly intellectual, and there is often irony in Aurobindo's voice. But he is serious when, in the next few sentences, he contrasts 'inner' and 'outer.' The 'outer' is the province of social interaction and morality.

> A moral law can be imposed as a rule or an ideal on numbers of men who have not attained that level of consciousness or that fineness of mind and will and psychic sense in which it [a spiritual influence] can become a reality to them and a living force. As an ideal it can be revered without any need of practice. As a rule it can be observed in its outsides even if the inner sense is missed altogether. The supramental and spiritual life cannot be mechanized in this way; it cannot be turned into a mental ideal or an external rule. It has its own great lines, but these must be made real, must be the workings of an active Power felt in the individual's consciousness and the transcriptions of an eternal Truth powerful to transform mind, life and body.[8]

8 Ibid., pp. 192-93.

Individual growth is chequered, and the ways human souls arrive at yogic readiness are various. Yoga is of course the main topic of the *Synthesis*, and these quotations and our chapter on ethical standards have as their immediate context instruction in yoga, as a science and an art. The Sanskrit word *yoga* translates as 'self-discipline,' and, in Aurobindo's usages, often 'conscious interaction with the Divine.' Yoga does have its requirements, 'its own great lines,' he says here. But these lines are less requirements rigidly formulable than stages in the development of skills, i.e. of meditation as of carpentry, indeed of powers of concentration that, it is claimed, could improve one's carpentry. 'Yoga is skill in works,' is a line Aurobindo quotes favourably from the *Gītā*.

Consciousness Supramental

The positive message of the passages cited is to urge development of consciousness on analogy to the development of skills or the exercising of talents. The having of a full-bodied 'knowledge how,' the having of special mystic powers (*siddhi*), is endorsed, as opposed to a life guided by what Aurobindo thinks of as a morality, a thin gruel of 'belief that,' or, as he says, 'mental construction.' Aurobindo envisages possibilities of what he calls a supramental organization of consciousness that would integrate and reshape the 'lower' instruments of 'mind, life and body.' Elsewhere he uses the analogy of ways mind reshapes forces of life. A dramatic example is romantic love, which is mentally transformed sexual desire according to his psychological theory.

The possibility of such a higher instrumentality of spirit or consciousness – the supramental, like the mental, is conceived as an instrument (compare the classical Sāṃkhya and Yoga understanding of *manas* and even *buddhi*, 'sense mind' and 'rational intelligence,' as external to consciousness) – is worth more than pursuit of an ethical ideal. Indeed, true societal harmony would normally be more likely through a person's working on herself as opposed to trying to live a moral life, Aurobindo suggests.

Thus one could argue that the really right thing to do, the genuinely moral life, on Aurobindo's premises, is not to aim at a moral life but at self-improvement. This is not, I think, a paradox. Nor, I admit, is it strictly correct, for Aurobindo does not hold that everyone should try yoga. Still, the gist of his advice is: change yourself, heighten your consciousness, and everything, including your relation to other persons, will be for the better.

In that [a supramental consciousness of the One and the unity of all] alone can all these lower discords resolve themselves into a victorious harmony of the true relations between manifested beings who are portions of the one Godhead and children of one universal Mother.[9]

In Aurobindo's view, everything is Brahman, whether figured as a transcendent consciousness or as Earth, Nature, the Goddess, the 'universal Mother.'

9 Ibid., p. 193.

Aurobindo's moral skepticism

Aurobindo's moral skepticism, although perhaps odd for neo-Vedānta as also against the backdrop of mainstream classical Indian philosophy, is not so surprising in the context of yogic mysticism. Several brands of skepticism have flourished in connection with yogic teaching in the Subcontinent. The Buddha is interpreted as having refused to answer philosophical questions because even adequate answers would not help an unenlightened questioner to make spiritual progress. The polemicist Nāgārjuna (c. 150 CE) apparently saw rival, non-Buddhist (and even Buddhist) reasoners as idly spinning mental wheels. Deftly he discredits their theories, apparently out of compassion, viewing the Buddhist path to require less intellectualization and more mindfulness. The Advaitin Śrīharṣa (c. 1150) refutes point by point positions of realists and logicians, apparently again with a spiritual motive, to help us hear the mystic message of the Upaniṣads. (Once you lose confidence in your own beliefs, you presumably become open to a perspective that is radically different.) Ethical skepticism is rare but nevertheless instanced. The great Advaitin Śaṅkara (c. 700) explains at length why duties spelled out as the *karma-khaṇḍa* portion of the Veda do not apply to those following the *jñāna-khaṇḍa*, the portion devoted to mystical knowledge. Classical Vedāntins do not say that societal norms are temporary mental constructions. But they do say that the novitiate must put aside prior allegiances and conceptions of duties – at least this is part of the message of more than a few Vedantic texts.

Furthermore, the mystic call has commonly been understood to conflict with special duties of one's station (as father, son, mother, daughter, and so on). Renunciants and mystic seekers probably have often been at odds with mores of society. Śaivites are reputed to drink *bhāṅg*, a cannabis product, and Tantrics are apparently, or were, notorious for purposely breaking societal prohibitions, meat-eating, drinking, and extramarital sex (euphemized as 'ritual intercourse'). Of course, offending societal norms must be distinguished from ethical skepticism. But the spirit of Aurobindo's skepticism is found, I think, in what we might call mystic experimentalism, an openness to novel experiences in line with yoga teaching and practice.

But Aurobindo's life-affirmativeness is unusual even in the Indian mystical context. Moreover, his skepticism about ethical formula seems to flow as much from his view of Brahman as expressing itself through desires and life as it does from principles of yogic coaching.

To try to locate Aurobindo's views among current philosophic conversations is difficult. Compatible with his peculiar variety of skepticism are important ethical theses that he, it could be argued, would endorse, though not by him explicitly stated. Aurobindo sometimes writes as though he subscribes to an ethical intuitionism, that what is right is known by insight particular to a situation. By 'insight' would be meant not just past experiences as mentally determinate, but also spontaneous intuition of the moment, a feeling of 'right desire' flowing from one's emerging spirituality. 'Right desire' is more important a concept for Aurobindo than 'choice.' One acts rightly, according to this reading, when one acts out of one's highest consciousness.

That one should develop the character to which a high consciousness would be natural seems a prescription ascribable to him. For him, the 'highest consciousness' would be a consciousness of a mysterious unity about which I will not speculate. But any such consciousness would, I presume, include respect for life and sensitivity to prosperity, happiness, and various cultural values. Informally, in letters and essays on poetry in particular, he seems to endorse standards that are not only high but also probably for most decidedly too high.[10]

In fact, by focusing on Aurobindo's ethical skepticism, I may do an injustice to the thrust of his value themes. At the heart of much of virtue ethics are such dicta as to *be* courageous, not merely to be able to *recognize* courage. To know the criteria for what counts as courageous is less central to right action than traits of character, so it is felt. Aurobindo fits in nicely with ethicists of such a persuasion. For Aurobindo, right action flows from right desire, more than from a choice made according to an ethical rule. Indeed, his emphasis on character seems to extend to the epistemic thesis that one needs to develop a certain character to sustain the consciousness that can spontaneously choose what is right and best. In any case, Aurobindo talks less about right choice than right desire: spiritualized desire would prompt the best course of action, according to him.

The problem with this analysis is less that it borders on conflict with Aurobindo's stated skepticism than that Aurobindo was not a professional philosopher. He does not speak the language of the ethical and meta-ethical conversations of university-trained professors. To respond from his perspective to objections to the theses I would attribute to him would soon be beyond my ability.

The deep questions with Aurobindo concern the value of yogic practices, as well as, of course, the truth or warrantedness of his world picture.

Regarding the value of yogic practices, there are issues such as the relative weight of intellectual qualities versus powers of concentration with respect to, say, a craft such as carpentry. It is not clear that yoga, if it excludes the intellectual element in our psychology, our 'knowledge that,' would be sufficient for excellence, since knowing various facts about materials, measurements, tools, and so forth appears just as necessary as the dexterity not to smash your thumb. Even in avoiding the thumb, and especially in details such as setting a nail correctly, internalized intellectual norms – and aesthetic norms, in addition – appear to be crucial, not only with regard to excellence but the very nature of the activity. Exercising some of our best skills does not require conscious verbalization – think of riding a bicycle. But norms that are verbalizable, and thus mental, appear to be nonetheless internalized in learned behaviour. Practicing may be far more important than talk in developing a skill or craft. But we are able to coach the unexperienced and warn not to turn the wheels too sharply or to hammer a nail flush that we want to set. Aurobindo is hardly pellucid about what it is to reject the intellectual in favour of alternative modes of consciousness, particularly as guides for action.

---

10 Sri Aurobindo (Ghose), *Letters on Yoga*, Pondicherry: Sri Aurobindo Ashram Trust, 1973, 3 vols, *passim*.

Regarding the truth of Aurobindo's worldview, my sense is that his advocacy of a mystic life would be well-founded only if his neo-Vedāntic metaphysics is at least roughly right, including the theories of rebirth and of a developing psychic being. Objections to these ideas are not hard to come by. Contemporary psychology is dominated by a materialist paradigm. The inwardness of yoga as well as its power for health and happiness are perhaps rallying points for the anti-materialist. This is not the place to make the argument. But clearly a metaphysics centred on consciousness will be at odds with all the prominent versions of scientific materialism. One should read Aurobindo against this backdrop with a sense of 'paradigm conflict.' So let us end with the remark that if materialism is right, Aurobindo is wrong, and conversely.

Index